Lecture Notes in Computer Science 10009

Commenced Publication in 1973
Founding and Former Series Editors:
Gerhard Goos, Juris Hartmanis, and Jan van Leeuwen

More information about this series at http://www.springer.com/series/7408

Kazuhiro Ogata · Mark Lawford
Shaoying Liu (Eds.)

Formal Methods and Software Engineering

18th International Conference
on Formal Engineering Methods, ICFEM 2016
Tokyo, Japan, November 14–18, 2016
Proceedings

 Springer

Editors
Kazuhiro Ogata
School of Information Science
Japan Advanced Institute of Science and
  Technology (JAIST)
Nomi
Japan

Shaoying Liu
Department of Computer Science
Hosei University
Tokyo
Japan

Mark Lawford
Department of Computing and Software
McMaster University
Hamilton, ON
Canada

ISSN 0302-9743   ISSN 1611-3349   (electronic)
Lecture Notes in Computer Science
ISBN 978-3-319-47845-6   ISBN 978-3-319-47846-3   (eBook)
DOI 10.1007/978-3-319-47846-3

Library of Congress Control Number: 2016954467

LNCS Sublibrary: SL2 – Programming and Software Engineering

Printed on acid-free paper

This Springer imprint is published by Springer Nature
The registered company is Springer International Publishing AG
The registered company address is: Gewerbestrasse 11, 6330 Cham, Switzerland

Preface

The International Conference on Formal Engineering Methods (ICFEM) is a premier conference for research in all areas related to formal engineering methods, such as verification and validation, software engineering, formal specification and modeling, software security, and software reliability. Since 1997, ICFEM has been serving as an international forum for researchers and practitioners who have been seriously applying formal methods to practical applications. Researchers and practitioners, from industry, academia, and government, are encouraged to attend, present their research, and help advance the state of the art. We are interested in work that has been incorporated into real production systems, and in theoretical work that promises to bring practical and tangible benefit.

In recent years, ICFEM has taken place in Paris, France (2015), Luxembourg (2014), Queenstown, New Zealand (2013), Kyoto, Japan (2012), Durham, UK (2011) and Shanghai, China (2010). The 18th edition of ICFEM took place in Tokyo during November 16–18, 2015. The Program Committee (PC) received 64 full research papers. Each paper received at least three reports from PC members or external reviewers. On the basis of these reports, each submission was extensively discussed in the virtual meeting of the PC, and the PC decided to accept 27 papers. The proceedings also include a full paper and two short summary papers from the three keynote speakers, Tom Maibaum (McMaster University), W. Eric Wong (University of Texas at Dallas), and Keijiro Araki (Kyushu University).

ICFEM 2016 was organized and supported by Hosei University. The conference would not have been possible without the contributions and the support of the following organizations: the Institute of Electronics, Information and Communication Engineers (IEICE), Japan Society for Software Science and Technology (JSSST), and The Murata Science Foundation. We thank also the Local Organizing Committee for their hard work in making ICFEM 2016 a successful and exciting event.

The main event was preceded by three workshops and a tutorial: the 5th International Workshop on Formal Techniques for Safety-Critical Systems (FTSCS 2016), the 6th International Workshop SOFL+MSVL, the Workshop on Formal and Model-Driven Techniques for Developing Trustworthy Systems, and a one day tutorial on formal specification and verification with CafeOBJ.

We would like to thank the numerous people who contributed to the success of ICFEM 2016: the Steering Committee members, the PC members and the additional reviewers for their support in selecting papers and composing the conference program, and the authors and the invited speakers for their contributions without which, of course, these proceedings would not exist. We would like also to thank Springer for their help during the production of this proceedings volume and the EasyChair team for their great conference system.

August 2016

Kazuhiro Ogata
Mark Lawford
Shaoying Liu

Organization

Program Committee

Bernhard K. Aichernig	TU Graz, Austria
Étienne André	Université Paris 13, France
Toshiaki Aoki	JAIST, Japan
Christian Attiogbe	University of Nantes, France
Richard Banach	University of Manchester, UK
Ezio Bartocci	TU Wien, Austria
Michael Butler	University of Southampton, UK
Ana Cavalcanti	University of York, UK
Sungdeok Cha	Korea University, South Korea
Yuting Chen	Shanghai Jiao Tong University, China
Sylvain Conchon	Université Paris-Sud, France
Frank De Boer	CWI, The Netherlands
Zhenhua Duan	Xidian University, China
Jeremy Gibbons	University of Oxford, UK
Stefania Gnesi	ISTI-CNR, Italy
Lindsay Groves	Victoria University of Wellington, New Zealand
Ian J. Hayes	University of Queensland, Australia
Michaela Huhn	TU Clausthal, Germany
Alexei Iliasov	Newcastle University, UK
Fuyuki Ishikawa	National Institute of Informatics, Japan
Weiqiang Kong	Dalian University of Technology, China
Fabrice Kordon	LIP6/UPMC, France
Mark Lawford	McMaster University, Canada
Xiaoshan Li	University of Macau, SAR China
Shaoying Liu	Hosei University, Japan
Yang Liu	Nanyang Technological University, Singapore
Larissa Meinicke	University of Queensland, Australia
Stephan Merz	Inria Nancy, France
Huaikou Miao	Shanghai University, China
Mohammadreza Mousavi	Halmstad University, Sweden
Shin Nakajima	National Institute of Informatics, Japan
Akio Nakata	Hiroshima City University, Japan
Manuel Nuñez	UC, Spain
Kazuhiro Ogata	JAIST, Japan
Kozo Okano	Shinshu University, Japan
Jun Pang	University of Luxembourg
Jan Peleska	TZI, Universität Bremen, Germany

Ion Petre	Åbo Akademi University, Finland
Shengchao Qin	Teesside University, UK
Silvio Ranise	FBK-Irst, Italy
Adrian Riesco	Universidad Complutense de Madrid, Spain
Jing Sun	University of Auckland, New Zealand
Kenji Taguchi	AIST, Japan
Jaco van de Pol	University of Twente, The Netherlands
Thomas Wahl	Northeastern University, USA
Xi Wang	Hosei University, Japan
Alan Wassyng	McMaster University, Canada
Fatiha Zaidi	Université Paris-Sud, France
Jian Zhang	Institute of Software, Chinese Academy of Sciences, China
Min Zhang	East China Normal University, China
Hong Zhu	Oxford Brookes University, UK
Huibiao Zhu	Software Engineering Institute, East China Normal University, China

Additional Reviewers

Aiguier, Marc	Millet, Laure
Azadbakht, Keyvan	Oh, Hakjoo
Basile, Davide	Patcas, Lucian
Bloemen, Vincent	Petre, Luigia
Briday, Mikaël	Renault, Etienne
Ciancia, Vincenzo	Ribeiro, Pedro
Colley, John	Salehi Fathabadi, Asieh
De Masellis, Riccardo	Semini, Laura
Dokter, Kasper	Souma, Daisuke
Fei, Yuan	Steel, Jim
Frehse, Goran	Su, Wen
Gao, Honghao	Sznajder, Nathalie
Hartmanns, Arnd	Tappler, Martin
He, Mengda	Taromirad, Masoumeh
Hoang, Thai Son	Traverso, Riccardo
Kamali, Mojgan	Wang, Luyao
Khakpour, Narges	Winter, Kirsten
Kitamura, Takashi	Wu, Xingming
Konnov, Igor	Xu, Zhiwu
Kuruma, Hironobu	Yang, Yilong
Laarman, Alfons	Yuan, Qixia
Li, Li	Zheng, Zheng
Lorber, Florian	

Abstracts of Keynotes

Combinatorial Testing and Its Applications

W. Eric Wong

Advanced Research Center for Software Testing and Quality Assurance,
Department of Computer Science, University of Texas at Dallas,
Richardson, USA
http://www.utdallas.edu/~ewong
ewong@utdallas.edu

Studies have shown that combinatorial testing can help programs detect hard-to-find software bugs that may not be revealed by test cases generated using other testing techniques. The first part of this talk focuses on traditional black-box requirements-based combinatorial testing. In particular, I will discuss results and lessons learned from two real-life industry applications: a control panel of a rail-road system and a Linux system. The second part extends the concept of combinatorial testing to a white-box structure-based setting. I will present an advanced coverage criterion, *Combinatorial Decision Coverage*, in conjunction with symbolic execution to achieve high coverage cost-effectively without suffering from potential space exploration. Finally, I will explain how combinatorial testing can be applied to a graph-based methodology for testing IoT (Internet of Things).

Bio

W. Eric Wong received his M.S. and Ph.D. in Computer Science from Purdue University, West Lafayette, Indiana, USA. He is a Full Professor, the Director of International Outreach, and the Founding Director of Advanced Research Center for Software Testing and Quality Assurance (http://paris.utdallas.edu/stqa) in Computer Science at the University of Texas at Dallas (UTD). He also has an appointment as a guest researcher at the National Institute of Standards and Technology, an agency of the U.S. Department of Commerce. Prior to joining UTD, he was with Telcordia Technologies (formerly Bellcore) as a senior research scientist and the project manager in charge of Dependable Telecom Software Development.

Dr. Wong is the recipient of the 2014 IEEE Reliability Society Engineer of the Year. He is also the Edit-in-Chief of the IEEE Transactions on Reliability. His research focuses on helping practitioners improve software quality while reducing production cost. In particular, he is working on software testing, program debugging, risk analysis, safety, and reliability. Dr. Wong has published more than 180 papers and edited 2 books.

Dr. Wong is also the Founding Steering Committee Chair of the IEEE International Conference on Software Security and Reliability (SERE) and the IEEE International

Workshop on Program Debugging. In 2015, the SERE conference and the QSIC conference (International Conference on Quality Software) merged into one large conference, QRS, with Q representing *Quality*, R for *Reliability*, and S for *Security*. Dr. Wong continues to be the Steering Committee Chair of this new conference (http://paris.utdallas.edu/qrs).

A (Proto) Logical Basis for the Notion of a Structured Argument in a Safety Case

Valentín Cassano[✉], Thomas S.E. Maibaum, and Silviya Grigorova

McMaster Centre for Software Certification, McMaster University,
Hamilton, Canada.
{cassanv,grigorsb}@mcmaster.ca, tom@maibaum.org

Abstract. The introduction of safety cases was a step in the right direction in regards to safety assurance. As presently practiced, safety cases aim at making a serious attempt to explicate, and to provide some structure for, the reasoning involved in assuring that a system is safe, generally in terms of so-called structured arguments. However, the fact current notations for expressing these structured arguments have no formal semantics and, at best, are loosely linked to goal structuring ideas and to Toulmin's notion of an argument pattern, is a crucial issue to be addressed. History clearly demonstrates that languages that have no formal semantics are deficient in relation to the requirements of a serious approach to engineering. In other words, one can only go so far with intuition, and certainly not far enough to justify the safety of complex systems, such as Cyber Physical Systems or autonomous cars. By rehearsing Gentzen's program for formalizing mathematical reasoning, his famous Calculus of Natural Deduction, we show how we can begin a program of formalizing safety reasoning by developing a working definition of a structured argument in a safety case and a calculus for safety reasoning.

Promotion of Formal Approaches in Japanese Software Industry and a Best Practice of FeliCa's Case (Extended Abstract)

Keijiro Araki[1(✉)] and Taro Kurita[2]

[1] Kyushu University, 744 Motooka, Nishi-ku, Fukuoka 819-0395, Japan
araki@ait.kyushu-u.ac.jp
[2] Sony Corporation, 2-10-1 Osaki, Shinagawa-ku, Tokyo 141-8610, Japan

Abstract. We have been making much effort to promote formal methods in Japan, especially Japanese IT companies. This paper describes our activities in Japan for almost twenty years, and shows typical reactions from such Japanese companies for application of formal methods. We mention about the obstacles they think to adopting formal methods in their real software development projects. On the other hand we also present a case of FeliCa Networks, Inc. as a best practice of applying formal methods in Japan. We discuss the lessons learned from our efforts of promoting formal methods and the FeliCa's case. Finally, we briefly introduce our research project to support software developers in adopting formal approaches to real projects.

Keywords: Formal methods · Rigorous specification · Practice · Development process · FeliCa IC Chip · VDM · VDMPad · ViennaTalk

Contents

A (Proto) Logical Basis for the Notion of a Structured Argument in a Safety Case

Valentín Cassano$^{(\boxtimes)}$, Thomas S.E. Maibaum, and Silviya Grigorova

McMaster Centre for Software Certification, McMaster University, Hamilton, Canada
{cassanv,grigorsb}@mcmaster.ca, tom@maibaum.org

Abstract. The introduction of safety cases was a step in the right direction in regards to safety assurance. As presently practiced, safety cases aim at making a serious attempt to explicate, and to provide some structure for, the reasoning involved in assuring that a system is safe, generally in terms of so-called structured arguments. However, the fact current notations for expressing these structured arguments have no formal semantics and, at best, are loosely linked to goal structuring ideas and to Toulmin's notion of an argument pattern, is a crucial issue to be addressed. History clearly demonstrates that languages that have no formal semantics are deficient in relation to the requirements of a serious approach to engineering. In other words, one can only go so far with intuition, and certainly not far enough to justify the safety of complex systems, such as Cyber Physical Systems or autonomous cars. By rehearsing Gentzen's program for formalizing mathematical reasoning, his famous Calculus of Natural Deduction, we show how we can begin a program of formalizing safety reasoning by developing a working definition of a structured argument in a safety case and a calculus for safety reasoning.

1 Introduction

Safety cases were introduced into safety practice as a way of making explicit and organizing the justification for a claim that some engineered artifact is safe. Initially, safety cases were cast as natural language documents whose nature and structure were only informally defined, complicating the knowing of what is required of them. The introduction of the idea that a safety case is a structured argument, with references to Toulmin's notion of an argument pattern (see [1]), was a big step forward in providing a more rigorous definition of a safety case. A lot of very useful work has been done in developing these ideas into useful methods and notations and software based tools to support the development of safety cases. To make further progress in transforming safety cases into a properly grounded engineering tool, enabling a systematic and scientific construction and analysis, we need to develop a more formal, logically principled basis for them.

What exactly do we mean by "more logically principled"? Firstly, to date, existing notations and languages for safety cases do not have a rigorous logical semantics. When presented with a safety case, say in GSN or CAE notation (see [2,3]), we have no mean for deciding whether the safety case is syntactically well

© Springer International Publishing AG 2016
K. Ogata et al. (Eds.): ICFEM 2016, LNCS 10009, pp. 1–17, 2016.
DOI: 10.1007/978-3-319-47846-3_1

formed, never mind whether the reasoning it purports to represent is sound, in the usual sense of properly defined logical systems. Though this state of affairs has persisted for 25 years and people have developed and used safety cases with some success, it is time to take action. The present practice of safety cases seems to be supported by intuition and experience rather than science. This brings with it a number of worrisome difficulties. The complexity of new systems, such as Cyber Physical Systems or autonomous cars, increases as time goes on. How can we expect to deal with this increase in complexity solely based on intuition? We know that, in the end, intuition always fails us when confronted by complexity. Would we have entrusted the lives of astronauts in our missions into space if they were engineered based on intuition and not science? The answer is a clear NO. So it must be with the development of safety cases for complex systems. Lastly, there is the problem of education: How do we teach new safety professionals the necessary rigour required in safety engineering without a scientific basis? Do we appeal to intuition and experience?

The aim of this paper is to set off on the long road to developing a logical calculus in which to incorporate the kind of reasoning involved in safety assurance. Though we will not be presenting such a logical calculus, we do not yet know enough to do so, we will attempt a *working definition* of a structured argument in a safety case in said logical calculus. Our goal is twofold. First, to lay out a foundation for systematization. Second, to set a standard against which progress can be measured. Working definitions are the basis of science and engineering and are an essential tool against which to measure scientific progress. Scientific progress will enable us to systematize, and make more measurable, our approach to making safety case practice more rigorous, if not yet fully formalized. We will happily make changes as we learn more and are able to justify their necessity.

2   Preliminary Observations

We will begin by outlining some of our observations about important elements of safety case reasoning. Perhaps the first point to make is that notations for presenting so called structured arguments in safety cases, such as GSN or CAE diagrams (see [2,3]; to save us from having to continually refer to all of them, we will use GSN as a witness of a set of similar notations) do not present arguments as such, they present safety goal decomposition structures, goal G can be achieved via its decomposition into sub-goals $G_1, \ldots, G_n$, with some reference to goal decomposition justification. In GSN diagrams, this justification takes the form of *strategies*: They justify why the proposed goal decomposition achieves the goal G, if appropriately combined. This is reminiscent of problem solving by decomposition (see [4]), where solutions to sub-problems can be combined in a prescribed way to solve the original problem, and also of goal structured requirements approaches such as KAOS (see [5]), which applies problem decomposition ideas to requirements definition. However, goal decomposition and structured arguments in safety cases are completely different things: Goal decomposition serves as a way of breaking down the structure of complex goals into more manageable ones, in contrast, safety arguments serve as a way of substantiating the notion that a safety claim follows from others. For us, notations like GSN fall short at presenting arguments, and what they do well at representing, goal decomposition, while very important, is hindered by not having a properly defined semantics (in comparison, KAOS trees enjoy of a formal semantics, well defined decomposition patterns, etc., making them better suited for engineering use.)

To further complicate things, attempts at supporting safety reasoning by casting it into First Order Logic (FOL) and using FOL automated deduction support (see [6]) are bound to face a great obstacle to overcome: Safety reasoning is not that of FOL (and, more generally, it is quite different from that captured by classical deductive logics). There are several reasons for this, but we will focus only on some of them. Firstly, some of the inference licenses used in safety reasoning are textbook examples of fallacies in FOL (e.g., judgments from expert opinions). Secondly, some of the inference licenses used in safety reasoning are inductive in nature (as in inductive reasoning). An obvious example of the latter occurs in reasoning about test cases: Concluding from a test set where every test case is successful that the corresponding program is correct for all input data, a proper generalization, requires a truly inductive reasoning step. Thirdly, safety case reasoning includes elements of defeasible reasoning, i.e., reasoning in which conclusions are open to revision or annulment (as discussed in the field of non-monotonic logics; see [7]). We make contingent inferences in the absence of certain information. They are contingent because further investigation may invalidate the conclusions drawn from them. Fourthly, safety case reasoning sometimes also uses a form of reasoning called eliminative induction (see [8]). Eliminative induction, first developed by Francis Bacon, and taken up by philosophers such as John Stuart Mill, John Maynard Keynes, Karl Popper, et al., works like this: Suppose that we want to conclude property A and we have identified that A may not be true if one or more properties $B_1, \ldots, B_n$ are true; if we can prove that no B_i holds, then we can conclude that A holds. This form of reasoning is in fact an example of a form of probabilistic reasoning that departs from the frequentist based reasoning of probability and is more related to confidence (as in confidence in a scientific theory). Confidence underlies reasoning about scientific theories, legal cases, and in other domains. For example, it is the basis on which semantics for statements in law like "beyond a reasonable doubt" or "on the balance of probabilities" can be defined. In safety reasoning confidence is absolutely necessary for it manifests the conventional wisdom that safety cannot be absolutely guaranteed. Lastly, safety reasoning has a global rather than a localized inductive nature (as in mathematical induction). Defeasible and probabilistic reasoning exhibit this particularity. In defeasible and probabilistic reasoning it is in general not possible to just add another branch to a proof in a soundness-preserving way (see [9]). This has grave consequences for the possibility of devising incremental safety approaches that support the well tried and understood concept of incremental design improvement (see [10]). The above combined lead to the observation that FOL, and, more generally, classical deductive settings, may be unfit for the purposes of safety reasoning.

In summary, to no one's surprise, safety reasoning presents a challenging topic for research with important practical implications. Taking on this challenge, we proceed by outlining and justifying a working definition of a structured argument in a safety case that, in our view, has some chance of having a well defined logical semantics. We illustrate with an example how the ideas may be used in practice.

3 Safety Cases, Structured Arguments, and Evidence

The commonly found definition of a safety case reads: "A safety case is a structured argument [. . .] that provides a compelling, comprehensible, and valid case that a system is safe for a given application in a given operating environment" (see [11]). On the one hand, safety cases are a step in the right direction in regards to safety assurance. They make a serious attempt to explicate, and to provide some structure for, the inference licenses used in guaranteeing that a system is safe. On the other hand, a striking feature of the definition of a safety case just given is its logical vagueness. It is unclear what is to be taken as constituting a structured argument, i.e., what are its defining characteristics, and how is such a structured argument to be assessed in terms of the soundness of the reasoning it involves. We discuss these issues from a logical point of view.

3.1 Gentzen's Calculus of Natural Deduction

To provide some context for discussion, and to fix the terminology we will use in what follows, let us recall some basic facts about Gentzen's Calculus of Natural Deduction for Classical First Order Logic ($\mathcal{NK}$ for short; see [12–14]). In brief, with his $\mathcal{NK}$, Gentzen aimed at developing: "A formalism that reflects as accurately as possible the actual logical reasoning involved in mathematical proofs" (see [12, p. 291]). Gentzen offers as an example of this kind of reasoning:

"$(\exists x \forall y F x y) \supset (\forall y \exists x F x y)$. The argument runs as follows: Suppose there is an x such that for all y Fxy holds. Let a be such an x. Then for all y: Fay. Now let b be an arbitrary object. Then Fab holds. Thus there is an x, viz., a, such that Fxb holds. Since b was arbitrary, our result therefore holds for all objects, i.e., for all y there is an x, such that Fxy holds. This yields our assertion" (see [12, p. 292]).

Gentzen's program consists of the integration of the kind of mathematical proofs carried out in an exactly defined calculus: The $\mathcal{NK}$. Towards this end, Gentzen provides precise definitions of so-called symbols, expressions, and figures. Symbols are the alphabet of Classical First Order Logic (FOL for short). Expressions are the language of FOL, i.e., the set of all formulæ defined recursively over the alphabet of FOL. Figures are inference or proof figures. The former are written

$$\frac{\mathbf{A}_1, \ldots, \mathbf{A}_n}{\mathbf{B}}$$

where $\mathbf{A}_1, \ldots, \mathbf{A}_n, \mathbf{B}$ are formulæ. The formulæ $\mathbf{A}_1, \ldots, \mathbf{A}_n$ appearing in an inference figure such as the one given above are called upper formulæ and the formula $\mathbf{B}$ is called a lower formula. Regarding inference figures Gentzen explains: "We shall have inference figures and they will be stated for each calculus as they arise" (see [12, p. 291]). The permissible inference figures which make up the $\mathcal{NK}$ correspond to the well-known rules of introduction and elimination of the logical connectives of the alphabet of FOL and the law of the excluded middle (see [12, pp. 292–295]). Gentzen states these permissible inference figures via inference figure schemata, such as

$$\frac{\genfrac{}{}{0pt}{}{[\mathbf{A}]}{\mathbf{B}}}{\mathbf{A} \supset \mathbf{B}} \supset\!-I$$

An inference figure schemata is to be understood as: The permissible inference figure obtains from the inference figure schemata by instantiating the syntactical variables for formulæ by corresponding formulæ. Proof figures, also called derivations, consist of a number of formulæ which are combined to form inference figures such that: "Each formula is a lower formula of at most one inference figure; each formula (with the exception of exactly one: the *endformula*) is an upper formula of at least one inference figure; and the system of inference figures is non-circular, i.e., there is in the derivation no cycle (no series whose last member is again succeeded by its first member) of formulæ of which each upper formula of an inference figure has the lower formula as the next figure one in the series" (see [12, p. 291]). The following derivation illustrates the result of incorporating the mathematical proof given above in $\mathcal{NK}$.

$$\frac{[\exists x \forall y F x y]^2 \quad \dfrac{\dfrac{\dfrac{[\forall y F a y]^1}{F a b} \forall\!-E}{\exists x F x b} \exists\!-I}{\forall y \exists x F x y} \forall\!-I}{\dfrac{\dfrac{\forall y \exists x F x y}{(\exists x \forall y F x y) \supset (\forall y \exists x F x y)}}{} \substack{\exists\!-E_1 \\ \supset\!-I_2}}$$

(Numbering annotations above are used to identify instances of permissible inference figures and discharged assumptions.) Introducing some further terminology that we will use later on, Gentzen calls the formulæ of a derivation that are not lower formulæ of an inference figure, initial; the formulæ of a derivation, D-formulæ; the inference figures of a derivation, D-inferences; and a branch in a derivation, a series of D-formulae whose first formula is an initial one and whose last formula is the endformula, and of which each formula but the last is an upper formula of a D-inference figure whose lower formula is next in the branch.

3.2 Structured Arguments in Safety Cases

Why recall some basic facts about $\mathcal{NK}$? First, because, indirectly via the integration of mathematical proofs into $\mathcal{NK}$, Gentzen provides a precise definition of what is a mathematical proof, enabling an analysis of its scope and limits. Second, because we consider that the notion of a mathematical proof stands somewhat in analogy with that of a structured argument in a safety case: While the former aims at capturing the kind of reasoning involved in mathematics, the latter aims at capturing the kind of reasoning involved in safety assurance. Third, because we consider that the notion of a structured argument in a safety case should be given a definition akin to the one that Gentzen provides for the notion of a mathematical proof: Without such a definition it is impossible to judge whether a proposed structured argument in a safety case is indeed such. Fourth, because we consider that if logic, logical methods, and their history have taught us anything at all, it is that only through the provision of precise definitions and their analyses can we avoid fallacious reasoning steps: Two of the most important results about Gentzen's definition of a derivation are the Soundness and Completeness Theorems (see [14]).

As an aside in light of the previous paragraph, we offer some clarifications to avoid any subsequent confusion. We are not saying that the kind of reasoning involved in mathematics and the kind of reasoning involved in safety assurance are one and the same. There are most definitely some points of departure between the two, some of which we referred to above and will further make clear below. Moreover, we are not saying that without a definition of a structured argument in a safety case that stands on grounds analogous to Gentzen's definition of a derivation, safety reasoning is vacuous. Though with some reservations, even in the absence of such a definition of a structured argument in a safety case, we see no major reason preempting logical progress in safety reasoning. (After all, it is not as if mathematical reasoning was impaired before Gentzen's definition of derivation.) Lastly, we are not saying that the aforementioned definition of a structured argument in a safety case shall be given from the outset. This would be a clear impossibility given the current state of the art of safety reasoning. Instead, our remarks are oriented towards the formulation of a working definition of a structured argument in a safety case that is (i) suitable for capturing as accurately as possible the actual logical reasoning involved in safety assurance, and (ii) amenable for the logical analyses that are needed to establish the well-formedness and the soundness of the inference licenses to be used in safety assurance. It is our hope that by discussing and refining such a working definition we can establish a strong logical foundation on which to improve safety reasoning.

How to cope with the issues mentioned above? Similarly to Gentzen's aim of incorporating mathematical proofs into a well defined calculus, what we have in mind is the integration of structured arguments in safety cases, safety arguments for short, in an exactly defined calculus, which we refer to as $\mathcal{SK}$. We consider this integration provides the sought after definition of a safety argument. Thus, we make precise first the concept of a s-derivation. Reminiscent of Gentzen's derivations, s-derivations consist of a number of s-formulæ which are combined to form s-inference figures in a way such that: Each s-formula is a lower s-formula of at most one s-inference figure; each s-formula (with the exception of exactly one: the s-endformula) is an upper s-formula of at least one s-inference figure; and the system of s-inference figures is non-circular. We write a s-inference figure

$$\frac{\mathbf{A}_1, \ldots, \mathbf{A}_n}{\mathbf{B}} \ \langle \mathbf{R} \rangle$$

where $\mathbf{A}_1, \ldots, \mathbf{A}_n, \mathbf{B}, \mathbf{R}$ are s-formulæ. In a s-inference step figure the s-formula $\mathbf{R}$ is optional. Following Gentzen's terminology, for a s-inference figure such as the one given above, we call $\mathbf{A}_1, \ldots, \mathbf{A}_n$ upper s-formulæ and $\mathbf{B}$ lower s-formula. $\mathbf{R}$ occupies a special place in s-derivations. We will return to it later on. We call the s-formulæ participating in a s-derivation S-formulæ and the s-inference figures participating in a s-derivation S-inference figures. Moreover, we call the s-formulæ of a s-derivation that are not lower formulæ of a S-inference figure initial s-formulæ. By way of example, the figure below illustrates a s-derivation

$$\mathbf{I}_1 \frac{\dfrac{\mathbf{I}_2, \mathbf{I}_3}{\mathbf{S}_1} \ \langle \mathbf{R}_1 \rangle \qquad \mathbf{I}_4}{\mathbf{S}_3} \ \langle \mathbf{R}_3 \rangle \qquad \mathbf{I}_5 \frac{\mathbf{I}_6}{\mathbf{S}_2} \ \langle \mathbf{R}_2 \rangle$$

where $\mathbf{I}_i, \mathbf{S}_j, \mathbf{R}_k, \mathbf{E}$ are the S-formulæ of the s-derivation, $\mathbf{I}_i$ are its initial s-formulæ, $\mathbf{E}$ is its s-endformula, and

$$\frac{\mathbf{I}_2, \mathbf{I}_3}{\mathbf{S}_1} \ \langle \mathbf{R}_1 \rangle, \quad \frac{\mathbf{I}_6}{\mathbf{S}_2} \ \langle \mathbf{R}_2 \rangle, \quad \frac{\mathbf{S}_1, \mathbf{I}_4}{\mathbf{S}_3} \ \langle \mathbf{R}_3 \rangle, \quad \frac{\mathbf{I}_5, \mathbf{S}_2}{\mathbf{S}_4}, \quad \frac{\mathbf{I}_1, \mathbf{S}_3, \mathbf{S}_4}{\mathbf{E}} \ \langle \mathbf{R}_4 \rangle$$

are its S-inference figures. When there is no place for ambiguities, we write a s-derivation with initial s-formulæ $\mathbf{I}_1, \ldots, \mathbf{I}_n$ and s-endformula $\mathbf{E}$, $\mathbf{I}_1, \ldots, \mathbf{I}_n \ \mathscr{D} \ \mathbf{E}$. The definition of $\mathcal{SK}$ concludes with the definition of the language of s-formulæ and the formulation of the permitted s-inference figures via s-inference figure schemata. We envision the language of s-formulæ as the $\mathcal{SK}$ counterpart of the claims involved in safety arguments, safety claims for short, and the permitted s-inference figures as the $\mathcal{SK}$ counterpart of the inference licenses used in the formulation of safety arguments. Their precise formulation is, however, an open research question and part of what makes the definition of a safety argument, via its integration into an exactly defined calculus, a working definition.

3.3 Some Comments on the Logical Basis of Safety Arguments

A significant part of our working definition of a safety argument needs to be completed. We need to provide a formal definition of s-formulæ; we need to formulate the s-inference figure schemata for the permissible s-inference figures of $\mathcal{SK}$; and, more importantly, we need to integrate a basic stock of safety arguments into $\mathcal{SK}$. Three important reasons for use of 'Proto' in the main title. Nevertheless, even at this early stage, the initial definition of a s-derivation allows us to discuss technically certain important issues regarding safety reasoning.

Regarding s-Formulæ. To provide some context for discussion: It is noted by Gentzen in [12] that in the formalization of mathematics, to the concept of 'object', 'function', 'predicate', 'variable', 'proposition', and so on, there corresponds certain symbols or combinations thereof. What Gentzen then assumes implicitly is the translation of some ordinary language of mathematics into a formal language. In Gentzen's world, this formal language is that of FOL: The set of all formulæ defined in the standard recursive way over an alphabet of so-called logical and non-logical symbols; logical symbols are symbols for the logical operators of universal truth ($\top$), universal falsehood ($\bot$), conjunction ($\wedge$), disjunction ($\vee$), material implication ($\supset$), and the universal ($\forall$) and existential ($\exists$) quantifiers; non-logical symbols are symbols for variables, constants, predicates, and functions (with their corresponding arity). There is, in Gentzen's world, no danger in assuming the translation of statements in the ordinary language of mathematics into that of FOL. First, because, to a large extent, the language of FOL has been designed having in mind the ordinary language of mathematics. Second, because mathematical statements are rigorously precise and unambiguous. For instance, no one will doubt that to the ordinary statement of mathematics 'There is no natural number whose successor is zero' there corresponds the formula $\forall n S(n) \neq 0$ in the standardly defined way.

More generally, the faithfulness of the translation of an ordinary language, such as English, into a formal language, such as that of FOL, depends on a systematic understanding of the formal language and on the suitability of such a formal language for the problem at hand. Is there a formal language in which to provide a precise definition for a s-formula that caters for a faithful translation of safety claims formulated, say, in plain English? Keeping in mind that what we are after is the integration of safety arguments into a precisely defined calculus, this question is of great relevance. The answer, however, is nontrivial. First, because it is not at all clear how to faithfully translate logical connectives in an ordinary language, such as English, into a formal language. Second, because a quick perusal of some safety claims reveals a heavy use of modal logical connectives ('acceptably', 'sufficiently', 'adequately') in combination with quantifiers of a restricted nature ('All identified hazards'). It is well known in classical logical studies that modal logical connectives and logical quantifiers are not easily dealt with. Following from these observations, perhaps Carnap's distinction between the observable and the theoretical in the language of science (see [15, ch. 23]) provides a better foundation than classical logical languages for formally defining the concept of a s-formula. But this thesis needs of further investigation.

Why should we even bother in giving a formal definition of s-formulæ? First, because formal languages are often unambiguous, easier to provide a clear semantics for, and, ultimately, more amenable to analyses and tool support. Second, because the unrestricted use of an ordinary language, such as English, is likely to be prone to paradoxes of self-reference: 'This sentence has five words' or the more hideous 'This sentence is false'. Regarding problems of self-reference, we consider that a version of a problem of this kind is already present in safety claims. To explain this consideration, let us recall some basic facts of Hoare's

Calculus (see [16]). Hoare's Calculus is a formalism enabling us to prove deductively that a program is correct. There is, however, no expression of the formal language of Hoare's Calculus which captures the expression 'The program S is correct'. The formal language of Hoare's Calculus consists of triples $\{P\}$ S $\{Q\}$ capturing expressions of the form: 'If (the precondition) P is true before the initiation of (the program) S, then, (the postcondition) Q will be true upon the completion of S'. 'The program S is correct' is a statement which is formulated outside of Hoare's Calculus and that corresponds to the concept of a derivation which has the triple $\{P\}$ S $\{Q\}$ as an endformula inside the calculus. The formulation of the claim 'The program S is correct' inside Hoare's Calculus yields a calculus which can assert its own provability. This gives rise to all sorts of logical problems. Here is our observation: Though programs and systems are distinct entities, and so is correctness and safety and the kind of reasoning they involve, we consider that in the same way that the correctness of a program S is to be established with respect to a property Q about S under the proviso P, the safety of a system S is to be established with respect to a property $\mathbf{E}$ about S under certain provisos $\mathbf{I}_i$. A safety argument would then be in place to structure the inference licenses which would lead us from $\mathbf{I}_i$ to $\mathbf{E}$. This understood, a claim such as 'The system S is (acceptably/sufficiently/adequately) safe' is about the calculus for safety reasoning, our $\mathcal{SK}$, and, as such, it should not belong to the calculus itself. This is precisely the kind of problems we wish to avoid. Fallacious reasoning begins with the use of formulæ that are, from the point of view of the candidate calculus, already logically problematic.

In summary, we should exercise great care in the formulation of safety claims, and what they are about, to avoid the kind of problems mentioned above, or others of a similarly problematic logical nature. To being with, we may restrict the formulation of safety claims to fragments of ordinary languages, such as English, that are expressive enough to capture the safety claims we need, but that maintain a reasonable degree of logical tractability. In doing so, we may be able to provide a precise definition of the language of s-formulæ, and a corresponding formal semantics, which caters for a faithful translation of safety claims.

Regarding s-Inference Figures. The definition of a s-inference figure given in Sect. 3.2 provides a necessary level of technicality for putting in context an important topic present in notations in which to formulate safety arguments: The appeal to Toulmin's argument patterns (see [1]) in the formulation of a safety argument. We begin by setting up the context in which we discuss our ideas. One of the research questions posited by Toumin in [1] is: How should we lay an argument out, if we want to show the sources of its validity? In answering this question, Toulmin identifies the following elements: claim (C), data (D), warrant (W), qualifier (Q), rebuttal (R), and backing (B). Resorting to this basic stock of concepts, Toulmin lays out his famous argument pattern in the following "form"

$$
\text{D} \xrightarrow{\hspace{4cm}} \text{So}, \text{Q}, \text{C}
$$

On account of B — Since W   Unless R

As is explained in [17], Toulmin articulates his argument patterns in the context of justifying an assertion in response to a challenge. The challenge starts with the assertion of a claim (C), of which we may be asked: What have we got to go on? To which we would answer with the data (D). Following the acceptance of D, we may be asked: How do you get there? (How do we get from D to C?) Our answer to this second question would be the warrant (W). The warrant is, thus, what allows us to infer the claim from the data. Warrants may be qualified by modalities (Q) such as 'probably', 'generally', 'necessarily, or 'presumably'. If the warrant is defeasible, i.e., open to revision or annulment, then, we ought to state the conditions of rebuttal (R). Finally, we may be asked for a justification of the warrant itself. Our answer to this last question would be the backing (B).

It is easy to see that, though with some restrictions, our formulation of a s-inference figure borrows elements from Toulmin's argument patterns and articulates them in Gentzen's terminology. More precisely, incorporating the modalities (Q) into the logical connectives of the language of s-formulæ, an inference figure

$$\frac{\mathbf{A}_1, \dots, \mathbf{A}_n}{\mathbf{B}} \langle \mathbf{R} \rangle$$

may be viewed as standing in analogy with Toulmin's triple of claim (C), data (D), and rebuttal (R) in the obvious way, i.e., D stands in analogy with the upper s-formulæ $\mathbf{A}_1, \dots, \mathbf{A}_n$, C stands in analogy with the lower s-formula $\mathbf{B}$, and R stands in analogy with the s-formula $\mathbf{R}$; for the latter reason, we also call the s-formula $\mathbf{R}$ a rebuttal. Rebuttals occupy a special place in s-inference figures and we will return to them immediately below. Moreover, Toulmin's notion of a warrant may be viewed as standing in analogy with a s-inference figure scheme. (If viewed in this light, [17] provides some insight into what a proper formulation of a s-inference figure scheme may look like.) Lastly, Toulmin's notion of a backing may be viewed as standing in analogy with a soundness statement about a s-inference figure scheme. The restrictions that we refer to are linguistic and logical constraints on the kind of rebuttals allowed. To provide some context for discussion: According to Toulmin, rebuttals indicate circumstances in which the general authority of the warrant would have to be set aside (see [1, p. 94]). In this respect, there are, at least, two possible ways in which Toulmin's view of a rebuttal may be understood: (i) As indicating a set of circumstances in which the *claim* licensed by the warrant would have to be set aside; (ii) As indicating a set of circumstances in which the *warrant itself* would have to be set aside. The analogy between a warrant and a s-inference figure scheme allows for the following clarification: (i) Implies that an instance of the s-inference scheme cannot be used in a particular s-derivation; (ii) Implies that the s-inference scheme cannot be part of the s-inference figure schemata defining our proposed calculus, $\mathcal{SK}$. If understood in this sense, (i) speaks to the defeasible aspect of s-derivations, a point that we will return to later on, whereas (ii) results in a denial of the proposed calculus (the so-called paradoxes of deontic logic present examples of the second kind of rebuttals; see [18]). In defining rebuttals as s-formulæ, and under the proviso that the language for s-formulæ cannot refer to properties of the $\mathcal{SK}$, we preempt the formulation of rebutals of the second kind. In principle, such a restriction is not necessary and could be lifted. However, at this point, it presents a firmer basis on which to start building a calculus for safety reasoning.

The relation between Toulmin's argument patterns and s-inference figures places the work of Toulmin in the context of safety reasoning: Toulmin's argument patterns present an interesting framework in which to formulate what s-inference figures, or s-figure schemata, may look like. However, in and of themselves, Toulmin's argument patterns are not s-inference figures nor s-figure schemata. This means that Toulmin's argument patterns do not define, at least not obviously, a calculus for safety reasoning, our sought after $\mathcal{SK}$. Such a calculus, which we view as a fundamental tool for analyzing the logical well-formedness of safety arguments, is only defined by the provision and justification of a sensible set of s-inference figures via s-inference figure schemata. In other words, the appeal to Toumin's argument patterns in the context of safety reasoning is rather limited, it serves as a way of showing the sources of validity of a safety argument, but it does not propose a way of assessing the validity of said sources.

Regarding s-Derivations. The following two questions immediately arise: (i) Are s-derivations suitable for formalizing the kind of reasoning involved in safety assurance? (ii) Do they support the logical analyses needed to establish the well-formedness and soundness of the inference licenses used in said kind of reasoning?

Our answer to question (i) is, at this point, mostly an expression of desire. Evidently, we consider that s-derivations present a suitable framework for the formalization of safety arguments and the kind of reasoning involved in safety assurance. This view is partly justified by safety arguments expressed as GSN or CAE diagrams. However, whether this view is fully justified is certainly open for debate, in particular, because we have been unable to produce an example of the incorporation of a safety argument as a s-derivation. This inability is (a) partly due to our own limitations and to the logical rigour that we intend to put in place in the integration of a safety argument into a s-derivation, we refer back to our discussion on the definition of s-formulæ and s-inference figures, and to the upcoming discussion on s-derivations, and (b) partly due to the logical havoc reigning over the handful of examples of safety arguments that we have taken a close look at, a situation to reverse and that we expect to shed some light on.

Our answer to question (ii) is, even at this point, more satisfactory, in particular, in relation to the well-formedness of a s-derivation $\mathbf{I}_1, \ldots, \mathbf{I}_n \mathcal{D} \mathbf{E}$. More precisely, given a s-derivation $\mathbf{I}_1, \ldots, \mathbf{I}_n \mathcal{D} \mathbf{E}$, we call another s-derivation $\mathbf{I}_i, \ldots, \mathbf{I}_j \mathcal{D} \mathbf{R}$, for $\mathbf{I}_i, \ldots, \mathbf{I}_j$ a subset of $\mathbf{I}_1, \ldots, \mathbf{I}_n$ and $\mathbf{R}$ a rebuttal of one of the S-inference figures of $\mathbf{I}_1, \ldots, \mathbf{I}_n \mathcal{D} \mathbf{E}$, a rebutting s-derivation for $\mathbf{I}_1, \ldots, \mathbf{I}_n \mathcal{D} \mathbf{E}$. A s-derivation is internally coherent in the absence of a rebutting s-derivation for it. (Note that we are calling a s-derivation coherent in the absence of a rebutting s-derivation for it and not in the presence of a proof that such a rebutting s-derivation does not exist; the latter is far more difficult to establish.) It is obvious that s-derivations that are internally incoherent are logically ill-formed.

Moreover, the notion of internal coherence speaks to the defeasible aspects of a s-derivation, i.e., the conditions under which a s-derivation is open to revision or annulment. By way of example, consider the following two s-derivations

$$\dfrac{\dfrac{\mathbf{I}_1,\mathbf{I}_2}{\mathbf{S}_1}\ \langle\mathbf{R}_1\rangle \quad \mathbf{I}_3}{\mathbf{E}}\ \langle\mathbf{R}_2\rangle \qquad\qquad \dfrac{\mathbf{I}_1\ \dfrac{\mathbf{I}_3}{\mathbf{S}_2}\ \langle\mathbf{R}_3\rangle}{\mathbf{R}_2}$$

If taken on its own accord, $\mathbf{I}_1,\mathbf{I}_2,\mathbf{I}_3\ \mathscr{D}\ \mathbf{E}$ is coherent. However, $\mathbf{I}_1,\mathbf{I}_2,\mathbf{I}_3\ \mathscr{D}\ \mathbf{E}$ is incoherent when paired up with $\mathbf{I}_1,\mathbf{I}_3\ \mathscr{D}\ \mathbf{R}_2$ (for the reason that $\mathbf{I}_1,\mathbf{I}_3\ \mathscr{D}\ \mathbf{R}_2$ establishes the rebuttal of one of the S-inference figures of $\mathbf{I}_1,\mathbf{I}_2,\mathbf{I}_3\ \mathscr{D}\ \mathbf{E}$, i.e., the S-inference figure which has $\mathbf{R}_2$ as its rebuttal). In the latter scenario, the use of the S-inference figure of $\mathbf{I}_1,\mathbf{I}_2,\mathbf{I}_3\ \mathscr{D}\ \mathbf{E}$ which has $\mathbf{R}_2$ as its rebuttal condition is locally unsound in $\mathbf{I}_1,\mathbf{I}_2,\mathbf{I}_3\ \mathscr{D}\ \mathbf{E}$; "locally unsound" for there may be other situations in which the use of such an inference figure is perfectly permissible, e.g., situations in which there is no s-derivation with $\mathbf{R}_2$ as its s-endformula. This calls for a revision of $\mathbf{I}_1,\mathbf{I}_2,\mathbf{I}_3\ \mathscr{D}\ \mathbf{E}$ as a whole, possibly establishing its annulment. Why possibly and not necessarily? Because, even in the presence of $\mathbf{I}_1,\mathbf{I}_3\ \mathscr{D}\ \mathbf{R}_2$, we may still be able to "repair" $\mathbf{I}_1,\mathbf{I}_2,\mathbf{I}_3\ \mathscr{D}\ \mathbf{E}$ by resorting to a s-inference figure which does not have $\mathbf{R}_2$ as a rebuttal. The discussion on the internal coherence of a s-derivation is important, not only because it clearly sets apart safety reasoning from mathematical reasoning but also, because it has a bearing on compositional safety argumentation: The composition of internally coherent s-derivations to form a larger s-derivation (a composition reminiscent of Gentzen's use of the cut rule) may result in a s-derivation that is incoherent.

4   Illustrating Some of Our Points

We proceed to illustrate some of the points that we made above by elaborating on some basic elements of a safety argument intended to make a case that a warning light is lit under certain conditions. Our emphasis will be placed on laying out explicitly the underlying logical structure that such a safety argument may have.

For the safety argument under consideration, we list the following representative elements. Firstly, the safety claim that the safety argument makes a case for: (E) 'Under certain critical conditions, the warning light is lit'. The critical conditions that E refers to will play no role in our example; we will refer to them as C. Moreover, we will refer to the claim 'The warning light is lit' as W. Secondly, an explicit inference license: $(\mathbb{L})$ 'E follows from W being the case, assuming that C is the case'; since E is of a conditional nature ('Under ..., ...'), we consider an inference license involving a hypothetical reasoning step. Thirdly, and completing the safety argument under consideration, a sub-safety argument making a case for W being the case assuming that C is the case. We consider this sub-safety argument to be developed from properties of an action t (or a combination thereof) described in the design and the implementation of the system that turns on the warning light. These properties may be: (T) 'The execution of t lights the warning light', together with $(Done(t))$ 't is executed'.

We are now in a position to make explicit part of the logical structure of the safety argument under consideration via a s-derivation. To be noted first is that the language of s-formulæ will need to cater for the faithful translation of E (and consequently C and W), T (and consequently t), and $Done(t)$. Let us suppose that in the language of s-formulæ, E is denoted by a s-formula $\mathbf{C} \rightsquigarrow \mathbf{W}$ (provided that C is denoted by a s-formula $\mathbf{C}$, W is denoted by a s-formula $\mathbf{W}$, and $\rightsquigarrow$ captures the meaning of the logical operator corresponding to the conditional in E); T is denoted by a s-formula $\langle t \rangle \mathbf{W}$ (provided that t is denoted by t', and $\langle \cdot \rangle$ captures the meaning of the logical modality in T); and $Done(t)$ is denoted by $\mathsf{Done}(\mathsf{t})$. On this basis, we may formulate $\mathbb{L}$ as a s-inference figure

$$\frac{\begin{array}{c} [\mathbf{C}] \\ \mathbf{W} \end{array}}{\mathbf{C} \rightsquigarrow \mathbf{W}} \rightsquigarrow -I$$

(As usual, square brackets indicate discharged assumptions.) The complete safety argument under consideration may be incorporated into a s-derivation such as

$$\frac{\begin{array}{c} [\mathbf{C}]^1, \langle t \rangle \mathbf{W}, \mathsf{Done}(\mathsf{t}) \\ \mathcal{D} \\ \mathbf{W} \end{array}}{\mathbf{C} \rightsquigarrow \mathbf{W}} \rightsquigarrow -I_1$$

where $[\mathbf{C}], \langle t \rangle \mathbf{W}, \mathsf{Done}(\mathsf{t}) \, \mathcal{D} \, \mathbf{W}$ is the s-derivation corresponding to the sub-safety argument referred to above.

5 Discussion

There are some points worth noting about the difference in nature between the s-derivation that we presented in the previous section, $\langle t \rangle \mathbf{W}, \mathsf{Done}(\mathsf{t}) \, \mathcal{D} \, \mathbf{C} \rightsquigarrow \mathbf{W}$, and the formulation of a safety arguments typically presented, say, as GSN diagrams. Firstly, there is a clear distinction between the formulation of the safety claim E from which $\mathbf{C} \rightsquigarrow \mathbf{W}$ obtains and the commonly found formulation of safety claims that play the same role. E is a specific property of the system that turns on a warning light, the warning light being lit under certain conditions, and $\mathbf{C} \rightsquigarrow \mathbf{W}$ is a s-formula. The relation between E, and/or $\mathbf{C} \rightsquigarrow \mathbf{W}$, and 'The system is (acceptably/adequately/sufficiently) safe', where 'system' refers to the system that turns on the warning light, is one of design intent: Presumably, the warning light being lit under certain critical conditions issues a warning so that an agent can take whatever appropriate actions are necessary, serving in this way as a safety mechanism, thus contributing to whatever conception of safety the designer had in mind. Now, as commented on in Sect. 3.3, $\mathbf{C} \rightsquigarrow \mathbf{W}$ is internal to the calculus of safety argumentation (compare program correctness), our sought after $\mathcal{SK}$, whereas 'The system is safe' is about the calculus, i.e., it corresponds to a claim about what $\langle t \rangle \mathbf{W}, \mathsf{Done}(\mathsf{t}) \, \mathcal{D} \, \mathbf{C} \rightsquigarrow \mathbf{W}$ represents to the designer, i.e., there has to be an agreement that 'The system is safe' can be made on the basis of $\mathbf{C} \rightsquigarrow \mathbf{W}$ and the s-derivation. Secondly, there is a clear cut distinction between

E and $\mathbb{L}$. Again, E is a property of the system that turns on the warning light. Instead, $\mathbb{L}$ is a consequence conducive statement about E seen as a safety claim, i.e., as part of a safety argument, and the safety claims from which it follows. This distinction is of utmost importance for the logical analysis of the soundness of inference licenses and s-inference figures. There is one last distinction between inference licenses such as $\mathbb{L}$ and the kind of strategies present in GSN diagrams that is worth noting: GSN strategies have no concept analogous to that of discharging an assumption. Unless other measures are taken, this limitation severely restricts most forms of conditional reasoning in the kind of Gentzen-like logical calculi that we have considered here, making it too severe a restriction.

There are also some important elements worth noting about the formulation of $\langle t \rangle \mathbf{W}, \mathsf{Done}(t) \; \mathcal{D} \; \mathbf{C} \rightsquigarrow \mathbf{W}$, in particular, in relation to the standard formalization of the logical concepts it involves. Firstly: Are we to interpret $\rightsquigarrow$ as the symbol for material implication? Thought it is known that material implication does not cope well with ordinary understandings of conditional statements, if we were to answer the question in the negative, say by interpreting $\rightsquigarrow$ as relevant or strict implication, then, we need to provide clarification as to how the s-inference figure corresponding to the introduction of $\rightsquigarrow$ differs from $\supset - I$ (see [13]). Secondly, the standard interpretation of $\langle t \rangle \mathbf{W}$ reads as: There is a possible execution of t which results in $\mathbf{W}$ being the case. Such an interpretation of $\langle t \rangle \mathbf{W}$ is seemingly appropriate for capturing T, i.e., 'The execution of t lights the warning light'. After all, it is not difficult to envision scenarios where t may be executed and yet the warning light might not be lit, e.g., scenarios where not all things went according to plan. At the same time, the standard reading of $\langle t \rangle \mathbf{W}$ preempts us from concluding $\mathbf{W}$ from the assumption that $\mathsf{Done}(t)$ is the case, for we would have to ensure that the execution of t referred to by $\mathsf{Done}(t)$ is one which lead us to $\mathbf{W}$ being the case and no other – a nontrivial matter. This said, there may be a formulation of a s-derivation which allows us to conclude $\mathbf{W}$ from $\langle t \rangle \mathbf{W}$ and $\mathsf{Done}(t)$ via appropriate s-inference figure schemata which include "scenarios where not all things went according to plan" as rebuttals. In such a s-derivation, the s-endformula $\mathbf{W}$ will be open to revision and potential annulment if things do not go according to plan. Altogether, the scheme of things just discussed is not a matter of logical pedantry, but rather they are important issues, and the leading causes of fallacies in safety reasoning, that are being brought into the foreground by the use of appropriate logical machinery.

There is a final issue to discuss: The use of evidence in s-derivations as a way of grounding initial s-formulæ. To provide some context for discussion, let us first recall some basic facts about the role of initial formulæ in $\mathcal{NK}$. According to Gentzen, a distinguishing feature of $\mathcal{NK}$ is that derivations start from assumptions, some of which may subsequently be discharged, to which logical deductions are then applied (see [12, p. 292]). These initial assumptions are the initial formulæ of a derivation. An important thing to notice about Gentzen's treatment of initial formulæ is their assumptive nature; they are, in a sense, "true" in themselves, given *deus ex machina*, and, as such, are accepted as the basis on which the derivation is built. In contrast, in safety reasoning, it is typically proposed that the safety claims from which a safety argument is built need to be provided with a rationale which justifies their postulation. This means that the initial s-formulæ in s-derivations lack the assumptive nature enjoyed by Gentzen's view of initial formulæ in derivations. Providing a rationale for justifying the postulation of a safety claim is reminiscent of the notion of justified belief in studies in epistemology or scientific explanation. It is at this point where evidence makes an appearance. Bringing in the concept of evidence in safety reasoning is a topic for research in its own right. In this respect, without elaborating at length, we cannot do more than offer some pointers to some of the literature which we consider provides a proper context for discussing the use of evidence in safety cases, and some of the challenges that this use presents (see classic texts such as [15,19], or more recent works such as [20–22]).

6   Conclusions

The present practice of safety cases, recorded in some notation, is the result of over 25 years of work. The object-oriented (OO) community and the Unified Modeling Language (UML) underwent a similar situation over a similar period. In both cases it has been pointed out that simply providing a loose syntax is not enough. Engineering disciplines rely on scientific theories and mathematics to enable precision in design and analyses to support sound design decisions. This was acknowledged by the OO comunity, who started incorporating mathematical precision into its notations some years ago, not without its hurdles and sometimes against the protests of the notation's inventors! The safety case community is slowly awakening to this; pushed by a need for proper engineering guarantees about safety, especially due to the increasing complexity of safety critical systems, and by the recognition that relying on the informal understanding and intuition of individuals, no matter how experienced, is not only unscientific, but a historic invitation to disaster.

In this paper, we have tried to take the first steps towards developing a proper scientific and logical basis for safety case understanding and construction: A working definition of a safety case via its incorporation in a precisely defined calculus. We start from two pillars. The first pillar, in line with other researchers in the area (see [23]), is the observation that assurance case reasoning is more akin to the argument based reasoning ideas of Toulmin than to the conventional deductive logic reasoning well known to mathematicians and software engineers (or computer scientists). This form of reasoning is already (more or less) well known in domains such as legal reasoning and scientific reasoning/explanation. The second pillar is Gentzen's program for formalizing mathematical reasoning in terms of a logical language, inference rules to support reasoning steps, and proofs to capture the "informal" notion of argument used by mathematicians. One can debate about the adequacy of Gentzen's formalization, but if one accepts it, and most mathematicians have, then one can make remarkable progress in analyzing mathematical reasoning, including developing automated tools such as theorem provers and model checkers. Though safety reasoning is very different in character from mathematical reasoning, we can use an analogous approach to that of Gentzen; in particular, we can focus on the same ingredients, i.e., a formalized logical language for expressing safety claims, a well defined notion of inference step (perhaps one based on Toulmin's idea of an argument step), a well defined notion of derivation (capturing the notion of safety argument), and a new ingredient, grounded proofs, i.e., the idea that all initial formulæ in a derivation cannot be taken for granted, i.e., gaining a proper understanding of the notion of evidence. We hope to have taken some steps in this direction.

References

1. Toulmin, S.: The Uses of Argument. Cambridge University Press, Cambridge (2003)
2. The GSN Working Group: Goal Structuring Notation. Version 1, November 2011
3. Adelard: Claim, Argument, Evidence Notation. Accessed 25 Jan 2016
4. Pólya, G.: How to Solve It, 2nd edn. Princeton University Press, Princeton (2004)
5. van Lamsweerde, A.: Requirements Engineering: From System Goals to UML Models to Software Specifications. Wiley, Hoboken (2009)
6. Rushby, J.: Logic and epistemology in safety cases. In: Bitsch, F., Guiochet, J., Kaâniche, M. (eds.) SAFECOMP 2013. LNCS, vol. 8153, pp. 1–7. Springer, Heidelberg (2013). doi:10.1007/978-3-642-40793-2_1
7. Bochman, A.: Non-monotonic reasoning. In: Gabbay, D., Woods, J. (eds.) Handbook of the History of Logic: The Many Valued and Nonmonotonic Turn in Logic, vol. 8, pp. 555–632. North-Holland, Amsterdam (2007)
8. Goodenough, J., Weinstock, C., Klein, A.: Eliminative induction: a basis for arguing system confidence. In: 35th International Conference on Software Engineering (ICSE 2013), pp. 1161–1164 (2013)
9. Bloomfield, R., Littlewood, B.: Multi-legged arguments: the impact of diversity upon confidence in dependability arguments. In: International Conference on Dependable Systems and Networks (DSN 2003), pp. 25–34 (2003)
10. Vincenti, W.: What Engineers Know and How They Know It: Analytical Studies from Aeronautical History. Johns Hopkins University Press, Baltimore (1993)
11. UK Ministry of Defense: Defence standard 00–56 issue 4: safety management requirements for defence systems (2007)
12. Gentzen, G.: Investigations into logical deduction. Am. Philos. Q. **1**(4), 288–306 (1964)
13. Prawitz, D.: Natural Deduction: A Proof-theoretical Study. AWE (1965)
14. van Dalen, D.: Logic and Structure, 5th edn. Springer, Heidelberg (2013)
15. Carnap, R.: An Introduction to the Philosophy of Science, 5th edn. Dover, Mineola (1966)
16. Hoare, C.: An axiomatic basis for computer programming. Commun. ACM **12**(10), 576–580 (1969)
17. Hitchcock, D.: Toulmin's warrants. In: van Eemeren, F., et al. (eds.) Anyone Who Has a View: Theoretical Contributions to the Study of Argumentation, vol. 8, pp. 69–82. Springer, Heidelberg (2003)
18. Åqvist, L.: Deontic logic. In: Gabbay, D., Guenthner, F. (eds.) Handbook of Philosophical Logic, vol. 8, 2nd edn, pp. 1–12. Springer, Heidelberg (2002)
19. Hempel, C.: Philosophy of Natural Science. Prentice Hall, Upper Saddle River (1966)

20. Achinstein, P.: The Book of Evidence. Oxford University Press, Oxford (2001)
21. Haack, S.: Evidence Matters: Science, Proof, and Truth in the Law. Cambridge University Press, Cambridge (2014)
22. Mayo, D., Spanos, A.: Error and Inference: Recent Exchanges on Experimental Reasoning, Reliability, and the Objectivity and Rationality of Science. Oxford University Press, Oxford (2010)
23. McDermid, J.: Safety arguments, software and system reliability. In: 2nd International Symposium on Software Reliability Engineering (ISSRE 1991), pp. 43–50 (1991)

Promotion of Formal Approaches in Japanese Software Industry and a Best Practice of FeliCa's Case (Extended Abstract)

Keijiro Araki[1](✉) and Taro Kurita[2]

[1] Kyushu University, 744 Motooka, Nishi-ku, Fukuoka 819-0395, Japan
araki@ait.kyushu-u.ac.jp
[2] Sony Corporation, 2-10-1 Osaki, Shinagawa-ku, Tokyo 141-8610, Japan

Abstract. We have been making much effort to promote formal methods in Japan, especially Japanese IT companies. This paper describes our activities in Japan for almost twenty years, and shows typical reactions from such Japanese companies for application of formal methods. We mention about the obstacles they think to adopting formal methods in their real software development projects. On the other hand we also present a case of FeliCa Networks, Inc. as a best practice of applying formal methods in Japan. We discuss the lessons learned from our efforts of promoting formal methods and the FeliCa's case. Finally, we briefly introduce our research project to support software developers in adopting formal approaches to real projects.

Keywords: Formal methods · Rigorous specification · Practice · Development process · FeliCa IC chip · VDM · VDMPad · ViennaTalk

1 Introduction

We promote formal methods in Japan, and reported the status of formal methods in Japan. [1,2] Many Japanese companies are interested in formal methods in development of software systems. Some companies introduce and apply formal approaches successfully in their own development processes. However, there are not so many companies apply formal methods in their real development projects.

In this paper, we report our activities to promote formal methods in Japan, and briefly introduce our current research project.

2 Promotion of Formal Methods in Japan

2.1 Seminars and Publications

We have a variety of activities to promote formal mthods under the collaboration with several kinds of organization such as SIG-FM of SEA (Software Engineers Association of Japan), IPA (Information-technology Promotion Agency,

© Springer International Publishing AG 2016
K. Ogata et al. (Eds.): ICFEM 2016, LNCS 10009, pp. 18–25, 2016.
DOI: 10.1007/978-3-319-47846-3_2

Japan)/SEC (Software Engineering Center/Software Reliability Enhancement Center), local public communities, private companies, universities, and so on. For example, we have had a series of seminars at Hiroshima, Kumamoto, Sapporo, Nagoya, Osaka, Tokyo, Okinawa, Ho Chi Minh City, Fukuoka, Nagano, Morioka, etc. We also made teaching materials for those seminars, and make them open on the IPA/SEC site. We published several reports on formal methods. Especially the report on successful cases of formal approaches to software development [6] focuses on eleven cases and presents many suggestions for applying formal methods in real systems.

2.2   Reactions from Japanese Companies

Many company people attend our seminars and become interested in formal methods. Especially the successful cases in Japan are quite attractive to them, and they want to know much in details about those cases. They also require to know more cases which may fit for their own projects. We survey such cases, and then they require much more. However, most of the companies will not adopt formal methods in their own projects.

The following is seven typical reactions from the Japanese companies:

- Real successful cases are interesting and attractive.
- Formal methods exist in the perfect formal world which seems unrelated to their everyday activities.
- Formal methods require highly trained mathematicians.
- Formal methods look difficult for them to apply by themselves.
- They need complete samples for their own problems.
- It is difficult to convince the top management of the benefits of formal methods.
- The cost-performance and effectiveness of formal methods are unknown.

Many of the above seem just excuse not to adopt formal methods.

3   A Best Practice of Formal Approach in Japan

Yes, we have applications of formal methods in Japan. Some of them adopt formal approaches to development of their final products. Some have continuous effort to learn formal methods with their own training courses and trials to apply formal methods to their projects.

We learn much about the practice of formal methods through the exchanges and collaborations with them. Especially, A best practice of formal approach to software development in Japan is the FeliCa's case to develop smart IC chips. [7,8] Fig. 1 shows the development process of FeliCa IC chip firmware with the formal specification in VDM++.

They only describe the specification in VDM++, and did not perform any formal proof nor code generation. The rigorous system description in VDM++ has good effects on the whole development process, and then they realized extremely high reliable products. No bug has appeared among more than 300 million chips which are used in a very wide variety of applications.

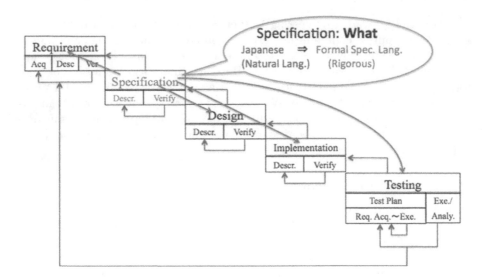

Fig. 1. VDM specification in the development process at FeliCa.

4   Formal Methods for Working Engineers

We aim to propose formal approaches applicable and effective in the real software development projects. We focus on the way how to incorporate formal development methodologies into the development process of each specific project in an IT company. We propose a development process for a specific purpose as a reference model. [9,10] We recommend the developers to customize our reference process model for their own project.

Figure 2 shows the overview of our current research project to propose formal approaches effective over the whole software life cycle. There exist many theories, methodologies, tools in formal methods. We believe each of them is applicable and effective for a specific purpose at some phase(s) in the software life cycle.

We have developed several tools to support construct rigorous descriptions for the target systems. Here we briefly introduce the following three tools:

- VDMPad: Interactive VDM-SL Tool
- ViennaTalk: IDE for Lightweight Formal Approach
- JOD: Dictional Tool Bridging Informal documents and Formal Documents

4.1   VDMPad

VDMPad is an interactive VDM-SL tool. [11] Fig. 3 shows a screen shot of VDM-Pad. A user writes a VDM-SL description in the top window. VDMPad performs the syntax and type checking for the VDM-SL description. If the state invariants are included in the description, VDMPad also check the invariants. In the second window, the user can write an expression to be evaluated by the VDMPad. And

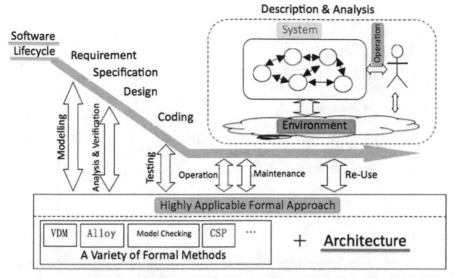

Formal Approach Effective at Each Stage in Software Lifecycle

Fig. 2. Overview of our research project.

then the result of the evaluation appears in the third window. If any error is detected, the message is output beneath the bottom line.

VDMPad is very useful to write VDM-SL description with a simple and interactive user interface. For beginners of VDM specification, VDMPad is easy to use and understand how to write VDM-SL specifications. It is also a nice tool for matured specifiers to describe components in VDM-SL and validate them with testing at the specification level.

The VDMPad service is available on the VDMPad Server [14].

4.2 ViennaTalk

ViennaTalk is an IDE (Integrated Development Environment) for lightweight formal approach which is a SmallTalk library to handle VDM-SL specifications. [12,15] Major components of ViennaTalk is as follows:

- VDMBrowser - A VDM-SL browser inspired by Smalltalk's class browsers and inspectors
- VDMPad - A lightweight web IDE for VDM-SL with animation and diagram presentation of data
- VDMC - A Smalltalk wrapper of VDM-SL animation
- Lively Walk-Through - A UI prototyping environment to animate UI prototype by VDM-SL specification
- Webly Walk-Through - A Web API server to publish VDM-SL specifications of web APIs.

Fig. 3. VDMPad: interactive VDM-SL tool.

- ViennaEngine - Animation engine wrapper
    - ViennaVDMJ - Animation engine by local VDMJ process
    - ViennaServer - Web server to publish animation engines
    - ViennaClient - Client module of ViennaServer/VDMPad
    - ViennaBankEngine - Aggregated animation engine
- ViennaTalk-Types - Smalltalk classes for VDM types
- ViennaTalk-Values - Smalltalk objects for VDM values
- ViennaTalk-Parsers - VDM parsers, Smalltalk code generators and VDM source formatter.

At brain storming and reviewing stages in a system development process, Informal descriptions like hand-drawn diagrams are often used. Those informal

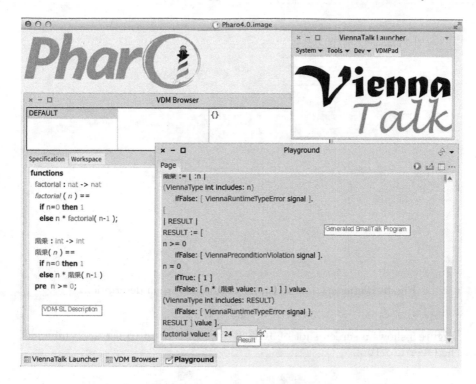

Fig. 4. ViennaTalk: IDE for lightweight formal approach.

description can be justified with VDM-SL easily on ViennaTalk. Lively Walk-Through and Webly Walk-Through support such work, and help the developers to clarify and share the ideas. The interactive animation of VDMPad also helps the validation of the ideas.

It can also generate a SmallTalk program from a VDM-SL description. The SmallTalk program is useful to test and validate the VDM specification with much wider data space. It also serves as a prototype of the specified system.

Figure 4 shows a screen shot of ViennaTalk. The left window shows a VDM-SL specification. The right window show the generated SmallTalk program for the VDM-SL specification. The small window with the value 24 is the result of the invocation of the SmallTalk program "factorial" with the parameter 4.

4.3   JOD Tool

The third tool is JOD, Dictionary Tool to Support Rigorous System Description. [13] It accepts informal documents written in a natural language, and manipulates the documents and provides useful information to clarify the system structures and functions. It bridges between informal documents and rigorous descriptions written in VDM-SL and VDL++.

Fig. 5. Dictionary tool to support rigorous system description.

Figure 5 shows a screen shot of JOD. This tool is open to use and embedded in the Overture Tool.

5   Concluding Remarks

We have promoted formal methods in Japan, and provided seminars, tutorial lectures, teaching materials, reports and support tools. We always cite the well-known "Seven Myths of Formal Methods" [5] and "Ten Commandments of Formal Methods." [3] We find many suggestions and insights to introduce and adopt formal methods in real system development processes. In the seminars and lectures, we tell those suggestions and insights with our own experiences and thinkings.

We found one more attractive concept "Preformal" [4] and regard it as a good guiding principle in formal approaches to system development. It is not easy for the beginners to construct formal description in their system development project. They need to understand the essential properties of formal methods as well as their own project. They also need to realize what are their purpose to apply formal methods. And then they may decide which formal method and how to apply to their project.

We intend to propose the purpose-oriented preformal approaches to construct rigorous/formal system description. We are sure that our tools described above work well along the preformal approaches.

Finally, we state messages to the Japanese IT companies.

- Know thyself.
- Heaven helps those who help themselves.

These are very common teachings. We will continue to promote formal methods in Japan and support IT engineers and users keeping the above commandments and teachings in mind.

Acknowledgments. This work is partly supported by Grant-in-Aid for Scientific Research (S) 2422001.

References

1. Araki, K.: Are formal methods relevant?: how to explode the seven myths in Japan. In: Proceedings of the APSEC 1995, pp. 514–515 (1995)
2. Araki, K., Chang, H.-M.: Formal methods in Japan: current state, problems and challenges. In: Proceedings of the Third VDM Workshop, VDM 2002 (2002)
3. Bowen, J.P., Hinchey, M.G.: Ten commandments of formal methods. IEEE Comput. **28**(4), 56–63 (1995)
4. Gmehlich, R., Jones, C.: Experience of deployment in the automotive industry. In: Romanovsky, A., Thomas, M. (eds.) Industrial Deployment of System Engineering Methods, pp. 13–26. Springer, Heidelberg (2013)
5. Hall, A.: Seven myths of formal methods. IEEE Softw. **7**(5), 11–19 (1990)
6. IPA/SEC: Report on Successful Cases of Formal Approaches with Rigorous Specification, WG on Rigorous Specification, IPA/SEC, Tokyo (2013) (in Japanese). http://sec.ipa.go.jp/reports/20130125.html
7. Kurita, T., Nakatsugawa, Y.: The application of VDM to the industrial development of firmware for a smart card IC chip. Int. J. Softw. Inf. **3**(2–3), 343–355 (2009)
8. Kurita, T., Ishikawa, F., Araki, K.: Practices for formal models as documents: evolution of VDM application to "Mobile FeliCa" IC chip firmware. In: Bjørner, N., Boer, F. (eds.) FM 2015. LNCS, vol. 9109, pp. 593–596. Springer, Heidelberg (2015)
9. Kusakabe, S., Lin, H.-H., Omori, Y., Araki, K.: Developing core software requirements of energy management system forsmart campus with advanced software engineering. Int. J. New Comput. Archit. Appl. **4**(1), 48–55 (2014)
10. Kusakabe, S., Lin, H.-H., Omori, Y., Araki, K.: Visualizing centrality of process area networks in CMMI-DEV. In: Proceedings of International Conference on Software and Systems Process (ICSSP 2015), pp. 173–174 (2015)
11. Oda, T., Araki, K., Larsen, P.G.: VDMPad: a lightweight IDE for exploratory VDM-SL specification. In: Proceedings of the 2015 IEEE/ACM 3rd FME Workshop on Formal Methods in Software Engineering, pp. 33–39 (2015)
12. Oda, T., Araki, K., Larsen, P.G.: ViennaTalk and assertch: building lightweight formal methods environments on pharo 4. In: Proceedings of the International Workshop on Smalltalk Technologies (2016, to appear)
13. Omori, Y., Araki, K., Larsen, P.G.: JODTool on the Overture Tool to manage formal requirement dictionaries. In: Proceedings of the 13th Overture Workshop, Co-located with FM 2015, pp. 3–17 (2015)
14. VDMPad Server: http://vdmpad.csce.kyushu-u.ac.jp/
15. ViennaTalk: https://github.com/tomooda/ViennaTalk-doc

Automated Requirements Validation for ATP Software via Specification Review and Testing

Weikai Miao[1](✉), Geguang Pu[1], Yinbo Yao[1], Ting Su[1],
Danzhu Bao[1], Yang Liu[1], Shuohao Chen[2], and Kunpeng Xiong[2]

[1] Shanghai Key Lab for Trustworthy Computing,
School of Computer Science and Software Engineering,
East China Normal University, No. 3663 North Zhongshan Rd, Shanghai, China
wkmiao@sei.ecnu.edu.cn
[2] Testing Departement, Casco Signal Ltd., Mingde International Plaza,
No. 158 Minde Road, Shanghai, China

Abstract. Complete and correct requirements specification is the foundation for developing high-quality Automatic Train Protection (ATP) software. Requirements validation aims at facilitating the completeness and correctness of the specification. In this paper, we propose a novel requirements validation approach combining diagram-guided specification review and scenario-based specification testing for ATP software. The specification is transformed into an executable prototype. Diagrams are generated from the prototype to visualize the interactions between variables for an effective review. To check whether the specification conforms to the user's concerned scenarios of train operation, the scenarios are specified as test cases for testing the prototype. The conformance is then determined via test analysis. Through the review and the testing, the requirements specification is validated. The case study and experiments show that the approach achieves a higher error detection rate and while it reduces the time costs comparing to the traditional review method used by our industrial partner.

1 Introduction

ATP (Automatic Train Protection) software is one of the kernel components of railway transportation system, which performs safety-critical functionalities of a train. The validation of the ATP software requirements must be considered for ensuring the quality of the ultimate software systems, since the requirements specification act as the foundation of the ATP software development.

Requirements validation focuses on checking the completeness and correctness of the requirements specification [1–3]. That is, the requirements specification needs to cover the user's expected functions as complete as possible. Potential scenarios of the target system should be satisfied by the specification. Meanwhile, the requirements specification should not contain logic errors (e.g., inconsistency). Research efforts have been devoted to the requirements validation from both the academic and the industrial communities, including specification review/inspection [4–7], specification testing [18–20] and animation [13, 17]. However, effective requirements validation for the industrial ATP software practitioners is still a challenge.

© Springer International Publishing AG 2016
K. Ogata et al. (Eds.): ICFEM 2016, LNCS 10009, pp. 26–40, 2016.
DOI: 10.1007/978-3-319-47846-3_3

One major problem is how to validate whether the user's (e.g., the train driver) concerned safety-critical scenarios (e.g., accelerate and then run at a designated velocity) of the train operation are completely and correctly satisfied by the requirements specification. Usually there is a gap between the concerned scenarios and the requirements specification. The specification is established by the requirements analyst and the ATP domain expert, which describes the ATP software from the functional perspective in terms of individual functions. However, such a specification does not explicitly specify the scenarios of running a train in the real world. The practitioner demands effective methods for validating whether the user's concerned scenarios can be satisfied by the specification.

In this paper, we propose a scenario-based specification testing approach to requirements validation of ATP software. The ATP analyst constructs the requirements document using a particular modeling language. To facilitate the automation of requirements validation, the specification is transformed into an equivalent executable ATP prototype. Since ATP software is a large-scale system that involves complex interactions among variables, directly reviewing the specification or the code of the prototype is tedious and error-prone. To tackle this problem, we provide an intuitive diagram-guided specification review technique. The variable dependency diagrams and the state transition diagrams are derived from the prototype. Potential errors of variable interactions are detected via the diagram-guided review. To validate whether the specification satisfies the user's concerned scenarios, we adopt the idea of "model-based testing". Specifically, concerned scenarios of train operations are defined in the scenario document using a designated scenario notation. Then the scenario document is transformed into an executable test script for running the prototype. The satisfaction of the prototype with respect to the scenarios can be evaluated via analyzing the test results. Through the static review and the dynamic testing, the requirements specification is rigorously validated.

To support the automation of the approach, we have developed a supporting tool for applying this approach in practice. We have also carried out a systematic case study for validating the efficacy of the approach in a real ATP software development project of our industrial partner, the CASCO Signal Ltd. of China. The feedback provided by the practitioner and the experimental results demonstrate that the approach can improve the efficacy of the requirements validation and lead to higher productivity of the ATP software development.

The rest of the paper is organized as follows. Section 2 overviews the state-of-art in the area of requirements validation. Section 3 presents the technical details of the approach. In Sect. 4, we present the case study and experiments for demonstrating the efficacy of the approach in real ATP software development. Section 5 summarizes the paper and points out our future research plans.

2 Related Work

Specification review is a classic technique for requirements validation, especially in the industry. To validate whether requirements specification really satisfies the given requirements, the authors of work [7] propose an approach based on the notion of querying a model, which is built from the requirements specification. Then scenario questions are raised and the results are analyzed for validating whether the derived model's behavior satisfies the given requirements. This work inherits the advantages of the review/inspection process. In the work [5], a mental model is introduced as the foundation for requirements validation. The requirements are aligned with the model and be reviews following certain criteria. A specification review approach based on virtual prototype is proposed in the work [22]. Specification in natural language is transformed into virtual prototype for structural and functional review. In practice, however, when the specification is in large-scale and the logics is complex, directly reviewing or inspecting textual requirements specification may be difficult. The efficacy, to a large extent, relies on the practitioner's experience. To facilitate the specification review, our approach recommends a diagram-based review strategy.

Animation of specification is also used for requirements validation. Specification animation is usually done through model checking and specification execution. ProB is a validation toolset for B formal specification that animates counter-examples by displaying its state transition paths [11, 12]. UPPAAL also animates dynamic behaviors of the target system by model checking [13, 14]. It allows system modeling with states and transitions and explores the state space automatically. In [15], the authors propose an approach to animating tabular specification. In [17], an animation-based inspection approach is proposed where animation is used to guide the inspection process. By demonstrating the relationship between input and output of the selected functional scenarios, the efficiency of the inspection activity can be improved. In fact, the effectiveness of animation relies on the understanding of the intended functions by human.

Specification testing is a promising technique for requirements validation. VDMTools is developed to support the analysis of VDM specifications [16]. It is able to execute a large subset of VDM notations. With test cases generated by certain criteria, VDMTools will show system behaviors by executing the concerned specifications. In [18], the authors propose a tool suite for testing software design specifications using dynamic slicing technology. In [19], the authors use testing modules to test formal specifications. The testing modules are described in the same formalism as the formal specification and can be automatically generated. Liu proposes a specification testing method for reviewing task trees of the target formal specifications [20]. It includes different strategies for generating test cases for different kinds of review task trees. Our approach differs from them in the way of test case generation and the automated test result analysis. The test cases in our approach are generated from dedicated scenarios. The scenario also acts as the foundation of the test oracle of specification testing.

Some researches adopt the formal methods for requirement validation. In the work [8, 9], the authors present the VDM++ specification validation of ATP software. [10] introduces a specification verification technique based on the SCADE platform. However, these approaches require that the practitioner construct the proof obligations using complex mathematics notations. Although in recent years formal methods have been reorganized by the industrial practitioners, exploiting these formal techniques including formal modeling and verification in industry is still challenging. In particular, how the formal methods can benefit traditional industrial software engineering activities such as specification review and inspection is still a problem. In our approach, we try to support the traditional specification review and testing using the formal specification written in a light-weight formal language for the ATP software. In this way, the precision of formal methods can help the requirements validation without change the practitioner's engineering processes radically.

3   The Approach

3.1   Main Framework of the Approach

Before a detailed illustration of the techniques involved in the approach, we first introduce the framework of the approach, which is described in Fig. 1.

In our approach, requirements are documented using the CASDL (Casco Accurate Description Language) language developed for ATP software modeling. The CASDL is a light-weight formal language for specifying the functions of an ATP system. In the textual specification, each function is specified in terms of the relations between the input and the output variables. In addition, there are some descriptions written in natural language in the specification.

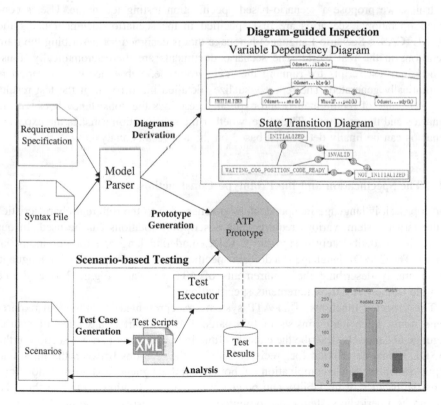

Fig. 1. Framework of the requirements validation approach

Requirements validation is performed via the stages of specification review and testing. To facilitate the automation of requirements validation, the specification needs to be processed into an executable model by removing the natural language comments for effective diagram generation and testing. To this end, we first transform the requirements specification into an equivalent executable model. Firstly, the analyst defines the syntax file for the specification language. Since the specification is basically written using the CASDL, the syntax file here defines the CASDL syntax. The syntax file and the requirements specification are accepted by a dedicated Model Parser. The parser can generate an executable CASDL requirement model, i.e., the prototype of the ultimate ATP software through analyzing the syntax file and the specification.

To facilitate a more effective specification review, we provide a diagram-guided review technique for specification validation. Two diagrams, variable dependency diagram (VDD) and state transition diagram (STD), are generated from the prototype to precisely visualize the interactions among variables and state transitions of individual variables, respectively. Through reviewing the VDDs, the analyst determines whether the relations among the involved variables conform to the expectations. Similarly, whether the state transitions of each concerned variable are correct can be checked via reviewing the STDs.

Specification review only checks the defined requirements statically. To validate whether the requirements specification satisfies the concerned operational scenarios of the trains, we propose a scenario-based specification testing technique. User's concerned operational scenarios are first specified in the scenario document using the CASSL (CASco Scenario Language) language that is designed for describing the train operations in the real world. The scenario documents are then automatically transformed into test scripts for running the ATP prototype. Subsequently, test report is automatically generated. The report visualizes detailed information of the test results (e.g., coverage of requirements) and explicitly describes the consistency between the scenarios and the prototype. Therefore, whether the specification satisfies the expected scenarios can be finally determined based on the test results analysis.

3.2   The Specification and the Prototype Construction

Our approach is language independent. In practice, due to the different characteristics of the target system, various requirements description notations can be used. In our approach, we deliberately design the CASDL modeling language for our industrial partner. The CASDL language is a domain specific requirements specification language for accurately describing the requirements of ATP software. Figure 2 is a simple example of the CASDL requirements specification.

The expected functions of an ATP system are represented by individual requirements items. Each item consists of two parts. The first part is a section of natural language to concisely describe the expected functions. The other part is a section of the CASDL formal description for precisely defining the relations between the input and output variables. Such combination of both natural language and formal notations keeps the balance of readability and precision of the specification. Note that the ATP software is a periodic system (i.e., computation tasks are driven according to the time

```
[iTC_CC_ATP-SwRS-0176]
//If OdometerState is NOT_INITIALIZED at period k, and if wheel stops at k,
then WheelMaximumMovement shall be set to zero.*/

if (OdometerState == NOT_INITIALIZED)
    if (WheelFilteredStopped(k) == True))
        WheelMaximumMovement = 0
    else:
        ...
if ((OdometerState(k-1) = NOT_INITIALIZED)
    and (not WheelFilteredStopped(k) and not UnconsistentSensorTest(k))
    and (WheelFilteredStopped(k-1))
    OdometerState = WAITING_COG_POSITION_CODE_READY
    ...
if ((OdometerState(k-1) = NOT_INITIALIZED) and UnconsistentSensorTest(k))
    OdometerState = INVALID
```

Fig. 2. The sample CASDL specification

period). In Fig. 2, the parameter k explicitly specifies the time period. The ATP software just runs in a sequential non-terminating execution cycle when the power is on. This specification describes the functionalities of the odometer monitoring component of the ATP software. The function is responsible for monitoring the speed of the train and the distance the train has passed. The odometer can switch between certain states. The state transitions of the variable *OdometerState* is regarded as a function in the specification. For instance, it can change from uninitialized state (i.e., *NOT INITIALIZED*) to the state that the meter is disabled or idled (i.e., *INVALID*). In this example, these functionalities are defined in terms of if-else control blocks.

Since the ATP software is a typical large-scale control system, the requirements validation should be automated. To this end, the textual requirements specification is transformed into an executable prototype for automated analysis and specification testing. The transformation focuses on removing all the natural language descriptions; meanwhile, the syntax errors in the specification are detected. We have implemented a Model Parser that uses the ANTLR tool [21] as the foundation for the transformation. Aided by the ANTRL (Another Tool for Language Recognition) tool, the parser can generate an executable CASDL requirement model. Given a language and its syntax, ANTLR can build the ASTs (Abstract Syntax Tree) for analyzing the target language. Our parser derives the prototype through analyzing the ASTs of the CASDL specification.

When the specification is processed, syntax errors of the CASDL specification can be detected. In particular, the circular dependency errors of variables can be automatically detected. Circular dependency error of variables is a typical logical error in ATP software, which refers to the situation that the relations among certain variables constitute a cycle. For instance, the value of variable A relies on the value of variable B. B relies on the value of variable C and C relies on the value of A. In this case, the variables A, B and C constitute a circular relation. From the perspective of data flow, a circular relation refers to a cycle of the data flows between certain variables. Such circular relations need to be detected. Otherwise, the system will be stuck in certain states. We have the additional criterion for detecting such errors.

Criterion 1. *Each variable V specified in the specification (i.e., the prototype) should be checked whether V is involved in any circular dependency relation.*

Let's consider the CASDL statement: *ImmediateNb = ImmediateNb + 1*. The value of *ImmediateNb* depends on itself and the value 1, which is obviously a circular dependency error. The intention of this statement is to add value 1 to the previous value of *ImmediateNb* and get the new value. The correct statement should be *ImmediateNb (k) = ImmediateNb(k-1) + 1* in which the state of *ImmediateNb* is explicitly differentiated. This is a special case that the circular relation occurs on a single variable.

3.3   Diagram-Based Specification Review

An ATP specification describes the train protection functions by defining the interactions between the variables. Some variables are crucial since they correspond to the kernel functions such as the speed monitoring. Therefore, the analyst needs to validate whether the interactions of these variables with other variables correctly represents the intended relations. Similarly, the state transitions of the individual variables also need to be considered. To this end, a careful and rigorous specification review is demanded.

The VDDs and the STDs are generated from the prototype for precisely visualizing the interactions among the concerned variables and the state transitions of each individual variable. The developer checks the diagrams and determines whether they conform to the expectation. Meanwhile, logic errors in the prototype are also detected.

Definition 1. *Avariable dependency diagram of a variable V is a tree structure in which the root node represents V. The child nodes of V is a set of variables ranging from V_child_1 to V_child_n(n > 0), which represents that the value of V depends on the n variables.*

The state transition diagrams of each concerned variable can also be derived from the prototype. For the sake of space, we omit the definition of the STD here since the definition is the same to the traditional definition of STD. The following criteria can be applied for the validation.

Criterion 2. *For each concerned variable V, generate the VDD for validating the intended relations between the involved variables.*

Criterion 3. *For each concerned variable V, generate the STD for validating the state transitions.*

Following the criteria, the analyst can validate the requirements from the perspectives of the relations among variables and the state transitions. We use the sample specification shown in Fig. 2 as an example to illustrate the review process. Figure 3 shows a part of the generated variable dependency diagram of the variable *OdometerState*.

The VDD shows that the value of this variable is determined by various variables such as *INITIALIZED*. If some relations conflict with the analyst's understanding of the requirements or some relations are missing, then the analyst can make decision that the

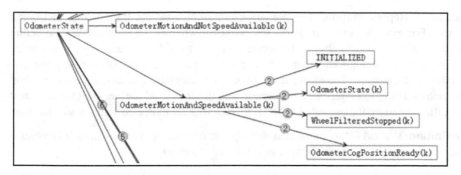

Fig. 3. The VDD of variable *OdometerState*

requirements are incorrect or incomplete. The VDD in this figure is in horizontal manner, since the structure is relatively too large to be displayed in vertical manner. Our tool provides both the horizontal and vertical views of the tree structures.

Similarly, the analyst can review the state transitions of a variable. Figure 4 describes the state transition of variable *OdometerState*.

The diagram shows that the variable cannot directly switch from the invalid state to the initialized state. The analyst and the ATP domain engineer found this missing transition after carefully reviewing the diagram.

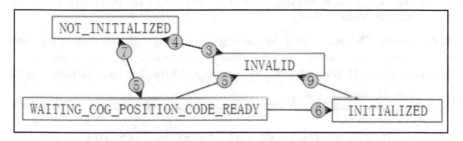

Fig. 4. The STD of variable *OdometerState*

3.4 Scenario-Based Specification Testing

The goal of the scenario-based specification testing is to dynamically check whether the user's concerned operational scenarios of the train are correctly and completely reflected by the specification. In other words, we try to check whether the specification satisfies the expected scenarios for running a train in the real world. The scenario-based testing is carried out in three steps. The first step is to describe the expected scenarios for operating the train. The second step is to transform the scenarios into executable test scripts for running the prototype. Finally, the test results are analyzed for checking the conformance of the prototype with respect to the scenarios. Therefore, whether the specification satisfies the scenario can be determined.

Scenario Representation. The scenarios represent how the train works in the real world. For example, the train driver may concern whether the train can stop at certain position after an acceleration. The scenarios are defined by the user based on domain knowledge. The domain engineer or the user may not familiar with software requirements modeling languages. Therefore, the scenario representation notation should be both precise and easy to understand. Our group and the industrial partner develop a domain specific scenario notation called CASSL for defining the expected scenarios of the train.

Definition 2. *An ATP scenario is a description of train operations, which consists of the train settings, the train actions and the event triggers.*

The train settings refer to the environment information for running the train, such as the routes and length of the train. The train actions are the primitive commands (e.g., stop or accelerate) for running a train. The event triggers refer to the configuration information for describing the reactions of the train with its external hardware (e.g., the signal equipment on the tracks).

The user can freely define the expected scenarios for running a train using the CASSL by setting the parameters values of each involved command. Figure 5 describes a scenario document in the CASSL language.

The train settings section defines the routes of the train using a sequence of blocks on the tracks. The "start" command in the train settings section represents that the train starts from the 0 position of the 247 block. In the train action section, the command *start(@0,30)* indicates that the train starts from the 0 position 30 s later after receiving the command. The train accelerates to the 4 speed units by the acceleration of 1 unit and then stops at position *@94*.

Test Execution. The user focuses on defining the physical variables such as the speed and the position information for the concerned scenarios. Then the scenarios are transformed into XML test scripts for testing the prototype. For each variable x in the

```
train{
  route: 247, 91, 92, 93, 94, 95, 96, 97, 98, 99, 100
  start: #(247,  0)
  length: 116066
  cog_dir: 1
  direction: 1
}

-> start(@0,  30)
-> acc(1,  4)
-> run(@84)
-> when(#(247, 116066)):
     ccnv.CCNVRuleEnable=1;
-> stop(@94)
```

Fig. 5. A scenario document for operating a train

scenario, there should be a set of corresponding variables denoted by $R(x)$ in the prototype. Function R represents the associations between the scenario variables and the prototype variables, which is pre-defined by the domain expert and saved as a file in the Test Executor of the tool. For each scenario, the Test Executor deduces the input values for running the prototype by referring to the association.

A scenario variable may correspond to several variables in the prototype.For instance, as shown by Fig. 5, the "run" action takes a variable as input for setting the speed of the train. This variable actually associates to the variables *TrainMaxSpeed*, *WheelMinSpeed* and other variables in the prototype. To run the prototype, we have implemented a CASDL execution engine as a component in the Test Executor.

Test Analysis. One major problem in automated test analysis is the construction of test oracle. That is, the expected outputs of the scenario need to be derived. By comparing the expected outputs of the scenario and the real outputs of the prototype, the consistency between the scenario and the prototype can be determined.

The expected values of the variables in the scenario are computed based the physics formulas stored in the Test Executor. The corresponding expected results of prototype can be deduced by referring to the association file. Formally, for each scenario, if the following condition holds, we say that the ATP prototype does not conforms to the scenario.

Condition 1. $\exists x \in S \bullet R(E(x)) \neq P(x)$

The above condition serves as the test oracle. For each variable x of the scenario S, its expected value is evaluated as $E(x)$. Function R represents the associations defined in the association file of the Test Executor. By referring to the associations, the expected values $R(E(x))$ of the corresponding variables of the prototype can be computed. $P(x)$ denotes the execution results produced by the prototype after running the test script. If $R(E(x))$ does not equal to $P(x)$, we say that the prototype does not satisfy the scenario S. Note that we linearise the computation of the kinematic behaviors such as the braking curves in our tool. That is, the engineer focuses on the concerned values at each time cycle.

For the previous example scenario, the expected speed of the train at the destination should be 0 based on the computation formulas. The expected value of its corresponding variable *TrainMaxSpeed* in the prototype should be 0 according to the association file. Figure 6 is the test results.

```
function TrainMaxSpeed(k) {
        if (OdometerSpeedAvailable(k)):
                return (round.ceil(abs(MaximumTrainMotion(k) / ATP_CYCLE_TIME)) +
        else:
                return round.ceil(abs(MaximumTrainMotion(k)) / ATP_CYCLE_TIME)

expected value: 0 real output: -594760564
```

Fig. 6. Test result of the scenario

The output value −594760564 after testing obviously violates the expected value 0. That is, the prototype does not implement the scenarios correctly.

4 Experiments

To validate the feasibility and demonstrate the efficacy of our approach, we have applied our approach and the tool in a real ATP software project. An ATP specification is established by the requirements analyst of our industrial partner. The specification is a Microsoft Word file which includes 455 requirements items. Two well-trained engineers participated in the experiments.

4.1 Specification Processing

Taking the syntax file and the textual specification as the inputs, the supporting tool performed the specification processing. The natural language descriptions were removed and the specification was transformed into an executable prototype. The average time for the tool to finish the overall specification (a 450 page document) transformation was about 3 min. During this transformation, 127 syntax errors were detected. Moreover, the tool identified 11 circular relations.

4.2 Diagram-Guided Specification Review

Since an ATP specification contains a huge amount of variables, in practice, the practitioner may only focus on the variables that correspond to the most important functions. In our case study, the practitioner selected 300 variables and generates the VDDs. The tool produced a 2 MB Excel file for storing the generated VDDs. The file contained 46174 rows to record the dependencies of the 300 concerned variables. That is, 300 tree structures were saved in the file. The degree of the deepest trees is 23. The generation of the STDs is similar to the VDDs generation. The engineers were more interested in those variables that associate to kernel functions of the ATP. In our case study, the analyst selected 8 variables to review their state transitions. The most complex state transition relation of a variable includes 5 states and 15 transitions.

4.3 Specification Testing

To sufficiently test the prototype derived from the specification, 317 scenario files were constructed by the ATP engineer. To sufficiently cover the potential operating scenarios of the train, we used real track maps in the case study. All the scenarios were automatically transformed into executable XML test scripts.

4.4 Experiment Results and Analysis

Errors detected from the requirements validation are categorized into four types: syntax error, variable circular error, functional error, and exceptions.

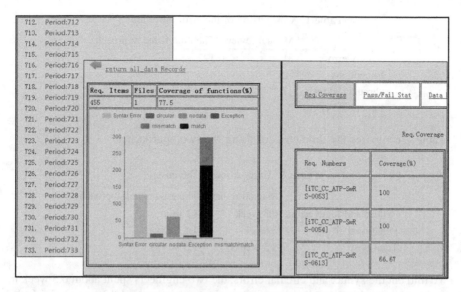

Fig. 7. Test result analysis of the case study

In particular, the functional errors refer to the errors related to the functions that are detected via specification review and testing. The exception errors are basically the unhandled code exception in the prototype. For instance, division by zero is an arithmetic exception. Figure 7 shows the statistics of the case study.

The tool generated both the textual test report and the visualized statistics. The chart shows 127 syntax errors, 11 circular errors, 83 functional errors, 5 exceptions and 61 no data errors were detected through the review and testing phases. Four of the exception errors were arithmetic errors (i.e., division by zero) and one was the out of bound of an array definition. There is a special type of error called *no data*, which is caused by the missing association definitions between the scenario variables and the variables in the prototype.

Our tool estimates the statement coverage of functions in the prototype. This figure shows that the statement coverage of the ATP prototype is 77.5 % after running a certain scenario. For the 317 scenarios used in the case study, the average statement coverage of the functions was approximately 82 %. Table 1 summarizes the comparison of the error detections achieved by the manual specification review and the automated approach.

In general, our proposed approach can reach higher error detection than the manual specification review method applied by the industrial partner. The two engineers reviewed the same specification manually and detected 81 syntax errors. They also detected 2 exceptions in the specification. Similarly, the engineers detect 7 circular errors of variables. For the functional errors, only 27 functional errors were detected through the manual review. Most of the functional errors detected by the engineers were the execution logic errors in individual functions, e.g., the missing of if-else branches.

Table 1. Comparison of the error detection

	Manual review	The automated approach
Syntax errors	81	127
Exceptions	2	5
Circular errors	7	11
Functional errors	27	83

Table 2 compares the time costs of using the two approaches.

Table 2. Comparison of the costs

	Manual review	The automated approach
Syntax and logic errors	0.5 week	12 min
Functional errors	3 weeks	1.5 weeks
Total cost	3.5 weeks	1.5 weeks

To find out the syntax and circular errors, the two engineers spent about 0.5 week in reviewing the specification. By the contrast, the tool only used 12 min to finish the static checking. Most of the time was spent on transforming the Word requirements specification to the executable CASDL prototype and the generation of the variable relations. They spent 3 weeks in identifying the functional errors by manual work while this task was performed within 1.5 weeks aided by the tool. When using the new approach, most of the human efforts were devoted to the construction of the concerned scenarios.

The results of the experiments have convinced us that the automated approach can significantly improve the efficacy and the productivity of the requirements validation for developing the ATP software.

5   Conclusion

Requirements validation is still a challenging problem for the ATP industrial practitioners due to the lack of effective methodologies and powerful tool support. To tackle this problem, in this paper we propose an automated requirements validation approach. Textual requirements specification is transformed into executable ATP prototype. In the static analysis phase, diagram-based review is conducted for validating the requirements from the perspective of variable interactions. The dynamic phase focuses on checking whether the requirements specification can satisfy the user's intended train operation scenarios. We have proposed a particular scenario description language. Test scripts are transformed from the scenarios for running the prototype. The conformance of the specification to the scenarios is evaluated via analyzing the test results. To facilitate the approach in practice, we have also developed a supporting tool for automating the activities involved in the approach.. The case study indicates that our approach is effective in requirements validation and can significantly improve the productivity of ATP software development.

We will continue to develop the approach as a long-term research project. Our future research will be devoted to the aspects including facilitating the association or traceability mechanism between the scenario variables and the prototype variables and the more effective technology for defining high-quality scenarios. The tool support will also be enhanced in our future research.

Acknowledgments. Weikai Miao is supported by NSFCs of China (No. 61402178, No. 61572306 and No. 91418203) and the STCSM Project (No. 14YF1404300). Geguang Pu is supported by China HGJ Project (No. 2014ZX01038-101-001) and STCSM Project No. 14511100400. This work is also partly supported by Japan JSPS KAKENHI (No. 26240008).

References

1. Kotonya, G., Sommerville, I.: Requirements Engineering. Wiley, Hoboken (1998)
2. Nuseibeh, B., Easterbrook, S.: Requirements engineering: a roadmap. In: Proceedings of International Conference on Software Engineering, pp. 35–41, April 2000
3. Wiegers, K.E.: Software Requirements. Microsoft Press, Redmond (2003)
4. Laitenberger, O., Beil, T., Schwinn, T.: An industrial case study to examine a non-traditional inspection implementation for requirements specifications. In: Proceedings of Eighth IEEE Symposium on Software Metrics, pp. 97–106 (2002)
5. Lee, G.Y.K., In, H.P., Kazman, R.: Customer requirements validation method based on mental models. In: 2014 21st Asia-Pacific Software Engineering Conference (APSEC), pp. 199–206, December 2014
6. Sinha, A., Sutton Jr., S.M., Paradkar, A.: Text2Test: automated inspection of natural language use cases. In: 2010 Third International Conference on Software Testing, Verification and Validation (ICST), pp. 155–164, April 2010
7. Aceituna, D., Do, H., Lee, S.W.: SQ2E: an approach to requirements validation with scenario question. In: 2010 17th Asia Pacific Software Engineering Conference (APSEC), pp. 33–42, November 2010
8. Xie, G., Hei, X., Mochizuki, H., Takahashi, S., Nakamura, H.: Model based specification validation for automatic train protection and block system. In: Proceedings of 7th International Conference on Computing and Convergence Technology, pp. 485–488, December 2012
9. Xie, G., Asano, A., Takahashi, S., Nakamura, H.: Study on formal specification of automatic train protection and block system for local line. In: Proceedings of 5th International Conference on Secure Software Integration Reliability Improvement Companion (SSIRI-C), pp. 35–40, June 2011
10. Wang, H., Liu, S., Gao, C.: Study on model-based safety verification of automatic train protection system. In: Proceedings of Asia-Pacific Conference on Computational Intelligence and Industrial Applications, pp. 467–470, November 2009
11. Leuschel, M., Butler, M.: ProB: a model checker for B. In: Araki, K., Gnesi, S., Mandrioli, D. (eds.) FME 2003. LNCS, vol. 2805, pp. 855–874. Springer, Heidelberg (2003)
12. Leuschel, M., Butler, M.: ProB: an automated analysis toolset for the B method. Int. J. Softw. Tools Technol. Transf. **10**(2), 185–203 (2008)
13. Behrmann, G., David, A., Larsen, K.G.: A tutorial on UPPAAL. In: Bernardo, M., Corradini, F. (eds.) SFM-RT 2004. LNCS, vol. 3185, pp. 200–236. Springer, Heidelberg (2004)
14. Vaandrager, F.: A first introduction to UPPAAL. Deliverable no.: D5. 12 Title of Deliverable: Industrial Handbook (2011)

15. Gargantini, A., Riccobene, E.: Automatic model driven animation of SCR specifications. In: Pezzé, M. (ed.) FASE 2003. LNCS, vol. 2621, pp. 294–309. Springer, Heidelberg (2003)

16. Fitzgerald, J., Larsen, P.G., Sahara, S.: VDMTools: Advances in support for formal modeling in VDM. ACM Sigplan Not. **43**(2), 3 (2008)

17. Li, M., Liu, S.: Integrating animation-based inspection into formal design specification construction for reliable software systems. IEEE Trans. Reliab. **65**(1), 88–106 (2016)

18. Li, J.J., Horgan, J.R.: A tool suite for diagnosis and testing of software design specifications. In: Proceedings of International Conference on Dependable Systems and Networks, New York, USA, pp. 295–304 (2000)

19. Brockmeyer, M.: Using modechart modules for testing formal specifications. In: Proceedings of 4th IEEE International Symposium on High-Assurance Systems Engineering, Washington, DC, USA, pp. 20–26 (1999)

20. Liu, S.: Utilizing specification testing in review task trees for rigorous review of formal specifications. In: Proceedings of Tenth Asia-Pacific Software Engineering Conference, pp. 510–519 (2003)

21. http://www.antlr.org/

22. Aceituna, D., Do, H., Lee, S.W.: Interactive requirements validation for reactive systems through virtual requirements prototype. In: Model-Driven Requirements Engineering Workshop (MoDRE), Trento, 2011, pp. 1–10 (2011)

Automatic Generation of Potentially Pathological Instances for Validating Alloy Models

Takaya Saeki[1]([⊠]), Fuyuki Ishikawa[2], and Shinichi Honiden[1,2]

[1] The University of Tokyo, Tokyo, Japan
{t-saeki,f-ishikawa,honiden}@nii.ac.jp
[2] National Institute of Informatics, Tokyo, Japan

Abstract. Alloy is a formal specification language that is widely used to verify software systems. However, while users can verify the properties of a specification with Alloy, it is not so easy for them to validate the specification, that is, to check that the specification is written just as the users intended. Alloy Analyzer, a tool supporting Alloy, has a feature to show concrete instances satisfying specifications that can be help in validation, but it does not control the order in which the instances are shown. Many studies have been conducted on ordering to help users explore instances in structured ways. However, not much prior research has focused on proper ways to explore instances for validating specifications. In this paper, we propose a method to assist users in validating specifications by displaying a set of instances that tend to include problems when their specifications have defects. In particular, the method applies pairwise testing to relations of Alloy specifications. We show effectiveness of the method in experiments using mutation analysis.

1 Introduction

Software has permeated society. Computers now control systems that in the past have had few or limited numbers of relations, such as automobile and train systems. As a result, it is becoming more and more important to ensure the reliability of software. A formal specification language is a technique for improving the reliability of software. It eliminates ambiguity from system specifications and makes it easy to get software assistance such as a machine-aided proof or model checking.

Alloy [5] is a formal specification language. It was developed by MIT and has widely been used in research and in practical applications. Alloy is often called a lightweight formal method. It brings the power of model checkers such as SPIN [4] to formal specification languages. Users write specifications in Alloy language based on first-order propositional logic. Alloy Analyzer, the official tool of the Alloy language, then verifies their properties automatically by model checking.

On the other hand, it is not easy to express exactly what users intend in the specification using the mathematical notation in the Alloy language. Properties

© Springer International Publishing AG 2016
K. Ogata et al. (Eds.): ICFEM 2016, LNCS 10009, pp. 41–56, 2016.
DOI: 10.1007/978-3-319-47846-3_4

are sometimes too weak or too strong, and the specification accepts or rejects unexpected instances. To tackle this difficulty, Alloy Analyzer offers a feature to show concrete instances. It gives users quick feedback on what they have written and helps them to understand the consequences of their models. Users can validate their models by checking instances, or *scenarios*, one by one. The process of checking concrete scenarios iteratively is called *scenario exploration*. The important role of this process is "debugging" of models. In exploring scenarios, users may find pathological instances where unexpected relations exist or instances where expected relations do not exist. In this way, they come to notice that new constraints should be added that they hadn't thought of before or that some of the current constraints are wrong.

Alloy Analyzer is useful tool for scenario exploration, but it has a problem with how it enumerates scenarios; the order of scenario generation is not tailored for validation. Alloy Analyzer shows possible scenarios one by one, and it "tends to" start generating them from small instances, but there is no further ordering control. During the scenario exploration process, Alloy Analyzer shows a scenario, and the user checks it; if it has no problem, the user pushes the "next" button and checks another scenario. This is not an effective way of model validation. All that the user can do is push the "next" button and hope for an interesting scenario to come along while iterating unordered scenarios one by one.

To solve this problem, some studies have proposed ways to provide users with methods to guide scenario generation; examples include Aluminum (2013) [10] and the work of Macedo et al. (2015) [8]. These studies help users to reach the scenarios they desire. For example, Aluminum offers an "augment" feature to guide scenario generation. It enables users to add relations interactively to current scenarios to reach the ones they want. In this way, users can explore scenarios they are interested in manually. However, users often even do not know what kinds of scenarios are useful to validate their models. Defects in models often arise from unnoticed problems such as under-constraints or over-constraints that did not come to their mind. In such cases, it is difficult for users to guide the scenario generation because the cause of the defects is an unnoticed gap between their intention and the actual models they write.

In this paper, we propose a way of automatically generating a set of scenarios that are likely to be pathological through heuristics based on pairwise testing. The method also presents unrealizable scenarios that are likely to be invalid when compared against the user's intention. We call it *Scenario Tour*; it generates a set of scenarios that should be checked for validation. In other words, it is test generation for scenario exploration. Scenario Tour helps users validate their models without all the trouble of manually guided scenario generation. We implemented Scenario Tour on top of Aluminum and evaluated its effectiveness by artificially adding defects to test models and checking whether the tour offered scenarios exposing the defects. In our experiments, Scenario Tour detected most of the mutation defects. It also detected a new defect not known before in an example model distributed with Alloy Analyzer.

2   Background and Motivation

2.1   Scenario Exploration in Alloy Analyzer

Alloy Analyzer has a feature to enumerate concrete instances that satisfy constraints in a given model in the form of a graph to visualize the relations in each instance. A simple gradebook model is illustrated in Fig. 1. This model is the same as the one in the original paper on Aluminum [10], but with a `gradedBy` relation added by us for the sake of explanation. There are four signatures, i.e., `Class`, `Student`, `Professor` and `Assignment`. A class has an instructor and sometimes has TAs. The classes may have assignments. The assignments always have students who submitted them and professors or students who grade them. The constraint of `gradedBy` states that the professor or students who grade them must be instructors or TAs of the classes they are submitted for. Figure 2 shows the scenario of the gradebook model.

This gradebook model has a defect. It lacks a constraint that prohibits students from being a TA of a class in which they have to submit their own assignments; that is, they can grade their own assignments. However, simply looking at scenarios such as in Fig. 2 does not help one to find this defect. Alloy Analyzer is not tailored to selectively show the most effective scenarios for validation.

2.2   Scenario Minimality Through Aluminum

It is believed that small instances are more likely to expose subtle defects [5]. Thus, presenting the smallest scenario first would be a desirable feature. Here, although Alloy Analyzer tends to present small scenarios first, this is not guaranteed and the order can change arbitrarily according to the situation. On the

```
abstract sig Subject {}
sig Student extends Subject {}
sig Professor extends Subject {}
sig Class {
  TAs: set Student,
  instructor: one Professor
}
sig Assignment {
  forClass: one Class,
  submittedBy: some Student,
  gradedBy: some Subject
} {
  gradedBy in (forClass.TAs + forClass.instructor)
}
run {}
```

Fig. 1. Simple grade book model

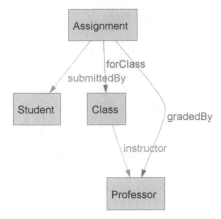

Fig. 2. Scenario of grade book model

other hand, Aluminum, an extension of Alloy Analyzer, presents only the *minimal* scenarios [10]. A minimal scenario is one that consists of the smallest number of Aluminum terms *tuples*, which roughly corresponds to the number of atoms or relations. Since the scenarios that Aluminum gives to users are always minimal ones, users can be sure that every one of their relations is necessary. Aluminum also offers a way to guide the scenario generation. It allows users to "augment" scenarios; users can add arbitrary relations to given minimal models. This enables them to explore scenarios they are interested in.

However, the manual guiding ability is not always useful. In the "debugging" phase, users often do not know what sorts of scenarios should be checked for defects. Model defects are often due to unnoticed gaps such as under-constraints or over-constraints that do not come to the user's mind. In such cases, it is difficult for users to guide the exploration towards pathological scenarios because the causes of the defects go unnoticed.

Therefore, it would be useful if we could generate a set of scenarios that are likely to be pathological automatically. By checking these generated scenarios, users would have more chance to find defects and increase their confidence in the validity of the models. Our approach tries to generate such scenario sets heuristically.

2.3   Other Related Work

Montaghami and Rayside (2012) suggested an Alloy extension with partial instance declaration [9]. It enables users to declare example scenarios that should or should not be consistent in the Alloy model. Such a feature could be useful for testing Alloy models. However, the user has to make a manual description and notice possible defects in advance. Thus, their extension has the same limitation as that of Aluminum.

There are studies that use Alloy to generate test suites for program code such as TestEra [7]. These studies, as well as ours, generate test suites using Alloy, but our study is different from them in that it generates test suites for an Alloy model itself instead of program code. There are also studies on random test generation for program code such as Randoop [11]. Whereas these studies generate many tests for random testing, our approach concentrates on generating a limited number of test cases by heuristics for manual checking.

As stated above, to the best of our knowledge, there has not been any research on generation of instance sets for finding defects by focusing on relations for first-order logic specification languages such as Alloy.

3 Method

3.1 Scenario Generation Heuristics Overview

We stated that for effective validation it would be useful to automatically generate a set of scenarios that are likely to have defects in Sect. 2.2. Our method generates such scenarios heuristically. The basic idea of our heuristics is that the gaps between the user's intention and the actual models tend to cause too weak or strong constraints, and they often appear in the form of unexpected co-occurrences of relations or absences of ones. We generate such scenarios that consist of many combinations of co-occurrences or absences of relations artificially. However, checking all combinations of relations amounts to a combinatorial explosion that is as impossible as to check as all possible scenarios. To avoid this problem and make the number of scenarios small enough to check, we apply pairwise testing. In addition, we assume that thorough co-occurrences or absences make especially pathological instances; our method generates such instances deliberately.

Our method also presents inconsistent scenarios, that is, scenarios that do not meet the given constraints. Incorrect under-constraints appear in scenarios in the form of pathological relation combinations. However, over-constraints do not appear in such form; users have to *notice* the absence of the scenarios they want, and that is more difficult than finding incorrect under-constrained scenarios. Thus, presenting inconsistent scenarios that are against the user's intention would be useful for validation. As described above, our method generates a set of scenarios through pairwise heuristics. Moreover, in the pairwise generation process, our method finds those scenarios that cannot meet the constraints. After that, it searches for the combinations of relations assigned by the pairwise process that make the scenarios inconsistent and presents the inconsistent scenarios to users for them to check if the combinations of relations actually should not meet their specifications.

3.2 Pairwise Scenario Generation

Scenario Tour generates sets of scenarios by applying pairwise test generation technique to combinations of relation co-occurrences. Pairwise testing, also known as all-pairs testing, is a combinatorial testing method in software engineering. In combinatorial testing, testers try to determine whether combinations of input parameter values cause a bug. Testing all such combinations naively leads to combinatorial explosion of test cases. Pairwise testing techniques dramatically decrease this number by only testing a test suite that covers all pairs of individual parameter values. That is, while every combination of two parameter values appears in at least one test case, all combinations of all values does not necessarily appear. Empirical studies have indicated that such pair combinations are sufficient for detecting a reasonable number of software errors [1,12].

As described before, inappropriate constraints cause gaps between the user's intention and the actual models, and they are likely to appear as unexpected combinations of relations or absences of expected relations in scenarios. Moreover, checking all such combinations leads to a combinatorial explosion. Thus, it is reasonable to apply pairwise testing to scenario generation. We take relations into or out of the signatures as parameters, and three elements about their quantifier as values of the parameters; `no`, `one`, and #`relations` ≥ 2. For example, Table 1 shows the combinatorial testing table of the gradebook model for inward relations. Those for outward relations go similarly, such as `None`, `One`, and `MTE2` for `Class` → `TAs`, `Class` → `Student`, and so on. By applying pairwise testing to them, all pairs of two relations statuses appear at least once in the scenario generation. For the gradebook model, all pairs such as (TAs → Student: None, gradeBy → Student: One) or (submittedBy → Student: MTE2, gradedBy → Professor: One) are surely included in the scenarios generated by Scenario Tour. Table 2 shows some of the test cases of pairwise testing for the gradebook model. We consider inward relations as examples here. Each line represents a scenario generated by Scenario Tour. For example, the scenario 1 in Table 2 represents an instance of the constraints shown in Fig. 3. It is visualized as graphical diagrams such as Fig. 4. In the figure, you can find "`checkThisFoo`" labels on some signatures. They indicate the key signatures of the scenario generated by pairwise testing.

Remember that this gradebook model has a defect, wherein the model lacks a constraint that prohibits students from being TAs for the class they attend. In Fig. 4, some of the assignments are graded by a student who also submitted them. This defect appears as a co-occurrence of `submittedBy` and `gradedBy` on

Table 1. Combinatorial table for inward relations: "MTE2" is short for "More Than or Equal to 2". This corresponds to the constraint "#`relations` ≥ 2"

TAs → Student	gradeBy → Student	submittedBy → Student	forClass → Class	instructor → Professor	gradedBy → Professor
None	None	None	None	None	None
One	One	One	One	One	One
MTE2	MTE2	MTE2	MTE2	MTE2	MTE2

Table 2. Part of the results of pairwise testing for Table 1

	TAs → Student	gradeBy → Student	submittedBy → Student	forClass → Class	instructor → Professor	gradedBy → Professor
Scenario 1	One	One	MTE2	MTE2	One	None
Scenario 2	One	None	None	None	One	One
Scenario 3	MTE2	MTE2	None	MTE2	MTE2	None

. . .

```
some checkThisStudent : Student |
  one TAs.checkThisStudent and
  one gradedBy.checkThisStudent and
  #submittedBy.checkThisStudent > 1
some checkThisClass : Class |
  #forClass.checkThisClass > 1
some checkThisProfessor : Professor |
  one instructor.checkThisProfessor and
  no gradedBy.checkThisProfessor
```

Fig. 3. Constraints that correspond to the scenario 1 of Table 2

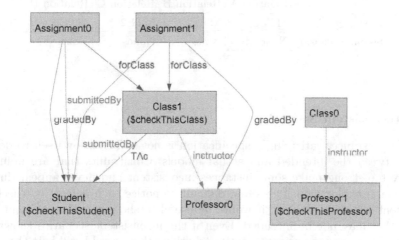

Fig. 4. Scenario represented by Fig. 3

some **Student**. Scenario Tour surely presents a case that includes the concurrent pair on a **Student** signature and points out the signature to users.

As this example for the gradebook model, we separate inward and outward relations for pairwise scenario generation because the consequent scenarios tend to be too complicated if we combine them. The latter pairwise testing would be more thorough, but our experiments indicated that the separated method is capable enough of finding the gaps. Thus, the pairwise scenario generation process is carried out twice for inward relations and outward relations.

3.3   Scenario Presentation Order

We stated that thorough maximization or minimization of the relations tends to make especially pathological situations. Scenario Tour follows this idea and presents a scenario with the maximal relations as the first presented scenario and one with the minimal relations next. Table 3 shows the first two presented scenarios with maximal and minimal relations for a case with four relations. Scenario Tour tries to generate these scenarios first. If these scenarios are not possible due to the constraints in the model, it tries to generate scenarios as close to them as possible (e.g., MTE2 for three relations and One for one relation as close as possible to the maximal). This presentation order enables users to notice most defects that emerge as inappropriate co-occurrences or absences of relations in the first or second scenario. For example, the defect of the gradebook model we explained in Sect. 3.1 will be detected in the first scenario. Common defects about incorrect multiplicity constraints of signatures will be detected in these scenarios, as well.

Table 3. The ideal first and second scenarios

	Relation A	Relation B	Relation C	Relation D
First scenario	MTE2	MTE2	MTE2	MTE2
Second scenario	None	None	None	None

3.4   Inconsistent Scenario

Checking instances satisfying a specification is not sufficient by itself to detect gaps between the intended and actual models. Constraints that are unintentionally too strong make some instances inconsistent and never appear during the scenario exploration. It is often difficult to notice such defects by checking consistent scenarios. Rather, it would be useful to show users inconsistent scenarios that may not be intended. Even if the inconsistent scenarios shown by Scenario Tour are not against intention, checking them would still help the users understand their model in a complementary way to scenario exploration with consistent scenarios.

   Our heuristic can naturally present inconsistent scenarios by extending consistent scenario presentation. Scenarios generated by pairwise testing sometimes are found to be impossible because of constraints in the specification. This is because some combinations of values assigned to parameters are not realizable under the constraints. In such cases, the generator tries to identify which factors in the pairwise setting make the scenario impossible. First, it checks whether each single value (No, One, MTE2) is possible in the specification. Then, it checks each pair (No-No, No-One, etc.). It tries to identify and present a combination of relations that makes the scenarios impossible in the minimal form if possible.

Then, Scenario Tour shows the combinations as inconsistent scenarios to users and asks them to confirm if they are exactly what they intend. After that, it eliminates the combination, regenerates pairwise test suites, and proceeds with the tour.

The current implementation stops searching for the cause of an inconsistency at pair combinations because a naive full search is not realistic (e.g., a combination of 7 factors is practically impossible). In our current implementation, Scenario Tour presents the inconsistent scenarios as "Non-minimal Inconsistent Scenarios" in such cases. Since these scenarios can include pairs that are irrelevant to the inconsistency, users have to find the core reason by themselves. In the future, we will try to improve how Scenario Tour handles non-minimal inconsistent scenarios.

4   Implementation

4.1   Alloy Engine

We implemented Scenario Tour on the top of Aluminum [10]. It generates scenarios by pairwise testing and converts them into Alloy constraints; then it gives them to Aluminum to solve. As we described in Sect. 2.2, Aluminum always gives minimal solutions. It enables Scenario Tour to show users minimal instances that meet the constraints of each scenario. This is a desirable feature because the consequent constraints tend to be somewhat complicated. Scenario Tour stresses the signatures to check by adding markers, but keeping instances small makes it much easier for users to check scenarios. It is also possible to use the augment feature of Aluminum to give users a manual exploration ability starting from the tour.

Aluminum is built on top of Alloy Analyzer. It includes both the original Alloy engine and the modified one for Aluminum features. We use the original engine during the scenario generation process because it is faster than the modified version. We use the modified one only for creating visualized scenarios for users. Therefore, we compared the performance of Scenario Tour with not Aluminum but Alloy Analyzer in the experiments (Sect. 5), despite that we built Scenario Tour on the latter.

4.2   Scenario Generation and Presentation

We explained that Scenario Tour tries to identify causal combinations of relations when it finds that the generated scenario is unrealizable. First, it checks whether each single value is possible; then it checks each pair. In our current implementation, Scenario Tour checks all single values in advance of the pairwise process. This makes the subsequent regular scenario generation process faster, but affects the execution time of the first scenario generation.

In the pairwise generation process, Scenario Tour generates two scenario sets: one for inward relations and the other for outward relations. The presentation order is arbitrary. In our current implementation, Scenario Tour shows two maximal scenarios for inward and outward relations in order at first, and two minimal scenarios for them next. After that, it presents the remaining scenario sets for inward relations first, and those for outward relations next.

4.3 Pairwise Combination Generation

Pairwise testing is a popular combinatorial testing technique that requires all combination of two values of each parameter to appear at least once. There are well-known algorithms for it, such as IPO strategy [13]. We did not implement it by ourselves and instead used PICT [2] as an external library. PICT is designed for speedy test generation, ease of use, and extensibility of the core engine. PICT offers useful features for Scenario Tour, such as support of complicated constraints.

5 Experimental Setting

5.1 Overview of the Experiment

The purpose of Scenario Tour is to show users a set of scenarios that may be against their intention. Users can find defects in their models or gain confidence in their correctness. To evaluate the effectiveness of Scenario Tour, we deliberately seeded valid models with defects and checked whether Scenario Tour generated scenarios that presented the defects.

The basic idea of the experiments is the same as that of mutation analysis for program code. Mutation analysis is a software testing technique that has been studied for three decades [6] to assess the quality of test suites for program code. It modifies programs according to some criteria and seeds them with faults. The modified program is called a *mutant*, and the quality of the test suite is assessed by how many mutants it can *kill* [3]. A rule of how to seed faults is called a mutation operator. The mutation operators represent mistakes programmers often make. Mutation operators for swapping < and > are common mutation operators for typical imperative programming languages.

Because we described Scenario Tour as test generation for modeling, it is natural that we should evaluate it by mutation analysis. We call an Alloy model into which we have deliberately added defects a mutant, in imitation of mutation analysis for software. We also say that Scenario Tour "kills mutants" when it generates scenarios that present invalid situation produced by mutants. We compared the effectiveness of Scenario Tour with that of Alloy Analyzer in terms of how many mutants they could kill and how many instances they required users to check before detecting defects. We also compared their execution times. We discuss the details in Sect. 6.

5.2   Mutation Operators

Because the mutation analysis for Alloy models is not common practice at present, there are no generally accepted mutation operators for it yet. Therefore, we defined mutation operators for our experiments by ourselves by referring to those for imperative programming languages. In our experiments, we applied the mutation operators in Tables 4 and 5 to the models.

Table 4 shows mutation operators that swap expressions of the models with modified ones. Especially common mistakes are writing incorrect multiplicity and quantifiers. This is because the core of the Alloy language is relations and first-order logic. The other mutation operators are mutations of binary operations. We define them so that we can apply mutations to most of the binary operations in the models of our experiments.

Table 4. Swapping mutation operators used in experiments

Swap each multiplicity operator: (lone — one — some — set)	
Swap each quantifier: (no — one — some — all)	
in	!in
=	!=
^	*
&	+

Table 5. Special mutation operators for alloy models

Remove a fact
Delete a single constraint
Replace a part of an expression with its type signature

The Alloy model below is an example of signature declaration with constraints.

```
sig sigForMutation {rel : some sigForMutation} {@rel = ~@rel}
```

The result of applying a mutation that changes the multiplicity some to one is as follows.

```
sig sigForMutation {rel : one sigForMutation} {@rel = ~@rel}
```

In addition to the swapping mutation operators, we also use the mutation operators for Alloy models listed in Table 5. These mutations apply semantic or rather large changes; they remove a whole fact, delete a single line constraint, or replace part of an expression with the superset type signature of it. We used these mutations to simulate situations where users have stronger constraints in mind but do not actually write them.

5.3   Experiment Environment

We conducted the experiments on a Microsoft Surface Pro 3/Windows 10 64 bit/Intel Core i7-4650U 1.70 – 2.30 GHz/8.00 Gb RAM. Aluminum was version 0.9. The underlying SAT solver of Aluminum was SAT4J. Microsoft PICT was the open source version, and the current revision hash of that is f58851e. The models were Filesystem, Grandpa, and Gradebook. Filesystem and Grandpa are distributed together with Alloy Analyzer as sample models. We have already presented Gradebook in Fig. 1. We chose these models because they are suited for validation by iteratively checking concrete scenarios one by one.

6   Experimental Results

6.1   Evaluation of Mutation Results

Tables 6 and 7 show the results of our experiments, while Tables 8 and 9 explain the table headings. The results of the mutation analysis shown in Table 6 suggest that Scenario Tour is useful for both quick incremental checks of Alloy specifications during the modeling process and careful validation of them at the end of the modeling process.

The **ST First** numbers are almost the same as the number of **Killed by next**, and this indicates that in Scenario Tour, users can notice invalid scenarios in earlier or as early scenarios as they can do in scenarios generated incrementally by Alloy Analyzer. This is accomplished by the scenario presentation order that shows the combinations of all MTE2 and all NONE first and second at the start points of the pairwise generation. In fact, the most of faults about multiplicity or quantifier are detected at the first or second scenario. This is a very useful feature for making quick checks in incremental modeling processes.

Killed by The Inconsistent indicates how many mutants were killed by inconsistent scenarios. We cannot evaluate the effect of inconsistent scenarios quantitatively since Alloy has no comparable feature. However, they killed many mutants that Alloy Analyzer could not. In addition, we found a new defect that was not known before in an official example model through an inconsistent

Table 6. Summary of results for kill rate and number of scenarios

Model Name	Mutant	Killed by next	Killed by ST	Killed by The Inconsistent	ST First	Consistent	Inconsistent	NMI
Grandpa	15	12	15	7	11	15.42	8.83	0
Filesystem	40	24	39	17	17	14.66	23.19	6.81
Gradebook	18	13	18	6	12	24.39	9.17	0

Table 7. Summary of results for running time

Model name	Inward relation		Outward relation		Alloy (ms)
	First scenario (ms)	Median (ms)	First scenario (ms)	Median (ms)	
Grandpa	1176.267	39	505.67	24	17
Filesystem	6708	68	2533.33	74	28.97
Gradebook	1275.67	29	369.17	25	11.94

Table 8. Explanation of Table 6

Heading	Description
Mutant	This shows the number of mutations applied to the model. We eliminate mutants that make a scenario unrealizable. Thus, Mutant means the number of valid mutants
Killed by next	This is the number of mutants killed by the **next** iteration, the regular scenario iteration feature of Alloy Analyzer. Note that **next** can iterate all possible scenarios. Thus, if Killed by next is smaller than Mutant, it means there are mutants that can be only killed by presenting inconsistent scenarios. For instance, such mutations that change the "set" multiplier to "some" never show their pathology through observable consistent scenarios because the defect caused by them is the absence of some relation
Killed by ST	"ST" means "Scenario Tour". This is the number of mutants killed by Scenario Tour
Killed by The Inconsistent	This is the number of mutants killed by the especially inconsistent scenario presentation in Scenario Tour. This number does not include mutants killed by NMI
ST First	This may be the most difficult one to grasp as to its meaning. This is the number of mutants that the number of instances Scenario Tour requires users to check before killing is smaller or as small as that of the regular Ally Analyzer scenario iteration feature
Consistent	This shows the average number of regular consistent scenarios generated by Scenario Tour for each model
Inconsistent	Similarly, this is the average number of inconsistent scenarios
NMI	"NMI" is an abbreviation for "Non-Minimal Inconsistent". This is the average number of non-minimal inconsistent scenarios for each model

scenario, as we will describe later. This fact also indicates the usefulness of presenting inconsistent scenarios. NMI scenarios are complex and inconsistent ones not showing minimal constraints. The **NMI** numbers indicate that the NMI scenarios are fewer by comparison with the inconsistent or (minimal) inconsistent cases.

Table 9. Explanation of Table 7

Heading	Description
Inward relation and outward relation	As we described in the Methods section, Scenario Tour generates two sets of scenarios; the first is based on pairwise inward relation combinations and the second is based on pairwise outward ones. Though Scenario Tour can take scenarios out of the two sets in arbitrary order, we measured the generation time for them separately
First scenario	This shows the time spent to generate the first scenario
Median	This is the median of the running times for generating scenarios. We used the median instead of the average since the very long running time for the first scenario affects the average too much
Alloy	This is the median of the running times of Alloy to generate scenarios by next

6.2 Evaluation of Running Time

Table 7 indicates that the running time of Scenario Tour is generally longer than that of the simple `next` iteration of Alloy Analyzer. This is natural because Scenario Tour generates scenarios by adding somewhat complicated constraints to the original models. The running time for the first scenarios of each tour is especially long. This must be because Scenario Tour checks for inconsistency in all single relation values in advance of the pairwise process, as we described before.

However, we think that the running time (a few seconds) is not too long for practical use. Even if it is not suitable for quick checks in incremental modeling, waiting for a few seconds does not seem to be problem for careful validation to complete the model.

6.3 Notable Finding

As we described before, Filesystem is an official example model distributed with Alloy Analyzer. In our evaluation experiments, we found a defect in it, which has not been noticed before. Filesystem is a simple model that consists of files, directories, a root directory, and a current directory. Scenario Tour showed us that the scenario represented by Fig. 5 is an inconsistent one. This means the current directory must be an entry of some directories. However, this would be a strange arrangement in most of the popular file systems because the situation would be fine when the current directory is the root directory. We investigated the model and found that both Cur and Root signatures are defined as below.

```
one sig Root extends Dir {} { no parent }
lone sig Cur extends Dir {}
```

Fig. 5. "Inconsistent" scenario of Filesystem

As can be seen, they both **extend** signature `Dir`. This makes them disjoint; thus, Scenario Tour reported that the current directory cannot be the root directory. For correct modeling of Filesystem, the author should have defined `Cur` by "in". After we fixed the definition, Scenario Tour told us that the situation was now a consistent scenario. Thus, we found an unnoticed defect of an official example model through our method. This indicates the usefulness of Scenario Tour.

7   Conclusion

We introduced "Scenario Tour", which helps users validate Alloy models by automatically generating scenarios that are likely to present gaps between the intentions of users and what actually they write. Scenario Tour also presents inconsistent scenarios that the regular scenario iteration feature of Alloy Analyzer never would present. Through this feature, we found a heretofore unnoticed defect in an example model distributed with Alloy Analyzer, and this suggests the usefulness of Scenario Tour in practice. Scenario Tour has a limitation as regards non-minimal inconsistent scenarios and its generation performance. However, mutation analysis suggests that it is powerful enough for practical use.

References

1. Cohen, D.M., Dalal, S.R., Fredman, M.L., Patton, G.C.: The AETG system: an approach to testing based on combinatorial design. IEEE Trans. Softw. Eng. **23**(7), 437–444 (1997)
2. Czerwonka, J.: Pairwise testing in the real world: practical extensions to test-case scenarios. In: Proceedings of 24th Pacific Northwest Software Quality Conference, pp. 419–430. Citeseer (2006)
3. DeMillo, R.A., Lipton, R.J., Sayward, F.G.: Hints on test data selection: help for the practicing programmer. Computer **4**, 34–41 (1978)
4. Holzmann, G.: Spin Model Checker, the: Primer and Reference Manual, 1st edn. Addison-Wesley Professional, Boston (2003)
5. Jackson, D.: Software Abstractions: Logic, Language, and Analysis. The MIT Press, Cambridge (2012)
6. Jia, Y., Harman, M.: An analysis and survey of the development of mutation testing. IEEE Trans. Softw. Eng. **37**(5), 649–678 (2011)
7. Khurshid, S., Marinov, D.: Testera: specification-based testing of Java programs using sat. Autom. Softw. Eng. **11**(4), 403–434 (2004). doi:10.1023/B:AUSE. 0000038938.10589.b9

8. Macedo, N., Cunha, A., Guimarães, T.: Exploring scenario exploration. In: Egyed, A., Schaefer, I. (eds.) FASE 2015. LNCS, vol. 9033, pp. 301–315. Springer, Heidelberg (2015)

9. Montaghami, V., Rayside, D.: Extending alloy with partial instances. In: Derrick, J., Fitzgerald, J., Gnesi, S., Khurshid, S., Leuschel, M., Reeves, S., Riccobene, E. (eds.) ABZ 2012. LNCS, vol. 7316, pp. 122–135. Springer, Heidelberg (2012). doi:10.1007/978-3-642-30885-7_9

10. Nelson, T., Saghafi, S., Dougherty, D.J., Fisler, K., Krishnamurthi, S.: Aluminum: principled scenario exploration through minimality. In: Proceedings of the 2013 International Conference on Software Engineering, pp. 232–241. IEEE Press (2013)

11. Pacheco, C., Ernst, M.D.: Randoop: feedback-directed random testing for Java. In: Companion to the 22nd ACM SIGPLAN Conference on Object-oriented Programming Systems and Applications Companion, OOPSLA 2007, pp. 815–816. ACM, New York (2007). http://doi.acm.org/10.1145/1297846.1297902

12. Smith, B.D., Feather, M.S., Muscettola, N.: Challenges and methods in testing the remote agent planner. In: AIPS, pp. 254–263 (2000)

13. Tai, K.C., Lie, Y.: A test generation strategy for pairwise testing. IEEE Trans. Software Eng. **28**(1), 109 (2002)

A General Lattice Model for Merging Symbolic Execution Branches

Dominic Scheurer[✉], Reiner Hähnle, and Richard Bubel

Department of Computer Science, TU Darmstadt, Darmstadt, Germany
{scheurer,haehnle,bubel}@cs.tu-darmstadt.de

Abstract. Symbolic execution is a software analysis technique that has been used with success in the past years in program testing and verification. A main bottleneck of symbolic execution is the path explosion problem: the number of paths in a symbolic execution tree is exponential in the number of static branches of the executed program. Here we put forward an abstraction-based framework for state merging in symbolic execution. We show that it subsumes existing approaches and prove soundness. The method was implemented in the verification system KeY. Our empirical evaluation shows that reductions in proof size of up to 80 % are possible by state merging when applied to complex verification problems; new proofs become feasible that were out of reach so far.

1 Introduction

Symbolic execution [7,20] is a classic program analysis technique that was used with considerable success in the past years, for example, in program testing [8] and program verification [4]. One of the main bottlenecks of symbolic execution is the path explosion problem [8]. It stems from the fact that symbolic execution must explore all symbolic paths of a program to achieve high coverage (in testing), respectively, soundness (in verification). As a consequence, the number of paths from the root to the leaves in a symbolic execution tree is usually exponential in the number of static branches of the executed program.

Various strategies are in use to mitigate path explosion, including subsumption [3,9], method contracts [5] and value summaries [23]. The last two allow one to perform symbolic execution per method: different symbolic execution paths are merged into the postcondition of a contract or a value summary (a conditional execution state over guard expressions). Summaries are computed on the fly and bottom-up, while contracts characterize all possible behaviors and must at least partially be written by hand. Unfortunately, even the use of rich contracts (instead of inlining) is insufficient to deal with complex problems [15].

A seemingly obvious technique to alleviate state explosion in symbolic execution trees consists of merging the states resulting from a symbolic execution step that caused a split (e.g., guard evaluation, statements that can throw exceptions, polymorphic method calls). After all, graph-based data structures are standard in model checking for the exploration of symbolic state spaces [10], as well as

© Springer International Publishing AG 2016
K. Ogata et al. (Eds.): ICFEM 2016, LNCS 10009, pp. 57–73, 2016.
DOI: 10.1007/978-3-319-47846-3_5

in other static software analyses. Indeed, several state merging variants were suggested for symbolic execution [18,21,23], but there are problems:

(1) State merging does not come for free, but creates considerable overhead: states must be merged, graph data structures are more complex than trees, path conditions as well as summaries tend to grow fast and must be simplified. Eager state merging can make things worse [18], therefore, it has to be carefully *controlled*. Simplification of intermediate expressions with the help of automated deduction is indispensable.

(2) All mentioned approaches assume that merged states are identical to corresponding unmerged states, possibly up to the differences encoded in value summaries. This is insufficient to merge large numbers of different behaviors.

In the present paper we address both issues. Regarding the second, we observe that instead of encoding merged states precisely into a conditional state, one might also *abstract* from the precise value of a variable. This results in a loss of precision, but reduces complexity. For example, consider symbolic execution of "**if** (b) x $= 1$ **else** x $= 2$;" in state σ. Precise state merging would result in a state identical to σ except the value of x is "x $\mapsto (1,$ if $\sigma(b) = true) \mid x \mapsto (2,$ if $\sigma(b) = false)$". This does not avoid path explosion, it only delays it. Now, assume that we define an abstract domain A for the possible values of x, where $\alpha(x)$ is the abstraction of x and A is an upper semilattice $\sqcup$. For example, A might be the sign lattice $\{\bot, -, 0, +, \top\}$. Then the merged state can be *over-approximated* by the partially abstract state that is identical to σ except x $\mapsto +$. Path explosion is avoided. We lost precision about the exact value of x, but for many analyses this is acceptable provided that the abstract lattice is suitably chosen.

Based on the theory of symbolic execution with abstract interpretation [6], in the present paper we put forward a general lattice-based framework for state merging in symbolic execution where a family of abstract lattices is defined by formulas of a program logic. Our framework preserves soundness of verification and we show that it subsumes earlier approaches to state merging [18,21,23].

Regarding issue (1) above, as a second contribution, we improved automation by implementing suitable proof macros for KeY as well as an extension of the Java Modeling Language (JML)[1] which allows software engineers to annotate Java source code with instructions on when to perform state merges.

We implemented the framework in the state-of-art verification system KeY[5], where contracts are available to mitigate state explosion. Since the latter must be partially written by hand, state merging is a complementary technique that promises a high degree of automation. We confirmed the usefulness of our approach empirically with an extensive evaluation: Results for small to medium sized programs are, as expected, mixed, because of the overhead of state merging. The strength of symbolic execution with state merging emerges when applied to complex verification problems like the TimSort implementation in the Java standard library [15], where we observe reductions in proof size of up to 80 %. Additionally, some proofs become feasible that were elusive before.

---

[1] http://www.eecs.ucf.edu/~leavens/JML//OldReleases/jmlrefman.pdf.

We continue with Sect. 2, which provides sufficient theoretical background to make the paper self-contained. Section 3 sets up our abstract lattice model. Section 4 defines the actual merge rules, states a soundness theorem and briefly mentions implementation issues. Section 5 contains the empirical evaluation, Sect. 6 lessons learned as well as future work, and Sect. 7 related work plus a brief conclusion.

2   Background

We formalize our theory in the program logic JavaDL [5], but the approach is easily adaptable to any program logic with an explicit notion of symbolic state.

2.1   Program Logic and Calculus

Our framework is realized in JavaDL, a sorted first-order dynamic logic [19] for sequential deterministic Java programs. For the sake of presentation, we restrict ourselves to a simplified JavaDL variant (simple imperative Java programs over primitive types **int, boolean**) and only give the essential definitions. The actual implementation is based on KeY which covers most sequential Java features: inheritance, dynamic dispatch, reference types, recursive methods, exceptions, and strings. Not covered are generic types (which are translated away), floating point types and lambda expressions. We refer the reader to [5] for a full account.

JavaDL extends sorted first-order logic by two modalities to express partial and total correctness of programs. For space reasons, we restrict ourselves to the former, the box modality $[\cdot]\cdot$. Its first argument is a program (more precisely, an executable sequence of Java statements); the second argument can be any JavaDL formula, possibly containing further modal operators. Given a program p and a JavaDL formula φ, the informal meaning of the formula $[p]\,\varphi$ is: *if* the program p terminates *then* the formula φ holds in the final state.

The syntax of terms and formulas is standard except for a few extra cases like modalities, conditional terms/formulas (Example 1) as well as *updates*. The set of all programs is *Prg*; the set of all program variables is denoted by PV. Updates represent state changes: an *elementary update* has the form $l \mathrel{:=} t$ with $l \in$ PV and t a term of a type compatible with l. Informally, an update has the same meaning as an assignment, where the program variable on the left-hand side is assigned the value of the right-hand side. Elementary updates are combined to parallel updates $U_1 \parallel \cdots \parallel U_n$ which represent simultaneous assignments. In case of a clash where the same variable l is assigned different values in a parallel update, the syntactically later assignment wins. The set of all updates is Upd, *skip* is the "empty update". Updates U can be applied to terms t, written $\{U\}t$, and formulas φ, written $\{U\}\varphi$. We give the non-standard cases of the inductive definitions of terms and formulas:

Definition 1 (Terms). *Let φ denote a formula, t_1, t_2 are terms of type T_1 and T_2 and U an update, then (i) $\{U\}t_1$ is a term of type T_1 (ii) if (φ) then (t_1) else (t_2) is a term of type T where T is the least common supertype of T_1 and T_2. The set of all terms is denoted by* Trm.

Definition 2 (Formulas). *Let φ, ψ_1, ψ_2 denote formulas, U an update and p a program, then each of (i) $[p]\,\varphi$ (ii) $\{U\}\varphi$ and (iii) if (φ) then (ψ_1) else (ψ_2) is a formula. For open formulas with free variables $\overline{v}$ we use the notation $\varphi_{\overline{v}}$ to make their occurrence explicit. The set of all formulas is denoted by* Fml.

Example 1. Let i, j be program variables and x, y logic variables, all of sort **int**.

- The formula $\forall x, y; \left(i \doteq x \;\wedge\; j \doteq y \rightarrow \{i := j \,\|\, j := i\}(i \doteq y \;\wedge\; j \doteq x)\right)$ uses a parallel update to exchange the values of i and j.
- The formula $i > j \rightarrow [i = i - j;]\,i > 0$ expresses that if program $[i = i - j;]$ is executed in a state where the value of i is greater than the value of j and it terminates, then in its final state i is positive.
- if $(i > j)$ then (i) else $(j) \geq 0$ means that the maximum of i and j is positive.

Formulas are evaluated in first-order structures with a non-empty domain D and an interpretation function I giving meaning to sort, function and predicate symbols. To reason about programs, we extend this to *Kripke structures* $K = (D, I, S, \rho)$. The values of program variables depend on the current program state and cannot be evaluated by the static interpretation function I. Instead they are assigned values by *Kripke states* $\sigma : \mathsf{PV} \rightarrow D \in S$. The state transition function $\rho : Prg \rightarrow (S \rightarrow 2^S)$ captures the program semantics (here: Java's semantics [14]).[2]

As our programs are deterministic, the value of $\rho(p)(\sigma)$ (for any program p and state σ) is either the empty set (p does not terminate when started in state σ) or a singleton. Formulas and terms are assigned meaning by an *evaluation function val* $(K, \sigma, \beta; \cdot)$, parametric in a Kripke structure K, a state σ and a variable assignment β. The evaluation function assigns terms a value in their domain and formulas one of the truth values tt, ff. Figure 1 shows some inductive definition cases. For expressions without free logic variables, we write *val* $(K, \sigma; \cdot)$; for sets of closed formulas C, we write *val* $(K, \sigma; C)$ meaning *val* $\left(K, \sigma; \bigwedge_{\varphi \in C} \varphi\right)$.

A sequent calculus [12], [5, Chap. 3] is used to prove the validity of JavaDL formulas. The rules for the first-order logic connectives are standard, those for programs follow the symbolic execution paradigm. Formulas with programs are transformed into pure first-order formulas by symbolically executing the programs in a forward manner and thereby computing the weakest precondition. Each execution step transforms or eliminates the first statement until the program is eliminated. We write $\vdash \varphi$ if a formula φ is *provable* using the calculus.

2.2 Symbolic Execution

We explain how the notions and concepts introduced in the standard literature [7] relate to our logic-based setting. Symbolic Execution (SE) of a program

---

[2] Our notion of Kripke structure is derived from that commonly used in modal logic [13] and slightly differs from the one often used in model checking. E.g., we require no fixed set of initial states, and the labeling function is given implicitly by the interpretation and Kripke state which is natural for imperative programs. There is no essential difference, however.

Programs $val\,(K,\sigma,\beta;\cdot) : Prg \rightarrow (S \rightarrow 2^S)$ with $val\,(K,\sigma,\beta;p)\,(\sigma_1) = \rho(p)(\sigma_1)$

Terms $val\,(K,\sigma,\beta;\cdot) : Trm \rightarrow D$ with

$$val\,(K,\sigma,\beta;(f(t_1,\ldots t_n)) = I(f)(val\,(K,\sigma,\beta;t_1),\ldots,val\,(K,\sigma,\beta;t_n))$$

$$val\,(K,\sigma,\beta;\text{if }(\varphi)\text{ then }(t_1)\text{ else }(t_2)) = \begin{cases} val\,(K,\sigma,\beta;t_1) & val\,(K,\sigma,\beta;\varphi) = tt \\ val\,(K,\sigma,\beta;t_2) & otherwise \end{cases}$$

$$val\,(K,\sigma,\beta;\{U\}t) = val\,(K,val\,(K,\sigma,\beta;U),\beta;t)$$

Formulas $val\,(K,\sigma,\beta;\cdot) : Fml \rightarrow \{tt,f\!f\}$ with

$$val\,(K,\sigma,\beta;[p]\varphi) = \begin{cases} val\,(K,\sigma',\beta;\varphi) & val\,(K,\sigma,\beta;p)\,(\sigma) = \{\sigma'\} \\ tt & otherwise \end{cases}$$

$$val\,(K,\sigma,\beta;\{U\}\varphi) = val\,(K,val\,(K,\sigma,\beta;U),\beta;\varphi)$$

Updates $val\,(K,\sigma,\beta;\cdot) : Upd \rightarrow S$ with

$$val\,(K,\sigma,\beta;1 := t) = \sigma' \quad \text{where } \sigma'(x) = \begin{cases} \sigma(x) & \text{if x} \neq 1 \\ val\,(K,\sigma,\beta;t) & otherwise \end{cases}$$

Fig. 1. Excerpt of the definition of $val\,(K,\sigma,\beta;\cdot)$

results in a Symbolic Execution Tree (SET) consisting of SE *states*, i.e., triples (U,C,φ) with (1) an update U, the *symbolic state*, capturing the changes made to program variables in the course of the execution, (2) the *path condition* C, a set of closed formulas comprising the decisions leading to this particular SE path as well as additional preconditions, and (3) the *program counter* φ, a closed formula, typically containing the remaining program to be executed as well as the postcondition to prove.

Please note that we generalize the usual notion of a *program counter*, which is normally only a pointer to a statement in the executed program. In our setting, a program counter may be an arbitrary closed formula. This generalization facilitates reasoning about the *validity* of SE states.

Definition 3 (Validity of SE States). *An SE state* $s = (U,C,\varphi)$ *is called valid iff for all Kripke structures* K *and states* σ *either* $val\,(K,\sigma;C) = f\!f$ *or* $val\,(K,\sigma;\{U\}\varphi) = tt$ *holds. We write valid* (s).

Consider an SE state $s = (U,C,[p]\varphi)$. Intuitively, if the path condition C does not hold in s, then the state is unreachable and trivially valid. Otherwise, all final state(s) reached when executing p in state $val\,(K,\sigma;U)$ must satisfy φ.

SET transitions are constrained by a rule-based *SE transition relation* $\delta : 2^{SEStates} \rightarrow 2^{SEStates}$, where *SEStates* is the set of all SE states. Again, this is a generalization of traditional SE, since the result of applying δ does not have to be a singleton. Based on Definition 3, we introduce a soundness notion for δ.

Definition 4 (Soundness of Symbolic Execution). *An SE transition relation* $\delta : 2^{SEStates} \rightarrow 2^{SEStates}$ *is called sound iff for each input-output pair* $(I,O) \in \delta$ *it is the case that* $\bigwedge_{o \in O} valid\,(o) \implies \bigwedge_{i \in I} valid\,(i)$.

The intuition behind the above definition is that, whenever one input state is not valid, also at least one output state must not be valid. Otherwise, it would be possible to derive an invalid property about a program.

2.3 Running Example

Listing 1. Distance of two positive integers

```
1  public int dist(int x, int y) {
2      if (y < x) {
3          int tmp = x;
4          x = y;
5          y = tmp;
6      } else {}
7      return y − x;
8  }
```

The program in Listing 1 is our running example. It computes the absolute difference (distance) between two positive numbers. Aiming to prove that the result is never negative, we start with the SE state below as initial SE state (the return value is assigned to the global program variable "result"):

$$\overbrace{(skip}^{U}, \overbrace{\{x > 0, y > 0\}}^{C}, \overbrace{[\textbf{if} (y < x) \{...\} \textbf{ else } \{\}\ \ \text{result} = y - x;]\ \text{result} \geq 0)}^{\varphi}$$

The *SE* state (U, C, φ) given above is valid iff for any *Kripke* state σ satisfying the path condition C, whenever we execute the program **if** (y<x) ... ; in σ, then in the reached final state the value of program variable result is non-negative.

We explain how the SET for the example is constructed by stepwise symbolic execution: Symbolic execution of the first statement (by applying the appropriate calculus rule) splits the SET into the following two new intermediate states:

$$(skip, \{x > 0,\ y > 0,\ y < x\}, [\{...\}\ \text{result} = y - x;]\ \text{result} \geq 0)$$
$$(skip, \{x > 0,\ y > 0,\ \neg y < x\}, [\{\}\ \text{result} = y - x;]\ \text{result} \geq 0)$$

On each branch, either the body of the then-branch or the else-branch has to be executed, followed by the remaining program. The remaining program is just a single assignment statement here, but could be arbitrarily complex in general. In addition, the path condition in each branch has been extended by the conjunct $y < x$ and its negation, respectively. Continuing symbolic execution on the first branch results in the state

$$((x \doteq y \parallel y \doteq x), \{x > 0,\ y > 0,\ y < x\}, [\text{result} = y - x;]\ \text{result} \geq 0)).$$

The motivation for state merging becomes very clear now: on each branch the same remaining program has to be executed.

3 The General Lattice Model

Symbolic Execution can be cast as *abstract interpretation* [11]. Each SE state describes a potentially infinite set of *concrete states*. As abstract interpretation demands a complete semilattice with join operation, partial order, least and top element, we define a concretization function from SE states to concrete states as well as a partial order relation between SE states.

Definition 5 (Concrete Execution States). *A concrete execution state is a pair* (σ, φ) *of a Kripke state* σ *and a formula* φ *(the program counter).*

A concrete execution state for a given program counter assigns to each program variable a concrete value of the universe. We define the semantics of SE states by stipulating a concretization function from SE states to concrete states based on the evaluation function $val\,(K, \sigma; \cdot)$ (β is not needed as formulas are closed).

Definition 6 (Concretization Function). *Let $s = (U, C, \varphi)$ be an SE state. The* concretization function *concr maps s to the set of concrete states*

$$concr\,(s) := \Big\{(\sigma', \varphi) : \sigma' = val\,(K, \sigma; U) \text{ and } K, \sigma \text{ is an arbitrary}$$

$$structure/Kripke \text{ state such that } val\,(K, \sigma; C) = tt\Big\}$$

The set of concrete states for a symbolic state s contains all pairs of Kripke states σ' and the program counter such that σ' can be reached via some state σ satisfying s's path condition in some Kripke structure. So the set $concr\,(s)$ contains exactly the concrete states that are described by the SE state s. Consider, for instance, the SE state $(\mathrm{x} := c, \{c > 0\}, \varphi)$: The set of concretizations for this state consists of all pairs (σ, φ), where σ is any function mapping the program variable x to a strictly positive integer.

Based on Definition 6, we define a *weakening relation* expressing that one symbolic execution state describes more concrete states than another one.

Definition 7 (Weakening Relation). *Let s_1, s_2 be two SE states. State s_2 is* weaker than *(a weakening of) s_1 (written: $s_1 \lesssim s_2$) iff $concr\,(s_1) \subseteq concr\,(s_2)$.*

Given a state s_1 with satisfiable path condition, Definitions 6 and 7 imply that a state s_2 can only be weaker than s_1 if both have syntactically the same program counter. States with unsatisfiable path condition have an empty set of concretizations and hence are stronger than any other state.

Consider the SE states $s_1 = (\mathrm{x} := c, \{c > 0\}, \varphi)$ and $s_2 = (\mathrm{x} := c, \{c \geq 0\}, \varphi)$. The set of concretizations of s_2 contains all concrete states of s_1 and additionally all concrete states that map x to zero, hence s_2 is a weakening of s_1 ($s_1 \lesssim s_2$).

Consider the SE state $s_3 = (\mathrm{x} := \mathsf{if}\,(\mathsf{true})\,\mathsf{then}\,(c)\,\mathsf{else}\,(t), \{c > 0\}, \varphi)$. Although s_1 and s_3 are syntactically different, all Kripke models coincide on the value of x and we would actually prefer to consider them as equal. Hence, we define an extensional equality $s_1 \overset{concr}{=} s_2 :\Leftrightarrow concr\,(s_1) = concr\,(s_2)$ stating that symbolic execution states are equal iff they evaluate to the same set of concrete execution states. Using $\overset{concr}{=}$ as equality, we can state the following lemma:

Lemma 1. *The weakening relation $\lesssim$ is a partial order relation.*

The core of our formal framework is a family of join-semilattices parametric in a join operation. The partial order induced by the join operation is constrained by the semantic weakening relation, see Definition 7.

Definition 8 (Induced Join-Semilattice of States). *Let $\varphi \in \mathrm{Fml}$ be a closed formula. The* carrier set S_φ *for φ is defined as*

$$S_\varphi := \{(U, C, \varphi) | (U, C, \varphi) \text{ is an SE state}\}.$$

A join-semilattice of SE states *is a structure* $(S_\varphi, \sqcup)$ *over* S_φ *with operator* $\sqcup$ *s.t. the semilattice properties (based on* $\overset{concr}{=}$*) (SEL1)–(SEL3) hold for all* $a, b, c \in S_\varphi$:

(*SEL1*) Idempotency: $a \sqcup a \overset{concr}{=} a$ (*SEL2*) Commutativity: $a \sqcup b \overset{concr}{=} b \sqcup a$
       (*SEL3*) Associativity: $(a \sqcup b) \sqcup c \overset{concr}{=} a \sqcup (b \sqcup c)$

Furthermore, we require that the partial order relation $\preceq$ *on* S_φ *defined as*

$$a \preceq b :\Leftrightarrow a \sqcup b \overset{concr}{=} b$$

satisfies (SEL4) and (SEL5)[3] *for* $a = (U_a, C_a, \varphi) \in S_\varphi$ *and* $b = (U_b, C_b, \varphi) \in S_\varphi$:

(SEL4)   Correctness: $a \preceq b$ *implies* $a \overset{\sim}{\lesssim} b$
(SEL5)   Conservativity: $a \preceq b$ *implies that* C_b *is logically equivalent to a formula* $C \wedge Ax_{\overline{v}}[\overline{c}/\overline{v}]$, *where (1)* $\overline{c}$ *are all uninterpreted Skolem constants occurring in* b *but not contained in* a, *(2)* C *does not contain any of the* $\overline{c}$, *(3)* $\bigwedge C_a \rightarrow C$ *is provable, and (4) the formula* $\exists \overline{v}; Ax_{\overline{v}}$ *is provable.*

We call $\{\mathbb{L}_\varphi\}_{\varphi \in \mathrm{Fml}} := \{(S_\varphi, \sqcup)\}_\varphi$ *the induced family of join-semilattices for* $\sqcup$.

We term (SEL4) *correctness* since it enables, together with (SEL5), to prove the correctness of our state merging rule (Theorem 1 below). The *conservativity* property (SEL5) imposes restrictions on merge operations that introduce Skolem constants (thus extending the signature), such as the abstraction technique introduced in Sect. 4.3. Property (SEL5) enforces that the path condition of a merged state is divisible into (1) a formula C without new constants which is implied by the states that are merged (for example, the disjunction of the path conditions of the merged states) and (2) a formula $Ax_{\overline{v}}[\overline{c}/\overline{v}]$ providing restrictions on the values of the new constants. In addition (3) it must be possible in every structure to assign values to the new constants such that $Ax_{\overline{v}}[\overline{c}/\overline{v}]$ holds. This is achieved by proving $\exists \overline{v}; Ax_{\overline{v}}$ in the unextended signature of the merged states. $Ax_{\overline{v}}$ may be seen as a (generalized) *defining axiom* [24] for the $\overline{c}$: we only demand the existence condition $\vdash \exists \overline{v}; Ax_{\overline{v}}$ and explicitly forgo the uniqueness condition to facilitate abstraction. In summary, (SEL5) allows only "conservative" extensions to a merged path condition. An example for a formula $Ax_{\overline{v}}[\overline{c}/\overline{v}]$ is $c > 0$, where c is a constant introduced in the merging step. Example 2 (Sect. 4.2) shows a fragment of a join-semilattice induced by a join operation based on the if $(\cdot)$ then $(\cdot)$ else $(\cdot)$ operator.

4   State Merging Techniques

We instantiate our framework with two join operations: the *If-Then-Else* (ITE) technique, a "classic" of state merging for symbolic execution (e.g., [18, 21, 23])

---

[3] $\psi_{\overline{v}}[\overline{t}/\overline{v}]$ denotes the substitution of the terms $\overline{t}$ for the free variables $\overline{v}$ in $\psi_{\overline{v}}$.

with full precision; and an abstraction-based technique which trades efficiency with potential loss of precision. To simplify specification of the join operations, we define a pattern that can be instantiated with specific merging techniques.

4.1 A State Merging Pattern

Definition 9. *Given two SE states* $s_j = (U_j, C_j, \varphi)$, $j = 1, 2$, *with program variables* $x_1, \ldots, x_n \in PV$ *of type* T *occurring in the* U_j. *A merge technique* M *defines two functions* $\mathsf{joinVal}\,(s_1, s_2; x, c_x)$ *and* $\mathsf{constraints}\,(s_1, s_2; x, c_x)$ *mapping* s_1, s_2, *program variable* x *and a fresh (for* x*) Skolem constant* c_x *to a closed term and a JavaDL formula, respectively. The join operation* $\sqcup_M$ *is defined by*

$$s_1 \,\dot\sqcup_M\, s_2 \coloneqq (U^*, C^*, \varphi) = ((U_1, C_1) \oplus (U_2, C_2), (U_1, C_1) \,ⓥ\, (U_2, C_2), \varphi)$$

where $U^* = (U_1, C_1) \oplus (U_2, C_2) \coloneqq (x_1 \coloneqq t_1 \,\|\, x_2 \coloneqq t_2 \,\|\, \cdots \,\|\, x_n \coloneqq t_n)$. *To define the terms* t_i, *let* $c_{x_1}, c_{x_2}, \ldots, c_{x_n}$ *be fresh Skolem constants of suitable types. Then*

$$t_i \coloneqq \begin{cases} \{U_1\} x_i & \text{if } (\star) \text{ holds} \\ \mathsf{joinVal}\,(s_1, s_2; x_i, c_{x_i}) & \text{otherwise} \end{cases}$$

Define $C^* = (U_1, C_1) \,ⓥ\, (U_2, C_2) \coloneqq (\bigwedge C_1 \vee \bigwedge C_2) \wedge \{U^*\}(\bigwedge C_i^{abs})$ *where*

$$C_i^{abs} \coloneqq \begin{cases} \text{true} & \text{if } (\star) \text{ holds} \\ \mathsf{constraints}\,(s_1, s_2; x_i, c_{x_i}) & \text{otherwise} \end{cases}$$

Condition $(\star)$ *holds if* x_i *is evaluated identically in either state and is defined as*

$$(\star) \quad \vdash (C_1 \rightarrow \{U_1\}\, P\,(x_i)) \leftrightarrow (C_2 \rightarrow \{U_2\}\, P\,(x_i))$$

where P *is a fresh (for* $U_1, U_2, C_1, C_2, \varphi$*) predicate symbol.*

The provability relation "$\vdash$" in $(\star)$ is undecidable, but it can be safely approximated in practice. For example, a prover may simply return "unprovable" after exceeding a fixed time limit. This way soundness is maintained at the cost of completeness due to overapproximation in some situations. The update application of $\{U^*\}$ to $(\bigwedge C_i^{abs})$ allows to take into account relations between values of program variables changed by the merge (e.g., the merge by predicate abstraction for the **dist** example in Sect. 5). Otherwise, only relations between constants and values before the merge would be reflected.

4.2 The If-Then-Else Technique

Definition 10 (If-Then-Else Merge). *Given two SE states* $s_j = (U_j, C_j, \varphi)$, $j = 1, 2$, *the join operation* $\sqcup_{ite}$ *is defined by*

$$\mathsf{joinVal}\,(s_1, s_2; x, c_x) \coloneqq \mathsf{if}\left(\bigwedge C_1\right) \mathsf{then}\,(\{U_1\}x)\,\mathsf{else}\,(\{U_2\}x)$$

$$\mathsf{constraints}\,(s_1, s_2; x, c_x) \coloneqq \text{true}$$

$$(\_x := \text{if } (y < x) \text{ then } (y) \text{ else } (x) \parallel \_y := \text{if } (y < x) \text{ then } (x) \text{ else } (y), \Gamma, \varphi)$$

$$(\_x := y \parallel \_y := x, \Gamma \cup \overbrace{\{y < x\}}, \varphi) \quad (\_x := x \parallel \_y := y, \Gamma \cup \{y \geq x\}, \varphi)$$

Fig. 2. Small excerpt of $(S_\varphi, \sqcup_{ite})$ for the `dist` example.

The definition can be generalized by allowing a *distinguishing formula* for the first argument of the if $(\cdot)$ then $(\cdot)$ else $(\cdot)$ term instead of $\bigwedge C_1$. It suffices to find a set of sub-conjuncts of C_1 whose negation implies C_2. Often one can simply choose the guard of the conditional statement which caused the SET to branch.

Proposition 1. *The "If-Then-Else Merge" technique induces a family of join-semilattices of SE states, i.e., the operation $\sqcup_{ite}$ and its associated partial order relation $\preceq$ satisfy axioms (SEL1)–(SEL5) of Definition 8.*

Example 2. Figure 2 depicts a fragment of the join-semilattice $(S_\varphi, \sqcup_{ite})$ induced by $\sqcup_{ite}$ for Listing 1. The two states at the bottom of the figure correspond to the outcome of the execution until the end of the if block, where Γ represents a common set of preconditions. Since the values for both $\_x$ and $\_y$ differ in those states, the If-Then-Else construction is applied. The differing formulas in the path conditions, $y < x$ and $y \geq x$, vanish in the path condition of the merged state since their disjunction can be simplified to `true`.

4.3   Abstract Weakening and Predicate Abstraction

Our General Lattice Framework, along with the state merging technique proposed below, at least partially closes the gap between symbolic execution and abstract interpretation [11] by facilitating merges based on abstract domain lattices. We first define the notion of abstract domain elements.

Definition 11 (Abstract Domain Element). *An* Abstract Domain Element *is a function defAx* $:$ Trm $\rightarrow$ Fml *mapping terms to* closed *formulas.*

Intuitively, an abstract domain element models an infinite set of *defining axioms* for JavaDL terms. If an axiom is true for a given term, then this term is described by the corresponding abstract domain element. This rather technical, syntactic definition is beneficial for the application in branch merging and allows for a straightforward embedding of predicate abstraction [16]. However, in contrast to predicate abstraction we allow infinite domains.

Definition 12 (Abstract Domain Lattice). *An* Abstract Domain Lattice *is a join-semilattice* $\mathcal{A}_T = (A_T, \sqcup)$ *with the induced partial order relation* $\sqsubseteq$ *for a countable set* A_T *of abstract domain elements accepting terms of some fixed type* T *as arguments. We impose the following requirements on* A_T *and* $\sqsubseteq$:

(1) A_T includes two elements with $\bot(t) = $ false, $\top(t) = $ true for any $t \in$ Trm.
(2) For $a, b \in A_T$ with $a \sqsubseteq b$, $\vdash a(t) \rightarrow b(t)$ holds for any term t of type T.
(3) For all $a \in A_T$ except for $\bot$, it holds that $\vdash \exists v; a(v)$.

Example 3 below illustrates the above definitions in the context of predicate abstraction. As usual, we have a bottom and a top element, where the bottom element is the only one that is not satisfiable. Furthermore, for each lattice element a that is more concrete than an element b ($a \sqsubseteq b$), also the defining axiom of a has to be stronger than that of b. Now we are in a position to generalize the "If-Then-Else Merge" technique: instead of using conditional terms for the result of joinVal $(s_1, s_2; \mathrm{x}, c_{\mathrm{x}})$ as in Definition 10, we compute a sound abstraction of the SE states to be merged. Technically, we employ the symbols c_{x} and constrain them by defining axioms computed from a suitable join in the join semi-lattice.

Definition 13 (Abstract Weakening Merge Method). *Let $\mathcal{A}_T = (A_T, \sqcup)$ be an abstract domain lattice. Given two SE states $s_j = (U_j, C_j, \varphi)$, $j = 1, 2$, the join operation $\sqcup_{abstr}$ is defined by*

$$\mathsf{joinVal}\,(s_1, s_2; \mathrm{x}, c_{\mathrm{x}}) \coloneqq c_{\mathrm{x}} \qquad \mathsf{constraints}\,(s_1, s_2; \mathrm{x}, c_{\mathrm{x}}) \coloneqq (defAx_1 \sqcup defAx_2)\,(c_{\mathrm{x}})$$

where, for $k \in 1, 2$, $defAx_k \in A_T$ are abstract domain elements such that $C_k \to defAx_k\,(\{U_k\}\,\mathrm{x})$ is provable and there is no element $defAx'_k \in A_T$ with $defAx'_k \neq defAx_k$ and $defAx'_k \sqsubseteq defAx_k$.

The constraints on $defAx_k$ state that they must be contained in the abstract domain lattice. There is not necessarily a *unique* element such that $C_k \to defAx_k\,(\{U_k\}\,\mathrm{x}_i)$ is provable. Any element for which there is no strictly smaller one suffices. For countable abstract lattices with an enumerable linearization, the functions $defAx_k$ are computable, in particular, for finite domains an enumeration is obtained by topological sorting. For the sign analysis domain, one enumeration is $\bot, -, 0, +, \top$. Generally, infinite domains should support *widening* [11] to ensure that suitable abstractions can be computed.

In Definition 13 we consider lattices with a uniform type. It is possible to use different lattices for different types in the merge technique. When no lattice is specified for some type, If-Then-Else merges are used as fallback. Depending on the situation, it may also be appropriate to define multiple lattices for the same type (see Example 3 and Fig. 3 for a concrete example for $\sqcup_{abstr}$).

Proposition 2. *The abstract weakening merge method induces a family of join-semilattices of SE states, i.e. the operation $\sqcup_{abstr}$ and its associated partial order relation $\preceq$ satisfy the axioms (SEL1)–(SEL5) of Definition 8.*

Predicate abstraction [16] is an instance of abstract weakening where the domain elements are constructed from combinations of a given finite set of unary predicates. The following example defines a domain for predicate abstraction that captures relations between program variables.

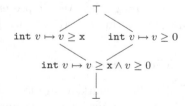

Fig. 3. Abstract domain for Example 3

Example 3 (Predicate Abstraction as Abstract Domain). Consider Listing 1. To prove that the result is non-negative, we need after the merge (line 7) the fact that the value of y is not smaller than the value of x. To capture this relation among the variables, we choose as abstraction predicates $v \geq x$ and $v \geq 0$, where v is a placeholder for the input term. The resulting abstract domain is built from the conjunctions of all subsets of those predicates, see Fig. 3.

State Merging with Join-Semilattices. The following theorem establishes the correctness of state merges with induced join-semilattices in the course of symbolic execution. We omit the proof for space reasons, and refer the reader to [22].

Theorem 1 (Correctness of Merging with Induced Join-Semilattices). *Let $\varphi \in$ Fml be a formula and $\mathbb{L}_\varphi$ an induced join-semilattice for a join operation $\sqcup$. Then, merging two SE states $s_i = (U_i, C_i, \varphi)$, $i = 1, 2$, to a state $s^* = s_1 \sqcup s_2$ is sound, i.e. if s^* is valid, then both s_1 and s_2 are valid.*

Example 4 (Continuation of Example 3). After symbolic execution of the conditional statement, we are left with two states that have identical program counters. So we can merge them using the abstraction predicates of Example 3 and end up in a single (valid) SE state as shown in Fig. 4.

$$
\begin{array}{cc}
\vdots & \vdots \\
(\_x := y \parallel \_y := x, \{C_1, y \leq -1 + x\}, \varphi) & (\_x := x \parallel \_y := y, \{C_2, y \geq x\}, \varphi)
\end{array}
$$

$$(\_x := c_1 \parallel \_y := c_2, \{(\bigwedge C_1) \vee (\bigwedge C_2),$$
$$\{\_x := c_1 \parallel \_y := c_2\}(c_1 \geq \_x \wedge c_1 \geq 0 \wedge c_2 \geq \_x \wedge c_2 \geq 0)\}, \varphi)$$

Fig. 4. Example: merging by predicate abstraction

5   Evaluation

To assess the efficacy of our state merging methods, we implemented them in the KeY verification system and applied them on a micro benchmark suite consisting of four Java programs. We also present the results of a highly complex case study on the TimSort method [15], which has been redone using our implementation.

5.1   Micro Benchmarks

Our micro benchmarks comprise the `dist` method ($\rightarrow$ Listing 1), method `abs` ($\rightarrow$ Listing 2) computing the absolute of a given integer parameter, method `gcd` ($\rightarrow$ Listing 4) computing the Greatest Common Divisor (GCD) of two integers, and method `posSum` computing the absolute of the sum of two positive integers

Listing 2. abs example

```
1  public int abs(int num) {
2      int  result ;
3      if (num < 0) { result = −num; }
4      else { result  = num; }
5      return result;
6  }
```

Listing 3. posSum example

```
1  public int posSum(int x, int y) {
2      while (x > 0) { y++; x−−; }
3      return abs(y);
4  }
```

Listing 4. gcd example

```
1   public static int gcd(int a, int b) {
2       if (a < 0) a = −a;
3       if (b < 0) b = −b;
4       int big, small;
5       if (a > b) {
6           big = a;
7           small = b;
8       } else {
9           big = b;
10          small = a;
11      }
12      return gcdHelp(big, small);
13  }
```

($\rightarrow$ Listing 3). In the dist example, the SE states after the execution of the if statement are suitable for merging. For abs, where the proof goal is to show that the result is positive, we use state merging after the execution of the if block before Line 5. In the case of gcd, we aim to prove that the returned result is actually the GCD of the input; state merging techniques are applied after Lines 2 and 3. Method posSum demonstrates the application of state merging for a while loop. Our goal is to prove that the returned result is the absolute of the sum of the inputs. To render the SET finite, we constrain the value of x by the upper bound 5. Thus, the loop is unwound five times during SE, giving the opportunity of four merges before the call to the method abs in Line 3.

For each example, we compare the number of rule applications in a proof without merging to the corresponding number in a proof containing merge rule applications on the basis of the If-Then-Else as well as the predicate abstraction technique. Results are shown in Table 1. In the last column, the predicates used for abstraction are listed; v is a placeholder for an input term of type int. The choice for abs induces a standard abstract domain for sign analysis of integers; in the other cases, the predicates are tailored to the specific situations.

The result for dist demonstrates that If-Then-Else merging can even increase the proof size when states are merged close to the end of SE. Merging with predicate abstraction was beneficial in all cases. However, If-Then-Else merging is easy to automate, whereas it is a harder problem to automatically infer abstraction predicates. Furthermore, the TimSort case study affirms that If-Then-Else merges can substantially decrease the sizes of larger proofs.

5.2 TimSort

In 2015, de Gouw et al. [15] discovered a bug in the TimSort implementation of the JDK library, Java's default sorting routine. The bug triggered, under certain circumstances, an uncaught exception. The authors fixed the bug and proved its absence as well as that of any other uncaught exception. An extended journal version of [15] is currently under preparation, where all verification proofs are being redone using the state merging approach presented in this paper. De Gouw

Table 1. Micro benchmark results

Example	# Rule Apps w/o merge	with merge	Diff. (%)	#Merges	Merge Techn.	Abstr. Predicates
dist	219	254	-15.98 %	1	ITE	–
dist	219	206	5.94 %	1	PRED (conj)	$\{v \geq 0, v \leq y\}$
abs	156	137	12.18 %	1	ITE	–
abs	156	132	15.38 %	1	PRED (disj)	$\{v > 0, v = 0, v < 0\}$
gcd	9,056	8,758	3.29 %	2	ITE	–
gcd	9,056	7,591	16.18 %	2	PRED (conj)	$\{v \geq 0, (v = a \vee v = -a)\}$ $\{v \geq 0, (v = b \vee v = -b)\}$
posSum	1,422	926	34.88 %	4	ITE	–
posSum	1,422	911	35.94 %	4	PRED	$\{v = x + y\}$

PRED (conj/disj): predicate abstraction with conjunctions/disjunctions of the predicates
ITE   : the If-Then-Else merge technique.

et al. kindly allowed us to include their current results as part of our evaluation.[4]
Table 2 provides a comparison of the proof sizes with and without merging. It shows that the proof sizes improved significantly for most proofs. All merges used, if not stated otherwise, the If-Then-Else technique and thus required no expert knowledge. In particular, state merging allowed to verify the method mergeHi which was out of reach in [15] due to the path explosion problem.

For `ensuresCapacity`, where merging with If-Then-Else actually increased the proof size, we created a new proof using a merge based on predicate abstraction. The resulting proof size is 15 % smaller compared to the version without merging and even 25 % smaller than the proof with If-Then-Else based merging.

Table 2. Statistics comparing proofs with and without state merging

Method	#Rule Apps (in [1])	#Rule Apps (with Merging)	#Merges	Percentage Changes with State Merging
ensuresCapacity	44,346	50,707	1	-14%
ensuresCapacity*	44,346	37,815	1	15%
mergeAt	279,155	63,309	6	77%
gallopLeft	303,716	88,332	6	71%
sort(a,lo,hi,c)	235,632	152,752	1	35%
mergeHi	N/A	460,409	5	NaN

*) Proof by authors of this paper, uses predicate abstraction rather than If-Then-Else.

6   Lessons Learned and Future Work

The proposed state merging approach transforms an SET into a connected and rooted Directed Acyclic Graph (DAG). Changing the underlying data structures in a complex verification system such as KeY would be a substantial undertaking. We implemented a different solution by adding the new merge node as a child to *only one of* the parents and *linking* the second parent to it. Our implementation

---

[4] Available at http://www.key-project.org/timsort/stats.html.

ensures that, if the subtree below a merge node is closed (or the merge node is pruned away), then the linked node is also closed (or "unlinked").

It is important to automate state merging as much as possible, in particular for less complex verification tasks that are otherwise fully automatic. To help this, we extended the specification language JML with the annotation $/ * @ \, merge\_proc < join\_operator > @ * /$. It is placed in front of a Java block after which the merge is supposed to happen. For certain join operators, for example the If-Then-Else join operator, this requires much less expert knowledge than the definition of a *block contract*, i.e. an annotation of a block of statements with pre- and postconditions, as an alternative way of tackling path explosion.

In our experiments, we discovered that state merging with the If-Then-Else technique is most beneficial when applied in situations where (1) a substantial amount of code remains to be executed, and thus a lot of repetition can be avoided, and (2) the difference between the states to be merged is as small as possible. "Difference" means the number of variables attaining different values in the symbolic states and the number of different formulas in the path conditions.

Predicate abstraction-based state merging is applicable to a wider range of constellations. However, to come up with suitable predicates requires a certain amount of expertise. An unsuitable choice of abstraction predicates can cause the unfeasibility of the proof goal, because abstraction loses precision. At this time, to merge states with predicate abstraction is comparable in difficulty to writing block contracts. Nevertheless, we think that state merging is more suitable for automation, because it can be performed on-the-fly *during* the proof process. Future work will aim at integrating heuristic approaches to improve the performance of If-Then-Else state merging [21] as well as methods developed for specification generation to automatically infer abstraction predicates [17, 25].

7 Related Work and Conclusion

Existing work on state merging in symbolic execution employs If-Then-Else based techniques [2, 18, 21, 23] or addresses the automatic generation of loop invariants by the means of abstraction [6, 25]. Kuznetsov et al. [21] try to assess the "cost-benefit ratio" of If-Then-Else based merges by heuristically trading off the reduction of states against the complexity of the resulting expressions. Bubel et al. [6] use value abstraction and Weiß et al. [25] use predicate abstraction for merging states in the course of the automatic generation of loop invariants.

In contrast to previous work, our approach is not limited to a particular state merging technique. We devised a general lattice-based framework for join operations and proved soundness of a state merging rule for join operations conforming to our framework. The two most popular state merging techniques in the literature, If-Then-Else and predicate abstraction, are instances of our framework. Our implementation is based on the state-of-the-art verification system KeY [1]. It has been extensively evaluated with the highly complex TimSort case study and it was demonstrated that significant improvements can be gained. This led to proofs that were out of reach before.

Acknowledgment. We would like to thank the authors of [15] for the permission to quote data from the extended journal version of their paper under preparation.

References

1. Ahrendt, W., et al.: The KeY platform for verification and analysis of Java programs. In: Giannakopoulou, D., Kroening, D. (eds.) VSTTE 2014. LNCS, vol. 8471, pp. 55–71. Springer, Heidelberg (2014)
2. Anand, S., Godefroid, P., Tillmann, N.: Demand-driven compositional symbolic execution. In: Ramakrishnan, C.R., Rehof, J. (eds.) TACAS 2008. LNCS, vol. 4963, pp. 367–381. Springer, Heidelberg (2008)
3. Anand, S., Păsăreanu, C.S., Visser, W.: Symbolic execution with abstract subsumption checking. In: Valmari, A. (ed.) SPIN 2006. LNCS, vol. 3925, pp. 163–181. Springer, Heidelberg (2006)
4. Beckert, B., Hähnle, R.: Reasoning and verification. IEEE Intell. Syst. **29**(1), 20–29 (2014)
5. Beckert, B., Hähnle, R. (eds.): Verification of Object-Oriented Software: The KeY Approach. Springer, Berlin (2006)
6. Bubel, R., Hähnle, R., Weiß, B.: Abstract interpretation of symbolic execution with explicit state updates. In: Boer, F.S., Bonsangue, M.M., Madelaine, E. (eds.) FMCO 2008. LNCS, vol. 5751, pp. 247–277. Springer, Heidelberg (2009)
7. Burstall, R.M.: Program proving as hand simulation with a little induction. In: Information Processing, pp. 308–312. Elsevier (1974)
8. Cadar, C., Sen, K.: Symbolic execution for software testing: three decades later. Commun. ACM **56**(2), 82–90 (2013)
9. Chu, D.-H., Jaffar, J., Murali, V.: Lazy symbolic execution for enhanced learning. In: Bonakdarpour, B., Smolka, S.A. (eds.) RV 2014. LNCS, vol. 8734, pp. 323–339. Springer, Heidelberg (2014)
10. Clarke, E.M., Grumberg, O., et al.: Model Checking. The MIT Press, Cambridge (1999)
11. Cousot, P., Cousot, R.: Abstract interpretation: a unified lattice model for static analysis of programs by construction or approximation of fixpoints. In: 4th Symposium of POPL, pp. 238–252. ACM Press, January 1977
12. Fitting, M.C.: First-Order Logic and Automated Theorem Proving, 2nd edn. Springer, Berlin (1996)
13. Fitting, M.C., Mendelsohn, R.: First-Order Modal Logic. Kluwer, Dordrecht (1998)
14. Gosling, J., Joy, B., et al.: The Java (TM) Language Specification, 3rd edn. Addison-Wesley Professional, Wokingham (2005). http://psc.informatik.uni-jena.de/languages/Java/javaspec-3.pdf
15. de Gouw, S., Rot, J., de Boer, F.S., Bubel, R., Hähnle, R.: OpenJDK's Java.utils.Collection.sort() is broken: the good, the bad and the worst case. In: Kroening, D., Păsăreanu, C.S. (eds.) CAV 2015. LNCS, vol. 9206, pp. 273–289. Springer, Heidelberg (2015)
16. Graf, S., Saidi, H.: Construction of abstract state graphs with PVS. In: Grumberg, O. (ed.) CAV 1997. LNCS, vol. 1254, pp. 72–83. Springer, Heidelberg (1997)
17. Hähnle, R., Wasser, N., et al.: Array abstraction with symbolic pivots. In: Ábrahám, E., Bonsangue, M., et al. (eds.) Theory and Practice of Formal Methods. LNCS, vol. 9660, pp. 104–121. Springer, Berlin (2016)

18. Hansen, T., Schachte, P., Søndergaard, H.: State joining and splitting for the symbolic execution of binaries. In: Bensalem, S., Peled, D.A. (eds.) RV 2009. LNCS, vol. 5779, pp. 76–92. Springer, Heidelberg (2009)
19. Harel, D., Tiuryn, J., et al.: Dynamic Logic. MIT Press, Cambridge (2000)
20. King, J.C.: Symbolic execution and program testing. Commun. ACM **19**(7), 385–394 (1976)
21. Kuznetsov, V., Kinder, J., et al.: Efficient state merging in symbolic execution. In: Proceedings of the 33rd Conference on PLDI, pp. 193–204. ACM (2012)
22. Scheurer, D.: From trees to DAGs: a general lattice model for symbolic execution. Master's thesis, Technische Universität Darmstadt (2015). http://tinyurl.com/Trees2DAGs
23. Sen, K., Necula, G., et al.: MultiSE: multi-path symbolic execution using value summaries. In: 10th Joint Meeting on Foundations of Software Engineering, pp. 842–853. ACM (2015)
24. Shoenfield, J.R.: Mathematical Logic. Addison-Wesley, Wokingham (1967)
25. Weiß, B.: Predicate abstraction in a program logic calculus. In: Leuschel, M., Wehrheim, H. (eds.) IFM 2009. LNCS, vol. 5423, pp. 136–150. Springer, Heidelberg (2009)

A Case Study of Formal Approach
to Dynamically Reconfigurable Systems
by Using Dynamic Linear Hybrid Automata

Ryo Yanase[1](✉), Tatsunori Sakai[1], Makoto Sakai[1], and Satoshi Yamane[2]

[1] Graduate School of Natural Science and Technology,
Kanazawa University, Kakuma-machi, Kanazawa, Ishikawa 920-1192, Japan
`ryanase@csl.ec.t.kanazawa-u.ac.jp`
[2] Institute of Science and Engineering, Kanazawa University,
Kakuma-machi, Kanazawa, Ishikawa 920-1192, Japan

Abstract. Networking systems and embedded systems are able to change their configuration, components and modules at run-time. Such a system is called dynamically reconfigurable system. For guaranteeing safety of the system, model checking is one of the effective methods. This paper presents a dynamic linear hybrid automaton (DLHA) as a specification language for designing dynamically reconfigurable systems. As a practical experiment, we describe an embedded cooperative system consisting of CPU and DRP by DLHAs and verify several properties for the system with a model checker that performs the reachability analysis by using monitor automata.

Keywords: Verification · Model checking and hybrid automata

1 Introduction

1.1 Background

Dynamically reconfigurable systems are being used in a number of areas [11,13,15]. The major methods of checking system safety include simulation and testing; however, it is often difficult for them to ensure safety precisely, since these methods don't check all states. In such cases, model checking is a more effective method. In this paper, we propose the *Dynamic Linear Hybrid Automaton* (DLHA) specification language for describing dynamically reconfigurable systems and provide a reachability analysis algorithm for verifying system safety.

1.2 Features of Dynamically Reconfigurable Systems Consisting of CPU and DRP

The target of our research is an embedded system in which a CPU and dynamically reconfigurable hardware, e.g., DRP or D-FPGA [3] operate cooperatively.

© Springer International Publishing AG 2016
K. Ogata et al. (Eds.): ICFEM 2016, LNCS 10009, pp. 74–89, 2016.
DOI: 10.1007/978-3-319-47846-3_6

The dynamically reconfigurable processor (DRP) is a coarse-grained programmable processor developed by NEC [15] and it manages both the power conservation and miniaturization. The DRP is used to accelerate the computations of a general purpose CPU with through cooperating operations, and it has the following features:

- Dynamically creation/destruction of the function: when a process occurs, the DRP constitutes a private circuit for processing it. The circuit configuration is released after the process finishes.
- Hybrid property: the operation frequency changes whenever a context switch occurs.
- Parallel execution: the DRP executes several processes on the same board at the same time.
- Queue for communication: the DRP asynchronously receives processing requests from the CPU.

For the experiments, we specified a dynamically reconfigurable embedded system consisting of a CPU and DRP, and verified the some of its important features. This is the first time that specification and verification of dynamic changes have been tried in a practical case.

1.3 Related Work

Specification. We developed a new specification language (DLHA) based on a linear hybrid automaton [2] with both creation/destruction events and unbounded FIFO queues. DLHA is different from existing research in the following points:

- Varshavsky and others proposed the GALA (Globally Asynchronous - Locally Arbitrary) modeling approach including timed guards [18]. This approach cannot describe hybrid systems since it is the specification language based on discrete systems. Thus, GALA cannot represent changes in operating frequency.
- Minami and others have specified a dynamically reconfigurable system using linear hybrid automata and have verified it by using a model checker, HYTECH [14]. Since linear hybrid automata cannot describe changes to the configuration and asynchronous communications by using unbounded FIFO queues, the system has been specified as a static system.
- Attie and Lynch specified systems whose components are dynamically created/destroyed by using I/O automata [4]. I/O automata cannot describe changes in variables, for example, changes in clock and operating frequency.
- Yamada and others proposed hierarchical linear hybrid automata for specifying dynamically reconfigurable systems [19]. They introduced concepts such as class, object, etc., to the specification language. However, as the scale of a system to be specified increases, the representation and method of analysis in the verification stage tend to be complex.

– Boigelot and Godefroid specified a communication protocol in terms of finite-state machines and unbounded FIFO buffers (queues), and they verified it [6]. Since the finite-state machine also cannot describe changes in variables, it is unsuitable in our case.
– Bouajjani and others proposed a reachability analysis for pushdown automata and symbolic reachability analysis for FIFO-channel systems [8,9]. However, since their analysis don't provide for continuous changes in variables, in languages cannot be used for designing hybrid systems.

Verification Method. The originality of our work on the verification method twofold:

– Our method targets systems that dynamically change their configurations, which is something the existing work, such as HYTECH, has studied. We extend the syntax and semantics of linear hybrid automata with special actions called *creation actions* and *destruction actions*. We define a state in which an automaton does not exist and transitions for creation and destruction.
– Our method is a comprehensive symbolic verification for hybrid properties, FIFO queues and creation/destruction of tasks.

2 Dynamic Linear Hybrid Automaton

2.1 Syntax

A dynamic linear hybrid automaton (DLHA) is an extended linear hybrid automaton and represented as a 8-tuple $(L, V, Inv, Flow, Act, T, t_0, T_d)$, where

– L is a finite set of nodes called locations.
– V is a finite set of variables.
– $Inv : L \rightarrow \Phi(V)$ is a function that assigns an invariant to each location, where $\Phi(V)$ is a set of all constraints over V.
– $Flow : L \rightarrow F(V)$ is a function that assigns a flow condition to each location, where $F(V)$ is a set of all flow conditions over V.
– $Act = Act_{in} \cup Act_{out} \cup Act_{\tau}$ is a finite set of *actions*.
  • Act_{in} is a finite set of *input actions*, and each input action has the form a?. An input action m? denotes receiving the message m.
  • Act_{out} is a finite set of *output actions*, and each output action has the form a!. An output action m! denotes broadcasting the message m to each DLHA.
  • Act_{τ} is a finite set of *internal actions* that denote other events.
  Moreover, we formalize the following special actions:
  • A *creation action* that has the form $Crt\_\mathcal{A}'$? or $Crt\_\mathcal{A}'$! denotes a message for creation of the DLHA $\mathcal{A}'$. $Crt\_\mathcal{A}'$? is an input action, and it represents that $\mathcal{A}'$ has been created. $Crt\_\mathcal{A}'! \in Act_{out}$ is an output action, and represents a request for creating $\mathcal{A}'$.

- A *destruction action* that has the form Dst_A'? or Crt_A'! denotes a message for a destruction of DLHA A'. Dst_A'? $\in Act_{in}$ is an input action that indicates A' has been destroyed.
- An *enqueue action* that has the form $q!m$ denotes enqueueing of message m into a queue q. This action is an internal one, that is, $q!m \in Act_\tau$.
- A *dequeue action* that has the form $q?m$ denotes dequeueing of message m from the top of queue q.

- $T \subseteq L \times \Phi(V) \times Act \times 2^{UPD(V)} \times L$ is a finite set of edges called *transitions*. Here, a constraint $\phi \in \Phi(V)$ is called a *guard condition*, and $\lambda \in 2^{UPD(V)}$ are called *update expressions*. Each update expression has the form $x := c$ or $x := x + c$, where $x \in V$ and $c \in \mathbb{Q}$.
- $t_0 \in L \times (Act_{in} \cup Act_\tau) \times 2^{UPD(V)}$ is an *initial transition*.
- $T_d \subseteq L \times \Phi(V) \times Act_{out}$ is a finite set of *destruction-transitions*.

2.2 Operational Semantics

A state σ of a DLHA $(L, V, Inv, Flow, A, T, t_0, T_d)$ is defined as $\perp \mid (l, \nu)$, where $l \in L$ is a location, $\nu : V \to \mathbb{R}$ is an assignment called *evaluation* of variables, and $\perp$ denotes an *undefined value*.

The semantics $\mathcal{M}$ of the DLHA is defined as $(\Sigma, \Rightarrow, \sigma_0)$, where Σ is a set of states, $\Rightarrow$ is a set of *time transitions* and *discrete transitions* and σ_0 is the initial state.

Time Transition. For arbitrary $\delta \in \mathbb{R}_{\geq 0}$,

- $\perp \Rightarrow_\delta \perp$,
- $(l, \nu) \Rightarrow_\delta (l, \nu')$ if $\nu' = \nu + \delta \cdot Flow(l) \in Inv(l)$,

where $\nu' = \nu + \delta \cdot Flow(l)$ denotes an evaluation such that $\forall x \in V.\nu'(x) = \nu(x) + \delta \cdot \dot{x} \cdot Flow(l)(x)$, and $\nu' \in Inv(l)$ denotes that $\nu'(x)$ satisfies the constraint $Inv(l)$ for any $x \in V$.

Discrete Transition. For an evaluation ν and update expressions $\lambda \in 2^{UPD(V)}$, $\nu[\lambda]$ denotes an evaluation updated by λ.

- For any transition $(l, \phi, a, \lambda, l') \in T$, $(l, \nu) \Rightarrow_a (l, \nu[\lambda])$ if $\nu \in \phi$ and $\nu[\lambda] \in Inv(l')$.
- (*Creation of a DLHA*) For the initial transition $t_0 = (l_0, a_0, \lambda_0)$, $\perp \Rightarrow_{a_0} (l_0, \mathbf{0}[\lambda_0])$ where $\mathbf{0}$ is an evaluation such that $\forall x \in V.[\mathbf{0}(x) = 0]$.
- (*Destruction of a DLHA*) For any destruction-transition $(l, \phi, a) \in T_d$, $(l, \nu) \Rightarrow_a \perp$ if $\nu \in \phi$.

For the initial transition (l_0, a_0, λ_0), the initial state σ_0 is defined as

$$\sigma_0 = \begin{cases} \perp & (a_0 \in Act_{in}) \\ (l_0, \mathbf{0}[\lambda_0]) & (otherwise). \end{cases}$$

3 Dynamically Reconfigurable Systems

To describe an asynchronous communication among DLHAs in a dynamically reconfigurable system, we use a queue (*unbounded* FIFO buffer) as a model of the communication channel. We assume that the system performs lossless transmission, so we can let the queue be unbounded.

A dynamically reconfigurable system $\mathcal{S} = (A, \mathcal{Q})$ consists of a finite set $A = \{\mathcal{A}_1, \ldots, \mathcal{A}_{|A|}\}$ of DLHAs and a finite set $\mathcal{Q} = \{q_1, \ldots, q_{|\mathcal{Q}|}\}$ of queues.

A state s of the dynamically reconfigurable system is a tuple $\langle \boldsymbol{\sigma}, \boldsymbol{w}_{\mathcal{Q}} \rangle$ where $\boldsymbol{\sigma}$ is a vector of states of DLHAs and $\boldsymbol{w}_{\mathcal{Q}}$ is a vector of contents of queues.

Time Transition. For an arbitrary $\delta \in \mathbb{R}_{\geq 0}$, the time transition is defined as

$$\langle \boldsymbol{\sigma}, \boldsymbol{w}_{\mathcal{Q}} \rangle \to_\delta \langle \boldsymbol{\sigma}', \boldsymbol{w}_{\mathcal{Q}} \rangle \iff \forall i.\sigma_i \Rightarrow_\delta \sigma_i.$$

Discrete Transition. Let $\boldsymbol{\sigma}, \boldsymbol{\sigma}', \boldsymbol{w}_{\mathcal{Q}}$ and $\boldsymbol{w}'_{\mathcal{Q}}$ be $\boldsymbol{\sigma} = (\sigma_1, \ldots, \sigma_{|A|})$, $\boldsymbol{\sigma}' = (\sigma'_1, \ldots, \sigma'_{|A|})$, $\boldsymbol{w}_{\mathcal{Q}} = (w_1, \ldots, w_{|\mathcal{Q}|})$ and $\boldsymbol{w}'_{\mathcal{Q}} = (w'_1, \ldots, w'_{|\mathcal{Q}|})$.

– For any output action $a!$, $\langle \boldsymbol{\sigma}, \boldsymbol{w}_{\mathcal{Q}} \rangle \to_a \langle \boldsymbol{\sigma}', \boldsymbol{w}_{\mathcal{Q}} \rangle$

  iff $\exists i.\sigma_i \Rightarrow_{a!} \sigma'_i \wedge \forall j \neq i.\sigma_j \Rightarrow_{a?} \sigma_j \vee ((\neg \exists \sigma'_j.\sigma_j \Rightarrow_{a?} \sigma'_j) \wedge \sigma_j = \sigma'_j).$

An output action is broadcasted to all DLHAs, and a DLHA receiving the action moves by synchronization if the guard condition holds in the state.

– For an internal action a_τ,
  • in the case of $a_\tau = q_k!w$, $\langle \boldsymbol{\sigma}, \boldsymbol{w}_{\mathcal{Q}} \rangle \to_{q_k!w} \langle \boldsymbol{\sigma}', \boldsymbol{w}'_{\mathcal{Q}} \rangle$,

    iff $\exists i.\sigma_i \Rightarrow_{q_k!w} \sigma'_i \wedge \forall j \neq i.\sigma_j = \sigma'_j \wedge w'_k = w_k w \wedge \forall l \neq k.w_k = w'_k,$

  • while in the case of $a_\tau = q_k?w$, $\langle \boldsymbol{\sigma}, \boldsymbol{w}_{\mathcal{Q}} \rangle \to_{q_k?w} \langle \boldsymbol{\sigma}', \boldsymbol{w}'_{\mathcal{Q}} \rangle$,

    iff $\exists i.\sigma_i \Rightarrow_{q_k?w} \sigma'_i \wedge \forall j \neq i.\sigma_j = \sigma'_j \wedge w_k = w w'_k \wedge \forall l \neq k.w_l = w'_l,$

  • otherwise, $\langle \boldsymbol{\sigma}, \boldsymbol{w}_{\mathcal{Q}} \rangle \to_{a_\tau} \langle \boldsymbol{\sigma}', \boldsymbol{w}_{\mathcal{Q}} \rangle$, iff $\exists i.\sigma_i \Rightarrow_{a_\tau} \sigma'_i \wedge \forall j \neq i.\sigma_j = \sigma'_j.$

A *run (or path)* ρ of the system $\mathcal{S}$ is the following finite (or infinite) sequence of states.

$$\rho : s_0 \to_{a_0}^{\delta_0} s_1 \to_{a_1}^{\delta_1} \cdots \to_{a_{i-1}}^{\delta_{i-1}} s_i \to_{a_i}^{\delta_i} \cdots$$

where $\to_{a_i}^{\delta_i}$ between s_i and s_{i+1} is defined as follows:

$$s_i \to_{a_i}^{\delta_i} s_{i+1} \iff \exists s'_i.s_i \to_{\delta_i} s'_i \wedge s'_i \to_{a_i} s_{i+1}.$$

The initial state s_0 is a tuple $\langle (\sigma_{01} \ldots, \sigma_{0|A|}), (w_{01}, \ldots, w_{0|\mathcal{Q}|}) \rangle$, where each σ_{0i} is the initial state of DLHA $\mathcal{A}_i$ and each w_{0j} is empty; that is, $\forall j.w_{0j} = \varepsilon$.

4   Reachability Analysis

4.1   Reachability Problem

We define reachability and the reachability problem for a dynamically reconfigurable system as follows:

Definition 1 (Reachability). *For a dynamically reconfigurable system $S = (A, Q)$ and a location l_t, S reaches l_t if there exists a path $s_0 \rightarrow^{\delta_0}_{a_0} \cdots \rightarrow^{\delta_{t-1}}_{a_{t-1}} s_t$ such that s_t has a DLHA-state which contains the location l_t.*

Definition 2 (Reachability Problem). *Given a dynamically reconfigurable system $S = (A, Q)$ and a location l_t, we output "yes" if S can reach l_t, and "no" otherwise.*

4.2   Algorithm of Reachability Analysis

Figure 1 show the algorithm of the reachability analysis. Our method introduces *convex polyhedra* for the reachability analysis in accordance with [12]. In this algorithm, we define a state s in the reachability analysis as (L, ζ, w_Q), where L is a finite set of locations, ζ is a convex polyhedron, and w_Q is a vector of contents of queues. Figure 1 is an overview of the reachability analysis, and this algorithm is performed by using the extended method of [1] with a set Q of queues. The analysis is performed as follows:

1. Compute the initial state s_0 of the system S (ll.1–3).
2. Initialize a traversed set Visit and a untraversed set Wait of states by $\varnothing$ and $\{s_0\}$ (line 4).
3. While Wait is not empty, repeat the following process (ll.5–16).
    (a) Take a state (L, ζ, w_Q) from Wait and remove the state from Wait (ll.6–7).
    (b) If the set L of locations contains the target location, return "yes" and terminate (ll.8–10).
    (c) If the state has not been traversed yet $((L, \zeta, w_Q) \notin \text{Visit})$ (line 11),
        i. add the state to Visit (line 12),
        ii. compute the set S_{post} of successors by using the subroutine Succ (line 13), and
        iii. add all components of S_{post} to Wait (line 14).

The subroutine Succ computes successors of a state. Successors for a state s together with a transition that has an output action are computed by the following procedures:

1. Initialize S_{post} by $\varnothing$.
2. Compute a convex polyhedron ζ_δ for time transition.
3. For each A_i in the system S, compute the set T_{si} of transitions that are outgoing from the state by using the input action $a_l?$.
4. Compute a set Δ of combinations of T_{si}.

5. For each combination $T = (t_1, \ldots, t_n) \in \Delta$, the successor $s' = (L'_T, \zeta'_T, \boldsymbol{w}_Q)$ is computed and $S_{post} := S_{post} \cup \{s'\}$.

The correctness of this algorithm is implied by Lemmas 1 and 2.

Lemma 1. *If this algorithm terminates and returns "l_t is not reachable", the system $\mathcal{S}$ holds the safety property.*

Lemma 2. *If this algorithm terminates and returns "l_t is reachable", the system $\mathcal{S}$ does not hold the safety property.*

By definition, all linear hybrid automata are DLHAs. Our system dynamically changes its structure by sending and receiving messages. However, the messages statically determine the structure, and the system is a linear hybrid automaton with a set of queues. It is basically equivalent to the reachability analysis of a linear hybrid automaton. Therefore, the reachability problem of dynamically reconfigurable systems is undecidable, and this algorithm might not terminate [1].

Moreover, in some cases, a system will run into an abnormal state in which the length of a queue becomes infinitely long, and the verification procedure does not terminate.

Input: a system $\mathcal{S}$ and a target location l_t
Output: "yes" or "no"
1: $L_0 \leftarrow \{l_{0i} \mid t_{0i} = (l_{0i}, a_{0i}, \lambda_{0i}), a_{0i} \neq Crt\_A_i?\}$
2: $\lambda_0 \leftarrow \bigcup \{\lambda_{0i} \mid t_{0i} = (l_{0i}, a_{0i}, \lambda_{0i}), a_{0i} \neq Crt\_A_i?\}$
3: $s_0 \leftarrow (L_0, \mathbf{0}[\lambda_0], (\varepsilon, \ldots, \varepsilon))$ /* Compute the initial state */
4: Visit $\leftarrow \varnothing$, Wait $\leftarrow \{s_0\}$ /* Initialize */
5: **while** Wait $\neq \varnothing$ **do**
6:      $(L, \zeta, \boldsymbol{w}_Q) \leftarrow s \in$ Wait
7:      Wait $\leftarrow$ Wait $\setminus \{(L, \zeta, \boldsymbol{w}_Q)\}$
8:      **if** $l_t \in L$ **then**
9:          **return** "yes"
10:     **end if**
11:     **if** $(L, \zeta, \boldsymbol{w}_Q) \notin$ Visit **then**
12:         Visit $\leftarrow$ Visit $\cup \{(L, \zeta, \boldsymbol{w}_Q)\}$
13:         $S_{post} \leftarrow \mathrm{Succ}((L, \zeta, \boldsymbol{w}_Q), \mathcal{S})$ /* Compute the set of post-states */
14:         Wait $\leftarrow$ Wait $\cup S_{post}$
15:     **end if**
16: **end while**
17: **return** "no"

Fig. 1. Reachability analysis

5 Practical Experiment

5.1 Model Checker

We implemented a model checker of dynamically reconfigurable systems consisting of DLHAs in Java (about 1,600 lines of code) by using the LAS, PPL, and QDD external libraries [5–7,17]. For the verification, we input the DLHAs of the system, a *monitor automaton*, and the *error location* to the model checker, and it output "yes (reachable)" or "no (unreachable)". The monitor automaton had a special location (we call it the error location), and checked the system without changing the system's behavior [12]. The monitor automata had to be specified to reach the error location if the system didn't satisfy the properties.

For the specification of the input model, we extended the syntax and semantics of DLHA as follows:

- A transition between locations can have a label *asap* (that means 'as soon as possible'). For a transition labeled *asap*, a time transition does not occur just before the discrete transition.
- Each DLHA can have constraints and update expressions for the variables of another DLHA in the same system. That is, for each DLHA, invariants, guard conditions, update expressions and flow conditions can be used by all DLHAs.

5.2 Specification of Dynamically Reconfigurable Embedded System

A Cooperative System Including CPU and DRP. We have specified a dynamically reconfigurable embedded system consisting of a CPU and DRP for the model described in our previous research [14]. A DRP has computation resources called *tiles* (or *processing elements*), and it dynamically sets the context of a process if there are enough free tiles. In addition, a DRP can change the operating frequency in accordance with running processes. In this paper, we assume that the number of tiles and the operating frequency for each process have been set in advance and that the operating frequency of the DRP is always the minimum frequency of the running co-tasks.

Figure 2 shows an overview of the system. This system processes jobs submitted from the external environment through the cooperative operation of the CPU and DRP. The CPU Dispatcher creates a task when it receives a call message of the task from the external environment. When a task on the CPU uses the DRP, The CPU Dispatcher sends a message to the DRP Dispatcher. The DRP Dispatcher receives the message asynchronously and creates a *co-task* (it means 'cooperative task') in a first-come, first-served manner if there are enough free tiles. Here, we will assume that this system has two tasks and two co-tasks that have the parameters shown in Tables 1 and 2.

The system, whose components are illustrated in Fig. 3, consists of 11 DLHAs and 1 queue. The external environment consists of EnvA (Fig. 4) and EnvB (Fig. 5) that periodically create TaskA (Fig. 7) and TaskB (Fig. 8). That is, EnvA uses *Crt_taskA*! to create TaskA every 70 ms, and EnvB uses *Crt_taskB*! to create

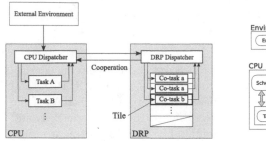

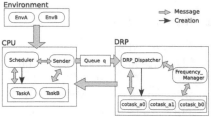

Fig. 2. Overview of the CPU-DRP embedded system

Fig. 3. Components of the system

Table 1. Parameters of tasks

Task	Period	Deadline	Priority	Process
A	70 ms	70 ms	High	20 ms, co-task a0,
				10 ms, co-task b0
B	200 ms	200 ms	Low	co-task a1, 97 ms

TaskB with every 200 ms. The Scheduler (Fig. 6) performs scheduling in accordance with the priority and actions for creation and destruction of DLHAs. For example, when TaskA is created by EnvA with *Crt_taskA*! and TaskB is already running, The Scheduler receives *Crt_taskA?* from EnvA and sends *Act_Preempt*! to TaskA and TaskB. Then, *Act_Preempt*! causes TaskA to move to *RunA* and TaskB to move to *WaitB*.

TaskA and TaskB send a message to The Sender if they need a co-task. The Sender (Fig. 9) enqueues the message to create a co-task to q when it receives a message from tasks. When TaskA sends *Act_Create_a0*! and moves to *RunA* from *WaitA*, The Sender receives *Act_Create_a0?* and enqueues *cotask_a0* in q with *q!cotask_a0*.

The DRP_Dispatcher (Fig. 10) dequeues a message and creates cotask_a0 (Fig. 12), cotask_a1 (Fig. 13), and cotask_b0 (Fig. 14) if there are enough free tiles. The Frequency_Manager (Fig. 11) is a module that manages the operating frequency of the DRP. When a DLHA of a co-task is created, The Frequency_Manager moves to the location that sets the frequency to the minimum value.

Table 2. Parameters of co-tasks

Co-task	Processing time	Deadline	Tiles	Rate of frequency
$a0, a1$	10 ms	15 ms	2	1
$b0$	5 ms	10 ms	6	1/2

Fig. 4. External environment: EnvA   **Fig. 5.** External environment: EnvB

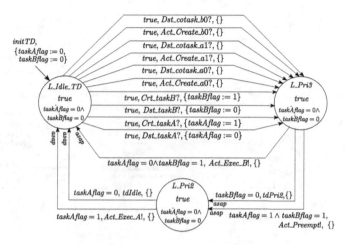

Fig. 6. CPU scheduler: scheduler

Other Cases. We have the parameters of the model in Subsect. 5.2 and conducted experiments with it.

- Modified Tasks: We modified the parameters of the tasks on the CPU as shown in Table 3. Here, the parameters of the co-tasks are the same as those in Table 2.
- Modified co-tasks: We modified the parameters of the co-tasks on the DRP, as shown in Table 4. Parameters of the tasks are the same as those in Table 1.

Table 3. Modified parameters of tasks

Task	Period	Deadline	Priority	Process
A	90 ms	80 ms	High	20 ms, co-task b0,
				20 ms, co-task a0
B	200 ms	150 ms	Low	co-task a1, 70 ms

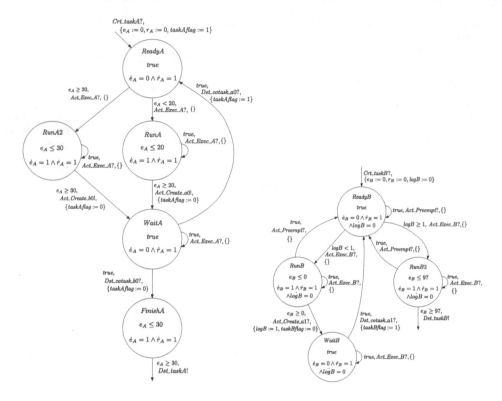

Fig. 7. Task: TaskA   **Fig. 8.** Task: TaskB

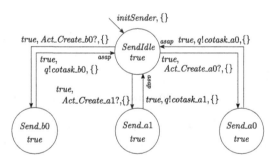

Fig. 9. Message sender to DRP: sender

5.3 Verification Experiment

We verified that the embedded systems described in Subsect. 5.2 provide the following properties by using monitor automata. The verification experiment was performed on a machine with an Intel (R) Core (TM) i7-3770 (3.40 GHz) CPU and 16 GB RAM running Gentoo Linux (3.10.25-gentoo).

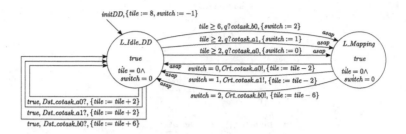

Fig. 10. DRP_Dispatcher

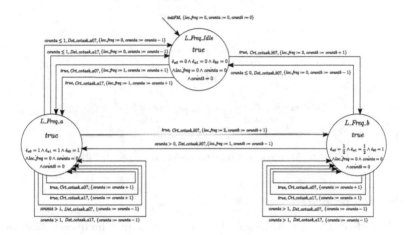

Fig. 11. Frequency_Manager

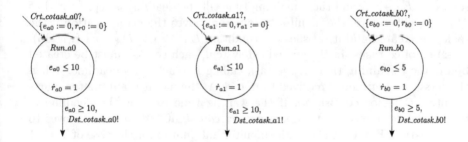

Fig. 12. cotask_a0   **Fig. 13.** cotask_a1   **Fig. 14.** cotask_b0

Table 4. Modified parameters of co-tasks

Co-task	Processing time	Deadline	Tiles	Rate of frequency
$a0, a1$	5 ms	10 ms	4	1
$b0$	10 ms	20 ms	5	1/3

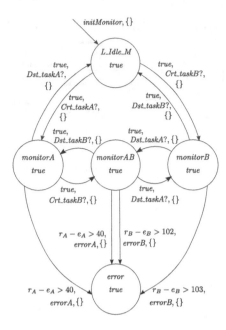

Fig. 15. Monitor automaton checking schedulability

Verification properties are below:

- Schedulability: Here, schedulability is a property in which each task of the system finishes before its deadline. Let E_A be the total processing time and D_A be the deadline in task A (Fig. 7); the remaining processing time is represented as $E_A - e_A$, and the remaining time till the deadline is represented as $D_A - r_A$. Therefore, the monitor automaton moves the error location if the task A is created and it satisfies the condition $E_A - e_A > D_A - r_A$ (Fig. 15).
- Creation of co-tasks: In the embedded system, each co-task must be created before the remaining time in the task calling it reaches its deadline. When the message $create\_a0$ is received from task A, the monitor automaton starts counting time for co-task $a0$. If the waiting time exceeds the deadline of task A before it receives the message Crt_cotask_a0, the monitor moves to error location. Figure 16 shows the monitor automaton for the case of Table 1 for co-task $a0$. Monitor automata for co-tasks $a1$ and $b0$ can be similarly described.
- Destruction of co-tasks: Each co-task must be destroyed before the waiting time reaches its deadline. For the co-task $a0$, when the message Crt_cotask_a0 is received from the dispatcher DRP_Dispatcher, the monitor automaton checks the message Dst_cotask_a0. Figure 17 shows the monitor automaton for the case of Table 2.
- Frequency management: Creating or destroying a co-task, the DRP changes the operating frequency corresponding to the co-tasks being processed. Since this system requires that the frequency is always at the minimum value, the

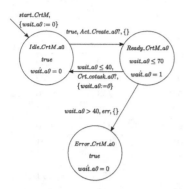

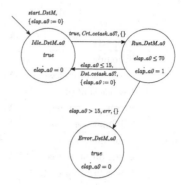

Fig. 16. Monitor automaton checking creation of co-task $a0$

Fig. 17. Monitor automaton checking destruction of co-task $a0$

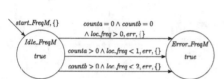

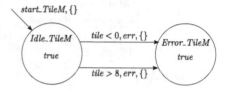

Fig. 18. Monitor automaton checking frequency management

Fig. 19. Monitor automaton checking tile management

monitor checks whether the frequency manager (Frequency_Manager) moves to the correct location when it receives a message for creating a co-task. For example, when co-task $a0$ and co-task $b0$ are running on the DRP, Frequency_Manager must be at location L_Freq_b. Figure 18 show the monitor automaton for the case of Table 2.

– Tile Management: When the DRP receives a message for creating of a co-task and the number of free tiles is enough to process it, the dispatcher creates the co-task. The dispatcher then updates the number of used tiles. The monitor automaton checks whether the number $tiles$ in DRP_Dispatcher is always between 0 and the maximum number, 8 in this case (Fig. 19).

The experimental results shown in Table 5 indicate that the modified tasks cases and the modified co-tasks cases were verified with less computation resources (memory and time) than were used by the original model. This reduction is likely due to the following reasons:

– Regarding the schedulability of the modified tasks model, the processing time is shorter than that of the original model since the verification terminates if a counterexample is found.
– In the cases of the modified co-tasks, the most obvious explanation is that the state-space is smaller than that of the original model since the number of branches in the search tree (i.e. nondeterministic transitions in this system)

Table 5. Experimental results

Model	Property	Satisfiability	Memory [MB]	Time [sec]	States
Original:	Schedulability	Yes	168	180	1220
	Creation of co-tasks	Yes	92	315	1220
	Destruction of co-tasks	Yes	154	233	1220
	Frequency management	Yes	173	265	1220
	Tile management	Yes	167	234	1220
Modified tasks:	Schedulability	No	105	10.2	91
	Creation of co-tasks	Yes	117	145	771
	Destruction of co-tasks	Yes	82	151	771
	Frequency management	Yes	197	115	771
	Tile management	Yes	135	107	771
Modified co-tasks:	Schedulability	Yes	83	141	768
	Creation of co-tasks	Yes	85	183	768
	Destruction of co-tasks	Yes	86	191	768
	Frequency management	Yes	104	141	768
	Tile management	Yes	119	134	768

is reduced by changing the start timings of the tasks and co-tasks with the parameters.

– In cases other than those of the modified tasks, it is considered that the state-space is smaller than that of the original model because this system is designed to stop processing when a task exceeds its deadline.

6   Conclusion and Future Work

In this paper, we proposed a dynamic linear hybrid automaton (DLHA) as a specification language for dynamically reconfigurable systems. We also devised an algorithm for reachability analysis and developed a model checker for verifying the system. Our future research will focus on a more effective method of verification, for example, model checking with CEGAR (Counterexample-guided abstraction refinement) and bounded model checking based on SMT (Satisfiability modulo theories) [10,16].

References

1. Alur, R., Courcoubetis, C., Halbwachs, N., Henzinger, T.A., Ho, P.H., Nicollin, X., Olivero, A., Sifakis, J., Yovine, S.: The algorithmic analysis of hybrid systems. Theor. Comput. Sci. **138**, 3–34 (1995)
2. Alur, R., Courcoubetis, C., Henzinger, T.A., Ho, P.-H.: Hybrid automata: an algorithmic approach to the specification and verification of hybrid systems. In: Grossman, R.L., Ravn, A.P., Rischel, H., Nerode, A. (eds.) HS 1991 and HS 1992. LNCS, vol. 736, pp. 209–229. Springer, Heidelberg (1993)

3. Amano, H., Adachi, Y., Tsutsumi, S., Ishikawa, K.: A context dependent clock control mechanism for dynamically reconfigurable processors. Technical report of IEICE, vol. 104, no. 589, pp. 13–16 (2005)
4. Attie, P.C., Lynch, N.A.: Dynamic input/output automata, a formal model for dynamic systems. In: Proceedings of the Twentieth Annual ACM Symposium on Principles of Distributed Computing, PODC 2001, pp. 314–316 (2001)
5. Bagnara, R., Hill, P.M., Zaffanella, E.: The parma polyhedra library: toward a complete set of numerical abstractions for the analysis and verification of hardware and software systems. Sci. Comput. Program. **72**(1–2), 3–21 (2008)
6. Boigelot, B., Godefroid, P.: Symbolic verification of communication protocols with infinite state spaces using QDDs. Form. Methods Syst. Des. **14**(3), 237–255 (1999)
7. Boigelot, B., Godefroid, P., Willems, B., Wolper, P.: The power of QDDs (extended abstract). In: Hentenryck, P. (ed.) SAS 1997. LNCS, vol. 1302, pp. 172–186. Springer, Heidelberg (1997). doi:10.1007/BFb0032741
8. Bouajjani, A., Esparza, J., Maler, O.: Reachability analysis of pushdown automata: application to model checking. In: Mazurkiewicz, A., Winkowski, J. (eds.) CONCUR 1997. LNCS, vol. 1243, pp. 135–150. Springer, Heidelberg (1997)
9. Bouajjani, A., Habermehl, P.: Symbolic reachability analysis of FIFO-channel systems with nonregular sets of configurations. In: Degano, P., Gorrieri, R., Marchetti-Spaccamela, A. (eds.) ICALP 1997. LNCS, vol. 1256, pp. 560–570. Springer, Heidelberg (1997)
10. Clarke, E.M., Grumberg, O., Jha, S., Lu, Y., Veith, H.: Counterexample-guided abstraction refinement. In: Emerson, E.A., Sistla, A.P. (eds.) CAV 2000. LNCS, vol. 1855, pp. 154–169. Springer, Heidelberg (2000)
11. Garcia, P., Compton, K., Schulte, M., Blem, E., Fu, W.: An overview of reconfigurable hardware in embedded systems. EURASIP J. Embed. Syst. **2006**(1), 1–19 (2006)
12. Henzinger, T.A., Ho, P.H., Wong-Toi, H.: HyTech: a model checker for hybrid. Softw. Tools Technol. Transf. **1**(Cav 97), 110–122 (1997)
13. Lockwood, J.W., Moscola, J., Kulig, M., Reddick, D., Brooks, T.: Internet worm and virus protection in dynamically reconfigurable hardware. In: Military and Aerospace Programmable Logic Device (MAPLD), p. F10 (2003)
14. Minami, S., Takinai, S., Sekoguchi, S., Nakai, Y., Yamane, S.: Modeling, specification and model checking of dynamically reconfigurable processors. Comput. Softw. **28**(1), 190–216 (2011). Japan Society for Software Science and Technology
15. Motomura, M., Fujii, T., Furuta, K., Anjo, K., Yabe, Y., Togawa, K., Yamada, J., Izawa, Y., Sasaki, R.: New generation microprocessor architecture (2): dynamically reconfigurable processor (DRP). IPSJ Mag. **46**(11), 1259–1265 (2005)
16. Nieuwenhuis, R., Oliveras, A., Tinelli, C.: Abstract DPLL and abstract DPLL modulo theories. In: Baader, F., Voronkov, A. (eds.) LPAR 2005. LNCS (LNAI), vol. 3452, pp. 36–50. Springer, Heidelberg (2005). doi:10.1007/978-3-540-32275-7_3
17. Ono, Y., Yamane, S.: Computation of quantifier elimination of linear inequalities of first order predicate logic. COMP Comput. **111**(20), 55–59 (2011). IEICE Technical report
18. Varshavsky, V., Marakhovsky, V.: GALA (Globally Asynchronous - Locally Arbitrary) design. In: Cortadella, J., Yakovlev, A., Rozenberg, G. (eds.) Concurrency and Hardware Design. LNCS, vol. 2549, pp. 61–107. Springer, Heidelberg (2002)
19. Yamada, H., Nakai, Y., Yamane, S.: Proposal of specification language and verification experiment for dynamically reconfigurable system. J. Inf. Process. Soc. Jpn. Program. **6**(3), 1–19 (2013)

Modelling Hybrid Systems in Event-B and Hybrid Event-B: A Comparison of Water Tanks

Richard Banach[1]([⊠]) and Michael Butler[2]

[1] School of Computer Science, University of Manchester,
Oxford Road, Manchester M13 9PL, UK
banach@cs.man.ac.uk
[2] School of Electronics and Computer Science, University of Southampton,
Highfield, Southampton SO17 1BJ, UK
mjb@ecs.soton.ac.uk

Abstract. Hybrid and cyberphysical systems pose significant challenges for a formal development formalism based on pure discrete events. This paper compares the capabilities of (conventional) Event-B for modelling such systems with the corresponding capabilities of the Hybrid Event-B formalism, whose design was intended expressly for such systems. We do the comparison in the context of a simple water tank example, in which filling and emptying take place at different rates, necessitating a control strategy to ensure that the safety invariants are maintained. The comparative case study is followed by a general discussion of issues in which the two approaches reveal different strengths and weaknesses. It is seen that restricting to Event-B means handling many more things at the meta level, i.e. by the user, than is the case with its Hybrid counterpart.

1 Introduction

Hybrid [9] and cyberphysical [10] systems pose significant challenges for a formal development formalism based on discrete events. A number of compromises are needed in order to allow a discrete event formalism to relate to the important continuous aspects of the behaviour of such systems. Formalisms that are more purpose built address such concerns more easily. This paper compares the capabilities of (conventional) Event-B (**EB**) for modelling such systems with the capabilities of the more purposely designed Hybrid Event-B (**HEB**). We do the comparison in the context of a simple water tank example, in which filling and emptying take place at different rates, necessitating a control strategy to ensure that the required safety invariants are maintained. This familiar scenario makes the discussion easier to follow. The example was modelled using **EB** in [8] using facilities built in **EB** for expressing certain continuous features of behaviour.

The rest of this paper is as follows. Section 2 overviews the **HEB** framework, and shows how **EB** results from forgetting the novel elements of **HEB**. Section 3 briefly recalls the water tank problem. Then Sect. 4 overviews the development in [8], which is a detailed study of the water tank example in the **EB** framework.

© Springer International Publishing AG 2016
K. Ogata et al. (Eds.): ICFEM 2016, LNCS 10009, pp. 90–105, 2016.
DOI: 10.1007/978-3-319-47846-3_7

Section 5 looks at a comparative (though on-paper-only) study of the same problem in **HEB**. Section 6 then embarks on a general comparison of the pros and cons of the **EB** and **HEB** approaches. Section 7 concludes.

2 An Outline of Hybrid Event-B, and of Event-B

In this section we outline Event-B and Hybrid Event-B for a single machine. Because it is more complex, we describe Hybrid Event-B first via Fig. 1, and show how it reduces to Event-B (which of course came earlier) by erasing the more recently added elements.

Figure 1 shows a schematic Hybrid Event-B machine. It starts with declarations of time and of a clock. Time is a first class citizen in that all variables are functions of time (which is read-only), explicitly or implicitly. Clocks are assumed to increase like time, but may be set during mode events. Variables are of two kinds. There are mode variables (like u) which take their values in discrete sets and change their values via discontinuous assignment in mode events. There are also pliant variables (such as x, y), declared in the PLIANT clause, which typically take their values in topologically dense sets (normally $\mathbb{R}$) and which are allowed to change continuously, such change being specified via pliant events.

Next are the invariants. These resemble invariants in discrete Event-B, in that the types of the variables are asserted to be the sets from which the variables' values *at any given moment of time* are drawn. More complex invariants similarly are predicates that are required to hold *at all moments of time* during a run.

Then, the events. The *INITIALISATION* has a guard that synchronises time with the start of any run, while all other variables are assigned their initial values as usual.

Mode events are analogues of events in discrete Event-B. They can assign all machine variables (except time). The schematic *MoEv* of Fig. 1, has parameters $i?, l, o!$, (input, local, and an output), and a guard *grd*. It also has the after-value assignment specified by the before-after predicate *BApred*, which can specify the after-values of all variables (except time, inputs and locals).

```
MACHINE HyEvBMch                    ... ...                  ... ...
TIME t                              MoEv                     PliEv
CLOCK clk                             STATUS ordinary          STATUS pliant
PLIANT x, y                           ANY i?, l, o!            INIT iv(x, y, t, clk)
VARIABLES u                           WHERE                    WHERE grd(u)
INVARIANTS                              grd(x, y, u, i?, l, t, clk)    ANY i?, l, o!
  x, y, u ∈ ℝ, ℝ, ℕ                   THEN                     COMPLY
EVENTS                                  x, y, u, clk, o! :|       BDApred(x, y, u,
  INITIALISATION                          BApred(x, y, u, i?, l, o!,    i?, l, o!, t, clk)
    STATUS ordinary                        t, clk, x', y', u', clk')  SOLVE
    WHEN                              END                        𝒟x =
      t = 0                         ... ...                        φ(x, y, u, i?, l, o!, t, clk)
    THEN                                                         y, o! :=
      clk, x, y, u := 1, x₀, y₀, u₀                                E(x, u, i?, l, t, clk)
    END                                                       END
... ...                                                     END
```

Fig. 1. A schematic Hybrid Event-B machine.

Pliant events are new. They specify the continuous evolution of the pliant variables over an interval of time. Figure 1 has a schematic pliant event $PliEv$. There are two guards: iv, for specifying enabling conditions on the pliant variables, clocks, and time; and grd, for specifying enabling conditions on the mode variables.

The body of a pliant event contains three parameters $i?, l, o!$, (input, local, and output, again) which are functions of time, defined over the duration of the pliant event. The behaviour of the event is defined by the COMPLY and SOLVE clauses. The SOLVE clause contains direct assignments, e.g. of y and output $o!$ (to time dependent functions); and differential equations, e.g. specifying x via an ODE (with $\mathcal{D}$ as the time derivative).

The COMPLY clause can be used to express any additional constraints that are required to hold during the pliant event via the before-during-and-after predicate $BDApred$. Typically, constraints on the permitted ranges of the pliant variables, can be placed here. The COMPLY clause can also specify at an abstract level, e.g. stating safety properties for the event without going into detail.

Briefly, the semantics of a Hybrid Event-B machine consists of a set of *system traces*, each of which is a collection of functions of time, expressing the value of each machine variable over the duration of a system run.

Time is modeled as an interval $\mathcal{T}$ of the reals. A run starts at some initial moment of time, t_0 say, and lasts either for a finite time, or indefinitely. The duration of the run $\mathcal{T}$, breaks up into a succession of left-closed right-open subintervals: $\mathcal{T} = [t_0 \ldots t_1), [t_1 \ldots t_2), [t_2 \ldots t_3), \ldots$. Mode events (with their discontinuous updates) take place at the isolated times corresponding to the common endpoints of these subintervals t_i, and in between, the mode variables are constant, and the pliant events stipulate continuous change in the pliant variables.

We insist that on every subinterval $[t_i \ldots t_{i+1})$ the behaviour is governed by a well posed initial value problem $\mathcal{D}xs = \phi(xs \ldots)$ (where xs is a relevant tuple of pliant variables). Within this interval, we seek the earliest time t_{i+1} at which a mode event becomes enabled, and this time becomes the preemption point beyond which the solution to the ODE system is abandoned, and the next solution is sought after the completion of the mode event.

In this manner, assuming that the $INITIALISATION$ event has achieved a suitable initial assignment to variables, a system run is *well formed*, and thus belongs to the semantics of the machine, provided that at runtime:

- Every enabled mode event is feasible, i.e. has an after-state, and on its completion enables a pliant event (but does not enable any mode event).[1]
- Every enabled pliant event is feasible, i.e. has a time-indexed family of after-states, and EITHER:
  (i) During the run of the pliant event a mode event becomes enabled. It preempts the pliant event, defining its end. ORELSE
  (ii) During the run of the pliant event it becomes infeasible: finite termination. ORELSE
  (iii) The pliant event continues indefinitely: nontermination.

---

[1] If a mode event has an input, the semantics assumes that its value only arrives at a time strictly later than the previous mode event, ensuring part of (1) automatically.

Thus in a well formed run mode events alternate with pliant events. The last event (if there is one) is a pliant event (whose duration may be finite or infinite). In reality, there are several semantic issues that we have glossed over in the framework just sketched. We refer to [5] for a more detailed presentation (and to [6] for the extension to multiple machines). The presentation just given is quite close to the modern formulation of hybrid systems. See e.g. [13,15], or [9] for a perspective stretching further back.

If, from Fig. 1, we erase time, clocks, pliant variables and pliant events, we arrive at a skeleton (conventional) Event-B machine. This simple erasure process illustrates (in reverse) the way that Hybrid Event-B has been designed as a clean extension of the original Event-B framework. The only difference of note is that now—at least according to the (conventional) way that Event-B is interpreted in the physical world—(the mode) events (left behind by the erasure) execute *lazily*, i.e. *not* at the instant they become enabled (which is, of course, the moment of execution of the previous event).[2]

3   The Water Tank Problem

The water tank problem is a familiar testing ground for approaches to control problems in event based frameworks like the B-Method. The purpose of the water tank controller is to maintain the water level in the tank between a low and a high level. There is a mechanism, assumed to act continually, by which water drains from the tank. To counteract this, there is a filling mechanism, acting faster than the draining mechanism, that can be activated at the behest of the controller to refill the tank when the water level has become too low—it is deactivated once the level has become high enough.

4   The Event-B Water Tank Development

In [8] there is a development of the water tank in **EB**. Since **EB** has no inbuilt continuous facilities, a considerable amount of continuous infrastructure had to be built behind the scenes using the theory plugin of the Rodin tool [3,14]. A fragment of this, the **EB** pattern for a pliant event in the style used in [8], is shown in Fig. 2. This treats update to continuous behaviour monolithically (i.e. by adding the whole piece from clk to t in a single action).

In more detail, there is a clock clk, and the presumption is that the event describes what happens

EB_PliEv
ANY t, f
WHERE
$t \geq clk + \epsilon$
$f \in ctsF(clk, t)$
$f(clk) = m(clk)$
$P(f)$
THEN
$clk, m := t, m \cup f$
END

Fig. 2. The **EB** pattern for representing a pliant event.

---

[2] We observe however, that it is considerably easier to simulate lazy execution semantics using eager semantics (e.g. via guards that depend on nondeterministically/probabilistically set auxiliary variables), than to achieve eager behaviour using lazy semantics.

MACHINE **EB**_*Tank*1	MACHINE **EB**_*Tank*2	MACHINE **EB**_*Tank*3
	REFINES **EB**_*Tank*1	REFINES **EB**_*Tank*2
VARIABLES *level*, *now*	VARIABLES *level*, *now*	VARIABLES *level*, *now*
INVARIANTS	INVARIANTS	
$\quad 0 \leq now$		
$\quad level \in ctsF(0, now)$		
$\quad \operatorname{ran} level \subseteq (L \ldots H)$		
$\quad now \in \operatorname{dom} level$		
	$\quad level(now) \in (L \ldots H)$	
EVENTS	EVENTS	EVENTS
INITIALISATION	*INITIALISATION*	*INITIALISATION*
	REFINES *INITIALISATION*	REFINES *INITIALISATION*
$\quad$ BEGIN	$\quad$ BEGIN	$\quad$ BEGIN
$\quad\quad now := 0$	$\quad\quad now := 0$	$\quad\quad now := 0$
$\quad\quad level := const(0, 0, L)$	$\quad\quad level := const(0, 0, L)$	$\quad\quad level := const(0, 0, L)$
$\quad$ END	$\quad$ END	$\quad$ END
ModeChange	*Fill*	*Fill*
	REFINES *ModeChange*	REFINES *Fill*
$\quad$ ANY t, l	$\quad$ ANY t, l	$\quad$ ANY t, l
$\quad$ WHERE	$\quad$ WHERE	$\quad$ WHERE
$\quad\quad now \leq t \wedge$	$\quad\quad now \leq t \wedge$	$\quad\quad now \leq t \wedge$
$\quad\quad \epsilon \leq t - now \wedge$	$\quad\quad \epsilon \leq t - now \wedge$	$\quad\quad \epsilon \leq t - now \wedge$
$\quad\quad l \in ctsF(now, t) \wedge$	$\quad\quad l \in ctsF(now, t) \wedge$	$\quad\quad l \in ctsF(now, t) \wedge$
$\quad\quad level(now) = l(now) \wedge$	$\quad\quad level(now) = l(now) \wedge$	$\quad\quad level(now) = l(now) \wedge$
$\quad\quad \operatorname{ran} l \subseteq (L \ldots H)$	$\quad\quad l(t) \subseteq (L \ldots H) \wedge$	$\quad\quad l(t) \subseteq (L \ldots H) \wedge$
	$\quad\quad l \in mono\_inc$	$\quad\quad der(l) = const(now, t, RU)$
$\quad$ THEN	$\quad$ THEN	$\quad$ THEN
$\quad\quad now, level := t, level \cup l$	$\quad\quad now, level := t, level \cup l$	$\quad\quad now, level := t, level \cup l$
$\quad$ END	$\quad$ END	$\quad$ END
END	*Empty*	*Empty*
	REFINES *ModeChange*	REFINES *Empty*
	$\quad$ ANY t, l	$\quad$ ANY t, l
	$\quad$ WHERE	$\quad$ WHERE
	$\quad\quad now \leq t \wedge$	$\quad\quad now \leq t \wedge$
	$\quad\quad \epsilon \leq t - now \wedge$	$\quad\quad \epsilon \leq t - now \wedge$
	$\quad\quad l \in ctsF(now, t) \wedge$	$\quad\quad l \in ctsF(now, t) \wedge$
	$\quad\quad level(now) = l(now) \wedge$	$\quad\quad level(now) = l(now) \wedge$
	$\quad\quad l(t) \subseteq (L \ldots H) \wedge$	$\quad\quad l(t) \subseteq (L \ldots H) \wedge$
	$\quad\quad l \in mono\_dec$	$\quad\quad der(l) = const(now, t, RD)$
	$\quad$ THEN	$\quad$ THEN
	$\quad\quad now, level := t, level \cup l$	$\quad\quad now, level := t, level \cup l$
	$\quad$ END	$\quad$ END
	END	END

Fig. 3. Event-B machines for the water tank.

in a time interval following clock value clk. A parameter t is introduced, greater than clk by at least ϵ (to prevent Zeno behaviour, though Zeno behaviour would not be detectable, nor cause any upset, in an Event-B proof). Another parameter f, describes the graph of a *continuousF*unction on the interval $[clk \ldots t]$ by which the function m, defined hitherto only on the interval $[0 \ldots clk]$, is to be extended. Defining functions set theoretically by their graphs, the extension of the function m is just the union of its previous value and f. Of course, clk must also be updated to t, ready for the next increment. For the function m to be continuous, its preceding final value must match the initial value of the increment f, as stated in the guard $m(clk) = f(clk)$. Finally, $P(f)$ expresses any further properties that the increment f is required to satisfy.

In Fig. 3 we see the main thread of the **EB** water tank, essentially as in [8]. Aside from what is shown, there are two contexts $c1$ and $c2$, which introduce various constants used in the development.

The Fig. 3 development starts with **EB_Tank1**. This introduces the water *level* variable, as well as the *now* variable (the analogue of *clk* in Fig. 2). Initialisation fixes *now* at 0 and *level* to the *const*ant function over the degenerate closed interval $[0 \ldots 0]$ with value L, the lower water level.

There is one event *ModeChange*, which illustrates how continuous behaviour is handled in the **EB** modelling style of [8]. As is clear, this is a simple instantiation of the pattern of Fig. 2.

From its name, one can infer that *ModeChange* is intended to model the transitions between filling and emptying episodes. However, there is nothing in its definition that forces this—the event merely extends the *level* function, defined by its graph, by some nonempty chunk into the future (that obeys the restriction on its range).

EB_Tank1 is refined to **EB_Tank2**. The variables are the same, and another invariant $level(now) \in (L \ldots H)$ is introduced to aid proof (of course, it follows mathematically from the earlier invariants $level \in ctsF(0, now)$ and ran $level \subseteq (L \ldots H)$). The previous event *ModeChange*, is refined to two separate events, *Fill* and *Empty*. These events have additional contraints in their guards, $l \in$ monotonically_increasing_functions for *Fill*, and $l \in$ monotonically_decreasing_functions for *Empty*. So each chunk that increments the *level* function is increasing or decreasing, but cannot oscillate.

Again, from their names, we might infer that *Fill* and *Empty* are intended to model the full filling and emptying episodes, which we expect to alternate. But there is no requirement that filling results in a *level* anywhere near H, nor analogously for emptying; also there is nothing to prevent successive filling, or successive emptying episodes.

EB_Tank2 is refined to **EB_Tank3**. The variables are the same, and there are no new invariants. The only change now is that monotonic behaviour is implemented by an axiomatic form of an ordinary differential equation. Thus, $l \in mono\_inc$ in *Fill* is replaced by $der(l) = const(now, t, RU)$, which says that the derivative of l is a constant function over the interval $[now \ldots t]$, with value $RateUp$. This, and the analogously modified *Empty*, covers what is shown in Fig. 3.

```
MACHINE EB_Tank30
REFINES EB_Tank2
VARIABLES
  level, now, step, slevel, mode
INVARIANTS
  step ∈ ℝ
  slevel ∈ ctsF(now, step)
  mode = UP ⇒
        slevel ∈ mono_inc
  mode = DOWN ⇒
        slevel ∈ mono_dec
  level(now) = slevel(now)
  slevel(step) = (L...H)
EVENTS
  INITIALISATION
    REFINES INITIALISATION
    BEGIN
      now := 0
      level := const(0, 0, L)
      step := 0
      slevel := const(0, 0, L)
      mode := UP
    END
  StepUp
    ANY l
    WHERE
      mode = UP ∧
      slevel(step) ≤ HT ∧
      l ∈ ctsF(step, step + P) ∧
      slevel(step) = l(step) ∧
      l ∈ mono_inc ∧
      l(step) ≤ l(step + P) ∧
      l(step + P) <
          l(step) + (RU × P) ∧
      l(step + P) ≤ H
    THEN
      step := step + P
      slevel := slevel ∪ l
    END
  EndFill
    REFINES Fill
    WHEN
      mode = UP ∧
      ¬ (slevel(step) ≤ HT)
    WITH
      l = slevel
      t = step
    THEN
      now := step
      level := level ∪ slevel
      mode := DOWN
      slevel := const(step, step,
                slevel(step))
    END
  StepDown  ...  ...
  EndEmpty  ...  ...
END
```

Fig. 4. The **EB_Tank30** machine.

Aside from the machines in Fig. 3, there is a further machine, $Tank30$, in the development discussed in [8]. This is also a refinement of **EB_$Tank2$**, although a different one. This one models a putative implementation of **EB_$Tank2$** using a time triggered loop. A new variable $step$ is introduced, whose job, like that of now, is to model increments of time, but on this occasion small ones, whose duration is determined by a constant P. Another new variable $slevel$ models the small increments or decrements to the water level accrued in each interval of length P. The events modelling these small increments or decrements also follow the pattern described earlier. Most of this machine is shown in Fig. 4 (the parts omitted are the details of events $StepDown$ and $EndEmpty$, which are straightforward analogues of events $StepUp$ and $EndFill$).

Unlike the models of Fig. 3, there is a variable $mode \in \{UP, DOWN\}$ to enforce filling or emptying behaviour until the boundary values are approached. And since, when using fixed time increments of length P, it is not realistic to expect filling and emptying to reach the limits H or L 'on the nose', thresholds HT and LT are introduced (respectively less than and greater than H and L), upon reaching which, the mode changes. Technically, the 'intermediate' filling and emptying events, $StepUp$ and $StepDown$, are 'new' events, refining a notional skip in **EB_$Tank2$**. The 'endpoint' events, $EndFill$ and $EndEmpty$, refine $Fill$ and $Empty$ in **EB_$Tank2$**, determining the needed values of now and $level$ to achieve refinement.[3]

Finally, we comment on the methodology used to arrive at these results. The properties of the reals, and of real functions, were axiomatised using the theory plugin of the Rodin tool [3, 14]. One aspect of this is that derivatives, expressed using axioms for der, are axiomatised as belonging to the continuous functions $ctsF$, for convenience (see [8]). If we then look at the way that these are used in **EB_$Tank3$**, we see that the derivatives specified are always constant functions. But filling episodes have a positive derivative of the l function, and emptying episodes give l a negative derivative. Joining two such episodes cannot yield a continuous derivative.

This apparent contradiction is resolved by noticing that each element of $ctsF$ is only defined with respect to its domain. Thus, a function f_1 defined on $[t_1 \ldots t_2]$ may have one continuous derivative, and a different function f_2 defined on $[t_2 \ldots t_3]$ may have a different continuous derivative. Even if f_1 and f_2 can be joined at t_2, the exclusive use of closed intervals for domains of continuous behaviour (which happens quite commonly in formulations of hybrid systems, see e.g. [9, 13, 15]) does not enable us to deduce that their derivatives can be joined at t_2. While consistent, the consequence of this is that the joined $f_1 \cup f_2$ cannot be regarded as a differentiable function on $[t_1 \ldots t_3]$, and in fact, an attempt

---

[3] The use of thresholds HT and LT rather than the precise limits H and L, correlates with the absence of guards to check reaching H or L in the corresponding **EB_$Tank1$** and **EB_$Tank2$** events. However, since the behaviour stipulated is *nondeterministic* monotonic, adding an extra constraint to demand that the behaviour exactly reached the required limit in events $EndFill$ and $EndEmpty$ would be perfectly feasible (mathematically, if perhaps not practically).

to regard it as such would lead to multiple values of the putative derivative at t_2. While relatively innocuous in the present example, it indicates a number of things. The first is that what is true can depend delicately on the axioms adopted. The second is that care needs to be taken in case the unexpected consequences of the axioms lead one astray. The third is a caution regarding the scalability of such an approach, as the number of counterintuitive cases proliferates.

5 The Hybrid Event-B Water Tank Development

In Fig. 5 we see a development of the water tank problem in **HEB**. It consists of three machines: **HEB_TankAbs**, an abstract formulation, which is refined by **HEB_TankMon** which includes the pump, and which is in turn refined by **HEB_TankODE**. These are relatively straightforward analogues of the machines **EB_Tank1**, **EB_Tank2**, **EB_Tank3** in the last section. The main difference between the two treatments is that in **HEB**, functions of time are manipulated solely using expressions for their values at any individual instant, and not *en bloc*, as graphs over (some portion of) their domain. This aligns the way that pliant and mode updates can be regarded, and simplifies many less trivial matters. For ease of comparison, we keep the names of constants in the two treatments the same, but alter other names to aid distinguishability.

HEB_TankAbs has only the water level variable wl, which is pliant, taking values in $\mathbb{R}$. The behaviour of wl is required to be CONTINUOUS (to prevent discontinuous jumps), and the nontrivial invariant $wl \in [L \ldots H]$ confines the water level to the real closed interval $[L \ldots H]$. In **HEB**, invariants are properties that have to hold at all times, so $wl \in [L \ldots H]$ is sufficient to express the safety property that wl is required to never leave $[L \ldots H]$. The only non-*INITIALISATION* event in **HEB_TankAbs** is the pliant event *WaterInRange*. This merely requires the behaviour to COMPLY (with the) *INVARIANTS*. So **HEB_TankAbs** specifies the required safety property and does not concern itself with how that safety property is to be maintained. The ability to do this properly in a hybrid/cyberphysical setting is an important feature of development in **HEB**. So **HEB_TankAbs** mirrors **EB_Tank1** quite closely.

The next machine **HEB_TankMon**, starts to engage with how the key invariant is maintained. It introduces the **EB**-style mode variable $pump \in \{ON, OFF\}$. The pump is turned on and off by mode events $PumpOn$ and $PumpOff$. These are like **EB** events aside from their eager behaviour—they execute as soon as their guards become true.

Again illustrating the ability to postpone implementation details, the behaviour of wl in the presence of the pump is merely specified to be MONotonically DECreasing when the pump is OFF, and to be MONotonically INCreasing when it is ON: in pliant events $WaterEmpty$ and $WaterFill$ respectively. Note that the $pump$ variable, introduced earlier than in **EB**, prevents successive filling or successive emptying episodes (unless we had additional mode events to interleave them, to conform with (1) and (2)).

```
MACHINE HEB_TankAbs

PLIANT wl

INVARIANTS
    wl ∈ [L . . . H]
    CONTINUOUS (wl)

EVENTS
    INITIALISATION

        STATUS ordinary
        BEGIN
            wl := L
        END
    WaterInRange
        STATUS pliant
        COMPLY INVARIANTS
        END
END
```

```
MACHINE HEB_TankMon
REFINES HEB_TankAbs
PLIANT wl
VARIABLES pump
INVARIANTS
    wl ∈ [L . . . H]
    CONTINUOUS (wl)
    pump ∈ {ON, OFF}
EVENTS
    INITIALISATION
        REFINES INITIALISATION
        STATUS ordinary
        BEGIN
            wl, pump := L, ON
        END
    WaterFill
        REFINES WaterInRange
        STATUS pliant
        WHEN pump = ON
        COMPLY MONINC(wl)
        END
    PumpOff

        STATUS ordinary
        WHEN
            wl = H ∧ pump = ON
        THEN pump := OFF
        END
    WaterEmpty
        REFINES WaterInRange
        STATUS pliant
        WHEN pump = OFF
        COMPLY MONDEC (wl)
        END
    PumpOn

        STATUS ordinary
        WHEN
            wl = L ∧ pump = OFF
        THEN pump := ON
        END
END
```

```
MACHINE HEB_TankODE
REFINES HEB_TankMon
PLIANT wl
VARIABLES pump
INVARIANTS
    wl ∈ [L . . . H]
    CONTINUOUS (wl)
    pump ∈ {ON, OFF}
EVENTS
    INITIALISATION
        REFINES INITIALISATION
        STATUS ordinary
        BEGIN
            wl, pump := L, ON
        END
    WaterFill
        REFINES WaterFill
        STATUS pliant
        WHEN pump = ON
        SOLVE D wl = RU
        END
    PumpOff
        REFINES PumpOff
        STATUS ordinary
        WHEN
            wl = H ∧ pump = ON
        THEN pump := OFF
        END
    WaterEmpty
        REFINES WaterEmpty
        STATUS pliant
        WHEN pump = OFF
        SOLVE D wl = RD
        END
    PumpOn
        REFINES PumpOn
        STATUS ordinary
        WHEN
            wl = L ∧ pump = OFF
        THEN pump := ON
        END
END
```

Fig. 5. Hybrid Event-B machines for the water tank.

Importantly, **HEB_TankMon** is a formal refinement of **HEB_TankAbs** according to the detailed definition in [5], as we would wish. Both of *WaterEmpty* and *WaterFill* refine the abstract *WaterInRange*, in that monotonic continuous behaviour is a refinement of continuous behaviour. The relevant PO expresses this by saying the following. For all times t during an execution of a concrete event, *WaterFill* say, that started at some time t_L say, if the value that wl reached at t due to executing *WaterFill* from its starting value $wl(t_L)$ was $wl(t)$, then the same value can be reached by executing the abstract event *WaterInRange* from t_L to t.

Mode events *PumpOn* and *PumpOff* are 'new' events in **EB** parlance, updating only the 'new' mode variable *pump*, so there is no change to abstract variable wl when they execute. However, there is no VARIANT that they decrease when they execute. The abstract event that they relinquish control to upon completion is the immediately succeeding pliant event, *WaterEmpty* for *PumpOff* or *WaterFill* for *PumpOn*. An auxiliary (pliant) variable could be introduced that was increased by these events and decreased by the mode events to create a variant, but this would clutter the model. Thus we see that **HEB_TankMon** mirrors **EB_Tank2** quite closely, aside from the presence of *pump* and its controlling events, which fix the durations of the monotonic episodes to be maximal, and ensures that switching takes place at the extreme values of the range.

Machine **HEB_TankODE** refines **EB_TankMon**. This time the various events are refined 1-1, so there are no 'new' events to worry about. The monotonic continuous behaviour of *WaterEmpty* and *WaterFill* is further refined to be given by ODEs in which the derivative of the water level variable *wl* is *RD* for *WaterEmpty* and *RU* for *WaterFill*, as in **EB**. This appears in the SOLVE clauses of these events. Once more, **HEB_TankODE** mirrors **EB_Tank3** quite closely, aside from issues concerning *pump*, which we have discussed already.

Supplementing the machines of Fig. 5, machines analogous to the **EB** *Tank*30 machine appear in Fig. 6. Machine **HEB_TankTTL** is a time triggered development of **HEB_TankMon**, and comparing it with *Tank*30 is instructive. Note that there are no new variables, just new behaviour of events. Thus *WaterFill* is refined to *WaterFillNormal* and to *WaterFillEnd*. The former of these is enabled when the water level is below the threshold *HT*. It demands increasing *wl* behaviour, but restricted to a filling rate no greater than *RU*. Occurrences of *WaterFillNormal* are interleaved by occurrences of mode event *WaterFillObs*, which runs at times that are multiples of *P*, provided the water level is not actually *H* itself. Since *WaterFillNormal* is increasing *wl*, *WaterFillObs* merely skips. Once above *HT*, *WaterFillEnd* runs. This is like *WaterFillNormal* except for an additional condition insisting that *wl* hits *H* at the end of the interval.[4] And once *wl* has reached *H*, *PumpOff* runs, as previously. While this design is unimpeachable mathematically, it is, of course, much more questionable from a practical perspective, as we pointed out in footnote 3. It does have the virtue though, of providing a straightforward refinement from **HEB_TankMon**. Machine **HEB_TankTTL** is completed by events *WaterEmptyNormal*, *WaterEmptyEnd*, *WaterEmptyObs*, *PumpOn*, which do the same as the preceding, but for the emptying phase.

Machine **HEB_TankTTL** is data refined to **HEB_TankIMP** on the right of Fig. 6. This 'implementation' machine illustrates the refinement of *pliant behaviour interleaved by mode skips, to pliant skips interleaved by mode updates*— a major aim of **HEB** is to allow such a passage from a high level continuous design to a discrete, digital implementation. A fresh variable *mwl* (monitored water level) is introduced, inc/decremented at each of the mode events. Observing *wl* and updating *mwl* at each multiple of *P* enables the invariant $|mwl - wl| \leq P \times \max(RU, RD)$ to be maintained, attesting to the reasonableness of the digital implementation.

What has been achieved by formulating the development in the **HEB** way compared to the **EB** way? Firstly, there is a certain fluency in referring to continuous behaviour via expressions that denote instantaneous values rather than

---

[4] The constraint is consistent provided the various constants are suitably related, of course.

```
MACHINE HEB_TankTTL
REFINES HEB_TankMon
TIME t
PLIANT wl
VARIABLES pump
INVARIANTS
  wl ∈ [L . . . H]
  CONTINUOUS (wl)
  pump ∈ {ON, OFF}
EVENTS
  INITIALISATION
    REFINES INITIALISATION
    STATUS ordinary
    BEGIN
      wl, pump := L, ON
    END
  WaterFillNormal
    REFINES WaterFill
    STATUS pliant
    INIT wl ≤ HT
    WHEN pump = ON
    COMPLY MONINC(wl) ∧
      wl(t) − wl(t_L) ≤
        RU × (t − t_L)
    END
  WaterFillObs
    STATUS ordinary
    WHEN
      pump = ON ∧ wl ≠ H ∧
        (∃ n • t = n × P)
    THEN skip
    END
. . .    . . .
```

```
. . .    . . .
  WaterFillEnd
    REFINES WaterFill
    STATUS pliant
    INIT wl > HT
    WHEN pump = ON
    COMPLY MONINC(wl) ∧
      wl(t) − wl(t_L) ≤
        RU × (t − t_L) ∧
      wl(t_L + P) = H
    END
  PumpOff
    STATUS ordinary
    WHEN
      wl = H ∧ pump = ON
    THEN pump := OFF
    END
  WaterEmptyNormal  . . .    . . .
  WaterEmptyEnd  . . .    . . .
  WaterEmptyObs  . . .    . . .
  PumpOn  . . .    . . .
END
```

```
MACHINE HEB_TankIMP
REFINES HEB_TankTTL
TIME t
VARIABLES mwl
INVARIANTS
  mwl ∈ [L . . . H]
  | mwl − wl | ≤
    P × max(RU, RD)
EVENTS
  INITIALISATION
    REFINES INITIALISATION
    STATUS ordinary
    BEGIN mwl := L END
. . .    . . .
```

```
. . .    . . .
  WaterFillNormal
    REFINES WaterFillNormal
    STATUS pliant
    INIT mwl = wl ∧ wl ≤ HT
    WHEN pump = ON
    COMPLY skip
    END
  WaterFillObs
    REFINES WaterFillObs
    STATUS ordinary
    WHEN
      pump = ON ∧ wl ≠ H ∧
        (∃ n • t = n × P)
    THEN mwl := wl
    END
  WaterFillEnd
    REFINES WaterFillEnd
    STATUS pliant
    INIT mwl = wl ∧ wl > HT
    WHEN pump = ON
    COMPLY skip
    END
  PumpOff
    STATUS ordinary
    WHEN
      wl = H ∧ pump = ON
    THEN
      pump, mwl := OFF, wl
    END
  WaterEmptyNormal  . . .    . . .
  WaterEmptyEnd  . . .    . . .
  WaterEmptyObs  . . .    . . .
  PumpOn  . . .    . . .
END
```

Fig. 6. The HEB_$TankTTL$ and HEB_$TankIMP$ machines.

having to assemble and disassemble graphs of functions (but only in the continuous case). Secondly, there are issues of potential semantic subtlety. We saw an example in the discussion of the differential properties of the *level* function in EB_$Tank3$: it was not formally differentiable globally, but consisted of differentiable monotonic pieces, leading to the join points having more than one derivative value, despite these being 'kink' points of the function. In HEB such matters are handled *ab inito* in the semantics, by the use of closed/open intervals and the Carathéodory formulation of differential equations and derivatives (which are only required to be defined almost everywhere). Thirdly, there is also the fluency of the passage from pliant behaviour interleaved by mode skips to pliant skips interleaved by mode updates. Discussion of further and more general matters appears in the next section.

6   Event-B Versus Hybrid Event-B

Based on the previous EB and HEB developments, we can draw some comparisons between the two approaches for modelling and formally refining hybrid systems.

1. First and foremost, **EB** has a well developed existing tool, whereas for **HEB**, tool development is, as yet, an aspiration. Having an existing tool is of inestimable benefit when you need to get the job done.

2. In an **EB** development, real time has to be modelled as a normal state variable. This imposes a responsibility on the model writer to not abuse the capabilities this offers. In truth, time is (in physical parlance) an *independent variable*—whereas other state variables correspond (physically) to *dependent variables*. From a linguistic formalism point of view, staying faithful to the physical reality means that time has to be a read-only variable, and that all other variables have to be functions of time. In an **EB** context, it is down to the self-discipline of the model writer to reflect these properties properly. Clearly it is possible to transgress them and to write unphysical models. In **HEB** these realities are hardwired into the syntax and semantics, making it impossible for the model writer to violate them.

3. An analogue of point **2** concerns the mathematical equipment of **EB** and **HEB**. In **EB** all mathematical objects beyond those needed for discrete modelling need to be axiomatised, typically using the theory plugin of the Rodin tool [3,14]. Although this framework is agnostic regarding the level of abstraction of the concepts being axiomatised, existing work emphasises a bottom up approach (as in the case study above). This potentially creates a lot of work before the level of abstraction needed for applications is reached, increasing risk.

The **HEB** perspective on this is to design the theoretical foundations of the semantics in a way that best suits the needs of applications engineering, giving system developers a mental model that is clear and easy to grasp, and, importantly, is free from unexpected surprises (such as the two-valued 'derivative' discussed earlier). The aim would be to internalise the world of continuous mathematics with the same level of care and consistency as the Rodin tool currently supplies for discrete mathematics and logic, and to supplement it via extensive imported support from external tools such as *Mathematica* [12] for calculational purposes. The facility for user designed rules and axiom schemes would be retained for specialised purposes, but would not be the default approach for continuous mathematics.

4. A specific example of the general remarks in the preceding point lies in the contrast between the explicit construction of functions as relations, manipulated via their graphs in Sect. 4 and their representation as expressions based on values of variables at a single (arbitrary) element of their time domain in Sect. 5.

5. Connected with the previous point is the observation that in **EB**, the discrete and continuous updates have to be handled by different means. Thus, discrete transitions are written down using (in effect, pairs of) state expressions, referred to via syntax such as $xs := E(xs)$, with the accepted conventions surrounding the syntactic machinery enabling the relevant expressions to be discerned. For continuous transitions though, because the **EB** framework offers no alternative syntax for update than that which is used for discrete transitions, updates to continuous behaviour have to be handled by updating the relation describing (the function of time that is) the continuous behaviour as a whole, in one action. Section 4 offers many examples. The discrete analogue of such an approach would be to update (in one action), for a discrete variable x, a non-trivial portion of its trace during an execution, i.e. to update say $\langle x_{i-1}, x_i \ldots x_{i+k}\rangle$, as a whole. (Aside from anything else, this would require the introduction into every model of an index variable (incremented at each event occurrence), as well as suitable history variables.)

By contrast, **HEB** provides special purpose syntactic machinery (via the COMPLY and SOLVE clauses) to specify continuous update incrementally and microscopically, rather than macroscopically, which is significant from an expressivity standpoint. As most physical models specify behaviour in a microscopic way (usually via differential equations etc.), being able to write these directly in the formal framework aids the ability to specify in a manner as close to application domain concerns as possible. Also, since the solutions to these microscopic specifications are macroscopic (describing properties of the solution over an extended portion of time/space), specifying in a microscopic way prevents forcing the move from microscopic to macroscopic from being done offline. In this way, discontinuous transitions and continuous transitions are handled in a consistent manner, via mode transitions and pliant transitions respectively, both of which are predominantly expression based ways of specifying updates.

6. Continuing from point **5**, when specifying the unavoidable handovers between continuous and discrete behaviours while using the macroscopic, relation based, way of specifying continuous behaviour, the endpoints of the periods of continuous behaviour need to be described within the relations themselves, so that the domain of the relevant relation can be specified. This is potentially an overhead for the model designer when the problem is complicated enough, since the handovers take place when prompted by physical law. In **HEB**, this job is taken over by a generic preemption mechanism, which is, in turn, much easier to handle in the expression based way of managing pliant behaviour, since all the details regarding the domain of applicability of the pliant behaviour do not need to be specified in advance.

7. Another consequence of point **5** concerns invariants. Invariants are normally expressions written in the state variables, that are expected to be true at all times. Now, when we only have the usual changes of discrete state, and we have the conventional interpretation of Event-B in the physical world in which discrete transitions occur at isolated times, then the state does not change in between these discrete transitions. Thus, once true at some point of an execution (e.g. at initialisation time), if invariants are reestablished at each discrete transition, then the invariants hold throughout the duration of the execution. Note that this reasoning takes place largely outside of the formal **EB** framework.

When the discrete **EB** transitions are extended to encompass updates to lumps of continuous behaviour, the preceding argument no longer holds. Straightforward safety properties built out of natural problem entities no longer correspond to equivalent expressions built on state variables, but need to be extracted from the relations containing pieces of continuous behaviour, potentially making the proof of safety properties more difficult.

The observation particularly concerns refinement. In relatively benign cases where refinement amounts to 'reduction of nondeterminism', it may be possible relatively straightforwardly to argue that, say, a continuous monotonic function is continuous, and thus, that a chunk of continuous monotonic function refines a continuous specification. But the challenge can get much harder when 'data refinement' is involved. Then, the chunks have to be unpacked and the pointwise expressions compared (in fact reflecting the **HEB** process), before anything can be deduced.

By contrast, the **HEB** approach expresses all instantaneous state update, both mode and pliant, via expressions in the state variables, which usually correspond to the natural variables of the problem. This enables the invariants to be built in the same straightforward way as in the purely discrete case. Refinement is rendered no harder than the discrete case, though the time parameter has to be carried around through the derivation (which, in the vast majority of cases, imposes no overhead).

While, in principle, any invariant written using the more transparent methods of **HEB** could, with effort, be translated into the more convoluted **EB** kind, as a general point, we should not underestimate the impact on those aspects of the application that are emphasised, made by the detailed formalism in which the models and properties of a given application are written. Thus: (a) properties in model based frameworks tend to be written as invariants on the state space, and behavioural properties remain implicit in the enabledness (or not) of events in the after-states of preceding events; (b) properties in behaviourally based frameworks tend to be written as temporal logic expressions, and say little or nothing about states or whether behaviours other than ones described are permissible; (c) the architectural structure of a system leads to an emphasis on the properties of the individual components, whether state based or behavioural, and properties of the system as a whole that depend on the correct execution of protocols by collections of components are downplayed (other than in approaches focused specifically on protocols), etc. So the difference between the **EB** and **HEB** approaches can lead to subtle bias in the safety properties that are written, and later checked during verification.

8. Although not a feature of the **EB** treatment here, a number of treatments of continuous phenomena using **EB**, describe continuous, time dependent phenomena via lambda expressions such as $\lambda \tau \bullet E(\tau)$. Extraction of a value is done via application of such an expression to a parameter. This technique makes even more distant (than in the **EB** technique used here) the connection between problem quantities and actual model variables, since there needs to be even more packing and unpacking of these lambda expressions to get at the juice inside (than in the present case). From a formal point of view, a binder like λ typically binds its variable: moreover, the bound variable is formally alpha convertible [7,11], which can change its name arbitrarily. If this is the case, the identification of the variable τ in the given expression with a problem domain quantity like the time, lies completely outside the formal framework—it becomes an application level convention. This contrasts with the practice in conventional descriptions of physical phenomena, of naming physical quantities using free variables, leading to the possibility of being able to correlate the mention of the same quantity at different places by simple lexical identity. Of course this practice is reflected in the design of **HEB**.

However, we have to be a little careful. In many similar formalisms, such as in the refinement calculus [4], alpha conversion is an intrinsic part of the machinery, leading precisely to the phenomenon being discussed. However in the logical language of **EB**, the *not-free-in* property is used instead when introducing binders. This is based on the idea that provided wise, non-clashing choices of bound variables are made at the point of introduction, those choices will never need to be overridden in the reasoning algorithms, precluding the need for formal alpha conversion. In the B-Book [1], the *not-free-in* property is explicitly correlated with the quantified variable in the predicate that specifies the lambda expression (B-Book p. 89, & *ff.*). In the **EB**-Book [2], the lambda variable is a *pattern*, and although the formalities of its role as bound variable are not explicitly discussed, similar properties may be inferred (**EB**-Book p. 331 & *ff.*). Thus, in the context of the *not-free-in* technique, *in theory*, it might be possible to use the free problem variables as lambda variables in sufficiently simple situations where this would cause no untoward clashes, but *in practice* this is not something that could be expected to be applicable with any generality.[5]

A genuine reconciliation of the issues just discussed would run as follows. A richer language of *type names* would be introduced. These names would be free identifiers. Complex (or built-in) types could be given a name, and name equivalence (rather than structural equivalence) would decide type equality and compatibility. That way, a type of time could be distinguished from a type of lengths, even though both are based on $\mathbb{R}$ under the bonnet. Alpha conversion would apply to lambda expressions etc. as usual, but not to the type name expressions that declared their types. We would have reinvented the free name convention of **HEB**, removed one level!

It is notable how most of the issues identified in the above list do not concern the details of the **EB** and **HEB** formalisms themselves, but engage with questions that surround how the formalism connects with the wider requirements and applications environment. This is another illustration of the observation that the more naturally a formal framework relates to the problem domain, the more useful its contribution to overall system dependability is likely to be.

7   Conclusions

In the previous sections we reviewed Event-B and its hybrid extension, and then summarised the water tank development in the two formalisms. This provided the background for a more thorough comparison of the two ways of developing hybrid systems in Sect. 6. What this showed was that although many issues

---

[5] Strictly speaking, *not-free-in* means 'does not occur free—*but may occur bound*—in'. Thus, the possibilities for alpha conversion are latent in the B-Method, even if they are downplayed.

that were rather natural to express in Hybrid Event-B could be handled, with some effort, in Event-B, doing it that way placed more and more reliance on conventions that lay outside the formal Event-B framework. Obviously, the aim of having a formal framework is to open the possibility of having a system whereby properties directly relevant to the application can be checked mechanically, instead of relying on informal conventions verified by humans for their enforcement. Thus the pure Event-B approach to hybrid system design and development will inevitably struggle increasingly, as the scale of the problem being tackled grows.

References

1. Abrial, J.R.: The B-Book: Assigning Programs to Meanings. Cambridge University Press, Cambridge (1996)
2. Abrial, J.R.: Modeling in Event-B: System and Software Engineering. Cambridge University Press, Cambridge (2010)
3. Abrial, J.R., Butler, M., Hallerstede, S., Hoang, T.S., Mehta, F., Voisin, L.: Rodin: an open toolset for modelling and reasoning in Event-B. STTT **12**, 447–466 (2010)
4. Back, R.J.R., von Wright, J.: Refinement Calculus: A Systematic Introduction. Springer, Heidelberg (1998)
5. Banach, R., Butler, M., Qin, S., Verma, N., Zhu, H.: Core hybrid Event-B I: single hybrid Event-B machines. Sci. Comput. Program. **105**, 92–123 (2015)
6. Banach, R., Butler, M., Qin, S., Zhu, H.: Core Hybrid Event-B II: Multiple Cooperating Hybrid Event-B Machines (2015, submitted)
7. Barendregt, H.: The Lambda Calculus its Syntax and Semantics. Elsevier, Amsterdam (1981)
8. Butler, M., Abrial, J.R., Banach, R.: Modelling and refining hybrid systems in Event-B and Rodin. In: Petre, S. (ed.) From Action System to Distributed Systems: The Refinement Approach. Dedicated to Kaisa Sere, pp. 29–42. CRC Press/Taylor and Francis, Oxford/Boca Raton (2015)
9. Carloni, L., Passerone, R., Pinto, A., Sangiovanni-Vincentelli, A.: Languages and tools for hybrid systems design. Found. Trends Electron. Des. Autom. **1**, 1–193 (2006)
10. Geisberger, E., Broy (eds.), M.: Living in a Networked World. Integrated Research AgendaCyber-Physical Systems (agendaCPS) (2015). http://www.acatech.de/fileadmin/user_upload/Baumstruktur_nach_Website/Acatech/root/de/Publikationen/Projektberichte/acaetch_STUDIE_agendaCPS_eng_WEB.pdf
11. Hindley, R., Seldin, J.: Introduction to Combinators and λ-Calculus. Cambridge University Press, Cambridge (1986)
12. Mathematica. http://www.wolfram.com
13. Platzer, A.: Logical Analysis of Hybrid Systems: Proving Theorems for Complex Dynamics. Springer, Heidelberg (2010)
14. RODIN Tool. http://www.event-b.org/, http://sourceforge.net/projects/rodin-b-sharp/
15. Tabuada, P.: Verification and Control of Hybrid Systems: A Symbolic Approach. Springer, Heidelberg (2009)

A System Substitution Mechanism for Hybrid Systems in Event-B

Guillaume Babin, Yamine Aït-Ameur$^{(\boxtimes)}$, Neeraj Kumar Singh,
and Marc Pantel

Université de Toulouse, IRIT/INPT-ENSEEIHT,
2 Rue Charles Camichel, Toulouse, France
`guillaume.babin@irit.fr`, `{yamine,nsingh,marc.pantel}@enseeiht.fr`

Abstract. Changes like failure or loss of QoS are key aspects of hybrid systems that must be handled during their design. Preserving the system state is a common requirement that can be ensured by reconfiguration relying on system substitution. The specification and design of these systems usually rely on continuous functions whereas their implementation is discrete. Moreover, the associated safety properties are characterized by a safety envelope defining safe system states. This paper presents a novel approach for formalizing the system substitution mechanism for hybrid systems, in which the system substitution maintains a safety envelope of the given hybrid system during system failure or switching from one supporting system to another. Proving the correctness of the discrete implementation of the defined reconfiguration mechanism for hybrid systems is a challenging problem. In this purpose, we propose to combine system substitution and incremental system modeling to ensure correct discretization. We rely on the Event-B method and the Rodin Platform with the *Theory* plug-in to develop the system models and carry out the proofs on dense real numbers.

Keywords: System reconfiguration and substitution · Continuous and discrete behaviors · Formal methods · Refinement and proof · Event-B

1 Introduction

Context. Cyber Physical Systems refer to the tight integration and coordination between computational and physical resources [18]. In these systems, a software component, the controller, manages the physical parts of the system. The early models for such systems usually rely on continuous functions. The controller is then implemented in a discrete manner thus combining continuous environment models with discrete controller models, building an hybrid system.

Proving the correctness of discrete implementations of continuous controllers is a challenging problem. Formal methods allow checking the correctness of such system functional requirements, including the required safety properties. Due to these core benefits, they have been adopted for designing and developing

© Springer International Publishing AG 2016
K. Ogata et al. (Eds.): ICFEM 2016, LNCS 10009, pp. 106–121, 2016.
DOI: 10.1007/978-3-319-47846-3_8

the new age of discrete controllers that must satisfy their original continuous specification [19] for building safe and reliable hybrid systems.

To prevent a system failure, controllers must react according to environment changes to keep a desired state or to meet minimum requirements that maintain a safety envelope for the system. A safety envelope is a safe over-approximation of system states. It can be modeled as invariants that define a set containing all possible system states under its nominal conditions. One key property studied in system engineering is the ability to take actions according to an evolving behavior. It may occur in different situations (e.g. failures, quality of service change, context evolution, maintenance, etc.). Most safety critical systems, such as avionics, nuclear, automotive and medical devices, whose failure could result in loss of life, including reputation and economical damage, use reconfiguration or substitution mechanisms to prevent losing the quality of system services required for system stability when a random failure occurs.

In our earlier work, we proposed both a correct by construction system substitution mechanism [8,9] and a strategy to derive discrete controllers from continuous specifications [6]. In [8,9], we defined the reconfiguration mechanism to maintain a safety property for a system (defined as a state-transitions system) during failure or to switch from one supporting system to another. The defined approach has been successfully applied, for the discrete case, on web services [7]. But it is not applicable straightforwardly for hybrid systems which need to handle continuous features. In [6], we presented the formal development of a continuous controller that is refined by a discrete one preserving the continuous functional behavior and the required safety properties. This work helped us formulating more general strategies, that we aim to develop in this paper, for the development of system substitution for hybrid systems using formal techniques.

Objective of this Paper. We target modeling hybrid systems, and providing modeling patterns for reconfiguration, using a correct by construction approach. We provide a generic system substitution mechanism for hybrid systems that allows maintaining a safety envelope during the system failure or switching from one supporting system to another using stepwise refinement in Event-B [3]. Moreover, we show how the defined substitution or reconfiguration mechanism applies to handle hybrid systems characterized by continuous functions using discrete functions. More precisely, we investigate the modeling of continuous systems in discrete form by preserving the continuous behavior. For hybrid systems, the system substitution is usually not instantaneous as it takes time to restore the state of the substituted system. We propose a special treatment to handle it. The primary use of the models is to assist in the construction, clarification, and validation of the continuous controller requirements to build a digital controller in case of system reconfiguration or system substitution. In this development, we use the Rodin Platform [4,16] to manage model development, refinement, proofs checking, verification and validation.

Paper Organization. The remainder of this paper is organized as follows. Section 2 presents preliminary details for system substitution mechanisms and the required modeling framework. Section 3 summarizes the studied systems and associated problems, including the informal requirements of the selected system. Section 4 explores an incremental proof-based formal development of system substitution for hybrid systems. Section 5 discusses our approach, and Sect. 6 presents related work and compares the results of this work with existing work. Finally, Sect. 7 concludes the paper with some future research directions.

2   Preliminaries

This section provides a comprehensive overview on system substitution mechanisms, for both continuous and discrete functions, that illustrates our proposal, and a basic overview on the Event-B modeling framework.

2.1   System Substitution Mechanism

System substitution allows to replace a system by another system that provides the same service. It can be used to ensure high availability in case of failure as required for safety critical systems such as avionics, nuclear, automotive and medical devices, where failure could result in loss of life, including reputation and economical damage. In general, system substitution can occur in any state of the system. We focus on *warm start* tagged as *Dynamic substitution*, where the substitute system will recover as much data and state variable values as possible from the halting state of the original system. *Dynamic substitution* allows replacing a failed system Sys_S with a new one Sys_T starting from the last running state of Sys_S. Thus, Sys_T must be initialized according to the last running state of Sys_S. In order to ensure that both systems provide the same services, they must implement the same specification *Spec* according to the recovery states.

2.2   The Modeling Framework

Event-B [3] is a formal modeling notation, in which the event-driven approach extends the B-method [2]. The Event-B language has two main components, *context* and *machine*, to characterize the systems. A *context* describes the static structure of a system using *carrier sets, constants, axioms* and *theorems*, and a *machine* describes the dynamic structure of a system using *variables, invariants, theorems, variants* and *events*. Table 1 shows a formal organization of a model, in which various clauses (i.e. VARIABLES, EVENTS) are used to introduce the required modeling components for specifying the given system requirements. For instance, the clause VARIABLES represents the state and the clause EVENTS represents the transitions (defined by a Before-After predicate (BA)) of a system. A list of events can be used to model possible system behaviors that modify the state variables by providing appropriate *guards* in a *machine*. A model also

Table 1. Model structure

CONTEXT	MACHINE
ctxt_id_2	*machine_id_2*
EXTENDS	**REFINES**
ctxt_id_1	*machine_id_1*
SETS	**SEES**
s	*ctxt_id_2*
CONSTANTS	**VARIABLES**
c	*v*
AXIOMS	**INVARIANTS**
$A(s,c)$	$I(s,c,v)$
THEOREMS	**THEOREMS**
$T_c(s,c)$	$T_m(s,c,v)$
END	**VARIANT**
	$V(s,c,v)$
	EVENTS
	Event $evt \triangleq$
	any x
	where $G(s,c,v,x)$
	then
	$v : |BA(s,c,v,x,v')$
	end
	END

Table 2. Proof obligations

Theorems	$A(s,c) \Rightarrow T_c(s,c)$ $A(s,c) \wedge I(s,c,v)$ $\Rightarrow T_m(s,c,v)$
Invariant preservation	$A(s,c) \wedge I(s,c,v)$ $\wedge G(s,c,v,x)$ $\wedge BA(s,c,v,x,v')$ $\Rightarrow I(s,c,v')$
Event feasibility	$A(s,c) \wedge I(s,c,v)$ $\wedge G(s,c,v,x)$ $\Rightarrow \exists v'.BA(s,c,v,x,v')$
Variant progress	$A(s,c) \wedge I(s,c,v)$ $\wedge G(s,c,v,x)$ $\wedge BA(s,c,v,x,v')$ $\Rightarrow V(s,c,v') < V(s,c,v)$

contains INVARIANTS and THEOREMS clauses to represent its relevant properties to check the correctness of the formalized behavior. A VARIANT clause can be used to introduce convergence properties in a machine. Moreover, the terms like *refines*, *extends*, and *sees* are mainly used to describe the relation between components of Event-B models.

The Event-B modeling language supports a *correct by construction* approach to design an abstract model and a series of refined models for developing any large and complex system. The refinement, introduced by the REFINES clause, decomposes a model (thus a transition system) into another transition system containing more design decisions when moving from an abstract level to a less abstract one. Refinement supports modeling a system gradually by introducing safety properties at various refinement levels. New variables and new events may be introduced in a new refinement level. These refinements preserve the relation between the abstract model and its corresponding refined concrete model, while introducing new events and variables to specify more concrete behaviors of the system. The defined abstract and concrete state variables are linked by introducing *gluing invariants*.

The Rodin Platform provides rich tool support for model development using the Event-B language. It includes project management, model development, proof assistance, model checking, animation and automatic code generation. Once an Event-B model is modeled and syntactically checked in the Rodin Platform, then a set of proof obligations is generated with the help of the Rodin tools. Theses generated proof obligations are further passed to the inbuilt Rodin prover. The main proof obligations associated to an Event-B model are listed in Table 2, in which the prime notation is used to denote the value of a variable after an event is triggered. More details on proof obligations can be found in [3].

The Theory Plug-In. A recent extension of the Event-B language allows extending it with theories [5] similar to algebraic specifications. In the Rodin Platform, this is provided by the *Theory* plug-in [13]. We formalize and analyze a system substitution mechanism applied to hybrid systems, that use the REAL datatype for state variables. Thus, we rely on the *Real* theory, written by Abrial and Butler[1] that provides a dense mathematical REAL datatype with arithmetic operators, an axiomatic semantics and proof rules.

3   Studied Systems

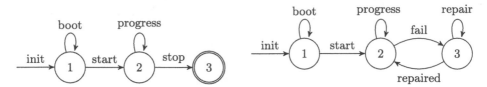

Fig. 1. Behavior of studied systems   **Fig. 2.** System substitution

In this section, we describe the studied family of simple systems as patterns including the mechanism for system substitution. These ones are depicted in Fig. 1 for the system and Fig. 2 for the substitution mechanism. They are formalized as state-transition systems. Their behaviors are characterized by three states: *boot* (1), *progress* (2) and *stopped* (3). The *boot* state is the initial state, and the *progress* state is the nominal running state. According to Fig. 1, after initialization, a system enters the *booting* state, denoted as *state 1*, which may take a certain amount of time. If a system does not require the booting phase, then the system initialization is followed by a *start* transition without any delay. After this one, the system moves into the *progress* state, denoted as *state 2*. If the system stops, it switches into the *stopped* state, denoted as *state 3*.

3.1   Problem Statement

The substitution mechanism allows maintaining the running state of a given system in case of failure or decreasing QoS by replacing it with another one that provides the required behavior. A basic substitution pattern is defined by the state-transitions system of Fig. 2. When a failure occurs, the running system is halted (*fail* transition), then repaired in *state 3* where the state of the substitute system is restored from the halted system. Finally, the control is given to the substitute system (transition *repaired* from *state 3* to *state 2*). The substitution correctness has been studied in different cases (equivalent, degraded or upgraded cases). This mechanism (Fig. 2) shall satisfy the following requirements: (1) Preserving the required system behavior of the original system; (2) Restoring the halted system correctly.

---

[1] http://wiki.event-b.org/index.php/Theory_Plug-in#Standard_Library.

Refinement is used to fulfill the first requirement. Several refinements may implement the same specification thus providing a class of systems that are candidate for substitution. The second requirement is expressed as a relation restoring the state variables of the substituted and substitute systems that must preserve the invariant and properties of the original specification. Details can be found in [8,9]. Substitutions can be instantaneous when it consists in restoring state variables that fulfill the specification invariant as shown in the case of web services compensation from [7]. But, for hybrid systems, it may require some time. The *repair* transition on state 3 of Fig. 2 must handle the repair process duration. This case is adressed in this contribution and the system behavior must be preserved during that duration.

3.2   Informal System Requirements

The hybrid systems behaviors models usually rely on continuous functions over time. Figure 3a depicts such a function f whose nominal value (after initialization) must stay in the safety enveloppe $[m, M]$. The time intervals $[A, B],]B, C]$ and $]C, D]$ correspond respectively to state 1, 2 and 3 of Fig. 1. Any system controller, including a reconfiguration one, must observe the behavior of the system (here the function f) and act (preserve or change the system mode) to keep the observation in the safety enveloppe. Such observations and actions are usually implemented by a software that requires the discretization of the continuous functions. Figure 3b depicts such a discrete form for f. The time intervals $[E, F]$ $]F, H]$ and $]H, I]$ correspond respectively to state 1, 2 and 3 of Fig. 1. In the software that implements such controllers, time is observed according to specific clocks and periods. Therefore, it is mandatory to define a correct discretization of time that preserves the observed continuous behavior introduced previously. This preservation entails the introduction of other requirements on the defined continuous function. With respect to a time interval δt, the margin z is defined as respecting: $z \geq \max_{t, \delta t \in \mathbb{R}+} |f(t) - f(t + \delta t)|$ (the evolution of f is assumed to be bounded) and $m + z < M - z$ (for consistency). Note that, in practice, these

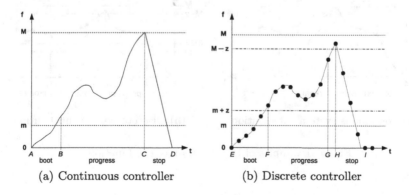

(a) Continuous controller   (b) Discrete controller

Fig. 3. Examples of the evolution of the function f

requirements are usually satisfied by the physical plant (f is usually a smooth continuous function).

Two continuous functions f and g characterize the behavior of two hybrid systems Sys_f and Sys_g. We assume that these systems maintain their observed output within the safety envelope $[m, M]$. Thus, they can substitute each other since they fulfill the same safety requirement. In this paper, we study the substitution of Sys_f by Sys_g after a failure occurrence (see requirements of Table 3).

Figure 4a and b show the substitution scenario in both continuous and discrete cases. The X axis describes time change and the vertical dashed lines model state transitions according to the behavior depicted in Fig. 2. Observe that during the repairing process (state 3 of Fig. 2) function f (associated with Sys_f) decreases due to its failure while function g (associated with Sys_g) is booting. The invariant states that $f + g$ belongs to the safety envelope $[m, M]$ during the repair (between C and D in the continuous case of Fig. 4a or G and H in the discrete case on Fig. 4b). Finally, the progress state 2 is reached a second time with Sys_g as the running system.

Table 3. Requirements in the abstract specification.

At any time, the feedback information value of the controlled system shall be less or equal to M in any mode	Req. 1
At any time, the feedback information value of the controlled system shall belong to the safety envelope $[m, M]$ in *progress* mode	Req. 2
The system feedback information value can be produced either by f, g or $f + g$ (f and g being associated to Sys_f and Sys_g)	Req. 3
The system Sys_f may have feedback information values outside $[m, M]$	Req. 4
At any time, in the *progress* mode, when using Sys_f, if the feedback information value of the controlled system equals to m or to M, Sys_f must is stopped	Req. 5

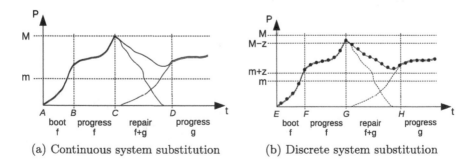

(a) Continuous system substitution   (b) Discrete system substitution

Fig. 4. Examples of the evolution of the function f

4   Formal Development

This section describes the stepwise formal development of studied systems in an abstract model and a sequence of refined models. The abstract model formalizes only the system initial behavior, while the refined models are used to define the concrete and more complex behaviors in a progressive manner that preserves the required safety properties at every refinement level.

Due to the limitation of the paper length, we only include a brief description of the model development and refinements. We invite readers to rely on the complete formal model available at [1] to understand the basic steps of the formal development, refinements and associated safety properties.

4.1   The Required Contexts

Contexts define the relevant concepts needed for our developments. The context *C_reals* (see Listing 1.1) defines the positive real numbers and theorems helpful for discharging the proofs. This context uses the REAL type for real numbers defined in the *Theory Real* by Abrial and Butler. Listing 1.2 introduces the constants $MODE\_X$ defining the different system modes (F, G and R for Sys_f, Sys_g and *Repair* modes) belonging to the *MODES* set.

```
CONTEXT C_reals -- Continuous functions
CONSTANTS
    REAL_POS, REAL_STR_POS
AXIOMS -- Axioms and theorems
       -- for continuous functions
    def01: REAL_POS = {x | x ∈ REAL ∧ 0≤ x)}
    ....

END
```

```
CONTEXT C_modes
SETS
    MODES
CONSTANTS
    MODE_F, MODE_R, MODE_G
AXIOMS
    axm1: partition(MODES, {MODE_F},
                    {MODE_R}, {MODE_G})

END
```

Listing 1.1. Context C_reals   **Listing 1.2.** Modes definition

The previous two contexts (*C_envelope* and *C_margin*) deal with the definition of a safety envelope. As mentioned in the requirements defined in Table 3, we define the interval of safe values as $[m, M]$ in the continuous case and $[m + z, M - z]$ with margin z in the discrete case.

```
CONTEXT C_envelope -- Safety envelope
EXTENDS C_reals
CONSTANTS
    m, M
AXIOMS
    axm01: m ∈ REAL_STR_POS
    axm02: M ∈ REAL_STR_POS
    axm03: smr(m,M)
THEOREMS
    thm01: m ≤ M
    thm02: 0 ≤ m
    thm06: 0 ≤ M
    thm03: ∀x · m ≤ x ⇒ x ∈ REAL_POS
    thm05: ∀a · m ≤ a ⇒ 0 ≤ a
END
```

```
CONTEXT C_margin -- Safety envelope margin
EXTENDS C_envelope
CONSTANTS
    z
AXIOMS
    axm01: z ∈ REAL_POS -- z ∈ R+
    axm02: M−m > 2∗z
THEOREMS
    thm03: 0 ≤ M−z
    thm06: z ≤ M−m
    thm07: m ≤ M−z
    thm08: m+z ≤ M
    thm10: m+z ≤ M−z
    ...
END
```

Listing 1.3. Context C_envelope   **Listing 1.4.** Context C_margin

4.2   Abstract Model: Definition of a Mode Controller

As shown in Fig. 2, we use three states to define a simple abstract controller (a mode automata) that models the system substitution through mode changes. Machine $M0$ (see Listing 1.5) describes the abstract specification of the reconfiguration state-transitions system depicted in Fig. 2. The modes are used in the events guards to switch from one state to another. At initialization, Sys_f is started ($MODE\_F$), it becomes active when the $active$ variable is true (Sys_f ended the booting phase). When a failure occurs, progress of Sys_f is stopped. The controller enters in the repairing mode $MODE\_R$. Once the system is repaired, the mode is switched to $MODE\_G$ and Sys_g enters the progress state.

```
MACHINE M0
SEES  C_modes
VARIABLES
    active    -- true when the system is started
    md        -- running mode of the system
INVARIANTS
    type01: active ∈ BOOL
    type03: md ∈ MODES
    tech01: active = FALSE ⇒ md = MODE_F
EVENTS
    INITIALISATION=
    THEN
        act1: active := FALSE
        act2: md := MODE_F
    END
    boot = WHERE
        grd1: active = FALSE
        grd2: md = MODE_F
    END
    start= WHERE
        grd1: active = FALSE
        grd2: md = MODE_F
    THEN
        act1: active := TRUE
    END
```

```
progress = WHERE
    grd2: active = TRUE
    grd1: md = MODE_F ∨ md = MODE_G
END
fail = WHERE
    grd2: active = TRUE
    grd1: md = MODE_F
THEN
    act1: md := MODE_R
END
repair= WHERE
    grd2: active = TRUE
    grd1: md = MODE_R
END
repaired = WHERE
    grd2: active = TRUE
    grd1: md = MODE_R
THEN
    act1: md := MODE_G
END
END
```

Listing 1.5. The mode automata

4.3   First Refinement: Introduction of the Safety Envelope

The first refinement introduces the safety envelope $[m, M]$: the main invariant satisfied by all functions: f initially, $f + g$ during substitution and g after substitution. Machine $M1$, defined in Listing 1.6, refines $M0$. It preserves the behavior defined in $M0$ and introduces two kinds of events: environment events (event name prefixed with ENV) and controller events (event name prefixed with $CTRL$) [23]. The ENV events produce the system feedback observed by the controller.

In this refinement, three new real variables f, g and p are introduced. f and g record the feedback information of Sys_f and Sys_g individually, while p records the feedback information of both systems before, during and after substitution. The variable p corresponds to f of Sys_f in $MODE\_F$, g of Sys_g in $MODE\_G$ and $f + g$ of combined Sys_f and Sys_g in $MODE\_R$ corresponding to the system reparation (invariants $mode01$ to $mode05$). In all cases, p shall belong to the safety envelope (invariants $envelope01$ and $envelope02$). The $CTRL$ events correspond to refinements of the abstract events of $M0$. They modify the control variable $active$ and md. The ENV events observe real values corresponding to the different situations where Sys_f and Sys_g are running or when Sys_f fails and Sys_g boots. This last situation corresponds to the reparation case.

```
MACHINE M1 REFINES M0                  CTRL_limit_detected_f REFINES fail =
SEES C_envelope, C_modes               WHERE
VARIABLES                                  grd5: f = m ∨ f = M
    active, md, p, f, g                END
INVARIANTS
                                       ENV_evolution_fg REFINES repair =
    envelope01: p ≤ M                  ANY new_f, new_g
    envelope02: active = TRUE ⇒ m ≤ p  WHERE
                                           grd3: m ≤ new_f + new_g
    mode01: md = MODE_F ⇒ p = f            grd4: new_f + new_g ≤ M
    mode04: md = MODE_F ⇒ g = 0           grd5: 0 ≤ new_f
    mode02: md = MODE_R ⇒ p = f + g       grd6: new_f ≤ f
    mode03: md = MODE_G ⇒ p = g           grd7: g ≤ new_g
    mode05: md = MODE_G ⇒ f = 0           grd8: new_g ≤ M
THEOREMS                               THEN
    ....                                   act1: f := new_f
EVENTS                                     act2: g := new_g
    INITIALISATION=                        act3: p := new_f + new_g
    ....                               END
    CTRL_started REFINES start =
    WHERE                              CTRL_repaired_g REFINES repaired =
        grd3: m ≤ p ∧ p ≤ M            WHERE
    END                                    grd3: m ≤ g
    ENV_evolution_f REFINES progress =     grd4: g ≤ M
    ANY new_f                              grd5: f = 0    -- f+g to g is continuous
    WHERE                              END
        grd2: active = TRUE ∧ md = MODE_F
        grd5: f ≠ m ∧ f ≠ M            ENV_evolution_g REFINES progress =
        grd3: m ≤ new_f                    ...
        grd4: new_f ≤ M                END
    THEN
        act1: f := new_f
        act2: p := new_f
    END
```

Listing 1.6. Refinement with ENV and CTRL events

4.4 Second Refinement: Continuous Behavior and Dense Time

The behaviors of continuous controllers defined on dense time are modelled by continuous functions introduced by this refinement. This behavior is modelled in Machine $M2$ (See Listing 1.7). It corresponds to Fig. 4a. Once the modes and the observed values are correctly set, the next refinements are straightforward. They correspond to a direct reuse of the development of a correct discretization of a continuous function proposed in [6].

Continuous functions f_c, g_c, p_c corresponding to variables f, g, p from $M1$ are introduced. A real positive variable now represents the current time. The gluing invariants ($glue01$ for example $p = p_c(now)$) connect the variables of machine $M1$ with the continuous functions values at time now. In the same way, each event of $M1$ is refined. Time steps dt are introduced and the continuous functions are updated by the environment ENV events. The continuous functions are updated on the interval $[now, now + dt]$ and now is updated to $now := now + dt$. The control $CTRL$ events observe the value $p_c(now)$ to decide whether specific actions on the mode md_c variable are performed or not. Listing 1.7 shows an extract of this machine and a detailed description of this refinement is given in [1, 6].

```
MACHINE M2 REFINES M1
SEES C_corridor, C_thms
VARIABLES
    now, p_c, f_c, g_c
    ...
INVARIANTS
    type01: now ∈ REAL_POS
    glue01: p = p_c(now)
    glue02: f = f_c(now)
    glue03: g = g_c(now)
    corridor01: ∀t · t ∈ [0,now] ⇒ p_c(t) ≤ M
    ...
EVENTS
    ...
    ENV_evolution_f
        REFINES ENV_evolution_f =
        ANY dt, new_f_c
        WHERE
            ...
            grd5: f_c(now) = new_f_c(now)
            grd6: ∀ t · t ∈ [now,now+dt] ⇒
                            new_f_c(t) ∈ [m,M]
        WITH
            new_f: new_f = new_f_c(now + dt)
        THEN
            act1: now := now + dt
            act2: p_c := p_c ⩤ new_f_c
            act3: f_c := f_c ⩤ new_f_c
            ...
        END
    ...
END
```

Listing 1.7. Machine M2

```
MACHINE M3 REFINES M2
SEES C_discrete, ...
VARIABLES
    p_d, f_d, g_d
    i   -- the current instant number
    et -- time elapsed from previous discrete
        --               value sampling time
    ...
INVARIANTS
    type01: f_d ∈ 0..i → REAL_POS
                 -- similar for p_d and g_d
    type04: i ∈ ℕ
    glue01: ∀ n· n ∈ 0..i ⇒ f_c(n∗tstep)=f_d(n)
                 -- similar for p_d and g_d
    glue02: now = i∗tstep + et
    ...
EVENTS
    ...
    ENV_evolution_f_on_tick
        REFINES ENV_evolution_f =
        ANY dt, new_f_c
        WHERE
            new_f_c ∈ [now,now+dt] → REAL_POS
            ...
        THEN
            act01: f := new_f
            act02: now := now + dt
            act03: f_c := f_c ⩤ new_f_c
            act04: i := i + 1
            act05: f_d(i+1) := new_f_c(now+dt)
            act06: et := 0
            ...
        END
    ...
END
```

Listing 1.8. Machine M3

4.5   Third Refinement: Discretization of the Continuous Behavior

This last refinement models a discrete controller. A discrete function is associated to values of the continuous function at each discrete time steps. The discrete behavior is given in Machine $M3$ (See Listing 1.8). It models the behavior from Fig. 4b following the work in [6]. Again, we follow the same approach as for the refinement of the continuous behavior. As mentioned in the context C_margin, the margin z is defined, such that $0 < z \wedge m + z < M - z \wedge M - m > 2 \times z$. This margin defines, at the discrete level, the new safety envelope $[m + z, M - z] \subset [m, M]$. The new discrete variables f_d, g_d, p_d of $M3$ are glued to f_c, g_c, p_c of $M2$. They correspond to discrete observations of f_c, g_c, p_c. The discretization step is defined as δt. Each environment event corresponding to a continuous event is refined into three events: the first one corresponds to discrete time now, the second one to discrete time $now + \delta t$ and the third one to any time in $]now, now + \delta t[$. In this discrete modeling, the last event ensures the correctness of refinement. Moreover, it must be $Zeno$ free, so we introduce a decreasing variant in this refinement. The discrete controller observes only the events on time jumps from now to $now + \delta t$. Note that due to the discretization and the introduction of the z margin, a possible failure can be detected when $p_d(now) \in [m, m + z[\vee p_d(now) \in]M - z, M]$. The predicted behavior is enforced by the discrete controller that detects a limit before the value of m or M is reached. This situation is depicted in Fig. 4b at instant G.

4.6 Model Analysis

This section gives the proof statistics through detailed data about generated proof obligations. Event-B supports *consistency checking* which shows that a list of events preserves the given invariants, and *refinement checking* which ensures that a concrete machine is a valid refinement of an abstract machine. The whole formal development is presented through one abstract model and a sequence of three refinement models to cover the possible operations of system substitution of hybrid systems.

Table 4. Proof Statistics

Model	Total number of POs	Automatic proof	Interactive proof
Abstract model (M0)	5	5 (100 %)	0 (0 %)
First refinement (M1)	93	48 (52 %)	45 (48 %)
Second refinement (M2)	209	71 (34 %)	138 (66 %)
Third refinement (M3)	425	78 (18 %)	347 (82 %)
Total	**732**	**202 (28 %)**	**530 (72 %)**

Table 4 gives the proof statistics for the development using the Rodin tool. To guarantee the correctness, we established various invariants in the incremental refinements. This development resulted in 732 (100 %) proof obligations, of which 202 (28 %) were proved automatically, and the remaining 530 (72 %) were proved interactively using the Rodin prover (see Table 4). These interactive proof obligations are mainly related to the complex mathematical expressions and the use of *Theory* plug-in for **REAL** datatype, which are simplified through interaction, providing additional information to assist the Rodin prover.

5 Discussion

System substitution is a mechanism that allows to maintain the running state of a given system in case of any failure by preserving the required behavior. Specially, for developing critical systems, it is highly required to mitigate any risk of failure. On the other hand, stepwise refinement always plays an important role in designing a complex and large system systematically through progressive development. For developing the system substitution mechanism for hybrid systems, the stepwise refinement played an important role to preserve the required behavior and safety properties. As mentioned earlier, refinement is a core concept in Event-B development, and applying the refinement steps in a systematic order is always useful for designers to know what decisions must be taken for introducing system behaviors in each new refinement level. We identified the following development steps to integrate our system substitution mechanism for hybrid systems: (1) Define a set of modes for the controller; (2) Define a safety envelope to preserve the desired behavior; (3) Handle the continuous behavior and dense time; (4) Model the discretization of the continuous function.

The proposed work is an extension of our previous work [6,8]. In [8], we have developed a generic formal model for system substitution and in [6], we have proposed the stepwise formal development for modeling continuous function using concrete functions. In this paper, we have used our existing approaches for addressing the challenges related to formal modeling and verification for the system substitution for hybrid systems. As far as we know, there are no similar published work. This work is a preliminary step for applying a system substitution mechanism for hybrid systems. We use the *Theory* plug-in for describing the hybrid systems and the required properties. In this experiment, we found that proof are quite complex and the existing Rodin tool support is not powerful enough to prove the generated proof obligation automatically. In fact, we need to assist the Rodin provers to find the required assumptions and predicates to discharge the generated proof obligations. On the other hand, we also found that the *Theory* plug-in is not yet complete. We have defined several assumptions and theorems in our model to help the proving process with the *Real* theory.

6   Related Work

Cyber-physical systems are strongly connected to their operating environment. Thus, the systems can adapt to environment changes to ensure the functional correctness. System reconfiguration is a key element to implement such kinds of systems that is proposed by several researchers. In [11], π-calculus and process algebra are used for system modeling, including reconfiguration, by exploiting behavioral matching based on bi-simulation. An Event-B approach was also proposed in [9]. The B-method is used for validating dynamic re-configuration of the component-based distributed systems using proofs techniques for consistency checking and temporal requirements [17]. Dynamic reconfiguration allows to stay in a system in a stable state using self-configuration and self-healing techniques. Rodrigues et al. [22] presented the dynamic membership mechanism as a key element of a reliable distributed storage system. Event-B is demonstrated in the specification of cooperative error recovery and dynamic reconfiguration for enabling the design of a fault-tolerant multi-agent system, and to develop dynamically reconfigurable systems to avoid redundancy [20]. Model checking of timed automata has been used by [15] to model and study the robustness of self-adaptive decentralized systems.

Cyber-physical systems belong to the class of hybrid systems, thus hybrid automata can be used to model the system requirements. The developed model can be verified through model checking tools, such as HyTech [14]. This approach enables automatic verification by exploring state space and required properties. Usually, model checking tools suffer from state explosion problem that impairs the use of any large model during verification process. Alternatively, theorem provers can be used to analyze and verify hybrid programs. The KeYmaera [21] tool, including an interactive theorem prover, is dedicated to hybrid system modeling and verification. In [12,23], the development of an hybrid system is proposed using the correct by construction approach, where first, it specifies the discrete model and then refines each event by introducing the continuous elements. It includes the use of a "now" variable, a "click" event that jumps in time to the next instant where an event can be triggered and simulated real numbers. In our work [6], we use this notion of "now" variable on dense time, and time progression is defined by events. We use the *Theory* plug-in to model the continuous functions, and another layer of refinement that introduces discretization of continuous elements. Banach et al. [10] proposed Hybrid Event-B that is an extension of Event-B, which contains pliant events to model continuous behavior by using differential equations during system modeling. However, there is currently no tool support for this extension, whereas our approach [6] enabled us to develop and to prove the models using available tools. In our work, we use real numbers defined by a minimal set of axioms without addressing floating-point numbers, which is out of the scope of this paper.

7   Conclusion

Hybrid systems are dynamic systems that combine continuous and discrete behaviors to model complex critical systems, such as avionics, medical, and automotive, where an error or a failure can lead to grave consequences. For critical systems, recovering from any software failure state and correcting the system behavior at runtime is mandatory. The substitution mechanism is an approach that can be used to recover from failure by replacing the failed system. Its use for hybrid systems is a challenging problem as it requires to maintain a safety envelope through discrete implementation of continuous functions. To address this problem, we have presented a refinement based formal modeling and verification of system reconfiguration or substitution for hybrid systems by proving the preservation of the required safety envelope during the process of system substitution. In this paper, we have extended our work on system substitution to handle systems characterized by continuous models. First, we formalized the system substitution at continuous level, then we developed a discrete model through refinement by preserving the original continuous behavior. The whole approach is supported by proofs and refinements based on the Event-B method. Refinements proved useful to build a stepwise development which allowed us to gradually handle the requirements. Moreover, the availability of a theory of real numbers allowed us to introduce continuous behaviors which usually raise from the description of the physics of the controlled plants. All the models have been encoded within the Rodin Platform [4]. These developments required many interactive proofs in particular after the introduction of real numbers. The interactive proofs mainly relate to the use of the *Theory* plug-in for handling real numbers. Up to our understanding, the lack of dedicated heuristics due to the representation of real numbers as an axiomatically-defined abstract data type, and not as a native Event-B type together with our limited experience in defining tactics led to this number of interactive proofs.

This work opened several research directions. First, the models defined in this work handled a single parameter for information feedback with a simple safety envelope (interval that the value must belong to). We plan to investigate the reformulation of this problem when several parameters will be considered. In this case, the safety envelope becomes a more complex expression (a constraint solving problem). The second possible extension of this work is related to parametrization of the safety envelope with time. In other words, instead of having constant interval bounds, we may define bound functions $m(t)$ and $M(t)$. Other properties like elasticity could be expressed. However, this extension requires a powerful prover on real numbers and constraint solving problems techniques. Another possible extension of this work is the development of simulation. The integration of simulation or co-simulation to validate the formal model hypotheses will undoubtedly strengthen the approach. Finally, studying particular systems through realistic case studies is another objective of our work.

References

1. Models. http://babin.perso.enseeiht.fr/r/ICFEM_2016_Models/
2. Abrial, J.R.: The B-Book: Assigning Programs to Meanings. Cambridge University Press, Cambridge (1996). http://ebooks.cambridge.org/ebook.jsf?bid= CBO9780511624162
3. Abrial, J.R.: Modeling in Event-B: System and Software Engineering, 1st edn. Cambridge University Press, New York (2010)
4. Abrial, J.R., Butler, M., Hallerstede, S., Hong, T.S., Mehta, F., Voisin, L.: Rodin: an open toolset for modelling and reasoning in Event-B. Int. J. Softw. Tools Technol. Transf. **12**(6), 447–466 (2010)
5. Abrial, J.R., Butler, M., Hallerstede, S., Leuschel, M., Schmalz, M., Voisin, L.: Proposals for mathematical extensions for Event-B. Technical report (2009)
6. Babin, G., Aït-Ameur, Y., Nakajima, S., Pantel, M.: Refinement and proof based development of systems characterized by continuous functions. In: Li, X., et al. (eds.) SETTA 2015. LNCS, vol. 9409, pp. 55–70. Springer, Heidelberg (2015). doi:10.1007/978-3-319-25942-0_4
7. Babin, G., Aït-Ameur, Y., Pantel, M.: Formal verification of runtime compensation of web service compositions: a refinement and proof based proposal with Event-B. In: IEEE International Conference on Services Computing, pp. 98–105 (2015)
8. Babin, G., Aït-Ameur, Y., Pantel, M.: Correct instantiation of a system reconfiguration pattern: a proof and refinement-based approach. In: IEEE International Symposium on High Assurance Systems Engineering (HASE), pp. 31–38 (2016)
9. Babin, G., Aït-Ameur, Y., Pantel, M.: Trustworthy cyber-physical systems engineering. In: Romanovsky, A., Ishikawa, F. (eds.) A Generic Model for System Substitution. Chapman and Hall/CRC, Boca Raton (2016)
10. Banach, R., Butler, M., Qin, S., Verma, N., Zhu, H.: Core hybrid Event-B I: single hybrid Event-B machines. Sci. Comput. Program. **105**, 92–123 (2015)
11. Bhattacharyya, A.: Formal modelling and analysis of dynamic reconfiguration of dependable systems. Ph.D. thesis, Newcastle University, January 2013
12. Butler, M., Abrial, J.R., Banach, R.: From Action Systems to Distributed Systems: The Refinement Approach, chap. Modelling and Refining Hybrid Systems in Event-B and Rodin, pp. 29–42. Chapman and Hall/CRC., April 2016

13. Butler, M., Maamria, I.: Practical theory extension in Event-B. In: Liu, Z., Woodcock, J., Zhu, H. (eds.) Theories of Programming and Formal Methods. LNCS, vol. 8051, pp. 67–81. Springer, Heidelberg (2013)
14. Henzinger, T.A., Ho, P.H., Wong-Toi, H.: HyTech: a model checker for hybrid systems. Int. J. Softw. Tools Technol. Transf. 1(1–2), 110–122 (1997). http://dx.doi.org/10.1007/s100090050008
15. Iftikhar, M.U., Weyns, D.: A case study on formal verification of self-adaptive behaviors in a decentralized system. In: Kokash, N., Ravara, A. (eds.) 11th International Workshop on Foundations of Coordination Languages and Self Adaptation (FOCLASA 2012), EPTCS, vol. 91, pp. 45–62 (2012)
16. Jastram, M., Butler, M.: Rodin User's Handbook: Covers Rodin V.2.8. CreateSpace Independent Publishing Platform, USA (2014). ISBN 10: 1495438147, ISBN 13: 9781495438141, http://handbook.event-b.org
17. Lanoix, A., Dormoy, J., Kouchnarenko, O.: Combining proof and model-checking to validate reconfigurable architectures. Electron. Notes Theor. Comput. Sci. 279(2), 43–57 (2011)
18. Lee, E.A., Seshia, S.A.: Introduction to Embedded Systems - A Cyber-Physical Systems Approach. LeeSeshia.org, 1.5 edn. (2014). http://leeseshia.org/
19. Lin, H.: Mission accomplished: an introduction to formal methods in mobile robot motion planning and control. Unmanned Syst. 02(02), 201–216 (2014)
20. Pereverzeva, I., Troubitsyna, E., Laibinis, L.: A refinement-based approach to developing critical multi-agent systems. Int. J. Crit. Comput.-Based Syst. 4(1), 69–91 (2013)
21. Platzer, A.: Logical Analysis of Hybrid Systems: Proving Theorems for Complex Dynamics. Springer, Heidelberg (2010). http://symbolaris.com/lahs/
22. Rodrigues, R., Liskov, B., Chen, K., Liskov, M., Schultz, D.: Automatic reconfiguration for large-scale reliable storage systems. IEEE Trans. Dependable Secure Comput. 9(2), 145–158 (2012)
23. Su, W., Abrial, J.R., Zhu, H.: Formalizing hybrid systems with Event-B and the Rodin platform. Sci. Comput. Program. 94, 164–202 (2014)

Service Adaptation with Probabilistic Partial Models

Manman Chen[1(✉)], Tian Huat Tan[1], Jun Sun[1], Jingyi Wang[1], Yang Liu[2], Jing Sun[3], and Jin Song Dong[4]

[1] Singapore University of Technology and Design, Singapore, Singapore
[2] Nanyang Technological University, Singapore, Singapore
manman_chen@sutd.edu.sg
[3] The University of Auckland, Auckland, New Zealand
[4] National University of Singapore, Singapore, Singapore

Abstract. Web service composition makes use of existing Web services to build complex business processes. Non-functional requirements are crucial for the Web service composition. In order to satisfy non-functional requirements when composing a Web service, one needs to rely on the estimated quality of the component services. However, estimation is seldom accurate especially in the dynamic environment. Hence, we propose a framework, ADFLOW, to monitor and adapt the workflow of the Web service composition when necessary to maximize its ability to satisfy the non-functional requirements automatically. To reduce the monitoring overhead, ADFLOW relies on asynchronous monitoring. ADFLOW has been implemented and the evaluation has shown the effectiveness and efficiency of our approach. Given a composite service, ADFLOW achieves 25 %–32 % of average improvement in the conformance of non-functional requirements, and only incurs 1 %–3 % of overhead with respect to the execution time.

1 Introduction

Service Oriented Architecture (SOA) is emerging as a methodology for building Web applications by using of existing Web services from different enterprises as components. Web services provide an affordable and adaptable framework that can produce a significantly lower cost of ownership for the enterprises over time. Web services make use of open standards, such as WSDL [8] and SOAP [14], which enable the interaction among heterogeneous applications.

The Web service composed by Web service composition is called a *composite service* (e.g., Travel Agency service) and the Web services that constitute the composite service are called *component services* (e.g., American Airline booking service). Non-functional requirements are an important class of requirements for Web services. They are concerned with quality of service (QoS) (e.g., response time, availability, cost) of Web services. The non-functional requirements are

This work is supported by research project T2MOE1303.

K. Ogata et al. (Eds.): ICFEM 2016, LNCS 10009, pp. 122–140, 2016.
DOI: 10.1007/978-3-319-47846-3_9

often an important clause in service-level agreements (SLAs), which is the contractual basis between service consumers and service providers on the expected QoS level. For example, nowadays, many big players in the market (e.g., Netflix, Amazon, and Microsoft Azure) have adopted microservice architecture [2]. It works by decomposing their existing monolithic applications into smaller, and highly decoupled services (also known as microservices). These microservices are then composed to fulfill their business requirements. For example, Netflix decomposed their monolithic DVD rental application into microservices that work together, and then stream digital entertainment to millions of Netflix customers every day.

In this work, the requirements of QoS for the composite service can be specified as *global constraints*. For example, an example of the global constraint is that the response time of the Web service composition must be less than 8 ms. To guarantee the SLAs between the Web service composition and its users, the design of Web service composition involves the estimation of QoS of component services. The QoS of component services could be solicited from the providers of component services either in the form of SLAs or based on past history of executions by making use of existing approaches (e.g., KAMI [9]).

However, due to the highly evolving and dynamic environment that the Web service composition is running, the design time assumptions for Web service composition, even if they are initially accurate, may later change during runtime. For example, the execution time of a component service may increase unexpectedly due to reasons such as network congestion, which could affect the response time of the composite service. Furthermore, at runtime, the non-functional properties of a composite service rely on the behaviors of component services offered by third-party partners. The distributed ownership makes the non-functional properties of Web service composition subject to changes. For instance, component service providers could modify existing component Web services, and usage profiles of the component Web services may change over time. These behaviors may result in potential violations of SLA of the composite Web service. Since estimations are seldom accurate, it is desirable that Web service compositions could *dynamically adapt* themselves to their environment with little or no human intervention in order to meet the guaranteed QoS levels. The loose coupling and binding features of SOA systems make them particularly suitable for runtime adaptation.

Existing works [5,15,17,18] address this problem by replacing component services or invoke component services adaptively, which we denote it as *point adaptation strategy*. *Point adaptation strategy* suffers several disadvantages. First, there are cases where such a strategy does not work. For example, there is no alternate service that can satisfy the non-functional requirements. In addition, there might not exist an alternating service that could be switched directly. Secondly, there maybe incur much cost as they may invoke another service to compensate it.

In this work, we propose the usage of *workflow adaptation strategy* to address this issue. A workflow adaptation strategy involves modifying the workflow to find a path for execution that can maximize the ability to satisfy the non-functional requirements. Therefore, we present *runtime ADaptation frame-work based on workFlow* (ADFLOW), a framework to alleviate the management problem of complex Web compositions that operate in rapidly changing environments. We propose the notion of *probabilistic partial model*, which is extended from the previous notion of partial model [11], to capture the *uncertainties* of system execution with probabilistic. The global constraints of the composite service are decomposed into local requirements for each state of a probabilistic partial model. When a possible violation of the global constraints is detected, adaptive actions are taken preemptively based on the probabilistic partial model, to avoid unsatisfactory behaviors or failures. In particular, the adaptive action chooses the execution that could maximize the likelihood of conformance of the global constraints.

Our contributions are summarized as follows.

1. We propose the probabilistic partial model to capture the runtime uncertainties of Web service composition.
2. We propose a runtime adaptation framework, ADFLOW for Web service composition. ADFLOW monitors the execution of Web service composition based on local requirements of the probabilistic partial model. If a possible violation of the global constraints of the composite service is detected, adaptive actions would be taken preemptively to prevent the violation.
3. To reduce the monitoring overhead, we propose to use *asynchronous monitoring* where the execution status is monitored asynchronously whenever possible. We show that this approach reduces the overhead significantly.
4. We have evaluated our method on real-world case studies, and we show that it significantly improves the chance of the composite service to conform to the global constraints.

Outline. The rest of paper is structured as follows. Section 2 describes a motivating example. Section 3 introduces the probabilistic partial model used for Web service compositions. Section 4 presents our ADFLOW adaptation framework for runtime adaptation. Section 5 evaluates the performance of our approach in several scenarios with the increasing complexity. Section 6 discusses related work. Section 7 concludes the paper and describes future work.

2   Motivating Example

In this work, we introduce four elementary compositional structures for composing the component services, i.e., the sequential ($\langle$sequence$\rangle$), parallel ($\langle$flow$\rangle$), loop ($\langle$while$\rangle$) and conditional ($\langle$if$\rangle$) compositions, which are all the essential structures of many programming languages; therefore, our work can be applied to other languages potentially. In addition, there are three basic activities to communicate with component services, i.e., receive ($\langle$receive$\rangle$), reply ($\langle$reply$\rangle$), and invocation ($\langle$invoke$\rangle$) activities. The $\langle$receive$\rangle$ and $\langle$reply$\rangle$ activities are used to receive requests from and reply results to the users of the composite service respectively. The $\langle$invoke$\rangle$ activity is used to invoke component services for their functionalities. There are two kinds of $\langle$invoke$\rangle$ activities, i.e., synchronous and asynchronous $\langle$invoke$\rangle$ activities. The *synchronous* $\langle$invoke$\rangle$ activity invokes the component service and wait for the reply, while the *asynchronous* $\langle$invoke$\rangle$ activity moves on after the invocation without waiting for the reply.

2.1 Running Example – Travel Booking Service

In this section, we introduce the Travel Booking Service (TBS) as a running example in this work. TBS is designed for providing a combined budget flight and hotel booking composite service by incorporating with several existing component services. The workflow of TBS is sketched in Fig. 1a.

TBS has five component Web services, namely a flight searching service (*FS*), three budget flight booking services (*BF$_1$*, *BF$_2$* and *BF$_3$*), and a hotel booking service (*HB*). Upon receiving the request from the customer (*Receive User*), a $\langle$flow$\rangle$ activity (denoted as ✧) is triggered, and *Invoke FS* and *Invoke HB* are executed concurrently; *Invoke HB* invokes the *HB* service to book the hotel (All invocation activities in this work are assumed to be synchronous, unless otherwise stated). *Invoke FS* invokes the *FS* service to search for budget flights. Upon receiving the reply from the *FS* service, a conditional activity (denoted as ◇) is followed. If the ticket price of *BF$_1$* is the lowest (represented by the guard condition g_1), *BF$_1$* is invoked (*Invoke BF$_1$*) to book the flight ticket. If the ticket price of *BF$_2$* is the lowest (represented by the guard condition g_2), then *BF$_2$* is invoked (*Invoke BF$_2$*) to book the ticket. Otherwise, *BF$_3$* is invoked to book the ticket (*Invoke BF$_3$*). Upon completion of the concurrent activities, TBS replies the user with a booking confirmation message (*Reply User*).

TBS provides an SLA for their service consumers such that it must respond within 600 ms upon any request with at least 95 % availability. The cost per invocation of TBS is 8 dollars – therefore TBS service provider needs to ensure it does not spend more than 8 dollars for its component services.

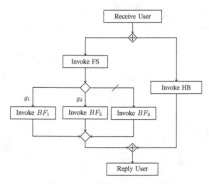

QoS Attribute	FS	HB	BF$_1$	BF$_2$	BF$_3$
Response Time (ms)	300	200	300	200	100
Availability	1	1	0.95	0.9	0.95
Cost ($)	2	1	2	2	1

(b) QoS for component services of TBS

(a) Travel Booking Service (TBS)

Fig. 1.

Now, let us consider a scenario where the flight searching service takes 500 ms. Classic point adaptation strategy may switch some service to an alternating service [5,15,17,18], which has been mentioned in the introduction, as it involves retrying or switching of a particular service. There are cases where such a strategy does not work. For example, there is no alternate service that can satisfy the non-functional requirements. In addition, there might not exist an alternating service that could be switched directly. In such a case, our workflow adaptation strategy, could be used.

2.2 Service Composition Notations

We use the syntax below to specify the workflow of a service composition succinctly.

- $P_1; P_2$ and $P_1|||P_2$ are used to denote sequential and concurrent executions of the activities P_1 and P_2 respectively.
- $C([g_1]P_1, [g_2]P_2, \cdots, [g_n]P_n, P_0)$ is used to denote the conditional activity, where g_i is a guard with $i \in \{1, 2, \cdots, n\}$. The guards are evaluated sequentially from g_0 to g_n, and activity P_i is executed for the first g_i that is evaluated to true. If all the guards are evaluated to false, the activity P_0 is executed.
- $sInv(P)$ and $aInv(P)$ are used to denote the synchronous and asynchronous invocations respectively of the activity P.
- $pick(S_1 \Rightarrow P_1, S_2 \Rightarrow P_2)$ is used to denote the pick activity, which contains two branches of *onMessage* activities where exactly one branch would be executed.

$$P_{TBS} = \{(\{[sInv(FS)]_4^6; C([g_1][sInv(BF_1)]_3^3, [g_2][sInv(BF_2)]_2^2, [sInv(BF_3)]_1^1\}_1^3\}_4^6|||[sInv(HB)]_2^2)_4^6; [reply]_0^0\}_4^6$$

(a) Process Description of TBS

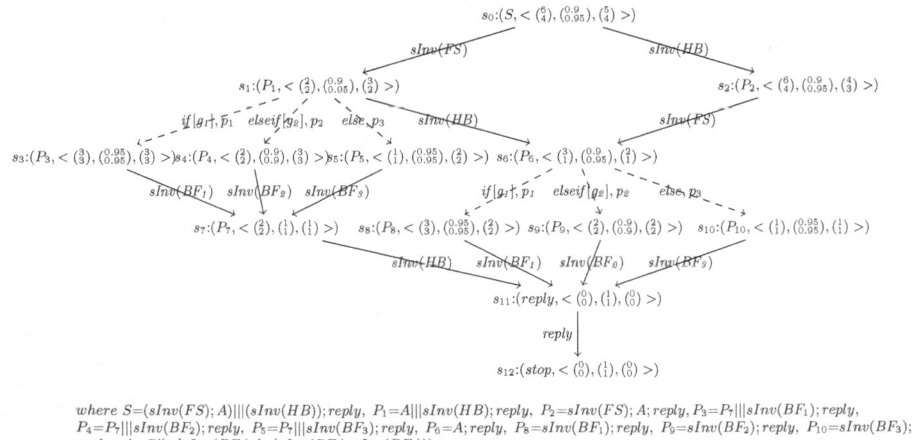

where $S=(sInv(FS); A)|||(sInv(HB)); reply$, $P_1=A|||sInv(HB); reply$, $P_2=sInv(FS); A; reply$, $P_3=P_7|||sInv(BF_1); reply$, $P_4=P_7|||sInv(BF_2); reply$, $P_5=P_7|||sInv(BF_3); reply$, $P_6=A; reply$, $P_8=sInv(BF_1); reply$, $P_9=sInv(BF_2); reply$, $P_{10}=sInv(BF_3); reply$, $A=C([g_1]sInv(BF_1), [g_2]sInv(BF_2), sInv(BF_3)))$

(b) Probabilistic Partial Model of TBS

Fig. 2. TBS example

Activity P_1 is activated when the message from the component service S_1 is received, while activity P_2 is activated if the message from the component service S_2 is received.

The process description of TBS, P_{TBS} is shown in Fig. 2a. The numbers annotated to each activity will be introduced in our technical report [3].

3 Preliminaries

In this section, we introduce various notions used in this work. A composite service CS is constructed using a finite number of component services. We use $S_{CS} = \langle s_1, s_2, \ldots, s_n \rangle$ to denote the set of all component services used in CS.

Table 1. Aggregation function

QoS attribute	Sequential	Parallel	Loop	Conditional
Response time	$\sum_{i=1}^{n} q(s_i)$	$\max_{i=1}^{n} q(s_i)$	$k * (q(s_1))$	$\sum_{i=1}^{n} p_i * q(s_i)$
Availability	$\prod_{i=1}^{n} q(s_i)$	$\prod_{i=1}^{n} q(s_i)$	$(q(s_1))^k$	$\sum_{i=1}^{n} p_i * q(s_i)$
Cost	$\sum_{i=1}^{n} q(s_i)$	$\sum_{i=1}^{n} q(s_i)$	$k * (q(s_1))$	$\sum_{i=1}^{n} p_i * q(s_i)$

3.1 QoS Attributes

In this work, we use three QoS attributes, i.e., response time, availability and cost as examples to demonstrate our approach. The response time $r \in \mathbb{R}_{\geq 0}$ of a service is defined as the delay between sending the request to the service and receiving the response from it. The availability $a \in \mathbb{R} \cap [0,1]$ of a service is the probability of the service being available. The cost of a service is the price that incurs by invoking the service. We use $R(a)$, $A(a)$ and $C(a)$ to denote the response time, availability and cost of the activity a respectively. Table 1 lists QoS values for component services of TBS, that will be used in the subsequent sections. There are two kinds of QoS attributes, positive and negative ones. Positive attributes, e.g., availability, provide good effect on the QoS; therefore, they need to be maximized. While negative attributes, e.g., response time and cost, need to be minimized. Our QoS attributes could be addressed similarly as these three QoS attributes. For example, reliability could be handled in the same way as availability.

3.2   QoS for Composite Services

The values of QoS attributes for composite service CS are aggregated from each component service based on internal compositional structures. There are four types of compositional structures: sequential, parallel, loop and conditional compositional structures. Table 1 shows the aggregation function for each compositional structure. In the parallel composition, the response time is the maximum one among response times of all participating component services since all participating component services execute concurrently. In the loop composition, it is aggregated by summing up the response time of the involved component service for k times where k is the number of maximum iteration of the loop and it could be inferred by using loop bound analysis tools (e.g., [10]). In the conditional composition, we use the expected value as the evaluation of guards is not known at the design time, where q_i is the probability for executing the service s_i.

3.3   Probabilistic Partial Models

Our approach is grounded on *probabilistic partial models*, which extend partial models introduced in [11]. In the following, we define various related notions before introducing the probabilistic partial model.

Definition 1 (State). *A state s is a tuple (P, V, Q), where P is a service process, V is a (partial) variable valuation that maps variables to their values, and Q is a vector which represents the* local estimation *of the state s, which will be discussed in Sect. 4.3. We introduce the details of local estimation in Sect. 4.3.*

Given a state $s = (P, V, Q)$, we use the notation $P(s)$, $V(s)$, and $Q(s)$ to denote the process, valuation, and local estimation of the state s respectively. Two states are said to be equal if and only if they have the same process P, the same valuation V and the same QoS attribute vector Q.

Definition 2 (Transition System). *A transition system is a tuple $\langle S, s_0, \Sigma, R \rangle$, where*

– *S is a set of states; $s_0 \in S$ is the initial state; Σ is a set of actions*
– *$R \subseteq S \times \Sigma \times S$ is a transition relation*

For convenience, we use $s \xrightarrow{a} s'$ to denote $(s, a, s') \in R$. Given a state $s \in S$, $Enable(s)$ denotes the set of states reachable from s by one transition, formally, $Enable(s) = \{s' | (s' \in S) \wedge (a \in \Sigma) \wedge (s \xrightarrow{a} s' \in R)\}$. An action a is enabled by s if there exists a state s' such that $s \xrightarrow{a} s'$. $Act(s)$ is denoted as the set of actions that can be triggered from s, formally, $Act(s) = \{a | (a \in \Sigma) \wedge (s' \in S) \wedge (s \xrightarrow{a} s' \in R)\}$. An *execution* π is a finite alternating sequence of states and actions $\langle s_0, a_1, s_1, \ldots, s_{n-1}, a_n, s_n \rangle$, where $\{s_0, \ldots, s_n\} \in S$ and $s_i \xrightarrow{a_{i+1}} s_{i+1}$ for all $0 \le i < n$. We denote the execution π by $s_0 \xrightarrow{a_1} s_1 \xrightarrow{\cdots} s_{n-1} \xrightarrow{a_n} s_n$. A state s is *reachable* if there exists an execution that starts from the initial state s_0 and ends in the state s. A state s is called a *terminal* state if $Act(s)$ is empty. Given an action $a \in \Sigma$, $A(a)$, $R(a)$ and $C(a)$ denote the availability, response time and cost of the action a. The transition system is generated based on the formal semantics of service process described in [12]. Given a composite service CS, we use $\mathcal{T}(CS)$ to denote the transition system of CS.

Definition 3 (Probabilistic Partial Models). *A probabilistic partial model is a tuple $\langle \mathcal{M}, \mathcal{F}, C_g, \mathcal{P} \rangle$, where $\mathcal{M} = \langle S, s_0, \Sigma, R \rangle$ is a transition system, $\mathcal{F}$ is a function: $S \times \Sigma \rightarrow \mathcal{B}$, where $\mathcal{B}$ is the set $\{True, False, Maybe\}$, and $C_g = \langle C_g^R, C_g^A, C_g^C \rangle$ is the global constraints for the model where C_g^R (resp., C_g^A, C_g^C) is the global response time (resp., availability, cost) constraint. $\mathcal{P}$ is a function: $S \times \Sigma \rightarrow p$ where $p \in \mathbb{R} \cap [0, 1]$.*

For convenience, given a composite service CS, we use $\mathcal{P}(CS)$ to denote the probabilistic partial model of CS. $\mathcal{P}(CS)$ is extended from $\mathcal{T}(CS)$ by mapping values (e.g., *True*, or *Maybe*, 0.5) for transitions on $\mathcal{T}(CS)$. We illustrate how the value on transitions of $\mathcal{P}(CS)$ are decided. Given an action $a \in Act(s)$, $F(s, a)$ denotes whether action $a \in \Sigma$ could be executed from state s, $P(s, a)$ provides the probability of executing the action $a \in \Sigma$ at the state s. Clearly, $F(s, a) = False$ and $P(s, a) = 0$ if $a \notin Act(s)$. $F(s, a) = True$ and $P(s, a) = 1$ if action $a \in Act(s)$ and could always be executed regardless the valuation of the variables. Otherwise, $F(s, a) = Maybe$ and $\sum_{a \in MAct(s)} P(s, a) = 1$ where $MAct(s) = \{a | a \in Act(s) \wedge (\mathcal{F}(s, a) = Maybe)\}$. $MAct(s)$ represents a set of *Maybe* actions from s, where exactly one of actions $a \in MAct(s)$ would be executed. The execution of a *Maybe* action depends on the evaluation of the guard (e.g., $\langle \text{if} \rangle$ activity), or dependent on the response from other component services (e.g., $\langle \text{pick} \rangle$ activity). We also use $TAct(s)$ to denote the set of *True* actions enabled by s; formally, $TAct(s) = \{a | a \in Act(s) \wedge (\mathcal{F}(s, a) = True)\}$. For example, actions $if[g_1]$, $elseif[g_2]$, and $else$ (with p_1, p_2 and p_3 as their respective probabilities) are *Maybe* actions, since the execution of these actions dependent on the evaluation of the guard conditions. In contrast, actions FS and HB are *True* actions, since both actions are triggered concurrently at state s_0.

Consider the probabilistic partial model of TBS, $\mathcal{P}(TBS)$, as shown in Fig. 2b. Recall that a state is represented as (P, V, Q). Since $V = \emptyset$ for all states in $\mathcal{P}(TBS)$, we represent states in $\mathcal{P}(TBS)$ as (P, Q) for simplicity. An edge is shown using solid (resp., dotted) arrow if the triggered action is a *True* (resp., *Maybe*) action, and an edge is labelled with probability if the triggered action is a *Maybe* action. Since the probability is 1 if the action is a *True* action, we omit the 1 in the $\mathcal{P}(TBS)$.

4   ADFlow Framework

In the following, we introduce a framework for supporting self-adaptation based on runtime information. The goal is to satisfy the system's global constraints with best efforts. We first introduce the architecture of the ADFLOW framework based on asynchronous monitoring. After that, we focus on the local estimation of probabilistic partial model and demonstrate how it can be used for the runtime adaptation.

In the following, Sect. 4.1 describes the architecture of ADFlow, Sect. 4.2 introduces the notion of *controllability* for activities. Section 4.3 introduces calculations for pessimistic and probabilistic estimation, and then Sect. 4.4 shows how the framework adaptively chooses an action based on the probabilistic estimation. Section 4.5 presents the asynchronous monitoring technique used in our approach.

4.1   Architecture of ADFlow

The architecture of ADFLOW is shown in Fig. 3b. ADFLOW consists of two essential components: the *Runtime Monitor and Adapter* (ADAPTER) and the *Runtime Execution Engine* (EXECUTOR). The ADAPTER monitors and keeps track of the execution of the programs using the probabilistic partial model, and provides adaptation if needed based on the local estimation of the probabilistic partial model. On the other hand, the EXECUTOR provides the environment for the execution of the service programs.

During the deployment of a composite service CS on EXECUTOR, the corresponding *probabilistic partial model* of CS, $\mathcal{P}(CS)$, will be automatically generated (before the execution of CS), stored and maintained by ADAPTER. As for each action execution of CS, ADAPTER will update the *active state pointer* that points to the current execution state $s_a \in S$ of $\mathcal{P}(CS)$. We call s_a the *active state* of $\mathcal{P}(CS)$. During the execution of CS, for every action performs by the EXECUTOR (e.g., invocation of a component service), a timer is used to record the duration of the action. Upon completion of the action, a *state update* message containing the information of the completed action and the duration is sent by the EXECUTOR to the ADAPTER, so that ADAPTER could update the current active state of the probabilistic partial model.

4.2   Controllability of Activity

Controllable activities are the activities that could be controlled by ADAPTER. They must be the activities that use *Maybe* actions (i.e., activities ⟨if⟩ and ⟨pick⟩). The reason for not controlling activities using *True* actions is that, *True* actions of an active state would definitely be executed at some point of the execution. Therefore, it will not provide any improvement for QoS of the composite service by controlling *True* actions. For example, consider TBS at the initial state s_0 in Fig. 2b, the enabled *True* actions $sInv(FS)$ and $sInv(HB)$, *must be* executed at some points for all executions that start from the initial state s_0 and end at the terminal state s_{12}. On the other hand, for *Maybe* actions (e.g., $if[g_1]$), they *may or may not be* executed (e.g., depends on the evaluation of their guards). Suppose ADAPTER detects the possible violation of the global constraints, and if the action to be executed next is controllable by ADAPTER, then ADAPTER could choose an action, that maximizes the chance of satisfying the global constraints, to be executed by EXECUTOR.

Consider TBS with active state at state s_1 in Fig. 2b, which has three *Maybe* actions, i.e., $if[g_1]$, $elseif[g_2]$, and *else*. For an $\langle if \rangle$ activity, it is the evaluation of guard conditions that decides which branch to execute. It is a violation of the semantics of the $\langle if \rangle$ activity if EXECUTOR, simply follows a different action (e.g., $elseif[g_2]$) chosen by ADAPTER, without checking the evaluation of the guard condition. For this purpose, we extend the $\langle if \rangle$ activity with an attribute ctr, so that users are allowed to specify whether the $\langle if \rangle$ activity is controllable by ADAPTER. If ctr is set to true, then EXECUTOR would send an *Adaptation Query* message to ADAPTER to consult which action to be executed next. ADAPTER would either select an action to be executed or decide not to control if there is no potential violation of the global constraints detected, and then replies to EXECUTOR. If ADAPTER chooses an action, EXECUTOR would disregard the valuation of guard condition and execute the action that is chosen by ADAPTER.

Given an activity P, $Ctrl(P) \in \{true, false\}$ denotes the controllability of P, which is defined recursively with Eq. (1). If P is a sequential activity $P_1; P_2$, the controllability of P is decided on the controllability of process P_1. For a concurrent activity $P = P_1|||P_2$, P is controllable if either activity P_1 or activity P_2 is controllable, since activities P_1 and P_2 are triggered at the same time. For conditional activity $P = C([g_1]P_1, [g_2]P_2, \ldots)$, the controllability is decided by the user-specified controllability of the conditional activity C.

$$Ctrl(P) = \begin{cases} Ctrl(P_1) & if \ P(s) = P_1; P_2 \\ Ctrl(P_1) \vee Ctrl(P_2) & if \ P(s) = P_1|||P_2 \\ Ctrl(C) \ if \ P(s) = C([g_1]P_1, [g_2]P_2, \ ) \end{cases} \qquad (1)$$

4.3   Local Estimation

In this section, we introduce the *local estimation* and the method to calculate it. The local estimation of a state s provides an estimation of QoS from two perspectives, pessimistic and probabilistic, for all executions starting from state s.

Pessimistic Estimation. The pessimistic estimation of a QoS attribute a provides a conservative estimation of the attribute a for all executions starting from the state s. For example, the pessimistic estimation of state s for the response time attribute is the maximum response time that is required for all executions starting from state s. The pessimistic estimation is used to help ADAPTER to decide whether to take over the composite service at the active state s_a. For example shown in Fig. 3a, suppose the total response time from the initial state s_0 to state s_a takes 1 s, and the global constraints for the response time is 2 s. If the pessimistic estimation of the response time at state s_a is r seconds, where $r > 1$, then the runtime adaptation is required. The reason is that since $1 + r > 2$ s, there exists an execution path that could violate the global constraint of the response time.

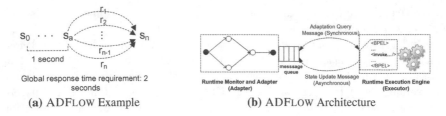

(a) ADFLOW Example   (b) ADFLOW Architecture

Fig. 3. ADFLOW

Probabilistic Estimation. The probabilistic estimation of the QoS attribute a provides the expected value for the attribute a for all possible executions starting from state s. The probabilistic estimation is used to guide the ADAPTER to choose an action to be executed next in order to maximize the chances to satisfy the global constraints. The local estimation $Q(s)$ of a state s is represented by a vector $\langle L_R(s), L_A(s), L_C(s) \rangle$, where $L_R(s)$, $L_A(s)$ and $L_C(s)$ represent the local estimation of response time, availability and cost for the state s respectively. The local estimation of a QoS attribute is a vector $\binom{pe}{pr}$, where $pe, pr \in \mathbb{R}$ represent the pessimistic and probabilistic estimation of the QoS attribute respectively. Henceforth, we denote the pessimistic and probabilistic estimation of the response time of a state s by $L_R^{pe}(s)$ and $L_R^{pr}(s)$ respectively. We define $L_A^{pe}(s)$, $L_A^{pr}(s)$, $L_C^{pe}(s)$, and $L_C^{pr}(s)$ in a similar manner.

Different QoS attributes might have different aggregation functions for different compositional structures. For QoS attributes (e.g., cost, availability) that only make use of summation and multiplication aggregation functions, we only require *backward value propagation* (discussed in our technical report [3]) for calculating the local estimation. For QoS attributes (e.g., response time) that involve the usage of maximization or minimization aggregation functions, *backward tagging propagation* (discussed in our technical report [3]) need to be applied, before backward value propagation.

4.4   Runtime Adaptation

Given a set of *Maybe* actions, ADAPTER needs a metric to decide the best action for execution. The *local optimality value* of an action a, denoted by $L(a)$ is used to provide a value that represents the worthiness of choosing the action a. In this section, we introduce the calculation of local optimality value, and the adaptation algorithm.

Local Optimality Value. We first introduce the notion of QoS optimality value of an action a which will be used for calculation of local optimality value for the action a.

Given a state s, and an action $a \in MAct(s)$, the *QoS optimality value* of the action a, denoted by $Q(a)$, is the expected QoS of all (finite) executions by executing the action a at s. It is calculated using a Simple Additive Weighting (SAW) method [24]. For the purpose of normalization, the action a compares the

---

Algorithm 1. Algorithm *ChooseAction*

---

    input : s, the active state
    input : *ctime*, current time
    input : *stime*, execution start time
    input : c, cost that has been incurred so far
    output: a, the next action to execute

1 **if** $Ctrl(P(s))$ **then**
2     $S_r \leftarrow ((ctime - stime + L_R^{pe}(s)) \leq C_g^R)$;
3     $S_a \leftarrow (L_A^{pe}(s) \geq C_g^A)$; $S_c \leftarrow ((c + L_C^{pe}(s)) \geq C_g^C)$;
4   **if** $\neg(S_r \wedge S_a \wedge S_c)$ **then**
5   **return** $\underset{a \in MAct(s)}{\operatorname{argmax}} (0.5{\cdot}Q(a) + 0.5{\cdot}f_b(S_r(a) \wedge S_a(a) \wedge S_c(a)))$;

6 **return** $\emptyset$;

---

probabilistic estimations of its QoS attributes with the maximum and minimum probabilistic estimations of all enabled *Maybe* actions. The calculation of $Q(a)$ is provided in Eq. (2), where $w_i \in \mathbb{R}^+$ is the weight with $\sum_{i=1}^{3} w_i = 1$. The *local optimality value* of an action a, denoted by $L(a)$, is calculated using Eq. (3), where $S_r(a), S_a(a), S_c(a) \in \{true, false\}$ denote whether the execution of action a could allow potential satisfaction of global constraints of response time, availability and cost respectively. Function $f_b(b)$ takes an input $b \in \{true, false\}$. When b is true, $f_b(b)=1$, otherwise, $f_b(b)=0$. The local optimality value of the action a ranges from 0.5 to 1 if $S_r(a) \wedge S_a(a) \wedge S_c(a)$, otherwise $L(a)$ ranges from 0 to 0.5. Therefore, it could guarantee that the local optimality values of actions that could possibly satisfy the global constraints are higher than the one that could not.

$$
\begin{aligned}
Q(a) = w_1 \cdot &\frac{U_{Max}^{(r)}(s) - a.probtag}{U_{Max}^{(r)}(s) - U_{Min}^{(r)}(s)} \\
+ w_2 \cdot &\frac{A(a) \cdot L_A^{pr}(s') - U_{Min}^{(a)}(s)}{U_{Max}^{(a)}(s) - U_{Min}^{(a)}(s)} \quad with \\
+ w_3 \cdot &\frac{U_{Max}^{(c)}(s) - (C(a) + L_C^{pr}(s'))}{U_{Max}^{(c)}(s) - U_{Min}^{(c)}(s)}
\end{aligned}
\qquad
\begin{aligned}
U_M^{(r)}(s) &= \underset{a \in MAct(s)}{M} (a.probtag) \\
U_M^{(a)}(s) &= \underset{a \in MAct(s)}{M} (A(a) \cdot L_A^{pr}(s')) \\
U_M^{(c)}(s) &= \underset{a \in MAct(s)}{M} (C(a) + L_C^{pr}(s')) \\
M &\in \{\min, \max\}
\end{aligned}
$$

$$\tag{2}$$

$$L(a) = 0.5{\cdot}Q(a) + 0.5{\cdot}f_b(S_r(a) \wedge S_a(a) \wedge S_c(a)) \tag{3}$$

Adaptation Algorithm. The adaptation algorithm is shown in Algorithm 1, which is used to choose the action to execute next. In Algorithm 1, the variable $s \in S$ is the active state reached by the execution, *ctime* and *stime* are the current time and start time of the execution respectively, and $c \in \mathbb{R}_{\geq 0}$ is the cost that has been incurred from the initial state to state s. Line 1 checks whether Runtime Adapter could control the activity $P(s)$. If $P(s)$ is controllable, then the algorithm proceeds in checking the potential satisfaction of global constraints. In line 2, it calculates the potential satisfaction of global constraint of response time, S_r, by checking that the duration of execution so far ($ctime - stime$) added with the pessimistic estimation of state s ($L_R^{pe}(s)$) is not larger than the global constraint of response time C_g^R. If the result is false, then there exists an execution that could violate C_g^R; otherwise, any execution from state s would allow satisfaction of C_g^R. The calculation of S_a and S_c (line 3) can be described in a similar manner.

If not all the global constraints for response time, availability and cost are detected to be satisfiable based on the pessimistic estimation (line 4), then the algorithm will return a best action with the highest local optimality value (line 5). Otherwise, the algorithm will return an empty action (line 6), which signals that an adaptation is not required.

4.5   Asynchronous Monitoring

ADAPTER might require to deal with multiple concurrent state update messages due to the concurrent execution of activities in the composite service (recall that service composition supports the parallel composition). Synchronous communication between the ADAPTER and the EXECUTOR for each state update message could result in high overhead and the parallel execution in the EXECUTOR can be "sequentialized". To be efficient, ADFLOW adopts an *asynchronous monitoring* mechanism. That is, asynchronous communication is used between the ADAPTER and the EXECUTOR during normal situations, and synchronous communication is used when it is necessary. In particular, all the state update messages are sent *asynchronously* to the message queue, and the ADAPTER updates states in batches on the probabilistic partial model. Synchronous communication is used only when the EXECUTOR encounters controllable activities. In such a case, an *adaptation query* message is sent to the message queue synchronously (i.e., the EXECUTOR waits for the reply before continuing execution) to consult whether there is a need for adaptation before their execution. The asynchronous monitoring of ADFLOW is shown in Fig. 3b. We have shown that synchronous monitoring has effectively reduced the overhead for monitoring (see Sect. 5 for the evaluation).

5   Evaluation

To reduce the external noise and control the non-functional aspect of a service, we make use of controlled experiment to evaluate our approach. We aim to answer the following research questions:

RQ 1. What is the *overhead* of ADFLOW?
RQ 2. What is the *improvement* provided by ADFLOW on the conformance of global constraints?
RQ 3. How is the *scalability* of ADFLOW?

The evaluation was conducted using two different physical machines, which are connected by a 100 Mbit LAN. One machine is running ApacheODE [1] to host the Runtime Engine to execute the service program, configured with Intel Core I5 2410M CPU with 4 GiB RAM. The other machine is to host the Runtime Adapter, configured with Intel I7 3520M CPU with 8 GiB RAM.

We use two case studies in this paper to evaluate our approach: Travel Booking Services and Large Service. Component services used in both services are real-world services that are set up on the server.

Travel Booking Service (TBS). This is the running example that has been used through out the paper.

Large Service (LS). To evaluate the scalability of our approach, we construct a large service LS with sequential execution of k *base activities*. The base activity is constructed by sequential execution of a synchronous invocation, followed by a controllable conditional activity with three branches which one branch has a better QoS, and subsequently followed by a concurrent activity. We denote the composite service with sequential execution of k base activities as *LS(k)*, which would consult ADAPTER for adaptation for k times since there are k controllable conditional activities.

5.1   Setup of Controlled Experiments

Given a composite service CS, we denote all component services that are used by CS as S_{CS}. Given a component service $s_i \in S_{CS}$, we use $R_e(s_i)$, $A_e(s_i)$, and $C_e(s_i)$ to denote the estimated response time, availability and cost of the component service s_i, which are either recorded in SLA or predicted based on historical data.

To test the composite service under controlled situation, we introduce the notion of *execution configuration*. An execution configuration which defines a particular execution scenario for the composite service. Formally, an execution configuration E is a tuple $\langle M, Q \rangle$, where M decides which path to choose for $\langle \text{if} \rangle$ and $\langle \text{pick} \rangle$ activities and Q is a function that maps a component service $s_i \in S_{CS}$, to a vector $\langle R(s_i), A(s_i), C(s_i) \rangle$. $R(s_i)$, $A(s_i)$ and $C(s_i)$ are QoS values for response time, availability, and cost of s_i. We discuss how an execution configuration $E = (M, Q)$ is generated. M is generated based on the probabilities of each branch of the conditional activities. Q is generated based on conformance parameter $p_c \in \mathbb{R} \cap [0, 1]$ and the estimated QoS attribute values. Given a composite service CS, we denote the estimated value of response time for a component service $s_i \in S_{CS}$ as $R_e(s_i)$. $R(s_i)$ will be assigned with a value from $[0, R_e(s_i)]$ normally with the probability of p_c, and assigned with a value from $[R_e(s_i), 3 \cdot R_e(s_i)]$ normally with the probability of $1 - p_c$. Values $A(s_i)$ and $C(s_i)$ are generated similarly.

Given a composite service CS, and an *execution configuration* E, we denote a run as $r(CS, A, E)$, where the second argument $A \in \{\text{ADFLOW}, \emptyset\}$ is the adaptive mechanism where $\emptyset$ denotes no adaptation. Two runs $r(CS, A, E)$ and $r(CS', A', E')$, are *equal*, iff $CS = CS'$, $A = A'$ and $E = E'$. Noted that all equal runs have the *same* execution paths, aggregated response times, availabilities costs.

5.2   Evaluation

We conduct three experiments **E1**, **E2**, and **E3**, to answer the research question **RQ1**, **RQ2**, and **RQ3**, respectively. Each experiment is repeated for 10000 times, and a configuration generation E is randomly generated for each repetition. We show the experiments and their results in the following.

E1: The overhead of our approach mainly comes from two sources: the asynchronous monitoring and synchronous adaptation. Given a composite service CS, in order to measure the overhead, we first generate an execution configuration $E = (M, Q)$ for an adaptive run $r(CS, \text{ADFLOW}, E)$. Adaptive run may not select a branch according to M, since the selection of a branch could also be decided by the ADAPTER, in the case where ADAPTER decides to control a controllable conditional structure. Therefore, after the adaptive run, we modifies M to M', according to the actual conditional branch selected by the ADAPTER. Then, using the M', we perform the non-adaptive run $r(CS, \emptyset, E')$, where $E' = (M', Q)$. These ensure that both adaptive run and non-adaptive run have the same execution, which allow effective measurement of the overhead introduced by ADFLOW. In this experiment, we set the conformance of each component service to 0.8. We compare the overhead of the following:

No Adaptation. Execution of the service program without the adaptation, for which we append the name of case studies with a subscript N, i.e., TBS_N, $LS(10)_N$.

Synchronous Adaptation. Runtime adaptation using synchronous monitoring (in contrast to our asynchronous monitoring approach) with ADFLOW, for which we append the name of case studies with a subscript S, e.g., TBS_S, $LS(10)_S$.

ADFLOW Approach. Runtime adaptation using ADFLOW, for which the case studies are specified without any subscript, e.g., TBS, $LS(10)$.

Results. The experiment results can be found in Fig. 4a. Note that due to the space constraint, the result of $LS(10)_S$ is not shown in our results. The average running time of TAS with adaptation is 278.28 ms and the average running time of TAS without adaptation is 271.69 ms; therefore the overhead is only 6.59 ms, 2.3 % of the running time. In contrast, the overhead for synchronous monitoring is 179.12 ms for TAS. On the other hand, the average running time of LS(10) is 457.65 ms and the average running time of LS(10) without adaptation is 450.66 ms; therefore, average overhead is 6.99 ms. In contrast, the overhead for the adaptation using synchronous monitoring is around 1100 ms. The results show that our approach has a little overhead, and compared to the adaptation using synchronous monitoring, our approach reduces the overhead noticeably.

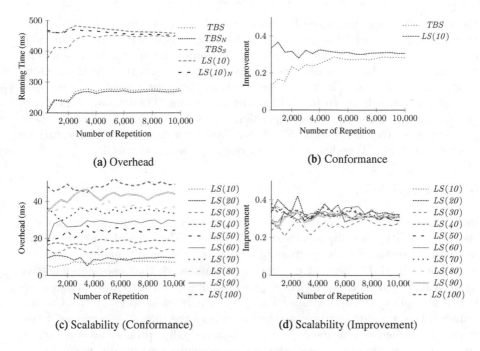

Fig. 4. Experiment results

E2: In this experiment, we measure the improvement for the conformance of global constraints due to ADFLOW. Given a composite service CS, a randomly generated execution configuration E, two runs $r(CS, \text{ADFLOW}, E)$ and $r(CS, \emptyset, E)$ are conducted. N_{se} is the number of executions that satisfy global constraints for composite service with ADFLOW, and N_e is the number of executions that satisfy global constraints for composite service without ADFLOW. The improvement is calculated by the formula $Improvement = (N_{se} - N_e)/10000$. We perform the experiment for 10000 times.

Results. The experiment results can be found in Fig. 4b. We notice that although the improvement fluctuates at the beginning, ADFLOW always provides an improvement, compared to no adaptation. We also notice that the improvement provided by ADFLOW starts to converge when the number of repetition grows. Overall, our approach improves 0.283 over TBS_N and improves 0.3 over $LS(10)_N$. The experiment results show that our approach noticeably improves the conformance of global constraints.

E3: We compare the overhead and improvement with respect to the size of LS, ranging from 10 to 100.

Results. The experiment results can be found in Fig. 4c and d. In Fig. 4c, the overhead increases with the size of LS, due to the reason that more synchronous adaptations are required with the size of the composite service increases. Nevertheless, we still have low overhead compared to the total running time, which is around 1%–3%. In Fig. 4c, we observe that the improvement for each case studies fluctuates between 0.2–0.42 at the beginning. The improvement starts to converge when the number of repetition grows. On average, the improvement for the case studies is between 25%–32%. This is consistent to our observations in experiment **E2**. Together, these show our approach scales well.

6   Related Work

In [5], Cardellini *et al.* propose to use a set of service components to implement the functionality of a component service adaptively. Their work focuses on adapting a single service for the purpose of decreasing response time and increasing availability. In [17], Moser *et al.* propose a framework that uses non-intrusive monitoring based on aspect-oriented programming (AOP), to detect failure service and replace them at runtime. In [15], Irmert *et al.* present the CoBRA framework to provide runtime adaptation, where the infeasible component services are replaced at runtime. In [18], Mukhija and Glinz propose an approach to adapt an application by recomposing its components dynamically, which implemented by providing alternative component compositions for different states of the execution environment. This work is orthogonal to our approach, they adopt point adaptation strategy, while we adopt workflow adaptation strategy.

Our work is also related to the non-functional aspect of Web service composition. In [13], Fung *et al.* propose a message model tracking model to support QoS end-to-end management. In [16], Koizumi and Koyama present a business process performance model which integrates the Timed Petri model and statistical model to estimate process execution time. Epifani et al. [9] present the KAMI approach to update model parameters by exploiting Bayesian estimators on collected runtime data. These aforementioned works are concerned with the prediction of QoS attributes, while our work focuses on runtime adaptation based on QoS attributes. In [20], given the response time requirement of the composite service, Tan *et al.* propose a technique to synthesize the local time requirement for component services that are used to compose the service. In [6,7,19,23], we focus on verification of combined functional and non-functional properties of the web service composition based on QoS of each component service. In [21,22], we propose to solve the optimal selection problem and recovery problem so that it could satisfy the requirements. The aforementioned works are orthogonal to this work.

7   Conclusion

In this paper, we have presented ADFLOW, a novel approach for monitoring and self-adapting the running of Web service composition to maximize its ability to satisfy the global constraints. ADFLOW uses workflow adaptation strategy, by selecting the best path for execution when necessary. In addition, ADFLOW adopts asynchronous monitoring to reduce the overhead. The evaluation has shown the efficiency and effectiveness of our approach. In particular, given a composite service, we achieve 25 %–32 % of average improvement in the conformance of non-functional requirements, and only incur 1 %–3 % of overhead with respect to the execution time. For future work, we plan to investigate the applicability our approach to other domains such as sensor networks [4].

References

1. Apache ODE. http://ode.apache.org/
2. Microservices. http://microservices.io/patterns/microservices.html
3. Technical report. http://tianhuat.bitbucket.org/technicalReport.pdf
4. Akyildiz, I.F., Su, W., Sankarasubramaniam, Y., Cayirci, E., et al.: A survey on sensor networks. IEEE Commun. Mag. **40**(8), 102–114 (2002)
5. Cardellini, V., Casalicchio, E., Grassi, V., Iannucci, S., Presti, F.L., Mirandola, R.: Moses: a framework for qos driven runtime adaptation of service-oriented systems. TSE **38**(5), 1138–1159 (2012)
6. Chen, M., Tan, T.H., Sun, J., Liu, Y., Dong, J.S.: VeriWS: a tool for verification of combined functional and non-functional requirements of web service composition. In: ICSE, pp. 564–567 (2014)
7. Chen, M., Tan, T.H., Sun, J., Liu, Y., Pang, J., Li, X.: Verification of functional and non-functional requirements of web service composition. In: ICFEM, pp. 313–328 (2013)
8. Chinnici, R., Moreau, J.-J., Ryman, A., Weerawarana, S.: Web services description language (WSDL) version 2.0. http://www.w3.org/TR/wsdl20/
9. Epifani, I., Ghezzi, C., Mirandola, R., Tamburrelli, G.: Model evolution by runtime parameter adaptation. In: ICSE, pp. 111–121 (2009)
10. Ermedahl, A., Sandberg, C., Gustafsson, J., Bygde, S., Lisper, B.: Loop bound analysis based on a combination of program slicing, abstract interpretation, and invariant analysis. In: WCET (2007)
11. Famelis, M., Salay, R., Chechik, M.: Partial models: towards modeling and reasoning with uncertainty. In: ICSE, pp. 573–583 (2012)
12. Foster, H.: A rigorous approach to engineering web service compositions. Ph.D. thesis, Citeseer (2006)
13. Fung, C.K., Hung, P.C.K., Wang, G., Linger, R.C., Walton, G.H.: A study of service composition with QoS management. In: ICWS, pp. 717–724 (2005)
14. Gudgin, M., Hadley, M., Mendelsohn, N., Moreau, J.-J., Nielsen, H.F., Karmarkar, A., Lafon. Y.: Simple object access protocol (SOAP) version 1.2. http://www.w3.org/TR/soap12/
15. Irmert, F., Fischer, T., Meyer-Wegener, K.: Runtime adaptation in a service-oriented component model. In: SEAMS, pp. 97–104. ACM (2008)
16. Koizumi, S., Koyama, K.: Workload-aware business process simulation with statistical service analysis and timed Petri Net. In: ICWS, pp. 70–77 (2007)
17. Moser, O., Rosenberg, F., Dustdar, S.: Non-intrusive monitoring and service adaptation for WS-BPEL. In: WWW, pp. 815–824 (2008)
18. Mukhija, A., Glinz, M.: Runtime adaptation of applications through dynamic recomposition of components. In: ARCS, pp. 124–138 (2005)

19. Tan, T.H.: Towards verification of a service orchestration language. In: ISSRE, pp. 36–37 (2010)
20. Tan, T.H., André, É., Sun, J., Liu, Y., Dong, J.S., Chen, M.: Dynamic synthesis of local time requirement for service composition. In: ICSE, pp. 542–551 (2013)
21. Tan, T.H., Chen, M., André, É., Sun, J., Liu, Y., Dong, J.S.: Automated runtime recovery for QoS-based service composition. In: 23rd International World Wide Web Conference, WWW 2014, Seoul, Republic of Korea, 7–11 April 2014, pp. 563–574 (2014)
22. Tan, T.H., Chen, M., Sun, J., Liu, Y., André, É., Xue, Y., Dong, J.S.: Optimizing selection of competing services with probabilistic hierarchical refinement. In: ICSE, pp. 85–95 (2016)
23. Tan, T.H., Liu, Y., Sun, J., Dong, J.S.: Verification of orchestration systems using compositional partial order reduction. In: Qin, S., Qiu, Z. (eds.) ICFEM 2011. LNCS, vol. 6991, pp. 98–114. Springer, Heidelberg (2011)
24. Yoon, K., Hwang, C.: Multiple Attribute Decision Making: An Introduction. Sage Publications, Incorporated, Thousand Oaks (1995)

A Formal Approach to Identifying Security Vulnerabilities in Telecommunication Networks

Linas Laibinis[1](✉), Elena Troubitsyna[1], Inna Pereverzeva[1], Ian Oliver[2], and Silke Holtmanns[2]

[1] Åbo Akademi University, Turku, Finland
{linas.laibinis,elena.troubitsyna,inna.pereverzeva}@abo.fi
[2] Nokia Corporation, Espoo, Finland
{ian.oliver,silke.holtmanns}@nokia.com

Abstract. The number of security attacks on the telecommunication networks is constantly increasing. To prevent them, the telecom sector is looking for new automated techniques facilitating a discovery of potential network vulnerabilities and rectification of them. In this paper, we propose an approach for identifying potential attack scenarios and defining recommendations for preventing them. The approach is formalised in the Event-B framework. It allows us to not only formalise the analysed part of the network architecture and verify consistency of the control and data flow of the associated services but also employ model checking to generate and analyse attack scenarios. By applying the proposed approach, the designers can systematically explore network vulnerabilities and propose recommendations for attack prevention.

1 Introduction

Over the last few years the number of attacks on the telecom networks has increased. The network operators observe the attempts of call and SMS interceptions, unauthorised call re-directions or alternations of billing information, etc. By using the services provided by the standard network protocols, e.g., such as SS7-MAP [16], the attackers can masquerade themselves as trusted network components and exploit network vulnerabilities with malicious intent. To prevent further escalation of the number of attacks, the telecom sector is looking for novel techniques that can help systematically, in a highly automated manner, analyse the existing network protocols, identify potential vulnerabilities, and propose recommendations for rectifying them.

In this paper, we propose a formal approach that allows the designers to automatically generate a set of potentially harmful scenarios and analyse possibilities for their prevention. Our approach consists of four steps: a representation of the standardised telecom operations and aggregated services in terms of input and output data, consistency analysis of such a representation, generation of feasible execution scenarios and identification of the harmful ones, and finally, suggesting recommendations for hardening the system against the identified attacks.

© Springer International Publishing AG 2016
K. Ogata et al. (Eds.): ICFEM 2016, LNCS 10009, pp. 141–158, 2016.
DOI: 10.1007/978-3-319-47846-3_10

Our approach is formalised in Event-B [1] – a state-based formalism that is particularly suitable for rigorous modelling of complex distributed systems. A specification in Event-B consists of two parts: a context and a (state) machine. A context constitutes the static model part specifying the desired data structures and their properties. Hence the context is suitable for defining the architectures of the analysed services in terms of the types of input and output parameters as well as internally generated data. Such a formalisation of service architectures allows us to rely on proofs to verify their consistency. The machine part specifies the dynamic behaviour of the system. In our approach, a state machine is used to define a generic pattern for modelling the dynamics of aggregated service execution. Model checking is used to generate all feasible execution traces under the constraints defined in the context. Each generated scenario can either match a valid scenario implementing a particular service or represent a potentially harmful scenario allowing an attacker to gain access to some sensitive data.

The recommendations for attack prevention are formulated as changes in definition of telecom operations in terms of the involved data. The recommendation feasibility is established by proving consistency of the modified service architectures and ensuring by model checking that no desired service is disabled.

The Rodin platform provides us with an automatic support for both proof-based verification and model checking in Event-B [12]. In particular, the model checking and animation extension of Rodin (called ProB [17]) helps us to identify the attack scenarios and then "replay" them to facilitate formulating the recommendations for system hardening, i.e., explore different ways of breaking the identified harmful execution sequences.

The rest of the paper is organised as follows. In Sect. 2 we present motivation as well as our formal view on security hardening of telecom networks. In Sect. 3 we give a short overview of the Event-B formalism and its associated model checker ProB. In Sect. 4 we present our formal approach for identifying security vulnerabilities. Finally, in Sect. 5 we provide an overview of related work and present some concluding remarks.

2   Identifying and Rectifying Network Vulnerabilities

2.1   Motivation: Security in Telecommunication Protocols

Telecommunication networks consist of heterogeneous components executing specific operations that can be composed to implement complex aggregated services. The SS7 protocol suite [15] standardises interfaces of the services and operations that guarantees interoperability of services from different providers. The mobile application part (MAP) [16] of SS7 defines an application layer – a set of standard operations – used to build a variety of services that support the GSM network including such services as billing, roaming, text messaging, etc.

The SS7 protocol suite was standardised under the assumption that only the trusted parties (government and large companies) would be operating telecom networks. Hence, the protocol suit does not have any in-built authentication and security protection. However, nowadays the situation has drastically changed: it

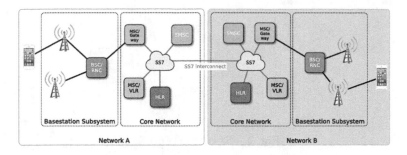

Fig. 1. Network architecture

became easy to get access to the network services, which has attracted not only a variety of small service providers but also attackers. The network operators report on increasing number of denial of service (DOS) attacks, call and SMS interception or re-direction, illegal alternation of the user profile data, etc.

Let us consider the component interaction while executing the "Provide roaming number" service. Figure 1 shows a (simplified) architecture of two cellular networks – A and B. Assume that a subscriber – a holder of a mobile phone – is "native" to A, i.e., his/her data are stored in Home Location Register (HLR) of A. This data includes a mobile subscriber's id, the user profile data (including the subscription details and billing address), current location, etc. Assume also that the user moves from A to B. When a base station in the B network detects a new foreign id, it contacts the Gateway of Mobile Switch Centre (MSC/Gateway) of B. In its turn, MSC/Gateway of B identifies the id origins and sends a request to the MSC/Gateway of A. MSC/Gateway of A checks the subscription info for the given id in HLR of A and replies to MSC/Gateway of B with the confirmation of user validity or notification of the invalid request. In the case of success, MSC/Gateway of B makes a request to Visitor Location Register (MSC/VLR) of B to associate a roaming number with the given id. Once this number is obtained, the services of B become available to the subscriber.

Since the protocol assumes the presence of trusted parties only, each request sent by a network element with a valid id is replied either with the requested data or an error diagnostic message. Nowadays an attacker can relatively easy obtain a valid network element id that allows him/her to intrude the trusted environment. Once it is done, the attacker can start to send requests to the network components, collect and analyse responses, and thus accumulate sufficient information to masquerade himself as a trusted party with the corresponding privileges and rights. For instance, it can result in associating a random (victim) subscriber id with the attacker's phone and interception of sensitive data.

Even if we only focus on the SS7 Core network shown on Fig. 2, it is possible to construct such attack scenarios. For instance, if the attacker obtains the id (called *global title*) of the SMS-C (Short Message Service Center) component, this may eventually, e.g., by subsequent requests to MSC/VLR and HLR, lead to getting access to the user profile and changing such sensitive data as the address

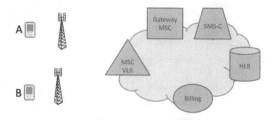

Fig. 2. SS7 core network

of the component responsible for customer billing. We will consider this scenario in more detail, while presenting our formal approach in Sect. 4.

A seemingly obvious solution is to introduce an authentication for each request. However, since a typical scenario consists of several steps, the resulting performance deterioration will be unacceptable. Hence, to harden the protocol, we should explore other ways to prevent an intruder from accumulating sufficient knowledge for an attack. A combination of such accumulated data and the command sequence represents a potential attack vector. To disable the execution of the identified scenario, we may try alter the associated data flow, i.e., to augment commands with additional inputs available only for trusted parties or remove some (redundant) outputs. In both cases, however, we should ensure that no valid execution scenarios are disabled as a result of such hardening.

2.2   A Formal Outlook on Security Hardening

Let us now take a more formal view on security hardening of telecommunication networks. A telecommunication network is a typical example of a complex distributed system composed of heterogeneous components. The network components interact with each other by sending and receiving a number of standardised telecommunication commands. We assume that every such command uniquely determines (the types of) the involved sending and receiving components.

We introduce the set C to represent all commands defined in the SS7-MAP standard. For each $c \in C$, we can define the associated data types used as its inputs, outputs, and other data[1]. Suppose that *DataTypes* is a collection of such data types. Then the command inputs and outputs can be defined as the functions

$$Inputs \in C \to \mathbb{P}(DataTypes) \quad \text{and} \quad Outputs \in C \to \mathbb{P}(DataTypes),$$

where $\mathbb{P}$ is the powerset constructor.

In general, certain commands, called *composite*, represent aggregated services, i.e., they encapsulate sequences of commands executed by different components. A component requested to execute a composite command becomes a service director. It requests execution of different commands from other components, forwards the necessary inputs, and collects the intermediate results to

---

[1] Examples of such data types could be User ID, Global Title, etc.

produce the (final) output of the composite command, i.e., it orchestrates the service execution and data flow. We introduce the function

$$CommSeq \in C \rightarrow seq(C),$$

where seq is a sequence constructor to represent composite commands. In such a way, most of protocol scenarios (starting with a particular command) may be formalised. If, for some $c \in C$, $CommSeq(c) = \varnothing$, we call such a command *single*.

For composite commands, it is sometimes important to refer to additional data elements that are produced by the associated service director and then forwarded as extra inputs to the lower layer commands or returned as extra outputs. We define this as the function

$$Produced \in C \rightarrow \mathbb{P}(DataTypes).$$

If a command is *single*, its produced data elements coincide with its outputs.

The introduced definitions of the command inputs, outputs and produced data elements allows us to explicitly formulate the properties for consistency of a particular data flow. We aim at ensuring that, for composite commands, there is always a component associated with each produced output or forwarded input. Formally, for all $c \in C$, $i \in 1..n(c)$,

$$Inputs(c[i]) \subseteq Inputs(c) \cup Produced(c) \cup \bigcup_{j \in 1..i-1} (Outputs(c[j])) \qquad (1)$$

$$Outputs(c) \subseteq Produced(c) \cup \bigcup_{j \in 1..n(c)} (Outputs(c[j])), \qquad (2)$$

where $c[i] = CommSeq(c)(i)$ and $n(c) = size(CommSeq(c))$.

Essentially, we require that a service director accumulates the necessary knowledge (consisting of its inputs, the internally produced values, and the intermediate results of the supervised lower layer commands) to ensure the overall data flow consistency of such execution. The first property requires that any lower layer command should be *collectively enabled* by such knowledge to be executed. The second property describes the consistency of completing the predefined scenario encoded by a composite command.

The above definitions allow us to formalise commands of SS7-MAP protocols, their interrelationships, and their collaborative execution. The formulated data consistency conditions can be also used to describe the requirements for building possible scenarios (command sequences) from the set of standardised commands.

Let us consider such a scenario $S \in seq(C)$, the initial user knowledge *Initials* and the target results *Finals*. We can denote the fact that the results *Finals* are reachable from the initial knowledge *Initials* by the scenario S as

$$Initials \rightsquigarrow^S Finals$$

provided that

$$\forall i \in 1..n(S).\ Inputs(S[i]) \subseteq Initials \cup \bigcup_{1..i-1} (Outputs(S[j])),$$

and
$$\forall i \in 1..n(S). \ Finals(c) \subseteq \bigcup_{1..n(c)} (Outputs(c[j])),$$

where $S[i] = CommSeq(S)(i)$ and $n(S) = size(CommSeq(S))$.

We assume that we can distinguish the critical knowledge (specific combinations of data type elements) that is not supposed to be leaked to an unauthorised external user. Accessing such a knowledge in many cases would indicate scenarios that can be used for malicious purposes by the intruder. Moreover, we assume that all such scenarios where this knowledge is accessed safely and legally or the scenarios that we want to exclude from consideration are known beforehand.

Let us introduce two constants –

$$Critical \in \mathbb{P}(DataTypes) \qquad \text{and} \qquad KnownSequences \in seq(C),$$

formalising the described notions. We also assume the presumed initial knowledge given in the constant $Initials \in \mathbb{P}(DataTypes)$.

Our goal is to identify a scenario S such that $S \notin KnownSequences$ and

$$Initials \rightsquigarrow^S Critical.$$

This scenario indicates a possible intruder attack. To prevent such an attack, we need to break this sequence by modifying one of the involved commands. Specifically, we may try to add inputs, removing some (redundant) outputs, adding a combination of internally produced data and lower layer inputs, etc.

The attempted modification of a specific command should not preclude all the situations it is validly used. In other words, for the identified "weak link", say the command $c1 \in S$, we have to first show that,

$$\neg (Initials \rightsquigarrow^{S[c1/c1']} Critical),$$

where $S[c1/c1']$ denotes a sequence where $c1$ was substituted with the modified command $c1'$. Moreover, the above data consistency conditions 1 and 2 should be shown to hold for the modified set $C[c1/c1']$. This ensures that all the other commands that rely on the substituted command $c1$ are still functional.

The proposed command modifications together with the consistency conditions 1 and 2 define the basis for system hardening against attacks. In Sect. 4, after a short Event-B background description given in the next section, we demonstrate how it can be implemented within the Event-B framework.

3   Background: Event-B and ProB

Event-B is a state-based formal approach that promotes the correct-by-construction development and formal verification by theorem proving [1]. In Event-B, a system model is specified as an *abstract state machine*. An abstract state machine encapsulates the model state, represented as a collection of variables, and defines state operations, i.e., it describes the dynamic system behaviour. The variables are strongly typed by the constraining predicates that, together with other important system properties, are defined as model *invariants*. Usually, a machine has an accompanying component, called a *context*, which includes user-defined sets, constants and their properties given as a list of model axioms.

The dynamic behaviour of the system is defined by a collection of atomic *events*. Generally, an event has the following form:

$$e \;\widehat{=}\; \textbf{any } a \textbf{ where } G_e \textbf{ then } R_e \textbf{ end,}$$

where e is the event's name, a is the list of local variables, G_e is the event *guard*, and R_e is the event action.

The guard is a state predicate that defines the conditions under which the action can be executed, i.e., when the event is *enabled*. If several events are enabled at the same time, any of them can be chosen for execution non-deterministically. If none of the events is enabled then the system deadlocks. The occurrence of events represents the observable behaviour of the system.

In general, the action of an event is a parallel composition of deterministic or non-deterministic assignments. In Event-B, this assignment is semantically defined as the next-state relation R_e. A deterministic assignment, $x := E(x, y)$, has the standard syntax and meaning. A non-deterministic assignment is denoted either as $x :\in S$, where S is a set of values, or $x :| P(x, y, x')$, where P is a predicate relating initial values of x, y to some final value of x'. As a result of such an assignment, x can get any value belonging to S or according to P.

Event-B employs a top-down refinement-based approach to system development. A development starts from an abstract specification that nondeterministically models most essential functional requirements. In a sequence of refinement steps, we gradually reduce nondeterminism and introduce detailed design decisions. The consistency of Event-B models, i.e., verification of well-formedness, invariant preservation as well as correctness of refinement steps, is demonstrated by proving the relevant verification theorems – proof obligations [1].

Modelling, refinement and verification in Event-B is supported by an automated tool – Rodin platform [12]. The platform provides the designers with an integrated modelling environment, supporting automatic generation and proving of the proof obligations. Moreover, various Rodin extensions allow the modeller to transform models from one representation to another. They also give access to various verification engines (theorem provers, model checkers, SMT solvers).

For instance, the ProB extension [17] of Rodin supports automated consistency checking of Event-B machines via model checking, constraint based checking, and animation. ProB supports analysis of liveness properties (expressed in linear or computational tree logic (LTL/CTL)), invariant violations as well as the absence of deadlocks.

4   Identifying and Preventing Security Attacks by Formal Verification and Model Checking

4.1   Overview of the Approach

In this paper, we propose a formal approach for identifying and preventing possible security attacks based on formal modelling and model checking in Event-B. In Sect. 2.2 we discussed how we can formally reason about telecommunication commands, their execution scenarios, the involved data and control flows, the critical knowledge, "leakage" of which should be prevented, etc. We will show how to capture these notions in the Event-B framework.

We start by giving a short outline of the overall approach. We propose an iterative method consisting of four phases (see Fig. 3), discussed in detail below.

In **Phase 1**, we create or subsequently modify the Event-B context component, containing the (types of) involved data elements and the definitions of protocol commands of interest. The structure of the commands (inputs, outputs, internally produced values, the lower layer commands) corresponds to the one described in Sect. 2.2. The context also introduces the initial knowledge of the attacker as well as the critical knowledge that should not be "leaked".

In **Phase 2**, we rely on the created Event-B (machine) model to simulate execution of all the defined above commands and then model check this model in ProB looking for inconsistencies or gaps in their execution. Essentially, any violations of the data flow consistency conditions 1 and 2 lead to deadlocking the model, which in turn indicate such inconsistencies in the command definitions.

If such a deadlock is found, we return to the first phase for necessary modifications of one or several commands. Otherwise, we proceed to Phase 3.

In **Phase 3**, we rely on other created Event-B (machine) model that simulates random "intruder" attacks, trying to access the predefined critical knowledge.

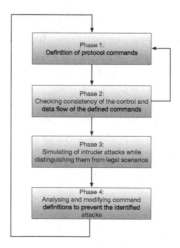

Fig. 3. Phases of the approach

A "successful attack" is stored as the corresponding command sequence. We also rely on the given valid or known scenarios to filter out some of these found sequences. The construction of such random attacks and filtering out known command sequences is done by the model checker ProB. A found invariant violation indicates a possible successful attack (a sequence of protocol commands).

In **Phase** 4, the obtained sequence of a possible attack is analysed. The purpose of such an analysis is to come up with one or several recommendations for command modifications. These recommendation in turn would become an input for the first phase, thus starting a new iteration of the proposed method. Let us now describe in detail the corresponding formalisation in Event-B.

4.2   Phase 1

Phase 1 focuses on introducing (or modifying) existing definitions of the target telecommunication commands, which will be used as the basis for the subsequent phases. In the corresponding Event-B formalisation, the involved data elements and commands are defined as a number of the respective sets and constants in the Event-B context component, presented in Figs. 4 and 6.

We assume that the specified commands have the predefined structure, as described in Sect. 2.2. The structure is expressed in terms of the involved data as well as other related commands (see Fig. 4). The underlying sets of all possible commands and data elements are introduced as the abstract sets *Commands* and *Data*. For each command, the functions *Inputs*, *Outputs* and *Produced* return the respective associated collections of data elements, while the function *CommSeq* returns the sequence of the involved lower layer commands. The data structures *Critical*, *KnownSequences*, and *Initial* define respectively the critical knowledge (data elements), the valid or already known command sequences that may lead to such data, and the presumed initial knowledge of the intruder.

To illustrate our methodology and, in particular, the application of model checking technique, we use a simple running example involving a small subset of commands. The hierarchical structure on the involved commands and their corresponding inputs and outputs is depicted in Fig. 5.

CONTEXT CommData
SETS *Commands, Data*
CONSTANTS *Inputs, Outputs, Produced, CommSeq, KnownSequences, Initial, Critical, ...*
AXIOMS
   axm1: $Inputs \in Commands \rightarrow \mathbb{P}(Data)$
   axm2: $Outputs \in Commands \rightarrow \mathbb{P}(Data)$
   axm3: $Produced \in Commands \rightarrow \mathbb{P}(Data)$
   axm4: $CommSeq \in Commands \rightarrow (\mathbb{N} \nrightarrow Commands)$
   axm5: $KnownSequences \in \mathbb{P}(\mathbb{N} \nrightarrow Commands)$
   axm6: $Initial \in \mathbb{P}(Data)$
   axm7: $Critical \in \mathbb{P}(Data) ...$
END

Fig. 4. The context CommData (part 1)

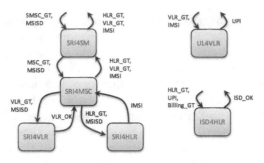

Fig. 5. Running example

The first command, SRI4SM, stands for a composite service "Send Routing Info", sent by SMS-C to MSC/Gateway. The required inputs are SMSC_GT, the global title (id) of SMS-C, and MSISD, the customer's mobile number. The command results are IMSI, International Mobile Subscriber Identity, as well as HLR_GT and VLR_GT – global titles of the involved HLR and MSC/VLR network components. The SRI4SM request is further decomposed to the respective lower layer commands (subservices) to the MSC/VLR and HLR components.

The second command, UL4SM, stands for a single service "Update Location", sent by MSC/VLR to HLR. As a result, a snapshot of the user profile information, UPI, is returned, including user services, forwarding settings, as well as the billing platform address. Finally, the third command, ISD4HLR, stands for a single service "Insert Subscriber Data", sent by HLR to MSC/VLR. The last input parameter, Billing_GT, is a new billing platform address to update the current one. The command result is simply a confirmation of successful update.

All three commands are internal services provided within a trusted network. However, as we will see later, they can be combined by the attacker to access and update sensitive information. In the remaining part of the context component (see Fig. 6), we instantiate the abstract data structures (e.g., *Commands*, *Data*, *Inputs*, *Outputs*, *Produced*, and *CommSeq*) for the chosen example.

---

axm8: $Commands = \{SRI4SM, SRI4MSC, SRI4VLR, SRI4HLR, UL4VLR, ISD4HLR\}$
axm9: $Data = \{SMSC\_GT, MSISD, MSC\_GT, VLR\_GT, VLR\_OK, HLR\_GT, IMSI,$
$\qquad UPI, Billing\_GT, ISD\_OK\}$
axm10: $Inputs = \{SRI4SM \mapsto \{SMSC\_GT, MSISD\}, SRI4MSC \mapsto \{MSISD, MSC\_GT\},$
$\qquad SRI4VLR \mapsto \{VLR\_GT, MSISD\}, SRI4HLR \mapsto \{HLR\_GT, MSISD\},$
$\qquad UL4VLR \mapsto \{VLR\_GT, MSCI\}, ISD4HLR \mapsto \{HLR\_GT, UPI, Billing\_GT\}\}$
axm11: $Outputs = \{SRI4SM \mapsto \{HLR\_GT, VLR\_GT, IMSI\},$
$\qquad SRI4MSC \mapsto \{HLR\_GT, VLR\_GT, IMSI\}, UL4VLR \mapsto \{UPI\},$
$\qquad SRI4VLR \mapsto \{VLR\_OK\}, SRI4HLR \mapsto \{IMSI\}, ISD4HLR \mapsto \{ISD\_OK\}\}$
axm12: $Produced = \{SRI4SM \mapsto \{MSC\_GT\}, SRI4MSC \mapsto \{VLR\_GT\},$
$\qquad SRI4VLR \mapsto \varnothing, SRI4HLR \mapsto \varnothing, UL4VLR \mapsto \varnothing, ISD4HLR \mapsto \varnothing\}$
axm13: $CommSeq = \{SRI4SM \mapsto \{1 \mapsto SRI4MSC\}, SRI4MSC \mapsto \{1 \mapsto SRI4VLR, 2 \mapsto$
$\qquad SRI4HLR\}, SRI4VLR \mapsto \varnothing, SRI4HLR \mapsto \varnothing, UL4VLR \mapsto \varnothing, ISD4HLR \mapsto \varnothing\}$
axm14: $KnownSequences = \varnothing$
axm15: $Initial = \{SMSC\_GT, MSISD\} \wedge Critical = \{UPI, ISD\_OK\}$

Fig. 6. The context CommData (part 2)

The internally produced data elements are instantiated using the following principle: all the data that are passed to the lower layer or returned to the higher layer can be either one of the command inputs, received outputs, or internally produced values. In other words, to guarantee consistency of the data flow, no data can come from nowhere. The only exception is for the lowest layer commands, where all their outputs coincide with internally produced ones.

4.3   Phase 2

The results of Phase 1 serve as a basis for the subsequent Phases 2 and 3. Before identification of possible intruder attacks (which will be the focus of Phase 3), we need to check/ensure that the given (or modified) command definitions are consistent, e.g., they do not contain loops and gaps in their execution.

To ensure such consistency, we employ the interplay of formal verification and model checking in Event-B. We model the process of intended command execution in general and then rely on model checking techniques (checking for deadlocks in Phase 2 and invariant violations in Phase 3) to find inconsistencies, incompleteness and security holes in the given concrete command definitions.

Specifically, in Phase 2 we rely on the Event-B model (machine) that

- non-deterministically picks a (still unchecked) command from the concrete collection defined in the context component;
- simulates execution of this command. The command can be either single or composite. In the latter case, its execution is decomposed into a sequence of commands of the lower layer.
- maintains what is "known" at each execution layer (for the component calling a command) and checks both data and control flow consistency;
- terminates when all the defined commands are successfully checked.

Then, for the created model, we employ model checking to find deadlocks. The presence of such deadlocks would mean that the hierarchy of commands is broken because some required inputs, outputs or produced data are missing.

Let us consider the Event-B model in more detail. Its overall structure is given in Fig. 7. The model introduces five variables. The variable *chosen* indicates whether a particular command is currently chosen for simulated execution,

```
MACHINE Phase_2 SEES CommData
  VARIABLES chosen, stacklevel, step, knows, Sequence
  INVARIANT
      chosen ∈ BOOL ∧ stacklevel ∈ N ∧ step ∈ N ⇸ N1 ∧ knows ∈ N ⇸ P(Data) ∧
      Sequence ∈ N ⇸ (N ⇸ Commands) ∧ dom(step) = 0..stacklevel ∧
      dom(knows) = 0..stacklevel ∧ dom(Sequence) = 0..stacklevel ∧
      chosen = FALSE  ⇒  stacklevel = 0 ...
  EVENTS
      choose  = ...          execute_single  = ...          start_seq  = ...
      finish_seq  = ...       finish  = ...
  END
```

Fig. 7. The machine Phase_2

while *stacklevel* models the current stack level of command execution. The function variables *step*, *knows*, and *Sequence* respectively store, for each stack level, the current execution step, the accumulated knowledge (in terms of received or produced data), and the sequence of the lower layer commands to be executed.

The model events specify choosing a new command (the event choose), executing a single lowest layer command (execute_single), starting execution of a sequence of the lower layer commands (start_seq), thus increasing *stacklevel*, and finishing execution of a sequence of the lower layer commands (finish_seq), thus decreasing *stacklevel*. Finally, the event finish checks that the whole command hierarchy has been executed and thus a new command may be chosen.

Below we present the specifications of a couple of model events. The event execute_single models execution of a single command. In that case, the knowledge of the calling command is updated with the produced outputs, while the execution step in the considered command sequence is increased.

```
execute_single  =
    any curr_comm where
        chosen = TRUE ∧ step(stacklevel) ∈ dom(Sequence(stacklevel)) ∧
        curr_comm = Sequence(stacklevel)(step(stacklevel)) ∧
        CommSeq(curr_comm) = ∅ ∧ Inputs(curr_comm) ⊆ knows(stacklevel) ∧
    then
        knows(stacklevel) := knows(stacklevel) ∪ Outputs(curr_comm) ∥
        step(stacklevel) := step(stacklevel) + 1
    end
```

Note that the guard $Inputs(curr\_comm) \subseteq knows(stacklevel)$ serves here as a data flow consistency condition, violation of which would lead to a model deadlock.

The event start_seq models the opposite situation, i.e., when the execution moves to the higher stack level. The affected variables *knows*, *step*, and *Sequence* are updated accordingly. The dual event finish_seq decreases the stack level and updates the affected values associated with the higher level.

```
start_seq =
    any curr_comm where
        chosen = TRUE ∧  step(stacklevel) ∈ dom(Sequence(stacklevel)) ∧
        curr_comm = Sequence(stacklevel)(step(stacklevel)) ∧ CommSeq(curr_comm) ≠ ∅ ∧
        Inputs(CommSeq(curr_comm)(1)) ⊆ Inputs(curr_comm) ∪ Produced(curr_comm)
    then
        knows(stacklevel + 1) := Inputs(curr_comm) ∪ Produced(curr_comm)  ∥
        step(stacklevel + 1) := 1  ∥  stacklevel := stacklevel + 1  ∥
        Sequence(stacklevel + 1) := CommSeq(curr_comm)
    end
```

The required data flow consistency condition (for start_seq) is given as the guard

$$Inputs(CommSeq(curr\_comm)(1)) \subseteq Inputs(curr\_comm) \cup Produced(curr\_comm).$$

The interplay between verification by theorem proving and model checking allows us to achieve "separation of concerns". Verification by theorem proving is employed to ensure the correctness of the modelled process of command execution. This correctness (as model invariants) can be proved for an arbitrary collection of commands following the pre-defined structure (see Fig. 4), thus disregarding concrete command instantiations for the chosen example (Fig. 6). Model checking, on the other hand, is predominantly used to find inconsistencies and gaps (as deadlocks) in the concrete command definitions of Fig. 6.

4.4   Phase 3

The main focus of Phase 3 is the identification of possible intruder attacks. This phase is based on the results of the previous phases. We build a formal model simulating different service scenarios and then rely on model checking to check for invariant violations indicating possible intruder attacks.

The Event-B model that we rely on in Phase 3

- simulates intruder attacks trying to obtain the predefined critical data. The attack is represented as the corresponding command sequence. This sequence is built by starting from the critical knowledge and simulating random command execution leading to it. The building process is completed when the presumed initial knowledge (data) of the intruder is reached;
- reverses the resulting command sequence in order to represent it in the form convenient for further analysis (i.e., a command sequence that starts with the initial data as an input and reaches the critical data);
- distinguishes whether the found command sequence is already known or not. If the found sequence matches one of the predefined known sequences, the search for intruder attack scenarios continues until all scenarios are analysed.

Further, for the created Event-B model, we employ model checking to find possible invariant violations. We formulate the invariant property stating that the collective critical data can be obtained only by executing the known sequences. In the case, when the resulting command sequence does not belong to the set of such sequences, a violation is found by model checking. Consequently, a found sequence becomes an input to Phase 4. If a command sequence matches a known one, the model checker continues to build another sequence, if possible. If no invariant violation is found, then, for the current command definitions, no attack scenarios can be constructed to obtain the predefined critical data.

The overall Event-B model structure described above is presented in Fig. 8. Due to the lack of space, we will only highlight the most interesting aspects of it. The variable *to_be_obtained* defines the knowledge of the intruder that he/she still needs to obtain for a successful attack. The constructed attack is stored as the corresponding command sequence in the variable *commands*.

Overall, Phase 3 is split into the sequential execution of several steps: constructing an attack (represented as a backward command sequence), reversing of the found sequence, and checking whether it is already known or not. The boolean variables *found*, *reversed*, *finished* enforce this predefined event order.

Next we briefly describe some machine events modelling steps of Phase 3. The event search (shown below) models finding the backward command sequence of the intruder attacks trying to obtain the critical data. Specifically, we start with

```
MACHINE Phase_3 SEES CommData
   VARIABLES commands, to_be_obtained, found, reversed, finished, result, ...
   INVARIANT
      commands ∈ ℕ ⇸ Commands ∧ to_be_obtained ⊆ Data ∧ found ∈ BOOL ∧
      reversed ∈ BOOL ∧ finished ∈ BOOL ∧ result ∈ BOOL ∧
      reversed = TRUE ⇒ found = TRUE ∧ finished = TRUE ⇒ reversed = TRUE ∧
      finished = TRUE ⇒ result = TRUE ∧ found = TRUE ⇒ to_be_obtained ⊆ Initial ...
   EVENTS
      search  =  ...              reverse  =  ...              comparison  =  ...
END
```

Fig. 8. The machine Phase_3

the *Critical* data as the initial value of the variable *to_be_obtained* and look which commands can produce one or more items from it. If such a command is found, the critical data it produces are removed from *to_be_obtained* and replaced with the required command inputs. We repeat this process until all required data from *to_be_obtained* belong to *Initial*. This condition is repeatedly re-checked and the corresponding boolean value is assigned to the variable *found*.

```
search =
   any comm, var where
      found = FALSE ∧ comm ∈ dom(Inputs) ∧ comm ∉ ran(commands) ∧
      Outputs(comm) ∩ to_be_obtained ≠ ∅ ∧ var = Outputs(comm) ∩ to_be_obtained
   then
      to_be_obtained := (to_be_obtained \ var) ∪ Inputs(comm)  ‖  num := num + 1  ‖
      commands := commands ∪ {num ↦ comm}  ‖  jj := num  ‖
      found := bool(((to_be_obtained \ var) ∪ Inputs(comm)) ⊆ Initial)
   end
```

The second step of the Phase 3 (the event **reverse**) is used to reverse the obtained command sequence stored in the variable *commands*. Specifically, the resulting sequence will be the command sequence that the first command inputs uses the initial data and outputs of the last command lead to the critical data.

Finally, the event **comparison** specifies checking whether the obtained command sequence is known or not. The command sequence is considered as known if it matches one of the predefined known sequences, i.e., belongs to *KnownSequences*. The comparison outcome is stored in *result*.

The resulting Event-B model is model checked against invariant violations. In particular, in Phase 3 we are interested to find possible new command sequences leading to the critical knowledge. Therefore, we check the created Event-B model against the property stating that the collective critical data elements can be obtained only by the given known sequences. This property is formulated as the following model invariant: *finished = TRUE ⇒ result = TRUE*.

The result of model checking indicating a violation of this invariant is the command sequence that leads to the critical knowledge. If such an illegal command sequence leading to critical knowledge is found, it becomes an input to Phase 4. To try model checking techniques on our running example (see Fig. 5), we instantiated the initial and critical data with concrete values in the Event-B model context. Namely, we assumed that the attacker initially knows the global title of SMS-C as well as the phone number of the user he/she wants to defraud, i.e., $Initial = \{SMSC\_GT, MSISD\}$. The successful attack would be obtaining the access of the user profile and updating this profile with the attacker supplied billing address, i.e., $Critical = \{UPI, ISD\_OK\}$.

Then we checked the Event-B model for invariant violations. For the given values of our running example, the result of such verification was the following command sequence: $\{1 \mapsto SRI4SM, 2 \mapsto UL4VLR, 3 \mapsto ISD4HLR\}$, indicating a specific command chain to obtain the predefined critical data.

4.5   Phase 4

In Phase 4, we analyse the identified attack vector to propose the recommendations for hardening. Our goal is to identify the feasible ways to modify the data flow associated with the analysed scenario. The feasibility is checked by repeating Phase 1 of our approach with the modified service definitions as the input. Currently we assume that the recommendations for hardening rely on the manual inspection of the identified attack vectors. However, model animation can significantly facilitate this process by allowing us to replay the identified attack scenario and considering inputs and outputs of each command individually.

At the current stage, we have experimented with a subset of SS7-MAP standard proposed by our industrial partners. Model animation has allowed us to visualise the attack scenarios that, in turn, facilitated discussion of the possible ways to harden the system by modifying the data flow. In the future we are planning to automate this stage as well. The automation may rely on, e.g., introducing additional information about the minimal sufficient types of inputs and outputs for each command and consequent automatic alternations of the command inputs and outputs. An automated analysis would allow us to significantly speed up identification of possible combinations for system hardening.

A few simple guidelines that we propose below can also serve as a basis of future automation of this task. Specifically, to break the identified command sequence constituting a possible attack scenario, we may try to (i) add extra input to some command, thus requiring extra information before executing the command, (ii) remove some redundant output from a command, because it may be possibly used for malicious purposes, (iii) add new produced data for some command together with some extra input for one of its (sub)commands it relies on (e.g., special data element that is added to guarantee that a couple of commands are used only in that particular way, by one calling the other).

It is easy to check that proposed command modifications (i.e., the results of Phase 4) indeed break the obtained harmful sequence. However, since any command may be a part of some predefined execution scenarios, we also need to check that the modifications are feasible, i.e., they do not disable any defined valid scenarios. To ensure that, we need to go through Phases 1–2. If Phase 2 demonstrates that some predefined command execution scenario is broken, then we have to return to Phase 4 and reconsider the suggested command modifications. If the proposed modifications do not affect the valid scenarios, then we can proceed to Phase 3 to find new possible attacker sequences and so on.

5 Related Work and Conclusions

Related Work. The problem of analysis of security protocols has been studied over several decades [2, 13] in the different application domains: web services [4, 14], mobile and sensor networks [11], operating systems [5], etc. There are several approaches proposed to model attacks and perform security evaluation for main types of attacks [3, 6, 8–10]. For instance, Armando et al. [3] demonstrate how to relate a specification of security protocols and their implementations to enable model-based security testing. In particular, they show how to use the traces of potential attacks found by a model checker to generate the corresponding test suits for verifying a protocol implementation. Our approach also employs model checking to generate possible attack scenarios. However, we also go further and propose recommendations for rectifying the found vulnerabilities. By combining proofs and model checking, we can verify that the proposed recommendations are feasible and correct, i.e., they do not disable the execution of the intended services yet prevent an execution of attack scenarios.

A cyber attack modelling and assessment of their impact are investigated in the work by Kotenko and Chechulin [9]. The authors introduce a framework that comprises an explicit representation of the intruder's behaviour, generation of attack graphs, as well as calculation of different security metrics. In our work, we rather focus on analysing the attack possibilities that the system architecture opens for an intruder. We assume that, e.g., by using social engineering, an intruder can gain an access to different data about the network components. By relying on formal modelling and verification, we construct an attack vector and identify the ways to prevent it.

There are several works that rely on Event-B or the B method to reason about security. For instance, the B4MSecure platform proposed in [7] introduces facilities for graphical modelling of access control policies as UML class diagrams and automates a translation of the graphical models into B specifications. Event-B has been also combined with Alloy to formally verify a security model of an operating system [5]. The authors investigate verification of integrity and confidentiality requirements. In our approach, we address these requirements by identifying possible ways an intruder can masquerade himself as a trusted party and get access or even alter sensitive data. Currently, the attack scenarios are analysed using model animation. However, we are planning to extend our approach to support graphical representation of scenarios as sequence diagrams.

Conclusions. In this paper, we have proposed a formal approach to identifying security vulnerabilities in the telecommunication protocols and defining the recommendations for rectifying them. The approach relies on formal modelling in Event-B that allowed us, in a unified way, to not only generate potentially harmful scenarios but also explore various alternatives for rectifying the identified vulnerabilities. The proposed approach is iterative: it enables a systematic analysis of all potential vulnerabilities and provides an immediate feedback on feasibility of the proposed hardening actions.

Event-B and the Rodin platform have offered us a suitable basis for the formalisation and automation of our approach. Event-B supports a separate treatment of static and dynamic parts of the model. In the static part of the model – the context – we defined the architectures of the analysed services. To verify feasibility of the proposed recommendations, we had to modify the context only. The dynamic part remained essentially unchanged and represented a generic pattern of service execution under the given constraints. Such a separation of concerns allowed us to significantly reduce the involved efforts.

The availability of the automated tool support – the Rodin platform – has been critical for ensuring applicability of our approach. The provers have been used to verify consistency of the architectures and the Pro-B model checker to find attack scenarios. Moreover, model animation has facilitated analysis of the scenarios as well as the recommendations for hardening. We believe that integration of these techniques allowed us to create a powerful support for security analysis of complex telecommunication protocols.

The proposed approach can be also used to provide an input for standardisation activities, and in particular for the currently on-going evolution of the SS7 protocol suite. As a future work, we are planning to investigate the idea of generating test suits on the basis of the identified attack scenarios.

References

1. Abrial, J.R.: Modeling in Event-B. Cambridge University Press, Cambridge (2010)
2. Armando, A., et al.: The AVISPA tool for the automated validation of internet security protocols and applications. In: Etessami, K., Rajamani, S.K. (eds.) CAV 2005. LNCS, vol. 3576, pp. 281–285. Springer, Heidelberg (2005). doi:10.1007/11513988_27
3. Armando, A., Pellegrino, G., Carbone, R., Merlo, A., Balzarotti, D.: From model-checking to automated testing of security protocols: bridging the gap. In: Brucker, A.D., Julliand, J. (eds.) TAP 2012. LNCS, vol. 7305, pp. 3–18. Springer, Heidelberg (2012). doi:10.1007/978-3-642-30473-6_3
4. Backes, M., Mödersheim, S., Pfitzmann, B., Viganò, L.: Symbolic and cryptographic analysis of the secure WS-ReliableMessaging scenario. In: Aceto, L., Ingólfsdóttir, A. (eds.) FoSSaCS 2006. LNCS, vol. 3921, pp. 428–445. Springer, Heidelberg (2006). doi:10.1007/11690634_29
5. Devyanin, P.N., Khoroshilov, A.V., Kuliamin, V.V., Petrenko, A.K., Shchepetkov, I.V.: Formal verification of OS security model with alloy and event-B. In: Ait Ameur, Y., Schewe, K.-D. (eds.) ABZ 2014. LNCS, vol. 8477, pp. 309–313. Springer, Heidelberg (2014)
6. Goldman, R.P.: A stochastic model for intrusions. In: Wespi, A., Vigna, G., Deri, L. (eds.) RAID 2002. LNCS, vol. 2516, pp. 199–218. Springer, Heidelberg (2002). doi:10.1007/3-540-36084-0_11
7. Idani, A., Ledru, Y.: B for modeling secure information systems. In: Butler, M., Conchon, S., Zaïdi, F. (eds.) ICFEM 2015. LNCS, vol. 9407, pp. 312–318. Springer, Heidelberg (2015). doi:10.1007/978-3-319-25423-4_20
8. Ingols, K., Chu, M., Lippmann, R., Webster, S.E., Boyer, S.W.: Modeling modern network attacks and countermeasures using attack graphs. In: 25th Annual Computer Security Applications Conference (ACSAC), pp. 117–126. IEEE (2009)

9. Kotenko, I., Chechulin, A.: A cyber attack modelling and impact assessment framework. In: Proceedings of the 5th International Conference on Cyber Conflict. NATO CCD COE Publications (2013)
10. Noel, S., Wang, L., Singhal, A., Jajodia, S.: Measuring security risk of networks using attack graphs. IJNGC **1**(1), 135–147 (2010)
11. Rekhis, S., Boudriga, N.: Formal reconstruction of attack scenarios in mobile ad hoc and sensor networks. J. Wirel. Commun. Netw. **39** (2011)
12. Rodin: Event-B Platform. http://www.event-b.org/
13. Ryan, P.Y.A., Schneider, S.A.: Modelling and Analysis of Security Protocols. Addison-Wesley-Longman, Boston (2001)
14. Salaün, G., Bordeaux, L., Schaerf, M.: Describing and reasoning on web services using process algebra. In: Proceedings of the IEEE International Conference on Web Services (ICWS 2004), p. 43. IEEE Computer Society (2004)
15. SS7: Signalling System No.7. http://www.informit.com/library/content.aspx?b=Signaling_System_No_7&seqNum=15/
16. SS7-MAP: SS7 - Mobile Application Part. http://www.informit.com/library/content.aspx?b=Signaling_System_No_7&seqNum=114/
17. The ProB Animator and Model Checker. http://www.stups.uni-duesseldorf.de/ProB/index.php.5/

Multi-threaded On-the-Fly Model Generation of Malware with Hash Compaction

Nguyen Minh Hai[1(✉)], Quan Thanh Tho[1], and Le Duc Anh[2]

[1] HoChiMinh City University of Technology, Ho Chi Minh City, Vietnam
{hainmmt,qttho}@cse.hcmut.edu.vn
[2] Tokyo University of Agriculture and Technology, Tokyo, Japan

Abstract. This paper introduces multi-threaded implementation of our binary code analyzer BE-PUM for malware. On-the-fly model generation by BE-PUM is combined with duplication detection and hash compaction method to minimize the resource consumption. The method operates in three phases including parallel expansion of states, duplication detection and update of the state space. A notable feature of our algorithm is that it requires very little synchronization or cooperation between threads, which is often a bottleneck of multi-threading, due to our strategy of local resource management. The experiments on 125 real-world malware show good performance improvement.

Keywords: Concolic testing · Pushdown system · Malware detection · Binary code analysis · Hash compaction · Multi-threaded

1 Introduction

Model checking is one of the main approaches for detecting malware [10]. The underlying idea consists of two steps including *model generation* and *model checking*. Model generation phase disassembles the infected executables and extracts the *control flow graph* (CFG) which contains nodes presenting all explored instructions in targeted file and edges linking between them. After a CFG (abstract model) is generated, the second phase is applied with popular analysis techniques like model checking [2,10]. Among them, model generation phase takes a very important task.

However, this model generation phase is not easy. The main drawback of this phase bases on the problem of obfuscation techniques, e.g. indirect jump, Structured Exception Handling (SEH) and self-modifying code. Model generation is implemented in many binary analysis tools, e.g. CodeSurfer/x86 [1], McVeto [18], JakStab [9], and a commercial product, IDA Pro[1] which is claimed to be one of the most popular and powerful tools for binary code analysis. However, they are quite limited when dealing with obfuscation techniques, e.g. indirect jumps. In [15,16], we propose a new tool, BE-PUM which applies an on-the-fly pushdown model generation of x86 binaries based on dynamic symbolic execution.

---

[1] http://www.datarescue.com/idabase/.

© Springer International Publishing AG 2016
K. Ogata et al. (Eds.): ICFEM 2016, LNCS 10009, pp. 159–174, 2016.
DOI: 10.1007/978-3-319-47846-3_11

BE-PUM traces precise control flow against obfuscation techniques including indirect jump, self-modifying code.

However, the symbolic simulation process of x86 instructions and Windows APIs in BE-PUM implies a significant resource consumption which causes this tool running quite slowly when dealing with real-world malware. Thus, speeding up BE-PUM by means of multiple threads to parallelize its operations comes as a natural approach. Nevertheless, as BE-PUM explores the CFG in an on-the-fly manner, it is necessary to synchronize all of sub-CFGs explored by all the threads, which supposedly causes a bottleneck issue. In addition, the problem of overlapping states explored by threads also results in redundant resource consumption.

Contributions. Inspired by [5], this paper studies an approach for reducing the processing time of exploring states in BE-PUM by applying the computational power of multiple threads. Our key contributions are summarized as follows.

1. We propose an algorithm of using multiple threads for speeding up the process of exploring states in BE-PUM. Our algorithm needs very little synchronization or cooperation between threads due to our strategy to handle local resources.
2. We combine our parallel algorithm with hash compaction method [7,8] to minimize the amount of memory necessary for storing the table of visited states.
3. We apply a method of duplication detection for eliminating redundant threads i.e. ones that cannot traverse new nodes.

The rest of this paper is organized as follows. Section 2 briefly introduces basic concepts of BE-PUM and presents the hash compaction method. Section 3 describes the high-level overview of our algorithm using a small example. An implementation of our approach is introduced in Sect. 4. Section 5 shows our experiment evaluation on 125 real-world malwares mainly collected from Virus-Total[2]. Section 6 presents the related works. Finally, the Sect. 7 discusses the conclusion and some future works.

2   Background

2.1   On-the-Fly Pushdown Model Generation of BE-PUM

BE-PUM [15,16] (Binary Emulation for PUshdown Model generation) targets on generating the precise CFG from binary code of malware. It applies an on-the-fly pushdown model generation of x86 binaries based on dynamic symbolic execution. BE-PUM traces precise control flow against obfuscation techniques. The current version of BE-PUM supports 300 of the most frequently occurring x86 (32bit) instructions and 450 of the most frequently occurring Win32 APIs.

---

[2] https://www.virustotal.com/en/.

Pushdown Systems. As described in [13], many obfuscation techniques in malware adopt the operation over the stack via the effects of *call*, *push* and *pop* instruction. Therefore, modeling the stack of the program is very important for analyzing precisely malware. In this part, we formulate the pushdown system adopted by BE-PUM. There are two approaches for a context-sensitive model, i.e. context-cloning and context-stacking. BE-PUM chooses context-stacking with the assumption that malware mainly modifies the top stack frame (i.e. return address/value).

Definition 1. *A pushdown system (PDS) is a triplet* $\langle P, \Gamma, \Delta \rangle$ *where*

- *P is a finite set of states,*
- *Γ is finite stack alphabet, and*
- *$\Delta \subseteq P \times \Gamma^{\leq 2} \times P \times \Gamma^{\leq 2}$ is a finite set of transitions, where $(p, v, q, w) \in \Delta$ is denoted by $(p, v \to q, w)$.*

We use $\alpha, \beta, \gamma, \cdots$ to range over Γ, and $w, v, \cdots$ over words in Γ^*. A *configuration* $\langle p, w \rangle$ is a pair of a state p and a stack content (word) w. As convention, we denote configurations by $c_1, c_2, \cdots$. One step transition $\hookrightarrow$ between configurations is defined as follows. $\hookrightarrow^*$ is the reflexive transitive closure of $\hookrightarrow$.

$$\frac{\langle p, \gamma w \rangle \hookrightarrow \langle p', \gamma' w \rangle}{(p, \gamma \to p', \gamma') \in \Delta} \; inter \qquad \frac{\langle p, \gamma w \rangle \hookrightarrow \langle p', \alpha\beta w \rangle}{(p, \gamma \to p', \alpha\beta) \in \Delta} \; push \qquad \frac{\langle p, \gamma w \rangle \hookrightarrow \langle p', w \rangle}{(p, \gamma \to p', \epsilon) \in \Delta} \; pop$$

A PDS enjoys decidable *configuration reachability*, i.e., given configurations $\langle p, w \rangle$, $\langle q, v \rangle$ with $p, q \in P$ and $w, v \in \Gamma^*$, decide whether $\langle p, w \rangle \hookrightarrow^* \langle q, v \rangle$.

On-the-Fly CFG Generation. The CFG construction in BE-PUM is designed in an on-the-fly manner. As described in the figure below, when encountering a conditional jump, BE-PUM applies concolic testing to decide next destinations.

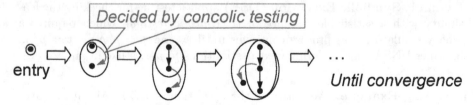

Let us formulate the notation as follows.

- k is an address in M and k_0 is the entry address,
- *asm* is an x86 assembly instruction,
- *asm*, obtained by disassembly of a binary sequence starting from $k \in M$, is referred by $asm = instr(Env_M, k)$,

The state of program can be represented by a pair $\langle (k, asm), Env \rangle$ with an address k, an x86 instruction asm and an environment Env consisting of values of registers R, flags F, and a memory status M (which includes the status of the stack S) after the execution starting from the entry point. When self-modifying code appears, which modifies the assembly code at k from asm to asm', BE-PUM introduces a new CFG node as a pair (k, asm'). Thus, BE-PUM distinguishes (k, asm) and (k, asm') as different CFG nodes. This idea is also presented in McVeto [18].

Concolic Testing. BE-PUM applies the concolic testing, a combination of static analysis and symbolic execution for calculating the next address when encountering indirect jump. The main idea of *symbolic execution* [11] (SE) is to symbolically execute a program. SE maintains a symbolic state $\langle p, \psi \rangle$ with a CFG node $p = (k, asm)$ and a path formula ψ which accumulates the precondition of the execution of the path starting from the entry CFG node to p. BE-PUM verifies the satisfiability of ψ by SAT/SMT solvers.

After solving the path condition ψ, BE-PUM generates test-cases and continues to explore multiple destinations. The figure below describes two ways to explore possibly multiple destinations of BE-PUM.

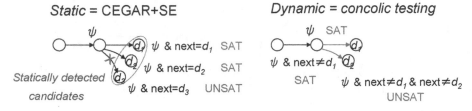

- **Static Symbolic Execution (SSE)** applies the static detection for next destination candidates and the feasibility of each destination p' is checked by the satisfiability of $\psi \wedge \texttt{next} = p'$.
- **Dynamic Symbolic Execution (DSE)** applies testing for checking the feasibility with a satisfiable instance of ψ (*concolic testing*), which requires a binary emulator. This process continues until $\psi \wedge \texttt{next} = p' \wedge \texttt{next} = p''$.... becomes UNSAT for exploring next destinations $p', p'', ...$, like in [4].

Motivating Example. We illustrate the operation of BE-PUM with a small example in Fig. 1. This example depicts BE-PUM's advantage of handling self-modification, system API invocation and indirect jump. Also, the problem when multi-thread issue is concerned is also discussed.

At a first look, the execution follows the looping path $P = (start \rightarrow 0 \rightarrow 1 \rightarrow 2 \rightarrow 3 \rightarrow 4 \rightarrow 1)$. However, the instruction at the location 3 overwrites the code at $offset\ L1 + 1$, which modifies the opcode at 1 from $EB\ 00$ to $EB\ 0A$. This means that $jmp\ L2$ at 1 is updated to $jmp\ L3$. This is a basic

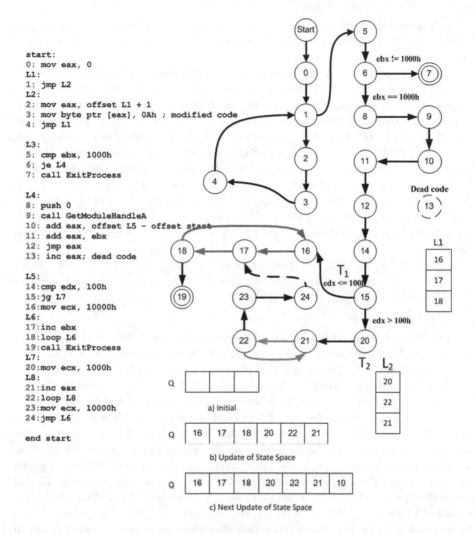

Fig. 1. The running example

self-modification technique. *JakStab, IDA Pro, MetaASM*[3] and *Hooper*[4] fail to trace this technique, whereas BE-PUM correctly generates

$(0,''\text{xor eax eax}'') \rightarrow (1,''\text{jmp L2}'')\rightarrow(2,''\text{mov eax, offset l1 + 1}'')$
$\rightarrow (3,''\text{mov byte ptr [eax], 0Eh}'')\rightarrow(4,''\text{jmp L1}'')\rightarrow(1,''\text{jmp L3}'')\rightarrow\cdots$

At each location, BE-PUM applies a single-step disassembly i.e. the instruction at this location is generated dynamically when a path reaches there. This feature enables BE-PUM to handle self-modification.

---

[3] http://metasm.cr0.org/.
[4] http://www.hopperapp.com/.

Following the path from location 8, one can observe that at 9, there is a system call of the API $GetModuleHandleA$. Then, there is an indirect jump at 12.

Currently, most of binary analysis tools suffer from difficulties when dealing with such system API invocation and indirect jump. BE-PUM successfully tackles those obstacles due to its mechanism of dynamic symbolic simulation. In BE-PUM, $GetModuleHandleA$ at 9 is invoked with parameter 0. BE-PUM simulates its symbolic execution using JNA[5]. The return value by executing this API is the base address of this program and stored in register eax. In the meantime, BE-PUM also evaluates the corresponding path formula as $(start \rightarrow 0 \rightarrow 1 \rightarrow 2 \rightarrow 3 \rightarrow 4 \rightarrow 1 \rightarrow 5 \rightarrow 6 \rightarrow 8 \rightarrow 9 \rightarrow 10 \rightarrow 11 \rightarrow 12)$ is $(ebx == 1000)$. To decide the next destination at 12, BE-PUM applies concolic testing by setting the value $(ebx = 1000)$ (as a satisfiable instance detected by $Z3\ 4.3$), and finds a new destination 14 (13 is dead node described with dotted line).

From 15, BE-PUM follows two paths $P_1 = (15 \rightarrow 16 \rightarrow 17 \rightarrow 18 \rightarrow 16 \rightarrow$ $... \rightarrow 18 \rightarrow 19)$ and $P_2 = (15 \rightarrow 20 \rightarrow 21 \rightarrow 22 \rightarrow 21 \rightarrow ... \rightarrow 22 \rightarrow 23 \rightarrow 24 \rightarrow$ $17 \rightarrow 18 \rightarrow 16 \rightarrow 17 \rightarrow ... \rightarrow 18 \rightarrow 19)$.

Issues Raised from the Motivating Example. Since BE-PUM operates in single thread, its processing time is the sum of processing time for executing the two paths P_1 and P_2. This is the first problem, which can be potentially solved by applying multiple-thread mechanism.

However, in order to apply this approach, one needs to handle the issue of unnecessary duplication when BE-PUM explores states in different paths using different threads. For example, assume that there is one thread executing the first path P_1 and reaches the final node at 19. In the meantime, another thread is executing the second path P_2. After unrolling the loop described in green line, the second thread reaches 24. From 24, it continues with the node 17 and processes the loop $(17 \rightarrow 18 \rightarrow 16 \rightarrow 17 \rightarrow ...)$. However, as this loop is already explored in P_1 by the first thread, to continue exploring this loop again should be a waste of resources. For solving this problem, we propose a mechanism of duplicate detection to significantly reduce the chance that that one thread visits states already visited by other threads. To achieve that, we need to collect all of states visited by all concurrent threads and store those states in multiple local lists. Obviously, it is important to reduce the memory consumption used for state storage in those lists. We handle this problem by applying the well-known hash compaction method [7,8].

2.2   Hash Compaction

Hash compaction [7,8,19] is well-known method introduced by Holzmann for minimizing the memory consumption in storing the visited states. The main idea

---

[5] https://jna.java.net/.

of this approach is to apply a *hash function* H which maps from *state vector* V to the fixed length of *bit strings* B. The length of B can be typically 32 or 64 bits. V is a data structure which unambiguously represents a state. For each visited state s stored in a list, instead of storing full state descriptor, only the hash value $H(s)$ is stored. Clearly, the main drawback of this method is that the hash function can produce the same output for different inputs. It implies that the two different state vectors can be mapped to the same value. The problem of hash collision can be alleviated by applying multiple hash functions [17,19]. Although this approach cannot guarantee collision-free, the probability of collision can be kept small enough to be applied in practice.

3   Algorithm of Multi-threaded On-the-Fly Model Generation

3.1   Running Example

We start this section by a running example showing how our approach can handle the problems pointed out in the motivating example. It is illustrated again by Fig. 1 but now we focus on the execution flow starting from 15, where two possible paths are generated and to be explored by two individual threads. In the naive design, when BE-PUM explores multiple paths, it sequentially traverses one by one. In this new design, BE-PUM supports multiple threads for exploring multiple paths at the same time, hence speeding up the process of CFG generation.

In this multi-threaded approach, we use global list Q for keeping all explored states of all threads and local list L_i for storing all visited states in each thread T_i. From 15, BE-PUM follows two paths $P_1 = (15 \rightarrow 16 \rightarrow 17 \rightarrow 18 \rightarrow 16 \rightarrow ... \rightarrow 18 \rightarrow 19)$ and $P_2 = (15 \rightarrow 20 \rightarrow 21 \rightarrow 22 \rightarrow 21 \rightarrow ... \rightarrow 22 \rightarrow 23 \rightarrow 24 \rightarrow 17 \rightarrow 18 \rightarrow 16 \rightarrow 17 \rightarrow ... \rightarrow 18 \rightarrow 19)$. Let us assume that at this time there are two threads, T_1 and T_2, which explore P_1 and P_2 respectively. Those threads explore states in depth-first manner and update new visited states in their corresponding local lists, L_1 and L_2. As described in Fig. 1, when T_1 explores states 16, 17 and 18, these states are stored in the local list L_1.

When a local list is full, we will update the states in the local list to the global list. If there is a state in the local list already kept in the global list, it means this state is already visited by another thread previously. Thus, the corresponding thread will be terminated.

For example, we assume that after T_1 explores 16, 17 and 18 and T_2 explores 20, 21 and 22, their local lists are full. Then, two threads update their internal states into the global list Q, resulting in Q keeping all of 6 those states, as presented in Fig. 1(b). Next, T_2 continues explores 23, 24, 17 and its local list L_2 is full again. At this point, T_2 again updates its internal states into Q and finds out that its internal state 17 is already in Q as depicted in Fig. 1(c) (since it is explored by T_1 beforehand). Thus, T_2 is terminated with no further exploration.

Remarks. There are two remarks for the approach we just describe as follows. First, to minimize the memory consumption of storing states in global list and local list, we implement the hash compaction mechanism as previously discussed in Sect. 2.2. Secondly, when applied in real program, the chance that two local lists are updated into the global list at the same time is quite relatively small, since each thread is basically exploring a different path in the CFG. That is why our approach requires very little synchronization or cooperation between threads when handling real malware samples.

3.2 Algorithm Overview

Let us consider state $S = (k, asm, H_1(Env), H_2(Env))$ with k is location and asm is instruction. Given $H_1(Env)$ and $H_2(Env)$ are hash functions which map the environment Env denoted in Sect. 2 to 32 bit fixed size string. We use two hash functions for minimizing the probability of hash collision as described in Sect. 2.2.

Let $T = (t_1, t_2, ..., t_n)$ be the set of threads participating in the exploration of states. We denote $L = (l_1, l_2, ..., l_n)$ as the set of local list which is stored in each thread.

In our proposed parallel approach, the primary data structures include the global list Q containing all explored states of all threads and local lists l_i storing all visited states in each thread t_i. As depicted in Fig. 2, each thread operates in three phases. In the first phase, thread t_i explores state in depth-first manner and updates new state in local list l_i. When local list is full, the second phase performs duplication detection to find duplicated states, i.e. states in l_i that are represented in Q. If duplication is detected, t_i is halted. If there is no state of l_i stored in Q, the thread starts the third phase which moves all the states of l_i into Q.

Within each phase, all threads work independently and it does not need to synchronize or cooperate before the algorithm proceeds to the next phase. This is the main feature of our algorithm.

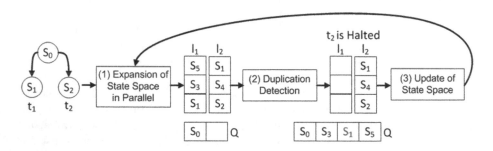

Fig. 2. Overview of three phases

3.3   Algorithm Details

This section describes three phases of our algorithm in details. Figure 3 illustrates the partial state space where the initial state s_0 is assumed to have three new successors of s_1, s_2 and s_3. These states are handled by three threads, t_1, t_2 and t_3 respectively.

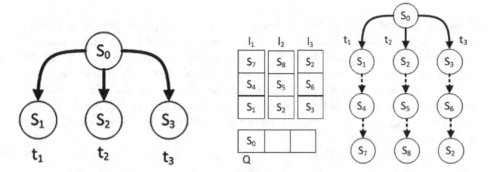

Fig. 3. Initial tree   **Fig. 4.** Expansion of state

Phase 1: Expansion of State Space. Threads explore state space using depth-first search algorithm. State tree is expanded and new states are put in local list corresponding to each thread. Since each thread t_i inserts states in the local list l_i only, there is no requirement of synchronization. Figure 4 depicts this first step of the algorithm. The dotted elements in Fig. 4 (right) describe the expansion of node. The final result of updating local list in each thread is also illustrated in Fig. 4 (left). This phase ends when local list is full. Although this figure just describes 3 threads, the expansion can be performed independently by any number of threads.

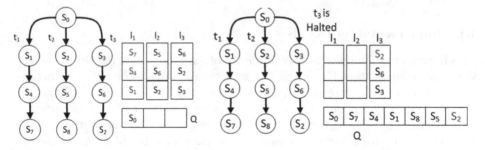

Fig. 5. Check for condition in   **Fig. 6.** Halting the thread
duplicate detection phase

Phase 2: Duplication Detection. The second phase starts when local list l_i of thread t_i is full. It first check whether any states in l_i are stored in Q. Note that two states are duplicated if the values of location k, instruction asm and two hash value of environment $H_1(Env), H_2(Env)$ are the same. If no duplication detected, thread starts Phase 3. In Fig. 5, s_1, s_4 and s_7 of l_1 are not in Q, thus thread t_1 starts Phase 3. In contrast, a thread is halted if duplication occurs. A halted thread discards the visited states and can be assigned new exploring task later. For instance, let us consider the example in Fig. 6, thread t_3 is halted since state s_2 of the local list l_3 is contained in global list Q.

Phase 3: Update of the State Space. In this third phase, thread moves all the state in local list to global list. Then, Phase 1 starts all over again. Figures 7 and 8 illustrate this phase. In Fig. 7, t_1 moves s_7, s_4 and s_1 from l_1 to Q. In Fig. 8, t_2 moves s_8, s_5 and s_2 from l_2 to Q. Note that each thread basically explores a different path in the CFG. Thus, the chance that their local lists are updated into the global lists at the same time is quite relatively small. Hence, each thread can perform its three phases independently, without concern of the status of other threads.

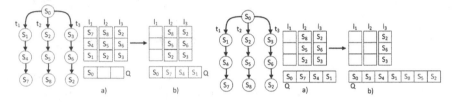

Fig. 7. Update of t_1 **Fig. 8.** Update of t_2

4   Implementation Issues

We have implemented our approach in the new version of BE-PUM. This section discusses the most important aspects in our implementation.

4.1   Implementation Details

This implementation inherits *Thread* library of Java to execute multiple threads. We implement a thread manager for monitoring threads operations, including creation of new thread, suspension, condition verification or deletion of thread. The thread manager just allows a certain number of threads running concurrently at the same time. For performance balance, the allowed maximum number of activating threads is equal to number of cores of CPU. However, this value can be manually modified. When a branch in the graph has to be explored but all threads are already used, the thread manager will store the position of this branch for assigning to free thread. The thread manager class is designed to be a singleton pattern and each thread is only allowed to interact with this single object for centralized management. An important requirement is the implementation of the primary data structure, i.e. global list and local list. We implemented them using *HashSet* library in Java. The main advantage of HashSet is that it provides constant time performance for the basic operations (addition, removal). Moreover, seeking operation of HashSet requires $O(1)$ time. In worst case, it produces $O(n)$ times when all elements have the same hash value. At some points, many threads can access HashSet concurrently. For resolving the concurrency, we declare the external synchronization using the *Collections.synchronizedSet* method.

4.2   Empirical Study on Deciding the Size of Local List

A notable feature of our algorithm is that it requires very little synchronization or cooperation between threads, which is often a bottleneck of multi-threading. The main reason of this characteristics is that we adopt the local list for preventing the persistent synchronization between threads when accessing global list. Note that thread examines global list when its local list is full. However, the size of local list requires much study since it has significant influence on performance of our algorithm. If the size of local list is too small, threads continuously update global list which easily causes conflict. If the size of local list is too large, threads stay too long in the first phase. For solving this problem, we have performed experiments on 8 small toy examples. These samples have the number of reachable states ranging from thousands to millions of states e.g. *demo*1 contains 21 states, *demo*8 stores more than 1000000 states. Table 1 presented our results. The second column *Processing Time* shows the computational time in seconds

Table 1. Experimental results on deciding size of local list

Buffer Size	Processing Time (ms)							
	Demo 1 ($\approx 21(s)$)	Demo 2 ($\approx 272(s)$)	Demo 3 ($\approx 4120(s)$)	Demo 4 ($\approx 65540(s)$)	*Demo*5 ($\approx 1048580(s)$)	Demo 6 ($\approx 16112143(s)$)	Demo 7 ($\approx 16515071(s)$)	Demo 8 ($\approx 16777221(s)$)
10	2172	2188	2563	8329	98953	1625562	1645547	1552906
20	2172	2203	2578	8281	99485	1527421	1598438	1570156
30	2172	2203	2594	8218	100312	1537157	1593218	1563516
40	2172	2188	2593	8250	98485	1610703	1645218	1562469
50	2172	2203	2579	8531	99406	1599312	1635500	1555171
60	2172	2219	2578	8250	99235	1561719	1582953	1570281
70	2172	2219	2562	8203	98954	1519828	1552016	1565406
80	2234	2203	2610	8250	99078	1518015	1577485	1550953
90	2187	2219	2625	8281	99219	1514421	1537172	1566032
100	2172	2219	2578	8203	99813	1506063	1540875	1559641
120	2219	2234	2579	8141	99922	1520391	1556547	1560000
150	**2172**	**2203**	**2578**	**8234**	**92094**	**1413203**	**1462031**	**1499609**
170	2187	2204	2579	8235	98313	1523453	1547282	1553453
200	2171	2234	2594	8234	98781	1535859	1562922	1563078
250	2172	2204	2578	8343	99781	1513812	1542609	1543468
300	2172	2219	2578	8297	98734	1517641	1541672	1558547
350	2171	2204	2578	8219	99234	1515328	1547390	1543297
400	2187	2219	2579	8234	99313	1500062	1538734	1555094
450	2204	2250	2578	8219	101047	1508828	1537344	1552453
500	2157	2203	2578	8234	100734	1479438	1544359	1553359
550	2156	2204	2578	8156	98641	1509984	1544812	1552812
600	2156	2203	2609	8250	99312	1510860	1558109	1546656
650	2172	2204	2563	8437	101391	1481281	1544297	1551547
700	2188	2219	2625	8235	100437	1500610	1543843	1566360

of our approach with different buffer size. Empirical results show that best result achieves when the size of local list is 150.

4.3   On-Demand Hashing Generation

In this implementation, one major priority is choosing hashing algorithms which maintain uniqueness and high speed performance in calculating. For achieving these goals, BE-PUM implements Murmur3[6] and FNV-1[7] hashing algorithms due to the balance between collision-resistant property and speed performance.

Hashing generation often takes a lot of time. For tackling this problem, BE-PUM uses on-demand hashing generation strategy. That is, it adopts a local cache for storing the last result of hashing generation. If there is no change in the environment, i.e. the values of registers, flags, stacks and memory do not change, BE-PUM returns the value of cache as the hash result. If there is modification of environment, it generates the new hash value and stores it in cache.

5   Experiments

5.1   Experimental Setup

For evaluating our approach, we have preformed our experiments on 125 real-world malwares collected mainly from VirusTotal[8]. Their sizes mostly range from a few to hundreds of kilobyte. All experiments are performed on 4-core machine, Windows XP with 2.9 GHz and 8 GB memory. We have conducted our algorithm on each malware with 1 to 4 worker threads and no multicore. Note that, in the case of no multicore, our approach reduces to the sequential algorithm which is implemented in the old version of BE-PUM.

5.2   Experimental Results

Figure 9 presents our experimental results. Malwares identified by the hash value are described on the vertical axis of the figure. The horizontal axis presents the execution time (in seconds) when applying our algorithm with different number of working threads on each malware. Our approach produces the better results in processing time when the number of worker threads increases.

Table 2 extracts some examples from Fig. 9. In Table 2, the second column *Malware* indicates the short presentation of unique hash value of malware. The third column *Processing Time* shows the computational time in seconds of our approach with 4 cores, 3 cores, 2 cores, 1 core and no multicore respectively. Clearly, this table shows a stable speed-up as the number of threads increases.

---

[6] http://docs.guava-libraries.googlecode.com/git/javadoc/com/google/common/ hash/Hashing.html.

[7] http://www.java2s.com/Code/Java/Development-Class/FNVHash.htm.

[8] https://www.virustotal.com/en/.

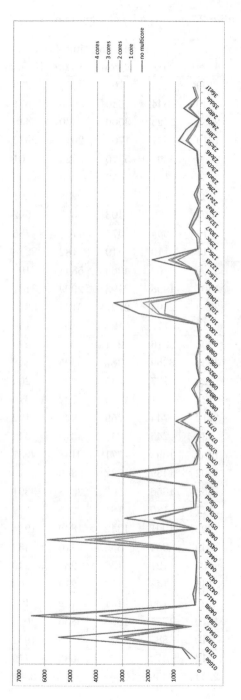

Fig. 9. Experimental results

Table 2. Some results of experiments

Num	Malware	Processing time (s)				
		4 cores	3 cores	2 cores	1 core	No multicore
1	0166e	160	165	168	360	378
2	021f0	640	644	646	666	671
3	033f9	2951	3323	3509	5430	5445
4	034d7	1310	1571	1702	2617	2672
5	038a9	3806	3891	5770	6424	6501
6	040f8	150	151	152	160	194
7	041cf	135	150	158	238	301
8	042b2	309	372	403	623	692
9	042ea	313	354	375	725	785
10	044c4	117	119	119	182	218
11	045ba	3300	3809	4063	5843	6192
12	051ab	1607	1998	2193	2909	3101
13	053eb	2359	2604	2727	3176	3327
14	056ad	113	117	120	157	184
15	060a6	204	216	221	250	219
16	066b9	3033	3269	3387	3505	3548
17	067dc	120	137	145	230	264
18	070f0	134	151	159	302	319
19	073cf	712	744	759	923	1192
20	089d5	239	245	247	319	342
21	096e8	1632	1691	1721	2148	2237
22	101a0	1392	1489	1537	2360	2410
23	102ad	1363	1656	1803	3318	3391
24	116c1	177	180	181	205	219
25	122d3	992	1091	1342	1849	1904
26	130a7	349	354	356	416	432
27	132a6	107	127	136	237	249
28	22e1f	140	148	152	219	299
29	23c46	128	130	131	149	192
30	23c95	1510	1775	1908	2836	3012
31	23ff6	810	885	922	1558	1932
32	24f09	413	479	512	633	779
33	36e1f	2234	2438	2540	3255	3394

In some cases, the increase is significant e.g. in analyzing malware $038a9^9$, the processing time reduces approximately 59 % from 6501 (s) for no multicore to 3806 (s) for 4 cores.

However, looking at the results closely, there are some cases in which the increase of working threads does not reduce the processing time, e.g. $040f8$. The reason is that this malware just traces one path which is not suitable for multiple threads. However, this case does not commonly happen in real-life malware.

6   Related Works

There is a considerable model generation tools from binary executables, e.g. CodeSurfer/x86 [1], McVeto [18], JakStab [9], BIRD [14], and BINCOA/OS-MOSE [3]. However, to the best of our knowledge, we are not aware of existing research on multi-threaded model generation.

Many approaches have been designed for multi-threaded model checking or reachability analysis [5,12]. All of them avoid to use the locks. Among them, our approach is the most similar to [5] as it adopts the idea of state compression and duplicate detection. However, our algorithm has a notorious advantage over [5]. In [5], threads operates in three phases. Within each phase, all threads must synchronize and cooperate before moving to the next phase. This is a significant bottleneck of multi-threading. As presented in Sect. 3, our approach requires very little cooperation between threads. Each thread can work independently without synchronization.

7   Conclusion

This paper proposes a logical continuation of our previous work based on an approach of using multiple thread for reducing the processing time. It is combined with hash compaction method and duplicate detection for minimizing the resource consumption. The main feature of our algorithm is that it requires very little synchronization between threads. The method is implemented as an option of BE-PUM (Binary Emulator for PUshdown Model generation). Experiments and observation confirm that this new version of BE-PUM explores state with significant increase in processing time. However, hash compaction is an incomplete method. Since two states can be mapped to the same value, our approach can ignore some parts of the state space. In the future work, we intend to apply the idea of Comback Method [6] for solving this problem.

Acknowledgments. This research is funded by Vietnam National Foundation for Science and Technology Development (NAFOSTED) under grant number 102.01-2015.16.

---

[9] The real malware's name is $038a994d075553b5cbc6b46ad033bf893b3ddc889d8c713c3c$ $245e320c693d36$. For short presentation, we use the first 5 bytes of malware's name.

References

1. Balakrishnan, G., Reps, T.: Analyzing memory accesses in x86 executables. In: Duesterwald, E. (ed.) CC 2004. LNCS, vol. 2985, pp. 5–23. Springer, Heidelberg (2004)
2. Balakrishnan, G., Reps, T., Kidd, N., Lal, A.K., Lim, J., Melski, D., Gruian, R., Yong, S., Chen, C.-H., Teitelbaum, T.: Model checking x86 executables with codeSurfer/x86 and WPDS++. In: Etessami, K., Rajamani, S.K. (eds.) CAV 2005. LNCS, vol. 3576, pp. 158–163. Springer, Heidelberg (2005)
3. Bardin, S., Herrmann, P., Leroux, J., Ly, O., Tabary, R., Vincent, A.: The BINCOA framework for binary code analysis. In: Gopalakrishnan, G., Qadeer, S. (eds.) CAV 2011. LNCS, vol. 6806, pp. 165–170. Springer, Heidelberg (2011)
4. Moser, A., et al.: Exploring multiple execution paths for malware analysis. In: SP, pp. 231–245 (2007)
5. Evangelista, S., Kristensen, L.M., Petrucci, L.: Multi-threaded explicit state space exploration with state reconstruction. In: Hung, D., Ogawa, M. (eds.) ATVA 2013. LNCS, vol. 8172, pp. 208–223. Springer, Heidelberg (2013)
6. Evangelista, S., Westergaard, M., Kristensen, L.M.: The ComBack method revisited: caching strategies and extension with delayed duplicate detection. In: Jensen, K., Billington, J., Koutny, M. (eds.) Transactions on Petri Nets and Other Models of Concurrency III. LNCS, vol. 5800, pp. 189–215. Springer, Heidelberg (2009)
7. Holzmann, G.: Design and Validation of Computer Protocols. Prentice-Hall, Upper Saddle River (1991). International Editions
8. Holzmann, G.: An improved protocol reachability analysis technique. Softw. Pract. Exp. 2, 137–161 (1988)
9. Kinder, J., Kravchenko, D.: Alternating control flow reconstruction. In: Kuncak, V., Rybalchenko, A. (eds.) VMCAI 2012. LNCS, vol. 7148, pp. 267–282. Springer, Heidelberg (2012)
10. Kinder, J., Katzenbeisser, S., Schallhart, C., Veith, H.: Detecting malicious code by model checking. In: Julisch, K., Kruegel, C. (eds.) DIMVA 2005. LNCS, vol. 3548, pp. 174–187. Springer, Heidelberg (2005)
11. King, J.C.: Symbolic execution and program testing. CACM 19(7), 385–394 (1976)
12. Laarman, A., van de Pol, J., Weber, M.: Boosting multi-core reachability performance with shared hash tables. In: FMCAD 2010, pp. 247–255. IEEE (2010)
13. Lakhotia, A., Kumar, E.U., Venable, M.: A method for detecting obfuscated calls in malicious binaries. IEEE Trans. Softw. Eng. 31(11), 165–170 (2005)
14. Nanda, S., Li, W., Lam, L., Chiueh, T.: BIRD: binary interpretation using runtime disassembly. In: 4th CGO, pp. 358–370 (2006)
15. Nguyen, M.H., Nguyen, T.B., Quan, T.T., Ogawa, M.: A hybrid approach for control flow graph construction from binary code. In: APSEC, pp. 159–164 (2013)
16. Hai, N.M., Ogawa, M., Tho, Q.T.: Obfuscation code localization based on CFG generation of malware. In: Garcia-Alfaro, J., et al. (eds.) FPS 2015. LNCS, vol. 9482, pp. 229–247. Springer, Heidelberg (2016). doi:10.1007/978-3-319-30303-1_14
17. Stern, U., Dill, D.L.: Improved probabilistic verification by hash compaction. In: Camurati, P.E., Eveking, H. (eds.) CHARME 1995. LNCS, vol. 987, pp. 206–224. Springer, Heidelberg (1995)
18. Thakur, A., Lim, J., Lal, A., Burton, A., Driscoll, E., Elder, M., Andersen, T., Reps, T.: Directed proof generation for machine code. In: Touili, T., Cook, B., Jackson, P. (eds.) CAV 2010. LNCS, vol. 6174, pp. 288–305. Springer, Heidelberg (2010)
19. Wolper, P., Leroy, D.: Reliable hashing without collision detection. In: Courcoubetis, C. (ed.) CAV 1993. LNCS, vol. 697, pp. 59–70. Springer, Heidelberg (1993)

CPDY: Extending the Dolev-Yao Attacker with Physical-Layer Interactions

Marco Rocchetto[1] and Nils Ole Tippenhauer[2(✉)]

[1] SnT, University of Luxembourg, Esch-sur-Alzette, Luxembourg
marco_rocchetto@stud.edu.sg
[2] ISTD, Singapore University of Technology and Design, Singapore, Singapore
nils_tippenhauer@sutd.edu.sg

Abstract. We propose extensions to the Dolev-Yao attacker model to make it suitable for arguments about security of Cyber-Physical Systems. The Dolev-Yao attacker model uses a set of rules to define potential actions by an attacker with respect to messages (i.e. information) exchanged between parties during a protocol execution. As the traditional Dolev-Yao model considers only information (exchanged over a channel controlled by the attacker), the model cannot directly be used to argue about the security of cyber-physical systems where physical-layer interactions are possible. Our Dolev-Yao extension, called Cyber-Physical Dolev-Yao (CPDY), allows additional orthogonal interaction channels between the parties. In particular, such orthogonal channels can be used to model physical-layer mechanical, chemical, or electrical interactions between components. In addition, we discuss the inclusion of physical properties such as location or distance in the rule set. We present an example set of additional rules for the Dolev-Yao attacker, using those we are able to formally discover physical attacks that previously could only be found by empirical methods or detailed physical process models.

1 Introduction

In recent years, security of Cyber-Physical systems (CPS) has received increasing attention by researchers from the domain of computer science, electrical engineering, and control theory [20,29]. We use the term CPS to refer to systems that consist of networked embedded systems, which are used to sense, actuate, and control physical processes. Examples for such CPS include industrial water treatment facilities, electrical power plants, public transportation infrastructure, or even smart cars. All those systems have seen a rapid increase in automation and connectivity, which threatens to increase vulnerability to malicious attacks.

Security analysis of any system relies on well-defined attacker and system models [3,16]. While the system model provides an appropriate abstraction of the system under attack, the attacker model ideally fully defines the possible interactions between the attacker and the attacked system. In particular, the model

---

M. Rocchetto—The work was carried out while Marco was with iTrust at Singapore University of Technology and Design.

K. Ogata et al. (Eds.): ICFEM 2016, LNCS 10009, pp. 175–192, 2016.
DOI: 10.1007/978-3-319-47846-3_12

will also define constraints for the attacker (e.g. finite computational resources, no access to shared keys).

In contrast to the domain of information security, where the Dolev-Yao attacker model [16] (DY) is widely used for protocol analysis, the state-of-the-art for CPS security does not have a common terminology for attacker models. Even if the topic has been broadly discussed in the CPS research community, e.g., in [12], only a small number of tentative works (e.g., [18,35]) have addressed that problem. The DY model used by the information security community represents a very strong attacker, who can access and manipulate all network traffic arbitrarily. One could directly translate this attacker to CPS by allowing the attacker to intercept any communication in a real system (e.g. local fieldbus communication), or to be within physical proximity of all (unprotected) devices. However, such an attacker would only be capable of finding attacks on the network level of the CPS. Since the network traffic of CPS does not contain information about all interactions possible in a CPS, it is not sufficient for comprehensive analysis. As a result, there likely are (physical-layer) interactions between the attacker and the system that cannot be captured by the DY paradigm.

In this paper, we investigate the application of the DY attacker model for security analysis of CPS. We present a set of extensions to allow for a more general attacker model for CPS, that we named CPDY (Cyber-Physical Dolev-Yao) [24]. The CPDY attacker model allows us to consider the interaction of an attacker on the communication network, the physical presence of attackers, and the physical interaction with the mechatronics component of the CPS.

We summarize our contributions as follows:

- We discuss the general limitations of the DY attacker model for analysis of CPS, and physical layer interactions between the attacker and the attacked system.
- We propose a number of rule extensions to analyze CPS using the DY model.
- We implement these rule extensions in the ASLan++ [37] formal language, and present use case examples.

Structure. In Sect. 2, we summarize the DY attacker model. We discuss the use of the DY model in the context of CPS in Sect. 3, and show that the traditional attacker and system model is only able to represent a subset of possible interactions. We propose extensions to the DY attacker model in Sect. 4, and show our results on a real word water treatment plant use case in Sect. 5. We summarize the related work in Sect. 6 and we conclude the paper in Sect. 7.

2   Background

2.1   Modeling Systems and Communications

Level of Modeling Detail. Formal languages, e.g. HLPSL [36] and ASLan++ [37], permit a modeler to define not only the exchanged messages but also the behavior of entities involved in the communication. Some of the security validation tools allow a modeler to benefit of some algebraic properties (e.g., [8,27]) but these are typically represented symbolically by a set of constraints. Intuitively, a high level of details (e.g., a concrete highly detailed representation of the behavior of an agent) may result in non-termination problems while performing the analysis. In addition, even if we could afford such a level of details, it might not be useful to analyze security protocols against security properties at that level of detail. Some of the most common attacks (such as man-in-the-middle and replay attacks) that violate confidentiality or authentication can be found without the need of detailing the encryption scheme in the protocol.

Modeling Simplifications. In the so called *perfect cryptography* assumption, the security encryption scheme is suppose to be "perfect", without any exploitable flaw, and so the only way for the attacker to decrypt a message is by using the proper key. That assumption is widely accepted in the security protocol community, and most of the formal reasoning tools for the analysis of security protocols abstract away the mathematical and implementation details of the encryption scheme [4,8,25,32].

Modeling Architectures. Following the same line of reasoning, when one considers more complicated architecture representation, such as web applications or Service Oriented Architecture (SOA), some of the components are commonly assumed to be "perfect", in the same way as encryption schemes. Several examples are shown by the case studies of the AVANTSSAR and SPaCIoS projects [3,34] where researchers have developed several abstract models of SOAs and web applications using the ASLan++ language, e.g., in [5]. In order to give some specific examples, databases in SQLi analysis in [10], CSRF token generation in [23] are assumed to be "perfect". This is due to the fact that (as the security of security protocols is not guaranteed only by encryption schemes) the security of web applications is not guaranteed only by store procedures or perfect random generation of token. Another example has been presented in [11], where authors search for attacks in zero-knowledge proof systems abstracting away some of the mathematical and implementation details of the zero-knowledge algorithms.

2.2 Cyber-Physical Systems

In this work, we use the term Cyber-Physical System (CPS) to refer to systems that consist of networked embedded systems, which are used to sense, actuate, and control physical processes. Examples for such CPS include industrial water treatment facilities, electrical power plants, public transportation infrastructure, or even smart cars. All those systems have seen a rapid increase in automation and connectivity, which threatens to increase vulnerability to malicious attacks. While details on network topology, protocols, and control differ between engineering domains, the fundamental architecture is similar. We now explain that architecture using an industrial control system (ICS).

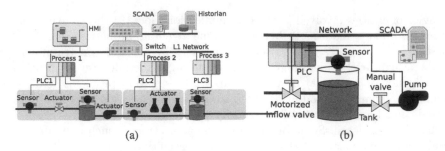

Fig. 1. (a) Example CPS architecture. (b) Use case scenario of water tank with motorized valve and pump controlled by a PLC. A level meter reports to the PLC. A manual valve is placed between tank and pump.

A modern industrial control system typically consists of several layers of networks. An example industrial control network is illustrated in Fig. 1a. The physical process is measured by distributed sensors, and manipulated by actuators. These sensors and actuators operate by receiving and sending analog signals. The analog signals are converted into digital signals by Programmable Logic Controllers (PLCs). The digital signals are then exchanged between PLCs and a central supervisory control system (SCADA) using industrial communication protocols (e.g. Modbus/TCP).

Modeling CPS. CPS can also be seen as a set of communicating agents [12] (often with one node acting as a controller), and related work focuses on the representation of the concrete behavior of the CPS [1,2,31,33]. This is believed to help the discovery the new attacks specific for CPS, e.g. resonance attacks [12]. However, that can lead researchers to over-complicating the system models even when searching for security attacks.

2.3   The Dolev-Yao Model

The DY attacker model [16] is a de-facto standard for the formal analysis of information security. The usage of such an attacker model is usually employed for the identification of cyber-related attacks, e.g., Web applications and Service-Oriented architectures as proposed in [3,23]. Attacker models à la DY have been proposed [26,30] to reason on CPS. In this work, we consider the standard DY [16] model of an active attacker who controls the network but cannot break cryptography.

The attacker can intercept messages and analyze them if he possesses the corresponding keys for decryption, and he can generate messages from his knowledge and send them under any agent name. As usual, for a set M of messages, we define DY (for "Dolev-Yao" knowledge) to be the smallest set closed under the *generation (G)* and *analysis (A) rules* of the *system* given in Fig. 2. The G rules express that the attacker can compose messages from known messages using pairing, asymmetric and symmetric encryption. The A rules describe how the attacker can decompose messages.

$$\frac{M_1 \in M}{M_1 \in DY} \, G_{\text{axiom}} \qquad \frac{M_1 \in DY \quad M_2 \in DY}{[M_1, M_2] \in DY} \, G_{\text{pair}} \qquad \frac{M_1 \in DY \quad M_2 \in DY}{\{M_1\}_{M_2} \in DY} \, G_{\text{crypt}}$$

$$\frac{M_1 \in DY \quad M_2 \in DY}{\{\![M_1]\!\}_{M_2} \in DY} \, G_{\text{scrypt}} \qquad \frac{[M_1, M_2] \in DY}{M_i \in DY} \, A_{\text{pair}_i} \qquad \frac{\{\![M_1]\!\}_{M_2} \in DY \quad M_2 \in DY}{M_1 \in DY} \, A_{\text{scrypt}}$$

$$\frac{\{M_1\}_{M_2} \in DY \quad inv(M_2) \in DY}{M_1 \in DY} \, A_{\text{crypt}} \qquad \frac{\{M_1\}_{inv(M_2)} \in DY \quad M_2 \in DY}{M_1 \in DY} \, A_{\text{crypt}}^{-1}$$

Fig. 2. The system of rules of the Dolev-Yao attacker

The *algebra of messages*, which tells us how messages are constructed, is defined following [8], in the standard way. In this paper, we consider the following operations:

- $\{M_1\}_{M_2}$ represents the *asymmetric encryption* of M_1 with public key M_2;
- $\{M_1\}_{inv(M_2)}$ represents the *asymmetric encryption* of M_1 with private key $inv(M_2)$ (the mapping $inv(\cdot)$ is discussed below);
- $\{\![M_1]\!\}_{M_2}$ represents the symmetric encryption of M_1 with symmetric key M_2;
- $[M_1, M_2]$ represents the concatenation of M_1 and M_2.
- $inv(M)$ gives the private key that corresponds to public key M

3 The Dolev-Yao Model Is Not Enough

Although the classic DY model can be applied to CPS security analysis straight away, we argue that it will not be able to detect a large set of attacks possible in that context (i.e. those that involve physical-layer interactions). To illustrate that argument, we now provide three example scenarios. For the sake of simplicity, we start by presenting the intuition behind the model and the goal. Further details on the ASLan++ prototype of these scenarios along with our results are provided in Sect. 5 and [24].

3.1 Application of Dolev-Yao for CPS

We base our example on a minimal setup in a water treatment system (see Fig. 1b). In particular, we use a subprocess of a real water treatment testbed depicted in Fig. 6 (the SWaT testbed [1,33]). A similar scenario has been considered in [21,22]. The scenario we considered contains five different components and a PLC:

1. A *motorized inflow valve*, initially open, let water flows into a tank through a pipe
2. A *tank* is equipped with a *sensor* which checks the level of the water inside the tank
3. The sensor communicates its reading of the level of the water inside the tank to a *PLC*

4. When the level of the water reaches a certain upper threshold, the PLC communicates to the motorized inflow valve to close and to the *pump* to start
5. Symmetrically, when the water reaches a certain lower threshold, the PLC communicates to the inflow valve to open and to the pump to stop
6. A *manual valve* (placed between the tank and the pump) can be manually opened/closed, e.g., to prevent the water to flow into the rest of the testbed in case the water in the tank is contaminated or the pump broken
7. A central *SCADA* control that communicates with the PLC over the network

In the following, we assume that the attacker's goal is to cause a water spillage (or burst) in the tank component. The abstract messages exchanged over the network are quite simple (see Fig. 3a). The valve controls the inflow of the water to the tank. The sensor of the tank reports the current fill state to the PLC as analog signals. The PLC converts the analog signals into digital messages (value in the picture) that it sends to the SCADA. If the water level in the tank has crossed certain high/low thresholds, the SCADA sends a close/open message to the inflow valve and on/off to the pump. We note that in this setting, there is no distinction between the tank and the sensor. Nothing prevents us in considering them as two separate entities, but this would complicate the model without benefit in terms of attacks.

We analyzed the ASLan++ model using the AVANTSSAR platform, and found a simple attack (as expected). In that attack, the attacker drops the messages from the PLC to the SCADA. As result, the tank will overflow and the attacker will achieve his goal. Even if the attack is simple, it shows that one can easily use state-of-the-art verification tools and the standard DY attacker model to search for attacks on a CPS model. This basic example demonstrates that it is possible to reason on similar scenarios without considering the (fluid) mechanics of the process under attack. In particular, even in such a simple example the equations describing the flow of the water are far from trivial and are usually considered when reasoning on similar scenarios. In the remainder of this section, we consider a modification of this scenario in which the network-only DY attacker model cannot find the attack.

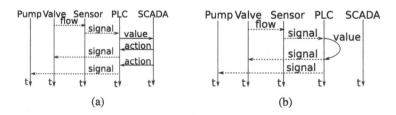

Fig. 3. (a) Physical interaction (dashed line) and digital interaction (solid line) between components in the first example. (b) Example interactions, with direct (out-of-band) communication between PLC, sensor, and actuator.

3.2   Limitations of Dolev-Yao for CPS

The previous examples demonstrates that the DY attacker model can be used to reason on network-related security aspects of CPS. We now consider a scenario in which the agents also interact through physical-layer interactions. In particular, in real-world CPS the communication between PLCs, sensors and actuators usually uses analog signals. When a distributed control scheme is used, the logic of the system is usually integrated directly into the PLC, instead of relying on the SCADA component. In addition, components can interact though the physical layer directly (e.g. by exchanging water from a pipe into a tank). To reflect such a setting, we modify the system in the previous example as follows: the inflow valve and the pump are now directly controlled by the PLC based on analog signals from the sensor. In other words, the valve and the pump operate without interrogating the SCADA. As a result, the messages on the network and SCADA are not directly involved in the operations of the valve and the pump. We can consider the setting as one in which there is just one entity whose internal behavior encapsulate the behaviors of the valves, sensor, tank, pump and PLC (see Fig. 3b). Since there is no communication over the network related to the opening/closing of the valve or to the level of the water, there is no way for the DY attacker model to achieve the goal, i.e., overflowing the tank. We confirmed this intuition with a related model in ASLan++ and evaluation in the AVANTSSAR platform. No successful attack is found.

Nevertheless, it could be expected that attacks by a physically present attacker are possible in the given setting, in particular if a physically present attacker can manually open or close the valves. Our ASLan++ model does not find such an attack because potential malicious physical-layer interactions with the system have not been considered.

3.3   Proposed Approach

We claim that, (so far) the related work generally models the operation of a CPS as a set of messages exchanged between entities over a network (see Sect. 6). For that reason, we consider prior work as limited modification of the DY attacker model. However, consideration of the physical actions is often crucial to find real-world attacks on CPS (e.g. attacks such as Stuxnet [38]). For that reason, we propose an extension of the DY attacker model with new physical interaction rules to support reasoning on the physical-layer security of CPS. We will introduce those rules in Sect. 4. Before that, we briefly discuss two aspects of our proposed approach in more detail: abstraction of physical process behavior, and whether verification tools or model checkers are better suited.

Abstraction of Physical Processes. In our proposed approach, physical layer interactions will be modeled as abstract interactions between components. In particular, we do not model all the details of the behavior of an agent for CPS. We believe that it will be very challenging for a security verification tool (or a model checker in general) to consider all details of the behavior of an agent for

CPS. For example, differential equations that model the behavior of an ultra-filtration process will be difficult to consider by the DY model or verification tool.

In this work, we abstract away all these details, similar to the way that perfect cryptography is used for security protocols analysis where we abstract from cryptographic primitives (see [15] for more details). In security protocols, that abstraction is justified by the observation that most of the attacks rely on the logical aspects of the protocol. Encryption schemes are treated as black box and the attacker cannot learn any useful information from an encrypted message without the proper decryption key. As such, a generic predicate over a term defines the encryption as $\{M_1\}_{M_2}$ in Sect. 2. In CPS, we assume that all the physical processes can be abstractly represented.

Verification Tools vs. Model Checkers. In particular, we propose to use a DY verification tool, and not a general model checker. Our argument for that is the following: in order to model a CPS to formally validate it against an attacker model, CPS (or subparts) are often modeled with languages supported by tools which do not implement the DY attacker model, e.g. NuSMV, SPIN [14]. However, it has been shown [7] that an ad-hoc implementation of the DY is more advanced in terms of efficiency and coverage than using a "general purpose" model checker with the DY model-hard coded in the specification. That is particularly evident when considering the numerous amount of verification tools developed specifically to reason on the security aspects of various systems, e.g., [4,8,9,17,32].

4   Physical-Layer Interactions for the Dolev-Yao Attacker

In this section, we present our proposed extensions of the DY model in order to make it suitable to argue about security of Cyber-Physical Systems. In particular, we discuss the introduction of additional rules for the DY attacker model to describe physical-layer interactions.

4.1   New Rules for the DY Attacker and System

New Rules for the System. The new rules for our system model aim to capture the diverse physical-layer interactions between components in the system under attack. The interactions are usually constrained by the laws of physics, which will never be violated. A very exhaustive coverage of all kinds of physical layer interactions and laws of physics would potentially result into a large set of additional rules (potentially automatically extracted from a system specification, e.g., [28]). In the following, we will consider only few additional rules to model specific interactions. In Fig. 4, we present rules that represent laws of physics related to our example (Fig. 1b). With a slightly abuse of notation, each rule represents a modification of the system status Sys from preconditions

$$\frac{Tank(level,value) \in Sys \quad Pump(status,off) \quad InflwoValve(status,open) \in Sys}{Tank(level,value') \in Sys \wedge (value' > value)} \; raise_1(Tank)$$

$$\frac{Tank(level,value) \in Sys \quad ManualValve(status,close) \in Sys \quad InflowValve(status,open) \in Sys}{Tank(level,value') \in Sys \wedge (value' > value)} \; raise_2(Tank)$$

$$\frac{C(status,damaged) \in Sys \quad C(contains,water) \in Sys \quad C(level,value) \in Sys}{C(level,value') \in Sys \wedge (value' < value)} \; damaged(C)$$

$$\frac{C(operate,manual) \in Sys \quad C(status,open) \vee C(status,close) \in Sys}{C(status,close) \in Sys} \; close(C)$$

$$\frac{C(operate,manual) \in Sys \quad C(status,open) \vee C(status,close) \in Sys}{C(status,open) \in Sys} \; open(C)$$

Fig. 4. Examples of rules that represent physical-layer interactions in the system

(top) to postconditions (bottom). *Sys* is a set collecting all the physical properties of the systems (e.g., water level, temperature, pressure) for each component in the system (e.g., tank). The properties are expressed with the predicate $C(property, value)$ (C($\cdot$) as short form of Component($\cdot$)). In Fig. 4, $raise_1(Tank)$ and $raise_2(Tank)$ relates a system configuration with its physical effects, i.e., the increase of the water level in the tank. $damaged(C)$ expresses the effect of the burst of the tank, and $close(C)$ and $open(C)$ defines the effect of physical interactions with a component (e.g., a valve) which can be manually operated to change its status.

Rules for DY Attacker. The new rules for our attacker model aim to capture the diverse physical-layer interactions between the attacker and the system (see Fig. 5). Similar to the system specification rules, the interactions between attacker and system are usually constrained by the laws of physics—even a strong attacker would not be able to create or consume arbitrary amounts of energy, move at infinite speed, or similar.

$$\frac{DYProp(distance,physical\_access) \quad DYProp(tool,damage)}{C(status,damaged) \in Sys} \; damage_{DY}$$

$$\frac{DYProp(distance,physical\_access) \quad C(operate,manual) \in Sys \quad C(status,open) \in Sys}{C(status,close) \in Sys} \; manualClose_{DY}$$

$$\frac{DYProp(distance,physical\_access) \quad C(operate,manual) \in Sys \quad C(status,close) \in Sys}{C(status,open) \in Sys} \; manualOpen_{DY}$$

Fig. 5. Examples of rules that represent physical-layer capabilities of attacker

4.2   Implementation of New Rules for DY

We base our attacker model on a review of related work that aims to profile attackers for CPS [12,13,18,33]. We found that they all share the idea of defining the attacker by means of a set of *dimensions*. These dimensions can be seen as *properties of the attacker*, e.g., distance with respect to the CPS, knowledge of the physics of the components of the system, tools (software and hardware) available to the attacker, financial support, and preference to stay hidden. We can use dimensions together with *physical properties of the system* to define new rules for the attacker as follows.

$$\frac{attacker\_property \quad system\_property}{result\ of\ action}\ action$$

where one or more attacker's properties along with the knowledge of one or more system property (that might be related to the knowledge of some physical laws connected to the system property) are the precondition to perform an action *action* which results are expressed as postconditions. In other words, an attacker is a malicious agent that can take advantage from the improper use of some device of the system.

In our first example, we can add the $damage_{DY}$ in Fig. 5 which express that an attacker who has physical access to the CPS could damage or manually operate a component, for example, a tank. Other examples are rules expressing that if the attacker has physical access to the CPS can (as we will discuss in Sect. 5.3) heat the tank and increase its pressure. In Sect. 5, we will show how we can leverage those attacker rules to find new attacks on a CPS which involve physical-layer interactions.

4.3 DY Rule Extension Using Horn Clauses

In order to apply our idea to a concrete example, we require a verification tool such that: (i) allows modification to the DY rules, and (ii) provides a language expressive enough to model a CPS. It is not easy to find a security verification tool with such constraints and, to the best of our knowledge, there is no tools in the literature.

In this work, we propose the following two workarounds that allow us to implement our additional rules even without a tool that satisfies the mentioned requirements: (i) we have used Horn Clauses (HC) to add extra rules to the DY attacker model, and (ii) we have used databases (shared memories) to store the state of the components the system, e.g., the level of the water of a tank. Using both ideas, we require only a tool that supports Horn Clauses and Shared Memories. We chose the ASLan++ specification language [37] which supports both HC and shared memories. Using ASLan++, we have implemented several case studies and obtained preliminary results that support our proposed approach.

5   Case Studies

In this section, we first show that a DY verification tool can be used to check security goals in CPS models. We have used the ASLan++ specification language [37] to define our examples which are based on a process of the SWaT

Fig. 6. Process P1 (raw water treatment) – SWaT testbed

testbed [19] depicted in Fig. 6 (see Fig. 3a for the message sequence chart). We start by providing more details on the example summarized in Sect. 3. In particular, we present a network-only modeling of the CPS and potential attacks, which shows that the DY model can be used to find attacks similar to ones discussed in related work (e.g., man-in-the-middle attacks in [2,33]). For that analysis, we abstract away the implementation details of the CPS and detect the same (network related) security flaw of most of the approaches we have found in the literature. We then modify the specification (as depicted in Fig. 3b) to show that when some physical operations (which are the at very core of a CPS) are involved in the process, the standard DY attacker model might not be able to find all attacks. To mitigate this, we modify the DY model to let him physically interact with the system under certain constraints. This allows the attacker to detect new attacks which involves physical interaction with the system. We show that almost all the attacks which relay on attackers' physical actions cannot be found. We propose a first investigation on how to extend the DY model in order to capture both cyber and physical attacks. Our results, along with timing, are summarized in Table 1.

Table 1. Summary of the analysis on the use cases

	Attack found		Timing	
	DY	CPDY	Analysis	Total
Network (Sect. 5.1)	✓	✓	220 ms	1.7 s
Manual (Sect. 5.2)		✓	8 ms	1.3 s
Heating (Sect. 5.3)		✓	4 ms	1.0 s

Total includes time for translation, analysis and attack trace generation

5.1   Network-Based Communication Use Case

This section briefly summarizes an implementation of the scenario proposed in Sect. 3.1. We focus on three aspects:

- The *status* of the system (e.g., the level of water and measurements of sensors)
- The *behavior* of each entity (i.e., tank, valves, pump, PLC and SCADA)
- The *communication* between various entities (analog and network channels)

In this example, the PLC converts the analog signals to digital messages and sends them to the SCADA control. To be coherent with the example, we model an analog channel (e.g., by using a database) between the inflow valve, the tank, the pump, and the PLC. The PLC then translates and communicates the tank/valve/pump status over a network channel with the SCADA. For the sake of readability, we assume the PLC automatically converts and sends the tank/valve/pump status. As a result, the valve, the tank, and the pump directly communicate with the SCADA over a network channel. The full implementation is reported in [24].

System Status. CPS can be seen as communicating over two channels: one is the network channel (maybe itself divided into several layers or regions) and the other is the physical flow of the events, e.g., electricity in power grids or water in water treatment or distribution CPS. We believe that an understanding on how to model the physical flow of a CPS, integration of that with the network (in such a way that an attacker model can concretely find new attacks) is still not well defined in the literature.

In this work, the status of the system is defined by a database *systemStatus*, shared between all the entities (but hidden to the DY attacker). The database is defined as a set of pairs (*agent, status*) that keeps track of the status of all entities of the specification.

Inflow Valve/Pump. The valve/pump specification describes a scenario where a SCADA changes the status of the valve/pump, e.g., from open/on to close/off, by sending to the valve a message through the PLC.

Manual Valve. The behavior of the manual valve is the same as the inflow valve. The only difference is that the manual valve can only be manually operated (e.g., to change its status from open to close), i.e., cannot be operated using network messages.

Tank. In the real testbed the PLC interrogates the sensor of the tank in order to obtain the level of the water inside the tank. For simplicity, we do not distinguish between the tank as a container and its sensors. We also assume that the sensor sends the sensed data of the level of the water whenever the level is above or below a certain threshold. We can obviously consider the more complicated and realistic tank specification containing a sensor that waits for the PLC to interrogate it. This complicates the analysis but the performance of the validation phase does not change order of magnitude (there is a variation of some milliseconds) and the result of the analysis remains the same. We recall that messages are directly sent to the SCADA instead of PLC for readability.

The tank model checks for two, mutually exclusive, status of the tank.

- If the level of the water has reached an upper threshold $overT$, the inflow valve is closed, the pump is on, and the manual valve is open, the $systemStatus$ database is updated as if the water level had lowered to a lower threshold $underT$. After the status update, the tank communicates its new status $underT$ to the SCADA.
- Symmetrically, if the level of the water has reached a threshold $underT$, the inflow valve is open, and either the manual valve is closed or the pump is off, the $systemStatus$ database is updated as if the water level had reached the upper threshold $overT$.

SCADA. As for the valve entity, we have defined the behavior of the SCADA waiting for incoming messages from the tank entity. When the tank communicates to the SCADA that the water has reached the upper threshold $overT$, the SCADA closes the inflow valve and turns on the pump. Symmetrically, when the tank reaches the lower threshold, the SCADA opens the inflow valve and turns off the pump.

Initial Status of the System. The initial status of the specification is defined with the tank empty (i.e., the level of the water is $underT$ in the $systemStatus$ database), the inflow and the manual valve are open, and the pump is off.

Goal. The goal is to overflow the tank and in ASLan++ we can define our goal as the following LTL (Linear Temporal Logic) formula.

$$\Box(inflowValve(status, open) \in Sys \Rightarrow$$
$$manualValve(status, open) \in Sys \wedge (tank(status, underT) \in Sys \vee pump(status, on) \in Sys))$$

In the formula, we define that whenever the inflow valve is open, i.e. the $systemStatus$ database contains $valve(status, open)$, then the manual valve is open, and either the tank must be empty or the pump turned on. In other words, if we find a configuration of the system such that the inflow valve is opened, the tank is full of water, and the pump is off, then the tank is overflowing. The $\Box$ at the beginning of the goal states that the goal must hold in every state of the system (i.e., LTL global operator).

Security Analysis. The AVANTSSAR platform finds a violation of the goal (i.e., a states where the goal does not hold). The goal is violated because there is a state of the system in which the tank has reached the $overT$ but the valve is still open and the pump is switched off. In order to achieve the goal, an attacker have to drop the packet, communicating the $overT$ status, sent from the tank to the SCADA.

5.2   Physics-Based Interaction Use Case

We now modify the scenario by removing the communication of the level of the water between the PLC and the SCADA, i.e., between tank/valve/pump and SCADA in the previous specification. For that reason, we assume that the PLC automatically close the inflow valve when the level of the water inside the tank reaches the threshold level $overT$. The DY attacker cannot spoof or eavesdrop the communication between entities anymore since there is no more network communication with the SCADA.

Security Analysis. Against the DY model, the AVANTSSAR platform does not report any attack on the specification with respect to the goal defined in Sect. 5.1. This result is straightforward since the attacker does not receives any message and there is no interactions over network between various entities.

As we are considering a CPS, an attacker who could have physical access to the system could most likely find a number of ways to overflow the tank. Being in close proximity of the CPS could give to the attacker an advantage with respect to a cyber-attacker who can only access the system through the network. For example, an attacker could manually operates the valves to increase the level of the water in the tank and burst the tank. In this perspective, it is fair to assume that there are some attacker properties, e.g., distance, that can be exploited by an attacker to perform some actions (or even attacks) that leads to some physical consequences in the CPS. As a simple motivating example, the following rule has been added to the specification (as a Horn clause as discussed in Sect. 5).

$$\frac{DYProp(distance, physical\_access) \land C(status, open) \in Sys \land C(operate, manual) \in Sys}{C(status, close) \in Sys}$$

The clause states that whenever the attacker has physical access to the CPS, he can close any valve which can be manually operated. We also modeled the opening of a valve.

When we run the AVANTSSAR platform searching for a state of the system in which the level of the water in the tank has reached the upper threshold $overT$ (defined as a goal), we (unsurprisingly) find an attack. To perform the attack, the attacker manually opens the inflow valve and closes the manual valve.

5.3   Physics-Based Interaction Use Case – A Stronger Attacker

This use case is a variation of the one in Sect. 5.2, where we add extra rules to the attacker. In particular, we have modeled that whenever the attacker has physical access to the CPS, he can physically interact with the system and heat up the water in tank (e.g., through microwave or fire).

$$\frac{DYProp(Distance, physical\_access) \quad DYProp(Tool, heating)}{C(status, heating) \in Sys} \; heat_{DY}$$

Note here that some system properties should hold, e.g., the tank should contain a liquid but for the sake of simplicity we abstract away system properties in this example.

We have modeled the corresponding physical laws and we report three examples in Fig. 7. $heat_1(C)$ and $heat_2(C)$ express the temperature and pressure increase when heating a generic component containing water respectively. $heat_3(C)$ defines the direct proportionality between temperature and pressure in the presence of water inside a component.

$$\frac{C(status,heating) \in Sys \quad C(contains,water) \in Sys \quad C(temperature,Level) \in Sys}{C(temperature,Level') \in Sys \wedge Level' > Level} \; heat_1(C)$$

$$\frac{C(status,heating) \in Sys \quad C(contains,water) \in Sys \quad C(pressure,Level) \in Sys}{C(pressure,Level') \in Sys \wedge Level' > Level} \; heat_2(C)$$

$$\frac{C(status,heating) \in Sys \quad C(contains,water) \in Sys \quad C(temperature,TLevel) \in Sys \quad C(pressure,PLevel) \in Sys}{C(temperature,TLevel') \in Sys \wedge C(pressure,PLevel') \in Sys \wedge (PLevel' > PLevel) \wedge (TLevel' > TLevel)} \; heat_3(C)$$

Fig. 7. Rules that represent physical laws in use case of Sect. 5.3

Goal. We check if the attacker can burst the tank, increasing the pressure of the tank.

$$\Box(\,Tank(pressure,\,overT) \notin Sys)$$

Security Analysis. The AVANTSSAR platform reports a violation of the goal. The two clauses $heat_2$ and $heat_{DY}$ have been used to heat the tank component and then to raise its pressure, bursting the tank.

6   Related Work

The formal verification of security properties of CPS is a non trivial task, as CPS introduce physical properties to the system under analysis. SAT/SMT solvers used by security analysis tools (e.g.,[3]) do not support such properties. In order to overcome this limitation, one could simulate the process (e.g., [2]) or adapt the level of abstraction of CPS components. In [35], the author presents a formal definition of an attacker model for CPS. The attacker is defined as a set of pairs representing locations and capabilities. Capabilities are defined as a set of tuples expressing actions, cost (energy/time) and range (with respect to the topology) of the attacker. The attacker is assumed to perform two types of attacks: *physical*, against a device and *cyber* against the communications; where the first requires physical access while the second proximity to the node. The actions of the attacker are *WSN actions* (remove, read/write, reveal, reprogram, starve) and *cyber actions* (block, eavesdrop, inject).

In [6,26], the authors present a formalization to reason on security properties of wireless networks (including a considerations of physical properties related to those networks). The authors present an attacker model as a variation of the DY attacker model. The attacker is a malicious agent of the network who cannot break cryptography. He has a fixed location, while the usual DY controls the entire network, a set of transmitters and receivers, an initial knowledge with his private/public keys which can use to create and analyze messages. The authors also consider constraints on the distance of communicating parties. An attacker can only intercept messages at his location and colluding attackers do not instantaneously exchange knowledge, they are constrained by the network topology.

7   Conclusions and Future Work

In this paper, we argued that (to the best of our knowledge) current approaches for the formal reasoning on the security of CPS do not consider most of the physical interaction between the attacker and the system. Instead, the works we reviewed only focus on the network interaction between components of a CPS, which is indeed important but not sufficient for an extensive security analysis. One of the main difficulties of considering physical interaction of the CPS is that usually this leads to the definition of the physical processes of various components of the CPS.

We proposed several basic uses cases in which the physical behavior of both the CPS and the attacker can be used to produce attacks that rely on physical actions of the attacker that are outside the normal behavior of the CPS. To alleviate that problem, we presented the idea of extending the DY attacker to a CPDY attacker model that allows to include physical-layer interaction. We implemented that CPDY model in ASlan++ and used the AVANTSSAR platform to show that our extended attacker model is indeed able to discover the physical-layer attacks in CPS.

Acknowledgments. This work was supported by the National Research Foundation of Singapore under grant NRF2014NCR-NCR001-40.

References

1. Adepu, S., Mathur, A.: An investigation into the response of a water treatment system into cyber attacks. In: IEEE Symposium on High Assurance Systems Engineering (HASE) (2015)
2. Antonioli, D., Tippenhauer, N.O., MiniCPS: a toolkit for security research on CPS networks. In: Proceedings of Workshop on Cyber-Physical Systems Security & Privay (SPC-CPS), co-located with CCS, October 2015
3. Armando, A., et al.: The AVANTSSAR platform for the automated validation of trust and security of service-oriented architectures. In: Flanagan, C., König, B. (eds.) TACAS 2012. LNCS, vol. 7214, pp. 267–282. Springer, Heidelberg (2012)
4. Armando, A., Compagna, L.: SATMC: a SAT-based model checker for security protocols. In: Alferes, J.J., Leite, J. (eds.) JELIA 2004. LNCS (LNAI), vol. 3229, pp. 730–733. Springer, Heidelberg (2004)
5. AVANTSSAR. Deliverable 5.3: AVANTSSAR Library of validated problem cases (2010). www.avantssar.eu
6. Basin, D., Capkun, S., Schaller, P., Schmidt, B.: Formal reasoning about physical properties of security protocols. Trans. Inf. Syst. Secur. (TISSEC) **14**(2), 16 (2011)
7. Basin, D., Cremers, C., Meadows, C.: Model checking security protocols. In: Handbook of Model Checking (2011)
8. Basin, D., Mödersheim, S., Viganò, L.: OFMC: a symbolic model checker for security protocols. J. Inf. Secur. **4**(3), 181–208 (2005)
9. Blanchet, B.: An efficient cryptographic protocol verifier based on prolog rules. In: Computer Security Foundation Workshop (CSFW). IEEE (2001)

10. Buchler, M., Hossen, K., Mihancea, P., Minea, M., Groz, R., Oriat, C.: Model inference and security testing in the spacios project. In: IEEE Conference on Software Maintenance, Reengineering and Reverse Engineering (CSMR-WCRE) (2014)

11. Camenisch, J., Mödersheim, S., Sommer, D.: A formal model of identity mixer. In: Kowalewski, S., Roveri, M. (eds.) FMICS 2010. LNCS, vol. 6371, pp. 198–214. Springer, Heidelberg (2010)

12. Cárdenas, A.A., Amin, S.M., Sinopoli, B., Giani, A., Perrig, A., Sastry, S.S.: Challenges for securing cyber physical systems. In: Workshop on Future Directions in Cyber-physical Systems Security. DHS, July 2009

13. Cárdenas, A.A., Roosta, T., Sastry, S.: Rethinking security properties, threat models, and the design space in sensor networks: a case study in scada systems. Ad Hoc Netw. **7**(8), 1434–1447 (2009)

14. Choi, Y.: From NuSMV to SPIN: experiences with model checking flight guidance systems. Formal Methods Syst. Des. **30**(3), 199–216 (2007)

15. Cortier, V., Delaune, S., Lafourcade, P.: A survey of algebraic properties used in cryptographic protocols. J. Comput. Secur. **14**(1), 1–43 (2006)

16. Dolev, D., Yao, A.C.: On the security of public key protocols. IEEE Trans. Inf. Theor. **29**(2), 198–207 (1983)

17. Escobar, S., Meadows, C., Meseguer, J.: Maude-NPA: cryptographic protocol analysis modulo equational properties. In: Aldini, A., Barthe, G., Gorrieri, R. (eds.) FOSAD 2009. LNCS, vol. 5705, pp. 1–50. Springer, Heidelberg (2009)

18. LeMay, E., Ford, M.D., Keefe, K., Sanders, W.H., Muehrcke, C.: Model-based security metrics using adversary view security evaluation (ADVISE). In: Proceedings of Conference on Quantitative Evaluation of Systems, QEST (2011)

19. Mathur, A., Tippenhauer, N.O.: A water treatment testbed for research and training on ICS security. In: Proceedings of Workshop on Cyber-Physical Systems for Smart Water Networks (CySWater), April 2016

20. Mo, Y., Kim, T.-H., Brancik, K., Dickinson, D., Lee, H., Perrig, A., Sinopoli, B.: Cyber-physical security of a smart grid infrastructure. Proc. IEEE **100**(1), 195–209 (2012)

21. Morris, T., Srivastava, A., Reaves, B., Gao, W., Pavurapu, K., Reddi, R.: A control system testbed to validate critical infrastructure protection concepts. J. Crit. Infrastruct. Prot. **4**(2), 88–103 (2011)

22. Reaves, B., Morris, T.: An open virtual testbed for industrial control system security research. J. Inf. Secur. **11**(4), 215–229 (2012)

23. Rocchetto, M., Ochoa, M., Torabi Dashti, M.: Model-based detection of CSRF. In: Cuppens-Boulahia, N., Cuppens, F., Jajodia, S., Abou El Kalam, A., Sans, T. (eds.) SEC 2014. IFIP AICT, vol. 428, pp. 30–43. Springer, Heidelberg (2014)

24. Rocchetto, M., Tippenhauer, N.O.: CPDY (Cyber-Physical Dolev-Yao) (2016). http://research.scy-phy.net/cpdy/

25. Rocchetto, M., Viganò, L., Volpe, M., Vedove, G.D.: Using interpolation for the verification of security protocols. In: Accorsi, R., Ranise, S. (eds.) STM 2013. LNCS, vol. 8203, pp. 99–114. Springer, Heidelberg (2013)

26. Schaller, P., Schmidt, B., Basin, D.A., Capkun, S.: Modeling and verifying physical properties of security protocols for wireless networks. In: Computer Security Foundations Symposium (CSF), pp. 109–123 (2009)

27. Schmidt, B., Sasse, R., Cremers, C., Basin, D.A.: Automated verification of group key agreement protocols. In: Symposium on Security and Privacy (S&P), pp. 179–194 (2014)

28. Schmidt, M., Lipson, H.: Distilling free-form natural laws from experimental data. Science **324**(5923), 81–85 (2009)

29. SPaCIoS. Deliverable 3.3.2: Methodology and technology forvulnerability-driven security testing (final version) (2014). http://www.spacios.eu
30. Steinmetzer, D., Schulz, M., Hollick, M.: Lockpicking physical layer key exchange: weak adversary models invite the thief. In: Proceedings of ACM Conference Wireless Security (WiSeC) (2015)
31. Taormina, R., Galelli, S., Tippenhauer, N.O., Salomons, E., Ostfeld, A.: Simulation of cyber-physical attacks on water distribution systems with EPANET. In: Proceedings of Singapore Cyber Security R&D Conference (SG-CRC), January 2016
32. Turuani, M.: The CL-Atse protocol analyser. In: Pfenning, F. (ed.) RTA 2006. LNCS, vol. 4098, pp. 277–286. Springer, Heidelberg (2006)
33. Urbina, D., Giraldo, J., Tippenhauer, N.O., Cardenas, A.: Attacking fieldbus communications in ICS: applications to the SWaT testbed. In: Proceedings of Singapore Cyber Security R&D Conference (SG-CRC), January 2016
34. Viganò, L.: The spacios project: secure provision and consumption in the internet of services. In: Software Testing, Verification and Validation (ICST), pp. 497–498. IEEE (2013)
35. Vigo, R.: The cyber-physical attacker. In: Ortmeier, F., Daniel, P. (eds.) SAFE-COMP Workshops 2012. LNCS, vol. 7613, pp. 347–356. Springer, Heidelberg (2012)
36. von Oheimb, D.: The high-level protocol specification language HLPSL developed in the EU project AVISPA. In: Proceedings of APPSEM 2005 workshop, pp. 1–17 (2005)
37. von Oheimb, D., Mödersheim, S.: ASLan++ — a formal security specification language for distributed systems. In: Aichernig, B.K., Boer, F.S., Bonsangue, M.M. (eds.) Formal Methods for Components and Objects. LNCS, vol. 6957, pp. 1–22. Springer, Heidelberg (2011)
38. Weinberger, S.: Computer security: is this the start of cyberwarfare? Nature **174**, 142–145 (2011)

Towards the Formal Verification of Data-Intensive Applications Through Metric Temporal Logic

Francesco Marconi[1], Marcello M. Bersani[1(✉)], Madalina Erascu[2], and Matteo Rossi[1]

[1] DEIB, Politecnico di Milano, Milan, Italy
{francesco.marconi,marcellomaria.bersani,matteo.rossi}@polimi.it
[2] Institute e-Austria Timisoara and West University of Timisoara, Timisoara, Romania
merascu@info.uvt.ro

Abstract. We present an approach for the automated formal verification of distributed systems based on the Storm technology. The approach is based on a formal model of the behavior of Storm topologies given in terms of the CLTLoc metric temporal logic extended with counters. We present a tool-supported mechanism to automatically generate formal models from high-level description of Storm topologies. The Zot formal verification tool is then used to check whether some desired properties hold for the modeled system or not. The analyzed properties concern the growth of the queues of the nodes of the Storm topology. Some experiments performed on example topologies show how the timing features of the modeled system influence the behavior of the queues of the nodes.

Keywords: Data-intensive applications · Distributed systems · Formal verification · Storm technology · Metric temporal logic

1 Introduction

Big Data is a prominent area, involving both academia and industry, researching innovative solutions to support the entire life-cycle (from design to deployment) of so-called data-intensive applications (DIAs), which are able to process huge amounts of information. Hence, defining frameworks for the development of DIAs that leverage Big Data technologies is nowadays of major importance.

The DICE project [9] defines techniques and tools for the data-aware quality-driven development of DIAs. In the DICE approach, designers model DIAs through UML diagrams tagged with suitable annotations capturing the features of Big Data applications, and in particular their *topology*. A topology provides an abstract representation of a DIA through directed graphs, where nodes are of two kinds: *computational nodes* implement the logic of the application by elaborating information and producing an outcome, whereas *input nodes* bring information into the application from the environment.

© Springer International Publishing AG 2016
K. Ogata et al. (Eds.): ICFEM 2016, LNCS 10009, pp. 193–209, 2016.
DOI: 10.1007/978-3-319-47846-3_13

The semantics underlying the topology typically changes depending on the target Big Data technology. In this paper we focus on the Apache Storm [1] technology—in which computational nodes are called *bolts*, and input nodes are called *spouts*—a framework which is widely used in applications that need reliable processing of unbounded streams of data, e.g. Groupon (www.groupon.com), The Weather Channel (www.weather.com), Spotify (www.spotify.com), etc. In Apache Storm applications, one of the key concerns is that time-related parameters such as emission rates of data do not induce an excessive load on the topology by accumulating data in nodes' queues. The latest version of the framework offers options to adapt these parameters at runtime (e.g., by slowing down the input nodes) to mitigate the issue, but this might negatively and unpredictably impact other features of the application. Hence, one would like to design the topology from the beginning in a way that run-time adaptation is not necessary.

In this paper, we approach such design with three contributions.

We define a formal model of DIAs based on the Storm technology. This model, which we call the *timed counter networks* model, is expressed through the Constraint LTL over clocks (CLTLoc) [7] metric temporal logic enriched with positive counters. CLTLoc allows users to express time delays, and the addition of positive counters allows for the description of memory usage issues such the evolution of the length of nodes' queues.

We allow for the automated verification of such formal models through the **D-VerT** (DICE Verification Tool) prototype tool. By performing formal verification tasks through **D-VerT**, designers can detect bad configurations producing undesired consequences, such as data processing delays causing an unbounded use of memory.

We define sufficient conditions for guaranteeing the soundness of the verification results obtained through **D-VerT**. In fact, the extension of CLTLoc with unbounded counters makes the logic undecidable in general, so we must guarantee that the conditions and abstractions introduced to make the verification technique applicable in practice do not generate spurious results.

The rest of the paper is structured as follows. Section 2 presents some related works and Sect. 3 gives an overview of the Apache Storm technology. Section 4 introduces CLTLoc extended with counters, and a sufficient condition guaranteeing the soundness of its satisfiability checking procedure. Section 5 introduces the formal model of Storm topologies, and Sect. 6 describes some experimental results carried out with the **D-VerT** tool. Section 7 concludes.

2   Related Works

Formal verification of distributed systems has been the focus of several decades of software engineering research. Challenging tasks in this context are: (i) finding the right abstraction for the formal model of the real world (*formalization*); (ii) developing techniques to prove the correctness of the modeled systems (*verification*); and (iii) bridging the gap between formalization and verification, since the formal model is often too complex to be tackled by the verification methods. Various approaches exist for the formalization of distributed systems; however, to the best of our knowledge none focuses on Storm-like streaming technologies.

Timed counter networks, the novel model of Storm topologies introduced in this paper, are inspired from *vector addition systems with states* (VASS) [14] and Timed Petri Nets [13]. VASS are a subclass of *counter systems*; that is, they are finite-state automata augmented with counters, whose values are non-negative integers, and which can be incremented and decremented. VASS are also equivalent to Petri nets for decision problems such as boundedness, covering and reachability [15]. Since distributed systems have unreliable communication, timed counter networks are also similar to lossy VASS [8], an abstraction of FIFO-channel systems, when only the number of messages is relevant, but not their ordering. Unlike (lossy) VASS, timed counter networks can express timing constraints along system executions through the notion of clocks.

Timed counter networks are inherently non-deterministic, and their behavior is effectively captured through formalisms such as the counter-augmented CLT-Loc. At first glance they also seem expressible in terms of formalisms such as Timed Petri Nets (TPN) [13]. However, CLTLoc is more suitable to this end because, typically, TPN-based models adopt, both in theory and in practice, an *urgent* semantics for the firing of transitions [4], where an enabled transition *must* fire when it reaches its upper time bound if it is not disabled earlier. This makes modeling the *possible* occurrence of events in timed counter networks (e.g., failures in Storm topologies) less natural. Moreover, the typical semantics of the firings of transitions in TPNs does not allow for the modeling of a policy such as the following: *dequeuing always removes the maximum number of available elements in the queue, but never more than k elements at the same time*. The model in Sect. 5, instead, makes use of this abstraction to represent the behavior of a node when it extracts new elements from its queue to process them.

Concerning formal verification issues, the reachability problem is decidable for lossy unbounded FIFO-channel models [3,12] which implies the decidability of the verification problem of safety properties for lossy VASS. To the best of our knowledge, lossy VASS have been investigated only from a theoretical point of view, and no verification tools handling them currently exist.

3 Overview of Apache Storm

Apache Storm [1] is a stream processing system that allows parallel, distributed, real-time processing of large-scale streaming data on horizontally scalable systems.

The key concepts in Storm applications are *streams* and *topologies*. Streams are infinite sequences of tuples that are processed by the application. Topologies are directed graphs of computation, whose nodes correspond to the operations performed over the data flowing through the application, and whose edges indicate how such operations are combined, i.e., the streaming paths between nodes.

There are two kinds of nodes, *spouts* and *bolts* (in the following also referred to as *topology components*). Spouts are stream sources. They generally get data

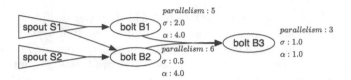

Fig. 1. Example of storm topology. Parameters σ and α are described in Sec. 5.

from external systems such as queuing brokers (e.g., Kafka, RabbitMQ, Kestrel) or from other data sources, e.g., Twitter Streaming APIs. Bolts apply transformations over the incoming data streams and generate new output streams to be processed by the connected bolts. When a topology component generates new data into an output stream, it is said to *emit* tuples. Connections are defined at design time by the subscription of the bolts to other spouts or bolts. Figure 1 shows an example of Storm topology that will be used in Sect. 6.

Spouts can be reliable or unreliable. The former keep track of all the tuples they emit, and if one of them fails to be processed by the entire topology within a certain timeout, then the spout re-emits it into the topology. The latter, instead, always emit each tuple only once, without checking for successful processing. Single bolts usually perform simple operations, such as filtering, join, functions, database interaction, which are combined in the topology to apply more complex transformations. IRichBolt and IRichSpout are the main Java interfaces to use for implementing the components of a topology. `execute()` is the method of IRichBolt defining the functionality of bolts; it reads the input tuples, processes the data, and emits (via the `emit()` method) the transformed tuples on the output streams. When the spouts are reliable, bolts have to acknowledge the successful or failed processing of each tuple at the end of the execution.

The Storm runtime is designed to leverage the computational power of distributed clusters. At a high level, its architecture is composed of one *master node*, and several *worker nodes*. One or more *worker processes* can be instantiated on a worker node, each of them executing different parts of the same topology. Each worker process runs a JVM where one or more *executors* (i.e. threads) are spawned. Executors can run one or more *tasks* which, in turn, can execute a spout or a bolt. The configuration of the topology defines the number of worker processes and, for each component (spout or bolt), the number of executors running it in parallel (the value of *parallelism* in Fig. 1) and the total number of tasks over those executors. Since each executor corresponds to a single thread, multiple tasks run serially on the same executor. However, each executor usually runs exactly one task (default option). Intra-worker and inter-worker communications are managed through queues. Each executor has its own input queue and output queue. Tuples are read from the input queue and processed by the thread handling the spout/bolt logic; they are emitted on the outgoing queue and then are moved to the parent worker's transfer queue by a send thread.

4 Constraint LTL over Clocks with Counters

The temporal logic model of Sect. 5 is expressed in terms of the CLTLoc logic [7] enriched with discrete unbounded counters, an extension of LTL allowing arithmetical variables to occur in atomic formulae and be incremented or decremented by an integer value. The decision procedure for determining whether a CLTLoc formula with counters is satisfiable or not is at the basis of the prototype tool used in Sect. 6 to formally verify Storm topologies. In this section we define the logic and we provide a method to check the soundness of the outcome of the satisfiability procedure for the defined logic when a trace is returned. The assessment is partial, in the sense that if the produced trace does not pass the soundness check, then nothing can be said of the satisfiability of the formula until a model passing the check is found.

The logic allows for two kinds of atomic formulae. Atomic formulae over $(\mathbb{R}, \{<, =\})$ contain arithmetical variables which behave as clocks of Timed Automata [13]. For instance, a possible atomic formula over clock x is $x < 4$, where $x \in \mathbb{R}$. Atomic formulae over $(\mathbb{N}, \{<, =\}, +, 0, 1)$ predicate over arithmetical variables that have no semantic restrictions. For instance, an atomic formula of this second kind is $y + z < 4$, where both y and z are in $\mathbb{N}$.

A clock x measures the time elapsed since the last "reset" of x, which occurs when $x = 0$. Since the values of clocks can be compared with constants in constraints of the form $x \sim c$ (where $c \in \mathbb{N}$ and $\sim \in \{<, =\}$), clocks are used to constrain the time elapsing between relevant events of topologies. A counter y, instead, stores a value that can be incremented, decremented and tested against a constant value. We use counters to represent the size of bolts' queues. We also exploit the modality X applied to integer variables, introduced in [10]: if y is an integer variable, term Xy represents the value of y in the next position of time.

Let V be a finite set of variables over $\mathbb{N}$. Atomic formulae θ over V are quantifier-free Presburger formulae over terms α of the form y or Xy, with $y \in V$.

Then, if C is a finite set of clock variables over $\mathbb{R}$, and AP is a finite set of atomic propositions, CLTLoc formulae with counters are defined as follows:

$$\phi := p \mid x \sim c \mid \theta \mid \phi \wedge \phi \mid \neg\phi \mid \mathbf{X}\phi \mid \mathbf{Y}\phi \mid \phi\mathbf{U}\phi \mid \phi\mathbf{S}\phi$$

where $p \in AP$, $x \in C$, $c \in \mathbb{N}$, $\sim \in \{<, =\}$, and $\mathbf{X}$, $\mathbf{Y}$, $\mathbf{U}$ and $\mathbf{S}$ are the usual "next", "previous", "until" and "since" operators of LTL [13].

An *interpretation* of a formula is a pair (π, σ), where $\pi : \mathbb{N} \to \wp(AP)$, and $\sigma : \mathbb{N} \times \{C \cup V\} \to \mathbb{R}$ is a mapping associating every variable in $C \cup V$ with a value in $\mathbb{R}$, but restricting values of the elements in V to $\mathbb{N}$. The semantics of CLTLoc is defined as for LTL, except for formulae $x \sim c$ and θ. Let A_V be the ordered set of all terms of the form y and Xy, with $y \in V$, and let $n-1$ be its cardinality; for each $\alpha_j \in A_V$, its depth $|\alpha_j|$ is such that $|\alpha_j| = 0$ if $\alpha_j = y$, and $|\alpha_j| = 1$ if $\alpha_i = Xy$ for some $y \in V$. Given a mapping $v : A_V \to \mathbb{N}$, $\theta[v(\alpha_0), \ldots, v(\alpha_{n-1})]$ is the valuation of θ through v, which is obtained by replacing each term α_j occurring in θ with value $v(\alpha_j)$. If $\theta[v(\alpha_0), \ldots, v(\alpha_{n-1})]$ is true we write $v \models \theta$. Let $t(\alpha_j) = y$ if α_j is either y or Xy. The following holds for each $i \in \mathbb{N}$, where the underlying assignment v is such that $v(\alpha_j) = \sigma(i + |\alpha_j|, t(\alpha_j))$:

$$(\pi, \sigma), i \models x \sim c \text{ iff } \sigma(i, x) \sim c$$
$$(\pi, \sigma), i \models \theta \qquad \text{iff } \theta[\sigma(i + |\alpha_0|, t(\alpha_0)), \ldots, \sigma(i + |\alpha_{n-1}|, t(\alpha_{n-1}))]$$

If ϕ is a formula, interpretation (π, σ) is a *model* for ϕ if $(\pi, \sigma), 0 \models \phi$ holds.

The satisfiability problem for CLTL and CLTLoc is decidable [7,10] and can be practically computed through the Bounded Satisfiability Checking (BSC) technique [6,7]. In general, a BSC decision procedure, given a formula ϕ, looks for an ultimately periodic model of ϕ of the form $\alpha(s\beta)^\omega$, where $|\alpha s\beta| = k$. To achieve this, it looks to build a bounded structure of the form $\alpha s\beta s$, i.e., where a state s is repeated. In the case of LTL formulae, a state corresponds to a set of subformulae of ϕ. For CLTL (resp., CLTLoc) formulae, a state includes also arithmetic constraints capturing the relationships among variables (resp., clocks), even those that do not appear explicitly in the formula as atomic formulae. For these logics it is guaranteed that, when the decision procedure finds a structure of the form $\alpha s\beta s$ for formula ϕ, this can be extended to an infinite model of the form $\alpha(s\beta)^\omega$. These results, however, cannot be extended to CLT-Loc augmented with counters, since the logic is in general undecidable, as it contains CLTL over quantifier-free Presburger formulae [11], i.e., the absence of ultimately periodic models for a formula does not entail its unsatisfiability.

As a consequence, we pursue a limited approach that stems from the analysis of the shape of the formulae defining the semantics of Sect. 5, which is still meaningful to discover possible dangerous executions of a Storm topology, i.e., those originated from a periodic behavior of its abstract model and representing undesired executions of running topologies (see Sect. 6). More precisely, we adapt the techniques developed in [6,7] into a procedure that, given a CLTLoc formula with counters and a bound k, tries to build a suitable structure $\alpha s\beta s$, with $|\alpha s\beta| = k$ and: (i) if no such structure is found, it concludes that no ultimately periodic models of length smaller than k exist; (ii) if a structure is found, it performs a check to determine whether the structure can be extended to an infinite model $\alpha(s\beta)^\omega$ and, if the check succeeds, it returns $\alpha s\beta$ as representative of the infinite model. If the check fails, the result is inconclusive, and a new structure must be looked for.

First of all, we remark that, since clocks and counters cannot be compared against each other, we can deal with them separately. In particular, the extend-ability *ad infinitum* of the assignments of values to clocks is guaranteed through the results of [7]. In the rest of this section, we outline a sufficient condition for extending *ad infinitum* a bounded assignment of values to counters.

In [6,10] the key abstraction that allows us to deal with the fact that variables have infinite domains is the notion of *symbolic valuation*, which captures the relationships between the values of the variables in a symbolic way. For example, if x, y, z are the variables appearing in formula ϕ, an example of symbolic valuation is the set of formulae $\{x < y, y < z, x < z\}$. In fact, symbolic valuations take into account also the fact that a CLTL formula can relate the values of variables at different time instants through the X operator. For example, if

$x, \mathrm{X}y$ are the terms appearing in formula ϕ, an example of symbolic valuation is $\{x < y, x = \mathrm{X}x, \mathrm{X}x < y, \mathrm{X}x < \mathrm{X}y, y < \mathrm{X}y\}$. Notice that a symbolic valuation can contain formulae (and even terms) that do not appear explicitly in ϕ, such as $x = \mathrm{X}x$ in the previous example, in order to provide a complete picture of the relationships among variables over a sufficient horizon. Since in CLTLoc with counters we allow for richer constraints on variables (e.g., we can write formulae such as $\mathrm{X}x = 2x + y$), we cannot exhaustively capture the relationships among possible terms. Hence, we introduce the notion of *partial symbolic valuation* (p.s.v.). More precisely, given a formula ϕ such that Θ_ϕ is the set of all its atomic formulae over counters, its set of *partial symbolic valuations* pSV_ϕ is simply $\wp(\Theta_\phi)$. For example, if $\Theta_\phi = \{x < y, \mathrm{X}x = y + z, \mathrm{X}y < x + \mathrm{X}z\}$, an example of partial symbolic valuation is set $\{x < y, \mathrm{X}x = y + z\}$. Given a p.s.v. ρ_i, it *symbolically satisfies* an atomic formula θ iff $\theta \in \rho_i$, in which case we write $\rho_i \models_{psv} \theta$. We can extend the notion of symbolic satisfaction to sequences of p.s.v.'s and CLTLoc formulae with counters in a straightforward way; for example, if $\rho = \rho_0 \rho_1 \dots$ is a sequence of p.s.v.'s, $\rho, 0 \models_{psv} \mathrm{X}(\mathrm{X}x = y + z)$ iff $\rho_1 \models_{psv} \mathrm{X}x = y + z$. In addition, given a set A_V of terms, a mapping $v : A_V \to \mathbb{N}$, and a p.s.v. ρ_i, we say that v satisfies ρ_i, written $v \models \rho_i$ iff for each $\theta \in \rho_i$ it holds that $v \models \theta$. Notice that, given a mapping v and a set of formulae Θ_ϕ, v induces a maximal p.s.v., which is simply the set of all $\theta \in \Theta_\phi$ such that $v \models \theta$.

The goal of our decision procedure is, given a formula ϕ, to find a bounded sequence $\sigma_k : [0, k] \times V \to \mathbb{N}$ of assignments to variables—which in turn corresponds to a sequence of mappings $v_0 v_1 \dots v_{k-1}$ such that $v_i(y) = \sigma(i, y)$ and $v_i(\mathrm{X}y) = \sigma(i+1, y)$ for all $y, \mathrm{X}y \in A_V$—such that, if $\rho_0 \rho_1 \dots \rho_{k-1}$ is the sequence of maximal p.s.v.'s induced by $v_0 v_1 \dots v_{k-1}$: (i) there is $0 \le l < k$ such that $\rho_0 \dots \rho_{l-1} (\rho_l \dots \rho_{k-1})^\omega, 0 \models_{psv} \phi$; (ii) σ_k can be extended to an infinite sequence of assignments $\sigma : \mathbb{N} \times V \to \mathbb{N}$, whose corresponding sequence of mappings $v_0 v_1 \dots$ is such that, for all $i \ge k$, it holds that $v_i \models \rho_{l+(i-k) \mod (k-l)}$.

This corresponds to finding a bounded sequence $\sigma_{k+1} : [0, k+1] \times V \to \mathbb{N}$, whose induced sequence of maximal p.s.v.'s $\rho_0 \rho_1 \dots \rho_k$ is such that $\rho_k = \rho_l$, and all subformulae of ϕ that hold at position l also hold at position k. In addition, as sufficient condition for the finite sequence of assignments to be extendable to an infinite one, we require that in the loop the evolution of each variable $y \in V$ has the same shape, as exemplified in Fig. 2. This entails that, for example, in the second iteration the value of y is the same as in the first iteration, plus the offset between the value of y in the first positions of the two iterations, represented as Δ_y in Fig. 2. Notice that, for the loop to be repeated *ad infinitum* with the same shape, Δ_y cannot be negative, since $y \in \mathbb{N}$.

For a bounded sequence σ_{k+1} to be extendable we check that, for each position i inside the loop (i.e., such that $l \le i < k$), for each successive iteration n, with $n > 0$, for each $y \in V$, each atomic formula θ of ϕ has the same value whether y is $\sigma_{k+1}(i, y)$ or $\sigma_{k+1}(i, y) + n\Delta_y$ (for example, if $\theta = y > 3$, $\sigma_{k+1}(i, y) = 5$, and $\Delta_y = 2$, both $\sigma_{k+1}(i, y) > 3$ and $\sigma_{k+1}(i, y) + n\Delta_y > 3$ hold).

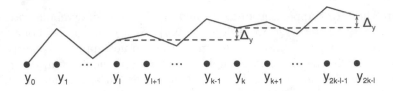

Fig. 2. Example of repeated shape for the evolution of variable y.

To perform the check, we ask whether Presburger formula (1) is satisfiable.

$$\forall n \begin{pmatrix} n > 0 \Rightarrow \\ \bigwedge_{\substack{l \leq i < k \\ \theta \in \Theta_\phi}} \begin{pmatrix} \theta[\sigma_{k+1}(i, y_1), \sigma_{k+1}(i+1, y_1), \ldots, \sigma_{k+1}(i, y_m), \sigma_{k+1}(i+1, y_m)] \\ \Leftrightarrow \\ \theta[\sigma_{k+1}(i, y_1) + n\Delta_{y_1}, \ldots, \sigma_{k+1}(i+1, y_m) + n\Delta_{y_m}] \end{pmatrix} \end{pmatrix} \tag{1}$$

In Formula (1), the set of variables V is $\{y_1, \ldots, y_m\}$; the terms $\sigma_{k+1}(i, y_j)$ are constants defined by the sequence of assignments σ_{k+1} to check; $\theta[\sigma_{k+1}(i, y_1), \sigma_{k+1}(i+1, y_1), \ldots, \sigma_{k+1}(i, y_m), \sigma_{k+1}(i+1, y_m)]$ (resp. $\theta[\sigma_{k+1}(i, y_1) + n\Delta_{y_1}, \ldots, \sigma_{k+1}(i+1, y_m) + n\Delta_{y_m}]$) is the value of atomic formula θ when each term of the set A_V is replaced by its assigned value, where $A_V = \{y_1, Xy_1, \ldots, y_m, Xy_m\}$; and for each $y_j \in V$, $\Delta_{y_j} = \sigma_{k+1}(k, y_j) - \sigma_{k+1}(l, y_j)$. As mentioned above, if Formula (1) is false, then we cannot conclude that σ_{k+1} can be extended to an infinite model, nor that formula ϕ admits a model.

5   Formal Model of Storm Topologies

This section describes the CLTLoc (with counters)-based model of Storm topologies. We first outline the chosen abstraction level and assumptions and then we introduce the temporal logic model of each component. The model focuses on the behavior of the queues of the bolts of Storm topologies. It describes how the timing parameters of the topology, such as the delays with which tuples are input to the topology by spouts and the processing time of tuples for each bolt, affect the accumulation of tuples in the queues. We use clocks to capture timing features and counters to describe the evolution of the size of the queues.

Although the model refers to Storm topologies, for example in the assumptions made, it essentially consists of a set of nodes processing and exchanging information—more precisely, tuples—and storing incoming data in queues, formalized through counters. For this reason, we call this model an example of *timed counter network*, an abstraction for the behavior of Storm-like topologies.

The formal model allows for the definition of topologies in a compositional way, similarly to how topologies are created by code developers. We formalized the behavior of the relevant features and parameters of spouts and bolts by reverse-engineering the IRichSpout and IRichBolt interfaces and we used them as building blocks for creating topologies, under the following assumptions:

- Deployment details, such as the number of worker nodes and the features of the (possibly) underlying cluster are abstracted away; topologies are assumed to run on a single worker process and each executor runs a single task, which is the default configuration of the runtime, as described at the end of Sect. 3.
- Each bolt has a single receive queue for all its parallel instances and no sending queue, while the workers' queues are not represented, since we assume to be in a single-worker scenario. For generality, all queues have unbounded size.
- We do not detail the contents of tuples, but only their quantities, since we measure the size of queues by the number of tuples they contain.
- The external sources of information from which spouts pull data are not explicitly represented, since they are outside of the perimeter of the application. Then, spouts are sources of tuples, so their queues are not represented.
- For each component, the duration of each operation or the permanence in a given state has a minimum and a maximum time.

A Storm topology is a directed graph $\mathbf{G} = \{\mathbf{N}, Sub\}$ where the set of nodes $\mathbf{N} = \mathbf{S} \bigcup \mathbf{B}$ includes in the sets of spouts ($\mathbf{S}$) and bolts ($\mathbf{B}$), and $Sub \subset \mathbf{B} \times \mathbf{N}$ captures the subscription relation defining how the nodes are connected to one another. If it holds that $(i, j) \in Sub$, this indicates that "bolt i subscribes to the streams emitted by spout/bolt j".

The behavior of both spouts and bolts can be illustrated by means of finite state automata (see Fig. 3). Spouts can be either emitting tuples or idle, therefore the corresponding automaton only has two states, *idle* and *emit*. Different emit actions (whose occurrence is captured by the system being in the *emit* state) can happen consecutively; also, the spout can be in the *idle* state for consecutive time instants. The possible execution sequences are determined by the timing constraints, as discussed in detail later. A bolt can alternatively be processing tuples, idle or in a failure state. The *process* macro-state is composed of three states, namely *take*, *execute* and *emit*. If a bolt is idle and its queue is not empty, it eventually reads tuples from the queue, performing an instantaneous *take* action, that is captured by the *take* state of the related finite state automaton. Immediately after a *take*, each bolt starts processing the tuples, an operation which lasts α time units, with α a parameter of the bolt, a positive real value which represents the amount of time that a bolt requires to process one tuple. This corresponds to the state *execute* in the automaton. Once the execution is completed, the bolt emits output tuples. This instantaneous action corresponds to the *emit* state. Bolts may fail and failures may occur at any moment; upon

(a)   (b)

Fig. 3. Finite state automata describing the states of spout (a) and bolt (b).

a bolt failure, the system goes to the *fail* state and all tuples stored, at that moment, in the queue of the failed bolt are lost, or replayed in case of a reliable topology. If no failure occurs, after an *emit* a bolt goes to *idle*, where it stays until it reads new tuples. Spout failures are not modeled; their effect is irrelevant for the growth analysis of bolt queues as they would reduce the workload on the topology. Hence, our approach focuses only on the analysis of topologies processing a full workload, i.e., where spouts never fail.

We model the behavior of Storm topologies through a set of formulae of CLTLoc with counters. We refer to this logic-based model as *timed counter network*. We break this model down in four parts: (i) the evolution of the state of the nodes; (ii) the behavior of the counters (i.e., the queues); (iii) timing constraints; (iv) failures. We present here only some highlights of the model, whose full version can be found in [5].

State Evolution. Each state is described through a combination of propositional variables. For example, a bolt j is in the macro-state *process* when process_j holds. In addition, it is in *take* (resp. *emit*) state when take_j (resp., emit_j) holds. The *execute* state, instead, corresponds to the configuration where process_j is true while both take_j and emit_j are false. Formula (2) defines the conditions for process_j to hold.

$$\bigwedge_{j \in \mathbf{B}} \left(\text{process}_j \Rightarrow \left(\begin{matrix} \text{process}_j \, \mathbf{S} \, (\text{take}_j \vee (\text{orig} \wedge \text{process}_j)) \wedge \\ \text{process}_j \, \mathbf{U} \, (\text{emit}_j \vee \text{fail}_j) \wedge \neg \text{fail}_j \end{matrix} \right) \right) \quad (2)$$

Queue Behavior. We use $\mathbb{N}$-valued discrete counters to represent the amounts of tuples moving through the topology. Whenever a component is emitting tuples or reading from its queue, the related counters are updated according to several constraints. Every time emit_j holds for a component j, r_{emit_j} tuples are added to the queues of all bolts subscribing to j (i.e., the variables q_i representing the occupancy level of those queues are incremented by r_{emit_j}). When multiple components subscribed by a bolt emit tuples simultaneously, the increment on its queue is equal to the sum of all the tuples emitted, corresponding to the value of r_{add_j}. Dually, when take_j holds, the occupancy level q_j is decremented by r_{process_j} (number of tuples read by bolt j). Formulae (3)–(4) describe these situations. Notice that add_j holds when at least one of the components subscribed by j is emitting, whereas startFail_j is true in the first instant of a failure state.

$$\text{add}_j \wedge \neg \text{take}_j \wedge \neg \text{startFail}_j \Rightarrow (\mathbf{X} q_j = q_j + r_{\text{add}_j}) \quad (3)$$

$$\text{take}_j \Rightarrow (\mathbf{X} q_j = q_j + r_{\text{add}_j} - r_{\text{process}_j}) \quad (4)$$

The number of tuples extracted from the queue depends on the parallelism level of the bolt (i.e., the number of parallel executors as described in Sect. 3), that is represented in the model by the value of $\hat{r}_{\text{take}_j}$. When a *take* occurs, if the number of elements in the queue plus the ones being added in the current time instant is greater than $\hat{r}_{\text{take}_j}$, the variable representing the number of tuples that will be processed (r_{process_j}) is equal to $\hat{r}_{\text{take}_j}$, otherwise it is equal to $q_j + r_{\text{add}_j}$

(i.e., the bolt takes all elements from the queue). This captures how each bolt is able to concurrently process a number of tuples that is at most equal to the number of its executors.

$$(\mathtt{take}_j \wedge \hat{r}_{\mathtt{take}_j} \geq q_j + r_{\mathtt{add}_j}) \Rightarrow (r_{\mathtt{process}_j} = q_j + r_{\mathtt{add}_j}) \tag{5}$$

$$(\mathtt{take}_j \wedge \hat{r}_{\mathtt{take}_j} < q_j + r_{\mathtt{add}_j}) \Rightarrow (r_{\mathtt{process}_j} = \hat{r}_{\mathtt{take}_j}) \tag{6}$$

The number of tuples emitted by the bolt j ($r_{\mathtt{emit}_j}$) at the end of the processing phase depends on parameter σ_j (a constant in $\mathbb{R}$), representing the ratio between output and input tuples. That is, given n_{in} input tuples, the total number of output tuples is equal to $\sigma \cdot n_{in}$. The value of σ is either measured by monitoring a deployed application, or defined by making assumptions based on the kind of operation performed by the bolt. Since $r_{\mathtt{emit}_j} \in \mathbb{N}$, simply imposing $r_{\mathtt{emit}_j} = \lfloor \sigma \cdot r_{\mathtt{process}_j} \rfloor$ (resp., $r_{\mathtt{emit}_j} = \lceil \sigma \cdot r_{\mathtt{process}_j} \rceil$) may lead to excessive under- (resp., over-) approximation, especially when $0 \leq \sigma \cdot r_{\mathtt{process}} \ll 1$. For this reason we keep track of the number of tuples processed, but not leading to the emission of output tuples. This is achieved through the auxiliary variable $\mathtt{buffer}_j$, which is incremented as new tuples are correctly processed by the bolt. As formalized in Formula (7), when an *emit* occurs on bolt j, $r_{\mathtt{emit}_j}$ is equal to $\lfloor \sigma \cdot \mathtt{buffer}_j \rfloor$, and $\mathtt{buffer}_j$ is then decremented by $\lfloor \frac{r_{\mathtt{emit}_j}}{\sigma} \rfloor$. Conversely, Formula (8) defines that when the bolt is not emitting, $\mathtt{buffer}$ keeps its value until the next *emit*.

$$\bigwedge_{\substack{j \in B \\ \neg final(j)}} \left(\mathtt{emit}_j \Rightarrow \begin{pmatrix} \mathtt{buffer}_j = Y\mathtt{buffer}_j + r_{\mathtt{process}_j} & \wedge \\ r_{\mathtt{emit}_j} \leq \sigma_j \mathtt{buffer}_j & \wedge \\ r_{\mathtt{emit}_j} > \sigma_j \mathtt{buffer}_j - 1 & \wedge \\ X\mathtt{buffer}_j \geq \mathtt{buffer}_j - \frac{r_{\mathtt{emit}_j}}{\sigma} & \wedge \\ X\mathtt{buffer}_j < \mathtt{buffer}_j - \frac{r_{\mathtt{emit}_j}}{\sigma} + 1 \end{pmatrix} \right) \tag{7}$$

$$\bigwedge_{j \in B, \neg final(j)} (\neg \mathtt{emit}_j \Rightarrow (r_{\mathtt{emit}_j} = 0 \wedge (X\mathtt{buffer}_j = \mathtt{buffer}_j)\mathbf{U}X\mathtt{emit}_j)) \tag{8}$$

Notice that some of the variables appearing in Formulae (3)–(8) have infinite domains, but some range over finite domains. More precisely, variables q_j for each bolt j, $r_{\mathtt{add}_j}$ for bolts subscribing to spouts, and $r_{\mathtt{emit}_i}$ for each spout i, are infinite counters. Variables $r_{\mathtt{process}_j}$, instead, are finite counters since they have values between 0 and $\hat{r}_{\mathtt{take}_j}$. Variables $\mathtt{buffer}_j$ and $r_{\mathtt{emit}_j}$ for each bolt, as well as $r_{\mathtt{add}_j}$ for all bolts not subscribing to spout streams, are also finite counters. In fact, $\mathtt{buffer}_j$, whose behavior is defined by Formulae (7) and (8), is finite since its value is always less than $\hat{r}_{\mathtt{take}_j} + \frac{1}{\sigma} + 1$. We do not show the reasoning that allows us to conclude the finiteness of the aforementioned counters for lack of space. The finiteness of some of the counters allows us to write succinct formulae where multiplications and divisions are abbreviations for long case formulae.

Timing Constraints. To measure the time spent in each state, and to impose timing constraints between different events, for each topology component we define a set of clock variables. Specifically, the duration of adjacent mutually exclusive processing phases (such as *idle*, *process* and *fail* for a bolt, *idle* and *emit* for a spout) is measured through two clocks, as done in [7]. At each instant only one of the two clocks is relevant to measure the time spent in the current processing phase; when the next phase starts, the second clock is reset and becomes the new relevant clock, while at the same time the value of the former is tested to verify if the measured delay satisfies the desired bound. In the following, we use a shorthand t_{phase} to indicate the currently relevant clock. Formula (9) defines the conditions for resetting t_{phase} for a bolt: in the origin, when a *take* occurs, when a failure starts and when an *idle* phase starts.

$$t_{\text{phase}} = 0 \Leftrightarrow \text{orig} \vee \text{take} \vee (\text{fail} \wedge \neg \mathbf{Y}\text{fail}) \vee (\text{idle} \wedge \neg \mathbf{Y}\text{idle}) \quad (9)$$

Formula (10) imposes that when *emit* occurs, the duration of the current processing phase is between $\alpha - \epsilon$ and $\alpha + \epsilon$, where $\epsilon \ll \alpha$ is a positive constant that captures possible (small) variations in the duration of the processing.

$$\text{process} \wedge \text{emit} \Rightarrow (t_{\text{phase}} \geq \alpha - \epsilon) \wedge (t_{\text{phase}} \leq \alpha + \epsilon) \quad (10)$$

Measuring non-adjacent time intervals, such as the time between the end of a failure and the start of the next one (i.e., time to failure), can be done using a single clock, which does not need to be tested at the same time it is reset.

Failures. In our model, whenever a node fails, the tuples being processed by the node, together with the tuples in its receive queue, are considered as failed (not fully processed by the topology). According to the reliable implementation of Storm, the spout tuples that generated them must be resubmitted to the topology. Since we do not keep track of single tuples, but we only consider quantities of tuples throughout the topology, given an arbitrary amount of failed tuples we can estimate the amount of spout tuples that have to be re-emitted by the connected spouts. In order to express this relationship between the failing tuples in a specific (failing) node and the new tuples having to be re-emitted, we introduce the concept of *impact* of the node failure with respect to another (connected) node. $Imp(j, i)$ ("impact of node j failure on node i") is the coefficient expressing the ratio $\frac{tuples\_to\_be\_replayed(i)}{failed\_tuples(j)}$ where $j \in \mathbf{B}$ is the failing bolt and $i \in \{\mathbf{S} \bigcup \mathbf{B}\}$ is another node in the topology. If there exists a path $\{p_0, \ldots, p_n | n > 0, p_0 = i, p_n = j\}$ in the topology connecting the two nodes such that $\forall k \in [0, n - 1] Sub(p_k, p_{k+1})$ holds, then a failure of node j has an impact on node i and $Imp(j, i) > 0$. If such a path does not exist, then $Imp(j, i) = 0$. The procedure to obtain the values of $Imp(j, i)$ for each bolt is described in [5]. Once this coefficient is calculated for all pairs of (*bolt*, *spout*) in the topology, it allows us to determine r_{replay_i}, (i.e., the number of tuples to be re-emitted by spout i after a bolt failure) by simply multiplying the number of failed tuples by the appropriate coefficient, as $\bigwedge_{i \in \mathbf{S}} (r_{\text{replay}_i} = \sum_{j \in \mathbf{B}} r_{\text{fail}_{ji}} \cdot Imp(j, i))$, where $r_{\text{fail}_{ji}}$ expresses "the number of failed tuples in bolt j affecting spout i". This value is incremented as in Formula (11) whenever a failure starts and is reset after all the $r_{\text{fail}_{ji}} \cdot Imp(j, i)$ tuples are emitted by the spout. Interested readers can refer to [5] for the complete model.

$$\bigwedge_{i \in \mathbf{S}, j \in \mathbf{B}} (\texttt{startFail}_j \wedge \neg \texttt{emit}_i \Rightarrow X r_{\texttt{fail}_{ji}} = r_{\texttt{fail}_{ji}} + q_j + r_{\texttt{process}_j} + r_{\texttt{add}_j}) \quad (11)$$

6   Experimental Results

We present some experimental results obtained with our prototype tool **D-VerT**[1], whose architecture is described in [5]. As shown in Fig. 4, **D-VerT** takes as input the description of a Storm topology, through a suitable JSON format, and implements the model-to-model transformation which produces the corresponding instance of timed counter network representing the topology. The resulting model is fed to the Zot formal verification tool [2], which has been modified to deal with CLTLoc formulae including unbounded counters. The property is violated if a non-spurious counterexample (i.e. a run of the system violating the property) is found. In this case, Zot returns the violating trace (*SAT* result), that is processed back and displayed graphically by **D-VerT**. If the verification terminates without providing counterexamples (*UNSAT* result), then the property holds limited to ultimately periodic executions represented by a prefix $\alpha s \beta s$ of bounded length.

We consider two different topologies: a simple DIA and a more complex topology (named "focused-crawler") provided by an industrial partner within the DICE consortium. In both cases, we verify the property "*all bolt queues have a bounded occupation level*". If the property holds, then we claim that all bolts are able to process the incoming tuples in a timely manner. Otherwise, there exists a counterexample that violates (i.e., disproves) the property and that corresponds to an unwanted execution of the topology where at least one queue grows with an unbounded trend. This behavior can be expressed in the k-satisfiability problem with a formula constraining the size of the queues. Over ultimately periodic executions, defined through a k-bounded model, a queue q grows indefinitely if its size at position k is strictly greater than the size at position l. Therefore, to enforce the construction of models satisfying such a constraint, we add to the formulae defining the k-satisfiability the conjunct $\bigvee_{j \in \mathbf{B}} q_j(l) + c < q_j(k)$, where c is a non-negative constant.

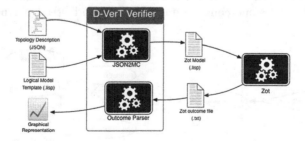

Fig. 4. D-VerT verification flow.

---

[1] github.com/dice-project/DICE-Verification.

The first use case (depicted in Fig. 1) allowed us to test some basic structures that may appear in a Storm topology, such as split and join of multiple streams. On this topology, we experimented on how modifying the parallelism level of a bolt affects its ability of processing incoming tuples. In the first analysis, run with the configuration in Fig. 1, Zot produces a trace showing that the adopted configuration leads to an unbounded increase of the queue occupation of B_2 and B_3. By changing the parallelism level of the bolts (setting it to, respectively, 8 for B_2 and 5 for B_3) we obtain a configuration showing no counterexample (up to length $k = 15$) of unbounded queue increase (timings of the two configurations – *simple-DIA-cfg-1* and *simple-DIA-cfg-2* – are reported in Table 1).

Table 1. Experimental analysis on commodity hardware (MacBook Air running MacOSX 10.11.4. with Intel i7 1.7 GHz, 8 GB 1600 MHz DDR3 RAM; SMT solver used by Zot was z3 v.4.4.1). The complete results and experimental configurations can be found at dice-project.github.io/DICE-Verification.

Topology	Bolts	Time	Max Memory	Outcome	Spurious
simple-DIA-cfg-1	3	60 s	104 MB	SAT	No
simple-DIA-cfg-2	3	1058 s	150 MB	UNSAT	N/A
focused-crawler-complete	8	2664 s	448 MB	SAT	No
focused-crawler-reduced-cfg-1	4	95 s	142 MB	SAT	No
focused-crawler-reduced-cfg-2	4	253 s	195 MB	SAT	No
focused-crawler-reduced-cfg-3	4	327 s	215 MB	SAT	No
focused-crawler-reduced-cfg-4	4	333 s	206 MB	SAT	No
focused-crawler-reduced-cfg-5	4	3184 s	317 MB	SAT	Yes
focused-crawler-reduced-cfg-6	4	1060 s	229 MB	SAT	Yes

The second use case represents a typical usage of Storm in big data applications. As part of a social network analysis framework, the topology depicted in Fig. 5 is in charge of fetching and indexing articles and multimedia items from multiple web sources. The formal analysis of the "focused-crawler" topology is motivated by some concerns raised by the industrial partner that were

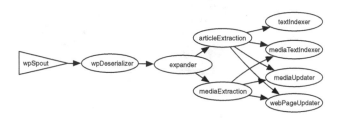

Fig. 5. "Focused-crawler" topology.

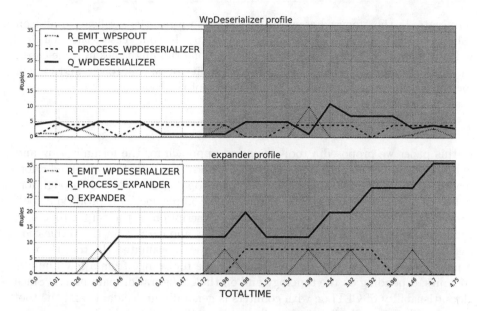

Fig. 6. D-VerT output trace of bolts *expander* and *wpDeserializer*. Black solid lines represent the number of tuples in each bolt queue over time. Dashed lines show the processing activity of the bolt, and dotted lines show the *emits* from the component upstream. Gray background highlights the suffix of the trace, that is repeated infinitely many times.

witnessed by monitoring the deployed application. After running the verification on the topology we pointed out the critical role of the *expander* bolt. Some output traces show possible system executions, even without failures, where the queue occupation level of such component is unbounded. Figure 6 shows two of the graphical output traces provided by **D-VerT** (referring to bolts *expander* and *wpDeserializer*). It can be noticed, by looking at the number of tuples in the queues (black solid lines) over time, how they both represent a periodic model in which a suffix (in gray) of a finite sequence of events is repeated infinitely many times after a prefix. After ensuring that the trace is not a spurious model, we concluded that the expander queue, having an increasing trend in the suffix, is unbounded. In order to evaluate the performance and the scalability of the tool, we carried out many experiments on the presented topologies, by varying the topology parameters and the number of bolts considered. Table 1 shows some of the time and memory consumptions statistics we collected. It can be noticed how the running time is strongly affected by both the number of bolts and their configurations, while the memory consumption is mainly correlated to the topology size (therefore, the number of formulae in the model). In the simple-DIA case study, we obtained counterexamples (*SAT* results) with very different timings depending on the configuration. The configuration leading to the *UNSAT* result, discussed previously, took considerably more time to terminate. In the "focused-crawler" case study, we ran the verification also on subsets of the topology (*focused-crawler-reduced*). In some cases, the tool provided a spurious counterexample. Despite the long running times in some cases, we think that the experiments show the feasibility of our approach, and we will focus in the future to optimizing the efficiency of the tool.

7   Conclusions and Future Work

In this paper we proposed a tool-supported approach for the formalization and automated verification of DIAs based on Storm technology. We presented a formal model of the temporal behavior of Storm topologies expressed through formulae of CLTLoc extended with counters. We implemented a prototype tool, **D-VerT**, which takes as input a high-level description of the target topology, produces the corresponding set of logic formulae, and carries out the verification task via the Zot bounded satisfiability checker. We evaluated the tool through a pair of case studies. The running times of the tool range from a few minutes to hours, depending on the topology and on the configuration parameters. Since the satisfiability of CLTLoc with counters is generally undecidable and the tool introduces some approximations to make the verification feasible in practice, we provided a procedure to determine, given a trace returned by the tool, whether this is spurious or not.

Future extensions and improvements of this work will follow several directions. In particular, we plan to: *(i)* extend the range of properties to be analyzed for the target topologies; *(ii)* pursue a finer-grained modeling approach, for example representing the internal messaging system with higher detail, to support more precise analyses; *(iii)* model other relevant technologies, such as Apache Spark and Apache Tez, by extending the current framework; *(iv)* further study the current model from a theoretical point of view, to achieve new results on the soundness and completeness of the analysis of timed counter networks.

Acknowledgment. Work supported by Horizon 2020 project no. 644869 (DICE).

References

1. Apache Storm. http://storm.apache.org/
2. The Zot bounded satisfiability checker. github.com/fm-polimi/zot
3. Abdulla, P.A., Jonsson, B.: Verifying programs with unreliable channels. In: Proceedings of LICS, pp. 160–170 (1993)
4. Bérard, B., Cassez, F., Haddad, S., Lime, D., Roux, O.H.: Comparison of the expressiveness of timed automata and time Petri nets. In: Pettersson, P., Yi, W. (eds.) FORMATS 2005. LNCS, vol. 3829, pp. 211–225. Springer, Heidelberg (2005). doi:10.1007/11603009_17
5. Bersani, M., Erascu, M., Marconi, F., Rossi, M.: DICE verification tool - initial version. Technical report, DICE Consortium (2016). www.dice-h2020.eu
6. Bersani, M.M., Frigeri, A., Morzenti, A., Pradella, M., Rossi, M., Pietro, P.S.: Constraint LTL satisfiability checking without automata. J. Appl. Log. **12**(4), 522–557 (2014)

7. Bersani, M.M., Rossi, M., San Pietro, P.: A tool for deciding the satisfiability of continuous-time metric temporal logic. Acta Informatica **53**(2), 171–206 (2016)
8. Bouajjani, A., Mayr, R.: Model checking lossy vector addition systems. In: Meinel, C., Tison, S. (eds.) STACS 1999. LNCS, vol. 1563, pp. 323–333. Springer, Heidelberg (1999). doi:10.1007/3-540-49116-3_30
9. Casale, G., Ardagna, D., Artac, M., Barbier, F., Nitto, E.D., Henry, A., Iuhasz, G., Joubert, C., Merseguer, J., Munteanu, V.I., Perez, J., Petcu, D., Rossi, M., Sheridan, C., Spais, I., Vladušič, D.: DICE: quality-driven development of data-intensive cloud applications. In: Proceedings of MiSE, pp. 78–83 (2015)
10. Demri, S., D'Souza, D.: An automata-theoretic approach to constraint LTL. Inf. Comput. **205**(3), 380–415 (2007)
11. Demri, S., Gascon, R.: The effects of bounding syntactic resources on Presburger LTL. Technical report LSV-06-5, LSV (2006)
12. Finkel, A.: Decidability of the termination problem for completely specified protocols. Distrib. Comput. **7**(3), 129–135 (1994)
13. Furia, C.A., Mandrioli, D., Morzenti, A., Rossi, M.: Modeling Time in Computing. Monographs in Theoretical Computer Science. An EATCS Series. Springer, Berlin (2012)
14. Karp, R.M., Miller, R.E.: Parallel program schemata. J. Comput. Syst. Sci. **3**(2), 147–195 (1969)
15. Reutenauer, C.: The Mathematics of Petri Nets. Masson and Prentice, Paris (1990)

Proving Event-B Models with Reusable Generic Lemmas

Alexei Iliasov, Paulius Stankaitis, and Alexander Romanovsky[✉]

Centre for Software Reliability, School of Computing Science, Newcastle University,
Newcastle upon Tyne, UK
{alexei.iliasov,paulius.stankaitis,alexander.romanovsky}@ncl.ac.uk

Abstract. Event-B is one of more popular notations for model-based, proof-driven specification. It offers a fairly high-level mathematical language based on FOL and ZF set theory and an economical yet expressive modelling notation. Model correctness is established by proving a number of conjectures constructed via a syntactic instantiation of schematic conditions. A significant part of provable conjectures requires proof hints from a user. For larger models this becomes extremely onerous as identical or similar proofs have to be repeated over and over, especially after model refactoring stages. In the paper we discuss an approach to making proofs more generic and thus less fragile and more reusable. The crux of the technique is offering an engineer an opportunity to complete a proof by positing and proving a generic lemma that may be reused in the same or even another project. To assess the technique potential we have developed a plug-in to the Rodin Platform and used it to prove a number of pre-existing Event-B models.

Keywords: Proofs · Automated theorem proving · Why3 · Rodin plug-in · Proof reusability · Schematic lemmas

1 Introduction

There was a concerted effort, funded by a succession of several EU research projects [12,15], to make Event-B [4] and its toolkit, the Rodin Platform [19], appealing and competitive in an industrial setting. One of the lessons of this mainly positive exercise is the general aversion of industrial users to interactive proof. It is possible, in principle, to learn, through experience and determination, the ways of underlying verification tools and master refinement and decomposition to minimise proof effort. The methodological implications are far more serious: building a good model is necessarily a trial and error process; one often has to start from a scratch or do considerable refactoring to produce an adequate model. This, obviously, necessitates redoing proofs and makes time spent proving dead-end efforts seem pointlessly wasted. Hence, proof-shy engineers too often do not make a good use of formal specification stage as they tend to hold on to the very first, often incoherent design.

© Springer International Publishing AG 2016
K. Ogata et al. (Eds.): ICFEM 2016, LNCS 10009, pp. 210–225, 2016.
DOI: 10.1007/978-3-319-47846-3_14

We want to change the way proofs are done, at least in an industrial setting. In place of an interactive proof - something that is inherently a one-off effort in Event-B and comparable model-based notations - we incite modellers to gradually accumulate a library of general support condition called a *schematic lemmas*. The principle here is that a fitting schematic lemma added to hypothesis set would discharge an open proof obligation. Such a lemma may not refer to any model variables or user-defined types and is, in essence, a property supporting the definition of the underlying mathematical language[1]. From our experience, a modelling project has a fairly distinctive usage of mathematical language and, we hypothesise, this leads to a distinctive set of supporting lemmas.

Since a schematic lemma does not reference model-specific variables or types it can be immediately reused in a new context and thus is a tangible and persistent outcome of a modelling effort, even an abortive one. It is not affected by model refactoring and restructuring of refinement steps. In a long term, we see schematic lemmas as a methodological tool promoting wider application of model restructuring (or even restarting from scratch) and thus helping engineers to construct better models and not feel constrained by the cost of a proof effort.

Another intriguing possibility, yet untested in practice, is that for a narrow application domain combined with tailored development patterns it is feasible to reach a point where a schematic lemma library makes modelling nearly free of interactive proofs.

The rest of the paper is organised as follows. In Sect. 2 we briefly present the Event-B modelling notation as well as its verification rules; we also introduce the Why3 plug-in that makes use of the Why3 umbrella prover [8]. Section 3 expands on the idea behind schematic lemmas and their potential role as a proof process. We present some experimental results in Sect. 4 and summarise the findings in Sect. 5.

2   Background

2.1   Event-B

Event-B [4] belongs to a family of state-based modelling languages that represent a design as a combination of state (a vector of variables) and state transformations (computations updating variables).

In general, a design in Event-B is abstract: it relies on data types and state transformations that are not directly realisable. This permits terse models abstracting away from insignificant details and enables one to capture various phenomena of a system with a varying degree of detail. Each statement about the effect of a certain computation is supported by a formal proof. In Event-B, one is able to make statements about safety (this incorporates the property of functional correctness) and progress. Safety properties ensure that a system

---

[1] There are, however, cases where the modeller's insight is critical in providing a witness or case split. These, we believe, should be handled at the specification as discussed, for instance, in [10].

never arrives at a state that is deemed unsafe (i.e., a shaft door is never open when a lift cab is on a different floor). Progress properties ensure that a system is able to achieve its operational goals (i.e., a lift cab eventually arrives).

Being a general-purpose formalism, Event-B does not attempt to fit any specific application domain. It has found applications in hardware modelling, validation of high-level use case scenarios, verification of business process logics and even as a friendly notation for a mathematician looking for a support from machine provers.

An Event-B development starts with the creation of a very abstract specification. A cornerstone of the Event-B method is the stepwise development that facilitates a gradual design of a system implementation through a number of correctness-preserving *refinement* steps. The general form of an Event-B model (or *machine*) is shown in Fig. 1. Such a model encapsulates a local state (program variables) and provides operations on the state. The actions (called *events*) are characterised by a list of local variables (parameters) vl, a state predicate g called *event guard*, and a next-state relation S called *substitution* or event *action*.

machine **M**
  sees **Context**
  variables v
  invariant $I(c, s, v)$
  initialisation $R(c, s, v')$
  events
    E_1 = any vl where $g(c, s, vl, v)$ then $S(c, s, vl, v, v')$ end
    $\cdots$
end

Fig. 1. Event-B machine structure

Event parameters and guards may be omitted leading to syntactic short-cuts starting with keywords **when** and **begin**.

Event guard g defines the condition when an event is *enabled*. Relation S is given as a generalised substitution statement [3] and is either deterministic ($x := 2$) or non-deterministic update of model variables. The latter kind comes in two notations: selection of a value from a set, written as $x :\in \{2, 3\}$; and a relational constraint on the next state v', e.g., $x :| x' \in \{2, 3\}$.

The **invariant** clause contains the properties of the system, expressed as state predicates, that must be preserved during system execution. These define the *safe states* of a system. In order for a model to be consistent, invariant preservation is formally demonstrated. Data types, constants and relevant axioms are defined in a separate component called *context*.

Model correctness is demonstrated by generating and discharging *proof obligations* - theorems in the first-order logic. There are proof obligations for model consistency and for a refinement link - the forward simulation relation - between the pair of *abstract* and *concrete* models.

More details on Event-B, its semantics, method and applications may be found in [4] and also on the Event-B community website [1]. A concise discussion of the Event-B proof obligations is given in [9].

2.2 Why3 Plug-In

Development in Event-B is supported by the Rodin Platform [1] that has been under active development since 2005. It has been long recognised that the Rodin Platform may significantly benefit from an interface between Event-B and TPTP [20] provers. To simplify translation we decided to use the Why3 [8] umbrella prover that offers a single and quite palatable input notation and also supports SMT-LIB compliant provers. Why3 supports 16 external automatic provers (not counting different versions of the same tool), these include all the state-of-the-art tools like Z3 [5], SPASS [25], Vampire [22] and Alt-Ergo [14].

Given that provers are CPU and memory intensive and there is a great potential for exploiting parallel processing, from the outset we were aiming at a provers-as-a-service cloud architecture. Indeed, running a collection of (distinct) provers on the same conjecture is a trivial and fairly effective way to speed up proofs given plentiful resources. Usability perception of interactive modelling methods such as Event-B is sensitive to peak performance when a burst of activity (new invariant) is followed by a relatively long period of idling (modeller thinking and entering model). The cloud paradigm, where only the actual CPU time is rented, seems well suited to such scenario. Also, the cloud's feature of scalability plays a critical role in this situation.

A plug-in to the Rodin Platform was realised [16] to map between the Event-B mathematical language and the Why3 *theory* input notation (we do not make use of its other part - a modelling language notation). The syntactic part of the translation is trivial: just one Tom/Java class mapping between Event-B and Why3 operators. The bulk of the effort is in the axioms and lemmas defining the properties of the numerous Event-B set-theoretic constructs. We have a working prototype able to discharge (via provers like SPASS and Alt-Ergo) a number of properties that previously required interactive proof. At the same time, we realise that axiomatisation of a complex mathematical language like the one of Event-B is likely to be an ever open problem. It is apparent that different provers prefer differing styles of operator definitions: some perform better with an inductive style (i.e., to define set cardinality one may say that the size of an empty set is zero, adding one element to a set increases its size by one) while others prefer regress to already known concepts (there exists a bijection such that ...). Since we do not know how to define one best axiomatization, even for any one given prover, we offer an open translator with which a user may define, with as many cross-checks as practically reasonable, a custom embedding of Event-B into the Why3.

The Why3 theory library we have developed in the support of the axiomatisation of the Event-B mathematical language does not appear optimal yet. For most cases the Why3 plug-in performs on a par with or better than the SMT plug-in [21] although it takes longer while using more provers at the back-end.

With one model (of a train control system), we had a disappointing result of 32 undischarged proof obligations with the Why3 plug-in against 5 left undischarged by the SMT plug-in.

3   Schematic Lemmas

There is a number of circumstances when existing interactive proofs become invalidated and a new version of an undischarged proof obligation appears.

On rare occasions a model or its sizeable part are changed significantly so that there is no or little connection between old and new proof obligations. Far more common are incremental changes that alter the goal, set of hypotheses, identifier names or types. During the refactoring of a refinement tree it is very common to lose a large proportion of manual proofs.

While there is a potential to improve the way the Rodin Platform handles interactive proofs, the fragility of such proofs has mainly to do with their nature. Unlike more traditional theorems and lemmas found in maths textbooks, model proof obligations have no meaning outside of the very narrow model context. And since Event-B relies on syntactic proof rules for invariant and refinement checks, even fairly superficial syntactic changes would result in new proof obligations which are, in fact, if not logically equivalent are often quite similar to the deleted ones.

Even in the case of a significant model change, it is, in our experience, likely that proof obligations similar to those requiring an interactive proof re-appear. In addition, there is a large number of essentially identical interactive proofs re-appearing in different projects due to specific weaknesses in the underlying automatic provers.

The key to our approach is understanding what 'similar' means in the relation to some two proof obligations. One interpretation is that similar conditions can be discharged by the same proof scripts. To make it practical, this has to be relaxed with some form of a proof script template [24]. The interpretation we take in this work is that two proof obligations are similar if they both can be discharged by adding same schematic lemma to the set of their hypotheses. This definition is rather intricately linked with the capabilities of underlying automated provers: adding a tautology (a proven lemma) to hypotheses does not change a conjecture but it might help to guide an automated prover to successful proof completion.

It is our experience that the existing the Rodin automatic provers do not benefit from adding a schematic lemma (with instantiated type variables, to make it first order) to hypotheses and they still need to be instantiated manually by manually by an engineer to have any effect. However, in the case of the Why3 plug-in, with which this approach has a close integration, it is different: a fitting schematic lemma in hypotheses makes proof nearly instantaneous.

There are situations when the only viable way to complete a proof is by providing a proof hint. One such case - refinement of event parameters - is adequately addressed at the modelling notation level where a user is requested to provide a witness as a part of a specification. There are proposals to generalise this, for the majority of situations, and define hints at the model level [10].

A schematic lemma considered on its own is of a little use. But if a proof obligation can be proven by adding a schematic lemma, then the construction of a schematic lemma in itself a proof process. As a simple illustration, consider the following (trivial) conjecture:

$$library \in \text{BOOKS} \to \mathbb{N}$$
$$b \in \text{BOOKS} \land c \in \mathbb{N}$$
$$\dots$$
$$\vdash$$
$$library \mathbin{\lhd\!\!\!-} \{b \mapsto c\} \in \text{BOOKS} \to \mathbb{N}$$

And suppose there were no automated prover capable of discharge it. It is clear that the crux of the statement is in the interaction of functional override, totality and functionality. The above can be rewritten as

$$f \in A \to B$$
$$\vdash$$
$$\forall x, y \cdot x \in A \land y \in B \Rightarrow f \mathbin{\lhd\!\!\!-} \{x \mapsto y\} \in A \to B$$

Since the Event-B mathematical language does not have type variables such a condition may only be defined either for specific A's and B's, or, in a slightly altered form, using the Theory plug-in [6]. But to discharge the original proof obligation one still needs to find this lemma and instantiates it. It is a tedious and error-prone process for a human but a fairly trivial task for a certain kind of automated provers.

The example above is quite generic in the sense it is potentially useful for in many other contexts. At times a schematic lemma need to be fairly concrete (see examples in Sect. 4. It is also easier to write a lemma that narrowly targets a proof obligation. This distinction between 'general' and 'specific' is, at the moment, completely subjective and relies on the modeller's intuition. To reflect the fact that a more general lemma is more likely to be reused, schematic lemmas are classified into three visibility classes: machine (single model), project (collection of models) and global. A machine-level lemma will be considered for a proof obligation of the machine with which the lemma is associated; similarly, for the project-level attachment. A global schematic lemma becomes a part of the Event-B mathematical language definition for the Why3 plug-in.

Just as model construction is often an iterative process, we have discovered during our experiments that finding a good schematic lemma may require several attempts. A common scenario is that an existing lemma may be relaxed so that while it is still strong enough to discharge conditions that were dependent on it, it can also discharge some new ones. For instance, we have seen several cases where a fairly narrow and detailed lemma would gradually slim down to a simple (and much more valuable) statement about distributivity of certain operators. It does require at times a considerable effort to come up with an abstract and minimal covering condition but the result is rewarding and reusable across projects.

3.1 Automatically Including Relevant Lemmas

Once there is a library of lemmas in place, it is vital that there is a way to automatically use them in every new proof obligation. Including all the lemmas in the hypotheses of every conjecture would simply overwhelm provers and effectively preclude automated proof. To discover relevant schematic lemmas we match the structure of a lemma against the structure of conjecture goals and hypotheses. Recall that a schematic lemma has no free identifiers and thus matching must be over structure.

Directly comparing a lemma and a conjecture is expensive: a straightforward algorithm (tree matching) is quadratic unless memory is not an issue. We use a computationally cheap proxy measure known as the Jaccard similarity which, as the first approximation, is defined as $JS(P, Q) = \mathrm{card}(P \cap Q)/\mathrm{card}(P \cup Q)$.

The key is in computing the number of overall and common elements and, in fact, defining what an "element" means for a formula. One immediate issue is that P and Q are sets and a formula, at a syntactic level, is a tree. One common way to match some two sequences (e.g., bits of text) using the Jaccard similarity is to use *shingles* of elements to attempt to capture some part of the ordering information. A shingle is a tuple preserving order of original elements but seen as an atomic element. Thus sequence $[a, b, c, d]$ could be characterised by two 3-shingles $P = \{[a, b, c], [b, c, d]\}$ (here $[b, c, d]$ is just a name) and matching based on these shingles would correctly show that $[a, b, c, d]$ is much closer to $[a, b, c, d, e]$ than to $[d, c, b, a]$. To account for trees structure we do matching on a set of paths from a root to all leaves and also on the the the set of sequences of the form $[p, c_1, \ldots, c_2]$ where p is a parent element and $c_1, \ldots, c_2$ are children. This immediately gives a set of n-shingles that might need to be converted into shorter m-shingles to make things practical.

As an example, consider the following expression $a * (b + c/d) + e * (f - d * 2)$. We are not interested in identifiers and literals so we remove them to obtain tree $+(*(+/))(*(-*))$ which has the following 3-shingles based on paths, $[*, +, /], [+, *, +], [+, *, -], [*, -, *]$, and only 1 3-shingle, $[+, *, *]$, based on the structure. The shingles are quite cheap to compute (linear to formula size) and match (fixed cost if we disregard low weight shingles, see below). Let $\mathrm{sd}(P)$ and $\mathrm{sw}(P)$ be set of depth and structure shingles of formula P. Then the similarity between some P and Q is computed as

$$s(P, Q) = \sum_{i \in I_1} \mathrm{w_d}(i) + c \sum_{i \in I_2} \mathrm{w_w}(i) \qquad I_1 = \mathrm{sd}(P) \cap \mathrm{sd}(Q), I_2 = \mathrm{sw}(P) \cap \mathrm{sw}(Q)$$

where $w_*(i) = \mathrm{cnt}(i)^{-1}$ and $\mathrm{cnt}(i)$ is number of times i occurs in all hypotheses and support lemmas. Very common shingles contribute little to the similarity assessment and may be disregarded so that there is some k such that $\mathrm{card}(I_1) < k, \mathrm{card}(I_2) < k$.

3.2   Schematic Lemma Plug-In

We have built a prototype implementation of the schematic lemma mechanism as a plug-in to the Rodin Platform. It integrates into the prover perspective and offers an alternative way to conduct an interactive proof either at a root node level or indeed for any open sub-branch of a proof obligation. At the moment, the notation employed is the native notation of Why3 but the first release will support entering a schematic lemma in the Event-B mathematical notation.

There are three main parts to the definition of a schematic lemma: identifiers, hypotheses and the goal. The identifier definition may use either one of the two built-in types (boolean and integer) or a fresh type variable (i.e., *type0* in Fig. 2). Hypotheses are defined by a list of predicates (while logically order should not matter, in practice it does and it is advantageous to have more constricting hypotheses first); these predicates may not mention any model variables but can refer to the identifiers defined in the lemma. And the goal is a predicate over the lemma identifiers.

The plug-in automatically constructs the first attempt at a schematic lemma through a simple syntactic transformation of a context proof obligation. All the identifiers occurring in either hypotheses or goal of the proof obligation are mapped into schematic lemma identifiers and then this mapping is used to translate hypotheses and the goal.

From this starting point it is up to the modeller to construct a promising lemma. A prepared lemma is *committed* where the Why3 plug-in is used to prove that the lemma holds, and also that adding it to the proof obligation in context

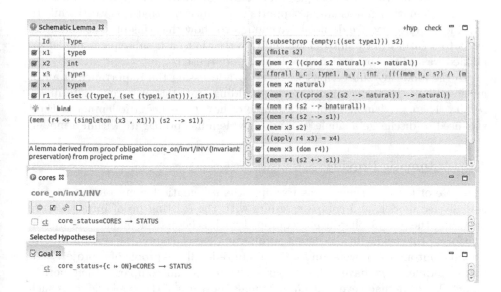

Fig. 2. Schematic lemma prover interface. Instead of working with the built-in interactive prover, a modeller attempts to construct a provable schematic lemma that would discharge the current proof obligation

discharges the proof obligation. If either fails, a user gets an indication of what has happened and it is not until both generic and concrete proofs are carried out that the schematic lemma may be used in the local library and assigned a binding level (machine, project or global). In the case of a success, the current open goal is closed.

To aid in the construction of a schematic lemma, the plug-in provides some simple productivity mechanisms. A hypotheses can be deselected without removing it to check whether both the lemma goal and the context proof obligation are still provable. An identifier may also be deselected and this automatically deselects all the hypotheses mentioning the identifier. It will take more experiments to arrive at methodological guidelines on constructing lemmas.

4   Case Study

In this section we discuss the experience of applying the schematic lemmas technique to prove several pre-existing models. Since this is an on-going project, we also discuss perceived advantages and disadvantages of doing proofs with our technique.

As the case study we consider four models, some of them fairly well known to the Event-B community. They are not very large but still have a reasonable number of proof obligations and make a good use of refinement and the Event-B modelling notation. Our intention was to take models from different domains constructed by different people to see how the technique performs in different settings. On the whole we were pleased to find that such diverse models still share a lot of schematic lemmas and it supports our conjecture that it is worthwhile to build lemma library. We do not have enough to show that this process definitely leads to a saturation point but we did observe that each subsequent model we tackled was a little bit easier since lemmas are reused.

In the following subsections we start by addressing the importance of automatic part of the verification process providing statistics on recent experiment results. Then we demonstrate an example of how the schematic lemma method was used to discharge a single goal and how lemmas propagate within a model.

4.1   Automatic Proving

The core of the experiment was to apply the schematic lemma plug-in to several diverse models and compare results with the existing proof infrastructure including the Why3 plug-in not equipped with schematic lemmas. The Rodin Platform provides facility to define automatic tactics, combining certain rewrite rule and automatic provers, and apply them redo all the proofs of a project. For this experiment, we have defined four such tactics and compared their performance. We have made every attempt to make best use of the available tools such as the Atelier-B ML prover, built-in PP and nPP provers, and, of course, the SMT plug-in that relies on some of the same back-end SMT provers.

Table 1. Comparative performance of four proof tactics; the first column is the overall number of generated proof obligations, the following four columns give the number of proof obligations remaining open (undischarged) after applying, from a scratch (that is, purging any previous proofs) the certain proof tactic. The final column gives in brackets the number of schematic lemmas used in the model (but not necessarily defined specifically for the model).

Model	Proof obligations	Open, Tactic[1]	Open, Tactic[2]	Open, Why3	Open, Why3 (+SL)
Order/supply communication [2]	276	24	4	8	4 (+2)
Fisher's algorithm [11]	82	16	4	1	0 (+1)
Train control system [4] (Chap. 17)	133	36	5	32	32 (+0)
B2B communication prot. [18]	498	63	25	20	8 (+5)
Automated teller machine [17]	962	77	28	1	0 (+1)
Total	1951	216	66	62	44

Table 1 summarises the results of our experiment. We use two tactics that are commonly available to the Rodin users. Tactic[1] applies a number of rewrite rules and then tries nPP, PP and ML provers; Tactic[2] does the same with addition of the SMT plug-in. The Why3 tactic is similar to Tactic[1] but with the Why3 plug-in as the sole automatic prover. This tactic does not use any schematic lemmas and relies solely on the basic axiomatisation library defining various Event-B operators. In the last column, the Why3 plug-in is able to locate an include suitable schematic lemmas. This is a completely automatic process: one can define a number of schematic lemmas (when doing interactive proofs), then purge all the proofs and the lemmas will be picked up automatically when relevant. The last number (+x) is the number of used schematic lemmas.

With one of the models (Train Control System) not only the Why3 plug in showed a lacklustre performance compared to the SMT plug-in but we also found it hard to come up with any useful schematic lemmas. Two of the remaining models were not proven completely as we have found it quite hard to read large proof obligations and deduce what is really happening there. It should, we hope, easier for a modeller who has a ready intuition as to what is the underlying meaning of a given proof obligation.

4.2   Nesting Lemmas

In this subsection we go a bit a deeper and discuss one specific example where a schematic lemma is used to complete a proof. We approached the experiment in a more or less blind style where a model itself was not analysed in any detail and we were generally concerned only with the specifics of a proof obligation - its goal and hypothesis, - in an attempt to deduce a schematic lemma strong enough to discharge the condition.

There are situations where a suitable schematic lemma, which we believed to be correct, and which as well discharged the context proof obligation could not be proven by the Why3 plug-in. Initially, this was a puzzling scenario as one would not want to comprise on the form of a schematic lemma. A possible back-door solution is to add (in a safe way, with a proof) a lemma to the Why3 library of the Event-B axiomatisation and include the lemma in every single proof obligation. However, we knew from the earlier experiments with the Why3 plug-in that a large number of supporting lemmas may overwhelm provers and then, in an extreme, pretty much nothing is provable.

The solution is to allow a modeller to construct chains of lemmas of which only the last one is used in the capacity of a schematic lemma and the rest help to prove it. With extra support lemmas one should be able to handle pretty much any case of forward or backward proof. These additional lemmas are visible in the context and saved with the schematic lemma so that one is able to redo all the proofs strictly on the basis of the Why3 axiomatisation library. Another possibility, offered by the Why3 itself, is to transition to a far more capable environment of Isabelle or Coq and complete a proof there. We have not tried this route so far and it is not clear how to embed an external proof script in a schematic lemma.

One example where we discovered a need for nesting lemmas is a relatively common case of proving that an overridden restricted relation is a member of a function. The effect of overriding $f \mathbin{\vartriangleleft} \{x \mapsto y\}$ is replacing mapping $\{x \mapsto f(x)\}$ with $\{x \mapsto y\}$ in f. In example below, function $database$ is overridden by a singleton pair and one needs to check it remains a total function.

$$\cdots \vdash database \mathbin{\vartriangleleft} \{ai \mapsto a\} \in Attr\_id \to Attrs$$

After unsuccessful attempts to prove it automatically, we used a schematic lemma technique to discharge it. Firstly, we added a schematic lemma shown below.

```
lemma lemma_total_overriding:
  forall f:rel 'a 'b, s:set 'a, t:set 'b, x: 'a, y : 'b.
    mem f (s --> t) /\ mem x s /\ mem y t ->
      mem (f <+ singleton (x, y)) (s --> t)
```

It seems to be a promising start as the original proof obligation was now discharged by Alt-Ergo (among others) in just 0.03 s. Yet the lemma itself could not be proven.

We discovered two new lemmas that should be added in the context of the schematic lemma and are enough to discharge it. They state some simple properties about domain overriding, and the functionality of an overridden function.

```
lemma lemma_total_overriding_help0:
  forall f : rel 'a 'b, x : 'a, y : 'b.
    subset  (dom f) (dom (f <+ (singleton (x, y))))

lemma lemma_total_overriding_help1:
  forall f:rel 'a 'b, s:set 'a, t:set 'b, x: 'a, y : 'b.
```

```
mem f (s --> t) /\ mem x s /\ mem y t ->
   mem (f <+ singleton (x, y)) (s +-> t)
```

Both statements were proven. For Alt-Ergo the times are 1.74 s and 1.08 s respectively. It is important to note that these lemmas only appear in the context of proving lemma_total_overriding.

4.3 Lemma Reuse

As we have stated previously, it has been one of the goals of this research to establish to what degree schematic lemmas are reusable at least within the same project. Clearly, it would not make any sense to write a dedicated lemma for each open proof obligation.

In this experiment, we address the problem of proof re-usability by shifting the focus from proving a single verification condition to validating remaining undischarged proof obligations of the model. We use a publicly available model Buyer/Seller B2B Communication protocol [18]. In our view, it is a fairly typical example of a model not constructed solely for illustration purposes, i.e., there is some scale and purpose to it.

A Buyer/Seller B2B Communication protocol model has 11 refinement steps and 498 verification conditions. Combining all the default tactics with all the available automatic provers and the SMT plug-in results in 25 undischarged verification conditions (63 without the SMT plug-in).

Our standard routine based on the Why3 plug-in consists in first applying the plug-in without any schematic lemmas with increasingly longer timeouts and only afterwards reviewing remaining conditions for the purpose of writing schematic lemmas.

For this specific experiment, we used an incremental timeout tactic with three theorem provers: Z3, EProver and Alt-Ergo. The initial timeout was set to 5 s then to 15 s and finally 45 s which roughly the point when provers start to run out of memory. The vast majority of conditions were proven under 5 s, only few more between 5 and 15 s, and no new conditions were proven with the 45 s timeout. The Why3 plug-in on its own has discharged a significant part of the obligations: only 4.6 % of the 498 open verification conditions were not automatically proven which is better than the SMT plug-in.

One immediately satisfying result that the schematic lemmas defined for two other models (Order/Supply Communication and Fisher's Algorithm) - completely unrelated in terms of domain and provenance - discharged ten proof obligations of the B2B model. After that, we have added further five schematic lemmas each discharging between 2 and four proof obligations. Table 2 shows the proof progress taking the model from 20 POs to 8 via five schematic lemmas. The remaining 8 could not be easily done with this approach. We have not arrived at a definite conclusion of whether there is a sizeable class of proof obligations for which one cannot construct meaningful lemmas or if it is just the case of unfamiliarity with the model making writing schematic lemmas inordinately difficult.

Table 2. The dynamics of proving the B2B communication protocol model using the schematic lemma technique. The numbers show how each next lemma (L_1, L_2, ...) affects the overall number of open proof obligations.

Model	Open, Why3	Open, $+L_1$	Open, $+L_2$	Open, $+L_3$	Open, $+L_4$	Open, $+L_5$
B2B Communication prot.	20	16	14	12	10	8

To pick but few simpler examples we show again a variation of reasoning about functional override and finiteness. Some lemmas coming from previous models were useful although some properties were still missing, i.e., overridden functions domain and range properties. Nonetheless, we managed to narrow down few of these properties and reduce the number of unsatisfied verification conditions by 10. The fundamental idea behind this proving style is to virtually break down a statement into pieces and consider what basic properties that could be missing.

For instance, the following trivial condition has discharged a large of seemingly unrelated proof obligations in several models.

```
lemma lemma_natural_increment:
  forall x, n : int.
    mem x bnatural1 /\ n >= 0 ->
      mem (x + n) bnatural1
```

A fairly common tactic in the schematic lemma approach, when not familiar with the model, and the condition appears to be true, is to try and identify the few key hypothesis and come up with a lemma that would bridge them to the goal. Although it sounds fairly trivial, proof obligations may contain tens if not hundreds hypotheses so just visually spotting the right few one might be tricky. We are working on heuristics to automatically filter and rank schematic lemma hypotheses.

As an illustration of the finiteness properties consider the following simple example.

$$\text{finite}(B\_2\_S\_proposal)$$
$$B\_2\_S\_counter\_proposal \in B\_2\_S\_proposal \twoheadrightarrow \text{dom}(B\_2\_S\_rejection)$$
$$\vdash$$
$$\text{finite}(B\_2\_S\_counter\_proposal)$$

It is not hard to prove it by hand by it is tedious to do it over an over again. So we added the following schematic lemma and all such and similar cases are now instantly discharged.

```
lemma lemma_finite_partial_domain:
  forall f : rel 'a 'b, s : set 'a, t : set 'b.
    finite (dom f) /\ mem f (s +-> t) ->
      finite f
```

There is a fine interplay between the functioning of the schematic lemmas plug-in and the Why3 plug-in filtering mechanism. The Why3 plug-in uses the shingles technique to rank and filter hypothesis and originally aimed at just filtering out irrelevant hypothesis. We had to slightly adjust matching weights as there are no common identifiers between a proof obligation and a schematic lemma so a bigger emphasise has to be made on structural patterns.

Throughout experiments with a collection of the Why3 back-end provers we noticed that not only different provers are better for certain problems, but they also prefer specific style of a writing a lemma. For instance, the order clauses in the conjunction in the left-hand side of an implication may have discernible effect not only on a proof time but also on proof success for some provers. Therefore, it is, to some extent, an experimental process requiring trying out different forms of the same argument.

5 Discussion

Completely automating a verification process is a largely debatable idea and a grand challenge for automated reasoning community. Nonetheless, we were keen to experiment with a handful of models and our tool, which exploits modern state-of-the-art theorem provers and identify on how far are we from the ultimate objective.

The models we have chosen for the case study are not particularly large. We have on purpose avoided taking some of the large industry-constructed as they have unusually high proportion of interactive proofs and may argue that Event-B abstraction mechanisms were not used to full extend to manage complexity and reduce the proof workload. In the longer term, however, we would want to tailor our technique to the needs of an industrial user. We believe, and this is supported by our experiments, that with a carefully lemma library and a domain-specific modelling guidance document, industrial user will be able to construct large and useful models without doing a single interactive proof. Failed proof obligations will still be reported, in slightly different style from now, to inform a modeller what is wrong and how it can be fixed. Any proof obligation remaining undischarged after throwing at it all possible automatic provers will be treated as a modelling error irrespective of whether the condition can be potentially proven or not. A similar mindset of restricting the usage of modelling notation in order to gain productivity has been with some great success for the Classical B refinement process [13].

The schematic lemma technique has the potential to significantly alter the way models are proved while proof persistence encourages frequent and deep model refactoring. We also hypothesise that at a certain stage accumulated schematic lemma make automatic proof support so complete that interactive proofs are no longer necessary and an undischarged proof is treated as failed and must be dealt with at a model level.

The idea of generalisation for the purpose of proof reuse has been explored in different settings. Perhaps the most well-known example to aspire to is the tactic or meta-proof language supported by general purpose interactive theorem provers such as Isabelle [23]. It is far more flexible and powerful technique but also requires a different level of expertise from a user. A much simpler technique is having a customisable set of rewrite or simplification rules. In principle, this is offered to some extent by the Theory plug-in; the Atelier-B interactive prover allows a modeller to define custom rewrite rules although this is can be extremely unsafe [7]. Reusable theory components with embedded lemmas, tautologies and rewrite rules are widely used in many verification tools from Maude to ACL2 and also recently available, thanks to the Theory plug-in, in Event-B. Schematic lemmas are far less topical than such theory components but then their inclusion is triggered automatically via syntactic matching rather than through direct instructions from a user.

As one extension of this work we see investigation of guidelines on schematic lemma construction to help an engineer decide when and what kind of a schematic might be used. The Why3 plug-in may optionally record all the proof attempts in a database. We would like to explore whether a form of automated data mining of failed proof obligations may be employed to automatically synthesise schematic lemma candidates.

In this work we have tried to weave the process of constructing generalised proofs into the very process of model construction and address two long standing challenges of model-based design: turning proofs into tangible artefacts that can survive deep model refactoring, and making interactive proof on organic part of model construction rather than an unfortunate side activity.

Acknowledgments. This work is supported by the RSSB/UK project SafeCap+: SafeCap for integrated optimum capacity, safety and energy strategies at multiple nodes, the EPSRC/UK project STRATA: Layers for Structuring Trustworthy Ambient Systems and the EPSRC IAA account project on Formal Data Analytics in Railway.

References

1. Event-B and the Rodin Platform. http://www.event-b.org/
2. Furst, A.: Event-B model of the Order/Supply Chain A2A Communication. http://deploy-eprints.ecs.soton.ac.uk/129/
3. Abrial, J.-R.: The B-Book. Cambridge University Press, Cambridge (1996)
4. Abrial, J.-R.: Modelling in Event-B. Cambridge University Press, Cambridge (2010)
5. de Moura, L., Bjørner, N.S.: Z3: an efficient SMT solver. In: Ramakrishnan, C.R., Rehof, J. (eds.) TACAS 2008. LNCS, vol. 4963, pp. 337–340. Springer, Heidelberg (2008)
6. Butler, M., Maamria, I.: Practical theory extension in Event-B. In: Liu, Z., Woodcock, J., Zhu, H. (eds.) Theories of Programming and Formal Methods. LNCS, vol. 8051, pp. 67–81. Springer, Heidelberg (2013)
7. Clearsy. Atelier B.: User and Reference Manuals. http://www.atelierb.societe.com/index_uk.html
8. Marché, C., Paskevich, A., Bobot, F., Filliâtre, J.-C.: Why3: shepherd your herd of provers. In: Boogie 2011: First International Workshop on Intermediate Verification Languages, pp. 53–64, August 2011

9. Hallerstede, S.: On the purpose of Event-B proof obligations. In: Börger, E., Butler, M., Bowen, J.P., Boca, P. (eds.) ABZ 2008. LNCS, vol. 5238, pp. 125–138. Springer, Heidelberg (2008)

10. Hoang, T.S.: Proof hints for Event-B (2012). CoRR, abs/1211.1172

11. Iliasov, A., Bryans, J.: A proof-based method for modelling timed systems. In: Voronkov, A., Virbitskaite, I. (eds.) PSI 2014. LNCS, vol. 8974, pp. 161–176. Springer, Heidelberg (2015)

12. Industrial deployment of system engineering methods providing high dependability and productivity (DEPLOY), IST FP7 project. http://www.deploy-project.eu/

13. Burdy, L.: Automatic refinement. In: Proceedings of BUGM at FM 1999 (1999)

14. Conchon, S., Contejean, É., Kanig, J., Lescuyer, S.: CC(X): semantical combination of congruence closure with solvable theories. In: Post-proceedings of the 5th International Workshop on Satisfiability Modulo Theories (SMT 2007), vol. 198, no. 2 of Electronic Notes in Computer Science, pp. 51–69. Elsevier Science Publishers (2008)

15. Rigorous Open Development Environment for Complex Systems (RODIN), IST FP6 STREP project. http://rodin.cs.ncl.ac.uk/

16. Iliasov, A., Stankaitis, P., Adjepon-Yamoah, D., Romanovsky, A.: Rodin platform Why3 plug-in. In: Butler, M., Schewe, K.-D., Mashkoor, A., Biro, M. (eds.) ABZ 2016. LNCS, vol. 9675, pp. 275–281. Springer, Heidelberg (2016). doi:10.1007/978-3-319-33600-8_21

17. Said, M.Y., Butler, M., Snook, C.: Language and tool support for class and state machine refinement in UML-B. In: Cavalcanti, A., Dams, D.R. (eds.) FM 2009. LNCS, vol. 5850, pp. 579–595. Springer, Heidelberg (2009)

18. Hoang, T.S.: Event-B model of the Buyer/Seller B2B Communication. http://deploy-eprints.ecs.soton.ac.uk/128/

19. The RODIN platform. http://rodin-b-sharp.sourceforge.net/

20. TPTP: Thousands of Problems for Theorem Provers. www.tptp.org/

21. Deharbe, D., Fontaine, P., Guyot, Y., Voisin, L.: Integrating SMT solvers in Rodin. Sci. Comput. Program. **94**(Part 2), 130–143 (2014)

22. Kovács, L., Voronkov, A.: First-order theorem proving and VAMPIRE. In: Sharygina, N., Veith, H. (eds.) CAV 2013. LNCS, vol. 8044, pp. 1–35. Springer, Heidelberg (2013)

23. Nipkow, T., Paulson, L.C., Wenzel, M.: Isabelle/HOL - A Proof Assistant for Higher-Order Logic. LNCS, vol. 2283. Springer, Heidelberg (2002)

24. Freitas, L., Whiteside, I.: Proof patterns for formal methods. In: Proceedings of FM 2014: Formal Methods - 19th International Symposium, Singapore, 12–16 May 2014, pp. 279–295 (2014)

25. Weidenbach, C., Dimova, D., Fietzke, A., Kumar, R., Suda, M., Wischnewski, P.: SPASS version 3.5. In: Schmidt, R.A. (ed.) CADE-22. LNCS, vol. 5663, pp. 140–145. Springer, Heidelberg (2009)

Formal Availability Analysis Using Theorem Proving

Waqar Ahmad[✉] and Osman Hasan

School of Electrical Engineering and Computer Science,
National University of Sciences and Technology (NUST), Islamabad, Pakistan
{waqar.ahmad,osman.hasan}@seecs.nust.edu.pk

Abstract. Availability analysis is used to assess the possible failures and their restoration process for a given system. This analysis involves the calculation of instantaneous and steady-state availabilities of the individual system components and the usage of this information along with the commonly used availability modeling techniques, such as Availability Block Diagrams (ABD) and Fault Trees (FTs) to determine the system-level availability. Traditionally, availability analyses are conducted using paper-and-pencil methods and simulation tools but they cannot ascertain absolute correctness due to their inaccuracy limitations. As a complementary approach, we propose to use the higher-order-logic theorem prover HOL4 to conduct the availability analysis of safety-critical systems. For this purpose, we present a higher-order-logic formalization of instantaneous and steady-state availability, ABD configurations and generic unavailability FT gates. For illustration purposes, these formalizations are utilized to conduct formal availability analysis of a satellite solar array, which is used as the main source of power for the Dong Fang Hong-3 (DFH-3) satellite.

Keywords: Higher-order logic · Unavailability fault tree · Availability Block Diagram · Theorem proving

1 Introduction

Availability analysis is used to identify and assess the causes and frequencies of system failures. The outcomes of availability analysis play a vital role in ensuring failure-free operation of the given system. Due to the rapid increase in the usage of technological systems in safety and mission-critical domains, such as transportation and healthcare, the demand of their availability and thus availability analysis is also growing dramatically.

The first step, in the availability analysis, is the evaluation of basic metrics of reliability and maintainability, such as mean-time to failure (MTTF) [1], mean-time between failure (MTBF) [1] and mean-time to repair (MTTR) [1], at the

---

The original version of this chapter was revised. The spelling of the author Waqar Ahmad has been corrected. The erratum to this chapter is available at DOI: 10.1007/978-3-319-47846-3_30

© Springer International Publishing AG 2016
K. Ogata et al. (Eds.): ICFEM 2016, LNCS 10009, pp. 226–242, 2016.
DOI: 10.1007/978-3-319-47846-3_15

individual *component level* of the given system. These metrics are then used to calculate the availability of each component of the system by using the reliability and the maintainability distributions, such as *Exponential* or *Weibull*, with failure and repair rates, $\lambda = \frac{1}{MTTF}$ and $\mu = \frac{1}{MTTR}$. The next step is the selection of an appropriate availability modeling technique, such as Availability Block Diagrams (ABD) [2] and unavailability Fault Trees (FT) [2]. These techniques are the extension of traditionally used reliability modeling techniques, such as Reliability Block Diagram (RBD) [1] and Fault Tree (FT) [1], for availability analysis purposes. Besides these two techniques, Markov chains [3] have also been used for availability assessment. In practice, it provides much more detailed analysis compared to ABD and UFT. However, the major problem with the Markov chain based availability analysis is its exponential growth in the state-space as the system complexity increases [3]. For instance, consider the large Multistage Interconnection Networks (MINs) [3] that are mainly used in the supercomputers and multi-process systems to realize communication among thousands of processors. To conduct the Markov chain based availability analysis of a 8×8 MIN consisting of 16 switching elements, we need to consider 2^{16} possible states [3]. Although, we can somewhat reduce the number of states by taking appropriate assumptions but it can compromise the accuracy of the availability results [3]. On the other hand, ABD and UFT are intuitive and transparent methods that can be used to describe the availability of large and complex systems, like MINs [4]. The ABD and UFT based modeling techniques also allow us to estimate the availability of the given system at the *system level* and play a particularly useful role at the design stages of the system to scrutinize the design alternatives without building the actual system. Once an appropriate availability model is obtained then the next step is to perform the *system level* availability analysis of the model using an appropriate analysis technique.

Traditionally, simulation tools, such as ReliaSoft [5] and ASENT [6], are used to analyze the availability models. However, these techniques cannot be termed as accurate due to their inherent incompleteness and the involvement of pseudorandom numbers and numerical methods. Given the safety and financial-critical nature of many technological systems these days, a slight unavailability of such a system, at a particular instant, may lead to disastrous situations, including the loss of human lives or heavy financial setbacks. For instance, it is reported that the Amazon Web Service (AWS) suffered an unavailability for 12 h, in April 21, 2011, causing hundreds of high-profile Web sites to go offline [7], which resulted in a loss of 66,240 US$ per minute downtime of its services.

Model checking techniques have been used to overcome the above-mentioned limitations for conducting the reliability analysis (e.g., [8,9]), which is in turn used to assess the failure free operation of a system in a given interval and is thus quite closely related to availability analysis. Stochastic Petri Nets (SPN) have also been utilized to formalize RBD and FT, which are then used to analyze the availability [10]. However, a major disadvantage of using these approaches is their inability to analyze large size systems. Moreover, the computation of probabilities in these methods [8,9] involves numerical methods, which compromises the accuracy of the results. Leveraging upon the high expressiveness of higher-order logic and a recent formalization of probability theory [11], the higher-order-logic theorem prover HOL4 has been recently used for the formalization of Reliability Block Diagrams (RBD) [12,13] and Fault trees (FT) [14]. These efforts clearly indicate the effectiveness of using a higher-order-logic (HOL) theorem prover for conducting reliability and failure analysis and, in the current paper, we develop the reasoning support for availability analysis by extending the HOL4 formalizations of RBD and FT. It is important to note that our proposed approach of using HOL theorem proving for availability analysis is primarily based on deductive reasoning. The availability properties are verified by using sound reasoning process and it is supported by the fact that every new theorem is derived from already verified theorems [15]. Therefore, the analysis is much more rigorous and accurate compared to computer algebra systems (CAS), such as Mathematica [16], which simplify the given closed form expressions and returns the results in the form of symbolic expressions. This fact can be illustrate with this example that the simplification of the expression $\frac{(x^2-1)}{(x-1)}$ by CAS yields $(x + 1)$ without explicitly mentioning $(x \neq 1)$ [17]. On the other hand, HOL theorem prover cannot verify the same expression without this premise.

The main contribution of the paper is to formalize the ABD, unavailability FT gates and steady-state availability to develop a formal library of availability theory foundations. This library can then be used to model and analyze both component and system level availability properties of any system within the sound core of a theorem prover. The main challenge faced in this formalization, compared to our earlier formalizations related to reliability theory, was to introduce the notion of an availability event that is associated with each system component. Each one of these availability events consists of a sequence of multiple random variables that are functioning over time. In order to illustrate the effectiveness of our proposed formalization, we present a formal availability analysis of a satellite solar array [18,19] that has been used as a main power source for the Dong Fang Hong-3 (DFH-3) satellite. In addition, we also provide some automated reasoning support for the availability analysis. This automation allows us to quantitatively compute the availability and unavailability of the DFH-3 satellite solar array from the given values of the failure and repair rates.

2   Probability and Reliability in HOL

Mathematically, a measure space is defined as a triple (Ω, Σ, μ), where Ω is a set, called the sample space, Σ represents a σ-algebra of subsets of Ω, where the subsets are usually referred to as measurable sets, and μ is a measure with domain Σ. A probability space is a measure space (Ω, Σ, Pr), such that the measure, referred to as the probability and denoted by Pr, of the sample space is 1. In the HOL formalization of probability theory [11], given a probability space p, the functions space, subsets and prob return the corresponding Ω, Σ and Pr, respectively. This formalization also includes the formal verification of some of the most widely used probability axioms, which play a pivotal role in formal reasoning about reliability properties. A random variable is a measurable function between a probability space and a measurable space. The measurable functions belong to a special class of functions, which preserves the property that the inverse image of each measurable set is also measurable. A measurable space refers to a pair $(S, \mathcal{A})$, where S denotes a set and $\mathcal{A}$ represents a nonempty collection of sub-sets of S. Now, if S is a set with finite elements, then the corresponding random variable is termed as a discrete random variable otherwise it is called a continuous one.

Now, reliability $R(t)$ is defined as the probability of a system or component performing its desired task over certain interval of time and expressed mathematically in terms of random variable as $R(t) = Pr(X > t)$. This concept can be formalized in HOL4 as follows:

$\vdash \forall$ p X t. Reliability p X t = distribution p X {y | Normal t < y}

where the variables $p : (\alpha \rightarrow bool)\#((\alpha \rightarrow bool) \rightarrow bool)\#((\alpha \rightarrow bool) \rightarrow real)$, $X : (\alpha \rightarrow extreal)$ and $t : real$ represent a probability space, a random variable and a $real$ number respectively. The function Normal takes a $real$ number as its inputs and converts it to its corresponding value in the $extended - real$ data-type, i.e., it is the $real$ data-type with the inclusion of positive and negative infinity. The function distribution takes three parameters: a probability space p, a random variable X and a set of $extended - real$ numbers and outputs the probability of a random variable X that acquires all the values of the given set in probability space p.

3   Instantaneous and Steady-State Availabilities

The instantaneous or point availability $A_{inst}(t)$ of a system or component can be defined as the probability that the given system or component is properly functioning at a given time instant t. If there are no repairs required after the fault has occurred then the availability $A(t)$ is simply equal to the reliability $R(t)$ of the system. However, if the system or component requires repair, then the availability can be considered as the function of two random variables, i.e., $X_i = T_i + D_i$, where T_i is the working time in the ith period and D_i is the repair time in the ith period. If the time when a system starts working in the kth period is $S_k = \sum_{i=1}^{k-1} X_i$ then the considered system is said to be available at time t when there exists a period such that $S_k \leq t < S_k + T_k$. Now, the corresponding availability event constituted by these random variables can be formalized in HOL4 as follows:

Definition 1. $\vdash \forall$ p X t. avail_event p L n t =
{x | SIGMA (λa. FST (EL a L) x + SND (EL a L) x) (count n) $\leq$ t $\wedge$
      t < SIGMA (λa. FST (EL a L) x + SND (EL a L) x) (count n) +
          FST (EL n L) x} $\cap$ p_space p

The above definition takes a probability space p, a list of random variable pairs L, representing the working and repair time random variables, a number n and a time variable t and returns the corresponding availability event. The function SIGMA takes an arbitrary function f and a set s and returns the sum of all the values obtained by applying the function f on each element of the given set. The HOL4 function count takes a number n and returns a set containing all the natural numbers less than the given number n. Similarly, the function EL takes an index variable and a list and retrieves the list element located at the given index number. The HOL4 functions FST and SND are primarily used to access the first and second elements in a pair. Definition 1 models the corresponding event of the ith working interval only. To cover all the working intervals, we take the union of these availability events, corresponding to the pairs of random variable in list L, in HOL4 as follows:

Definition 2. $\vdash \forall$ p L t. union_avail_events p L t = BIGUNION (IMAGE (λa. avail_event p L a t) (count (LENGTH L)))

An interesting property of the availability event is that its probability, also known as instantaneous availability, is always greater or equal to the corresponding reliability, i.e., $R_{T_1}(t) \leq A_{inst}(t)$, where T_1 is the first time-to-work random variable. This property can be formally verified, based on Definitions 1 and 2, in HOL4 as follows:

Theorem 1. $\vdash \forall$ p t L. prob_space p $\wedge$ (0 $\leq$ t) $\wedge$ ¬NULL L $\wedge$
($\forall$n. avail_event p L n t $\in$ events p) $\wedge$
($\forall$a b. (a $\neq$ b) $\Rightarrow$
 DISJOINT (avail_event p L a t) (avail_event p L b t)) $\Rightarrow$
 (Reliability p (FST (HD L)) t $\leq$ prob p (union_avail_events p L t))

The first two assumptions ensure that p is a valid probability space and time index t must be positive. The next two assumptions make sure that the given list of random variables must not be empty and the availability events are in the events space p. The last assumption ensures that the availability events are disjoint. The conclusion models the property that the instantaneous availability is always greater or equal to reliability. The function Reliability takes a probability space p, a random variable that is associated with the system or component and a time variable t and returns the reliability of the system or component [12].

Consider that the failure and repair random variables are exhibiting exponential distributions with failure and repair rates λ and μ, respectively, then the instantaneous availability at the component level can be expressed mathematically as follows [1]:

$$A_{inst}(t) = \frac{\mu}{\mu + \lambda} + \frac{\lambda}{\mu + \lambda} e^{-(\lambda + \mu)t} \tag{1}$$

where the failure and repair rates are the mean-time-to-failure (MTTF) and mean-time-to-repair (MTTR), i.e. $\lambda = \frac{1}{MTTF}$ and $\mu = \frac{1}{MTTR}$, which are basic metrics for reliability and maintainability, respectively.

Now, we can formalize the instantaneous availability, given in Eq. 1, as follows:

Definition 3. ⊢ ∀ p L m. inst_avail_exp p L m =
∀t. prob p (union_avail_events p L (&t)) =

$$\frac{\text{SND m}}{(\text{SND m} + \text{FST m})} + \frac{\text{FST m}}{(\text{SND m} + \text{FST m})} * \exp\ (-(\text{SND m} + \text{FST m}) * \&t)$$

where the variables FST m and SND m represent failure and repair rates, respectively.

The steady-state availability of any component, which reflects the long-term availability after the system becomes stable, can be evaluated by taking the limit as t approaches infinity in Eq. (1).

$$A_{steady} = \lim_{t \to \infty} A_{inst}(t) = \frac{\mu}{\mu + \lambda} \tag{2}$$

The above equation can be formally verified in HOL4 as follows:

Theorem 2. ⊢ ∀ p L m. prob_space p ∧ (0 < FST m ∧ 0 < SND m) ∧
(∀t. (∀a b. a ≠ b ⇒
DISJOINT (avail_event p L a t) (avail_event p L b t)) ∧
(∀n. avail_event p L n t ∈ events p)) ∧ inst_avail_exp p L m ⇒

$$(\text{lim } (\lambda t. \text{prob p (union\_avail\_events p L (\&t)))} = \frac{\text{SND m}}{(\text{SND m} + \text{FST m})})$$

The assumptions of the above theorem are quite similar to those used in Theorem 1. The proof of Theorem 2 is primarily based on the fact that the negative exponential function tends to zero as its exponent tends to infinity.

4   Availability Block Diagrams

Availability Block Diagram (ABD) are graphical structures that represent the system components and their interconnections in the form of blocks and connector lines, respectively. The system is termed as available, if at least one path of properly available components from the input to output exists.

The availability of a system with components connected in series is considered to be available at time instant t only if all of its components are available at time t, as depicted in Fig. 1(a). If $A_{inst_i}(t)$ is a mutually independent event that represents the instantaneous availability of the ith component of a serially connected system with N components at time instant t, then the steady-state availability of the complete system can be expressed as [20]:

$$\lim_{t \to \infty} Pr(\bigcap_{i=1}^{N} A_{inst_i}(t)) = \prod_{i=1}^{N} (\frac{\mu_i}{\mu_i + \lambda_i}) \tag{3}$$

The series ABD configuration can be formalized as:

Definition 4. ⊢ (∀ p. series_struct p [] = p_space p) ∧
(∀ p h t. series_struct p (h::t) = h ∩ series_struct p t)

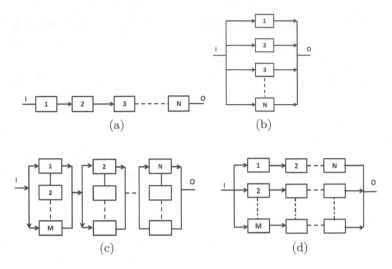

Fig. 1. ABDs (a) Series (b) Parallel (c) Series-Parallel (d) Parallel-Series

The above function takes a list of events corresponding to the availability of individual components of the given system and the probability space p and returns the intersection of all of the elements in a given list and the whole probability space, if the given list is empty. Based on this definition, Eq. (3) can be formally verified as follows:

Theorem 3. ⊢ ∀ p L M. (A1): prob_space p ∧ (A2): (0 ≤ t) ∧
(A3): (∀z. MEM z M ⇒ 0 < FST z ∧ 0 < SND z) ∧
(A4): (LENGTH L = LENGTH M) ∧
(A5): (∀t'. ¬NULL (union_avail_event_list p L (&t'))) ∧
(A6): (∀z. MEM z (union_avail_event_list p L (&t')) ⇒ z ∈ events p) ∧
(A7): mutual_indep p (union_avail_event_list p L (&t'))) ∧
(A8): inst_avail_exp_list p L M ⇒
(lim (λt. prob p (series_struct p (union_avail_event_list p L (&t)))) =
list_prod (steady_state_avail_list M))

where the function **union_avail_event_list** can be obtained by mapping the function **union_avail_event** on every element of the given random variable list. The function **list_prod** returns the product of given real number list. The first two assumptions (A1–A2) ensure that p is a valid probability space and the time t must be positive. The assumptions (A3–A4) guarantee that the failure and repair rates are positive and the length of failure-repair random variable and the corresponding rate lists are equal. The next two assumptions (A5–A6) make sure that the length of availability event list, representing the availability of individual components, must not be empty and each availability event in a **avail_event_list** is in events space p. The last two assumptions (A7–A8) provide the mutual independence among all the availability events and the instantaneous availability of each component. The conclusion of the theorem represents

Eq. (3) as the function `steady_state_avail_list` takes a list of pairs, representing the failure and repair rates, and returns a list of steady-state availabilities, corresponding to each component of the given system.

Similarly, the availability of a system with parallel connected components, depicted in Fig. 1(b), mainly depends on the component with the maximum availability. In other words, the system will continue functioning as long as at least one of its components remains functional. Mathematically [20]:

$$\lim_{t \to \infty} Pr(\bigcup_{i=1}^{N} A_{inst_i}(t)) = 1 - \prod_{i=1}^{N}(1 - \frac{\mu_i}{\mu_i + \lambda_i}) \tag{4}$$

Now, the availability of a system with a parallel structure is defined as:

Definition 5. ⊢ `(parallel_struct [] = {})` ∧
`(∀ h t. parallel_struct (h::t) = h ∪ parallel_struct t)`

The function `parallel_struct` accepts a list of reliability events and returns the parallel structure reliability event by recursively performing the union operation on the given list of reliability events or an empty set if the given list is empty. We can now verify Eq. (4) as follows:

Theorem 4. ⊢ ∀p L M.
`(lim (λt. prob p (parallel_struct p (union_avail_event_list p L (&t)))) =`
`1 - list_prod (one_minus_list (steady_state_avail_list M))`

The above theorem is verified under the same assumptions as Theorem 3. The conclusion of the theorem represents Eq. (4) where, the function `one_minus_list` accepts a list of *real* numbers $[x1, x2, \cdots, xn]$ and returns the list of *real* numbers such that each element of this list is 1 minus the corresponding element of the given list, i.e., $[1 - x1, 1 - x2 \cdots, 1 - xn]$. The proof of Theorem 4 is based on Theorem 3 along with the fact that given a list of n mutually independent events, the complement of these n events are also mutually independent.

If in each serial stage the components are connected in parallel, as shown in Fig. 1(c), then the configuration is termed as a series-parallel structure. If $A_{inst_{ij}}(t)$ is the event corresponding to the instantaneous availability of the jth component connected in an ith subsystem at time instant t, then the steady-state availability of the complete system can be expressed as follows [20]:

$$\lim_{t \to \infty} Pr(\bigcap_{i=1}^{N} \bigcup_{j=1}^{M} A_{inst_{ij}}(t)) = \prod_{i=1}^{N}(1 - \prod_{j=1}^{M}(1 - \frac{\mu_{ij}}{\mu_{ij} + \lambda_{ij}})) \tag{5}$$

By extending the ABD formalization approach, presented in Theorems 3 and 4, we formally verify the generic availability expression for series-parallel ABD configuration, given in Eq. (5), in HOL4 as follows:

Theorem 5. ⊢ ∀ p L M. `prob_space p ∧ (LENGTH L = LENGTH M) ∧`
`(∀z. MEM z (FLAT M) ⇒ 0 < FST z ∧ 0 < SND z) ∧`
`(∀n. n < LENGTH L ⇒ (LENGTH (EL n L) = LENGTH (EL n M))) ∧`
`(∀t'. (∀z. MEM z (list_union_avail_event_list p L (&t')) ⇒ ¬NULL z) ∧`

```
(∀z'. MEM z' (FLAT (list_union_avail_event_list p L (&t'))) ⇒
  z' ∈ events p) ∧
mutual_indep p (FLAT (list_union_avail_event_list p L (&t')))) ∧
two_dim_inst_avail_exp p L M ⇒
(lim (λt. prob p
  (series_parallel_struct p (list_union_avail_event_list p L (&t)))) =
  list_prod (one_minus_list (MAP (λa. compl_steady_state_avail a) M)))
```

where the function `list_union_avail_event_list` is obtained by mapping the function `union_avail_event_list` on each element of the given random variable list.

The function `series_parallel_struct` models the series-parallel ABD by first mapping the function `parallel_struct` on each element of the given event list and then applying the function `series_struct` to this obtained list. Similarly, the function `compl_steady_state_avail` returns a list of one minus steady-state availabilities.

The functions `list_prod` and `one_minus_list` are used to model the product and complement of steady-state availabilities, respectively. The assumptions are similar to the ones used in Theorems 3 and 4 with the extension that the given lists are two-dimensional lists. The HOL4 function `FLAT` is used to convert a two dimensional list into a single list. The conclusion models the right-hand-side of Eq. (5). The proof of the above theorem uses Theorems 3 and 4 and also requires a lemma that given the list of mutually independent reliability events, an event corresponding to the series-parallel structure and a reliability event are also independent in probability.

If the components in these reserved *subsystems* are connected serially then the structure is called a parallel-series structure, as depicted in Fig. 1(d). If $A_{ij}(t)$ is the event corresponding to the availability of the jth component connected in a ith subsystem at time t, then the steady-state availability becomes:

$$\lim_{t\to\infty} Pr(\bigcup_{i=1}^{M} \bigcap_{j=1}^{N} A_{ij}(t)) = 1 - \prod_{i=1}^{M}(1 - \prod_{j=1}^{N} \frac{\mu_{ij}}{\mu_{ij} + \lambda_{ij}}) \tag{6}$$

The above equation is also verified as a HOL4 theorem in our development and more details about it can be found in [21].

5   Unavailability Fault Trees

Unavailability FT is a graphical technique consisting of internal nodes, which are represented by gates like OR, AND and XOR, and the external nodes, that model the unavailability events, which are associated with the occurrence of faults in components of the given system. The generic nature of these gates allows us to construct an efficient and accurate unavailability fault tree (FT) model for any given system. This FT can in turn be used to investigate the potential causes of a fault occurrence, which makes the system unavailable, and the calculation of minimal number of unavailability events, known as minimal cut-set (MCS), that contribute towards the occurrence of a *top event*, i.e., a critical event, which can cause the whole system unavailable upon its occurrence.

We can formalize the unavailability event of a system by taking the complement of the availability event with respect to the probability space p.

Definition 6. ⊢∀ p X t.
union_unavail_events p L t = p_space p DIFF union_avail_events p L t

The instantaneous unavailability of the system can be expressed as follows:

$$\overline{A_{inst}}(t) = \frac{\lambda}{\mu+\lambda} - \frac{\lambda}{\mu+\lambda}e^{-(\lambda+\mu)t} \tag{7}$$

The HOL4 formalization of the above equation is as follows:

Definition 7. ⊢ ∀ p L m. inst_unavail_exp p L m =
∀t. prob p (union_unavail_events p L (&t)) =

$$\frac{\text{FST m}}{(\text{SND m + FST m})} - \frac{\text{FST m}}{(\text{SND m + FST m})} * \text{exp} \ (-(\text{SND m + FST m}) * \&t)$$

If the occurrence of the unavailability event at the output is caused by the occurrence of all the input unavailability events then this kind of behavior can be modeled by using the AND unavailability FT gate, as shown in Table 1.

$$Pr(\bigcap_{i=2}^{N} \overline{A_{inst_i}}(t)) = \prod_{i=2}^{N} \frac{\lambda_i}{\lambda_i + \mu_i} \tag{8}$$

The above equation can be formalized in HOL4 as follows:

Theorem 6. ⊢ ∀ p L M. prob_space p ∧
(∀z. MEM z M ⇒ 0 < FST z ∧ 0 < SND z) ∧ (LENGTH L = LENGTH M) ∧
(∀t'. ¬NULL (union_unavail_event_list p L (&t')) ∧
(∀z. MEM z (union_unavail_event_list p L (&t')) ⇒ z ∈ events p) ∧
mutual_indep p (union_unavail_event_list p L (&t'))) ∧
inst_unavail_exp_list p L M ⇒
  (lim (λt.
    prob p (AND_unavail_FT_gate p (union_avail_event_list p L (&t)))) =
  list_prod (steady_state_unavail_list M))

The assumptions of the above theorem are similar to the ones used in Theorem 2 and the conclusion of Theorem 5 represents Eq. (8).

In the OR unavailability FT gate, the occurrence of the output unavailability event depends upon the occurrence of any one of its input unavailability event. The function OR_unavail_FT_gate, given in Table 1, models this behavior as it returns the union of the input unavailability list L by using the recursive function union_list. The NOR unavailability FT gate, modeled by using the function NOR_unavail_FT_gate, given in Table 1, can be viewed as the complement of the OR unavailability FT gate and its output unavailability event occurs if none of the input unavailability event occurs.

Similarly, the NAND unavailability FT gate, represented by the function NAND_unavail_FT_gate in Table 1, models the behavior of the occurrence of an

Table 1. HOL formalization of fault tree gates

Unavail. FT Gates	HOL Formalization
AND	⊢ ∀ p L t. AND_unavail_FT_gate p L t = inter_list p (union_unavail_event_list p L t)
OR	⊢ ∀ p L t. OR_unavail_FT_gate p L t = union_list (union_unavail_event_list p L t)
NAND	⊢ ∀p L1 L2 t. NAND_unavail_FT_gate p L1 L2 t = inter_list p (compl_list p (union_unavail_event_list p L1 t)) ∩ inter_list p (union_unavail_event_list p L2 t)
NOR	⊢ ∀ p L t. NOR_unavail_FT_gate p L t = p_space p DIFF union_list (union_unavail_event_list p L t)
XOR	⊢ ∀ p A B. XOR_FT_unavail_gate p A B = ((p_space p DIFF A ∩ B) ∪ (A ∩ p_space p DIFF B))
NOT	⊢ ∀ p A. NOT_unavail_FT_gate p A = (p_space p DIFF A)

output unavailability event when at least one of the unavailability events at its input does not occur. This type of gate is used in unavailability FTs when the non-occurrence of the unavailability event in conjunction with the other unavailability events causes the top unavailability event to occur. This behavior can be expressed as the intersection of complementary and normal events, where the complementary events model the non-occurring unavailability events and the normal events model the occurring unavailability events. The output unavailability event occurs in the 2-input XOR unavailability FT gate if only one, and not both, of its input unavailability events occur. The HOL4 representation of the behaviour of the XOR_unavail_FT_gate is also presented in Table 1. The function NOT_unavail_FT_gate accepts an unavailability event A and probability space p and returns the complement to the probability space p of the given input unavailability event A. The verification of the corresponding unavailability expressions, of the above-mentioned unavailability FT gates, is presented in Table 2. These expressions are verified under the same assumptions as the ones used for Theorem 6 and the proofs are mainly based on some fundamental mutual independence properties of the given unavailability events along with some axioms of probability theory.

The principle of inclusion exclusion (PIE) forms an integral part of the reasoning involved in verifying the unavailability of a FT. In FT based unavailability analysis, firstly all the basic unavailability events are identified that can cause the

Table 2. Unavailability fault tree gates

Unavailability FT Gates	Conclusions of the formally verified Theorems
$\lim\limits_{t\to\infty} \overline{A}_{OR}(t) = \lim\limits_{t\to\infty} Pr(\bigcup\limits_{i=1}^{N} A_{inst_i}(t))$ $= 1 - \prod\limits_{i=2}^{N}(1 - \dfrac{\lambda_i}{\lambda_i + \mu_i})$	`lim (λt. prob p` `(OR_unavail_FT_gate p L &t) =` `1 - list_prod (one_minus_list` `(steady_state_unavail_list M)))`
$\lim\limits_{t\to\infty} \overline{A}_{NOR}(t) = 1 - \lim\limits_{t\to\infty} \overline{A}_{OR}(t)$ $= \prod\limits_{i=2}^{N}(1 - \dfrac{\lambda_i}{\lambda_i + \mu_i})$	`(lim (λt. prob p` `(NOR_unavail_FT_gate p L &t)) =` `list_prod (one_minus_list` `(steady_state_unavail_list M`
$\lim\limits_{t\to\infty} \overline{A}_{NAND}(t) =$ $\lim\limits_{t\to\infty} Pr(\bigcap\limits_{i=2}^{k} A_i(t) \cap \bigcap\limits_{j=k}^{N} \overline{A}_i(t)) =$ $\prod\limits_{i=2}^{k}(1 - \dfrac{\mu_i}{\mu_i + \lambda_i}) * \prod\limits_{j=k}^{N} \dfrac{\lambda_i}{\mu_i + \lambda_i}$	`(lim (λt. prob p` `(NAND_unavail_FT_gate p L1 L2 t) =` `list_prod (steady_state_avail M1) *` `list_prod (steady_state_unavail_list M2`
$\lim\limits_{t\to\infty} \overline{A}_{XOR}(t) =$ $\lim\limits_{t\to\infty} Pr(\overline{A}(t)B(t) \cup A(t)\overline{B}(t)) =$ $(1 - \dfrac{\lambda_1}{\lambda_1 + \mu_1}) * \dfrac{\lambda_2}{\lambda_2 + \mu_2} + \dfrac{\lambda_1}{\lambda_1 + \mu_1} *$ $(1 - \dfrac{\lambda_2}{\lambda_2 + \mu_2})$	`(lim (λt. prob p` `(XOR_unavail_FT_gate p A B &t)) =` `(1 - (steady_state_unavail M1))*` `(steady_state_unavail M2) +` `(steady_state_unavail M1)*` `(1 - (steady_state_unavail M2))`
$\lim\limits_{t\to\infty} \overline{A}_{NOT}(t) = Pr(A(t)) = (1 - \dfrac{\lambda}{\lambda + \mu})$	`lim (λt. prob p (NOT_FT_gate p A &t) =` `FST m / (FST m + SND m)`

occurrence of the system top unavailability event. These unavailability events are then combined to model the overall fault behavior of the given system by using the fault gates. These combinations of basic unavailability events, called cut sets, are then reduced to minimal cut sets (MCS) by using set-theory rules, such as idempotent, associative and commutative. The PIE is then used to evaluate the overall failure probability of the given system.

If $\overline{A}_i$ represent the ith basic unavailability event or a combination of unavailability events then the overall unavailability of the given system can be expressed in terms of the probabilistic inclusion-exclusion principle as follows:

$$\mathbb{P}(\bigcup_{i=1}^{n} \overline{A}_i) = \sum_{J \neq \{\}, J \subseteq \{1,2,...,n\}} (-1)^{|J|-1} \mathbb{P}(\bigcap_{j \in J} \overline{A}_j) \qquad (9)$$

The above equation has been formalized in HOL4 as follows [14]:

Theorem 7. ⊢ ∀ p L t. prob_space p ∧
(∀ x. MEM x (union_avail_event_list p L t) ⇒ x ∈ events p) ⇒
  (prob p (union_list (union_avail_event_list p L t)) =
    sum_set {y | y ⊆ set (union_avail_event_list p L t) ∧ y ≠ {}}
      (λt. -1 pow (CARD y - 1) * prob p (BIGINTER y)))

The function sum_set recursively sums the return value of the function f, which is applied on each element of the given set s. In the above theorem, the set s is represented by the term $\{x|C(x)\}$ that contains all the values of x, which satisfy condition C. Whereas, the λ abstraction function (λt. -1 pow (CARD t - 1) * prob p (BIGINTER t)) models $(-1)^{|J|-1}\mathbb{P}(\bigcap_{j \in J} \overline{A_j})$, such that the functions CARD and BIGINTER return the number of elements and the intersection of all the elements of the given set, respectively.

The proof script [21] of the above-mentioned formalizations of ABD and unavailability FT gates and the PIE principle is composed of more than 9000 lines of HOL script and took about 350 man-hours. The main outcome of this formalization is that the definitions and theorems of ABDs and FT gates can be used to capture the behavior of wide variety of real-world systems and analyze their corresponding availability in higher-order logic.

6   Application: Satellite Solar Arrays

As an illustrative application to demonstrate the effectiveness of our availability theory related formalization, we consider a solar array that has been used in the DFH-3 Satellite, which was launched by the People's Republic of China on May 12, 1997 [18,19]. Solar arrays are one of the most vital components of the satellites because the mission success heavily depends upon the continuous reliable source of power. The satellite's solar array is a mechanical system, which mainly consists of various mechanisms, including: deployable, synchronization, locking and orientation.

The solar array can be modeled by using series-parallel ABD configurations, shown in Fig. 2, and based on the availability of its individual components, such as electric detonator (ED), the cutting knife (CK), the starting spring (SS), hing bearing (HB) and hing of locking mechanism (HL), the overall availability of the solar array can be evaluated [18]. The HOL4 formalization of the solar array ABD (Fig. 2) is as follows:

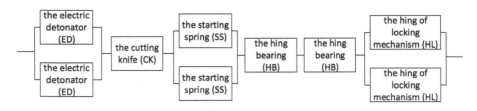

Fig. 2. Solar array ABD

Definition 8. ⊢ ∀p X_ED X_CK X_SS X_HB X_HL t .
RO_ABD p X_ED X_CK X_SS X_HB X_HL t =
series_parallel_struct p
    (list_union_avail_event_list
        ([[X_ED;X_ED];[X_CK];[X_SS;X_SS];[X_HB];[X_HB];[X_HL;X_HL]]) t)

We verified the following theorem for the availability of the satellite solar array:

Theorem 8. ⊢ ∀p X_ED X_CK X_SS X_HB X_HL.
(lim (λt. prob p (RO_ABD p X_ED X_CK X_SS X_HB X_HL &t)) =
(1 - (1 - steady_state_avail ED) pow 2) * steady_state_avail CK *
(1 - (1 - steady_state_avail SS) pow 2) *
((steady_state_avail HB) pow 2) * (1 - (1 - steady_state_avail HL) pow 2)

We have omitted the assumptions of this theorem here due to space limitations and the complete formalization is available at [21]. The proof of the above theorem is primarily based on Theorem 5 and is very straightforward.

An unavailability FT can be constructed by considering the faults in the solar array mechanical components, which are the fundamental causes of satellite' solar array mechanisms failure. The unavailability FT for the solar array of the DFH-3 Satellite that was launched by the People's Republic of China on May 12, 1997 [19] is depicted in Fig. 3 and we formally analyze this FT in this paper. The proposed FT formalization (functions OR_unavail_FT_gate and AND_unavail_FT_gate, given in Table 1) is used to model the MCS of the unavailability of the solar array as follows:

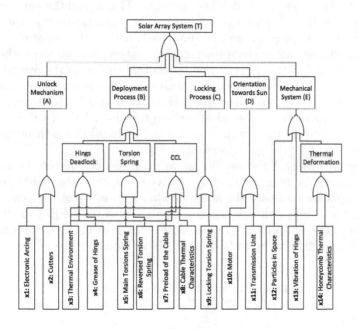

Fig. 3. Solar array unavailability FT

Definition 9. ⊢ ∀ p x1 x2 x3 x4 x5 x6 x7 x8 x9 x10 x11 x12 x13 x14 t.
Solar_unavail_FT p x1 x2 x3 x4 x5 x6 x7 x8 x9 x10 x11 x12 x13 x14 t =
OR_unavail_FT_gate

```
[OR_unavail_FT_gate (union_avail_event_list p [x1; x2; x3; x4] t);
AND_unavail_FT_gate p (union_avail_event_list p [x5; x6] t);
OR_unavail_FT_gate
   (union_avail_event_list p [x7; x8; x9; x10; x11; x12; x13; x14] t)]
```

The overall unavailability of a solar array can now be verified as follows:

Theorem 9. $\vdash \forall$ p x1 x2 x3 x4 x5 x6 x7 x8 x9 x10 x11 x12 x13 x14.
(lim(λt.

Solar_unavail_FT p x1 x2 x3 x4 x5 x6 x7 x8 x9 x10 x11 x12 x13 x14 &t)) =
1 - (list_prod (steady_state_unavail_list [x5;x6]) *
(1 - list_prod (one_minus_list (steady_state_unavail_list
      [c1;c2;c3;c4;c6;c7;c8;c9;c10;c11;c12;c13;c14])))))

Again all quantifiers and the assumptions of the above theorem have not been included due to space limitations and the complete theorem can be found at [21]. The proof of the above theorem utilizes the PIE principle (Theorem 7) and the unavailability FT gates with their corresponding mathematical expression, given in Tables 1 and 2.

The proof script [21] for Theorems 8 and 9 is composed of about 100 lines of HOL code compared to about 9000 lines of code that had to be written to formalize the foundational availability concepts. This straightforward reasoning clearly indicates the usefulness of our work. The distinguishing features of the formally verified Theorems 8 and 9, compared to the other existing availability analysis alternatives, include their generic nature, i.e., all the variables are universally quantified and thus can be specialized to obtain the availability for any given failure and repair rates, and their guaranteed correctness due to the involvement of a sound theorem prover in their verifications. Moreover, the usage of a theorem prover in their verification ensures that all the required assumptions for the validity of the results are explicitly included in the theorems, which is quite important for designing accurate systems.

In order to facilitate the use of our formally verified results by industrial design engineers for their availability analysis, we have also developed a set of SML scripts to automate the simplification step of these theorems for any given failure and repair rate values corresponding to the DFH-3 satellite solar array components. For instance, the auto_solar_RBD_avail script automatically computes the availability up to 12 decimal places based on Theorem 8 as follows:

```
⊢ prob_space p ∧
(∀t'. (∀z. MEM z (FLAT (list_union_avail_event_list
   [[X_ED;X_ED];[X_CK];[X_SS;X_SS];[X_HB];[X_HB];[X_HL;X_HL]] (&t'))) ⇒
z ∈ events p) ∧
mutual_indep p (FLAT
(list_union_avail_event_list
   [[X_ED;X_ED];[X_CK];[X_SS;X_SS];[X_HB];[X_HB];[X_HL;X_HL]] (&t')))) ∧
two_dim_inst_avail_exp p
[[X_ED;X_ED];[X_CK];[X_SS;X_SS];[X_HB];[X_HB];[X_HL;X_HL]]
[[(0.1,0.3);(0.1,0.3)];[(0.2,0.5)]; [(0.3,0.4); (0.3,0.4)]; [(0.7,0.8)];
[(0.7,0.8)]; [(0.5,0.5); (0.5,0.5)]] ⇒
lim (λt. prob p ( RO_ABD p X_ED X_CK X_SS X_HB X_HL &t)) = 0.116618075802
```

This `auto_solar_RBD_avail` script can be used for any values of the failure
and repair rates and can be easily extended to be used for the instantiation
of the generic result of Theorems 9 [21]. With a very little modification, these
kind of automation scripts can facilitate industrial design engineers to accurate
determine the availability of many other safety-critical systems.

7 Conclusion

The foremost requirements to conduct the formal availability analysis within a
theorem prover is to formalize the ABD configurations, i.e., series, parallel, series-
parallel and parallel-series, unavailability FT gates, such as AND, OR, NAND,
NOR, XOR and NOT, and instantaneous and steady-state availability. This
paper fulfills the above-mentioned requirement and thus provides a framework,
which can be used to carry out the formal availability analysis of any system
within a sound core of HOL4 theorem prover. For illustration, our formalizations
are utilized to conduct the formal availability analysis of an satellite solar array
and the results have been found to more rigorous than the existing availability
analysis alternatives. However, this formalization is only limited to static ABD
and UFT models and cannot express the time varying system states, dependent
systems and non-series-parallel topologies. This limitation can be removed by
extending the present formalization to dynamic ABD and dynamic UFT. This
can be done by combining this formalization of ABD and UFT with the recently
proposed Markov chain formalization [22] in HOL4.

References

1. Trivedi, K.S.: Probability and Statistics with Reliability, Queuing and Computer
   Science Applications, 2nd edn. Wiley, London (2002)
2. Stapelberg, R.F.: Handbook of Reliability, Availability, Maintainability and Safety
   in Engineering Design. Springer Science & Business Media, Berlin (2009)
3. Blake, J.T., Trivedi, K.S.: Multistage interconnection network reliability. Trans.
   Comput. **38**(11), 1600–1604 (1989)
4. Bistouni, F., Jahanshahi, M.: Analyzing the reliability of shuffle-exchange networks
   using reliability block diagrams. Reliab. Eng. Syst. Saf. **132**, 97–106 (2014)
5. ReliaSoft (2016). http://www.reliasoft.com/
6. ASENT (2016). https://www.raytheoneagle.com/asent/rbd.htm
7. Bailis, P., Kingsbury, K.: The network is reliable. Queue **12**(7), 20 (2014)
8. Robidoux, R., Xu, H., Xing, L., Zhou, M.: Automated modeling of dynamic reliability block diagrams using colored Petri nets. IEEE Trans. Syst. Man Cybern.
   Part A: Syst. Hum. **40**(2), 337–351 (2010)
9. Bozzano, M., Cimatti, A., Katoen, J.-P., Nguyen, V.Y., Noll, T., Roveri, M.: The
   COMPASS approach: correctness, modelling and performability of aerospace systems. In: Buth, B., Rabe, G., Seyfarth, T. (eds.) SAFECOMP 2009. LNCS, vol.
   5775, pp. 173–186. Springer, Heidelberg (2009)
10. Signoret, J.P., Dutuit, Y., Cacheux, P.J., Folleau, C., Collas, S., Thomas, P.: Make
    your Petri nets understandable: reliability block diagrams driven Petri nets. Reliab.
    Eng. Syst. Saf. **113**, 61–75 (2013)

11. Mhamdi, T., Hasan, O., Tahar, S.: On the formalization of the Lebesgue integration theory in HOL. In: Kaufmann, M., Paulson, L.C. (eds.) ITP 2010. LNCS, vol. 6172, pp. 387–402. Springer, Heidelberg (2010)
12. Ahmed, W., Hasan, O., Tahar, S., Hamdi, M.S.: Towards the formal reliability analysis of oil and gas pipelines. In: Watt, S.M., Davenport, J.H., Sexton, A.P., Sojka, P., Urban, J. (eds.) CICM 2014. LNCS, vol. 8543, pp. 30–44. Springer, Heidelberg (2014)
13. Ahmed, W., Hasan, O., Tahar, S.: Formal reliability analysis of wireless sensor network data transport protocols using HOL. In: Wireless and Mobile Computing, Networking and Communications, pp. 217–224. IEEE (2015)
14. Ahmed, W., Hasan, O.: Towards formal fault tree analysis using theorem proving. In: Kerber, M., Carette, J., Kaliszyk, C., Rabe, F., Sorge, V. (eds.) CICM 2015. LNCS, vol. 9150, pp. 39–54. Springer, Heidelberg (2015)
15. Gordon, M., Melham, T.: Introduction to HOL: A Theorem Proving Environment for Higher-Order Logic. Cambridge Press, Cambridge (1993)
16. Mathematica (2008). www.wolfram.com
17. Harrison, J., Théry, L.: Extending the HOL theorem prover with a computer algebra system to reason about the reals. In: Joyce, J.J., Seger, C.-J.H. (eds.) HUG 1993. LNCS, vol. 780, pp. 174–184. Springer, Heidelberg (1994)
18. Wu, H.C., Wang, C.J., Liu, P.: Reliability analysis of deployment mechanism of solar arrays. Appl. Mech. Mater. **42**, 139–142 (2011)
19. Wu, J., Yan, S., Xie, L.: Reliability analysis method of a solar array by using fault tree analysis and fuzzy reasoning Petri net. Acta Astronaut. **69**(11), 960–968 (2011)
20. Ebeling, C.E.: An Introduction to Reliability and Maintainability Engineering. Tata McGraw-Hill Education, Maidenherd (2004)
21. Ahmed, W.: Formalization of Availability Block Diagram and Unavailability FT (2016). http://save.seecs.nust.edu.pk/availability/
22. Liu, L.Y.: Formalization of discrete-time Markov chains in HOL. Ph.D. thesis, Concordia University (2013)

Formal Verification of the *rank* Algorithm for Succinct Data Structures

Akira Tanaka[1](✉), Reynald Affeldt[1], and Jacques Garrigue[2]

[1] National Institute of Advanced Industrial Science and Technology (AIST),
Tsukuba, Japan
`tanaka-akira@aist.go.jp`
[2] Nagoya University, Nagoya, Japan

Abstract. Succinct data structures are designed to use a minimal amount of computer memory in a time-efficient way. Their correct implementation is essential to big data analysis. Yet, succinct data structures are difficult to verify because they rely on bit-level manipulations better achieved with low-level languages. In this paper, we report on the formal verification of the standard Jacobson *rank* algorithm using the Coq proof-assistant and extract an OCaml implementation from it. This requires overcoming the mismatch between Coq being a purely functional programming language and succinct data structures being inherently imperative. To enjoy the best of both worlds, we propose to use code extraction from Coq to OCaml but with an original (tested but unverified) implementation of bitstrings. We can then use Coq to formalize correctness, including important claims about storage requirements, and still obtain efficient native code. To the best of our knowledge, this is the first application of formal verification to succinct data structures.

1 Towards Formal Verification for Succinct Data Structures

Succinct data structures are data structures designed to use an amount of computer memory close to the information-theoretic lower bound in a time-efficient way (see [18] for an introduction). They are used in particular to process big data. Concretely, succinct data structures make it possible to provide data analysis with a significantly reduced amount of memory (for example, one order of magnitude less memory for string search facilities in [2]). Thanks to an important amount of research, succinct data structures are now equipped with algorithms that are often as efficient as their classical counterparts. In this paper, we are concerned with the most basic one: the *rank* algorithm, which counts the number of 1 (or 0) in the prefixes of a bitstring (for example, *rank* is one of the few basic blocks in the implementation of [2]—see Appendix A of the technical report). The salient property of the *rank* algorithm is that it requires $o(n)$ storage for constant-time execution where n is the length of the bitstring (see Sect. 2 for background information).

© Springer International Publishing AG 2016
K. Ogata et al. (Eds.): ICFEM 2016, LNCS 10009, pp. 243–260, 2016.
DOI: 10.1007/978-3-319-47846-3_16

Our long-term goal is to provide formal verification of algorithms for succinct data structures. In particular, we aim at the construction of a realistic library of verified algorithms. Such a library could significantly improve the confidence in software implementation of big data analysis. However, software implementations of algorithms for succinct data structures are difficult to verify. Indeed, since these data structures are designed at the bit-level and since performance is a must-have, they are usually written in low-level languages (e.g., C++ for SDSL [16]). The direct verification of C-like languages is now possible [14] but it requires a substantial infrastructure (concretely, an instrumented formal semantics of the target language) whose development is orthogonal to the problem of verifying succinct data structures.

In this paper, we show how to develop a verified implementation of an algorithm for succinct data structures using the Coq proof-assistant [5]. Coq provides us with the ability to reason about the correctness of the algorithm: its functional correctness but also the important properties about storage requirements. We can also derive an efficient implementation thanks to the extraction facility from Coq to the OCaml language and the imperative features of the latter. The main issue when dealing with algorithms for succinct data structures in Coq is that, since Coq is a purely functional language, arrays are better represented as lists to perform formal verification. However, lists do not enjoy constant-time random-access, making it difficult to use the extraction facility of Coq to generate efficient OCaml algorithms. As a solution, we provide an OCaml library for bitstrings with constant-time random-access that matches the interface of Coq lists so that we can use real bitstrings in the extracted code. This approach augments the trusted base but in the form of a localized, reusable library of OCaml code whose formal verification can anyway be carried out at a later stage. We think that this is a reasonable price to pay compared to the benefits of carrying out formal verification in Coq.

Paper Overview. In this paper, we demonstrate our approach by building a verified implementation of the *rank* function using the Coq proof-assistant. More precisely, we provide formal verification for the *rank* function (formal proof of functional correctness in Sect. 5.2 and formal proof for storage requirements in Sect. 5.3) and extraction to executable OCaml code (by providing in particular a new library for bitstrings with constant-time random-access in Sects. 4.2 and 4.3). We will be able to check that the time-complexity of the extracted code is as expected (i.e., execution is constant-time, see Sect. 6.2). In the process, we discuss thoroughly the choices we made, in particular, the modular approach we took when formalizing the *rank* function in the Coq proof-assistant (generic version in Sect. 3.1 and its instantiation in Sect. 5.1).

2 A Formal Account of the *rank* Algorithm

We explain what the *rank* algorithm is supposed to achieve (its *functional correctness*, Sect. 2.1) and how Jacobson's *rank* actually achieves it (in particular, its storage requirements, Sect. 2.2). These points are addressed formally using Coq resp. in Sects. 5.2 and 5.3.

2.1 Specification of the Functional Correctness of the *rank* Algorithm

Given a bitstring s and an index i in s, $rank_s(i)$ counts the number of 1's up to i (excluded). For example, in Fig. 1 (the first and second-level directories will be explained in Sect. 2.2), s contains 26 1's, $rank_s(4) = 2$, $rank_s(36) = 17$, and $rank_s(58) = 26$.

The mathematically-inclined reader would formally specify the *rank* algorithm as $rank_s(i) = |\{k \in [0,\dots,i) \mid s[k] = b\}|$ where b is the query bit ($b = 1$ in the example above). Using the Coq proof-assistant, such a specification can be formalized directly. For bits, one can use the Coq type for Booleans `bool`. An input bitstring can be formalized as a list of Booleans (type `seq bool` in Coq). An index i is a natural number (type `nat` in Coq). A functional programmer would formally specify the *rank* algorithm as list surgery and filtering. For example:

```
Definition rank b i s := count_mem b (take i s).
```

We regard this Coq function as the specification of the functional correctness of the *rank* algorithm. Note that it does not provide an efficient implementation: it can be executed (both in Coq and as an extracted OCaml program) but computation would (hopefully) be linear-time. In this paper, we provide Coq functions that are more realistic in the sense that they can be extracted to executable OCaml code.

2.2 Jacobson's *rank* Algorithm and Its Space Complexity

Jacobson's *rank* algorithm [11] is a constant-time implementation of *rank*. It uses auxiliary data structures, in particular two arrays called the first and second-level directories that essentially contain pre-computed values of *rank* for substrings of the input bitstring s of size n (see Fig. 1). More precisely, each directory contains

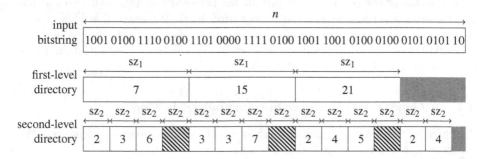

Fig. 1. Illustration for the *rank* algorithm ($sz_2 = 4$, $sz_1 = 4 \times sz_2$, $n = 58$). Example extended from [13].

fixed-size integers, whose bit-size is large enough to represent the intended values, so that the bit-size for each directory depends on n.

Let sz_2 be the size of the substrings used for the second-level directory. Hereafter, we refer to these substrings as the "small blocks". The size of the substrings used for the first-level directory is $sz_1 = k \times sz_2$ for some k. We refer to these substrings as the "big blocks". The first-level directory is precisely an array of n/sz_1 integers such that the ith integer is $rank_s((i+1) \times sz_1)$. The second-level directory is also an array of integers. It has n/sz_2 entries and is such that the ith entry is the number of bits among the $(i\%k + 1) \times sz_2$ bits starting from the $((i/k) \times sz_1)$th bit ($/$ is integer division and $\%$ is the remainder operation). One can observe that when $i\%k = k - 1$, the ith entry of the second-level directory (the hatched rectangles in Fig. 1) can be computed from the first-level directory and therefore does not need to be remembered.

Given an index i, Jacobson's $rank$ algorithm decomposes i such that $rank_s(i)$ can be computed by adding the results of (1) one lookup into the first-level directory, (2) one lookup into the second-level directory, and (3) direct computation of $rank$ for a substring shorter than sz_2. For example, in Fig. 1, $rank_s(36) = rank_s(2 \times 16 + 1 \times 4 + 0)$ is computed as $15 + 2$ and $rank_s(58) = rank_s(3 \times 16 + 2 \times 4 + 2)$, as $21 + 4 + 1$. Since the computation of $rank$ for a substring shorter than sz_2 in (3) can also be tabulated or computed with a single instruction on some platforms, $rank$'s computation is constant-time.

It can be shown (and we will do it formally in Sect. 5.3) that the directories require only $\frac{n}{\log_2 n} + \frac{2n \log_2 \log_2 n}{\log_2 n} \in o(n)$ bits with integers of the appropriate size (not necessarily the word size of the underlying architecture).

3   Our Approach: Extraction from a Generic *rank* Function

In a nutshell, our approach consists in (1) providing a generic implementation of the *rank* algorithm to keep formal proofs as high-level as possible and (2) extracting OCaml code from a concrete instantiation of the *rank* algorithm. As explained in Sect. 1, this approach makes it difficult to obtain efficient OCaml code because of the conflicting requirements between the data structures at the formal proof level and at the implementation level. We make this idea clearer in Sect. 3.2 where we also justify our approach. Before that, we explain the (generic) *rank* algorithm that we will verify and extract (instantiation to be found in Sect. 5.1).

3.1   A Generic Rank Algorithm Formalized in Coq

The generic version essentially consists of two functions: one that constructs the directories and one that performs the lookup.

To simplify the presentation, we first explain a function that counts bits in a naive way[1]. bcount b i l s counts the number of bits b (0 or 1) inside the slice $[i, \ldots, i + l]$ of the bitstring s (essentially a list of booleans—see Sect. 4.1):

```
Definition bcount b i l s := count_mem b (take l (drop i s))
```

In the code below, we use notations from the Mathematical Components [7] library: .+1 is the successor function, %/ and %% are the integer division and modulo operators, and if x is xp.+1 then e1 else e2 means: if x is greater than 0 then return e1 with xp bound to $x - 1$, else return e2.

Construction of the Directories. The function buildDir computes both directories in one pass (it returns a pair). It has been written with extraction in mind. In particular, it uses tail calls, and indexing instead of list pattern-matching.

j is a counter for small blocks (we start counting from nn, the total number of small blocks, i.e., n/sz_2). i is a counter to count small blocks in one big block. n1 contains the number of bits counted so far for the current big block. n2 contains the number of bits counted so far for the current small block. D1 (resp. D2) are abstract data types meant for the first-level (resp. second-level) directory (so that emptyD1, pushD1, etc. are meant to be instantiated with concrete functions later).

The function buildDir iterates over the number of small blocks. At each iteration, the number of bits in the current small block is stored in m (line 2) (b is the query bit, sz2 is the size of small blocks, inbits is the input bitstring). For each small block, n2 is stored in the second-level directory (line 4). After a big block has been scanned, the number of bits counted so far for the current big block n1 + n2 is stored in the first-level directory (line 8). The number of small blocks in one big block (kp plus 1) is used to control the iteration inside a big block (line 10).

Observe that the directories built by buildDir are slightly different from the data structures explained in Sect. 2.2: they start with a 0 (stored at line 8 for the first-level directory and stored at line 9 for each group of small blocks) which is of course not necessary but this simplifies the lookup function.

```
1  Fixpoint buildDir j i n1 n2 D1 D2 :=
2    let m := bcount b ((nn - j) * sz2) sz2 inbits in
3    if i is ip.+1 then
4      let D2' := pushD2 D2 n2 in
5      if j is jp.+1 then buildDir jp ip n1 (n2 + m) D1 D2'
6      else (D1, D2')
7    else
8      let D1' := pushD1 D1 (n1 + n2) in
9      let D2' := pushD2 D2 0 in
10     if j is jp.+1 then buildDir jp kp (n1 + n2) m D1' D2'
11     else (D1', D2').
12 Definition rank_init_gen := buildDir nn 0 0 0 emptyD1 emptyD2.
```

---

[1] The function bcount is not intended to be extracted as it is but replaced by a more efficient function. It could be tabulated as explained in Sect. 2.2, but in this paper, it will be replaced by a single gcc built-in operation (see Sect. 4.2).

Lookup. The function `rank_lookup_gen` is a generic implementation of the lookup function. It computes the rank for index `i`:

```
Definition rank_lookup_gen i :=
  let j2 := i %/ sz2 in (* index in the second-level directory *)
  let j3 := i %% sz2 in (* index in a small block *)
  let j1 := j2 %/ k in (* index in the first-level directory *)
  lookupD1 j1 D1 + lookupD2 j2 D2 + bcount b (j2 * sz2) j3 inbits.
```

`j1` (resp. `j2`) is the index of the block in the first-level directory (resp. second-level directory). They are computed using the size of small blocks `sz2` and the ratio between the size of big and small blocks `k` (or in other words, `sz1 = k * sz2`). `lookupD1` (resp. `lookupD2`) is meant to perform array lookup; it will be instantiated later.

3.2 Our Approach w.r.t Extraction

In the code above, lookup in the directories is meant to be performed by the functions `lookupD1` and `lookupD2`. Constant-time execution for these functions is required for Jacobson's *rank* function to be efficient. If we implement these functions with `nth`-like access to standard `lists` (which is linear-time), Coq will not generate OCaml functions with the desired time complexity. At first, one may think of looking for an ingenious implementation scheme that may cause Coq to generate efficient OCaml code. This approach seems to us too optimistic as a first step towards the goal of providing a verified library of functions for succinct data structures for the following two reasons:

- Coming up with new implementation schemes is likely to make more difficult the task of proving formally the functional correctness and the storage requirements of algorithms.
- The code extraction facility of Coq is not optimized in any way (by design, because it is part of the trusted base). In practice, it tends to generate inefficient code for convoluted formalizations. As a matter of fact, previous work shows that Coq requires significant engineering to handle imperative features and native data structures (e.g., [3]).

Instead, our approach consists in (1) making the best we can out of list-like data structures in Coq and (2) providing an efficient OCaml implementation of the list interface that we will substitute to Coq-generated functions.

4 An OCaml Bitstring Library for Coq Lists of Booleans

Direct extraction of Coq lists and list functions suffers two major problems w.r.t. succinct data structures: (1) memory usage is very inefficient (assuming 64-bit machine words, it would take 192 bits to represent one Boolean), (2) random-access will be linear-time instead of the required constant-time complexity. We now explain an OCaml implementation for the interface of Coq lists that solves above problems.

4.1 Bitstrings Formalized in Coq

We define bitstrings as an inductive type which wraps Coq lists:

```
Inductive bits : Type := bseq of seq bool.
```

The type `bits` is isomorphic to the type of lists of booleans. In consequence, many functions for `bits` are easily derivable from Coq standard functions `size`, `nth`, `++` (concatenation), etc. In particular, we equip our formalization with a *coercion* that transparently turns the type `bits` into the type `seq bool`. Concretely, this coercion is the function `Definition seq_of_bits s := match s with bseq l => l end.` that is automatically inserted by Coq to make types match. For example, `size s` below should actually read as `size (seq_of_bits s)`.

```
Definition bnil := bseq nil.
Definition bsize (s : bits) := size s.
Definition bnth (s : bits) i := nth false s i.
Definition bappend (s1 s2 : bits) := bseq (s1 ++ s2).
```

However, code extracted from above functions does not achieve the desired complexity. For example, the code extracted from `bsize`, `bnth`, and `bcount` (Sect. 3.1) would be linear-time because these functions scan the lists obtained from `bits`[2]. Regarding memory usage, the list constructor `cons` would allocate one memory block per argument (see Fig. 2, on the left, for an illustration). In addition, OCaml needs one more word for each block to manage memory. Assuming the machine word is 64 bits, `cons` would therefore need 192 bits to represent a Coq `bool`, that was supposed to represent a single bit...

In the next section (Sect. 4.2), we provide OCaml definitions to replace the Coq type `bits`, its constant `bnil` and the functions `bsize`, `bnth`, `bappend`, etc. How the OCaml definitions are substituted for the Coq definitions is explained in Sect. 6.1.

4.2 Bitstrings Implemented in OCaml

The main idea to achieve linear-time construction and constant-time random-access in OCaml is to implement bitstrings using a datatype that allows for random-access of bits. For this purpose, we use the type `bytes` introduced in OCaml 4.02.0[3]. The resulting OCaml type is as follows[4]:

```
type bits_buffer = { mutable used : int; data : bytes; }
type bits = Bdummy0 | Bdummy1 | Bref of int * bits_buffer (* len, buf *)
```

---

[2] Let s be a bitstring of length n. `bsize` s is $O(n)$, `bnth` i s is $O(i)$, `bcount` b i l s is $O(i + l)$. `bcount` requires an additional $O(i)$ because of the `drop` function (see Sect. 3.1).

[3] Currently, `bytes` is the same as `string`; OCaml plans to change `string` to immutable.

[4] The OCaml definitions below belong to the module `Pbits`; the prefix `Pbits.` is omitted when no confusion is possible.

Fig. 2. A Coq `bits` on the left and the corresponding OCaml `bits` on the right

Bitstrings are stored in a `bits_buffer` as a value of type `bytes` together with the number of bits `used` so far. (The first bit is the least significant bit of the first byte in the `bytes`.) Let us first explain the constructor for arbitrary-length bitstrings (`Bref`) and then explain how short bitstrings are implemented as unboxed integers (this will explain `Bdummy0` and `Bdummy1`).

bits Represented with `Bref`. The data structure `Bref`(*len, buf*) (depicted on the right of Fig. 2) represents the prefix of size *len* of the bitstring *buf*. Let us call *used* the value of the field `used` of the corresponding `bits_buffer` data structure.

The dynamics of `Bref` is as follows. Initially, a `Bref` has 0 as *len* and references a `bits_buffer` with *used* as 0, which means that the bitstring is empty. When a bit is appended to the `Bref`, the `bits_buffer` is destructively updated and a new `Bref` is allocated. The bit is assigned to the $used^{th}$ bit in `data` and *used* is incremented. A new `Bref` is allocated with incremented *len* and reference the `bits_buffer`. (When the `bits_buffer` is full (i.e., $8 \times |\text{data}| = used$), `data` is copied into a new `bytes` with a doubled length before the bit is appended.) Array construction always append a bit to `Bref` which *len* is equal to *used*.

The constructor `Bref` can represent any bitstring but it requires memory allocation for each value, even to represent an empty bitstring, a single boolean, etc. We can improve efficiency by avoiding memory allocation for bitstring that fit in machine words. Note that there is no soundness problem in losing sharing of bitstrings, because bitstrings `bits` are immutable in Coq.

bits Represented with Unboxed Integers. In summary, we use the unboxed integers of OCaml to represent short bitstrings. In OCaml, values are represented by w-bit integers, w being the number of bits in a machine word (32 or 64). These integers represent either (1) a $(w - 1)$-bit unboxed integer or (2) a pointer to a block allocated in the heap. OCaml datatypes use unboxed integers for constant constructors, and pointers to blocks otherwise. Therefore, we can represent short bitstrings by unboxed integers. More precisely, we represent bitstrings of length $u \leq w-2$ as a $(w-1)$-bit integer using the following format: $\overbrace{0\ldots0}^{w-u-2} 1b_{u-1}\ldots b_1 b_0 1$ (the position of the topmost 1 represents the length of the bitstring and the trailing 1 is a tag bit to distinguish unboxed integers from pointers). To treat the latter integers as `bits` we use `Obj.magic`. For example, `bnil` $(0\ldots011)$ is defined as follows.

```
let bits_from_int bn = ((Obj.magic (bn : int)) : bits)
let bnil = bits_from_int 1 (* the tag bit is invisible in OCaml *)
```

The reason for adding the constructors Bdummy0 and Bdummy1 to the datatype bits is technical. Without them, OCaml optimizes pattern-matching (discrimination of values with match) if a datatype has no constant constructor (assuming that the value must be a pointer), or if it has only one constant constructor (assuming that any non-zero value must be a pointer). Adding two constant constructors disables these optimizations, and allows us to safely use pattern-matching to discriminate unboxed integers from Bref blocks.

OCaml Functions for Bitstrings. Using the OCaml bits datatype, we have implemented OCaml functions that match the Coq functions of Sect. 4.1 but with better complexities, as summarized in Table 1. For this purpose, we make use of OCaml imperative features such as destructive update and random access in bytes.

Table 1. Time complexity of OCaml functions w.r.t. their Coq counterparts (n and n' are the lengths of s and s')

Function	Complexity in Coq	Complexity in OCaml
bsize s	$O(n)$	$O(1)$
bnth s i	$O(i)$	$O(1)$
bappend s s'	$O(n)$	$O(n')$ (amortized, for array construction)
bcount b i l s	$O(i+l)$	$O(l)$

4.3   From Natural Numbers to Fixed-Size Integers

At the abstract level, the *rank* algorithm stores natural numbers in directories but a concrete implementation manipulates fixed-size integers instead. For this reason, we extend our Coq formalization and OCaml implementation of bitstrings with functions to manipulate fixed-size integers:

Table 2. Interface and implementation of the first-level directory using generic array functions

Interface	Implementation
D1Arr	bits
emptyD1 : D1Arr	bnil
pushD1 w1 s n : D1Arr	bappend s (bword w1 n)
lookupD1 w1 i s : nat	getword (i * w1) w1 s

- `bword u n` builds a short bitstring from the lower $u \leq w - 2$ bits of a natural number `n` in constant-time. In OCaml, a natural number is formatted as $b_{w-2} \ldots b_1 b_0 1$, where w is the number of bits in a machine word. In order to construct short bitstrings as unboxed integers following the format explained in Sect. 4.2, we use simple bit operations: clear the higher bits, $b_{w-2} \ldots b_{u+1}$, and set the topmost bit, b_u.
- `getword i u s` looks for the $u \leq w - 2$ bits (ordered with least significant bit first) starting from index `i` in `s`, regarding them as a natural number. In OCaml, this function is implemented by accessing data at the level of bytes (not bits) to reduce the overhead (number of bit operations and number of loops).

Using these functions, it becomes possible to provide a concrete instantiation of directories. For example, let us consider the first-level directory, that stores fixed-size integers of size `w1`. Its implementation is summarized in Table 2. Let `D1Arr` be the type of the first-level directory. An empty first-level directory is implemented by an empty array `emptyD1` that is just an empty bitstring `bnil`. The result of appending an unboxed integer `n` (seen as a `w1`-bit bitstring) to the first-level directory `s` is implemented by the array `pushD1 w1 s n`. `lookupD1 w1 i s` is the ith pushed in the first-level directory `s`.

5   Formal Verification of an Instance of the Generic *rank* Algorithm

We instantiate the generic *rank* function of Sect. 3.1 to obtain a concrete implementation of Jacobson's *rank* algorithm. Then, we prove that this implementation indeed computes *rank* (as specified in Sect. 2.1) and fulfills storage requirements (as seen at the end of Sect. 2.2).

5.1   Instantiation of the *rank* Algorithm

We instantiate the functions from Sect. 3.1 (`rank_lookup_gen` and `rank_init_gen`) with the array of bits from Sect. 4.3. The parameters of this instantiation (number and size of blocks in the directories, etc.) are important because they need to be properly set to achieve the storage requirements specified in Sect. 2.2. For the sake of clarity, we isolate these parameters by means of two datatypes. `Record Param` carries the parameters of Jacobson's algorithm. `Record Aux` essentially carries the results of the execution of the initialization phase:

```
1  Record Param : Set := mkParam     7  Record Aux : Set := mkAux
2  { kp_of  : nat ;                   8  { query_bit: bool;
3    sz2p_of : nat ;                  9    input_bits: bits;
4    nn_of  : nat ;                  10    parameter: Param;
5    w1_of  : nat ;                  11    directories: D1Arr * D2Arr }.
6    w2_of  : nat }.
```

Jacobson's algorithm is parameterized by the number of small blocks (minus 1) in a big block (or $sz_1/sz_2 - 1$) (field kp_of, line 2), the number of bits (minus 1) in a small block (or $sz_2 - 1$) (line 3), the number of small blocks (line 4), and the bit-size of fixed-size integers for each directory (lines 5–6). The instantiation of rank_init_gen returns the query bit (line 8), the input bitstring (line 9), the parameters of Jacobson's algorithm (line 10), the first and second-level directories themselves (line 11).

The instantiation of rank_init_gen is a matter of passing the appropriate parameters and the functions D1Arr, D2Arr, etc. that we explained in Sect. 4.3:

```
Definition rank_init b s : Aux :=
  let param := rank_param (bsize s) in
  let w1 := w1_of param in let w2 := w2_of param in
  mkAux b s param
    (rank_init_gen b s param
       D1Arr emptyD1 (pushD1 w1) D2Arr emptyD2 (pushD2 w2)).
```

Similarly, rank_lookup_gen is instantiated with the parameters resulting from the execution of rank_init together with the functions D1Arr, D2Arr, etc. from Sect. 4.3:

```
Definition rank_lookup aux i :=
  let b := query_bit aux in
  let param := parameter aux in
  let w1 := w1_of param in let w2 := w2_of param in
  rank_lookup_gen b (input_bits aux) param
    D1Arr (lookupD1 w1) D2Arr (lookupD2 w2)
    (directories aux) i.
```

5.2 Functional Correctness of Jacobson's Algorithm in Coq

The functional correctness of Jacobson's algorithm is stated using the generic *rank* function (rank_lookup_gen, Sect. 3.1) with its formal specification (rank, Sect. 2.1). As a matter of fact, we do not need to assume any concrete instantiation of the directories to establish functional correctness, the generic properties of arrays are sufficient.

```
Lemma rank_lookup_gen_ok_to_spec : forall i dirpair,
  i <= size inbits ->
  dirpair = rank_init_gen b inbits param
    D1Arr emptyD1 pushD1 D2Arr emptyD2 pushD2 ->
  rank_lookup_gen b input_b param
    D1Arr lookupD1 D2Arr lookupD2 dirpair i = rank b i inbits.
```

The many parameters D1Arr, D2Arr, etc. come from the array interface that we implemented using the Section mechanism of Coq.

5.3 Space Complexity of Auxiliary Data Structures

The required storage depends on the parameters of Jacobson's algorithm explained in Sect. 5.1. They should be chosen appropriately to achieve $o(n)$ space complexity. We use the following parameters. They are taken from [4, Sect. 2.2.1]. We add 1 to sz_2 and k to make them strictly positive for all $n \geq 0$.

$$k = \lceil \log_2(n+1) \rceil + 1 \qquad\qquad w_1 = \lceil \log_2(\lfloor n/sz_2 \rfloor \times sz_2 + 1) \rceil$$
$$sz_2 = \lceil \log_2(n+1) \rceil + 1 \qquad\qquad w_2 = \lceil \log_2((k-1) \times sz_2 + 1) \rceil$$
$$sz_1 = k \times sz_2 = (\lceil \log_2(n+1) \rceil + 1)^2$$

The formalization in Coq of above parameters is direct. Below, `bitlen n`[5] is Coq code for $\lceil \log_2(n+1) \rceil$:

```
Definition rank_default_param n :=
  let kp   := bitlen n in (* k-1 *)
  let sz2p := bitlen n in (* sz2-1 *)
  let sz2  := sz2p.+1 in
  let nn   := n %/ sz2 in
  let w1   := bitlen (n %/ sz2 * sz2) in
  let w2   := bitlen (kp * sz2) in
  mkParam kp sz2p nn w1 w2.
```

Using these parameters, we showed that the asymptotic storage requirement for the auxiliary data structures is indeed $o(n)$, more precisely $\frac{n}{\log_2 n} + \frac{2n \log_2 \log_2 n}{\log_2 n}$, similarly to [4, Theorem 2.1].

For the sake of illustration, let us show how we prove in Coq that the contribution of the first-level directory to space complexity is $\frac{n}{\log_2 n}$. First, we fix *rank*'s parameters using the following declaration:

```
Definition rank_param n := rank_param_w_neq0 (rank_default_param n).
```

`rank_default_param` has been explained just above. `rank_param_w_neq0` is just a technicality to take care of the uninteresting case where the length of input bitstring is zero[6]. The contribution of the first-level directory to space complexity is the length of the bitstring that represents it, i.e., `size (directories (rank_init b s)).1` (`.1` stands for the first projection of a pair). In Coq, we proved the following lemma about this length:

```
Lemma rank_spaceD1 b s :
  size (directories (rank_init b s)).1 =
  let n := size s in let m := bitlen n in
  ((n %/ m.+1) %/ m.+1).+1 * (bitlen (n %/ m.+1 * m.+1)).-1.+1.
```

(`.-1` is notation for the predecessor function.)

For the sake of readability, we write this Coq expression using mathematical notations (in the case where $n \geq 3$):

$$\left(\frac{\frac{n}{\lceil \log_2(n+1) \rceil + 1}}{m+1} + 1 \right) p$$

with :
$$m = \lceil \log_2(n+1) \rceil$$
$$p = \lceil \log_2(\frac{n}{m+1} \cdot (m+1) + 1) \rceil$$
where $\div$ is the Euclidean division

---

[5] This function is implemented in C using gcc's `__builtin_clzl` [6], which counts the number of leading zeros in a `long` value. gcc generates LZCNT instructions (since Intel AVX2 [8]).

[6] In this case, `w1` and `w2` become 0 and our word array cannot distinguish an empty array and non-empty array.

When n is large, we observe that $m \sim p$, thus the whole expression is asymptotically equal to $\frac{n}{\log_2 n}$, as desired. See [19] for the $\frac{2n \log_2 \log_2 n}{\log_2 n}$ contribution of the second-level directory to space complexity.

6 Final Extraction and Benchmark

We extract the *rank* function from Sect. 5.1 using the OCaml library for bit-strings from Sect. 4.2 and benchmark the result to check that its execution is constant-time.

6.1 Extraction of the Verified *rank* Function

Concretely, extraction from Coq is the matter of the command `Extraction` (see file `Extract.v` [19]).

Extraction of Coq Lists. To replace inductive types and functions with custom OCaml code, we provide the following hints:

```
1  Extract Inductive bits =>
2    "Pbits.bits" [ "Pbits.bseq" ] "Pbits.bmatch".
3  Extract Inlined Constant bnil => "Pbits.bnil".
4  Extract Inlined Constant bsize => "Pbits.bsize".
5  Extract Inlined Constant bnth => "Pbits.bnth".
6  Extract Inlined Constant bappend => "Pbits.bappend".
```

At line 1, we replace the Coq inductive type `bits` with the OCaml type `Pbits.bits` defined in OCaml. `Pbits.bseq` and `Pbits.bmatch` are specified to replace the constructor and pattern-matching expression which converts list of booleans to `Pbits.bits` and vice versa. `Pbits.bseq` and `Pbits.bmatch` are defined but our application doesn't use them to avoid memory inefficient list of booleans.

From line 3, the constant and functions `bnil`, `bsize`, `bnth`, etc. from Sect. 4.1 are replaced by `Pbits.bnil`, `Pbits.bsize`, `Pbits.bnth` etc. to be explained in Sect. 4.2.

Extraction of the *rank* Algorithm. Because we used abstractions in Coq, we must be careful about inlining at extraction-time to obtain OCaml code as efficient as possible. In particular, we need to ensure that the function parameters we have introduced for modularity using Coq's `Sections` are inlined. Concretely, we inline most function calls using the following Coq command: `Extraction Inline emptyD1 pushD1 lookupD1 ...` . As a result, `rank_lookup` looks like an hand-written program, prefix notations aside. As for the function `buildDir` in `rank_init`, we obtain a tail-recursive OCaml function, like the one we wrote in Coq, so that it should use constant-size stack independently of the input bitstring.

Since we obtain almost hand-written code, we can expect `ocamlopt` to provide us with all the usual optimizations. There are however specific issues due to Coq idiosyncrasies. For example, the pervasive usage of the successor function `.+1` for natural numbers is extracted to a call to the OCaml function `Pervasives.succ` that `ocamlopt` luckily turns into an integer increment. (One can check which inlining `ocamlopt` has performed by using `ocamlopt -dclambda`.) In contrast, anonymous function calls produced by extraction may be responsible for inefficiencies. For example, the mapping from Coq `nat` to OCaml `int` is defined as follows (file `ExtrOcamlNatInt.v` from the Coq standard library):

```
Extract Inductive nat => int [ "0" "Pervasives.succ" ]
 "(fun f0 fS n -> if n=0 then f0 () else fS (n-1))".
```

It is responsible for calls of the form `(fun f0 fS n -> ...)` `(fun _ -> E1)` `(fun jp -> E2)` that `ocamlopt` unfortunately cannot β-reduce.

6.2 Benchmarking of the Verified *rank* Function

Figure 3 shows the performance of a single lookup invocation for the *rank* function by measuring the time taken by `rank_lookup aux i` for inputs up to 1000Mbit (recall that the input string `s` is part of `aux`). We make measurements for 1000 values of the input size n. For each n, we make 10 measures for `i` between 0 and n. The measurement order is randomized (n and `i` are picked randomly).

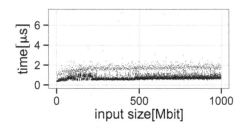

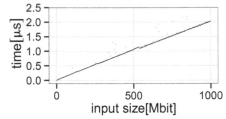

Fig. 3. Performance of rank lookup   **Fig. 4.** Performance of rank initialization

Execution seems constant-time ($0.83\,\mu s$ on average) w.r.t. the input size. One can observe that execution seems a bit faster for small inputs. We believe that this is the effect of memory cache. One can also observe that the result is noisy. We believe that this is because of memory cache with access patterns and some instructions, such as IDIV (integer division), that use a variable number of clock cycles [9].

Figure 4 shows the performance of initialization for the *rank* function by measuring the time taken by `rank_init` for inputs up to 1000 Mbit. We make measurements for 1000 values of the input size. As expected, the result seems linear. There are several small gaps, for input size 537 Mbit for example. This happens because the parameters for Jacobson's *rank* algorithm are changed at this point: sz_2 and k are changed from 30 bit to 31 bit, w1 is changed from 29 bit to 30 bit. As a result, the size of the first-level directory decreases from 17.3 Mbit to 16.8 Mbit and the second-level directory, from 179 Mbits to 174 Mbits, leading to a shorter initialization time.

Benchmark Environment. The operating system is Debian GNU/Linux 8.4 (Jessie) amd64 and the CPU is the Intel Core i7-4510U CPU (2.00 GHz, Haswell). The time is measured using the clock_gettime function with the CLOCK_PROCESS_CPUTIME_ID resolution set to 1 ns. The *rank* implementation is extracted by Coq 8.5pl1 and compiled to a native binary with ocamlopt version 4.02.3. C programs are compiled with gcc 4.9.2 with options -O -march=native (-march=native is used to enable POPCNT and LZCNT of recent Intel processors).

About OCaml's Garbage Collector. Gc.full_major and Gc.compact are invoked before each measurement to mitigate the GC effect. Garbage collection does not occur during lookup measurements (major_collections and minor_collections in Gc.stat are unchanged). During initialization measurements, the GC has a small impact. Indeed, in Fig. 4, major garbage collection happens at most 226 times during one initialization measurement. Moreover, using another experiment with gprof, we checked that the time spent by the GC (with Gc.full_major and Gc.compact disabled) during the rank_init benchmark accounts for less than 5 %.

7 Discussion and Perspectives

About Complexity. For the time being, we limited ourselves to benchmarking the extracted code for time-complexity. It would be more convincing to perform formal verification using a monadic approach (e.g., [15]). We have addressed the issue of space-complexity in Sect. 5.3. In general, one may also wonder about the space-complexity of intermediate data structures. In this paper, we obviously did not build any but this could also be addressed by counting the number of cons cells using a monad.

About Extraction of Natural Numbers. In this paper, there is no problem when we extract Coq nat to OCaml int, despite the fact that nat has no upper-bound. OCaml ints are $(w - 1)$-bit signed integers that can represent positive integers less than 2^{w-2} (w is the number of bits in a machine word) [12]. However, the maximum number of bits in an OCaml bytes is $2^{w-10}w$ bits because one OCaml block may not contain more than 2^{w-10} words [12]. Since $2^{w-10}w < 2^{w-2}$ for $w = 32$ and $w = 64$, an int can always represent the number of bits in a bytes. For this reason, nat arguments of functions such as bnth or intermediate values in the *rank* algorithm do not overflow when turned into int. This can be ensured during formal verification by using a type for fixed-size integers (such as int : nat -> Type in [1]) instead of natural numbers.

About Alignment. The extracted code can be further optimized by insisting on having the sizes (w1, w2 in this paper) of the integers in the directories to be multiples of 8. This removes the need for masking an shifting when reading entries from the directories. This can be enforced by modifying rank_default_param.

About the Correctness of OCaml Code. The OCaml part of the library has not been formally proved, but it has been extensively tested for functional correctness. We have implemented a test suite for the OCaml bitstring library using OUnit [17]. Concretely, we test functions for bits by comparison with list functions using random bitstrings. We also test the extracted *rank* function by comparison with the rank function defined in specification like style, i.e., count_mem b (drop i s). Since we plan to reuse this library for other functions, it will endure even more testing. Formal verification of the OCaml part would be interesting, but it seems difficult as of today, because we are relying on unspecified features regarding optimization, Obj.magic, and C.

Our rank function is careful to use bitstrings in a linear way (i.e., it never adds bits twice to the same bitstring), but the correctness of the OCaml bitstring library does not rely on this fact. Whenever it detects repeated addition to a shared buffer, which can be seen through a discrepancy between the used field of the bits_buffer and the *len* part of the Bref, it copies the first *len* bits to a new buffer before adding the extra bits.

Formal verification of the Coq library may be used to further guarantee the time-complexity properties of the OCaml library. For example, to achieve linear-time construction of arrays with bappend (Sect. 4.2), bappend s s' must be called on s at most once. The approach that we are currently exploring to ensure this property is to augment the *rank* function with an appropriate monad.

About Performance of the Extracted Implementation. We have not yet undertaken a thorough benchmark comparison with existing libraries for succinct data structures. This is mostly because the focus of this paper is first and foremost verification, but also because the libraries we have checked so far do not seem to implement the same *rank* algorithm, making comparison difficult. Nevertheless, we can already observe that extracted OCaml code does not suffer from any significant performance loss compared to existing libraries. For example, we have observed that the SDSL [16] *rank* function for H_0-compressed vectors executes in about $0.1 \sim 1.8\,\mu s$ depending on algorithm's parameters while our *rank* function executed in $0.83\,\mu s$ (see Sect. 6.2). (To be fair, it is likely that our *rank* function consumes more memory since Jacobson's algorithm does not compress its input.) We believe that this is an indication that our approach can indeed deliver acceptable performance with the benefit of formal verification.

8   Conclusion

We discussed the verification of an OCaml implementation of the *rank* function for succinct data structures. We carried out formal verification in the Coq proof-assistant, from which the implementation was automatically extracted. We assessed not only functional correctness but also storage requirements, thus ensuring that data structures are indeed succinct. To obtain efficient code, we developed a new OCaml library for bitstrings whose interface match the Coq lists used in formal verification. To the best of our knowledge, this is the first application of formal verification to succinct data structures.

We believe that the libraries developed for the purpose of our experiment are reusable: the OCaml library for bitstrings of course, the array interface for directories (that are used by other functions for succinct data structures), lemmas developed for the purpose of formal specification of *rank* (as we saw in Sect. 5.2, verification of functional correctness can be carried out at the abstract level). We also discussed a number of issues regarding extraction from Coq to OCaml: the interplay between inlining at extraction-time and by the OCaml compiler, the soundness of code replacement at extraction-time, etc. Based on the results of this paper, we are now tackling formal verification of *rank*'s counterpart function *select* and plan to address more advanced algorithms.

Acknowledgments. The authors are grateful to the anonymous reviewers for their helpful comments. This work is partially supported by a JSPS Grant-in-Aid for Scientific Research (Project Number: 15K12013).

References

1. Affeldt, R., Marti, N.: An approach to formal verification of arithmetic functions in assembly. In: Okada, M., Satoh, I. (eds.) ASIAN 2006. LNCS, vol. 4435, pp. 346–360. Springer, Heidelberg (2008)
2. Agarwal, R., Khandelwal, A., Stoica, I.: Succinct: enabling queries on compressed data. In: NSDI 2015, pp. 337–350. USENIX Association (2015). Technical report: http://people.eecs.berkeley.edu/~rachit/succinct-techreport.pdf
3. Armand, M., Grégoire, B., Spiwack, A., Théry, L.: Extending Coq with imperative features and its application to SAT verification. In: Kaufmann, M., Paulson, L.C. (eds.) ITP 2010. LNCS, vol. 6172, pp. 83–98. Springer, Heidelberg (2010)
4. Clark, D.: Compact pat trees. Doctoral dissertation, University of Waterloo (1996)
5. The Coq Development Team: Reference Manual. Version 8.5. INRIA (2004–2016). http://coq.inria.fr
6. Free Software Foundation: GCC 4.9.2 Manual (2014). http://gcc.gnu.org/onlinedocs/gcc-4.9.2/gcc
7. Gonthier, G., Mahboubi, A., Tassi, E.: A small scale reflection extension for the Coq system. Version 16. Technical report RR-6455, INRIA (2015)
8. Intel Advanced Vector Extensions Programming Reference, June 2011
9. Intel 64 and IA-32 Architectures Optimization Reference Manual, September 2015
10. Intel SSE4 Programming Reference, April 2007
11. Jacobson, G.: Succinct static data structures. Doctoral dissertation, Carnegie Mellon University (1988)

12. Jones, R.W.M.: A beginners guide to OCaml internals (2009). https://rwmj. wordpress.com/2009/08/04/ocaml-internals
13. Kim, D.-K., Na, J.C., Kim, J.E., Park, K.: Efficient implementation of rank and select functions for succinct representation. In: Nikoletseas, S.E. (ed.) WEA 2005. LNCS, vol. 3503, pp. 315–327. Springer, Heidelberg (2005)
14. Klein, G., Andronick, J., Elphinstone, K., Heiser, G., Cock, D., Derrin, P., Elkaduwe, D., Engelhardt, K., Kolanski, R., Norrish, M., Sewell, T., Tuch, H., Winwood, S.: seL4: formal verification of an operating-system kernel. Commun. ACM **53**(6), 107–115 (2010)
15. Nipkow, T.: Amortized complexity verified. In: Urban, C., Zhang, X. (eds.) ITP 2015. LNCS, vol. 9236, pp. 310–324. Springer, Berlin (2015)
16. SDSL: Succinct Data Structure Library. https://github.com/simongog/sdsl-lite
17. OUnit: Unit test framework for OCaml. http://ounit.forge.ocamlcore.org/
18. Okanohara, D.: The world of fast character string analysis. Iwanami Shoten (2012). (in Japanese)
19. Tanaka, A., Affeldt, R., Garrigue, J.: Formal Verification of the Rank Function for Succinct Data Structures. https://staff.aist.go.jp/tanaka-akira/succinct/index. html

Contextual Trace Refinement for Concurrent Objects: Safety and Progress

Brijesh Dongol[1]([envelope]) and Lindsay Groves[2]

[1] Brunel University London, London, UK
Brijesh.Dongol@brunel.ac.uk
[2] Victoria University of Wellington, Wellington, New Zealand
lindsay@ecs.vuw.ac.nz

Abstract. Correctness of concurrent objects of safety properties such as linearizability, sequential consistency, and quiescent consistency, and progress properties such as wait-, lock-, and obstruction-freedom. These properties, however, only refer to the behaviour of the object in isolation, which does not tell us what guarantees these correctness conditions on concurrent objects provide to their client programs. This paper investigates the links between safety and progress properties of concurrent objects and a form of trace refinement for client programs, called contextual trace refinement. In particular, we show that linearizability together with a minimal notion of progress are sufficient properties of concurrent objects to ensure contextual trace refinement, but sequential consistency and quiescent consistency are both too weak. Our reasoning is carried out in the action systems framework with procedure calls, which we extend to cope with non-atomic operations.

1 Introduction

Concurrent objects provide operations that can be executed simultaneously by multiple threads, and provide a layer of abstraction to programmers by managing thread synchronisation on behalf of client programs, which in turn improves safety and efficiency. Correctness of concurrent objects is usually defined in terms of the possible *histories* of invocation and response events generated by executing the operations of a sequential specification object. There are several notions of safety for concurrent objects [7,12]: sequential consistency, linearizability, and quiescent consistency being the most widely used. Similarly, there are many different notions of progress [12,13], e.g., wait-, lock- and obstruction-freedom are popular non-blocking conditions.

Both safety and progress properties are stated in terms of a concurrent object in isolation, and disregard their context, i.e., the client programs that use them. Programmers (i.e., client developers) have therefore relied on informal "folk theorems" to link correctness conditions on concurrent objects and substitutability of objects within client programs. We seek to provide a formal account of this relationship, addressing the question: "Provided concurrent object OC is correct with respect to sequential object OA, how are the behaviours of $C[OA]$ related

© Springer International Publishing AG 2016
K. Ogata et al. (Eds.): ICFEM 2016, LNCS 10009, pp. 261–278, 2016.
DOI: 10.1007/978-3-319-47846-3_17

to those of $\mathcal{C}[OC]$?", where $\mathcal{C}[O]$ denotes a client program $\mathcal{C}$ that uses object O, for different notions of correctness. One of the first answers to this question was given by *abstraction theorems* [9], linking safety properties: sequential consistency and linearizability to a contextual notion of correctness called *observational refinement*, which defines substitutability with respect to the initial and final state of a system's execution. For *terminating* clients, linearizability is shown to be equivalent to observational refinement, while sequential consistency is shown to be equivalent to observational refinement provided that clients do not communicate outside the given objects.

Since non-termination is common in many concurrent systems, e.g., operating systems and real-time controllers, our work aims to understand the link between concurrent correctness and substitutability for *potentially non-terminating* clients. Related to this aim is the work of Gotsman and Yang [10] and Liang et al. [15], who link observational refinement to safety and progress properties of concurrent objects. However, both [10,15] assume that the concurrent objects in question are already linearizable; in contrast, we do not assume linearizability. Further, [10] aims to understand *compositionality* of progress properties, while [15] develops *characterisations* of progress properties based on their observational guarantees.

The motivation for our work differs from [10,15] in that we take *contextual trace refinement* as the underlying correctness condition when substituting OC for OA in $\mathcal{C}$, then aim to understand the safety/progress properties on OC that are required to guarantee trace refinement between $\mathcal{C}[OA]$ and $\mathcal{C}[OC]$. To this end, we develop an *action systems* framework that integrates and extends existing work [1,18] from the literature, building on our preliminary results on this topic [8]. As part of our contributions we (i) extend Sere and Waldén's treatment of action systems with procedures [18] with *non-atomic procedures*; (ii) develop a theory for *contextual trace refinement*, adapting Back and von Wright's [1] theory for trace refinement of action systems, then reduce system-wide proof obligations (i.e., properties of the client and object together) to proof obligations on the objects only; (iii) show that linearizability [14] and minimal progress [13] together are sufficient to guarantee contextual trace refinement; and (iv) show that both sequential consistency and quiescent consistency are too weak to ensure contextual trace refinement, even in the presence of minimal progress.

2   Concurrent Objects and Their Clients

We motivate concurrent objects using Treiber's stack (Sect. 2.1). An example stack client (Sect. 2.2) is used to motivate contextual trace refinement (Sect. 2.3).

2.1   Client-Object Systems

We consider concurrent systems where a client consists of multiple threads which interact with one or more concurrent objects and shared variables. For example, the following client program consists of threads 1 and 2 using a shared stack s, and variables x, y and z.

```
Init x, y, z = 0, 0, 0
   Thread 1:                              Thread 2:
     T1: s.push(1);                         U1: s.pop(y);
     T2: s.push(2);                         U2: z := x;
     T3: s.pop(x);
```

Init: S = ⟨⟩

push(v) ==
atomic { S := ⟨v⟩⌢S }

pop ==
atomic {
  if S = ⟨⟩
  then return empty
  else
    lv := head(S);
    S := tail(S);
    return lv }

Fig. 1. Abstract stack

```
Init: Head = null

push(v) ==                    pop ==
H1: n := new(Node);             repeat
H2: n.val := v;           P1:   ss := Head;
    repeat                P2:   if ss = null
H3:   ss := Head;         P3:   then return empty
H4:   n.next := ss;             else
H5: until                 P4:     ssn := ss.next;
      CAS(Head,ss,n)      P5:     lv := ss.val
H6: return                P6:   until
                                  CAS(Head,ss,ssn);
                          P7:   return lv
```

Fig. 2. The Treiber stack

Thread 1 pushes 1 then 2 onto the stack s, then pops the top element of s and stores it in x. Concurrently, thread 2 pops the top element of s and stores it in y, then reads the value of x and stores it in z.

The abstract behaviour of a stack is defined in terms of a sequential object, as shown in Fig. 1. The abstract stack consists of a sequence of elements S together with two operations *push* and *pop* ('⟨' and '⟩' delimit sequences, '⟨⟩' denotes the empty sequence, and '⌢' denotes sequence concatenation). Note that when the stack is empty, *pop* returns a special value empty that cannot be pushed onto the stack.

If concurrent objects are implemented using fine-grained concurrency, the call statements in their clients are not necessarily atomic because they may invoke non-atomic operations. Furthermore, depending on the implementation of s, we will get different traces of the client program because the effects of the concurrent operations on s may take effect in different orders. For example, Fig. 2 presents a simplified version of a non-blocking stack example due to Treiber [19]. In this implementation, each line of the push and pop corresponds to a single atomic step. Synchronisation of push and pop operations is achieved using a compare-and-swap (CAS) instruction, which takes as input a *(shared) variable* gv, an *expected value* lv and a *new value* nv:

```
CAS(gv, lv, nv) ≙ atomic { if (gv = lv)
                           then gv := nv ; return true
                           else return false }
```

With this stack implementation, the executions of operations, say T1 and U1, in the above client may overlap, and different behaviours may be observed according to the order in which steps of the different threads are executed. Treiber's stack is linearizable with respect to the abstract stack in Fig. 1, so the effect of each operation call takes place between its invocation and its response. If a different stack implementation is used which satisfies a more permissive correctness condition, such as sequential consistency or quiescent consistency [12], a wider range of behaviours may be observed by its client.

2.2 Observability and Contextual Trace Refinement

With an example client-object system in place, we return to the main question for this paper: What guarantees do correctness conditions on concurrent objects provide to clients that use the objects? Furthermore, how can one address divergence, termination and reactivity of a client? To address these, we first pin down the aspects of the system being developed that are visible to an external observer. Following Filipović et al. [9], we take the state of the client variables to be observable, and the state of the objects they use to be unobservable. Therefore, for the client program in Sect. 2.1, variables x, y and z are observable, but none of the variables of the stack implementation s are observable. This allows us to reason about a client with respect to different implementations of s. Second, we define *when* a system may be observed. Unlike Filipović et al. [9] who only observe the client state at the beginning and end of a client's execution, we assume that the states *throughout* a client's execution are visible. This allows us to accommodate, for example, reactive clients, which interact with an observer in some way even if they are potentially non-terminating.

Therefore, our notion of correctness for the combined client-object system will be a form of *observational refinement* that holds iff every (observable) trace of a client using a concurrent object is equivalent to some (observable) trace of the same client using the corresponding abstract specification of the object. The end result is that from the perspective of a client program, it will be impossible to tell whether it is using the concurrent object, or its abstract (sequential) specification.

Example 1. Let $\mathcal{D}$ denote the client program in Sect. 2.1, TS denote the Treiber stack in Fig. 2, and AS denote the abstract stack in Fig. 1. Suppose the stack s in $\mathcal{D}$ is an instance of TS. Then the following is a possible observable trace of $\mathcal{D}[TS]$:

$$tr \mathrel{\hat{=}} \langle (x, y, z) \mapsto (0, 0, 0), (x, y, z) \mapsto (0, 2, 0), (x, y, z) \mapsto (1, 2, 0), (x, y, z) \mapsto (1, 2, 1) \rangle$$

where $(x, y, z) \mapsto (0, 0, 0)$ is shorthand for the state $\{x \mapsto 0, y \mapsto 0, z \mapsto 0\}$, and we ignore *stuttering*, i.e., consecutive states that leave the observable state unchanged. Trace tr is obtained by initialising as specified by Init, then executing T1, T2, U1, T3, then U2 to completion; i.e. they execute their operation call without interruption. It is straightforward to see that tr can also be generated by $\mathcal{D}[AS]$, i.e., when using the abstract stack for s. Thus tr can be accepted as being correct. Executions can, of course, be much more complicated than tr — because TS consists of non-atomic operations, executions of T1, T2 or T3 may overlap with U1 or U2.   □

We say that TS *contextually trace refines* AS *with respect to the client program* C iff every trace of $C[TS]$ is a possible trace of $C[AS]$. In this paper, we wish to know whether contextual refinement holds for every client program. To this end, we say TS *contextually trace refines* AS iff TS contextually trace refines AS with respect to every client program C.

2.3   Correctness Conditions on Concurrent Objects

There are many notions of correctness for concurrent objects, and these are defined in terms of *histories* of invocation and response events, corresponding to operation calls on the object [12] (see Sect. 5 for details).

Concurrent histories may consist of both overlapping and non-overlapping operation calls, inducing a partial order on events. Safety properties define how, if at all, this partial order is preserved by the corresponding abstract histories generated by the corresponding sequential object [7,12]. We will consider three different safety properties. *Sequential consistency* is a simple condition requiring the order of operation calls in a concrete history for a single process to be preserved. Operation calls performed by different processes may be reordered in the abstract history even if the operation calls do not overlap in the concrete history. *Linearizability* strengthens sequential consistency by requiring the order of non-overlapping operations to be preserved. Operation calls that overlap in the concrete history may be reordered when mapping to an abstract history. *Quiescent consistency* is weaker than linearizability, but is incomparable to sequential consistency. A concurrent object is said to be quiescent at some point in its history if none of its operations are executing at that point. Quiescent consistency requires the order of operation calls that are separated by a quiescent point to be preserved. Operation calls that are not separated by a quiescent point may be reordered, including operations performed by the same process.

Progress conditions on concurrent objects are necessary to ensure that clients will eventually be able to continue execution after calling operations on the objects they use. We consider a notion of progress called *minimal progress* [13], which guarantees that after some finite number of steps, some operation of the concurrent object terminates.

3   Modelling Client-Object Systems

Our formal framework for reasoning about contextual trace refinement is based on existing work on action systems with procedures [18], which we extend to cope with potentially non-atomic operations. We let Var and Val denote the types of variables and values, respectively. We distinguish between *unobservable* and *observable* variables using Var_U and Var_O, respectively, where $Var_U, Var_O \subseteq Var$ and $Var_U \cap Var_O = \varnothing$. A *state* is a function $\Sigma_V \cong V \rightarrow Val$, where

$V \subseteq Var$, and a *predicate* of type K is of type $\mathcal{P}K \; \widehat{=} \; K \to \mathbb{B}$, e.g., a *state predicate* over V is of type $\mathcal{P}\Sigma_V$.

The abstract syntax of an action system is of the form:

$$\mathscr{A} \; ::= \; \|[\, \mathbf{var_u} \; L; \; \mathbf{var_o} \; G; \; \mathbf{proc} \; ph_1 = P_1 \ldots \mathbf{proc} \; ph_n = P_n; \; I; \; \mathbf{do} \; A \; \mathbf{od}\,]\|$$

where $L \subseteq Var_U$ is a set of *unobservable variables* and $G \subseteq Var_O$ a set of *observable variables*; each $ph_i = P_i$ is a (non-recursive) procedure declaration; I is an action modelling initialisation; and A is the main action. Within each $ph_i = P_i$, P_i is an action and ph_i is a procedure heading $p_i(\mathbf{val} \; v, \mathbf{res} \; x)$ with procedure name p_i and optional call-by-value and call-by-result parameters v and x. Procedure declarations may additionally be parameterised by thread identifiers.

The abstract syntax of *actions* is of the form:

$$A \; ::= \; \mathbf{var} \; x \mid \mathbf{rav} \; x \mid \mathbf{skip} \mid x \;{\in\!\!\!\!\!\!\!\!\;}\; E \mid x := e \mid p(in, out) \mid A_1; \; A_2 \mid b \to A \mid A_1 \sqcap A_2$$

where x is a variable, E is a set-valued expression, e is an expression, p is a procedure name, in and out are inputs and outputs to a procedure (which may be a value or a variable), and b is a predicate. Actions $\mathbf{var} \; x$ and $\mathbf{rav} \; x$ introduce and remove variable x from the state space, respectively, $\mathbf{skip}$ is an action that leaves the state unchanged, $x \;{\in\!\!\!\!\!\!\!\!\;}\; E$ denotes non-deterministic assignment, $x := e$ denotes assignment, $p(e, x)$ is a procedure call with value parameter e and result parameter x, $A_1; \; A_2$ is sequential composition of A_1 and A_2, $b \to A$ is a guarded action, and $A_1 \sqcap A_2$ is (demonic) choice between A_1 and A_2.

The meaning of *parameterless procedures* is given by syntactically replacing each procedure call p in A by the procedure body, P. Procedure parameters are handled by introducing new local variables with the same name; for call-by-value, the new variable is initialised with the value of the actual parameter, while for call-by-results, the final value is copied to the variable passed as the parameter (see [18]). We give examples of these in Examples 2 and 3 below.

When invoking non-atomic operations, it will be important to detect when the invoked operation has terminated. To this end, we assume that a variable $\widehat{pc}_t$ is used to control the flow of execution within an operation; thus $\widehat{pc}_t$ must be declared whenever thread t is currently executing an operation. Formally, we use state predicate

$$dec.v \; \widehat{=} \; \lambda \sigma \bullet v \in dom(\sigma)$$

which holds iff variable v is declared in the domain of the given state. We use '.' for function application.

Example 2. Consider again the client program $\mathcal{D}$ from Sect. 2.1 and suppose it uses the abstract stack object AS in Fig. 1. The action system modelling the client-object system is $\mathcal{D}[AS]$, given below. The shared stack is a sequence modelled by an unobservable variable S. The client consists of variables x, y and z, as well as program counters pc_1 and pc_2 (which we distinguish from $\widehat{pc}_t$). We assume

$$npc_t(k) \; \widehat{=} \; (dec.\widehat{pc}_t \to \mathbf{skip}) \sqcap (\neg dec.\widehat{pc}_t \to pc_t := k)$$

is an action that sets pc_t to k if t completes the operation it is currently executing.

$|[$ **var**$_u$ S; **var**$_o$ x, y, z, pc_1, pc_2;

  proc $push_t(\textbf{val } in) = S := \langle in \rangle \frown S$

  proc $pop_t(\textbf{res } out) = \quad S = \langle \rangle \wedge \neg dec.\widehat{pc}_t \rightarrow \textbf{var } ret, \widehat{pc}_t; \ ret := empty; \ \widehat{pc}_t := 1$

                         $\sqcap \ S \neq \langle \rangle \wedge \neg dec.\widehat{pc}_t \rightarrow \textbf{var } ret, \widehat{pc}_t;$

                                         $ret, S := head.S, tail.S; \ \widehat{pc}_t := 1$

                    $\sqcap \ \widehat{pc}_t = 1 \rightarrow out := ret; \ \textbf{rav } ret, \widehat{pc}_t;$

  $S, pc_1, pc_2 := \langle \rangle, T1, U1; \ x, y, z := 0, 0, 0;$

  do $pc_1 = T1 \rightarrow push_1(1); \ npc_1(T2)$

     $\sqcap pc_1 = T2 \rightarrow push_1(2); \ npc_1(T3)$

     $\sqcap pc_1 = T3 \rightarrow pop_1(x); \ npc_1(\bot)$

     $\sqcap pc_2 = U1 \rightarrow pop_2(y); \ npc_2(U2)$

     $\sqcap pc_2 = U2 \rightarrow z, pc_2 := x, \bot \ \textbf{od} \,]|$

□

Example 3. The $push_t$ operation of the Treiber stack is defined as follows. We assume $newNode.n \ \widehat{=}\ n \ \Subset\ Nodes$; $Nodes := Nodes \backslash \{n\}$ assigns n to be a new node from the available set of nodes $Nodes$. For simplicity, we assume $Nodes$ is an infinite set (e.g., the natural numbers), so a new node is always available. Thus we have:

  proc $push_t(\textbf{val } in) = \quad \neg \ dec.\widehat{pc}_t \rightarrow \textbf{var } \widehat{pc}_t, v_t, n_t, ss_t; \ v_t := in; \ \widehat{pc}_t := H1$

                        $\sqcap \ \widehat{pc}_t = H1 \rightarrow newNode.n_t; \ \widehat{pc}_t := H2$

                        ...

                        $\sqcap \ \widehat{pc}_t = H6 \rightarrow \textbf{rav } \widehat{pc}_t, v_t, n_t, ss_t$

The *pop* operation is similar, except that it additionally sets the output variable to the returned value.

  proc $pop_t(\textbf{res } out) = \quad \neg \ dec.\widehat{pc}_t \rightarrow \textbf{var } \widehat{pc}_t, ss_t, ssn_t, lv_t; \ \widehat{pc}_t := P1$

                        ...

                    $\sqcap \ \widehat{pc}_t = P7 \rightarrow out := lv_t; \ \textbf{rav } \widehat{pc}_t, ss_t, ssn_t, lv_t$

The action system resulting from using the Treiber stack (which we will refer to as *TS*) as the shared concurrent object in Sect. 2.1 is $\mathcal{D}[TS]$. It is similar to the action system in Example 2, except that the unobservable variables are *Nodes* (the set of all available nodes), *Head* (a pointer to a node, or *null*), *val* (a partial function of type $Nodes \nrightarrow Val$), *next* (a partial function of type $Nodes \nrightarrow Node$); the procedure declarations above are used; and initialisation of the object is $Nodes, Head, val, next := \mathbb{N}, null, \varnothing, \varnothing$.

□

We now make the concept of an object and the notation $\mathcal{C}[O]$ for an object O and client $\mathcal{C}$ more precise. An *object* is a triple $O \ \widehat{=}\ (L, P, I)$, where L is a set of variables, $P \ \widehat{=}\ \{ph_{1,t} = P_{1,t}, \ldots, ph_{n,t} = P_{n,t}\}$ is a set of (potentially parameterised) procedure declarations, and I is an initialisation action. A *client* is a triple $\mathcal{C} \ \widehat{=}\ (G, A, J)$, where G is a set of variables, and A and J are the main and initialisation actions, respectively. Then $\mathcal{C}[O]$ is the action system

    $|[\textbf{var}_u \ L; \ \textbf{var}_o \ G; \ \textbf{proc } ph_{1,t} = P_{1,t} \ldots \textbf{proc } ph_{n,t} = P_{n,t}; \ I; \ J; \ \textbf{do } A \ \textbf{od} \,]|.$

    The next section formalises the semantics of action systems and defines our notion of contextual trace refinement for it.

4   Semantics and Contextual Trace Refinement

We now give the semantics for action systems and define contextual trace refinement, which extends the existing theory on trace refinement [1]. Note that we only use part of the action systems framework. In particular, to develop a more direct link to trace refinement, we only give a relational semantics for actions.

We assume that expressions are functions from states to values. A *relation* is of type $\mathcal{R}(K, K') \,\hat{=}\, K \to \mathcal{P}K'$, thus a *state relation* is of type $\mathcal{R}(\Sigma_V, \Sigma_{V'})$, where $V, V' \subseteq Var$. Assume r, r_1 and r_2 are state relations, b is a predicate and S is a set. We let

- $(r_1 \circ r_2).\gamma.\gamma' \,\hat{=}\, \exists \gamma'' \bullet r_1.\gamma.\gamma'' \wedge r_2.\gamma''.\gamma'$ denote *relational composition*,
- $(b \lhd r).\gamma.\gamma' \,\hat{=}\, b.\gamma \wedge r.\gamma.\gamma'$ denote *domain restriction*, and
- $S \lhd r = \{(\gamma, \gamma') \in r \mid \gamma \notin S\}$ denote domain anti-restriction.

For a function f, we let $f \oplus \{x \mapsto v\} \,\hat{=}\, \lambda z \in dom(f) \bullet$ **if** $z = x$ **then** v **else** $f.z$ denote *functional overriding*.

Definition 1. *The (relational) semantics of an action A is given by rel.A:*

$$rel.(\mathbf{var}\ x) \,\hat{=}\, \lambda \sigma \bullet \lambda \sigma' \bullet$$
$$(\{x\} \lhd \sigma') = \sigma \wedge dec.x.\sigma' \qquad\qquad rel.\mathbf{skip} \,\hat{=}\, id$$
$$rel.(\mathbf{rav}\ x) \,\hat{=}\, \lambda \sigma \bullet \lambda \sigma' \bullet (\{x\} \lhd \sigma) = \sigma' \qquad rel.(b \to A_1) \,\hat{=}\, b \lhd rel.A_1$$
$$rel.(x := e) \,\hat{=}\, \lambda \sigma \bullet \lambda \sigma' \bullet \sigma' = \sigma \oplus \{x \mapsto e.\sigma\} \qquad rel.(A_1;\ A_2) \,\hat{=}\, rel.A_1 \circ rel.A_2$$
$$rel.(x :\in E) \,\hat{=}\, \lambda \sigma \bullet \lambda \sigma' \bullet \qquad\qquad rel.(A_1 \sqcap A_2) \,\hat{=}\, rel.A_1 \vee rel.A_2$$
$$\exists k : E.\sigma \bullet \sigma' = \sigma \oplus \{x \mapsto k\}$$

Recall that the semantics of a procedure call is given by substitution as described in Sect. 3. We let $grd.A.\gamma \,\hat{=}\, \gamma \in dom(rel.A)$ denote the *guard* of A. Because an action system is a loop with a non-deterministic choice over actions [1], we frequently use iteration in our reasoning. Formally, finite iteration of relation r (denoted r^*) is defined as follows:

$$r^0 \,\hat{=}\, id \qquad\qquad r^{k+1} \,\hat{=}\, r \circ r^k \qquad\qquad r^* \,\hat{=}\, \exists k \in \mathbb{N} \bullet r^k$$

The semantics of an iterated action is defined by lifting from iteration defined on relations, namely, $rel.A^* \,\hat{=}\, (rel.A)^*$. We say an *iterated execution of A terminates from state γ* iff $term.A.\gamma \,\hat{=}\, \exists k \bullet \forall \gamma' \bullet (rel.A)^k.\gamma.\gamma' \Rightarrow \neg grd.A.\gamma'$. Note that $\neg grd.A.\gamma \Rightarrow term.A.\gamma$ holds for all actions A and states γ.

We use $\text{seq}\, X$ to denote (possibly infinite) sequences of elements of type X, and assume indices start from 0.

Definition 2. *A possibly infinite sequence of states s is a* trace *of action system $\mathscr{A}$ iff $\exists \sigma \bullet rel.I.\sigma.(s.0) \wedge \forall i : dom(s)\backslash\{0\} \bullet rel.A.(s.(i-1)).(s.i)$ holds.*

A *trace* is *complete* iff either the trace is of infinite length or the guard of A does not hold in the last state of the trace. The set of all *complete traces* of an action system $\mathscr{A}$ is denoted $[\![\mathscr{A}]\!]$.

Traces (Definition 2) provide a conceptually simple model for a system's execution, and trace refinement provides a conceptually simple notion of substitutability [1]. Typically, because a concrete system is more fine-grained than the abstract, one must remove stuttering from a trace. An action system may also exhibit *infinite stuttering* by generating a trace that ends with an infinite sequence of consecutive stuttering steps. After infinite stuttering, one will never be able to observe any state changes, and hence, we treat infinite stuttering as *divergence*, which is denoted by a special symbol '$\uparrow \notin \Sigma$'. For any trace $s \in [\![\mathscr{A}]\!]$, we define $Tr.s$ to be the non-stuttering observable sequence of states, possibly followed by $\uparrow$, which is obtained from s as follows. First, we obtain a sequence s' by removing all finite stuttering in s and replacing any infinite stuttering in s by $\uparrow$. Second, for each $i \in dom(s')$, we let $(Tr.s').i = \textbf{if } s'.i \neq \uparrow \textbf{ then } Var_U \lhd s'.i \textbf{ else } \uparrow$. It is straightforward to define functions that formalise both the steps above (see for example [6]).

Definition 3. *Abstract action system $\mathscr{A}$ is* trace refined *by concrete action system $\mathscr{C}$ (denoted $\mathscr{A} \sqsubseteq \mathscr{C}$) iff $\forall s' \in [\![\mathscr{C}]\!] \bullet \exists s \in [\![\mathscr{A}]\!] \bullet Tr.s = Tr.s'$ holds.*

Back and von Wright have developed simulation rules (details elided due to lack of space) for verifying trace refinement of action systems [1], which we adapt to reason about client-object systems in Lemmas 1 and 2. First, we formalise the meaning of contextual trace refinement. The notion is similar to the notion of data refinement given by He et al. [3,11], but extended to traces, which enables one to cope with non-terminating reactive systems.

Definition 4. *An abstract object OA is* contextually trace refined *by a concrete object OC, denoted $OA \sqsubseteq OC$, iff for any client $\mathcal{C}$ we have $\mathcal{C}[OA] \sqsubseteq \mathcal{C}[OC]$.*

In this paper, for simplicity, we assume that (atomic) actions do not abort [3], therefore the proof obligations for aborting actions do not appear in Lemmas 1 and 2 below – it is straightforward to extend our results to take aborting behaviour into account. However, like Back and von Wright [1], our notion of refinement ensures *total correctness* of the systems we develop, i.e., the concrete system may only deadlock (or diverge) if the abstract system deadlocks (or diverges). Thus, in addition to the standard step correspondence proof obligations for ensuring safety of the concrete system, we include Back and von Wright's proof obligations that ensure progress.

Because the entire state of the client is observable, the proof obligations pertaining to the client can be trivially discharged, leaving one with proof obligations that only refer to the object. For procedure declarations $P \mathrel{\widehat{=}} \{ph_{1,t} = P_{1,t}, \ldots, ph_{n,t} = P_{n,t}\}$, we let $tact.v.x.t.P \mathrel{\widehat{=}} p_{1,t}(v,x) \sqcap \cdots \sqcap p_{n,t}(v,x)$ denote the choice between procedures in P for inputs v and x and thread t then define:

$$act.P \mathrel{\widehat{=}} \textstyle\bigsqcap_{v,x,t} tact.v.x.t.P \qquad\qquad rem.P \mathrel{\widehat{=}} \textstyle\bigsqcap_{v,x,t} dec.\widehat{pc}_t \rightarrow tact.v.x.t.P$$

To simplify the syntax, we implicitly assume that in $tact.v.x.t.P$ the inputs v and x are of the correct type for each procedure. Guard $dec.\widehat{pc}_t$ is used to detect whether the procedure being executed by thread t has terminated — if t is executing a procedure, say $ph_{i,t}$, we know $dec.\widehat{pc}_t$ will hold and when this procedure terminates $\neg dec.\widehat{pc}_t$ will hold, which disables thread t. The intention is to use $rem.P$ in (4) below, which attempts to execute the remaining steps of the running operations by each thread to completion.

Lemma 1 (Forward Simulation). *If* $OA = (L_A, P_A, I_A)$ *and* $OC = (L_C, P_C, I_C)$ *are objects, then* $OA \sqsubseteq OC$ *if there exists a relation* R *and the following hold for any states* σ, τ *and* τ':

$$rel.I_C.\tau.\tau' \Rightarrow \exists \sigma' \bullet R.\sigma'.\tau' \wedge rel.I_A.\sigma.\sigma' \tag{1}$$

$$R.\sigma.\tau \wedge rel.(act.P_C).\tau.\tau' \Rightarrow \exists \sigma' \bullet R.\sigma'.\tau' \wedge rel.(act.P_A)^*.\sigma.\sigma' \tag{2}$$

$$R.\sigma.\tau \wedge \neg grd.(act.P_C).\tau \Rightarrow \neg grd.(act.P_A).\sigma \tag{3}$$

$$true \Rightarrow term.(rem.P_C).\tau \tag{4}$$

The first three proof obligations are straightforward. Proof obligation (4) requires that the main action of the concrete object OC terminates if threads do not invoke new operations after the operation currently being executed has terminated. Note that (4) does not rule out infinite stuttering within the program $\mathcal{C}[OC]$, but it does ensure that any infinite stuttering is caused by the client as opposed to the object OC, and hence, this infinite stuttering must also be present within $\mathcal{C}[OA]$. Therefore, if (4) holds, so does Back and von Wright's non-termination condition.

Dually to forward simulation, there exists a method of *backward simulation*, which requires that the abstract action system under consideration is *continuous*. An action system $\mathscr{A}$ with main action A is *continuous* iff for all σ, the set $\{\sigma' \mid rel.A.\sigma.\sigma'\}$ is finite, i.e., A does not exhibit infinite non-determinism.

Lemma 2 (Backward Simulation). *Suppose* $OA = (L_A, P_A, I_A)$ *and* $OC = (L_C, P_C, I_C)$ *are objects and* $\mathcal{C}$ *is a client such that* $\mathcal{C}[OA]$ *is continuous. Then* $\mathcal{C}[OA] \sqsubseteq \mathcal{C}[OC]$ *holds if there exists a total relation* R *and for any states* σ' *and* τ, τ' *condition* (4) *as well as each of the following hold:*

$$rel.I_C.\tau.\tau' \wedge R.\sigma'.\tau' \Rightarrow \exists \sigma \bullet rel.I_A.\sigma.\sigma' \tag{5}$$

$$rel.(act.P_C).\tau.\tau' \wedge R.\sigma'.\tau' \Rightarrow \exists \sigma \bullet R.\sigma.\tau \wedge rel.(act.P_A)^*.\sigma.\sigma' \tag{6}$$

$$\neg grd.(act.P_C).\tau \Rightarrow \exists \sigma \bullet R.\sigma.\tau \wedge \neg grd.(act.P_A).\sigma \tag{7}$$

Lemmas 1 and 2 reduce the proof obligations for trace refinement of client-object systems to the level of objects only. This allows one to explore properties of objects in isolation to guarantee contextual trace refinement.

5   Events and Histories

This section provides background for defining safety (e.g., linearizability) and progress (e.g., lock-freedom) properties of concurrent objects [12]. We define both types of properties in terms of *histories* of invocation and response events [12,14] that record the externally visible interaction between a client and the object it uses. The type of an event is *Event*, which is defined as follows [4]:

$$Event ::= inv \langle\!\langle \mathbb{N} \times Op \times (Val \cup \{\bot\}) \rangle\!\rangle \mid ret \langle\!\langle \mathbb{N} \times Op \times (Val \cup \{\bot\}) \rangle\!\rangle$$

The components of each event are the thread identifier, the operation name and input/output values. We use $\bot \notin Val$ to denote an invocation (return) event that has no input (output). Thus, for example, $inv(1, push, 2)$ denotes an $push$ invocation by thread 1 with value 2, and $ret(1, push, \perp)$ denotes a return from this invocation.

The history of an object is a (potentially infinite) sequence of events, i.e., $History \mathrel{\widehat{=}} \text{seq}\,Event$. A history of an object is generated by an execution of a *most-general client* for the object [5]. We formalise the concept of a most general client in our framework in Definition 5 below, but first we describe how invocations and responses are recorded in a history. For an object $O \mathrel{\widehat{=}} (L, \{ph_{1,t} = P_{1,t}, \ldots, ph_{n,t} = P_{n,t}\}, I)$ assuming $H \notin L$ is a history variable, we let $P_{i,t}^H$ be the *history-extended* procedure derived from $P_{i,t}$ by additionally recording invocation and response events in H (also see [4]).

Example 4. The history-extended procedure for $push_t$ from Example 2 is:

$$H := H \mathbin{^\frown} \langle inv(t, push, in)\rangle;\ S := \langle in \rangle \mathbin{^\frown} S;\ H := H \mathbin{^\frown} \langle ret(t, push, \perp)\rangle$$

while the history-extended version of $push_t$ procedure from Example 3 is:

$$\neg\,dec.\widehat{pc}_t \rightarrow \mathbf{var}\ \widehat{pc}_t, v_t, n_t, ss_t;\ v_t := in;$$
$$H := H \mathbin{^\frown} \langle inv(t, push, in)\rangle;\ \widehat{pc}_t := H1$$
$$\ldots$$
$$\sqcap\,\widehat{pc}_t = H6 \rightarrow H := H \mathbin{^\frown} \langle ret(t, push, \perp)\rangle;\ \mathbf{rav}\ \widehat{pc}_t, v_t, n_t, ss_t$$

□

Definition 5. *The* most general client *of* $O \mathrel{\widehat{=}} (L, \{ph_{1,t} = P_{1,t}, \ldots, ph_{n,t} = P_{n,t}\}, I)$ *is the action system* $\mathcal{M}[O]$ *below, where* $H \notin L$ *is its history,* $tt \notin L$ *is a fresh variable that models termination and* $P^H \mathrel{\widehat{=}} \{ph_{1,t} = P_{1,t}^H \ldots ph_{n,t} = P_{n,t}^H\}$ *is the set of history extended procedures:*

$$\mathcal{M}[O] \mathrel{\widehat{=}} \|[\mathbf{var}_\mathbf{u}\ L \cup \{H, tt\};\ \mathbf{var}_\mathbf{o}\ Var_O;$$
$$\mathbf{proc}\ ph_{1,t} = P_{1,t}^H\ \ldots \mathbf{proc}\ ph_{n,t} = P_{n,t}^H\ ;$$
$$I;\ H := \langle \rangle;\ tt := false\ ;$$
$$\mathbf{do}\ \neg tt\ \rightarrow\ act.P^H \sqcap (\textstyle\bigsqcap_{w:V_O, a:Val}\ w := a) \sqcap tt := true\ \mathbf{od}]\|$$

Thus, $\mathcal{M}[O]$ includes unobservable variables H (initially $\langle\rangle$) and tt (initially $false$), which model the history and termination of $\mathcal{M}[O]$, respectively. Provided tt is false, at each iteration of the action system either

- a step of a history-extended procedures of O is executed, or
- some observable variable is set to a non-deterministically chosen value, or
- $\mathcal{M}[O]$ terminates by setting tt to $true$.

The intention of $\mathcal{M}[O]$ is to model all possible client behaviours, including for instance faults (where a thread stops running) or a divergence (where a thread repeatedly executes the same operation).

Definition 6. *The set of histories of an object* O *is given by*

$$\{h \in \text{seq}\,Event \mid \exists\,s : [\![\mathcal{M}[O]]\!] \bullet \exists\,i : dom(s) \bullet h = (s.i).H\}$$

6 Contextual Trace Refinement: Progress

The progress condition we will consider is *minimal progress*, which guarantees system-wide progress, even though there may be individual threads that may not make progress [13]. To formalise minimal progress, we say event e_1 *matches* e_2 iff $matches(e_1, e_2) \stackrel{\frown}{=} \exists t, o, u, v \bullet e_1 = inv(t, o, u) \wedge e_2 = ret(t, o, v)$ holds, i.e., e_1 is an invocation of an operation by a thread and e_2 is the corresponding return. We say $m \in dom(h)$ is a *pending invocation* iff $pi(m, h) \stackrel{\frown}{=} \forall n \in dom(h) \bullet m < n \Rightarrow \neg matches(h.m, h.n)$ holds.

An object O satisfies minimal progress iff for every trace tr of the $\mathcal{M}[O]$, it is always the case that in the future, either $\mathcal{M}[O]$ terminates, or there is some pending operation invocation that completes and returns.

Definition 7. *An object O satisfies* minimal progress *iff for every $s \in [\![\mathcal{M}[O]]\!]$ and $i \in dom(s)$, there exists a $j \in dom(s)$ such that $i \leqslant j$ and*

$$(s.j).tt \vee \exists m \bullet pi(m, (s.j).H) \wedge \neg pi(m, (s.(j+1)).H) .$$

That is, for any trace s of $\mathcal{M}[O]$ and index $i \in dom(s)$ there is a state $s.j$ (where $j \geqslant i$) from which some pending operation in $s.j$ completes. There are a variety of objects that satisfy minimal progress, e.g., wait-, lock-free objects under any scheduler, and obstruction-free objects under isolating schedulers (see [13] for details). Objects that do not satisfy minimal progress include obstruction free implementations that are executed using a weakly fair scheduler.

The lemma below states that any object that satisfies minimal progress does not suffer from deadlock, and is guaranteed to terminate if no additional operations are invoked.

Lemma 3. *If $O = (L, P, I)$ satisfies minimal progress, then for any $\gamma \in [\![\mathcal{M}[O]]\!]$ and $i \in dom(\gamma)$, both $grd.(act.P).(\gamma.i)$ and condition (4) hold.*

Using Lemma 3, we simplify and combine Lemmas 1 and 2. In particular, we are left with the proof obligations for safety only as in the theorem below.

Theorem 1. *Suppose $OA = (L_A, P_A, I_A)$ and $OC = (L_C, P_C, I_C)$ are objects, OC satisfies minimal progress, and $R \in \mathcal{R}(\Sigma_{L_A}, \Sigma_{L_C})$. Then*

1. *$OA \stackrel{\frown}{\sqsubseteq} OC$ if both (1) and (2) hold, and*
2. *for any client C such that $C[OA]$ is continuous, $C[OA] \sqsubseteq C[OC]$ holds if R is total and both (5) and (6) hold.*

7 Safety and Contextual Trace Refinement

We give the formal definition of safety properties using the nomenclature in [4,7]. We say $m, n \in dom(h)$ form a *matching pair* in h iff $mp(m, n, h)$ holds, where $mp(m, n, h) \stackrel{\frown}{=} m < n \wedge matches(h.m, h.n) \wedge \forall i \bullet m < i < n \Rightarrow \pi_1.(h.i) \neq \pi_1.(h.m)$ and π_i is the *projection function* returning the ith element of the given tuple.

Following [7], safety properties are defined in terms of a history h and a *mapping function* f between indices. The *sequential history* corresponding to h and f is obtained using $map(h, f) \mathrel{\hat{=}} \{f(k) \mapsto h(k) \mid k \in dom(f)\}$. Different safety properties are defined by placing different types of restrictions on f. The most basic restriction is validity of a mapping. We say a function f is a *valid mapping function* if, for any history h, (a) the domain of f is contained in the domain of h, (b) the range of f is a consecutive sequence starting from 0, (c) f only maps matching pairs in h, and (d) matching pairs in h are mapped to consecutive events in the target abstract history. Assuming $[m, n]$ is the set of integers from m to n inclusive, we formalise validity for mapping functions using $VMF(h, f)$, where

$$VMF(h, f) \mathrel{\hat{=}} dom(f) \subseteq dom(h) \wedge (\exists\, n : \mathbb{N} \bullet ran(f) = [0, n-1]) \wedge injective(f) \wedge$$
$$(\forall\, m, n : dom(h) \bullet mp(m, n, h) \Rightarrow (m \in dom(f) \Leftrightarrow n \in dom(f))) \wedge$$
$$(\forall\, m, n : dom(f) \bullet mp(m, n, h) \Rightarrow f.n = f.m + 1)$$

When formalising correctness conditions, one must also consider *incomplete histories*, which have pending operation invocations that may or may not have taken effect. To cope with these, like Herlihy and Wing [14], we use *history extensions*, which are constructed from a history h by concatenating a sequence of returns corresponding to some of the pending invocations of h. A *correctness condition* Z is a predicate on a history and a mapping function.

Definition 8. *A concurrent object OC implementing an abstract object OA is correct with respect to a correctness condition Z, denoted $OC \models_{OA} Z$, iff for any history h of OC, there exists an extension he of h, a valid mapping function f such that $VMF(he, f) \wedge Z(he, f)$ holds and $map(he, f)$ is a history of OA.*

7.1 Linearizability

We now show that linearizability is a sufficient safety condition for discharging the proof obligations in Theorem 1. Linearizability is a *total* condition, which means that all completed (i.e., returned) operation calls in a given history h must be mapped by f.[1] In addition, it must satisfy an *order* condition lin, which states that the return of an operation may not be reordered with an invocation that occurs after it. We use $inv?(e) \mathrel{\hat{=}} \exists\, t, o, v \bullet e = inv(t, o, v)$ if e is an invocation event and $ret?(e) \mathrel{\hat{=}} \exists\, t, o, v \bullet e = ret(t, o, v)$ if e is a response.

$$total(h, f) \mathrel{\hat{=}} \forall\, m : dom(h) \bullet \neg pi(m, h) \Rightarrow m \in dom(f)$$
$$lin(h, f) \mathrel{\hat{=}} \forall\, m, n : dom(f) \bullet m < n \wedge ret?(h.m) \wedge inv?(h.n) \Rightarrow f.m < f.n$$

Definition 9. *We say OC is* linearizable *with respect to OA iff $OC \models_{OA} lin \wedge total$.*

First, we show contextual trace refinement for a *canonical implementation* [2, 16, 17], which splits each sequential abstract operation call into three actions: an *invocation*, an *effect action* and a *response*.

---

[1] This is in contrast to *partial* conditions defined for relaxed memory (see [7] for details).

Definition 10. *For an abstract procedure* $ph_t(\mathbf{val}\ in, \mathbf{res}\ out) = P_t$, *the canonical implementation of the procedure is:*

$$
\begin{array}{ll}
\neg dec.\widehat{pc}_t \rightarrow & \mathbf{var}\ \widehat{pc}_t;\ \widehat{pc}_t := 1;\ H \frown \langle inv(t, p, in) \rangle \\
\sqcap \widehat{pc}_t = 1 \rightarrow & ph_t(in, out);\ \widehat{pc}_t := 2 \\
\sqcap \widehat{pc}_t = 2 \rightarrow & \mathbf{rav}\ \widehat{pc}_t;\ H \frown \langle ret(t, p, out) \rangle
\end{array}
$$

Invocation and response actions modify the auxiliary history variable by recording the corresponding event, while the effect action has the same effect as the abstract operation call. Unlike the abstract object, the histories of a canonical implementation are potentially concurrent.

Theorem 2 (Canonical Contextual Trace Refinement). *Suppose OA and OB are objects, where OB is a canonical implementation of OA. Then* $OA \widehat{\sqsubseteq} OB$.

Proof. We use Lemma 1 because OB may not satisfy minimal progress. Here, $rel.act.OB$ trivially satisfies (4) because by nature each procedure of a canonical object terminates. The proof of (3) requires further consideration because $rel.act.OB$ may deadlock. For example, OB may be a stack with a *pop* operation that blocks when the stack is empty. In such cases, because no data refinement is performed, the guard of the canonical object is false when the guard of the abstract object is false, allowing one to discharge (3). The remaining proof obligations are straightforward.   □

Next, we restate a completeness result by Schellhorn et al. [17], who have shown completeness of backward simulation for verifying linearizability. In particular, provided OC is a linearizable implementation of OA, they show that it is always possible to construct a backward simulation relation between the OC and the canonical implementation of OA.

Lemma 4 (Completeness of Backward Simulation [17]). *Suppose OA, OB and OC are objects and* $\mathcal{M}[OA]$ *is continuous. If* $OC \models_{OA} lin \wedge total$ *and OB is a canonical implementation of OA, then there exists a total relation R such that both (5) and (6) hold between* $\mathcal{M}[OB]$ *and* $\mathcal{M}[OC]$.

Finally, we prove our main result for linearizability, i.e., that linearizability and minimal progress together preserves contextual trace refinement.

Theorem 3. *Suppose object OC is linearizable with respect to OA, OC satisfies minimal progress, and* $\mathcal{M}[OA]$ *is continuous. If C is a client such that* $\mathcal{C}[OA]$ *is continuous then* $\mathcal{C}[OA] \sqsubseteq \mathcal{C}[OC]$.

Proof. Construct a canonical implementation OB of OA. By transitivity of $\sqsubseteq$, the proof holds if both (a) $\mathcal{C}[OA] \sqsubseteq \mathcal{C}[OB]$ and (b) $\mathcal{C}[OB] \sqsubseteq \mathcal{C}[OC]$. Condition (a) holds by Theorem 2, and (b) holds by Theorem 1 (part 2), followed by Lemma 4. Application of Theorem 1 (part 2) is allowed because if $\mathcal{C}[OA]$ is continuous then $\mathcal{C}[OB]$ is continuous, whereas application of Lemma 4 is allowed because if R satisfies (5) and (6) for $\mathcal{M}[OB]$ and $\mathcal{M}[OC]$, then R also satisfies (5) and (6) for $\mathcal{C}[OB]$ and $\mathcal{C}[OC]$.   □

7.2   Sequential and Quiescent Consistency

We now consider contextual trace refinement for concurrent objects that satisfy sequential consistency and quiescent consistency, both of which are weaker than linearizability. Both conditions are total [7]. Additionally, sequential consistency disallows reordering of operation calls within a thread (see sc below), while quiescent consistency (see qc below) disallows reordering across a quiescent point (defined by qp below).

$$sc(h, f) \cong \forall m, n : dom(f) \bullet m < n \wedge \pi_1.(h.m) = \pi_1.(h.n) \wedge$$
$$ret?(h.m) \wedge inv?(h.n) \Rightarrow f.m < f.n$$
$$qp(m, h) \cong \forall n : dom(h) \bullet n \leq m \Rightarrow \neg pi(n, h[0..m])$$
$$qc(h, f) \cong \forall m, k, n : dom(f) \bullet m < k < n \wedge qp(k, h) \Rightarrow f.m < f.n$$

Definition 11. *An object OC is* sequentially consistent *with respect to OA iff OC $\models_{OA} sc \wedge total$, and OC is* quiescent consistent *with respect to OA iff OC $\models_{OA} qc \wedge total$.*

Our results for sequential consistency and quiescent consistency are negative — neither condition guarantees trace refinement of the underlying clients, regardless of whether the client program in question is *data independent*, i.e., the state spaces of the client threads outside the shared object are pairwise disjoint.

Theorem 4. *Suppose object OC is sequentially consistent with respect to object OA. Then it is not necessarily the case that OA $\sqsubseteq$ OC holds.*

Proof. Consider the program in Fig. 3, where the client threads are data independent — x is local to thread 1, while y and z are local to thread 2 — and s is assumed to be sequentially consistent. Suppose thread 1 is executed to completion, and then thread 2 is executed to completion. Because s is sequentially consistent, the first pop (at T3) may set x to 1, the second (at U2) may set y to 2. This gives the execution:

$$\langle (x, y, z) \mapsto (0, 0, 0),\ (x, y, z) \mapsto (1, 0, 0),\ (x, y, z) \mapsto (1, 0, 1),\ (x, y, z) \mapsto (1, 2, 1) \rangle$$

that cannot be generated when using the abstract stack AS from Fig. 1 for s. $\square$

Theorem 4 differs from the results of Filipović et al. [9], who show that for data independent clients, sequential consistency implies observational refinement. In essence, their result holds because observational refinement only considers the initial and final states of a client program — the intermediate states of a client's execution are ignored. Thus, internal reorderings due to sequentially consistent objects have no effect when only observing pre/post states. One can develop hiding conditions so that observational refinement becomes a special case of contextual trace refinement, allowing one to obtain the result by Filipović et al. [9]. Further development of this theory is left for future work. We now give our result for quiescent consistency.

```
                                 Init x, y, z = 0;
                                 Thread 1 ==        Thread 2 ==
Init x, y, z = 0;                T1: s.push(1);     U1: s.pop(z)
Thread 1 ==       Thread 2 ==    T2: s.push(2);
T1: s.push(1);    U1: z := 1;    T3: s.pop(x);
T2: s.push(2);    U2: s.pop(y);  T4: s.pop(y);
T3: s.pop(x);                    T5: s.push(3);
```

Fig. 3. Counter example for contextual trace refinement and sequential consistency

Fig. 4. Counter example for contextual trace refinement and quiescent consistency

Theorem 5. *Suppose object OC is quiescent consistent with respect to object OA. Then it is not necessarily the case that $OA \sqsubseteq OC$ holds.*

Proof. Consider the program Fig. 4, where the client threads are data independent — x and y are local to thread 1, while z is local to thread 2 — and s is a quiescent consistent stack. The concrete program may generate the following observable trace:

$$\langle (x,y,z) \mapsto (0,0,0), \quad (x,y,z) \mapsto (1,0,0), \quad (x,y,z) \mapsto (1,2,0), \quad (x,y,z) \mapsto (1,2,3) \rangle$$

Note that the *pop* operations at T3 and T4 have been reordered, which could happen if the execution of *pop* at $U1$ overlaps with T1, T2, T3 and T4. The trace above is not possible when the client uses the abstract stack AS from Fig. 1. □

8   Conclusions

In this paper, we have developed a framework, based on action systems with procedures, for studying the link between the correctness conditions for concurrent objects and contextual trace refinement, which guarantees substitutability of objects within potentially non-terminating reactive clients. Thus, we bring together the previously disconnected worlds of correctness for concurrent objects and trace refinement within action systems. We have shown that linearizability and minimal progress together ensure contextual trace refinement, but sequential consistency and quiescent consistency are inadequate for guaranteeing contextual trace refinement regardless of whether clients communicate outside the concurrent object. The sequential consistency result contrasts earlier results for observational refinement, where sequential consistency is adequate when clients only communicate through shared objects [9].

We have derived the sufficient conditions for contextual trace refinement using the proof obligations for forwards and backward simulation. However, neither of these conditions have been shown to be necessary, leaving open the possibility of using weaker correctness conditions on the underlying concurrent objects. Studying this relationship remains part of future work — areas of interest include the study of how the correctness conditions for safety of concurrent objects under relaxed memory models [7] can be combined with different scheduler implementations for progress (e.g., extending [13,15]) to ensure contextual trace refinement.

Acknowledgements. We thank John Derrick and Graeme Smith for helpful discussions. Brijesh Dongol is supported by EPSRC grant EP/N016661/1. "Verifiably correct high-performance concurrency libraries for multi-core computing systems".

References

1. Back, R.J.R., Wright, J.: Trace refinement of action systems. In: Jonsson, B., Parrow, J. (eds.) CONCUR 1994. LNCS, vol. 836, pp. 367–384. Springer, Heidelberg (1994). doi:10.1007/978-3-540-48654-1_28
2. Colvin, R., Doherty, S., Groves, L.: Verifying concurrent data structures by simulation. Electr. Notes Theor. Comput. Sci. **137**(2), 93–110 (2005)
3. de Roever, W.P., Engelhardt, K.: Data Refinement: Model-Oriented Proof Methods and Their Comparison. Cambridge Tracts in Theoretical Computer Science. Cambridge Univ. Press, Cambridge (1996)
4. Derrick, J., Schellhorn, G., Wehrheim, H.: Mechanically verified proof obligations for linearizability. ACM Trans. Program. Lang. Syst. **33**(1), 4 (2011)
5. Doherty, S.: Modelling and verifying non-blocking algorithms that use dynamically allocated memory. Master's thesis, Victoria University of Wellington (2003)
6. Dongol, B.: Progress-based verification and derivation of concurrent programs. Ph.D. thesis, The University of Queensland (2009)
7. Dongol, B., Derrick, J., Smith, G., Groves, L.: Defining correctness conditions for concurrent objects in multicore architectures. In: Boyland, J.T. (ed.) ECOOP. LIPIcs, vol. 37, pp. 470–494. Dagstuhl (2015)
8. Dongol, B., Groves, L.: Towards linking correctness conditions for concurrent objects and contextual trace refinement. In: REFINE Workshop (2015 to appear)
9. Filipović, I., O'Hearn, P.W., Rinetzky, N., Yang, H.: Abstraction for concurrent objects. Theor. Comput. Sci. **411**(51 52), 4379 4398 (2010)
10. Gotsman, A., Yang, H.: Liveness-preserving atomicity abstraction. In: Aceto, L., Henzinger, M., Sgall, J. (eds.) ICALP 2011. LNCS, vol. 6756, pp. 453–465 Springer, Heidelberg (2011). doi:10.1007/978-3-642-22012-8_36
11. He, J., Hoare, C.A.R.: Data refinement refined resume. In: Robinet, B., Wilhelm, R. (eds.) ESOP 86. LNCS, vol. 213, pp. 187–196. Springer, Heidelberg (1986)
12. Herlihy, M., Shavit, N.: The Art of Multiprocessor Programming. Morg. Kauf., Burlington (2008)
13. Herlihy, M., Shavit, N.: On the nature of progress. In: Fernàndez Anta, A., Lipari, G., Roy, M. (eds.) OPODIS 2011. LNCS, vol. 7109, pp. 313–328. Springer, Heidelberg (2011). doi:10.1007/978-3-642-25873-2_22
14. Herlihy, M.P., Wing, J.M.: Linearizability: a correctness condition for concurrent objects. ACM Trans. Program. Lang. Syst. **12**(3), 463–492 (1990)
15. Liang, H., Hoffmann, J., Feng, X., Shao, Z.: Characterizing progress properties of concurrent objects via contextual refinements. In: D'Argenio, P.R., Melgratti, H. (eds.) CONCUR 2013. LNCS, vol. 8052, pp. 227–241. Springer, Heidelberg (2013). doi:10.1007/978-3-642-40184-8_17
16. Lynch, N.A.: Distributed Algorithms. Morgan Kaufmann, Burlington (1996)

17. Schellhorn, G., Derrick, J., Wehrheim, H.: A sound and complete proof technique for linearizability of concurrent data structures. ACM TOCL **15**(4), 31:1–31:37 (2014)
18. Sere, K., Waldén, M.A.: Data refinement of remote procedures. Formal Asp. Comput. **12**(4), 278–297 (2000)
19. Treiber, R.K.: Systems programming: coping with parallelism. Technical report RJ 5118, IBM Almaden Res. Ctr. (1986)

Local Livelock Analysis of Component-Based Models

Madiel S. Conserva Filho[1], Marcel Vinicius Medeiros Oliveira[1($\boxtimes$)],
Augusto Sampaio[2], and Ana Cavalcanti[3]

[1] Universidade Federal do Rio Grande do Norte, Natal, Brazil
madiel@ppgsc.ufrn.br, marcel@dimap.ufrn.br
[2] Universidade Federal de Pernambuco, Recife, Brazil
[3] University of York, York, UK

Abstract. In previous work we have proposed a correct-by-construction approach for building deadlock-free CSP models. It contains a comprehensive set of composition rules that capture safe steps in the development of concurrent systems. In this paper, we extend that work by proposing and implementing a strategy for establishing livelock freedom based on constructive rules similar to those that ensure the absence of deadlock. Our method is based solely on the local analysis of the minimum sequences that lead the CSP model back to its initial state. The effectiveness of our livelock-analysis technique is demonstrated via three case studies. We compare the performance of our approach with that of two other techniques for livelock freedom verification: FDR2 and SLAP.

Keywords: Component-based systems · Local analysis · Livelock

1 Introduction

Component-based System Development (CBSD) has been used to deal with the increasing complexity of software. It focuses on the construction of systems from reusable and independent components [1]. Its correct application, however, relies on the trust in the behaviour of the components and in the emergent behaviour of the composed components because failures may arise if the composition does not preserve essential properties, especially in concurrent systems.

In [9], we have proposed a systematic design of CBSD that integrates components via asynchronous compositions, mediated by buffers, considering a grey-box style of composition [2], in which services that cannot be accessed by other components remain visible to the environment. This strategy is based on safe composition rules that guarantee, by construction, deadlock freedom. The absence of livelock is trivially ensured since the basic components are, by definition, livelock-free, and no operator that may introduce such a behaviour is used. The approach is underpinned by the process algebra CSP [4,10], a well established formal notation for modelling and verifying concurrent systems. We

© Springer International Publishing AG 2016
K. Ogata et al. (Eds.): ICFEM 2016, LNCS 10009, pp. 279–295, 2016.
DOI: 10.1007/978-3-319-47846-3_18

provided a component model, $\mathcal{BRIC}$, that imposes constraints on the components and their interactions. Each component is represented by a tuple, where one of the elements is the behaviour of the system described as a CSP process.

This paper focuses on livelock analysis for asynchronous CSP models that perform black-box compositions. It defines a component notion that seems better aligned to CBSD, in which the internal services of components are hidden from its environment. This, however, may introduce livelock, a clearly undesirable behaviour. A system is livelock-free if there exists no state from which it may perform an infinite sequence of internal actions. The traditional livelock analysis performs a global analysis of an internal representation of a model as a labelled transition system, in order to verify that such a state cannot be reached [10]. This strategy is fully automated, for instance, in FDR2 [5]. One alternative is to make a static analysis of the syntactic structure of a system, proposing syntactic rules either to classify CSP systems as livelock-free or to report an inconclusive result. This strategy is implemented in SLAP [7]. Another promising strategy, which is the basis of compositional approaches, performs a local analysis that verifies only some parts of the system. It can identify problems before compositions, predicting, by construction, global properties based on known local properties of the composing components. Locality provides an alternative to circumvent the state explosion generated by the interaction of components and allows us to identify livelock before composition.

In this paper, we present a technique for constructing livelock free systems in $\mathcal{BRIC}$ using local analysis. We consider livelock freedom of $\mathcal{BRIC}$ components in the context of black-boxes rather than grey-boxes compositions adopted in [9]. We introduce side conditions that guarantee, by-construction, that the $\mathcal{BRIC}$ composition rules, which ensure deadlock freedom, also ensure livelock freedom. The verification of these conditions uses metadata that allow us to record partial results of verification, decreasing the overall analysis effort. Our strategy supports a systematic development that rules out designs with livelock. We consider two versions of $\mathcal{BRIC}$: $\mathcal{BRIC}^*$, in which asynchronicity is achieved using finite buffers, and $\mathcal{BRIC}^\infty$, which uses infinite buffers. The possibility of introducing livelock is directly related to the finiteness of the buffer. We also present a comparative analysis of the performance of our strategy with respect to those implemented in FDR2 and in SLAP, based on three case studies.

In the next section, we introduce CSP. Section 3 presents the component model $\mathcal{BRIC}$ that defines the building blocks of our systematic development approach. In Sect. 4, we introduce our approach for livelock-free composition in $\mathcal{BRIC}$ based on local analysis. Its performance is evaluated in Sect. 5. Finally, we draw our conclusions, and discuss future work in Sect. 6.

2   CSP

CSP is one of the most important formalisms for modelling and verifying concurrent reactive systems. This process algebra can be used to describe systems as interacting components: independent entities called processes that interact with each other exchanging atomic, instantaneous and synchronous messages, represented by events. The main CSP constructs used in this paper are presented below. Further information can be found in [4,10].

There are two basic CSP processes: *SKIP* and *STOP*. The former represents the terminating process, and the latter deadlocks. The prefixing $c \to P$ is initially able to perform only the simple event c, and behaves like process P after that. Events may also be compound. For instance, $c.n$ is composed by the channel c and the value n. If we assume that the type of c is the set $\{1, 2\}$, the production $\{\!| \; c \; |\!\}$ returns the set of all events on c, $\{c.1, c.2\}$. Communications may be considered as outputs and inputs: $c!x$ represents an output on some channel c, and $c?x$ is the syntax for an input. The process $g \,\&\, P$ behaves as P if the predicate g is true. Otherwise, it behaves like *STOP*.

The process $P \,\square\, Q$ is an external choice between process P and Q: the environment needs to make the choice by communicating an initial event to one of the processes. When the environment has no control over the choice, we have an internal choice $P \,\sqcap\, Q$. The process $P; \; Q$ combines the processes P and Q in sequence. The process **if** b **then** P **else** Q behaves as P if b holds and as Q otherwise. The parallel composition $P \parallel_X Q$ synchronises P and Q on the events in the set X; events that are not listed in X occur independently. The interleaving $P \,|||\, Q$ runs the processes independently.

The process $P[[a \leftarrow b]]$ behaves like P except that all occurrences of a in P are replaced by b. The hiding process $P \setminus X$ behaves like P, but all events in the set X are hidden and turned into internal actions, which are not visible to the environment. For example, $P = (a \to P) \setminus \{a\}$ is a divergent process that indefinitely performs the event a without communicating with its environment.

In order to illustrate some CSP constructs, we use a classical example of a concurrent system, the dining philosophers [10], which is used throughout this paper. It consists of philosophers that try to acquire a pair of shared forks in order to eat. The philosophers are sat at a table and there is a fork between each pair of philosophers. Each philosopher must pick up both forks before eating.

> *datatype EV = up | down*
> *datatype LF = thinks | eats*
> *channel fk1, fk2, pfk1, pfk2 : EV*
> *channel life : LF*
> *Fork = (fk1.up → fk1.down → Fork) □ (fk2.up → fk2.down → Fork)*
> *Phil = life.thinks → pfk1.up → pfk2.up → life.eats →*
> *   pfk1.down → pfk2.down → Phil*

The process *Fork* ensures that two philosophers cannot hold a fork simultaneously. It offers a deterministic choice between the events $fk1.up$ and $fk2.up$, where $fk1$ and $fk2$ are channels of type EV. The process *Phil* represents the life cycle of a philosopher: before eating, the philosopher thinks and picks the forks up. After eating, the philosopher puts the forks down.

There are three well-established semantic models of CSP: traces $(\mathcal{T})$, stable failures $(\mathcal{F})$, and failures-divergences $(\mathcal{FD})$ [10]. The set $traces(P)$ contains all possible sequences of events in which P can engage. The set $failures(P)$ contains all the failures of P, that is, pairs (s, X), where s is a trace of P and X is a set of events which P may refuse after performing s. The failures-divergences is the most satisfactory model for analysing liveness properties of a CSP process. In $\mathcal{FD}$, a process P is represented by the pair $(failures_\perp(P), divergences(P))$. The set $failures_\perp(P)$ contains all failures of P, and additional failures that record that P can refuse anything after diverging. The set $divergences(P)$ contains all traces of P that lead it to a divergent behaviour and all extensions of those traces. A process P is divergence-free if, and only if, $divergences(P) = \emptyset$.

3 $\mathcal{BRIC}$

The $\mathcal{BRIC}$ component model [9] has been originally proposed to ensure, by construction, the absence of deadlock. It is an algebra that has contracts as operands and composition rules as operators. A component contract, whose definition is presented below, is a tuple and encapsulates a component in $\mathcal{BRIC}$.

Definition 1 (Component Contract). *A component contract $Ctr:\langle \mathcal{B}, \mathcal{R}, \mathcal{I}, \mathcal{C} \rangle$ comprises its behaviour $\mathcal{B}$, which is described as a restricted form of CSP process, I/O process, described below, a set of channels $\mathcal{C}$, a set of data types $\mathcal{I}$, and a total function $\mathcal{R} : \mathcal{C} \to \mathcal{I}$ from channels to their types.*

We use $\mathcal{B}_{Ctr}$, $\mathcal{R}_{Ctr}$, $\mathcal{I}_{Ctr}$ and $\mathcal{C}_{Ctr}$ to denote the elements of the contract Ctr. The behaviour $\mathcal{B}_{Ctr}$ is represented by an I/O process, which is defined as follows, where we use α_P to denote the set of events that P can communicate.

Definition 2 (I/O Process). *We say a CSP process P is an I/O process if:*

- *whenever $c.x \in \alpha_P$, then c is either an input or an output channel;*
- *P has infinite traces (but finite state space);*
- *P is divergence free;*
- *P is input deterministic, that is, after every trace of P, if a set of input events of P may be offered to the environment, they may not be refused by P after the same trace;*
- *P is strongly output decisive, that is, all choices (if any) among output events on a given channel in P are internal.*

All channels of an I/O process are either input or output channels. I/O processes are also non-terminating processes but, for practical purposes in model checking, they have finite state spaces, and are divergence free. Input determinism and strong output decisiveness are not relevant in the context of livelock analysis. For this reason, we omit their formal definitions, which can be found in [8].

We illustrate the compositional development of $\mathcal{BRIC}$ with the construction of an asymmetric dining table with 2 philosophers and 2 forks. The behaviour of each philosopher and each fork is represented as a process $Phil_i$ or $Fork_i$, where $i \in \{1, 2\}$. The channels fk, pfk, both of type $ID.ID.EV$, and lf of type $ID.LF$, where $ID : \{1, 2\}$, distinguish each philosopher and each fork, whose behaviours are described as an instantiation of *Phil* and *Fork* described in Sect. 2.

$Fork_1 = Fork\,[[fk1 \leftarrow fk.1.1, fk2 \leftarrow fk.1.2]]$
$Fork_2 = Fork\,[[fk1 \leftarrow fk.2.2, fk2 \leftarrow fk.2.1]]$
$Phil_1 = Phil\,[[life \leftarrow lf.1, pfk1 \leftarrow pfk.1.1, pfk2 \leftarrow pfk.2.1]]$
$Phil_2 = Phil\,[[life \leftarrow lf.2, pfk1 \leftarrow pfk.2.2, pfk2 \leftarrow pfk.1.2]]$

As all forks and philosophers are represented by one process with indices on its channels, there is a separate definition for each component contract. For example, the contracts Ctr_{Fork_1} and Ctr_{Phil_1} are:

$Ctr_{Fork_1} = \langle Fork_1, \{fk.1.1 \rightarrow EV, fk.1.2 \rightarrow EV\}, \{EV\}, \{fk.1.1, fk.1.2\}\rangle$
$Ctr_{Phil1} = \langle Phil_1, \{lf.1 \rightarrow LF, pfk.1.1 \rightarrow EV, pfk.2.1 \rightarrow EV\}, \{LF, EV\},$
$\qquad\qquad \{lf.1, pfk.1.1, pfk.2.1\}\rangle$

The contract Ctr_{Fork_1} has a behaviour defined by $Fork_1$, and two channels: $fk.1.1$ and $fk.1.2$, both of type EV. The behaviour of the contract Ctr_{Phil_1} is $Phil_1$. This contract has three channels, $lf.1$ of type LF, and $pfk.1.1$ and $pfk.2.1$ of type EV.

In $\mathcal{BRIC}$, we have two types of component composition: binary composition and unary composition. The former is defined below. It provides an asynchronous interaction on channels ic and oc between two contracts Ctr_1 and Ctr_2 mediated by a (possibly infinite) bi-directional buffer $(BUFF_{IO})$.

Definition 3 (Asynchronous Binary Composition). *Let Ctr_1 and Ctr_2 be two distinct component contracts with disjoint sets of channels ($\mathcal{C}_{Ctr_1} \cap \mathcal{C}_{Ctr_2} = \emptyset$), and ic and oc be channels within $\mathcal{C}_{Ctr_1}$ and $\mathcal{C}_{Ctr_2}$, respectively. The asynchronous binary composition of Ctr_1 and Ctr_2 is given by:*

$$Ctr_1\,{}_{\langle ic \rangle} \asymp {}_{\langle oc \rangle}\, Ctr_2 = \langle(((\mathcal{B}_{Ctr_1} \;|||\; \mathcal{B}_{Ctr_2}) \;||_{\{|ic, oc|\}}\; BUFF_{IO}), \mathcal{R}_{Ctr_3}, \mathcal{I}_{Ctr_3}, \mathcal{C}_{Ctr_3}\rangle$$

where $\mathcal{C}_{Ctr_3} = (\mathcal{C}_{Ctr_1} \cup \mathcal{C}_{Ctr_2}) \setminus \{ic, oc\}$, $\mathcal{R}_{Ctr_3} - \mathcal{C}_{Ctr_3} \lhd (\mathcal{R}_{Ctr_1} \cup \mathcal{R}_{Ctr_2})$, and $\mathcal{I}_{Ctr_3} = ran(\mathcal{R}_{Ctr_3})$.

The behaviour of a binary composition is defined as the synchronisation of the behaviour of Ctr_1 and Ctr_2 via a (possibly infinite) bi-directional buffer. The channels used in the composition are not offered to the environment in further compositions ($\mathcal{C}_{Ctr_3}$). The operator $\lhd$ stands for domain restriction and is used to restrict the mapping from channels to interfaces ($\mathcal{R}_{Ctr_3}$) and, furthermore, to restrict the set of interfaces of the resulting contract ($\mathcal{I}_{Ctr_3}$).

Unary compositions are used to assemble channels of a single component Ctr.

Definition 4 (Asynchronous Unary Composition). *Let Ctr be a component contract, and ic and oc be two distinct channels within $\mathcal{C}_{Ctr}$. The asynchronous unary composition of Ctr is defined as:*

$$Ctr \asymp \big|_{\langle ic \rangle}^{\langle oc \rangle} = \langle(\mathcal{B}_{Ctr} \;||_{\{|ic, oc|\}}\; BUFF_{IO}), \mathcal{R}_{Ctr}, \mathcal{I}_{Ctr}, \mathcal{C}_{Ctr}\rangle$$

where $\mathcal{C}_{Ctr} = (\mathcal{C}_{Ctr} \setminus \{ic, oc\})$, $\mathcal{R}_{Ctr} = \mathcal{C}_{Ctr} \lhd \mathcal{R}_{Ctr}$, and $\mathcal{I}_{Ctr} = ran\,\mathcal{R}_{Ctr}$.

The $\mathcal{BRIC}$ composition rules proposed to ensure deadlock freedom by construction are: interleave, communication, feedback and reflexive. The interleave composition aggregates two independent contracts such that, after composition, they do not communicate with each other.

Definition 5 (Interleave Composition). *Let Ctr_1 and Ctr_2 be two component contracts, such that $\mathcal{C}_{Ctr_1} \cap \mathcal{C}_{Ctr_2} = \emptyset$. The interleave composition of Ctr_1 and Ctr_2 is given by $Ctr_1 [|||] Ctr_2 = Ctr_{1\langle\rangle} \asymp {}_{\langle\rangle} Ctr_2$.*

In this composition, components do not share any channel and no synchronisation is enforced. It is a particular kind of composition that involves no communication. In our example, philosophers and forks can be interleaved separately: $Forks = Ctr_{Fork_1} [|||] Ctr_{Fork_2}$ and $Phils = Ctr_{Phil_1} [|||] Ctr_{Phil_2}$. These compositions are valid since the contracts have disjoint channels.

The second rule is based on the traditional way to compose two components, attaching two components connecting two channels, one from each component. Here, Σ is the finite set of all events and $P \upharpoonright X = P \setminus (\Sigma \setminus X)$ restricts the behaviour of P to a set of events X by hiding all events but those in X.

Definition 6 (Communication Composition). *Let Ctr_1 and Ctr_2 be two component contracts, and ic and oc two channels, such that $ic \in \mathcal{C}_{Ctr_1}$ and $oc \in \mathcal{C}_{Ctr_2}$, $\mathcal{C}_{Ctr_1} \cap \mathcal{C}_{Ctr_2} = \emptyset$, and $\mathcal{B}_{Ctr_1} \upharpoonright \{ic\}$ and $\mathcal{B}_{Ctr_2} \upharpoonright \{oc\}$ are strong compatible. The communication composition of Ctr_1 and Ctr_2 is defined as*

$$Ctr_1[ic \leftrightarrow oc] Ctr_2 = Ctr_{1\langle ic\rangle} \asymp {}_{\langle oc\rangle} Ctr_2$$

The proviso of strong compatibility ensures that the outputs of each process are always accepted by the other process. Formally, considering that I_P^s and O_P^s denote the inputs and outputs of a process P after a trace s, respectively, P and Q are strong compatible if, and only if:

$$\forall s : traces(P) \cap traces(Q) \bullet (O_P^s \neq \emptyset \vee O_Q^s \neq \emptyset) \wedge O_P^s \subseteq I_Q^s \wedge O_Q^s \subseteq I_P^s$$

In our example, we are able to compose the contracts $Forks$ and $Phils$ using the communication composition: $PComm = Forks[fk.1.1 \leftrightarrow pfk.1.1]Phils$. The resulting contract includes all philosophers and forks. The remaining connections that are needed to complete the dining table require the connection of two channels of the same component. For this reason, $\mathcal{BRIC}$ also provides unary compositions that can be used for such connections and enables the construction of systems with cyclic topologies. Due to the existence of possible cycles, however, new conditions are required to preserve deadlock freedom.

The unary composition rules are feedback and reflexive. The feedback composition represents the simpler unary composition case, where two channels of the same component are assembled, but do not introduce a new cycle [9]. The requirement on the independence of the channels guarantees that no cycles are introduced. A channel c_1 is independent of a channel c_2 in a process when any communication on c_1 does not interfere with the communications on c_2, and vice-versa; hence, both channels are independently offered to the environment.

Definition 7 (Feedback Composition). *Let Ctr be a component contract, and ic and oc two communication channels from C_{Ctr} that are independent in B_{Ctr}, and such that $B_{Ctr} \upharpoonright ic$ and $B_{Ctr} \upharpoonright oc$ are strong compatible. The feedback composition of Ctr hooking oc to ic is defined as $Ctr[oc \hookrightarrow ic] = Ctr \bowtie|_{\langle oc \rangle}^{\langle ic \rangle}$.*

The contract *PComm* contains all forks and philosophers. The channels *fk.2.2* and *pfk*.1.2, however, are independent in *PComm* because they occur in the interleaved sub-components *Forks* and *Phils*, respectively. We may, therefore, connect these channels using feedback: $PFeed_1 = PComm[pfk.1.2 \hookrightarrow fk.2.2]$. The channels *fk*.2.1 and *pfk*.2.1 are also independent in *PFeed$_1$*. Intuitively, their connection do not introduce a cycle; we may, therefore, connect these channels using the feedback composition: $PFeed_2 = PFeed_1[pfk.2.1 \hookrightarrow fk.2.1]$.

The reflexive composition deals with more complex compositions that introduce cycles of dependencies in the topology of the system structure, some of which may be undesirable because they introduce divergence.

Definition 8 (Reflexive Composition). *Let Ctr be a component contract, and ic and oc two communication channels from C_{Ctr} such that $B_{Ctr} \upharpoonright \{ic, oc\}$ is buffering self-injection compatible. The reflexive composition is defined as $Ctr[ic \hookrightarrow oc] = Ctr \bowtie|_{\langle oc \rangle}^{\langle ic \rangle}$.*

The definition of the reflexive composition is similar to that of the feedback composition. It, however, has a stronger proviso that requires buffering self-injection compatibility, which allows one to assembly two dependent channels of a process via a buffer, without introducing deadlocks. This property is similar to the notion of strong compatibility, except for the fact that two distinct channels of the same process must be compatible. Its formalisation can be found in [8].

In our example, we conclude the design of our system using the reflexive composition to connect channels *fk*.1.2 and *pfk*.2.2.

$$PSystem = PFeed_2[fk.1.2 \hookrightarrow pfk.2.2]$$

This connection could not be achieved using feedback because the two channels are not independent in *PFeed$_2$*. Intuitively, their connection introduces a cycle that causes the dependence between these channels.

4   Livelock Analysis for $\mathcal{BRIC}$

In the $\mathcal{BRIC}$ approach livelock is not an issue because the rules do not hide the composed channels in the CSP behaviour of the resulting contract; they are just removed from the communication channel set, preventing further compositions on them. This gives us a grey-box style of abstraction [2]. We extend the possibilities of performing compositions in $\mathcal{BRIC}$, providing a constructive strategy to perform black-box compositions [11], where the components encapsulate functionality, increasing the abstraction level of the system.

In [9], the concept of livelock is not defined at the component contract level. We define the notion of livelock-free component contract that considers $\mathcal{BRIC}$

components as black-boxes. For that, we consider the component behaviour and the communication channels that are in the component set of visible channels, which are eligible for future compositions. As a result, a component contract Ctr is livelock-free if the CSP process resulting from hiding all channels that are not in the set C_{Ctr} in the behaviour B_{Ctr} is divergence free.

Definition 9 (Livelock-free Component Contract). *A component contract $Ctr = \langle B, R, I, C \rangle$ is livelock-free if, and only if, $divergences(B_{Ctr} \restriction C_{Ctr}) = \emptyset$.*

In what follows, we present the definitions used in our livelock analysis technique and describe the local conditions that guarantee livelock-free $BRIC$ compositions at the component contract level. We make a clear distinction of asynchronous compositions via finite and infinite buffers because the finiteness of the buffer is relevant for detecting the possibility of livelock in asynchronous systems. We consider $BRIC^*$, which achieves asynchronous compositions via finite buffers, and $BRIC^\infty$, in which asynchronicity is achieved using infinite buffers.

4.1   Basic Definitions

A livelock-free contract never performs an infinite sequence of internal events without communicating with its environment. Hence, reasoning about divergences requires reasoning about infinite behaviours. Therefore, the first step of our approach identifies the infinite behaviours of a given component. The function $IP(P)$ returns the traces that lead a given process P to a recursion.

Definition 10 (Interaction Patterns). *Let P be a CSP process. The set of interaction patterns is defined as: $IP(P) = \{t : traces(P) \mid P \equiv_{\mathcal{FD}} (P/t)\}$.*

The process P/t (pronounced P after t) represents the behaviour of P after the trace t is performed. The set $IP(P)$ contains all traces of P after which the process (P/t) has the same failures and divergences of P: they are equivalent in the failures-divergences model. Hence, $IP(P)$ gives an infinite set of traces that leads the process P back to its initial state. In our example, the set of interaction patterns of $IP(Fork_1)$ contains the traces that lead this fork to a recursion:

$$\{\langle fk.1.1.up, fk.1.1.down \rangle, \langle fk.1.2.up, fk.1.2.down \rangle,$$
$$\langle fk.1.1.up, fk.1.1.down, fk.1.1.up, fk.1.1.down \rangle, \ldots \}$$

This set is infinite. Our strategy, however, only needs the set of minimal interaction patterns, which only contains the traces that lead the process to its first recursion. In what follows, we use the function S°, which, given a set of traces S (in our case, interaction patterns), returns the concatenation closure on S, i.e., the set of all sequences we can obtain by taking any subset of traces from the original S and concatenating them together (possibly with repetitions).

$$S^\circ = \{t : \Sigma^* \mid (\exists ss : \text{seq}(\Sigma^*) \bullet \text{ran}(ss) \subseteq S \land t = ^\frown / ss)\}$$

Here, Σ^* is the set of finite sequences of elements of Σ, seq(Σ^*) is the set of finite sequences over Σ^*, $^\frown/\,ss$ is the distributed concatenation of all the elements of the sequence of sequences ss, and ran(ss) is the set of the elements of ss.

The set of Minimal Interaction Patterns of a process P, $MIP(P)$, is the minimal set from which we are able to generate the same traces that can be generated from $IP(P)$. Formally, it is a subset of any other subset of interaction patterns S of $IP(P)$, such that $S^\circ = IP(P)$.

Definition 11 (Minimal Interaction Patterns). *Let P be a CSP process. The set of minimal interaction patterns of P, $MIP(P)$, is a set such that*

$$(MIP(P))^\circ = IP(P) \ and \ \forall S : \mathbb{P}(\Sigma^*) \mid S^\circ = IP(P) \bullet MIP(P) \subseteq S.$$

The following constructive proposition is based on the calculation of *traces* proposed by Roscoe [10]. It calculates the *MIP* for CSP processes that describe the behaviour of the basic components, which are strictly sequential (possibly with choices) with no hiding. Parallelism is achieved by composing component contracts using the composition rules. We also consider only tail recursion (and no mutual recursion), in which recursive calls may only happen after at least one visible event (guarded tail recursions). In what follows, we use N to denote the process name and $\overline{P}$ to represent the CSP process expression that defines its behaviour. We also use W_1 and W_2 to denote CSP behaviours.

Proposition 1 (Minimal Interaction Patterns Calculation). *Let N be a process name, and $\overline{P}$ its behaviour. Then $MIP(N)$ is given by $MIP_N(\overline{P})$:*

$$MIP_N(N) = \{\langle\rangle\}$$
$$MIP_N(SKIP) = MIP_N(STOP) = \{\}$$
$$MIP_N(c \rightarrow W_1) = \{t : MIP_N(W_1); \ e : \{\!| \ c \ |\!\} \bullet \langle e \rangle ^\frown t\}$$
$$MIP_N(W_1 \mathbin{\square} W_2) - MIP_N(W_1 \sqcap W_2) = MIP_N(W_1) \cup MIP_N(W_2)$$
$$MIP_N(W_1[\![R]\!]) = \bigcup\{t : MIP_N(W_1) \bullet ren(t, R)\}$$
$$MIP_N(W_1; \ W_2) = \left\{ \begin{array}{l} t_1 : traces(W_1); \ t_2 : MIP_N(W_2) \mid last(t_1) = \checkmark \\ \qquad\qquad\qquad\qquad\qquad\quad \bullet front(t_1) ^\frown t_2 \end{array} \right\}$$
$$MIP_N(g \ \& \ W_1) = MIP_N(W_1)$$
$$MIP_N(\textbf{if} \ g \ \textbf{then} \ W_1 \ \textbf{else} \ W_2) = MIP_N(W_1) \cup MIP_N(W_2)$$

The sequence *front(t)* contains all elements of the sequence t but the last one, *last(t)* returns the last element of t, and the function *ren(t, R)*, presented below, applies the renaming relation on events R to the trace t. For functional renaming, this function returns a singleton set that contains a trace that corresponds to t but replaces every element in the domain of the renaming function by its image. However, relational renaming needs special care because it may turn simple prefixing into an external choice. By way of illustration, for $P = a \rightarrow P$, $P[\![a \leftarrow b, a \leftarrow c]\!] = a \rightarrow P \mathbin{\square} c \rightarrow P$. For this reason, the function *ren* presented below returns a set of traces and we need a distributed union ($\bigcup$) in the definition of MIP_N for renaming (see Proposition 1).

$ren(\langle\rangle, R) = \{\langle\rangle\}$
$ren(\langle e\rangle \frown t, R) = $ **if** $e \in \mathrm{dom}(R)$ **then** $\{e' : R[\{e\}]; \; s : ren(t, R) \bullet \langle e'\rangle \frown s\}$
        else $\{s : ren(t, R) \bullet \langle e\rangle \frown s\}$

In Proposition 1, when MIP_N is applied to N itself, the result is the empty sequence. With our assumption that the process is guarded tail recursive, this ensures that at this stage a minimum path is recorded. $SKIP$ and $STOP$ do not contain any MIP because they terminate (either successfully or not). The MIP_N of the prefix process $c \to W_1$ is formed by concatenating the sequence $\langle c\rangle$ to the front of the sequences of $MIP_N(W_1)$. The MIP of internal and external choices are the union of the MIP_N of the two operands. The MIP of $W_1[[R]]$ are those of W_1 replacing all occurrences of the events e in the domain of the renaming relation R by the relational image of $\{e\}$ in R. The $MIP_N(W_1; \; W_2)$ are the ones of W_2 prefixed by the traces of W_1 that lead to termination, but removing $\checkmark$. The calculation of the MIP_N of guarded processes $g \;\&\; W_1$ (and alternation **if** g **then** W_1 **else** W_2) simply ignores the guard g and takes $MIP_N(W_1)$ (and $MIP_N(W_2)$) as the result. As a consequence, our approach may find false negatives because we consider interaction patterns which may not be feasible depending on the evaluation of g. For instance, if we consider a process $P = g \;\&\; a \to P$, our approach indicates the possibility of divergence in $P \setminus \{a\}$ because we do not analyse the value of g, which determines the existence of either a divergence or a deadlock.

In our example, the calculation of the minimum interaction patterns for $Fork_1$ and $Phil_1$ yields the following result.

$MIP(Fork_1) = \{\langle fk.1.1.up, fk.1.1.down\rangle, \langle fk.1.2.up, fk.1.2.down\rangle\}$
$MIP(Phil_1) = \{\langle lf.1.thinks, pfk.1.1.up, pfk.2.1.up, lf.1.eats,$
        $pfk.1.1.down, pfk.2.1.down\rangle\}$

We are now able to infer which channels can be used to compose a livelock-free contract in $\mathcal{BRIC}$. The function $Allowed$ identifies all communication channels that can be individually hidden with no introduction of contract livelock.

Definition 12 (*Allowed*). *Let Ctr be a livelock-free component contract. The set of communication channels of $\mathcal{C}_{Ctr}$ that can be individually hidden with no introduction of divergence is given by Allowed(Ctr) defined below:*

$Allowed(Ctr) =$
        $\mathcal{C}_{Ctr} \setminus \{c : \mathcal{C}_{Ctr} \mid \exists s : MIP(\mathcal{B}_{Ctr}) \bullet \mathrm{ran}(s) \cap evs(\mathcal{C}_{Ctr}) \subseteq evs(\{c\})\}$

The set $evs(cs) = \bigcup\{c : cs \bullet \{\!| \, c \, |\!\}\}$ contains all events produced by the channels in the set cs given as argument.

The set of *Allowed* channels of a given contract Ctr contains all communication channels c, such that there is no $MIP(\mathcal{B}_{Ctr})$ composed only by events on c. Using these channels on compositions does not introduce a contract livelock because even after individually hiding the communication on these channels, every member of $MIP(\mathcal{B}_{Ctr})$ still has at least one further external communication on a different channel with the environment. In our example, the sets of allowed channels are $Allowed(Ctr_{Phil_1}) = \{lf.1, pfk.1.1, pfk.2.1\}$ and $Allowed(Ctr_{Fork_1}) = \emptyset$. The latter is empty because every member of $MIP(Fork_1)$ either contains only interactions on $fk.1.1$ or only interactions on $fk.1.2$.

4.2   Conditions for Livelock Freedom in $\mathcal{BRIC}^*$

An interleave composition always results in a livelock-free contract, since the behaviour of both composing contracts are livelock-free by definition, and no communication channel is used in this composition. The proofs of the theorems in this paper can be found in [3].

In the communication composition via finite buffers, $Ctr_1[ic \leftrightarrow oc]^* Ctr_2$, a contract livelock may be introduced because we hide the channels ic and oc used in the composition, since they are removed from the set $\mathcal{C}$ of the resulting component. There are, however, conditions under which this composition is safe.

For instance, we consider the composition $Ctr_{Fork_1}[fk.1.1 \leftrightarrow pfk.1.1]^* Ctr_{Phil_1}$ previously presented. Since the communication is asynchronous, after sending the events $fk.1.1.up$ and $fk.1.1.down$ to the buffer, $Fork_1$ recurses and may send such events to the buffer again before the first ones have been consumed by $Phils_1$ via $pfk.1.1.up$ and $pfk.1.1.down$. This, however, may be done only a finite number of times because the buffer is finite and, at some point, the communications on $pfk.1.1.up$ and $pfk.1.1.down$ will be enforced causing the occurrences, for instance, of the visible events $lf.1.thinks$ and $lf.1.eats$. This composition is, therefore, livelock-free. Along with the finiteness of the buffer, the fact that one of the connecting channels is in the corresponding set of allowed channels $(pfk.1.1 \in Allowed(Ctr_{Phils_1}))$ guarantees a resulting livelock-free contract.

We establish below a condition that ensures that a contract livelock is not introduced in a communication composition in $\mathcal{BRIC}^*$.

Theorem 1 (*Livelock-free Finite Communication Compositions*). *Let Ctr_1 and Ctr_2 be two livelock-free component contracts, and ic and oc two channels in $\mathcal{C}_{Ctr_1}$ and $\mathcal{C}_{Ctr_2}$, respectively. The composition $Ctr_1[ic \leftrightarrow oc]^* Ctr_2$ is livelock-free if $ic \in Allowed(Ctr_1)$ **or** $oc \in Allowed(Ctr_2)$.*

Regarding unary compositions, due to the finiteness of the buffer, we also only need to check if at least one of the communication channels used in the composition belongs to the set of *Allowed* channels of the contract.

Theorem 2 (*Livelock-free Finite Unary Compositions*). *Let Ctr be a livelock-free component contract, and ic and oc two channels in $\mathcal{C}_{Ctr}$. The compositions $Ctr[ic \hookrightarrow oc]^*$ and $Ctr[ic \hookleftarrow oc]^*$ are livelock-free if $ic \in Allowed(Ctr)$ **or** $oc \in Allowed(Ctr)$.*

We now turn our attention to the cases in which neither of the connecting channels are in the set of *Allowed*. For example, let us consider three simple livelock-free contracts Ctr_1, Ctr_2 and Ctr_3 defined as follows.

$$C_1 : \langle \mathcal{B}_{C_1}, \{a \to \mathbb{N}\}, \{\mathbb{N}\}, \{a\}\rangle, where\ \mathcal{B}_{C_1} = a.1 \to a.2 \to \mathcal{B}_{C_1}$$
$$C_2 : \langle \mathcal{B}_{C_2}, \{b \to \mathbb{N}\}, \{\mathbb{N}\}, \{b\}\rangle, where\ \mathcal{B}_{C_2} = b.1 \to b.2 \to \mathcal{B}_{C_2}$$
$$C_3 : \langle \mathcal{B}_{C_3}, \{c \to \mathbb{N}\}, \{\mathbb{N}\}, \{c\}\rangle, where\ \mathcal{B}_{C_3} = c.2 \to c.3 \to \mathcal{B}_{C_3}$$

The composition $Ctr_1[a \leftrightarrow c]Ctr_3$ is valid in $\mathcal{BRIC}$ because a and c are strong compatible. However, neither a or c are allowed in the corresponding contracts; this composition yields a divergent contract. In general, however, this would not necessarily happen. For example, $Ctr_1[a \leftrightarrow b]Ctr_2$ would not introduce a contract livelock because the channels would not be able to synchronise. The $\mathcal{BRIC}$ rules, however, require the connecting channels to be strong compatible, that is, at every state of a in $\mathcal{B}_{Ctr_1}$ if $a.n$ is offered, then $b.n$ is also offered by $\mathcal{B}_{Ctr_2}$. In $Ctr_1[a \leftrightarrow b]Ctr_2$, a and b are not strong compatible. As a consequence of the strong compatibility requirement, there is no case in which neither of the connecting channels are in $Allowed$ of their contracts and the $\mathcal{BRIC}$ compositions result in a livelock-free component contract.

In $\mathcal{BRIC}^\infty$, the assumption that communications with the buffer will halt at some point because the buffer is full is no longer valid because the buffers are infinite. We, therefore, need stronger conditions to ensure livelock freedom.

4.3   Conditions for Livelock Freedom in $\mathcal{BRIC}^\infty$

In the presence of infinite buffers, the conditions for safe compositions are necessarily stronger because one of the contracts may indefinitely interact with the buffer via the connecting channel. For example, let us revisit the example of Sect. 4.2 replacing the buffer by an infinite one. The communication composition $Ctr_{Fork_1}[fk.1.1 \leftrightarrow pfk.1.1]^\infty Ctr_{Phil_1}$ remains asynchronous. After sending $fk.1.1.up$ and $fk.1.1.down$ to the buffer, $Fork_1$ still recurses and may send such events to the buffer again before the first ones has been consumed by $Phils_1$ via $pfk.1.1.up$ and $pfk.1.1.down$. This, however, may now be done indefinitely because the buffer is infinite; there is no guarantee that $Phils_1$ ever consumes any message on $pfk.1.1.up$ and $pfk.1.1.down$ causing the occurrence, for instance, of the visible events $lf.1.thinks$ and $lf.1.eats$. For this reason, the divergence of $Fork_1$ affects the overall composition. Therefore, we need a stronger requirement to ensure contract livelock freedom in a communication composition in $\mathcal{BRIC}^\infty$.

Theorem 3 (*Livelock-free Infinite Communication Compositions*). *Let Ctr_1 and Ctr_2 be two livelock-free contracts, and ic and oc two channels in $\mathcal{C}_{Ctr_1}$ and $\mathcal{C}_{Ctr_2}$, respectively. The composition $Ctr_1[ic \leftrightarrow oc]^\infty Ctr_2$ is livelock-free if $ic \in Allowed(Ctr_1)$ **and** $oc \in Allowed(Ctr_2)$.*

Regarding the unary compositions in $\mathcal{BRIC}^\infty$, we have to ensure that the pair of connecting channels can be hidden together. We define the function $Allowed_{Bin}(Ctr)$, which is similar to $Allowed(Ctr)$, but characterises all pairs of channels that can be hidden together without generating a contract livelock.

Definition 13 (*$Allowed_{Bin}$*). *Let Ctr be a livelock-free contract. The set of pairs of channels of $\mathcal{C}_{Ctr}$ that can be hidden with no introduction of divergence is given by $Allowed_{Bin}(Ctr)$ defined as:*

$$Allowed_{Bin}(Ctr) =$$
$$\{c_1, c_2 : \mathcal{C}_{Ctr} \mid \neg (\exists s : MIP(\mathcal{B}_{Ctr}) \bullet ran(s) \cap evs(\mathcal{C}_{Ctr}) \subseteq \{\! |\, c_1, c_2 \,|\!\})\}$$

For the same reason, the infiniteness of the buffers, unary compositions in $\mathcal{BRIC}^\infty$ have a stronger condition for ensuring livelock freedom. We require both connecting channels to be allowed to be hidden together.

Theorem 4 (*Livelock-free Infinite Unary Compositions*). *Let Ctr be a livelock-free contract, and ic and oc two channels in C_{Ctr}. The compositions $Ctr[ic \hookrightarrow oc]^\infty$ and $Ctr[ic \stackrel{\cdot}{\hookrightarrow} oc]^\infty$ are livelock-free if $(ic, oc) \in Allowed_{Bin}(Ctr)$.*

The Theorems 1 to 4 establish the conditions under which we ensure that the result of any $\mathcal{BRIC}$ composition is a livelock-free component contract.

In order to be able to perform further compositions using the resulting contracts in an efficient manner, we calculate the new *MIP* after every livelock-free composition. This information is stored in the contracts as metadata that aims at alleviating further verifications in our method for component composition.

4.4 Dealing with Metadata

The calculation of the *MIP*s of composed components can be based on the function proposed in [10] that calculates the traces of a parallel composition as the combination of the traces of each argument process, where the synchronised events are shared and all other events are interleaved. In our strategy, however, we are not concerned with the *MIP* generated by the interleaving of the *MIP*s because livelock can only be introduced by hiding events of a basic component.

For instance, using the merge from [10] to calculate the new *MIP*s of the interleaving composition $Ctr_{Fork_1} [|||] Ctr_{Fork_2}$, we get all possible sequences resulting from merging $MIP(Fork_1)$ and $MIP(Fork_2)$:

$$\{\langle fk.1.1.up, fk.1.1.down, fk.2.2.up, fk.2.2.down\rangle$$
$$\langle fk.1.1.up, fk.2.2.up, fk.1.1.down, fk.2.2.down\rangle,$$
$$\langle fk.2.2.up, fk.2.2.up, fk.1.1.down, fk.1.1.down\rangle, \ldots \}$$

For any two minimum interaction patterns ip_1 and ip_2 from $MIP(Fork_1)$ and $MIP(Fork_2)$, respectively, this merge includes a large number of traces that communicate on the same channels from ip_1 and ip_2, which only differ in the order of the events. This order, however, is not relevant for our strategy because, using $\mathcal{BRIC}$, further compositions like, for instance, with a contract Ctr_3, will be made on a one channel to one channel basis. As a consequence, composing Ctr_3 with $Ctr_1 [|||] Ctr2$ will be a communication between Ctr_3 with either Ctr_1 or Ctr_2. Based on this analysis, we provide a variation of the merge function from [10]. This optimisation is extremely relevant to the scalability of our approach.

Definition 14 (Optimised Trace Merge). *Let xs be a set of events, x and x' denote members of xs, and y denote a typical member of $\Sigma \setminus xs$. The optimised trace merge is defined as follows.*

$$\langle\rangle \;\|_{xs}^{\langle s_0, t_0\rangle} \langle\rangle = \{\langle\rangle\} \tag{1}$$

$$\langle x\rangle \frown s \;\|_{xs}^{\langle s_0, t_0\rangle} \langle\rangle = \{u \mid u \in \langle x\rangle \frown s \;\|_{xs}^{\langle s_0, t_0\rangle} t_0\} \tag{2}$$

$$\langle\rangle \;\|_{xs}^{\langle s_0, t_0\rangle} \langle x\rangle \frown t = \{u \mid u \in s_0 \;\|_{xs}^{\langle s_0, t_0\rangle} \langle x\rangle \frown t\} \tag{3}$$

$$\langle y\rangle \frown s \;\|_{xs}^{\langle s_0, t_0\rangle} t = \{\langle y\rangle \frown u \mid u \in s \;\|_{xs}^{\langle s_0, t_0\rangle} t\} \tag{4}$$

$$s \;\|_{xs}^{\langle s_0, t_0\rangle} \langle y\rangle \frown t = \{\langle y\rangle \frown u \mid u \in s \;\|_{xs}^{\langle s_0, t_0\rangle} t\} \tag{5}$$

$$\langle x\rangle \frown s \;\|_{xs}^{\langle s_0, t_0\rangle} \langle x\rangle \frown t = \{u \mid u \in s \;\|_{xs}^{\langle s_0, t_0\rangle} t\} \tag{6}$$

$$\langle x\rangle \frown s \;\|_{xs}^{\langle s_0, t_0\rangle} \langle x'\rangle \frown t = \{\} \tag{7}$$

The differences between our definition for trace merging and that of [10] are: (1) Our merge function has the original traces s_0 and t_0 as arguments. This allows us to merge n concatenations of s_0 with m concatenations of t_0; (2) In the cases in which one side is willing to perform a synchronisation event x and the other side has finished (lines 2 and 3), we "reset" the side that has finished, enforcing at least one synchronisation on x and decreasing the size of one of the sequences by at least one; (3) In the cases in which one side is willing to perform an independent event (lines 4 and 5), we do not take all possible combinations of permuting the independent events for the reasons previously explained; and (4) In the cases in which the synchronisation is feasible (line 6), our merge function does not include the synchronised event in the result because they are hidden after composition. We define the merge function as follows.

Definition 15 (MIP Merge). *Let Ctr_1 and Ctr_2 be two livelock-free component contracts, ic and oc two communication channels in $\mathcal{C}_{Ctr_1}$ and $\mathcal{C}_{Ctr_2}$, respectively, and x a fresh channel name. The MIP merge is defined as follows.*

$$
\begin{aligned}
&MIPMerge(\,Ctr_1,\,Ctr_2, ic, oc) = \\
&\quad \{s : MIP(\mathcal{B}_{Ctr_1}) \mid \{\!|\; ic\;|\!\} \cap ran(s) = \emptyset\} \\
&\quad \cup\; \{t : MIP(\mathcal{B}_{Ctr_2}) \mid \{\!|\; oc\;|\!\} \cap ran(t) = \emptyset\} \\
&\quad \cup\; \bigcup \left\{
\begin{aligned}
& s : MIP(\mathcal{B}_{Ctr_1});\; t : MIP(\mathcal{B}_{Ctr_2});\; sx, tx : \Sigma^* \\
& \quad\mid \{\!|\; ic\;|\!\} \cap ran(s) \neq \emptyset \wedge \{\!|\; oc\;|\!\} \cap ran(t) \neq \emptyset \\
& \quad\wedge\; sx \in ren(s, \{v : extensions(ic) \bullet (ic.v, x.v)\}) \\
& \quad\wedge\; tx \in ren(t, \{v : extensions(oc) \bullet (oc.v, x.v)\}) \\
& \quad\bullet\; sx \;\|_{\{\!|x|\!\}}^{\langle sx, tx\rangle} tx
\end{aligned}
\right\}
\end{aligned}
$$

The resulting merge contains all *MIP*s from $\mathcal{B}_{Ctr_1}$ and $\mathcal{B}_{Ctr_2}$ that do not have events on the connecting channels ic and oc, respectively. The remaining *MIP*s are merged using the optimised trace merge. Before the merge, however, the *MIP*s have to be unified on the events of the connecting channels. For that, we use a fresh channel name x and the function ren to replace references to ic and oc in $\mathcal{B}_{Ctr_1}$ and $\mathcal{B}_{Ctr_2}$, respectively, by x. The function $extensions(c)$ returns the values which will 'complete' the channel yielding an event [10].

Next, the metadata calculation for the binary operators is as follows.

Proposition 2 (Binary Composition Metadata). *Let Ctr_1 and Ctr_2 be two livelock-free component contracts and ic and oc two channels in $\mathcal{C}_{Ctr_1}$ and $\mathcal{C}_{Ctr_2}$, respectively. The MIP of the binary compositions are defined as follows.*

$$MIP(Ctr_1 \, [\|\|] \, Ctr_2) = MIP(\mathcal{B}_{Ctr_1}) \cup MIP(\mathcal{B}_{Ctr_2})$$
$$MIP(Ctr_1[ic \leftrightarrow oc] \, Ctr_2) = MIPMerge(Ctr_1, Ctr_2, ic, oc)$$

Finally, we formalise the metadata calculation for the unary compositions.

Proposition 3 (Unary Composition Metadata). *Let Ctr be a livelock-free component contract and ic and oc two communication channels in $\mathcal{C}_{Ctr}$. The MIP of the unary compositions are presented as follows.*

$$MIP(Ctr[ic \hookrightarrow oc]) = \{s : MIP(\mathcal{B}_{Ctr}) \bullet s \setminus \{\!| \, ic, oc \, |\!\}\}$$
$$MIP(Ctr[ic \overset{\hookrightarrow}{} oc]) = \{s : MIP(\mathcal{B}_{Ctr}) \bullet s \setminus \{\!| \, ic, oc \, |\!\}\}$$

The calculation of the resulting *MIP* for unary compositions simply removes both connecting channels from the original *MIP*s.

5 Evaluation

In this section, we demonstrate that our constructive approach to build livelock free models can be applied in practice to large systems involving several compositions. We have developed three case studies: Milner's scheduler [6], which schedules a number of tasks and can be modelled as a ring of cell processes synchronised pairwisely, and two variations of the dining philosopher [10], a livelock-free version and a version in which we have deliberately included livelock. All case studies are developed using the $\mathcal{BRIC}$ methodology, hence, we worked with asynchronous versions of these three case studies.

For each case study, we provide a comparative analysis of three scenarios: the global analysis of FDR2, the static analysis of SLAP, and our local analysis. In these case studies, we have used a dedicated server with an 8 core Intel(R) Core(TM) i7-2600K, 16 GB of RAM and 160GB of SSD in an Ubuntu system. The CSP scripts of these case studies can be found at http://goo.gl/mAZWXq.

Table 1. Results of the livelock analysis for Milner's scheduler in $\mathcal{BRIC}^*$.

N	#	FDR2	SLAP (BDD)	SLAP (SAT)	LLA
5	5	0.123 s	0.045 s	4.196 s	0.177s
10	10	672.164 s	0.128 s	14.340 s	0.218 s
15	15	*	0.465 s	29.862 s	0.243 s
100	100	*	2428.308 s	**	0.559 s
1,000	1,000	*	*	**	3.959 s
3,000	3,000	*	*	**	7.578 s

Tables 1 and 2 summarise our results. The column N is the number of cells and philosophers for Milner's scheduler and dining philosophers, respectively.

Table 2. Results of the livelock analysis for the dining philosophers in $\mathcal{BRIC}^*$.

N	#	Livelock-free system				System with livelock			
		FDR2	SLAP (BDD)	SLAP (SAT)	LLA	FDR2	SLAP (BDD)	SLAP (SAT)	LLA
3	10	2.884s	0.342s	2.114s	0.219s	0.941s	0.252s	1.224s	0.215s
10	38	*	51.708s	383.884s	0.303s	*	26.259s	149.091s	0.297s
100	398	*	*	*	0.778s	*	*	**	0.769s
1,000	3,988	*	*	*	3.888s	*	*	**	3.431s
10,000	39,988	*	*	*	206.689s	*	*	**	185.209s

The column # is the number of compositions, and the columns FDR2, SLAP and LLA present the time cost of the global analysis in FDR2, SLAP Static Analysis (using BDD and SAT), and our local analysis (LLA). The * indicates one hour timeout and ** indicates memory overflow.

The results show that FDR2 and SLAP are unable to deal with large asynchronous configurations. On the other hand, our method provided successful results of livelock analysis for 10,000 philosophers and 10,000 forks (20,000 CSP processes and 39,988 $\mathcal{BRIC}^*$ compositions) in less than 4 min. This proved to be a very promising result in dealing with complex and large systems.

6   Conclusion

In this paper, we propose a correct-by-construction approach for ensuring livelock freedom in $\mathcal{BRIC}$ models built using four composition rules. The development of this strategy is based on the minimum sequences that represent patterns of interactions after which the system recurses. Considering only these finite sequences, we are able to locally assert livelock freedom before integrating components. Furthermore, we use metadata for storing information that alleviate verification conditions during component composition. To perform this analysis in $\mathcal{BRIC}$, we have provided a clear distinction of asynchronous compositions via finite and infinite buffers because the finiteness of the buffer is relevant for detecting the possibility of livelock in such systems.

We have used three case studies that demonstrate the scalability of our approach. For larger systems, the verification using FDR2 and SLAP may easily become costly and infeasible. On the other hand, our compositional livelock analysis seems promising as demonstrated in our case studies.

Our approach for local and compositional livelock analysis can still be improved. Parameters and non-tail recursion are not addressed here; they are, however, in our research agenda, which also includes additional case studies.

References

1. Beneken, G., Hammerschall, U., Broy, M., Cengarle, M., Jürjens, J., Rumpe, B., Schoenmakers, M.: Componentware - State of the Art 2003, October 2003
2. Bruin, H.: A grey-box approach to component composition. In: Czarnecki, K., Eisenecker, U.W. (eds.) GCSE 1999. LNCS, vol. 1799, pp. 195–209. Springer, Heidelberg (2000). doi:10.1007/3-540-40048-6_15
3. Filho, M., Oliveira, M., Sampaio, A., Cavalcanti, A.: Local livelock analysis of component-based models. Technical report, UFRN 2(016). http://goo.gl/zl1MQV
4. Hoare, C.A.R.: Communicating Sequential Processes. Prentice-Hall, Upper Saddle River (1985)
5. Formal Systems Ltd.: FDR2: User Manual, version 2.94 (2012)
6. Milner, R.: Communication and Concurrency. Prentice-Hall, Upper Saddle River (1989)
7. Ouaknine, J., Palikareva, H., Roscoe, A.W., Worrell, J.: A static analysis framework for livelock freedom in CSP. Log. Methods Comput. Sci. 9(3) (2013)
8. Ramos, R.T.: Systematic development of trustworthy component-based systems. Ph.D. thesis, Federal University of Pernambuco (2011)
9. Ramos, R., Sampaio, A., Mota, A.: Systematic development of trustworthy component systems. In: Cavalcanti, A., Dams, D.R. (eds.) FM 2009. LNCS, vol. 5850, pp. 140–156. Springer, Heidelberg (2009). doi:10.1007/978-3-642-05089-3_10
10. Roscoe, A.W.: The Theory and Practice of Concurrency. Prentice-Hall Series in Computer Science. Prentice-Hall, Upper Saddle River (1998)
11. Soni, P., Ratti, N.: Analysis of component composition approaches. Int. J. Comput. Sci. Commun. Eng. 2(1) (2013). ISSN: 2319-7080

Session-Based Compositional Analysis
for Actor-Based Languages Using Futures

Eduard Kamburjan[1]([⊠]), Crystal Chang Din[2], and Tzu-Chun Chen[1]

[1] Department of Computer Science, TU Darmstadt, Darmstadt, Germany
kamburjan@cs.tu-darmstadt.de, tc.chen@dsp.tu-darmstadt.de
[2] Department of Informatics, University of Oslo, Oslo, Norway
crystald@ifi.uio.no

Abstract. This paper proposes a simple yet concise framework to statically verify communication correctness in a concurrency model using futures. We consider the concurrency model of the core ABS language, which supports actor-style asynchronous communication using futures and cooperative scheduling. We provide a type discipline based on session types, which gives a high-level abstraction for structured interactions. By using it we statically verify if the local implementations comply with the communication correctness. We extend core ABS with sessions and annotations to express scheduling policies based on required communication ordering. The annotation is statically checked against the session automata derived from the session types.

1 Introduction

While distributed and concurrent systems are the pillars of modern IT infrastructures, it is non-trivial to model asynchronous interactions and statically guarantee communication correctness of such systems. This challenge motivates us to bring a compositional analysis framework, which models and locally verifies the behaviors of each distributed endpoints (i.e. components) from the specification of their global interactions. For modeling, we focus on core ABS [10,15], an object-oriented actor-based language designed to model distributed and concurrent systems with asynchronous communications. For verification, we establish a hybrid analysis, which statically type checks local objects' behaviors and, at the same time ensures that local schedulers obey to specified policies during runtime. We apply *session types* [12,21] to type interactions by abstracting structured communications as a global specification, and then automatically generating local specifications from the global one to locally type check endpoint behaviors.

The distinguishing features of the core ABS concurrency model are (1) *cooperative scheduling*, where methods explicitly control internal interleavings by explicit scheduling points, and (2) the usage of *futures* [11], which decouple the process invoking a method and the process reading the returned value. By

---

Every author contributed to this paper equally.

© Springer International Publishing AG 2016
K. Ogata et al. (Eds.): ICFEM 2016, LNCS 10009, pp. 296–312, 2016.
DOI: 10.1007/978-3-319-47846-3_19

sharing future identities, the caller enables other objects to wait for the same method results. Note that core ABS does not use channels. Communication between processes is restricted to method calls and return values.

The order of operations on futures is fixed: First a fresh future identity is created upon the caller invoking a method on the callee, then the callee starts the method execution. After method termination, the callee sends the result to the future, i.e. future is resolved. Finally, any object which can access the future can read the value from this future. Our session-based type system ensures that the specification respects this order. We have two kinds of communications: Caller invoking a method at a remote callee, and callee returning values via a future to those who know that future. The later is non-trivial since several endpoints can read more than once from the same resolved future at any time.

To the best of our knowledge, it is the first time that session types are considered for typing the concurrency model of core ABS. Our contributions include: (1) extending core ABS with sessions (SABS for short) by giving special annotations to specify the order of interactions among concurrent class instances, (2) establishing a session-based type system, and (3) generating session automata [2] from session types to represent scheduling policies and typestate [20]. To capture the interactions among objects, which are running several processes, we introduce a *two-fold notion of local types*: Object types defining behaviors (i.e. including scheduling behavior) among class instances, while method types defining behaviors that processes should follow.

Outline: Section 2 gives a motivating example which is used in the rest of the paper. Section 3 introduces the concurrency model of SABS. Section 4 defines session types for SABS (ABS-ST for short), while Sect. 5 gives a type system. Section 6 introduces session automata which are used to verify behaviors of schedulers. Section 7 gives the related works, while Sect. 8 concludes our work.

2   Motivating Example: A Grading System

Consider a service (illustrated in Fig. 1), called *grading system*, which offers an expensive computation on sensitive data, e.g. automatic evaluation of exams. This service consists of three endpoints: A computation server, denoted by c, and a service desk, denoted by d, where a student, denoted by s, can request their grades. The protocol is as follows: Once c finishes calculating the grades, it sends a *publish*

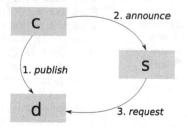

Fig. 1. A grading system

message containing the grades to d and an announcement, *announce* message, to a student. It is not desirable that d starts a new communication with c because c may be already computing the next exams; it is also not desirable that d communicates to s without any request from s.

If a student requests his/her grades before the service desk receives the grades from c by *publish*, the scheduler of d must postpone the process of *request* until *publish* has been executed and terminated. This is not possible for core ABS, because a scheduler in core ABS cannot be idle while waiting for a specific message when the process queue is non-empty. Thus we propose an extension of core ABS to ensure that the endpoints and their local schedulers behave well to the specified communication order.

3   The Session-Based ABS Language (SABS)

This section introduces the concept of *session* to core ABS [10,15]. The extended language is called session-based ABS, SABS in short. The goal of this extension is to equip the language's compiler with the ability to statically ensure communication correctness for applications written in core ABS.

3.1   Syntax and the Concurrency Model of Core ABS

The SABS language provides a combination of algebraic datatype, functional sublanguage, and a simple imperative object-oriented language. The former two kinds are kept the same in SABS as in core ABS. The imperative object-oriented layer is extended. The syntax of SABS can be found in Fig. 2, in which the new language extension is highlighted and will be explained in Sect. 3.2.

A SABS model, denoted by P, defines datatypes $\overline{Dd}$, functions $\overline{F}$, interfaces $\overline{IF}$, classes $\overline{CL}$, and main block $\{\overline{T}\ \overline{x};\ s\}$ to configure the initial state. In datatype declarations Dd, an abstract datatype D has at least one constructor $Cons$, which has a name Co and a list of generic types $\overline{A}$ for its arguments.

Syntactic categories	Definitions
T in Ground Type	$T ::= B \mid I \mid D \mid D\langle \overline{T}\rangle$ $B ::= $ Bool $\mid$ Int $\mid$ String $\mid$ Unit $\mid \cdots$
B in Basic Type	$A ::= N \mid T \mid D\langle\overline{A}\rangle$
A in Generic Type	$Dd ::= $ **data** $D[\langle\overline{A}\rangle] = Cons[\overline{\mid Cons}];$ $Cons ::= Co[(\overline{A})]$
N in Names	$F ::= $ **def** $A\ fn[\langle\overline{A}\rangle](\overline{A\ x}) = e;$
e in Expression	$e ::= b \mid x \mid t \mid$ **this** $\mid$ **destiny** $\mid Co[(\overline{e})] \mid fn(\overline{e}) \mid$ **case** $e\ \{\overline{br}\}$
x in Variable	$t ::= Co[(\overline{t})] \mid$ **null** $br ::= p \Rightarrow e;$ $p ::= \_ \mid x \mid t \mid Co[(\overline{p})]$
t in Ground Term	$P ::= \overline{Dd}\ \overline{F}\ \overline{IF}\ \overline{CL}\ \{\overline{T}\ \overline{x};\ s\}$
br in Branch	$IF ::= $ **interface** $I\ \{\overline{Sg}\ \}$ $Sg ::= T\ m\ (\overline{T\ x})$
p in Pattern	$CL ::= [[a]]$**class** $C\ [(\overline{T\ x})]\ [$**implements** $\overline{I}]\ \{\overline{T\ x};\ \overline{M}\}$
C, I, m in Names	$M ::= Sg\ \{\overline{T\ x};\ s\}$
L in Local Types	$a ::= $ **Scheduler:** L $ptc ::= $ **Protocol:** G $join ::= $ **Ses: String**
S in Session IDs	$rhs ::= e \mid e!m(\overline{e}) \mid e.$**get**
G in Global Types	$s ::= s; s \mid x = rhs \mid$ **skip** $\mid$ **return** e
s in Statement	$\qquad \mid$ **await** $e?\mid$ **if** $b\ \{s\}\ [$**else** $\{s\}] \mid$ **while** $b\ \{s\} \mid$ **case** $e\{\overline{p \Rightarrow s;}\}$
b in Bool Expression	$\qquad \mid [ptc]$ $\mathrm{x} = $ **new** $Session(e) \mid [join]\ x = $ **new** $C[(\overline{e})]$

Fig. 2. SABS syntax. Terms ⁻ denote possibly empty lists over corresponding syntactic categories, and [] optional elements. The highlighted ones are the new syntax added to core ABS.

A future of built-in type $\texttt{Fut}\langle T \rangle$ expresses that the value stored in the future is of type T. Function declarations F consist of a return type A, a function name fn, an optional list of parameters of types $\overline{A}$, a list of variable declarations $\overline{x}$ of types $\overline{A}$, and an expression e. Expressions e include boolean expressions b, variables x, (ground) terms t, the self-identifier this, the return address destiny of the method activation, constructor expressions $Co(\overline{e})$, function expressions $fn(\overline{e})$, and case expressions case e $\{\overline{br}\}$ where br is a branch. An interface $\overline{IF}$ has a name I and method signatures $\overline{Sg}$. A method signature Sg declares the return type T of a method with name m and formal parameters $\overline{x}$ of types $\overline{T}$. A class CL has a name C, the fields $\overline{x}$ of type $\overline{T}$ for formal parameters and state variables, implemented interfaces $\overline{I}$ and methods $\overline{M}$. The right-hand side expressions rhs include (pure) expressions e, asynchronous remote method invocation $e!m(\overline{e})$, and future fetching expression $e.\texttt{get}$. Statements s include sequential composition, assignment, session creation, object creation, guarding statement await e?, if, while, branching, skip and return statement.

The Concurrency Model. In SABS each object has one scheduler and one processor. It is possible to have more than one processes on an object, but at most one process is executed by the processor on an object at a time. For a method call, a fresh future identity, say f, is generated by the caller upon sending an asynchronous remote method invocation to the callee. A future can be seen as a placeholder for the method result. The callee creates a new process for the receiving call. If the processor of the callee is busy while the new message arrives, the created process will be put into the process pool and can later be chosen for execution by the scheduler. Upon method termination, the callee returns the result to f, i.e. f is resolved. Any object sharing the identity f can read the value from f by executing $f.\texttt{get}$. This statement blocks the current process until f is resolved and then returns the value. Since execution control is not transferred between objects and there is no direct access from one object to the fields of other objects, each object can be analyzed individually. SABS supports cooperative scheduling. Each object relies on its scheduler to select a process for execution at the explicit scheduling points, which can be upon termination of object initialization, at await statement, and upon method termination. When a process execution encounters statement await f?, if the future f is not resolved yet, the processor is released and the current process is suspended and put into the process pool. Then the processor is idle and the scheduler chooses a process from the pool for execution based on a scheduling policy (i.e. specified by a local specification). We say the chosen process from the pool is reactivated.

3.2   New Language Extension

SABS provides a set of new features in order to guide the scheduler to select the intended process for execution according to the required interaction ordering. In Fig. 2, the statement $[\texttt{Protocol}:\mathbf{G}]$ $x = \texttt{new}$ $Session(e)$ creates a new session with a fresh session id stored in x. The parameter e is the session name

of type *String*. The annotation [Protocol : **G**] describes the global communication specification **G**, which will be formalized in Sect. 4.1, that the newly
created session should obey. The statement [Ses : S] $x = $ **new** $C[(\overline{e})]$ creates a
new object with a fresh object *id* stored in x. The annotation [Ses : S] specifies
that the newly created object belongs to session S. Each object can belong to
at most one session. The annotation [Scheduler : **L**] is optional and can be
added in front of the class declarations. It provides the local communication
specification **L** to guide the scheduler of the current object.

The SABS implementation for the grading example in Sect. 2 is in Fig. 3, in
which we create a new session ses named Service. Type gradingSystem defines
this session's global communication specification (introduced later in Sect. 4.1).
Computer server c, student s and service desk d all belong to the same session ses.
The scheduling policy for the service desk is represented by a local specification
c?$_f$ *publish*.s?$_{f'}$ *request* (introduced later in Sect. 4.2), which specifies the method
request invoked by the student s can only be executed after the execution of
method publish invoked by the computer server c.

```
1   interface ServiceDesk{ Unit publish(Int g); Int request(); }
2   interface CompServer{ Unit pubGrd(ServiceDesk d, Student s, Int g); }
3   interface Student{ Unit announce(ServiceDesk d); }
4
5   [ Scheduler: c?f publish.s?f' request] // local protocol for SD
6   class SD(CompServer c, Student s) implements ServiceDesk{
7          Int grade = 0;
8          Unit publish(Int g){grade = g;}
9          Int request(){return grade;}}
10
11  class CS implements CompServer{
12         Unit pubGrd(ServiceDesk d, Student s, Int g){
13                Fut<Unit> f = d!publish(g,this);
14                Fut<Unit> f' = s!announce(d,this);
15         }}
16
17  class S implements Student{
18         Int grade = 0;
19         Unit announce(ServiceDesk d){
20                Fut<Int> f'' = d!request(this);
21                grade = f''.get;
22         }}
23
24  { [ Protocol: gradingSystem ] Ses ses = new Session("Service");
25    [ Ses: ses ] CompServer c = new CS;
26    [ Ses: ses ] Student s = new S;
27    [ Ses: ses ] ServiceDesk d = new SD(c,s);
28    Fut<Unit> f0 = c!pubGrd(d,s,85); }
```

Fig. 3. The ABS implementation for the example in Sect. 2.

4   Compositional Analysis Based on Session Types

Based on the approach of compositional analysis and the theory of session types [12], we introduce the ABS-ST (*ABS Session Types*) framework: Each object (i.e. component) is statically checked against its local specification, which are projected from a global specification, specifying the overall interactions among objects (i.e. composes objects). As multiparty session types type interactions consisting of simple sending and receiving actions among multiple processes, ABS-ST type interactions consisting of asynchronous remote method calls, scheduling, and futures among *objects*. This work extends [16], which contains proofs, full examples and definitions.

4.1   Global Types

Global types, denoted by $\mathbf{G}$, define global communication specifications within a closed system of objects. Contrary to session types [12,21], we do not specify the datatype of a message since the message is a method call or a method return and every method in SABS has a fixed signature. The syntax of $\mathbf{G}$ is defined:

Definition 1. Let $\mathbf{p}, \mathbf{q}$ range over objects, denoted by Ob, f over futures, m over method names and C over all constructors of all abstract datatypes.

$$\mathbf{G} ::= 0 \xrightarrow{f} \mathbf{q}:m \mid \mathbf{G}.\mathbf{g} \qquad \mathbf{g} ::= \mathbf{p} \xrightarrow{f} \mathbf{q}:m.\mathbf{g} \mid \mathbf{p}{\downarrow}f:(\mathsf{C}).\mathbf{g} \mid \mathbf{p}{\uparrow}f:(\mathsf{C}).\mathbf{g} \mid$$
$$\mathsf{Rel}(\mathbf{p}, f).\mathbf{g} \mid \mathbf{p}\{\mathbf{g}_j\}_{j \in J} \mid \mathsf{end} \mid \mathbf{g}^*$$

Initialization $0 \xrightarrow{f} \mathbf{q}:m$ starts interactions from the *main block* invoking object $\mathbf{q}$, e.g. we write $0 \xrightarrow{f_0} \mathbf{c}:pubGrd$ to specify the code in the *main block* in Fig. 3. We use . for sequential composition and write $\mathbf{G}.\mathbf{g}$ to mean interaction(s) $\mathbf{g}$ follows $\mathbf{G}$. Interaction $\mathbf{p} \xrightarrow{f} \mathbf{q}:m$ models a remote call, where object $\mathbf{p}$ asynchronously calls method m at object $\mathbf{q}$ via future f, and then $\mathbf{q}$ creates a new process for this method call. The resolving type $\mathbf{p}{\downarrow}f:(\mathsf{C})$ models object $\mathbf{p}$ resolving the future f. If the method has an algebraic datatype as its return type, then the return value has C as its outermost constructor; otherwise we simply write $\mathbf{p}{\downarrow}f$. The fetching type $\mathbf{p}{\uparrow}f:(\mathsf{C})$ models object $\mathbf{p}$ reading the future f. The usage of C here is similar to the one in $\mathbf{p}{\downarrow}f:(\mathsf{C})$. The releasing type $\mathsf{Rel}(\mathbf{p}, f)$ models $\mathbf{p}$ which releases the control until future f has been resolved. This type corresponds to **await** f? statement in SABS. The example below shows how $\mathsf{Rel}(\mathbf{p}, f)$ works:

Example 1. Consider $\mathbf{G}_{\text{release}} = 0 \xrightarrow{f_0} \mathbf{a}:m_0.\mathbf{a} \xrightarrow{f_1} \mathbf{b}:m_1.\mathbf{b} \xrightarrow{f_2} \mathbf{a}:m_2.\mathbf{g}$. It does not specify the usage of futures correctly: At the moment $\mathbf{b}$ makes a remote call on m_2 at $\mathbf{a}$, the process computing f_0 is still active at $\mathbf{a}$. We shall revise it to

$$\mathbf{G}'_{\text{release}} = 0 \xrightarrow{f_0} \mathbf{a}:m_0.\mathbf{a} \xrightarrow{f_1} \mathbf{b}:m_1.\mathsf{Rel}(\mathbf{a}, f_1).\mathbf{b} \xrightarrow{f_2} \mathbf{a}:m_2.\mathbf{g}$$

Here $\mathbf{a}$ suspends its first process computing f_0 until f_1 has been resolved; during this period, $\mathbf{a}$ can execute the call on m_2.

The branching type $\mathbf{p}\{\mathbf{g}_j\}_{j\in J}$ expresses that as $\mathbf{p}$ selects the jth branch, $\mathbf{g}_j$ guides the continuing interactions. The type end means termination.

Note that only a *self-contained* $\mathbf{g}$ can be repeatedly used. We say $\mathbf{g}$ is *self-contained* if (1) wherever there is a remote call or releasing, there is a corresponding resolving and visa versa; and (2) it contains no end, and (3) every repeated type within it is also *self-contained*. We say $A \in \mathbf{g}$ if A appears in $\mathbf{g}$ and $A \in \mathbf{G}$ if $A \in \mathbf{g}$ for some $\mathbf{g} \in \mathbf{G}$. E.g., we have $\mathbf{q} \xrightarrow{f} \mathbf{p}:m \in \mathbf{0} \xrightarrow{f_0} \mathbf{q}:m.\mathbf{q} \xrightarrow{f} \mathbf{p}:m$ and $\mathbf{q}\{\mathbf{g}_2\} \in \mathbf{q}\{\mathbf{g}_j\}_{j\in\{1,2,3\}}$ and its negation means the inverse. A future f is *introduced in* $\mathbf{g}$ (or $\mathbf{G}$) if $\mathbf{p} \xrightarrow{f} \mathbf{q} \in \mathbf{g}$ (or $\mathbf{G}$).

Now we define type $\mathbf{g}^* = \mathit{fresh}(\mathbf{g}).\mathbf{g}^*$ (in case $\mathit{fresh}(\mathbf{g})$ is a branching, we append $\mathbf{g}^*$ to the end of every branch), meaning finite repetition of a *self-contained* $\mathbf{g}$ by giving every repetition fresh future names:

$$\mathit{fresh}(\mathbf{g}) = \begin{cases} \mathbf{g}\{f_1'/f_1\}\cdots\{f_n'/f_n\} & \text{if } f_1, ..., f_n \text{ are } \textit{introduced in } \mathbf{g} \text{ and } f_1', .., f_n' \text{ fresh} \\ \mathbf{p}\{\mathit{fresh}(\mathbf{g}_j)\}_{j\in J} & \text{if } \mathbf{p}\{\mathbf{g}_j\}_{j\in J} \\ \text{Undefined} & \text{otherwise} \end{cases}$$

In other words, we need to keep *linearity* of futures for every iterations.

Example 2. We show how the global type gradingSystem, used in the code of Fig. 3, represents the grading system discussed in Sect. 2:

$$\text{gradingSystem} = \mathbf{0} \xrightarrow{f_0} \mathbf{c}:\mathit{pubGrd}.\mathbf{c} \xrightarrow{f} \mathbf{d}:\mathit{publish}.\mathbf{d}\downarrow f.\mathbf{c} \xrightarrow{f'} \mathbf{s}:\mathit{announce}.$$

$$\mathbf{s} \xrightarrow{f''} \mathbf{d}:\mathit{request}.\mathbf{d}\downarrow f''.\mathbf{s}\uparrow f''.\mathbf{s}\downarrow f'.\mathbf{c}\downarrow f_0.\text{end}$$

The session is started by a call on $\mathbf{c}.\mathit{pubGrd}$, while other objects are inactive at the moment. After the call $\mathbf{c} \xrightarrow{f} \mathbf{d}:\mathit{publish}$, the service desk $\mathbf{d}$ is active at computing f in a process running *publish*. We position $\mathbf{d} \downarrow f$ there to specify that $\mathbf{d}$ must resolve f after it is called by $\mathbf{c}$ and before it is called by $\mathbf{s}$ (i.e. $\mathbf{s} \xrightarrow{f''} \mathbf{d}:\mathit{request}$). For $\mathbf{c}$, it can have a second remote call $\mathbf{c} \xrightarrow{f'} \mathbf{s}:\mathit{announce}$ after its first call. Thus in this case it is no harm to move $\mathbf{d} \downarrow f$ right after $\mathbf{c} \xrightarrow{f'} \mathbf{s}:\mathit{announce}$. As $\mathbf{d}$ is called by $\mathbf{s}$, $\mathbf{d}$ can start computing f'' in a process running *request* only after $\mathbf{d}\downarrow f$, which means the process computing *publish* has terminated. $\mathbf{s}$ will fetch the result by $\mathbf{s}\uparrow f''$ after $\mathbf{d}$ resolves f''; then $\mathbf{s}$ resolves f'. Note that, since $\mathbf{c}$ does not need to get any response from $\mathbf{d}$ nor $\mathbf{s}$, $\mathbf{c}$ simply finishes the session by $\mathbf{c} \downarrow f_0$. The end is there to ensure all processes in the session terminate. The valid use of futures is examined during generating object types from a global type, a procedure introduced in Sect. 4.3. If $\mathbf{s}\uparrow f''$ is specified before $\mathbf{d} \downarrow f''$, the projection procedure will return *undefined* since f'' can not be read before being resolved.

4.2   Local Types

Besides global types, to statically check code, we define local types, which describe local specifications at object level. The syntax of local types is defined:

Definition 2

$$\mathbf{L} \ ::= \ \mathbf{p}!_f m.\mathbf{L} \ | \ \mathbf{p}?_f m.\mathbf{L} \ | \ \mathsf{Put} \ f:(\mathsf{C}).\mathbf{L} \ | \ \mathsf{Get} \ f:(\mathsf{C}).\mathbf{L} \ | \ \mathsf{Await}(f, f').\mathbf{L}$$
$$| \ \mathsf{React}(f).\mathbf{L} \ | \ \oplus\{\mathbf{L}_j\}_{j \in J} \ | \ \&_f\{\mathbf{L}_j\}_{j \in J} \ | \ \mathbf{L}^*.\mathbf{L} \ | \ \mathsf{skip}.\mathbf{L} \ | \ \mathsf{end}$$

We use . to denote sequential composition. The type $\mathbf{p}!_f m$ denotes a sending action via an asynchronous remote call on method m at endpoint $\mathbf{p}$. The type $\mathbf{p}?_f m$ denotes a receiving action which starts a new process computing f by executing method m after a call from $\mathbf{p}$. The resolving $\mathsf{Put} \ f:(\mathsf{C})$ and fetching $\mathsf{Get} \ f:(\mathsf{C})$ have the same intuitive meaning as their global counterparts. The suspension $\mathsf{Await}(f, f')$ means that the process computing f suspends its action until future f' is resolved. The reactivation $\mathsf{React}(f)$ means the process continues the execution with f. The choice operator $\oplus$ in $\oplus\{\mathbf{L}_j\}_{j \in J}$ denotes that the currently active process selects a branch to continue. The offer operator $\&_f$ in $\&_f\{\mathbf{L}_j\}_{j \in J}$ denotes that the object offers branches $\{\mathbf{L}_j\}_{j \in J}$ when f is resolved. The type skip denotes no action and we say $\mathbf{L}.\mathsf{skip} \equiv \mathbf{L} \equiv \mathsf{skip}.\mathbf{L}$.

In ABS-ST the communication happens among processes in different objects. We list three kinds of local types:

- A *method type* describes the execution of a single process on a particular future f. It has the following attributes: (1) Its first action is $\mathbf{p}?_f m$ for some $\mathbf{p}, m, f$, and (2) if it has a branching type, the final action in every branch is $\mathsf{Put} \ f:(\mathsf{C})$ for some C, f, and (3) it contains no further resolving action or receiving action, and (4) it contains no end.
- An *object type* is a type which is not a method type.
- A *condensed type*, denoted by $\hat{\mathbf{L}}$, where $\mathbf{L}$ is an object type, replaces every action, except receiving and reactivation actions, in $\mathbf{L}$ with skip.

Example 3 Consider object $\mathbf{d}$ in the *grading system* in Sect. 2. Its method type on future f, which is used for calling method *publish*, is $\mathbf{c}?_f publish.\mathsf{Put} \ f$. Its object type is $\mathbf{L} = \mathbf{c}?_f publish.\mathsf{Put} \ f.\mathbf{s}?_{f''} request.\mathsf{Put} \ f''.\mathsf{end}$, and its condensed type is $\hat{\mathbf{L}} = \mathbf{c}?_f publish.\mathsf{skip}.\mathbf{s}?_{f''} request.\mathsf{skip}.\mathsf{skip} \equiv \mathbf{c}?_f publish.\mathbf{s}?_{f''} request$.

4.3 Projection

Projection is the procedure to derive local types of endpoints from a global type. Since in SABS data is sent between different objects by active processes, the projection rules have two levels: (1) Projecting a global type on objects and resulting *object types* and (2) projecting *object types* on a *future* and resulting *method types*, which type the behavior of process for computing the target future.

4.4 Projecting a Global Type to Local Types

We say a global type is *projectable* if every projection on every of its participants is defined and every future is introduced exactly once (i.e. linearity).

A projectable global type implies that the futures appear in it are located correctly across multiple objects; thus the object types gained from it ensure the correct usage of futures.

We define $pre(\mathbf{G}, \mathbf{G}')$ as the set of prefixes of $\mathbf{G}$:

$$pre(\mathbf{G}, \mathbf{G}') = \{\mathbf{G}'' \mid \mathbf{G} \in \mathbf{G}' \text{ implies } \mathbf{G}''.\mathbf{G} \in \mathbf{G}'\}$$

and that a future f *introduced in* $\mathbf{G}'$ is *active* on object $\mathbf{o}$ in $\mathbf{G}$ iff (if and only if):

$$(\mathbf{p} \xrightarrow{f} \mathbf{o} \in pre(\mathbf{G}, \mathbf{G}')) \wedge (\mathbf{o} \downarrow f : (\mathsf{C}) \notin pre(\mathbf{G}, \mathbf{G}'))$$
$$\wedge \left((\mathsf{Rel}(\mathbf{p}, f') \in pre(\mathbf{G}, \mathbf{G}') \wedge f \text{ active in } \mathsf{Rel}(\mathbf{p}, f')) \rightarrow \mathbf{o} \downarrow f' \in pre(\mathbf{G}, \mathbf{G}') \right)$$

The first conjunct captures that after $\mathbf{p} \xrightarrow{f} \mathbf{o}$, f becomes active on $\mathbf{o}$, while after $\mathbf{o} \downarrow f : (\mathsf{C})$, f becomes inactive on $\mathbf{o}$; the second conjunct captures that if f has been suspended on f' (i.e. $\mathsf{Rel}(\mathbf{p}, f') \in pre(\mathbf{G}, \mathbf{G}') \wedge f$ active in $\mathsf{Rel}(\mathbf{p}, f')$), then f must have been reactivated by resolving f' (i.e. $\mathbf{o} \downarrow f' \in pre(\mathbf{G}, \mathbf{G}')$).

Figure 4 defines the projection rules as a function $pj(\mathbf{g}, \mathbf{o})_\mathbf{G}$ projecting $\mathbf{g}$ to object $\mathbf{o}$, where $\mathbf{g} \in \mathbf{G}$. We write $pj(\mathbf{G}, \mathbf{o})_\mathbf{G} = \mathbf{G} \upharpoonright \mathbf{o}$. The side-conditions verify the defined cases, where the futures are used correctly; others are undefined.

The interaction type projects a sending action on the caller side and a receiving action on the callee side. A resolving type gives an action for resolving f on the corresponding object, and generates a reactivation for every objects who are waiting for f; for others, it gives skip. A fetching type gives an action for fetching the result from f on the corresponding object and gives skip for others. Its side-condition ensures that a future is resolved before fetching it. This must be checked at a global level because resolving and fetching take place in different objects. A releasing type gives suspension for the corresponding object and gives skip for others. Its side-condition ensures that the releasing object does not have any other future waiting for the same resolving. A branching type gives a choice type for the active side and an offer for every one that either receives one of the calls invoked by the object making the choice or reads from the active future. For other objects, each branch should have the same behavior so that those objects always know how to proceed no matter which branch was selected. Termination type gives end, which means every future has been resolved and all objects are inactive. The repetition and concatenation are propagated down.

4.5   Projecting Object Types to Method Types

Figure 4 also defines the projection of an object type $\mathbf{L}$ to a method type on a future f, denoted by $pjm(\mathbf{L}, f)$. Since the correct usage of futures has been checked when we do $\mathbf{G} \upharpoonright \mathbf{o}$, $pjm(\mathbf{G} \upharpoonright \mathbf{o}, f)$ has ensured the valid usage of futures.

For a sending, receiving, resolving, fetching, suspending, or repetition object type which is active on future f, the projected method type is itself; otherwise the projection gives skip. A choice object type gives a choice method type when

Projection from global types to object types

$$pj(\mathbf{p} \xrightarrow{f} \mathbf{q}:m, \mathbf{o})_G = \begin{cases} \mathsf{q}!_f m & \text{if } (\mathbf{o} = \mathbf{p}) \wedge (f \text{ is fresh}) \\ \mathsf{p}?_f m & \text{if } (\mathbf{o} = \mathbf{q}) \wedge (f \text{ is fresh}) \wedge (\mathbf{q} \text{ is inactive}) \\ \mathsf{skip} & \text{if } (\mathbf{o} \neq \mathbf{q} \wedge \mathbf{o} \neq \mathbf{p}) \wedge (f \text{ is fresh}) \end{cases}$$

$$pj(\mathbf{p}{\downarrow}f:(\mathsf{C}), \mathbf{o})_G = \begin{cases} \mathsf{Put}\ f:(\mathsf{C}) & \text{if } (\mathbf{o} = \mathbf{p}) \wedge (f \text{ is active on } \mathbf{p}) \\ \mathsf{React}\ f' & \text{if } (\mathbf{o} \neq \mathbf{p}) \wedge (\mathsf{Rel}(\mathbf{o}, f) \in pre(\mathbf{p}{\downarrow}f:(\mathsf{C}), \mathbf{G})) \\ & \qquad \wedge (\ f' \text{ is active on } \mathbf{o} \text{ in } \mathsf{Rel}(\mathbf{o}, f)) \\ \mathsf{skip} & \text{otherwise} \end{cases}$$

$$pj(\mathbf{p}{\uparrow}f:(\mathsf{C}), \mathbf{o})_G = \begin{cases} \mathsf{Get}\ f:(\mathsf{C}) & \text{if } (\mathbf{o} = \mathbf{p}) \wedge (\mathbf{q}{\downarrow}f:(\mathsf{C}) \in pre(\mathbf{p}{\uparrow}f:(\mathsf{C}), \mathbf{G})) \\ \mathsf{skip} & \text{if } (\mathbf{o} \neq \mathbf{p}) \wedge (\mathbf{q}{\downarrow}f:(\mathsf{C}) \in pre(\mathbf{p}{\uparrow}f:(\mathsf{C}), \mathbf{G})) \end{cases}$$

$$pj(\mathsf{Rel}(\mathbf{p}, f), \mathbf{o})_G = \begin{cases} \mathsf{Await}(f', f) & \text{if } (\mathbf{o} = \mathbf{p}) \wedge (f' \text{ is active on } \mathbf{p}) \\ & \qquad \wedge (\nexists\mathbf{p'}.\ \mathbf{p'}{\downarrow}f \in pre(\mathsf{Rel}(\mathbf{p}, f), \mathbf{G})) \\ \mathsf{skip} & \text{if}(\mathbf{o} \neq \mathbf{p}) \end{cases}$$

$$pj(\mathbf{p}\{\mathbf{g}_j\}_{j \in J}, \mathbf{o})_G = \begin{cases} \oplus\{pj(\mathbf{g}_j, \mathbf{o})_G\}_{j \in J} & \text{if } (\mathbf{o} = \mathbf{p}) \\ \&_f\{pj(\mathbf{g}_j, \mathbf{o})_G\}_{j \in J} & \text{if } (\mathbf{o} \neq \mathbf{p}) \wedge (f \text{ is active on } \mathbf{o}) \\ \mathbf{L} & \text{if } (\mathbf{o} \neq \mathbf{p}) \wedge (\forall j \in J.\ pj(\mathbf{g}_j, \mathbf{o})_G = \mathbf{L}) \end{cases}$$

$$pj(\mathsf{end}, \mathbf{o})_G = \mathsf{end} \qquad pj(\mathbf{g}^*, \mathbf{o})_G = (pj(\mathbf{g}, \mathbf{o})_G)^* \text{ if } \mathbf{g} \text{ is self-contained}$$

$$pj((\mathbf{G'}.\mathbf{g}), \mathbf{o})_G = \begin{cases} pj(\mathbf{G'}, \mathbf{o})_G & \text{if } (pj(\mathbf{G'}, \mathbf{o})_G = \mathsf{skip}) \\ pj(\mathbf{G'}, \mathbf{o})_G.pj(\mathbf{g}, \mathbf{o})_G & \text{otherwise} \end{cases}$$

Projection from object types to method types

$$\mathsf{SIMPLE} = \{\mathbf{p}!_{f'}m, \mathbf{p}?_f m, \mathsf{Put}\ f:(\mathsf{C}), \mathsf{Get}\ f':(\mathsf{C}), \mathsf{Await}(f, f')\}$$

$$pjm(\mathbf{L}, f) = \begin{cases} \mathbf{L} & \text{if } (\mathbf{L} \in \mathsf{SIMPLE}) \wedge (f \text{ is active}) \\ \mathsf{skip} & \text{if } (\mathbf{L} \in \mathsf{SIMPLE}) \wedge (\text{some other future is active}) \\ \mathsf{skip} & \text{if } (\mathbf{L} = \mathsf{React}(f)) \vee (\mathbf{L} = \mathsf{end}) \\ pjm(\mathbf{L}_1, f).pjm(\mathbf{L}_2, f) & \text{if } (\mathbf{L} = \mathbf{L}_1.\mathbf{L}_2) \\ pjm(\mathbf{L'}, f) & \text{if } (\mathbf{L} = (\mathbf{L'})^*) \wedge (\mathbf{p} \xrightarrow{f} \mathbf{q} \in \mathbf{L'}) \\ pjm(\mathbf{L'}, f)^* & \text{if } (\mathbf{L} = (\mathbf{L'})^*) \wedge (\mathbf{p} \xrightarrow{f} \mathbf{q} \notin \mathbf{L'}) \\ pjm(\mathbf{L}_j, f) & \text{if } ((\mathbf{L} = \&_{f'}\{\mathbf{L}_j\}_{j \in J}) \vee (\mathbf{L} = \oplus\{\mathbf{L}_j\}_{j \in J})) \\ & \qquad \wedge (f \neq f') \wedge (\mathbf{p} \xrightarrow{f} \mathbf{o} \in \mathbf{L}_j) \\ \oplus\{pjm(\mathbf{L}_j, f)\}_{j \in J} & \text{if } (\mathbf{L} = \oplus\{\mathbf{L}_j\}_{j \in J}) \\ \&_{f'}\{pjm(\mathbf{L}_j, f)\}_{j \in J} & \text{if } (\mathbf{L} = \&_{f'}\{\mathbf{L}_j\}_{j \in J}) \wedge (\mathbf{L}_j \text{ are distinct}) \end{cases}$$

Fig. 4. Projection rules

it projects on an active future used by the target object, while gives a unique **L** when it projects on a future which only appears in one branch. Similarly for the case of offer object type. A reactivation object type gives a method type skip when it projects on any future because the next action after a suspension will always be a reactivation inside a method type. Termination object type also always gives skip for any future because it is not visible. A concatenation object type gives a concatenation method type on any future.

5   Type System

We say the objects involving in a sequence of communications, i.e. a session, satisfy *communication correctness* iff, during the interactions, they always comply with some pre-defined global type. To locally check endpoint implementations and statically ensure communication safety, which is currently not supported by core ABS, we here introduce a type system, which is defined in Fig. 5.

We use Θ as session environments, which contain sessions associating to global types that they follow, with information about the types of participants; we use Γ as shared environments mapping expressions to ground types, and Δ as channel environments mapping channels (composed by a session name and an object) to local types. Note that, channel environments *only exist in the type system*. When we write Θ, Θ', we mean $domain(\Theta) \cap domain(\Theta') = \emptyset$, so as for φ, Γ and Δ. Θ and Γ together store the shared information. For convenience, we define $role(\mathbf{G})$ returning the set of participants in $\mathbf{G}$, $ptypes(C)$ returning the types of parameters of C, $implements(C, I)$ returning true if C can implement interface I, $obj(C)$ returning an instance of class C, and $fields(C)$ returning a shared environment containing attributes of C. We only list the session-related typing rules related. Others are as same as those in core ABS [15].

Rule (T-New-Session) types a session creation by checking if $\mathbf{G}$ in the annotation is projectable (see Sect. 4.4), the session id s is fresh, and the type of e is String. If all conditions are satisfied, we create $\Theta = \{Any : \mathbf{0}\}_{s:\mathbf{G}}$ to record mappings of types to the participants in $\mathbf{G}$. The first mapping is Any : $\mathbf{0}$, in which Any types the session initializer. Also, a channel $s[\mathbf{0}]$ and its type $\mathbf{G} \upharpoonright \mathbf{0}$ is created in shared environments to specify this object playing $\mathbf{0}$ in $\mathbf{G}$. Rule (T-New-Join) types an object creation, which joins session s, which is a name (with type String) of a session. The object creation is valid if s has been created (i.e. $\Theta \vdash \{\varphi\}_{s:\mathbf{G}}$) and the type of $\bar{e}$ is $ptypes(C)$.

Rule (T-Scheduler) is the key rule to activate session-based typing. A class with annotation [Scheduler: L] is well-typed if its methods are well-typed (this part is as same as the rule (T-Class) in [15]) and, by given the fact that the instance of C has joined session s (i.e. $s[obj(C)] : \emptyset$), the local scheduler who specifies the behavior of $obj(C)$ against $\mathbf{L}$ should find $\mathbf{L} = \mathbf{G} \upharpoonright \mathbf{p}$ where $\mathbf{p} \in role(\mathbf{G})$, which implies that $obj(C)$, typed by I, plays as $\mathbf{p}$ in $\mathbf{G}$ when it joins s. Then we extend Θ to Θ' by adding $I : \mathbf{p}$ into $\{\varphi\}_{s:\mathbf{G}}$ to claim that $\mathbf{p}$ associates to interface I, and replacing $s[obj(C)] : \emptyset$ with $s[\mathbf{p}] : \mathbf{L}$ in the channel environment.

Rule (T-Send) types an asynchronous remote method call. The object is allowed to have such a call, specified by $s[\mathbf{p}] : \mathbf{q}!_f m$, when the object calls a method m using f (by checking $x : f$) at an object playing $\mathbf{q}$ in $\mathbf{G}$ (i.e. Θ has $\{\varphi, I : \mathbf{q}\}_{s:\mathbf{G}}$ and Γ has $e : I$) and its next statement s is also well-typed.

Θ(Session Environments) ::= $\emptyset \mid \Theta, \{\varphi\}_{\mathbf{s}:\mathbf{G}}$ $\varphi ::= \emptyset \mid \varphi, I : \mathbf{p} \mid \varphi, \mathsf{Any} : \mathbf{0}$
Γ(Shared Environments) ::= $\emptyset \mid \Gamma, e : T$
Δ(Channel Environments) ::= $\emptyset \mid \Delta, \mathbf{s}[\mathbf{p}] : \mathbf{L}$

$$\frac{\textbf{(T-New-Session)}}{\mathbf{G} \text{ is projectable } \ \mathbf{s} \text{ fresh } \ \Theta = \{\mathsf{Any} : \mathbf{0}\}_{\mathbf{s}:\mathbf{G}} \ \ \Gamma \vdash e : \mathsf{String}}$$
$$\Theta, \Gamma \vdash [\texttt{Protocol: G}] \ \mathtt{Ses} \ \mathbf{s} = \mathbf{new} \ Session(e) \rhd \Delta, \mathbf{s}[0] : \mathbf{G} \upharpoonright 0$$

(T-New-Join)
$$\frac{\Theta \vdash \{\varphi\}_{\mathbf{s}:\mathbf{G}} \text{ for some } \mathbf{G} \ \ \Gamma \vdash \overline{e} : ptypes(C) \ \ \Gamma \vdash c : I}{\Theta, \Gamma \vdash [\texttt{Ses: s}] \ c = \mathbf{new} \ C[(\overline{e})] \rhd \Delta, \mathbf{s}[c] : \emptyset}$$

(T-Scheduler)
$$\forall I \in \overline{I}.implements(C, I) \ \ \Theta, \Gamma[\mathbf{this} \mapsto C, fields(C)] \vdash \overline{M} \rhd \Delta, \mathbf{s}[obj(C)] : \emptyset$$
$$\frac{\Theta = \Theta'', \{\varphi\}_{\mathbf{s}:\mathbf{G}} \ \ \exists \mathbf{p} \in role(\mathbf{G}) \ s.t. \ \mathbf{G} \upharpoonright \mathbf{p} = \mathbf{L} \ \ \Theta' = \Theta'', \{\varphi, I : \mathbf{p}\}_{\mathbf{s}:\mathbf{G}}}{\Theta', \Gamma \vdash [\texttt{Scheduler: L}] \ \mathtt{class} \ C \ [(\overline{T} \ \overline{x})] \ [\mathtt{implements} \ \overline{I}] \ \{\overline{T} \ \overline{x}; \ \overline{M}\} \rhd \Delta, \mathbf{s}[\mathbf{p}] : \mathbf{L}}$$

(T-Send)
$$\frac{\Theta = \Theta', \{\varphi, I : \mathbf{q}\}_{\mathbf{s}:\mathbf{G}} \ \ \Gamma \vdash e : I \ \ \Gamma \vdash x : f \ \ \Gamma \vdash s \rhd \Delta, \mathbf{s}[\mathbf{p}] : \mathbf{L}}{\Theta, \Gamma \vdash x = e!m(\overline{e}); s \rhd \Delta, \mathbf{s}[\mathbf{p}] : \mathbf{q}!_f m.\mathbf{L}}$$

(T-Method)
$$(\Theta = \Theta', \{\varphi, T : \mathbf{q}\}_{\mathbf{s}:\mathbf{G}}) \wedge ((T = I) \vee (T = \mathsf{Any}))$$
$$\frac{T \in \overline{T} \ \ \Gamma' = \Gamma[\overline{x} \mapsto \overline{T}, \overline{x'} \mapsto \overline{T'}] \ \ \Gamma'[\mathbf{destiny} \mapsto f'] \vdash s \rhd \Delta, pjm(\mathbf{L}, f')}{\Theta, \Gamma \vdash T'' \ m \ (\overline{T} \ \overline{x})\{\overline{T'} \ \overline{x'}; s\} \rhd \Delta, \mathbf{s}[\mathbf{p}] : pjm(\mathbf{q}?_f m.\mathbf{L}, f')}$$

(T-Offer)
$$\frac{\Gamma \vdash e : T \ \ J = \{1..n\} \ \ \forall j \in J.\Gamma \vdash p_j : T \ \ \Gamma \vdash s_j \rhd \Delta, \mathbf{s}[\mathbf{p}] : \mathbf{L}_j \ \ f \text{ active on } \mathbf{p} \text{ in } \mathbf{L}_j}{\Gamma \vdash \mathbf{case} \ e\{p_1 \Rightarrow s_1, ..., p_n \Rightarrow s_n\} \rhd \Delta, \mathbf{s}[\mathbf{p}] : \&_f \{\mathbf{L}_j\}_{j \in J}}$$

(T-Choice)
$$\frac{\Gamma \vdash e : T \ \ \Gamma \vdash p : T \ \ J = \{1..n\} \ \ k \in J \ \ \Gamma \vdash s \rhd \Delta, \mathbf{s}[\mathbf{p}] : \mathbf{L}_k}{\Gamma \vdash \mathbf{case} \ e \ \{p \to s\} \rhd \Delta, \mathbf{s}[\mathbf{p}] . \oplus \{\mathbf{L}_j\}_{j \in J}}$$

(T-Await)
$$\frac{\mathbf{L} = \mathsf{React}(f).\mathbf{L'} \ \ f' \text{ inactive on } \mathbf{p} \text{ in } \mathbf{L'} \ \ \Gamma \vdash s \rhd \Delta, \mathbf{s}[\mathbf{p}] : \mathbf{L}}{\Gamma \vdash \mathbf{await} \ e?; s \rhd \Delta, \mathbf{s}[\mathbf{p}] : \mathsf{Await}(f, f').\mathbf{L}}$$

(T-Skip)
$$\frac{\Gamma \vdash s \rhd \Delta, \mathbf{s}[\mathbf{p}] : \mathbf{L}}{\Gamma \vdash \mathbf{skip}; s \rhd \Delta, \mathbf{s}[\mathbf{p}] : \mathsf{skip}.\mathbf{L}}$$

(T-Return)
$$\frac{\Gamma \vdash e : T \ \ \Gamma(\mathbf{destiny}) = f \ \ \Gamma \vdash s \rhd \Delta, \mathbf{s}[\mathbf{p}] : \mathbf{L}}{\Gamma \vdash \mathbf{return} \ e; s \rhd \Delta, \mathbf{s}[\mathbf{p}] : \mathsf{Put} \ f : (\mathsf{C}).\mathbf{L}}$$

(T-While)
$$\frac{\Gamma \vdash b : \mathsf{Bool} \ \ \Gamma \vdash s \rhd \Delta, \mathbf{s}[\mathbf{p}] : \mathbf{L}}{\Gamma \vdash \mathbf{while} \ b\{s\} \rhd \Delta, \mathbf{s}[\mathbf{p}] : \mathbf{L}^*}$$

(T-Get)
$$\frac{\Gamma \vdash s\{e.\mathbf{get}/x\} \rhd \Delta, \mathbf{s}[\mathbf{p}] : \mathbf{L}}{\Gamma \vdash x = e.\mathbf{get}; s \rhd \Delta, \mathbf{s}[\mathbf{p}] : \mathsf{Get} \ f : (\mathsf{C}).\mathbf{L}}$$

Fig. 5. The type system for the concurrent object level of ABS (Parts: Session-related)

Rule (**T-Method**) types a method execution. It is valid to do so if the method body is well-typed and the caller is an object playing $\mathbf{q}$ in $\mathbf{G}$, known by $\Theta = \Theta', \{\varphi, T : \mathbf{q}\}_{\mathbf{s}:\mathbf{G}}$ where T is either equal to I or Any. We use f' for returning the computation result as long as $f' = f$ (i.e. $pjm(\mathbf{q}?_f m.\mathbf{L}, f') = \mathbf{q}?_f m.pjm(\mathbf{L}, f')$.)

Rule (T-Offer) types `case` $e\{p_1 \Rightarrow s_1, ..., p_n \Rightarrow s_n\}$ with $\&_f\{\mathbf{L}_j\}_{j \in J}$ by checking if every branch $p_j \Rightarrow s_j$ is well-typed by $\mathbf{L}_j$ and checking if f is active in $\mathbf{L}_j$ on the object $\mathbf{p}$ in session $\mathbf{s}$. Rule (T-Choice) is the counterpart of (T-Offer). Rule (T-Await) types the await statement with $\mathsf{Await}(f, f')$. It checks if the next statament is well-typed by $\mathsf{React}(f).\mathbf{L}'$, which specifies the next action is to reactivate the usage of f and, since f' has been resolved, in $\mathbf{L}'$ we have f' inactive on $\mathbf{p}$. Other rules are straightforward.

After locally type checking every objects' implementations in a session based on their corresponding local types, which are projected from a global type that the session follows, our system ensures overall interactions among those objects comply with communication correctness:

Theorem 1 (Communication Correctness). *Let G be a projectable global type and S a closed system in which a session s obeys to G. Let $\mathbf{p}'_1, ..., \mathbf{p}'_n$ are objects in s and respectively act as $\mathbf{p}_1, ..., \mathbf{p}_n$ in G. If the objects' implementations are all well-typed by rules in Fig. 5, the interactions among $\mathbf{p}'_1, ..., \mathbf{p}'_n$ comply with communication correctness against G.*

6   Session Automata

As we type check a SABS program via rules in Fig. 5, by rule (T-Scheduler), a local type $\mathbf{L}$ is assigned as a *scheduling policy* to the scheduler of object $[\mathtt{Scheduler: L}]$ `class` C { ... }; the scheduler can (re)activate processes (i.e. by executing methods) based on $\mathbf{L}$. To ensure that the scheduler's behavior follows $\mathbf{L}$, we propose a verification mechanism where a scheduler uses a session automaton [2], as a *scheduling policy*, to model the possible sequence of events.

In this model, when the object is idle, the object's scheduler inputs the processes which can be (re)activated according to the session automaton, which is automatically generated by $\mathbf{L}$. If a labelled transition, which corresponds to an event, can fire in the automaton, the object (re)activates this event. If there are several processes which can run such transition, the scheduler randomly selects one of them. This mechanism is a variant of typestate [20].

Session automata, a subclass of register automata [17], only store fresh futures; it is decideable whether two session automata accept the same language [2]:

Definition 3 (k-Register Session Automata). *Let Σ be a finite set of labels, D be an infinite set of data equipped with equality, and $k \in \mathbb{N}$. A k-Register Session Automaton is a tuple (Q, q_0, Φ, F) where Q is the finite set of states, $q_0 \in Q$ is the initial state, $F \subseteq Q$ is the set of accepting states and $\Phi \subseteq (Q \times Q') \cup (Q \times \Sigma \times 2^{\{1,...,k\}} \times \{1, ..., k\} \times Q)$ is the transition relation.*

Data words are words over an alphabet $\Sigma \times D$. A data word automata has a data store, which can save k data values. A transition fires for a letter $(a, d) \in \Sigma \times D$ if a set of equalities of the form $d = r_i$ are satisfied, where r_i refers to the ith stored data value. After a transition fires, the data store records d.

Let $\sigma : \{1, \ldots, k\} \to D$ be the store. We define (q, a, I, i, q') as a transition in automaton from state q to state q' upon reading (a, d) if $\sigma[i] = d$ for all $i \in I$, $I = \{1..n\}$ by updating $\sigma[i]$ to d, and define (q, q') as an ϵ-transition that switches the state without reading the next letter:

Definition 4 (Runs of Session Automata). A *run* of a k-register session automaton $A = (Q, q_0, \Phi, F)$ on a data word $w = (a_1, d_1), \ldots, (a_k, d_k) \in (\Sigma \times D)^k$ is a sequence $s \in (Q \times \mathbb{N} \times (\{1, \ldots, k\} \to D))^*$. An element (q, j, σ) of the sequence denotes that A is at state q with store σ and reads (a_j, d_j). To be a run of A, the sequence $s = (q_0, j_0, \sigma_0), \ldots, (q_n, j_n, \sigma_n)$ must satisfy the following:

$$\Big((q_i, q_{i+1}) \in \Phi \wedge (j_i = j_{i+1}) \wedge (\sigma_i = \sigma_{i+1})\Big) \vee$$

$$\Big((q_i, (a_{j_i}, d_{j_i}), I, k, q_{i+1}) \in \Phi \wedge (j_{i+1} = j_i + 1) \wedge (\sigma_{i+1} = \sigma_i[k/d_{j_i}]) \wedge \forall l \in I.\ \sigma_i(l) = d_{j_i}\Big)$$

where $I = \{1..n\}$ and $\sigma_i[k/d_{j_i}]$ is a function mapping the kth stored data to d_{j_i}. Now we revise Σ to $\Sigma = \big((\{\texttt{invocREv}\} \times \mathsf{Met}) \cup \{\texttt{reactEv}\}\big)$ and $D = \mathsf{Fut}$, where $\texttt{invocREv}$ labels process activation and $\texttt{reactEv}$ labels process reactivation. Given an object type, we can build a session automaton.

Definition 5. Let **L** be an object type. Let k be number of futures in $\hat{\mathbf{L}}$. We assume the futures are ordered and $pos(f)$ refers to the number of f in the ordering. The k-register session automaton $A_{\mathbf{L}}$ is defined inductively as follows:

- $\mathbf{p}?_f m$ is mapped to a 2-state automaton which reads $(\texttt{invocREv}, m)$ and stores the future f in the $pos(f)$-th register on its sole transition.
- React f is mapped to a 2-state automaton which reads $\texttt{reactEV}$ and tests for equality with the $pos(f)$-th register on its sole transition.
- Concatenation, branching, and repetition using the standard construction for concatenation, union, and repetition for NFAs.

When a process is activated, the automaton stores the process's corresponding futures; when a process is reactivated, the automaton compares the process's corresponding futures with the specified register. As all repetitions in types projected from a global type are self-contained, after the repetition, the futures used there are resolved and thus the automaton can overwrite it safely. The example below shows how a session automaton works based on an object type.

Example 4. Consider the example from Sect. 2. A simple automaton describing the sequence for the **d** (Service Desk) is

The scheduler above does not need to use registers because it does not have reactivations. The following one must read the registers to schedule reactivations:

$$\mathbf{L} = (\mathbf{p}?_f m_1.\mathsf{Await}(f, f').\mathbf{p}?_{f''} m_3.\mathsf{Put}\ f''.\mathsf{React}(f).\mathsf{Put}\ f)^*$$

The generated 2-register session automaton is:

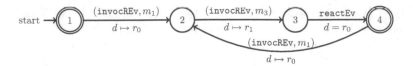

The following theorem states that the objects involving in a session are faithful to the session's protocol if their processes can be verified by the corresponding schedulers, whose behaviors follow the session automata.

Theorem 2 (Fidelity). *Let G be a projectable global type and S a closed system in which a session s obeys to G. Let $p'_1, ..., p'_n$ are objects interacting in s and respectively act as participants $p_1, ..., p_n$ in G. Let A_j be a session automaton generated from $G \upharpoonright p_j$. If every scheduler for p_j, $j \in \{1..n\}$ accepts the same language as A_j does, the implementations on objects are faithful to G.*

7   Related and Future Work

The compositional approach introduced in [5,6] proposed a four event semantics for core ABS. Their verification approach was bottom-up, i.e., class invariants are verified and composed into system property based on history wellformedness; while our approach is top-down, i.e., system property is specified in session types and projected into class invariants. We verify class invariants based on the scheduling policy type-checked by local session types. Besides, we introduce session types for process suspension and process reactivation.

Session types for object-oriented languages have been studied in [3,8] and implemented for libraries/extensions of mainstream languages like Java [13]. Also, lightweight session programming in Scala [19] was proposed by introducing a representation of session types as Scala types. However, they do not explore the valid usage of futures for modeling channel-based concurrency, neither verify cooperative scheduling against specified execution orders.

Schedulers with automata for actor-based models were studied by Jaghoori et al. [14], while user-defined schedulers for ABS were introduced by Bjørk et al. [1]. Our use of automata is similar to the *drivers* of [14], where drivers can not reject any process if the process queue is non-empty and do not consider reactivations. Our schedulers enable the object to wait for a method call to arrive.

Field et al. [7] used finite state automata (without registers) to encode typestate, Gay et al. [8] used typestate to guide session types with non-uniform objects, while Grigore et al. [9] established register automata for runtime verification. In their approach the automata monitor the order of method invocations in a sequential setting. The registers are used to store an unbounded amount of object identities. Our automata are extended to be able to check the specified orders of method calls. The schedulers thus can apply these automta to schedule specified activations and reactivations in a concurrent setting.

Neykova and Yoshida [18] also consider an actor model with channels, where processes are monitored by automata. Deniélou and Yoshida [4] used communicating automata to approximate processes and local types. However, their approaches do not consider scheduling and validating the usage of futures.

We plan to prove that our type system ensures that interactions among objects are deadlock-free and always progresses, and then implement a session-based extension for the core ABS language.

8   Conclusion

We establish a hybrid framework for compositional analysis. The system property is guaranteed by type checking each objects' behaviors against local session types, which are gained by projecting global types on endpoints. In summary, we statically ensure communication correctness for concurrent processing and, at the same time, ensure local schedulers' behaviors will follow the specified execution order among asynchronous communications at runtime.

Acknowledgments. We thank Reiner Hähnle and Patrick Eugster who provided the original idea and insightful discussions for this paper. We also thank the reviewers for their constructive comments. This work was supported by the ERC grant FP7-617805 *LiVeSoft: Lightweight Verification of Software* and the EU project FP7-610582 *Envisage: Engineering Virtualized Services*.

References

1. Bjørk, J., de Boer, F.S., Johnsen, E.B., Schlatte, R., Tarifa, S.L.T.: User-defined schedulers for real-time concurrent objects. ISSE **9**(1), 29–43 (2013)
2. Bollig, B., Habermehl, P., Leucker, M., Monmege, B.: A fresh approach to learning register automata. In: Béal, M.-P., Carton, O. (eds.) DLT 2013. LNCS, vol. 7907, pp. 118–130. Springer, Heidelberg (2013). doi:10.1007/978-3-642-38771-5_12
3. Campos, J., Vasconcelos, V.T.: Channels as objects in concurrent object-oriented programming. In: Honda, K., Mycroft, A. (eds.) PLACES 2010. EPTCS, vol. 69, pp. 12–28 (2010)
4. Deniélou, P.-M., Yoshida, N.: Multiparty session types meet communicating automata. In: Seidl, H. (ed.) ESOP 2012. LNCS, vol. 7211, pp. 194–213. Springer, Heidelberg (2012). doi:10.1007/978-3-642-28869-2_10
5. Din, C.C., Bubel, R., Hähnle, R.: KeY-ABS: a deductive verification tool for the concurrent modelling language ABS. In: Felty, A.P., Middeldorp, A. (eds.) CADE 2015. LNCS (LNAI), vol. 9195, pp. 517–526. Springer, Heidelberg (2015). doi:10.1007/978-3-319-21401-6_35
6. Din, C.C., Owe, O.: Compositional reasoning about active objects with shared futures. Formal Aspects Comput. **27**(3), 551–572 (2015)
7. Field, J., Goyal, D., Ramalingam, G., Yahav, E.: Typestate verification: abstraction techniques and complexity results. Sci. Comput. Program. **58**(1–2), 57–82 (2005)
8. Gay, S.J., Gesbert, N., Ravara, A., Vasconcelos, V.T.: Modular session types for objects. Logical Methods Comput. Sci. **11**(4), 1–76 (2015)

9. Grigore, R., Distefano, D., Petersen, R.L., Tzevelekos, N.: Runtime verification based on register automata. In: Piterman, N., Smolka, S.A. (eds.) TACAS 2013. LNCS, vol. 7795, pp. 260–276. Springer, Heidelberg (2013). doi:10.1007/978-3-642-36742-7_19

10. Hähnle, R.: The abstract behavioral specification language: a tutorial introduction. In: Giachino, E., Hähnle, R., Boer, F.S., Bonsangue, M.M. (eds.) FMCO 2012. LNCS, vol. 7866, pp. 1–37. Springer, Heidelberg (2013). doi:10.1007/978-3-642-40615-7_1

11. Halstead, R.H.: Multilisp: a language for concurrent symbolic computation. ACM TOPLAS 7(4), 501–538 (1985)

12. Honda, K., Yoshida, N., Carbone, M.: Multiparty asynchronous session types. In: Necula, G.C., Wadler, P. (eds.) POPL 2008, pp. 273–284. ACM (2008)

13. Hu, R., Yoshida, N., Honda, K.: Session-based distributed programming in Java. In: Vitek, J. (ed.) ECOOP 2008. LNCS, vol. 5142, pp. 516–541. Springer, Heidelberg (2008). doi:10.1007/978-3-540-70592-5_22

14. Jaghoori, M.M., de Boer, F.S., Chothia, T., Sirjani, M.: Schedulability of asynchronous real-time concurrent objects. J. Logic Algebraic Program. 78(5), 402–416 (2009)

15. Johnsen, E.B., Hähnle, R., Schäfer, J., Schlatte, R., Steffen, M.: ABS: a core language for abstract behavioral specification. In: Aichernig, B.K., Boer, F.S., Bonsangue, M.M. (eds.) FMCO 2010. LNCS, vol. 6957, pp. 142–164. Springer, Heidelberg (2011). doi:10.1007/978-3-642-25271-6_8

16. Kamburjan, E.: Session Types for ABS. Technical report (2016). www.se.tu-darmstadt.de/publications/details/?tx_bibtex_pi1[pub_id]=tud-cs-2016-0179

17. Kaminski, M., Francez, N.: Finite-memory automata. Theor. Comput. Sci. 134(2), 329–363 (1994)

18. Neykova, R., Yoshida, N.: Multiparty session actors. In: Kühn, E., Pugliese, R. (eds.) COORDINATION 2014. LNCS, vol. 8459, pp. 131–146. Springer, Heidelberg (2014). doi:10.1007/978-3-662-43376-8_9

19. Scalas, A., Yoshida, N.: Lightweight session programming in Scala. In: Krishnamurthi, S., Lerner, B.S. (eds.) ECOOP 2016. LIPIcs, vol. 56, pp. 21:1–21:28. Schloss Dagstuhl - Leibniz-Zentrum fuer Informatik (2016)

20. Strom, R.E., Yemini, S.: Typestate: a programming language concept for enhancing software reliability. IEEE Trans. Softw. Eng. 12(1), 157–171 (1986)

21. Takeuchi, K., Honda, K., Kubo, M.: An interaction-based language and its typing system. In: Halatsis, C., Maritsas, D., Philokyprou, G., Theodoridis, S. (eds.) PARLE 1994. LNCS, vol. 817, pp. 398–413. Springer, Heidelberg (1994). doi:10.1007/3-540-58184-7_118

An Event-B Development Process
for the Distributed BIP Framework

Badr Siala[1,2], Mohamed Tahar Bhiri[1], Jean-Paul Bodeveix[2],
and Mamoun Filali[2(✉)]

[1] Université de Sfax, Sfax, Tunisia
siala@irit.fr, tahar_bhiri@yahoo.fr
[2] IRIT CNRS UPS Université de Toulouse, Toulouse, France
{bodeveix,filali}@irit.fr

Abstract. We present a refinement-based methodology to design correct by construction distributed systems specified as Event-B models. Starting from an Event-B machine, the studied process proposes successive steps in order to split and schedule the computation of complex events and then to map them on subcomponents. The specification of these steps is done through two domain specific languages. From these specifications, two refinements are generated. Eventually, a distributed code architecture is also generated. The correctness of the process relies on the correctness of the refinements and the translation. We target the distributed BIP framework.

1 Introduction

In this paper, we are concerned with providing tool support to assist system design using a safe refinement-based process. The considered systems will be seen as a collection of interacting actors. The first levels of the process provides a centralized view of the system behavior. It will be built by taking into account system requirements incrementally, in the form of a series of abstract machines written in Event-B [3]. Then, we propose dedicated, user guided, refinement generators to take into account the distributed nature of the designed system. As a result, we obtain a set of interacting machines of which composition is proven to conform to the abstract levels. The system can then be executed on a distributed platform via a translation to the BIP (Behavior, Interaction, Priority) language [5]. By now, it should be clear that our aim is not to fully automate the distribution process but to assist it. While keeping modest, the difference is similar to that between a model checker where the proof of a judgement is automatic and a theorem proving assistant where the user ha s to compose basic strategies in order to make his proof. Actually, while a theorem proving assistant helps to construct the proof of a goal, we intend to help in the elaboration of a distributed model through refinement patterns [16].

The semantics of Event-B and BIP are based on labeled transition systems thereby promoting their coupling. Event-B is used for the formal specification and the decomposition of initially centralized reactive systems. BIP is used for

© Springer International Publishing AG 2016
K. Ogata et al. (Eds.): ICFEM 2016, LNCS 10009, pp. 313–328, 2016.
DOI: 10.1007/978-3-319-47846-3_20

the implementation and the deployment of distributed systems specified and verified in Event-B. The skeleton of the BIP code is automatically generated from Event-B.

Sections 2 and 3 present Event-B composition/decomposition techniques and the component-based model BIP. Section 4 proposes our development process of distributed systems by coupling Event-B and BIP. This process is illustrated by Fig. 1. Section 5 relates our distributed systems development approach to existing work. We conclude the paper in Sect. 6 and present some perspectives.

Fig. 1. Process steps

2   Event-B

The Event-B method allows the development of correct by construction systems and software [3]. To achieve this, it supports natively a formal development process based on a refinement mechanism with mathematical proofs. Figure 2 illustrates a refinement step where a machine M0 using a context C0 is refined by a machine M1 using an extension C1 of C0. Contexts define abstract data types through sets, constants and axioms while machines define symbolic labelled transition systems through variables and events specifying their evolution while preserving invariant properties.

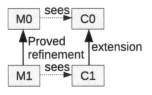

Fig. 2. Event-B development step

As a running example, we will consider the electronic hotel key system case study [15]¹. The context (Listing 1.1) introduces basic data structures: guests, rooms and cards defined as ordered pairs of keys². State variables (Listing 1.2) declare the current key of a room (`currk`), the rooms owned by a guest (`owns`), the cards issued by the hotel and cards owned by a guest.

```
context chotel
sets
    ROOM GUEST KEY
constants
    CARD
axioms
    @crd CARD = KEY × KEY
end
```

Listing 1.1. Hotel context

```
machine hotel sees chotel
variables
    currk owns issued cards
invariants
    @currk_ty currk ∈ ROOM → KEY
    @owns_ty owns ∈ ROOM → ℙ(GUEST)
    @issued_ty issued ∈ ℙ(CARD)
    @cards_ty cards ∈ GUEST → ℙ(CARD)
```

Listing 1.2. Hotel state variables

---

¹ The full code is available in https://dl.dropboxusercontent.com/u/98832434/hotelrefinements.html.

² prj1 returns the left projection of an ordered pair.

The dynamics of the system is described by events, one of which, named `register` being given in Listing 1.3.

This is a non-deterministic event, parametrized by the variables g for the incoming guest, r for the room to be chosen and c for the card to be issued. The `where` part specifies which of these triples are allowed: the room should be free (g1), the card should not have been issued (g2) and the card should open the door (g3). The `then` part specifies how the state space is updated: the current key of the room will be the second key of the card (a1), the card has been issued (a2), is owned by the guest (a3) which owns the room (a4).

```
event register
any g r c
where
  @tg g ∈ GUEST
  @tr r ∈ ROOM
  @tc c ∈ CARD
  @g1 owns(r) = ∅
  @g2 c ∉ issued
  @g3 prj1(c) = currk(r)
then
  @a1 currk(r) := prj2(c)
  @a2 issued := issued∪{c}
  @a3 cards(g) := cards(g)∪{c}
  @a4 owns(r) := {g}
end
```

Listing 1.3. Hotel register event

Recently, Event-B has been enhanced by reuse techniques such as genericity [17], abstraction [13], composition and decomposition [4,18]. In this paper, we are mainly concerned by composition and decomposition. They allow the formal combination of specifications through the refinement mechanism. Two methods of composition/decomposition were identified for Event-B: shared variable [19] and shared event [18]. Shared variable composition/decomposition is suitable for shared-memory parallel systems whereas shared event composition/decomposition is suitable for message-passing distributed systems. In this paper, we limit ourselves to the shared event composition/decomposition approach inspired by CSP where processes synchronize on the same event and may exchange messages. In Event-B, subcomponents (sub-specifications) can synchronize through shared events and exchange data specified by the common value of their parameters.

2.1 Shared Event Composition

The shared event composition of Event-B machines is represented by a new construct called **composed machine** [18]. This operation requires the disjointness of the sets of state variables of the machines to be composed. It is defined as a machine merging subcomponents' properties: conjunction of invariants, union of variables and parallel synchronisation of events. The composition of two events which have common parameters p is defined as follows [18]:

```
E1 ≜ any p,x where G(p,x,m1) then S(p,x,m1) end
E2 ≜ any p,y where H(p,y,m2) then T(p,y,m2) end
E1||E2 ≜ any p,x,y where G(p,x,m1)∧H(p,y,m2) then S(p,x,m1)||T(p,y,m2) end
```

where x, y, p are sets of parameters from the events E1 and E2 and m_1 and m_2 are the variables of the two subcomponents. Sending a value v can be modeled by using a guard of the form $p = v$. The other guards will constrain the sent value either at the sending point or at the receiving point. This design pattern originating from CSP has been proposed by Butler for action systems [7] and in [18] for Event-B.

The **composed machine** is supposed to satisfy the Event-B standard Proof Obligations (POs) related to invariants and refinements. Moreover, during the composition of several subcomponents, it is possible to add a composition invariant relating the states of subcomponents.

Like CSP parallel composition, Event-B shared event composition is monotonic under refinement [18]. Actually, the composition of refined subcomponents is a refinement of the composition of initial subcomponents.

Semantics. In the following we state the semantics of the product CM of machines M_i as a labelled transition over the variables of the subcomponents.

$$\frac{(e = \|_{i \in I} M_i.e) \in CM \quad (e = \textbf{any } X_i \textbf{ where } G_i(X_i) \textbf{ then } S_i(X_i)) \in M_i}{\langle v_1, \ldots, v_n \rangle \xrightarrow{e(p)} \langle v'_1, \ldots, v'_n \rangle}$$
$$\bigwedge_{i \in I} G_i(X_i \triangleleft p)(v_i), \ \bigwedge_{i \in I} v'_i = S_i(X_i \triangleleft p)(v_i), \ \bigwedge_{i \notin I} v'_i = v_i$$

where

- v_i is the valuation of the variables of the component M_i,
- p is the valuation of the union of the parameters of the component events.

2.2   Shared Event Decomposition

Decomposition is a mean to master the complexity (divide and conquer) or to introduce architectural aspects (see Sect. 4). It can be seen as the inverse of composition where an Event-B model is split into several simpler subcomponents. Concretely, decomposition is specified by a set of subcomponent names and a partition of variables, each class being mapped to a subcomponent. An important point is that the composition of subcomponents refines the initial centralized model. However, decomposition fails if a guard or an action refers to variables mapped to different locations. Within the scope of distributed systems, we propose a support to help solving these problems. Decomposition can also fail if the synthesized typing invariant is not strong enough. It could to badly formed expression where some partial functions are applied outside their definition domain. We do not consider this problem.

2.3   Shared Event Composition/Decomposition Tool

The Rodin platform provides an interactive tool [19] as a plugin allowing the shared event composition/decomposition of Event-B specifications. Composition is defined by editing a *composed machine* which designates the subcomponents and defines synchronization events as a product of subcomponent events. Conversely, decomposition is built by naming subcomponents and mapping variables on them. In case of success, the tool generates a machine for each subcomponent and a composed machine. Given that the decomposition of the invariants depends on the scope of the variables, invariants containing variables distributed over several subcomponents are discarded.

3   The BIP Component-Based Model

The BIP language [5] allows to build component-based systems. To achieve this, it offers a means to describe atomic components and composition operators describing composite components. In BIP, an architecture is a hierarchical model consisting of a structured collection of components obtained by composition of atomic components which represent the leaves of the hierarchical model.

3.1   Atomic Components

An atomic BIP component declares data, ports and a behavior. Data variables (**data**) are typed. Ports (**port**) give access to some variables and constitute the component **interface**. The behavior is defined by a port, a guard and a variable update function.

According to the component-based paradigm, a BIP component is a design-time concept (a type) and a runtime concept (an instance). This is also true for ports. Listings 1.4 and 1.5 present, respectively, the port types and an atomic component ty_Desk produced by our BIP code generator (see Sect. 4.3).

```
port type ty_empty_port()
port type ty_register_Desk (INT register_g , INT  register_c)
port type ty_register_Guest (INT register_g , INT  register_c)
```

Listing 1.4. Port types

```
atom type ty_Desk()
  /* state variables */
  data INT currk ...
  /* temporary variables */
  data INT register_g
  /* port instances */
  export port ty_empty_port compute_register_r ()
  export port ty_register_Desk register(register_g ,register_c)
  place P0
  initial to P0 do /* initialize variables */
  /* transitions */
  on compute_register_c from P0 to P0 provided register_g_computed
  on register from P0 to P0 provided register_g_computed do /* action */
end
```

Listing 1.5. Atomic component ty_Desk

3.2   Coordination Between BIP Components

The component-based model BIP has three layers called Behavior, Interaction and Priority. The *Behavior* layer describes the behavior of atomic components (see Sect. 3.1) whilst layers *Interaction* and *Priority* describe the architectural aspects of a component-based system. This separation between behavioral and architectural aspects is an asset in BIP [5]. The synchronization constraints between BIP components are expressed through interactions defined by the **connector** construct whereas scheduling constraints between these interactions are expressed through the *Priority* concept.

BIP Connectors. A connector is simultaneously a *design-time* and a *runtime* concept. A BIP connector is defined by:

- a set of ports $\{p_1, ..., p_n\}$ of subcomponents involved in an interaction.
- an optional port p with variables exported by the connector allowing to compose the connectors.
- a set of interactions which are subsets of $\{p_1, ..., p_n\}$. Every interaction can be annotated by a guard, an *upstream transfer functions* (**up**) and *downstream transfer functions* (**down**). The guards of the interactions involve variables in the scope of ports and connector variables. In this work, we limit ourselves to simple connectors restricted to data transfer (Sect. 4).

For example, Listing 1.6 defines two connector types[3]. The first one denotes a pure synchronization and the second one a synchronization with data exchange.

```
connector type ty_compute_register_r(ty_empty_port Desk, ty_empty_port Guest)
  define Desk Guest
  on Desk Guest down {}
end
connector type ty_register(ty_register_Desk Desk, ty_register_Guest Guest)
  define Desk Guest
  on Desk Guest down {
    Guest.register_c=Desk.register_c;Desk.register_g=Guest.register_g;
  }
end
```

Listing 1.6. Connector types

Composite Component. In BIP, a composite component is both present at design-time and runtime. It includes the following elements:

- atomic or composite components declared by the keyword **component**;
- connectors which connect the components forming the composite component declared by the keyword **connector**;
- priority rules declared by the keyword **priority**;
- exported ports that define the interface of the composite component.

Listing 1.7 presents a composite component. It contains two atomic components and a connector for coordinating them.

```
compound type ty_hotel_decomposition ()
  component ty_Desk Desk()
  component ty_Guest Guest()
  connector ty_register register(Desk.register , Guest.register)
  ...
end
```

Listing 1.7. The Hotel root component type

---

[3] produced by our BIP code generator in Sect. 4.3.

3.3   BIP Execution and Operational Semantics

The BIP execution engine starts with the calculation of executable interactions (Interaction layer). Then, it schedules these interactions, taking into account the priority constraints (Priority layer). Finally, the transitions of the atomic components involved in the interaction are executed (Behavior layer). We now give the operational semantics of the composition of a set of components $(C_i)_{i \in 1..n}$ connected through a set of connectors γ. First, we sum up the syntax of components and connectors as follows:

- $C_i = \langle \Sigma_i, P_i, X_i, \rightarrow_i \rangle$ where Σ_i are the locations of C_i, P_i its set of ports, X_i its set of variables, $\mathcal{G}(X_i)$ is a set predicates over X_i, $\mathcal{A}(X_i)$ is a set of actions over X_i and $\rightarrow_i \subseteq \Sigma_i \times P_i \times \mathcal{G}(X_i) \times \mathcal{A}(X_i) \times \Sigma_i$ its transitions labelled by a guard and an action. We will write $\sigma_i \xrightarrow{p_i/g_i/a_i}_i \sigma_i'$ for an element of $\rightarrow_i$.
- $\gamma \subseteq \{\langle I \subseteq 1..n, (p_i(x_i))_{i \in I} \in \Pi_{i \in I} P_i(X_i), p, G, (D_i)_{i \in I}, U \rangle\}$ is a set of connectors where for a given connector, I is the set indexes of interacting components, $(p_i(x_i))_{i \in I}$ the selected set of ports (one in each component) with their view x_i on component variables, p the outbound port, G the connector guard, D_i the set of *down* functions specifying the update of subcomponent states and U the *up* function specifying the outbound port data.

Then, the operational semantics of the composition is defined by the following transitions over locations and valuations v_i of the component variables. A connector over enabled ports is selected. The *down* actions D_i of the connector are performed before the local action a_i of each component.

$$\frac{\begin{array}{c} \langle I, (p_i)_{i \in I}, p, G, (D_i)_{i \in I}, U \rangle \in \gamma \\ \bigwedge_{i \in I} \sigma_i \xrightarrow{p_i/g_i/a_i}_i \sigma_i' \;\wedge\; \bigwedge_{i \notin I} \sigma_i' = \sigma_i \\ (\bigwedge_{i \in I} g_i(v_i)) \;\wedge\; G(\langle x_i \lhd v_i \mid i \in I \rangle) \\ \bigwedge_{i \in I} v_i' = a_i(v_i \;\lhdplus\; D_i(\langle x_j \lhd v_j \mid j \in I \rangle)) \;\wedge\; \bigwedge_{i \notin I} v_i' = v_i \end{array}}{\langle (\sigma_1, v_1), \ldots, (\sigma_n, v_n) \rangle \xrightarrow{p(U(\langle x_i \lhd v_i \mid i \in I \rangle))} \langle (\sigma_1', v_1'), \ldots, (\sigma_n', v_n') \rangle}$$

For readability reasons, priorities are not taken into account. We should add that the fired interaction is not hidden by ready interactions having a lower priority.

3.4   The BIP Tool-Chain

The BIP tool-chain includes translators from other languages to BIP, formal verification tools and code generators from a BIP model. The BIP language features a static checker called D-Finder [5]. It is a compositional verification tool (invariants, deadlock). Likewise, the BIP language has a runtime verification tool [11]. The code generators take the BIP model and generate single-threaded or multi-threaded code that can be executed and analyzed [14].

4   Towards a Distribution Process

Our goal is to provide a process for guiding the user refinements in order to map an initial "centralized" design (as explained in Sect. 2) on a distributed architecture. The proposed process can be seen as a continuation of the basic methodology which captures requirements as successive refinements of an initial specification. However, as we target a system engineering process, our aim is not to propose a fully automatic distribution tool. For example, in the hotel case study, the behavior of the guest should be mapped on a Guest component. Figure 1 illustrates the proposed process. It is based on three steps: a splitting step which splits events in order to allow the incremental and local resolution of non-determinism, a mapping step which introduces *components* and *mappings* of variables over these components and a distributed code generation step.

We reuse the *shared event decomposition* plugin [18]. However, it does not apply on models where guards or actions access variables mapped on different components as the tool would not know how to split them. Moreover, even if each guard or action refers to only one variable, the resulting components produced by this tool would not be usable. Consider two variables a and b mapped on components C_1 and C_2 and the event ev:

ev $\triangleq$ any p where @g1: a > p @g2: p < b then p1 := p end

Applying [18] is possible: each of C_1 and C_2 gets a copy of ev with respectively g_1 and g_2 as their unique guard, but this leads to another problem: we get two synchronized events specifying constraints over the parameter p. Their separate refinement could lead to incompatible choices and thus to a deadlock resulting from the assembly. The proposed transformations allow the user to avoid this problem by guiding the refinement process. For this purpose, the user can provide parameters to automatic refinement tools. As a result, the two constraints will be located on the same component, while variables will be possibly mapped to distinct subcomponents. Transformations are organized in three steps presented in Sects. 4.1, 4.2 and 4.3.

Moreover, as an implementation constraint, we consider that BIP connectors should not perform computations. Data usage in connectors will thus be restricted to data transfer. This property will lead to a specific refinement of the Event-B model during the mapping processing step (see Sect. 4.2). These steps can be automatically performed given some user annotations. In order to support such a process, we consider two domain specific languages (DSL), one for specifying event parameters computation order and the other for specifying the mapping of machine variables and possibly the location of guard computations. The transformation steps are explicitly specified through the proposed DSLs. These two specifications are used to generate refined models and projections to subcomponents automatically. The correctness of the refinements ensures the correctness of the development. Our process, applied to our example, is illustrated by Fig. 3.

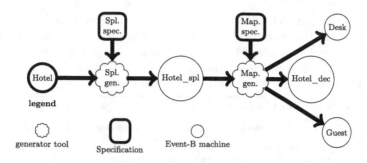

Fig. 3. Hotel transformations

4.1   The Event Splitting Step

The splitting step allows the user to inject heuristics for computing event parameters specified by a set of constraints: an event can be split in order to allow the incremental resolution of its non-determinism. This transformation can be useful if the event is non-deterministic and intended to be shared by several sub-components. Non-determinism will be constrained to occur on local events so that data exchanged will be locally computed before. This step is guided by the user as he may want to control the order in which non-determinism is resolved[4].

The Event Splitting Plugin.
Figure 4 illustrates the profile of the transformation implemented as a Rodin plugin. It takes as input an Event-B machine and a *splitting specification*, whose structure is described by a domain specific language.

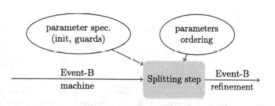

Fig. 4. Event splitting step

$$\text{event } ev \text{ when } p_1 \ \dots \ p_n \text{ parameter } p \text{ init } v \text{ with } g_1 \ \dots \ g_m$$
$$\quad \quad \text{ when } \dots \quad \quad \text{ parameter } \dots$$

We specify for some of the model events, e.g. ev, the parameters (p) to be computed, the parameters on which it depends (p_i), the default value v of p (for typing purposes) and the guards (g_i) acting as the specification of the value of p. The plugin generates a refinement of the input machine.

Such a specification provides a partial order on event parameters. It is used to schedule newly introduced events aiming at computing and storing in a state variable the value of their associated parameter. Ordering constraints are implemented through the introduction of one boolean variable for each parameter, its *computed state*. The machine invariant is extended by the properties of the newly introduced variables: if a variable has been computed, its specification, given by

---

[4] We consider here that non-determinism is only introduced through event parameters.

its guards, is satisfied. When all the parameters of an event have been computed as state variables, the event itself can be fired. The progress of parameters computation is ensured by a *variant* defined as the number of parameters remaining to be computed. More precisely, the previous specification for parameter p of event *ev* will produce the following machine contents:

```
machine generated refines input_machine
variables
  ev_p    ev_p_computed //witness and status for parameter p of event ev
invariants
  @ev_gi ev_p_computed ⇒ gi // where p is replaced by ev_p
variant  // count of the remaining parameters to compute
  {FALSE ↦ 1, TRUE ↦ 0}(ev_p_computed) + ...
events
  event INITIALISATION extends INITIALISATION
  then
    @ev_p ev_p := v
    @ev_p_comp ev_p_computed := FALSE
  end

  convergent event compute_ev_p // computes parameter p of event ev
  any p where
    @gi gi // guards acting as p specification
    @pi ev_pi_computed = TRUE //parameters, p depends on, have been computed
    @p ev_p_computed = FALSE // p remains to be computed
  then
    @a ev_p := p  //computed value stored in state variable ev_p
    @computed ev_p_computed := TRUE // makes the variant decrease
  end

  event ev refines ev
  when
    @p_comp ev_p_computed = TRUE
  with
    @p p = ev_p // parameter p of inherited event is refined to ev_p
  then
    @pi ev_pi_computed := FALSE // for all ev_pi with updated guards
    ...     // replace p by ev_p in actions of the refined event
  end
end
```

Listing 1.8. Generated machine for the splitting refinement

An important point is that we get a refinement of the input machine. It should be proved by the user by discharging the standard proof obligations generated by Rodin and has actually been proved for the hotel example. Three main properties should be established: convergent events refine skip as they do not modify inherited state variables and preserve the invariant. They cannot be launched indefinitely as they make the variant (a natural number) decrease. Lastly, the event ev is refined as new state variables which take place of the parameters of the inherited event satisfy their guards. The refined invariant is also preserved thanks to the reset of the *computed state* of parameters which depend on guards using updated variables. We can also prove that absence of deadlock is preserved: if the guards of an abstract event are true, the parameters of this event can be or have been computed and lastly the refined event itself can be launched.

Application to Our Example. With respect to our example, the `register` event (see Listing 1.3) has three parameters: `g,r,c`. We specify that the parameter `g` should be computed first as the arrival of a guest is supposed to trigger the various actions. Then, a room is chosen in `r` and its associated card is computed in `c`. For each parameter, we specify its initial value and the name of guards which constitute its specification. The dependencies for the `register` event (see Listing 1.3) are specified as follows:

```
splitting hotel_splitted
refines hotel
events
  event register
    parameter g init g0 with tg // tg does't depend on r,c
    when g parameter r init r0 with tr g1 // fired after computation of g
    when g r parameter c init c0 with tc g2 g3 // fired after g,r
end
```

Listing 1.9. Splitting specification

4.2 The Mapping Step

The aim of this step is to set a distributed implementation over subcomponents of an Event-B centralized model. As for the splitting step, the mapping step takes as input a machine and a *mapping specification* described using a dedicated domain specific language. The user can thus provide a set of subcomponent names and declare a mapping from machine variables and possibly event guards to subcomponents. Then, the tool generates a refinement of the input machine and one projection machine for each subcomponent. This step has two phases: the first one, called the *replication phase*, replicates the variables over the components in order to allow a local access to remote variables; the second one, called the *projection phase*, isolates each component as such. The first phase generates a refinement of the input machine which is in turn refined by the product of its projections, thanks to the shared event decomposition mechanism [19].

The Replication Phase. Given the mapping of machine variables to subcomponents, this phase builds a refinement of the input machine by introducing local copies of distant variables accessed by guards. It maps each guard or action to a component and performs some renaming.

We suppose in the following that variables v_i are mapped on components C_i. The convergent events are shared by source (C_i) and destinations (C_j) of variables remotely accessed by guards. Refinements of inherited events are shared by the sources (C_i) of local copies (on C_j) of variables accessed by guards and by components (C_k) owning variables remotely accessed by actions. Figure 5 presents a component-based view of the transformed model. The focus is put on event *ev* of

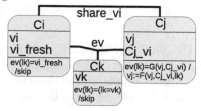

Fig. 5. Local copies and distant access

component C_j. Its guard reads the local copy of v_i while the action has remote access to v_k. Event synchronization ensures the local copy of v_i is up-to-date and gives access to v_k by constraining the event parameter (lk in the figure, local_vk in the code pattern).

Listing 1.10 presents the transformation pattern focused on component C_i. The resulting machine should refine the input machine. This is for the moment verified by discharging the proof obligations generated by Rodin. As previously, we plan to establish this result at the meta-level and the arguments will be very similar to those given for the splitting transformation.

```
machine generated refines input_machine
variables
    vi // inherited variables, on Ci
    Cj_vi // copy of vi mapped on Cj (used by a Cj guard)
    vi_fresh // true if vi has been copied, on Ci
invariants
    @Cj_vi_f vi_fresh = TRUE ⇒ Cj_vi = vi // copy is synchronized
variant
    {FALSE ↦ 1, TRUE ↦ 0}(vi_fresh) + ...
events
    convergent event share_vi // shared by Ci and Cj
    any local_vi
    where
        @g vi_fresh = FALSE // on Ci
        @l local_vi = vi // on Ci
    then
        @to_Cj Cj_vi := local_vi // on Cj
        @done vi_fresh := TRUE // on Ci
    end

    event ev refines ev // shared by Ci, Cj, Ck
    any local_vk
    where
        @vj_access local_vk = vk // on Ck, access to remote variables
        @vi_fresh vi_fresh = TRUE // on Ci, copy to Cj has been done
        @g [vi := Cj_vi]g // inherited guard on Cj, access to local copy of vi
    then
        @a vj := [vi := Cj_vi || vk := local_vk]e // on Cj
    end
end
```

Listing 1.10. replication phase

Furthermore, as for the splitting plugin, the freshness of copies is reset when the source variable is updated by an action.

The Projection Phase. It generates a machine for each component, as would do the *shared event decomposition* plugin [19]. However, thanks to the replication phase, guards and actions over remote variables are now accepted. For component C_j, we get the following code template:

```
machine Cj
variables vj Cj_vi
invariants  // keep only those referring vj and Cj_vi
events
  event share_vi // sync with Ci event, import vi
  any local_vi  then
    @to_Cj Cj_vi := local_vi
  end

  event share_vj // sync with Cl event, export vj
  any local_vj then
    @to_Cl local_vj := vj
  end

  event ev
  any local_vk // read by some Cj action
  where
    @vj_fresh vj_fresh = TRUE // needed by Cl, vj has been exported
    @g [vi := Cj_vi]g // mapped on Cj, access to copy of vi
  then
    @a vj := [vi := Cj_vi;vk=local_vk]e
  end
end
```

Listing 1.11. Projection phase

We have to note that some invariants may be lost: we only keep those who refer variables local to the considered component. It means that the correctness of the resulting machines (i.e. the fact that events preserve the remaining invariants) should be proven. If this is not possible, invariants should be added by the user. However, the composition of the projections, as defined in [19], to which lost invariants are added is, by construction, the machine we had before decomposition. As a consequence, thanks to the monotony of composition, the design process can be pursued on each component machine.

Application to Our Example. Listing 1.12 specifies hotel subcomponents and the mapping of the variables `currk owns issued` on the component `Desk` and the variable `cards` on the component `Guest`.

```
components Desk Guest
mappings
  variables currk owns issued ⟼ Desk;
  variable cards ⟼ Guest;
```

Listing 1.12. Hotel components and mapping specification

4.3 The Code Generation Step

This step assumes that the input Event-B model conforms to a subset of Event-B, we called Event-B0, which plays the role of the subset B0 of the B language that is translated to C. In the considered subset, shared events should be those resulting from the application of the replication phase of the mapping step. Furthermore, we suppose that subcomponent machines do not need to be refined. Events should be deterministic (parameters should have a value) and use a subset of the Event-B expression and predicate languages for which their exists a direct mapping to their BIP counterparts. For this purpose, we require that used set expressions and predicates have been refined to calls to a set library [10] of which signature has a C implementation within the BIP framework. Here, we present how the architectural part of the BIP code is generated. The generator takes as input the mapping specification (subcomponent names, variable and guards mappings) and the refined machine produced by the mapping step.

Port Type Generation. For each shared event and each component of which variables are referenced by this event, we generate a port type taking as parameter the type of exported variables (variables mapped to this component and used by guards or actions mapped to other components). A port type for synchronisation purpose only is generated for all events that do not export variables. Listing 1.5 provides port types generated for our example.

Connector Type Generation. For each event which uses variables of several components, we generate a connector type taking as parameters ports specified by the previously introduced port types. They are supposed to be synchronous. They define a **down** action which copies (via the ports) variables of one component to their copies located in components which need them. Listing 1.6 illustrates the application of this rule in our example.

Subcomponent Skeleton Generation. For each subcomponent, we generate an atomic BIP component. It contains:

- variables mapped to this component as well as variables of other components referenced by guards or actions mapped to this component.
- instances of the port types associated to this component
- for each event, a transition synchronized on the corresponding port instance, and the BIP translation of guards and actions mapped to this component.

As an illustration, Listing 1.5 gives an extract of the atomic component type ty_Desk generated by our plugin.

Composite Component Generation. The root component contains an instance of each subcomponent and connector. Each connector instance takes as parameter a port instance defined in one of the concerned subcomponents. Listing 1.7 provides the code of our example resulting from this step.

The generated BIP architecture should for now be completed manually by the data types and behaviors of atomic components. To achieve this, we envision to use the Theory component [10] of the Rodin platform. Indeed, the Theory component allows to develop proved mathematical theories (datatypes, operators, rewrite rules, inference rules). This allows the extension of Event-B by useful data structures such as arrays, linked lists and hash tables.

5   Related Work

Over the last years, several formalisms such as process algebra, input/output automata, UNITY and TLA$^+$ have been proposed to model and mostly to reason over concurrent and distributed systems. However, to the best of our knowledge, their effective use within development frameworks leading to a distributed implementation has not yet been a general tendency. The automatic generation of source code from formal specifications is supported by few formal methods such as B and Event-B. In [6], an approach is developed allowing the generation of efficient code from B formal developments by using an imperative intermediate language B0. Several Event-B source code generators have been proposed [9,12,20]. Indeed, an Event-B model can represent sequential, concurrent or distributed code as well as reactive, distributed or hybrid systems. The work described in [20] proposes a set of plugins for the Rodin development tool that automatically generate imperative sequential code from an Event-B formal specification. These works do not take into account Event-B composition. Whereas the works described in [9] generate concurrent Ada code restricted to binary synchronization. The automatic refinement of B machines is also possible thanks to the Bart tool [8]. Also, in Event-B, the atomicity decomposition plugin [16] defines a DSL to parametrize the refinement generator. However, the refinement pattern is dedicated to event splitting and does not apply to our problem.

6   Conclusion

In this paper, we have presented a distribution process for system designs formally expressed as Event-B models. Starting from an Event-B machine, the studied process proposes successively the splitting step and the mapping step. The specification of these two steps is done through two domain specific languages. Eventually, a distributed Event-B model and a distributed BIP code architecture are also automatically generated. As we said in the introduction, our primary aim is provide tools to assist the user in the design of distributed systems. Providing a fully automatic process is not in our objectives as we target system engineering and requirements may provide constraints in functions/data to component mapping. Each proposed step generates refinements. The proof obligations generated by Rodin for these refinements remain to be discharged in order to assert the correctness of the developed model.

As future work, we envision to enhance the tooling of our process. Currently, the splitting and mapping steps have been implemented with the xtext [2] language infrastructure, the refinements and the BIP code have been generated with the accompanying xtend language [1] which provides support for writing code generators[5]. We are interested in achieving a distributed code generator plugin for the Rodin platform by taking into account types and the translation of Event-B expression and predicate languages.

We are also interested in studying how the proof obligations generated by the refinements can be discharged definitively at the meta level. In the long term, we seek to enrich the set of transformations and to provide a library of certified transformations dedicated to the development of distributed systems for various architectures.

---

[5]   The generated code is available at
https://dl.dropboxusercontent.com/u/98832434/hotelrefinements.html.

References

1. Java 10, today! http://www.eclipse.org/xtend/. Accessed 16 Jan 2006
2. Language engineering for everyone! https://eclipse.org/Xtext. Accessed 16 Jan 2006
3. Abrial, J.-R.: Modeling in Event-B: System and Software Engineering, 1st edn. Cambridge University Press, New York (2010)
4. Abrial, J.-R., Hallerstede, S.: Refinement, decomposition, and instantiation of discrete models: application to Event-B. Fundam. Inf. **77**(1–2), 1–28 (2007)
5. Basu, A., Bensalem, S., Bozga, M., Combaz, J., Jaber, M., Nguyen, T.-H., Sifakis, J.: Rigorous component-based system design using the BIP framework. IEEE Softw. **28**(3), 41–48 (2011)
6. Bert, D., Boulmé, S., Potet, M.-L., Requet, A., Voisin, L.: Adaptable translator of B specifications to embedded C programs. In: Araki, K., Gnesi, S., Mandrioli, D. (eds.) FME 2003. LNCS, vol. 2805, pp. 94–113. Springer, Heidelberg (2003)
7. Butler, M.: A CSP approach to action systems. Ph.D. thesis, Oxford University (1992)
8. Clearsy. Bart (b automatic refinement tool). http://tools.clearsy.com/wp-content/uploads/sites/8/resources/BART_GUI_User_Manual.pdf
9. Edmunds, A., Butler, M.: Tasking Event-B: An extension to Event-B for generating concurrent code. Event Dates: 2nd April 2011, February 2011
10. Edmunds, A., Butler, M.J., Maamria, I., Silva, R., Lovell, C.: Event-B code generation: type extension with theories. In: ABZ Proceedings, pp. 365–368 (2012)
11. Falcone, Y., Jaber, M., Nguyen, T.-H., Bozga, M., Bensalem, S.: Runtime verification of component-based systems in the BIP framework with formally-proved sound and complete instrumentation. Softw. Syst. Model. **14**(1), 173–199 (2015)
12. Fürst, A., Hoang, T.S., Basin, D., Desai, K., Sato, N., Miyazaki, K.: Code generation for Event-B. In: Albert, E., Sekerinski, E. (eds.) IFM 2014. LNCS, vol. 8739, pp. 323–338. Springer, Heidelberg (2014)
13. Fürst, A., Hoang, T.S., Basin, D., Sato, N., Miyazaki, K.: Formal system modelling using abstract data types in Event-B. In: Ait Ameur, Y., Schewe, K.-D. (eds.) ABZ 2014. LNCS, vol. 8477, pp. 222–237. Springer, Heidelberg (2014)
14. Jaber, M.: Centralized and Distributed Implementations of Correct-by-construction Component-based Systems by using Source-to-source Transformations in BIP. Theses, Université Joseph-Fourier - Grenoble I, October 2010
15. Nipkow, T.: Verifying a hotel key card system. In: Barkaoui, K., Cavalcanti, A., Cerone, A. (eds.) ICTAC 2006. LNCS, vol. 4281, pp. 1–14. Springer, Heidelberg (2006)
16. Salehi Fathabadi, A., Butler, M., Rezazadeh, A.: A systematic approach to atomicity decomposition in Event-B. In: Eleftherakis, G., Hinchey, M., Holcombe, M. (eds.) SEFM 2012. LNCS, vol. 7504, pp. 78–93. Springer, Heidelberg (2012)
17. Silva, R., Butler, M.: Supporting reuse of Event-B developments through generic instantiation. In: Breitman, K., Cavalcanti, A. (eds.) ICFEM 2009. LNCS, vol. 5885, pp. 466–484. Springer, Heidelberg (2009)
18. Silva, R., Butler, M.: Shared event composition/decomposition in Event-B. In: Aichernig, B.K., Boer, F.S., Bonsangue, M.M. (eds.) Formal Methods for Components and Objects. LNCS, vol. 6957, pp. 122–141. Springer, Heidelberg (2011)
19. Silva, R., Pascal, C., Hoang, T.S., Butler, M.: Decomposition tool for Event-B. Softw. Pract. Experience **41**(2), 199–208 (2011)
20. Singh, N.K.: EB2ALL: an automatic code generation tool. In: Singh, N.K. (ed.) Using Event-B for Critical Device Software Systems, pp. 105–141. Springer, London (2013)

Partial Order Reduction for State/Event Systems

Shuanglong Kan[1,2]([✉]), Zhiqiu Huang[1,2], and Zhe Chen[1,2]

[1] College of Computer Science and Technology,
Nanjing University of Aeronautics and Astronautics, Nanjing, China
{kanshuanglong,zqhuang,zhechen}@nuaa.edu.cn
[2] Collaborative Innovation Center of Novel Software Technology
and Industrialization, Nanjing, China

Abstract. State/Event Linear Temporal Logic (SE-LTL) provides a concise and intuitive way to express properties incorporating both states and events. However, as SE-LTL is not preserved under classical stutter-equivalence, conventional Partial Order Reduction (POR) cannot be directly used to check them. In this paper, we propose a novel technique to exploit POR for checking SE-LTL. This technique detects a *"state part"* of a Büchi automaton (BA) translated from an SE-LTL formula. POR is integrated into the construction of the synchronous products of BAs and Labeled Kripke Structures (LKS), where *"state parts"* direct the use of POR. The integrated POR modifies conventional POR by introducing an identification of visible actions with respect to events. In addition, we compare our technique with the existing POR for weak SE-LTL and give a method to combine them to obtain more reduction. We have implemented our technique in the SPIN model checker. The experimental results illustrate the potential of the technique for reduction compared with pure state-based POR and SE-LTL model checking without POR.

1 Introduction

In modular and component-based software, communication proceeds via events and is commonly data-dependent. In order to apply existing model checking techniques [3,14] to such software, we need to provide formalisms which incorporate both *events* and *states*. Modeling techniques based on annotated finite state automata might be either *state-based* or *event-based*. Although these two frameworks are interchangeable, converting from one representation to the other often results in a significant enlargement of the state space. In addition, both approaches are not practical when it comes to modular software, in which events

This work was supported by the National High-tech R&D Program of China (863 Program) under Grant No. 2015AA015303, Funding of Jiangsu Innovation Program for Graduate Education KYLX_0315, the Fundamental Research Funds for the Central Universities, Joint Research Funds of National Natural Science Foundation of China and Civil Aviation Administration of China (U1533130).

© Springer International Publishing AG 2016
K. Ogata et al. (Eds.): ICFEM 2016, LNCS 10009, pp. 329–345, 2016.
DOI: 10.1007/978-3-319-47846-3_21

are often data-dependent. In order to address this issue, Chaki et al. [2] provided a framework in which both states and events can be expressed. In the framework, the behavior of a system is modeled by Labeled Kripke Structures (LKS). The property specification logic is *State/Event* Linear Temporal Logic (SE-LTL) which is an extension of standard LTL [9]. SE-LTL distinguishes it from LTL by introducing events as atomic propositions. Moreover, Chaki et al. [2] showed that standard automata-theoretic LTL model checking algorithms can be ported to the framework at no extra cost.

However, conventional Partial Order Reduction (POR) [6,13,16], which is one of the most successful state space reduction techniques, cannot be directly used to verify SE-LTL formulas. The reason is that most SE-LTL formulas are not preserved under stutter-equivalence. Chaki et al. [2] do not introduce POR into their framework, but they suggest it as a future direction. Benes et al. [1] provided a POR for SE-LTL by introducing a notion of state/event stutter-equivalence. However, the drawback of [1] is that most SE-LTL formulas are also, in general, not preserved under state/event stutter-equivalence. So they defined a new logic based on SE-LTL, called *weak state/event LTL* (wSE-LTL), which is invariant under the state/event stutter-equivalence. In fact, wSE-LTL is a subset of SE-LTL. Our previous work introduced a technique to exploit POR for checking LTL with *nexttime* operator [11]. As each SE-LTL formula can be converted into an LTL formula with *nexttime* operators, the SE-LTL formula could be checked with the POR in [11]. This technique is suitable for the full class of SE-LTL, but it is less efficient than the technique presented in this paper. There is work like [15], which transforms state/event systems into purely state-based ones and then uses conventional POR. However, this approach enlarges the state space (the number of both states and transitions can be in the worst case multiplied by the size of the alphabet). Lawford et al. [12] provided a technique for compositional model reduction of real-time systems with respect to real-time state-event temporal logic. This technique is based on state-event equivalent relations for runs in models. Our technique also retains equivalent runs in reduced models, but we also consider SE-LTL formulas to reduce more states.

In this paper, we propose a novel technique to exploit POR for checking SE-LTL. POR is integrated into the construction of the Synchronous Product (SP) of a BA translated from an SE-LTL formula (such a BA is called SE-BA in the sequel) and an LKS. Our technique needs some more insight into the SE-BAs. We aim at detecting a *"state part"* of an SE-BA. State parts indicate that the parts could be checked with POR. In other words, when checked against a *state part* of an SE-BA, an LKS could be reduced by POR. In addition, the conventional POR should also be modified to check SE-LTL. We need to reconsider the identification of visible actions in an LKS with respect to events. The core of our technique is the definition of a synchronous product of an SE-BA and an LKS with the integration of the modified POR. *State parts* direct the use of the modified POR during the construction of the SP. Our POR for SE-LTL is called SE-POR. Moreover, we also compare our work with existing POR for checking wSE-LTL [1] and show that SE-POR is also suitable for wSE-LTL. We give a technique to combine SE-POR with the POR for wSE-LTL [1] to obtain more reduction. We have implemented our technique into SPIN model checker [8] and the experimental results show that SE-POR is much more efficient than SE-LTL model checking without POR and pure state-based POR.

This paper is organized as follows. In Sect. 2, we present some preliminaries. In Sect. 3, some more insight into the translation from SE-LTL formulas into SE-BAs is presented. In Sect. 4, we introduce the POR for checking SE-LTL. In Sect. 5, we compare our technique with the POR for wSE-LTL and combine SE-POR with it to obtain greater state reduction. In Sect. 6, we present the implementation and experimental results. In Sect. 7, we draw some conclusions and discuss future work.

2 Preliminaries

In this section, we recall the basic idea of SE-LTL model checking [2] and give a brief description of conventional POR.

Labeled Kripke Structure. A labeled Kripke structure is defined as a 6-tuple $(S, Init, P, Act, T, \mathcal{L}_s)$, where (1) S is a finite set of states, (2) $Init \subseteq S$ is a set of initial states, (3) P is a finite set of *atomic state propositions*, (4) Act is a finite set of actions, (5) $T \subseteq S \times Act \times S$ is a transition relation over the sets of states and actions, (6) $\mathcal{L}_s : S \to 2^P$ is a state-labeling function, such that for a state s, $\mathcal{L}_s(s)$ denotes the set of atomic state propositions that are satisfied in s. For each transition $(s, a, s') \in T$, it is also written as $s \xrightarrow{a} s'$.

The behavior of an LKS can be described by runs. An infinite run $\sigma = \langle s_0, a_0, s_1, a_1, s_2, \ldots \rangle$ in an LKS is an infinite alternating sequence of states and actions subject to the following: for each $i \geqslant 0$, $(s_i, a_i, s_{i+1}) \in T$. We use the notation $L(s)$ to denote the set of infinite runs that start with s. For example, $\sigma \in L(s_0)$. An infinite run, which starts with a state in $Init$, is called an initial run of the LKS. The set of all initial runs of an LKS $\mathcal{M}$ is denoted as $L(\mathcal{M})$.

An LKS is different from a Kripke Structures (KS), which is for LTL model checking, that actions are also considered in an LKS. We inherit the notion of traces in KS. The trace of the run σ is defined as $\pi(\sigma) = \mathcal{L}_s(s_0), \mathcal{L}_s(s_1), \ldots$, which is obtained by applying the state-labeling function to each state in the sequence of the run and actions are ignored. Two runs are *stutter-equivalent* if and only if there exists a partitioning of the their traces, so that all sets of atomic propositions in both the *kth* block of one trace and the *kth* block of the other trace are same. *Stutter-equivalence* relation is the core of conventional POR.

State/Event Linear Temporal Logic. The syntax of SE-LTL is the following:

$$\psi ::= p \mid e \mid \neg\psi \mid \psi \wedge \psi \mid \mathsf{X}\psi \mid \psi \mathsf{U}\psi,$$

where e ranges over a set EP of events and p ranges over a set SP of atomic state propositions. Events and atomic state propositions are all called *atomic propositions*. The set of atomic propositions is denoted as AP, i.e., $AP = EP \cup SP$. The operators $\neg$ and $\wedge$ are standard Boolean operators. The operators X and U are temporal operators.

Note that, the terms *action* and *event* have distinct semantics in this paper, which is different from [1] and [2], where the two terms can be used interchangely. Actions in LKSs are responsible for the change of states while events in SE-LTL are for verification, and events have a higher abstraction level than actions. There is a partial map $\mathcal{E} : Act \rightharpoonup EP$ from an action to an event, which means that when the action is executed, the event is generated.

The semantics of SE-LTL is explained over runs of an LKS and a partial map $\mathcal{E}$. Let $\sigma = \langle s_0, a_0, s_1, a_1, \ldots \rangle$ be an infinite run. Let $\sigma^i = \langle s_i, a_i, \ldots \rangle$ be the ith suffix of σ starting with the state s_i. The semantics of SE-LTL is defined as follows:

($E1$) $\sigma \vDash p$ iff $p \in \mathcal{L}_s(s_0)$,   ($E2$) $\sigma \vDash e$ iff $\mathcal{E}(a_0) = e$,

($E3$) $\sigma \vDash \neg\psi$ iff $\sigma \nvDash \psi$,   ($E4$) $\sigma \vDash \psi_1 \wedge \psi_2$ iff $\sigma \vDash \psi_1$ and $\sigma \vDash \psi_2$,

($E5$) $\sigma \vDash \mathsf{X}\psi$ iff $\sigma^1 \vDash \psi$,   ($E6$) $\sigma \vDash \psi_1 \mathsf{U}\psi_2$ iff there is some $i \geqslant 0$ such that $\sigma^i \vDash \psi_2$ and, for all $0 \leqslant j \leqslant i - 1$, $\sigma^j \vDash \psi_1$

SE-LTL can be extended with derived operators: (1) $\mathsf{F}\psi \overset{def}{=} \top \mathsf{U}\psi$, (2) $\mathsf{G}\psi \overset{def}{=} \neg\mathsf{F}\neg\psi$, and (3) $\psi_1 \mathsf{R}\psi_2 \overset{def}{=} \neg(\neg\psi_1 \mathsf{U}\neg\psi_2)$, which is the dual of the operator U.

Büchi Automata. A Büchi automaton is a 5-tuple $\mathcal{B} = (Q, \Sigma, \mathcal{T}, I, F)$, where (1) Q is a finite set of states, (2) Σ is a finite alphabet, let $\Sigma' = 2^\Sigma$, (3) $\mathcal{T} \subseteq Q \times \Sigma' \times Q$ is a total transition function, $(q, \alpha, q') \in \mathcal{T}$ is also denoted as $q \xrightarrow{\alpha} q'$, $I \subseteq Q$ is a set of initial states, $F \subseteq Q$ is a set of accepting states. The definition of BAs is transition-based, that is, each transition in a BA is labeled by an element in Σ'. The alphabet Σ in a BA corresponds to the power set of AP of atomic propositions (i.e., $\Sigma = 2^{AP}$). For LTL, AP is equal to the set SP of atomic state propositions. For SE-LTL formulas, $AP = SP \cup EP$ as SE-LTL allows events in AP. BAs translated from SE-LTL formulas are called SE-BAs.

The translation from an SE-LTL formula into an SE-BA can reuse existing translations for LTL without any modification. But the semantics of SE-BAs is explained over runs of LKSs and is defined as follows: an infinite run σ of $\mathcal{B}$ over a run $\langle s_0, a_0, s_1, a_1, s_2, \ldots \rangle$ in an LKS is an alternating sequence $\sigma = \langle q_0, \alpha_0, q_1, \ldots \rangle$ of states and transitions in $\mathcal{B}$ such that $q_0 \in I$, $\forall i \geqslant 0, \widetilde{\mathcal{L}_s(s_i)} \wedge \widetilde{\mathcal{E}(a_i)} \vDash \alpha_i$, where $\widetilde{\mathcal{L}_s(s)} = \bigwedge \mathcal{L}_s(s) \wedge \bigwedge\{\neg p \mid p \in SP\backslash\mathcal{L}_s(s)\}$ and $\widetilde{\mathcal{E}(a_i)} = \mathcal{E}(a_i) \wedge \bigwedge\{\neg e' \mid e' \in EP\backslash\{\mathcal{E}(a_i)\}\}$, and $(q_i, \alpha_i, q_{i+1}) \in \mathcal{T}$. The run σ is accepting if it contains infinitely many states in F. A run in an LKS is accepted by $\mathcal{B}$ if and only if there exists an accepting run of $\mathcal{B}$ over it.

Synchronous Products of SE-BAs and LKSs. Chaki et al. [2] exploited standard automata-theoretic model checking algorithms to verify SE-LTL by proposing a definition of synchronous products of SE-BAs and LKSs.

Let $\mathcal{M} = (S, Init, P, Act, T, \mathcal{L}_s)$ be an LKS and $\mathcal{B} = (Q, \Sigma, \mathcal{T}, I, F)$ be an SE-BA. Let $\mathcal{E}$ be a partial map from actions to events. The synchronous product of $\mathcal{M}$ and $\mathcal{B}$ is defined as $\mathcal{M} \otimes \mathcal{B} = (Q_p, \Sigma, \mathcal{T}_p, I_p, F_p)$, where (1) $Q_p \subseteq S \times Q$, is a set of states. Each state in Q_p is denoted as a pair (s, q) where s is a state in S and q is a state in Q, (2) $T_p \subseteq Q_p \times Q_p$, is a transition function. A transition $((s, q), (s', q'))$ is in T_p iff there exists a transition (s, a, s') in T and a transition (q, α, q') in T such that $\widetilde{\mathcal{L}_s(s)} \wedge \widetilde{\mathcal{E}(a)} \vDash \alpha$, (3) $I_p \subseteq Q_p$ is a set of initial states. A state (s, q) is in I_p iff $s \in Init$ and $q \in I$, (4) $F_p \subseteq Q_p$ is a set of accepting states. A state (s, q) is an accepting state iff $q \in F$.

The product $\mathcal{M} \otimes \mathcal{B}$ is also a BA. Its set of initial accepting runs is denoted as $L(\mathcal{M} \otimes \mathcal{B})$. The following theorem from [2] illustrates that existing LTL model checking algorithms can be used to check SE-LTL formulas on LKSs.

Theorem 1. *Let $\mathcal{M}$ be an LKS and $\mathcal{B}_{\neg \psi}$ be an SE-BA translated from an SE-LTL formula $\neg \psi$. Then $M \vDash \psi$ iff $L(\mathcal{M} \otimes \mathcal{B}_{\neg \psi}) = \varnothing$.*

Partial Order Reduction. We give a rough description of the basic idea of conventional POR. As LKSs can be obtained by labeling actions on transitions in KS, here we use LKSs instead of KSs to describe conventional POR to facilitate the successive presentation. In fact, conventional POR also needs to consider the semantics of transitions in KSs.

For a state s in an LKS $\mathcal{M}$, whose transition relation is T, The notation $enable(s) = \{(s, a, s') \mid (s, a, s') \in T\}$ denotes the set of all transitions that are enabled at s. Conventional POR avoids searching redundant runs in $\mathcal{M}$ by only selecting a subset of $enable(s)$ to expand s and the subset is called the ample set, denoted as $ample(s)$. Since $ample(s)$ is a subset of $enable(s)$, only a subset of runs of $L(\mathcal{M})$ is checked, therefore some states are reduced. The core of conventional POR is the computation of ample sets. There are two important notions in conventional POR. For two transitions t_1 and t_2 in $enable(s)$, if they can execute concurrently then they are *independent*; otherwise they are *dependent*. The formal definition of *dependent* and *independent* can be found in the textbook [4]. An action $a \in Act$ is an *invisible action* if for each transition (s, a, s') in an LKS, $\mathcal{L}(s) - \mathcal{L}(s')$; otherwise a is a *visible action*. Conventional POR computes an ample set of a state s by selecting a subset of $enable(s)$ that satisfies the following 4 conditions:

C0 $ample(s) = \varnothing$ if and only if $enable(s) = \varnothing$,
C1 along every run in the full LKS that starts at s, the following condition holds: a transition that is dependent on a transition in $ample(s)$ cannot be executed without a transition in $ample(s)$ occurring first,
C2 if s is not fully expanded (i.e., $ample(s) \subset enable(s)$), then every transition $t \in ample(s)$ is labeled by an invisible action,
C3 for any cycle in the LKS, there exists at least one state along the cycle that is fully expanded.

3   More Insight into SE-BAs

SE-POR detects a *"state part"* of an SE-LTL formula. In this section, we detect a *"state part"* of an SE-LTL formula by detecting a *"state part"* of the SE-BA translated from the formula.

Our work concentrates on transition-based SE-BAs. There are various works discussing the translation from LTL formulas into transition-based BAs, such as LTL2BA [5] and the translation part of the SPIN model checker [8]. All of them could be exploited to detect *"state parts"*. But for our purpose, we present a new description of the translation. During the translation, we detect a *"state part"* of an SE-BA. This translation does not consider any optimization in order to facilitate the description of SE-POR.

We first introduce two notions derived from [5]. (1) The first one is *Negative Normal Form* (NNF). An LTL formula is in NNF if no operator appears in the scope of a negative operator. Every LTL formula can be transformed into its NNF. But pushing negations into Until (U) subformulas needs to use the operator Release (R), which is the dual of U operator. So the translation from SE-LTL formulas into SE-BAs also needs to consider the operator Release (R). Henceforth, we suppose that every SE-LTL formula is in NNF. (2) The second one is *temporal formulas*, which are the formulas, where the topmost operator is neither a conjunction nor a disjunction operator. Based on the notion of temporal formulas, we introduce an extension of Disjunction Normal Form (DNF) for SE-LTL formulas. It is different from classical DNF for propositional logic that temporal formulas are viewed as atomic propositions. For an SE-LTL formula ψ, it is in DNF if $\psi = \phi_1 \vee \ldots \vee \phi_n$, where ϕ_i with $1 \leqslant i \leqslant n$ is a conjunction of temporal formulas (atomic propositions are also temporal formulas).

The translation from SE-LTL into SE-BA consists of two steps: (1) translate an SE-LTL formula into a Generalized Büchi Automata (GBA) and then translate the GBA into an SE-BA. A GBA is a 5-tuple $\mathcal{G} = (Q_g, \Sigma, \mathcal{T}_g, I_g, F_g)$, where (1) Q_g is a finite set of states, (2) Σ is a finite alphabet, let $\Sigma' = 2^\Sigma$, (3) $\mathcal{T}_g \subseteq Q_g \times \Sigma' \times Q_g$ is a total transition function, $(q, \alpha, q') \in \mathcal{T}_g$ is also denoted as $q \xrightarrow{\alpha} q'$, $I_g \subseteq Q_g$ is a set of initial states, $F_g = \{T_1, \ldots, T_r\}$, where $T_j \subseteq \mathcal{T}_g$ is a set of accepting transitions. An infinite run in a GBA is an alternating sequence $\langle q_0, \alpha_0, q_1, \ldots \rangle$ of states and transitions in the GBA such that $q_0 \in I_g$ and $(q_i, \alpha_i, q_{i+1}) \in \mathcal{T}_g$ for $i \geqslant 0$. A run is an accepting run if for each $1 \leqslant j \leqslant r$, it uses infinitely many transitions from T_j.

3.1   Translation from SE-LTL into GBA

In order to translate an SE-LTL formula ψ into a GBA $(Q_g, \Sigma, \mathcal{T}_g, I_g, F_g)$, it is firstly converted to its NNF and then to its DNF. Assume its DNF is $\psi = \psi_1 \vee \ldots \vee \psi_n$, where ψ_i is a conjunction of temporal formulas. The set I_g of initial states is the n states identified with ψ_1 to ψ_n, respectively. In order to construct Q_g and the transition function $\mathcal{T}_g$, we first set $Q_g = I_g$ and then expand states in Q_g until no new state or transition is added to Q_g or $\mathcal{T}_g$, respectively. More precisely, for a state q in Q_g, we calculate all its outgoing transitions. For each outgoing transition (q, α, q'), it is added to $\mathcal{T}_g$ and q' is added to Q_g. Each state in Q_g is identified with a conjunction of temporal formulas.

We now describe the construction of outgoing transitions of a state. Let q be a state identified with ψ_i, assume $\psi_i = \phi_1 \wedge \ldots \wedge \phi_m$, where ϕ_j is a temporal formula. The conjunction is also denoted as a set $\psi_i = \{\phi_1, \ldots, \phi_m\}$.

The computation of outgoing transitions of q consists of two steps, which is presented as follows.

Step 1. The first step computes a set of pairs (P, N) for each temporal formula in $\{\phi_1, \ldots, \phi_m\}$, where P is a set of literals and N is a set of temporal formulas. A literal is an atomic proposition or its negation. Let ϕ be a temporal formula. The set of pairs for ϕ is denoted as $trans(\phi)$. We introduce an operator $\otimes$ for sets of pairs in order to compute $trans(\phi)$. Let S_1 and S_2 be two sets of pairs, then $S_1 \otimes S_2 = \{(P, N) \mid \exists (P_1, N_1) \in S_1.\exists (P_2, N_2) \in S_2.P = P_1 \cup P_2 \text{ and } N = N_1 \cup N_2\}$. The recursive computation of $trans(\phi)$ is presented as follows:

1. if $\phi = a$ or $\phi = \neg a$, where a is an atomic proposition (a is either an atomic state proposition or an event), then its set of pairs is $\{((\{a\}, \varnothing)\}$ or $\{((\{\neg a\}, \varnothing)\}$, respectively.
2. if $\phi = X\varphi$ and the DNF of φ is $\varphi_1 \vee \ldots \vee \varphi_k$ then the set of pairs is $\{(\varnothing, \varphi_1), \ldots (\varnothing, \varphi_k)\}$.
3. if $\phi = \varphi_1 U \varphi_2$ then its set of pairs is computed as $trans(\varphi_2) \cup (trans(\varphi_1) \otimes \{(\varnothing, \{\phi\})\})$. That is, we must first compute $trans(\varphi_1)$ and $trans(\varphi_2)$ in order to compute $trans(\phi)$.
4. if $\phi = \varphi_1 R \varphi_2$ then its set of pairs is computed as $trans(\varphi_2) \otimes (trans(\varphi_1) \cup \{(\varnothing, \{\phi\})\})$,
5. if $\phi = \varphi_1 \wedge \varphi_2$ then its set of pairs is computed as $trans(\varphi_1) \otimes trans(\varphi_2)$,
6. if $\phi = \varphi_1 \vee \varphi_2$ then its set of pairs is computed as $trans(\varphi_1) \cup trans(\varphi_2)$.

Step 2. This step constructs all outgoing transitions of q. The set of outgoing transitions of q is $trans(\phi_1) \times \ldots \times trans(\phi_m)$. More precisely, let $(P_l, N_l) \in trans(\phi_l)$ for $1 \leqslant l \leqslant m$. One outgoing transition of q is $(q, P_1 \cup \ldots \cup P_m, q')$, where q' is identified with $N' = N_1 \cup \ldots \cup N_m$, which is also a set of temporal formulas and q is identified with $\psi_i = \{\phi_1, \ldots, \phi_m\}$. The transition can be explained as follows: In order to satisfy the formula ψ_i identified with q, the transition selects to satisfy the conjunction of literals in $P_1 \cup \ldots \cup P_m$ at the current state in an LKS and satisfy the conjunction of temporal formulas in N' by a run starting from the next state. We use the notation $\mathcal{S}(q_i)$ to denote the conjunction that the state q_i is identified with. For example, $\mathcal{S}(q) = \psi_i$ and $\mathcal{S}(q') = N'$. For each state q_t in Q_g, we construct all its outgoing transitions. Let (q_t, α, q_t') be an outgoing transition. If q_t' is already in Q_g then we only add the transition to $\mathcal{T}_g$; otherwise we add q_t' and the transition to Q_g and $\mathcal{T}_g$, respectively.

At last, we construct the accepting condition F_g. Let U be the set of until subformulas of ψ, that is, the formula of type $\psi_1 U \psi_2$. The accepting condition is defined as $F_g = \{T_f \mid f \in U\}$, where $T_f = \{(q, \alpha, q') \mid f \notin \mathcal{S}(q) \text{ or } \exists (P, N) \in trans(f).P \subset \alpha \text{ and } f \notin N \subseteq \mathcal{S}(q')\}$. The definition of $\mathcal{T}_f$ is complex and it comes from [5]. But we should not be concerned about it, as it has less relation with our technique. We now define two kinds of transitions in a GBA. A literal is an *event literal* if it is an event or the negation of an event.

Definition 1. *Let (q, α, q') be a transition in a GBA. If there is at least one event literal in α then the transition is called an event-transition; otherwise it is a state-transition.*

3.2   Translation from GBA to SE-BA

Let $\mathcal{G} = (Q_g, \Sigma, \mathcal{T}_g, I_g, F_g)$ be a GBA with $F_g = \{T_1, \ldots, T_r\}$. We define the SE-BA $\mathcal{B} = (Q, \Sigma, \mathcal{T}, I, F)$, where: (1) $Q = Q_g \times \{0, \ldots, r\}$ is a set of states, (2) $I = I_g \times \{0\}$ is a set of initial states, (3) $F = Q_g \times \{r\}$ is a set of accepting states, (4) $\mathcal{T} = \{((q, j), \alpha, (q', j')) \mid (q, \alpha, q') \in \mathcal{T}_g \text{ and } j' = next(j, (q, \alpha, q'))\}$ with

$$next(j, t) = \begin{cases} max\{j \leqslant i \leqslant r \mid \forall j < k \leqslant i, t \in T_k\} & \text{if } j \neq r \\ max\{0 \leqslant i \leqslant r \mid \forall 0 < k \leqslant i, t \in T_k\} & \text{if } j = r \end{cases}$$

This translation comes from [5]. We now define event-transitions and state-transitions for SE-BA.

Definition 2. *Let $t = ((q, i), \alpha, (q', j))$ be a transition in an SE-BA. The transition t is an event-transition iff (q, α, q') is an event-transition. The transition t is a state-transition iff (q, α, q') is a state-transition.*

Figure 1 depicts an SE-BA translated from $p\mathsf{U}e$, where p is an atomic state proposition and e is an event. The set of initial states is $\{q_0\}$ and the set of accepting states is $\{q_1\}$. The transition $(q_0, \{p\}, q_0)$ is a state-transition and $(q_0, \{e\}, q_1)$ is an event-transition.

Let ST be the set of state-transitions. The state part of the SE-BA is the set ST. State-transitions only require that the system is in some states. In the following section, we will explain how to exploit state-transitions for SE-POR.

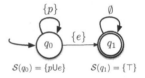

$S(q_0) = \{p\mathsf{U}e\}$ $S(q_1) = \{\top\}$

Fig. 1. An SE-BA translated from $p\mathsf{U}e$

4   Partial Order Reduction for SE-LTL Formulas

In this section, we consider SE-POR for checking SE-LTL without the X operator. The full version of this paper also considers SE-POR for SE-LTL with the X operator. It can be download at https://sourceforge.net/projects/se-spin/files/full_version_se_por.pdf/download. In conventional POR for LTL, we always select the ample set of a state s to expand s. But in SE-POR, the selection of $ample(s)$ or $enable(s)$ to expand s depends on whether s is checked against a *state part* of an SE-BA. In addition, since SE-LTL has atomic propositions of events, the computation of ample sets is different from conventional POR. In Subsect. 4.1, we introduce a synchronous product of an LKS and an SE-BA with the integration of POR. The synchronous product illustrates when ample sets are exploited during the verification. In Subsect. 4.2, we discuss the computation of ample sets for SE-LTL.

4.1   Synchronous Products of SE-BAs and LKSs with POR

The synchronous product of an LKS and an SE-BA with the integration of POR is defined as follows:

Definition 3. *Let* $\mathcal{M} = (S, Init, P, Act, T, \mathcal{L}_s)$ *be an LKS and* $\mathcal{B} = (Q, \Sigma, \mathcal{T}, I, F)$ *be an SE-BA. The synchronous product of* $\mathcal{M}$ *and* $\mathcal{B}$ *with the integration of POR is defined as a BA* $\mathcal{M} \otimes_s \mathcal{B} = (Q_p, \Sigma, \mathcal{T}_p, I_p, F_p)$, *where* (1) $Q_p = S \times Q$ *is a set of states,* (2) $I_p = \{(s, p) \in Q_p \mid s \in Init$ *and* $q \in I\}$ *is a set of initial states,* (3) $F_p = \{(s, q) \in Q_p \mid q \in F\}$ *is a set of accepting states, and* (4) $\mathcal{T}_p \in Q_p \times Q_p$ *is a transition function and a transition* $((s, q), (s', q'))$ *is in* $\mathcal{T}_p$ *iff one of the following two conditions holds:*

(1) *there exists an **event-transition** $q \xrightarrow{\alpha} q'$ in $\mathcal{B}$, and there exists a transition $s \xrightarrow{a} s'$ in enable(s) such that $\widehat{\mathcal{L}_s(s)} \wedge \widehat{\mathcal{E}(a)} \vDash \alpha$,*

(2) *there exists a **state-transition** $q \xrightarrow{\alpha} q'$ in $\mathcal{B}$, and there exists a transition $s \xrightarrow{a} s'$ in ample(s) such that $\widehat{\mathcal{L}_s(s)} \wedge \widehat{\mathcal{E}(a)} \vDash \alpha$.*

From the definition of $\mathcal{T}_p$, it can be observed that when a state s in $\mathcal{M}$ is checked against a state-transition in an SE-BA, it only selects the transitions in $ample(s)$ to construct the synchronous product. As $ample(s) \subseteq enable(s)$, we only select a subset of runs in $\mathcal{M}$ for checking, therefore some states are reduced from the synchronous product.

A infinite run in $\mathcal{M} \otimes_s \mathcal{B}$ is a sequence of states: $\sigma = \langle (s_0, q_0), (s_1, q_1), \ldots \rangle$. The projection of σ on $\mathcal{M}$ is denoted as $Pj_M(\sigma) = \langle s_0, a_0, s_1, \ldots \rangle$ and the projection of σ on $\mathcal{B}$ is denoted $Pj_B(\sigma) = \langle q_0, \alpha_0, q_1, \ldots \rangle$. The run σ is an accepting run if and only if $Pj_B(\sigma)$ is an accepting run of $\mathcal{B}$. The notation $L(\mathcal{M} \otimes_s \mathcal{B})$ denotes exactly the set of initial accepting runs in $\mathcal{M} \otimes_s \mathcal{B}$. We have $L(\mathcal{M} \otimes_s \mathcal{B}) \subseteq L(\mathcal{M} \otimes \mathcal{B})$.

Figure 2 illustrates the construction of $\mathcal{M} \otimes_s \mathcal{B}$. $\mathcal{M} \otimes_s \mathcal{B}$ is to expand (s_0, q_0) and q_0 has two outgoing transitions α and β. Firstly, consider the transition (q_0, α, q_1). Assume it is a state-transition and $\mathcal{L}(s_0) \vDash \alpha$. The state s_0 has three outgoing transitions, i.e., $enable(s_0) = \{(s_0, b, s_1), (s_0, a, s_2), (s_0, a, s_3)\}$. Assume $ample(s_0) = \{(s_0, b, s_1)\}$. According to (2) of Definition 3, we only need to select the transition in $ample(s_0)$ to synchronize with α, which constructs the transition $((s_0, q_0), (s_1, q_1))$ in Fig. 2(c). Secondly, we consider the transition (q_0, β, q_2), and assume it is

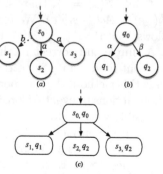

Fig. 2. An illustration of $\mathcal{M} \otimes_s \mathcal{B}$

an event-transition with $\beta = \alpha' \wedge e$, where α' only consists of atomic state propositions and $\mathcal{L}(s_0) \vDash \alpha'$, and e is an event. Since it is an event-transition, we select the three transitions in $enable(s_0)$ to expand (s_0, q_0). Assume that $\mathcal{E}(a) = e$ and $\mathcal{E}(b) \neq e$. So only two transitions can synchronize with (q_0, β, q_2).

The synchronized transitions are $((s_0, q_0), (s_2, q_2))$ and $((s_0, q_0), (s_3, q_2))$ shown in Fig. 2(c). Therefore $\mathcal{M} \otimes_s \mathcal{B}$ only expands (s_0, q_0) with 3 transitions, while $\mathcal{M} \otimes \mathcal{B}$ will expands (s_0, q_0) with 5 transitions.

4.2   Computation of Ample Sets

The computation of the ample set of a state s in conventional POR [16] is to select a subset of $enable(s)$ that satisfies the 4 conditions: C0, C1, C2, and C3, which are described in Sect. 2. The computation of ample sets in SE-POR, however, needs to reconsider the condition C2 in conventional POR. The conditions C0, C1, and C3 keep unchanged. More precisely, the identification of visible actions in SE-POR needs to consider both events and atomic state propositions, while conventional POR only needs to consider atomic state propositions. The identification of visible actions with respect to atomic state propositions in SE-POR is the same as conventional POR. We only focus on the identification of visible actions with respect to events.

For events appearing in an SE-LTL formula, the work introduced in [1] identifies all actions, which are mapped to the events, as visible actions. This method is suitable for the verification of weak SE-LTL [1], which is a subset of SE-LTL. But it cannot preserve the correctness of SE-POR, which is for the full class of SE-LTL. The work of [1] is only concerned with events but our work needs to be concerned with *event literals*.

Consider an LKS $\mathcal{M}$ and an SE-BA $\mathcal{B}$ translated from an SE-LTL formula ϕ. We want to check $\mathcal{M}$ against $\mathcal{B}$. Assume ϕ is in NNF. Some notations are first introduced. The notation $elit(\phi)$ is the set of event literals appearing in ϕ. For example, if $\phi = \mathsf{F}(e_1 \rightarrow \mathsf{G}(p \wedge \neg e_2))$, where e_1 and e_2 are two events and p is an atomic state proposition, then $elit(\phi) = \{e_1, \neg e_2\}$. Let e be an event and Act be the set of actions in $\mathcal{M}$. The notation $vib(e)$ is defined as $vib(e) = \{a \in Act \mid \mathcal{E}(a) = e\}$, that is, the set of all actions mapped to e. The notation $vib(\neg e) = Act - vib(e)$. We extend the use of vib to a set S of event literals as follows: $vib(S) = \bigcup_{l \in S} vib(l)$. For example, $vib(elit(\phi)) = \bigcup_{l \in elit(\phi)} vib(l)$.

A simple and correct method for identifying visible actions with respect to the event literals in ϕ is to detect all actions in $vib(elit(\phi))$ as visible actions. Using this method, the number of visible actions is dependent on the partial map $\mathcal{E}$ from actions to events. Consider the visible actions identified by the literal $\neg e$, i.e., visible actions are $vib(\neg e) = Act - vib(e)$. If there is only one action mapped to e then the only one action in $\mathcal{M}$ is identified as the unique invisible action. But if most actions in $\mathcal{M}$ are mapped to e then most actions are invisible actions with respect to $\neg e$. Even though we cannot say that more invisible actions always yield more reduction, but the number of invisible actions has an effect on the efficiency of the technique. In this paper, we propose a condition, which is a predicate, such that if an event literal l satisfies it then we can select either $vib(l)$ or $vib(\neg l)$ (we have $\neg\neg e \equiv e$) as visible actions. Then the efficiency of SE-POR is dependent on our selection of visible actions with respect to l.

Before introducing the predicate, we first present some notions. A formula ψ is in U-form iff $\psi = \psi_1 \mathsf{U} \psi_2$. A formula ψ is in R-form iff $\psi = \psi_1 \mathsf{R} \psi_2$. The notation

$UR(\phi)$ denotes the set of all subformulas of ϕ, which are either U-form or R-form. An event literal is said to be *uncovered* by U-form and R-form subformulas in an SE-LTL formula if it appears outside U-form and R-form subformulas. More formally, Let ϕ be an SE-LTL formula and l be an event literal appearing in ϕ. The DNF of ϕ is $\phi_1 \vee \ldots \vee \phi_n$, where ϕ_i is a conjunction of temporal formulas for $1 \leqslant i \leqslant n$. If there is a conjunction $\phi_i = \{\varphi_1, \ldots, \varphi_m\}$ such that there exists a temporal formula $\varphi_j \in \phi_i$ with $1 \leqslant j \leqslant m$ and φ_j is the literal l, then we say that l is *uncovered* by U-form and R-form subformulas in ϕ, or l is uncovered in ϕ for short. For example, let e be an event and p be an atomic state proposition. The event e is uncovered in $e \vee Gp$ and $e \wedge (pUe)$, but not uncovered in $p \wedge (eUp)$. We now introduce the predicate, denoted as $inst(\phi, l)$.

Definition 4. *Let ϕ be an SE-LTL formula, which is in NNF, and l be an event literal in ϕ. The predicate $inst(\phi, l)$ is false iff there exists a subformula f in $UR(\phi)$ such that the literal l satisfies (1) if $f = \phi_1 U \phi_2$ then l is uncovered in ϕ_2, and (2) if $f = \phi_1 R \phi_2$ then l is uncovered in ϕ_1; otherwise $inst(\phi, l)$ is true.*

For each event literal $l \in elit(\phi)$, if $inst(\phi, l) = true$, we can select either $vib(l)$ or $vib(\neg l)$ as visible actions. If $inst(\phi, l) = false$, we can only select $vib(l)$ as visible actions. For example, assume $\phi = F(e_1 \rightarrow G(p \wedge \neg e_2))$, where p is an atomic state proposition, and e_1 and e_2 are events. Let $f_1 = F(e_1 \rightarrow G(p \wedge \neg e_2)) \equiv TU(e_1 \rightarrow G(p \wedge \neg e_2))$ and $f_2 = G(p \wedge \neg e_2) \equiv \perp R(p \wedge \neg e_2)$, then $UR(\phi) = \{f_1, f_2\}$. For f_1, $\neg e_2$ is not uncovered in $(e_1 \rightarrow G(p \wedge \neg e_2))$ and for f_2, $\neg e_2$ does not appear in $\perp$, so $inst(\phi, \neg e_2) = true$. The visible actions identified by events in ϕ could be $vib(\{e_1, \neg e_2\})$ or $vib(\{e_1, e_2\})$. In this paper, if $vib(e)$ and $vib(\neg e)$ both could be detected as visible actions, where e is an event, our strategy always selects $vib(e)$. This strategy yields more reduction for the benchmarks of our experiments. The details of our strategy are introduced as follows. We first define the notation $c(l)$ for the literal l.

$$c(l) = \begin{cases} e, \text{ if } l = \neg e, \text{where } e \text{ is an event, and } inst(\phi, l) = true \\ l, \text{ otherwise} \end{cases} \tag{1}$$

The notation $elit'(\phi) = \{c(l) \mid l \in elit(\phi)\}$. For all event literals in ϕ, our strategy identifies all actions in $vib(elit'(\phi))$ as visible actions with respect to these event literals. We illustrate the strategy by an example. Consider the property that for all states in a system, if a process sends a message to other processes then it will eventually receive a response. It can be specified as $\phi = G(send \rightarrow F \ receive)$, where *send* and *receive* are events. We first translate its negation $\neg \phi \equiv F(send \wedge G \neg receive)$ into an SE-BA. As $inst(\neg \phi, \neg receive)$ is true, so all actions in $vib(\{send, receive\})$ are identified as visible actions. Based on $elit'$, we redefine state-transitions and event-transitions in SE-BAs (see Definition 2). The new definition yields more state-transitions, so we might obtain more reduction.

Definition 5. *Let (q, α, q') be a transition in an SE-BA translated from ϕ. If there exists at least one literal in both $elit'(\phi)$ and α then the transition is called an event-transition, otherwise it is a state-transition.*

The product $\otimes_s$ is also correct with respect to state-transitions defined by Definition 2. The new definition of event-transitions requires that there exists an event literal in both $elit'(\phi)$ and α, while the old definition of event-transitions only requires that there exists an event literal in α. So we can obtain more state-transitions and therefore more reduction. We only prove the correctness of $\otimes_s$ with respect to Definition 5 and $vib(elit'(\varphi))$.

Theorem 2. *Let $\mathcal{B}$ be an SE-BA translated from an SE-LTL formula $\neg\phi$ without X operators and $\mathcal{M}$ be an LKS. State-transitions are defined by Definition 5 and visible actions with respect to events are $vib(elit'(\neg\phi))$. Then $\mathcal{M} \vDash \phi$ iff $L(\mathcal{M} \otimes_s \mathcal{B}) = \varnothing$.*

5 Comparison and Combination with POR for wSE-LTL

In this section, we concentrate on the relation between SE-POR and the POR for weak SE-LTL [1], denoted as wSE-POR. Firstly, we recall the syntax and semantics of wSE-LTL. Secondly, we show that SE-POR is also suitable for the properties specified by wSE-LTL formulas. At last, we propose a technique to combine SE-POR and wSE-POR to obtain more reduction.

Weak SE-LTL is introduced to characterize a class of SE-LTL formulas that could be checked with wSE-POR. The syntax of wSE-LTL is defined as follows:

$$\psi :: = \widetilde{\mathcal{P}}(e) \mid p \mid \neg\psi \mid \psi \wedge \psi \mid \psi \mathsf{U}\psi \mid \widetilde{\mathsf{X}}\psi \mid \psi \mathsf{U}_e\psi$$

where e ranges over a set of events EP and p ranges over a set of atomic state propositions SP. Let $\sigma = \langle s_0, a_0, s_1, a_1, \ldots \rangle$ be an infinite run of an LKS. The semantics of wSE-LTL is explained over infinite runs of LKSs.

(1) $\sigma \vDash \widetilde{\mathcal{P}}(e)$ iff $\exists k \geqslant 0.\mathcal{E}(a_k) = e$ and $\forall 0 \leqslant j < k.\mathcal{E}(a_j) \notin EP$,
(2) $\sigma \vDash p$ iff $p \in \mathcal{L}_s(s_0)$,
(3) $\sigma \vDash \neg\psi$ iff $\sigma \nvDash \psi$,
(4) $\sigma \vDash \psi_1 \wedge \psi_2$ iff $\sigma \vDash \psi_1$ and $\sigma \vDash \psi_2$,
(5) $\sigma \vDash \psi_1 \mathsf{U}\psi_2$ iff $\exists k \geqslant 0.\sigma^k \vDash \psi_2$ and $\forall 0 \leqslant j < k.\sigma^j \vDash \psi_1$,
(6) $\sigma \vDash \widetilde{\mathsf{X}}\psi$ iff $\exists k \geqslant 0.\mathcal{E}(a_k) \in EP, \forall 0 \leqslant j < k.\mathcal{E}(a_j) \notin EP$ and $\sigma^{k+1} \vDash \psi$,
(7) $\sigma \vDash \psi_1 \mathsf{U}_e\psi_2$ iff $\exists k \geqslant 0.\mathcal{E}(a_k) = e, \sigma^{k+1} \vDash \psi_2$ and $\forall 0 \leqslant j < k + 1.\sigma^j \vDash \psi_1$.

The work of [1] illustrates that wSE-LTL is a subset of SE-LTL by proposing a translation from wSE-LTL formulas into equivalent SE-LTL formulas. Let $\xi = \bigwedge_{e \in EP} \neg e$. The notation $T(\psi)$ denotes the translation for the wSE-LTL formula ψ. Then $T(\psi)$ is the following:

$$T(p) := p \qquad\qquad T(\widetilde{\mathcal{P}}(e)) := \xi \mathsf{U}e$$
$$T(\widetilde{\mathsf{X}}\psi) := \xi \mathsf{U}(\neg\xi \wedge \mathsf{X}T(\psi)) \qquad\qquad T(\psi \mathsf{U}\phi) := T(\psi)\mathsf{U}T(\phi)$$
$$T(\psi \wedge \phi) := T(\psi) \wedge T(\phi) \qquad\qquad T(\neg\psi) := \neg T(\psi)$$
$$T(\psi \mathsf{U}_a\phi)] := T(\psi)\mathsf{U}(a \wedge T(\psi) \wedge \mathsf{X}T(\phi))$$

More details of wSE-LTL could be found in [1]. The method of wSE-POR computes an ample set for each state and use the ample set to expand the state.

The difference between wSE-POR and SE-POR is that wSE-POR always selects ample sets to expand states in LKSs, while SE-POR only selects ample sets to expand states when encountering state-transitions. The computation of ample sets in wSE-POR also reconsiders the condition C2 of conventional POR.

We now compare the identification of visible actions between SE-POR and wSE-POR. For a wSE-LTL formula ϕ, assume the set of *events* appearing in ϕ is $evt(\phi)$. In Subsect. 4.2, $elit(\phi)$ denotes the set of *event literals* appearing in ϕ. In wSE-POR, it detects the actions in $vib(evt(\phi))$ as visible actions. That is, the visible actions are $vib(evt(\phi)) = \{a \in Act \mid \exists e \in evt(\phi).\mathcal{E}(a) = e\}$. In SE-POR, we detect $vib(elit'(\phi))$ as the set of visible actions. We will show that, in fact, $vib(evt(\phi)) = vib(elit'(\phi))$ for any wSE-LTL formula ϕ (for SE-LTL formulas, which are not wSE-LTL, they may not have the same set of visible actions).

We only need to consider the identification of visible actions with respect to $\widetilde{\mathcal{P}}(e)$ and $\neg\widetilde{\mathcal{P}}(e)$ in a wSE-LTL formula ϕ. As $T(\widetilde{\mathcal{P}}(e)) \equiv \xi U e$, $inst(\xi U e, e) = true$, so SE-POR can select either $vib(e)$ or $vib(\neg e)$ as visible actions. According to $elit'(\phi)$, SE-POR always selects $vib(e)$. For $\neg\widetilde{\mathcal{P}}(e)$, as $T(\neg\widetilde{\mathcal{P}}(e)) \equiv (\bigvee_{e' \in EP} e')R\neg e$, $inst((\bigvee_{e' \in EP} e')R\neg e, \neg e) = true$, so we can select either $vib(e)$ or $vib(\neg e)$ as visible actions. According to $elit'(\phi)$, SE-POR always selects $vib(e)$. Therefore $vib(evt(\phi)) = vib(elit'(\phi))$. As both SE-POR and wSE-POR only modify the condition C2 of conventional POR, so they compute the same ample set for a state s. The following theorem illustrates that SE-POR could also be applied to check wSE-LTL formulas.

Theorem 3. *Let ψ be a wSE-LTL formula, ϕ be its equivalent SE-LTL formula, and $\mathcal{B}$ be the SE-BA translated from $\neg\phi$. Let $\mathcal{M}$ be an LKS. Then $\mathcal{M} \vDash \psi$ iff $L(\mathcal{M} \otimes_s \mathcal{B}) = \varnothing$.*

Theorem 3 illustrates that our technique is suitable for a larger class of SE-LTL formulas compared with the work introduced in [1]. For example, the SE-LTL formula FGe, where e is an event, could not be checked by wSE-POR. Since this formula is not preserved under state/event stutter-equivalence, which is introduced in [1], and wSE-POR requires SE-LTL formulas are preserved under state/event stutter-equivalence. But this formula can be checked by SE-POR.

However, we must admit that SE-POR is less efficient compared with wSE-POR when checking a wSE-LTL formula, since SE-POR checks a larger set of runs in LKSs in order to enable a larger class of SE-LTL. But as Theorem 3 indicates that our technique is also suitable for wSE-LTL, and SE-POR and wSE-POR compute the same ample set for a state s, we provide a technique to combine them to obtain more reduction for the formulas that incorporate both the notions of SE-LTL and wSE-LTL. The combined logic is called Combined State/Event LTL (cSE-LTL). The syntax of cSE-LTL is defined as follows:

$$\phi ::= p \mid e \mid \phi_w \mid \neg\phi \mid \phi \wedge \phi \mid \phi U \phi$$

where ϕ_w is a wSE-LTL formula, p ranges over a set SP of atomic state propositions, e ranges over a set EP of events. The operators $\neg, \wedge, U$ are same as the

definition of SE-LTL. The semantics of cSE-LTL is explained over infinite runs
of LKSs based on the semantics of SE-LTL and wSE-LTL.

In order to check a cSE-LTL formula ϕ, the formula should be translated into
a pure SE-LTL formula. Assume ϕ is translated into an SE-LTL ϕ'. We detect the
temporal subformulas of ϕ', that are translated from wSE-LTL subformulas of ϕ.
The notation $\mathcal{W}(\phi')$ denotes the set of temporal submformulas in ϕ' translated
from wSE-LTL subformulas. We introduce the notion of weak-states. Let $\mathcal{B}$ be
the BA translated from ϕ'. Let q be a state of $\mathcal{B}$ which is identified with $\mathcal{S}(q) =
\{\psi_1, \ldots, \psi_n\}$. If for all $\psi_i \in \mathcal{S}(q)$, $\psi_i \in \mathcal{W}(\phi')$, then q is called a *weak-state*. The
following definition of synchronous products illustrates how to exploit weak-
states to reduce the sizes of the synchronous products.

Definition 6. *Let* $\mathcal{M} = (S, Init, P, Act, T, \mathcal{L}_s)$ *be an LKS and* $\mathcal{B} =
(Q, \Sigma, \mathcal{T}, I, F)$ *be an SE-BA. The synchronous product of* $\mathcal{M}$ *and* $\mathcal{B}$ *with respect
to POR and weak-states is defined as* $\mathcal{M} \otimes_w \mathcal{B} = (Q_p, \Sigma, \mathcal{T}_p, I_p, F_p)$, *where*
Q_p, I_p, F_p *are same as the definition of* $\otimes_s$ *and* $\mathcal{T}_p$ *is defined as follows: a transition* $(s, q) \to (s', q')$ *is in* $\mathcal{T}_p$ *iff*

1. *if q is not a weak-state then either one of the following two conditions should
   hold: (1) there exists an event-transition $q \xrightarrow{\alpha} q'$ and there exists a transition
   $s \xrightarrow{a} s'$ in enable(s) such that $\widetilde{\mathcal{L}_s(s)} \wedge \widetilde{\mathcal{E}(a)} \vDash \alpha$, (2) there exists a state-
   transition $q \xrightarrow{\alpha} q'$ and there exists a transition $s \xrightarrow{a} s'$ in ample(s) such that
   $\widetilde{\mathcal{L}_s(s)} \wedge \widetilde{\mathcal{E}(a)} \vDash \alpha$.*
2. *if q is a weak-state then there exists a transition $q \xrightarrow{\alpha} q'$ and there exists a
   transition $s \xrightarrow{a} s'$ in ample(s) such that $\widetilde{\mathcal{L}_s(s)} \wedge \widetilde{\mathcal{E}(a)} \vDash \alpha$.*

The synchronous product $\mathcal{M} \otimes_w \mathcal{B}$ selects $ample(s)$ to expand s when the
state q is a weak-state or the outgoing transitions of s are synchronized with a
state-transition of q. The following theorem illustrates the correctness of $\otimes_w$ for
the checking of cSE-LTL formulas.

Theorem 4. *Let $\mathcal{M}$ be an LKS and $\mathcal{B}$ be an SE-BA translated from a cSE-LTL
formula. Then $L(\mathcal{M} \otimes_s \mathcal{B}) = \varnothing$ iff $L(\mathcal{M} \otimes_w \mathcal{B}) = \varnothing$.*

6   Implementation and Experimental Results

In order to evaluate the efficiency and effectiveness of our technique, we have
implemented a prototype tool for SE-POR based on the model checker SPIN,
called SE-SPIN. SPIN uses PROMELA [7] to model systems and LTL to specify
properties [8]. SE-SPIN extends SPIN by allowing the user to declare *event variables* in PROMELA models. Its syntax is as follows: [(*statement*)]@*event_name*,
where *statement* is a statement of a PROMELA model and *event_name* is the
name of an event. This event occurs when the statement is executed. An event
name can only be defined in PROMELA models and only be referenced in SE-
LTL formulas. Moreover, we modified the on-the-fly model checking of SPIN to

check SE-LTL formulas and integrated SE-POR into it. We conducted experiments on two benchmarks. All experiments were performed on a computer with Intel core i5, 4GB RAM and a 64-bit version of Mac OS X. The time limitation is one hour. The source code of SE-SPIN and benchmarks can be obtained at https://sourceforge.net/p/se-spin/code/ci/master/tree/.

Table 1. Experimental results for producer-consumer prototype

NC	NP	SQ	States NO-POR	Time (s)	States POR	Time (s)
2	2	5	1022333	2.56	585341	0.55
2	3	5	7984123	74.3	2858123	17.5
3	3	5	–	–	29184813	276

The first benchmark is a toy model of the *producer-consumer* problem. The checked property is that when an item is put into the queue, then the item will be obtained in the future. Here *put an item* into the queue and *get an item* from the queue are events. Experimental results are shown in Table 1, where **NC, NP**, and **SQ** denote the number of consumers, the number of producers, and the size of the queue, respectively. **States NO-POR** and **States POR** denote the number of states stored during SE-LTL model checking without SE-POR and the number of states stored during SE-LTL model checking with SE-POR. The symbol '–' means that SE-POR does not terminate within one hour. The experimental results show that SE-POR is more efficient than SE-LTL model checking without POR, especially increasing the numbers of producers and consumers.

The second benchmark comes from [10], which checks the General Inter-Orb Protocol (GIOP) of Common Object Request Broker Architecture. One of the properties in [10] needs events to express it. The property is that when a user sends a request message, it will finally receive a reply message. The property is called *S-R* and can be expressed in SE-LTL as $G(send \rightarrow (Freceive))$, where *send* and *receive* are the two events. [10] uses labels in PROMELA to indirectly denote events and it is a pure state-based representation. The experimental results are shown in Table 2, where **State-based POR, SE-based**, and **SE-based POR** denote state-based model checking with POR (used in [10]), SE-LTL model checking without POR and SE-LTL model checking with SE-POR, respectively. We select three models: giop1, giop2, and giop3 in [10]. The experimental results are expressed as pairs (*number of states,time*), where the first element is the number of states and the second element is the execution time in seconds. We can see that SE-POR is more efficient than state-based model checking with POR. The reason is that even though adding labels in PROMELA models could represent the meaning of events but it will introduce a lot of redundant search. The performance of SE-LTL model checking without POR is the worst.

Table 2. Experimental results for GIOP

Benchmark	Property	State-based POR (states, time)	SE-based (states, time)	SE-based POR (states, time)
giop1	S-R	(450006, 5.2)	(1195940, 26.4)	(196472, 1.93)
giop2	S-R	(161858, 2.74)	(651231, 26.4)	(62054, 1.09)
giop3	S-R	(261200, 3.76)	(1271334, 46.5)	(49473, 0.82)

7   Conclusion and Future Work

In this paper, we combine SE-LTL model checking with partial order reduction to improve the performance of the verification of systems incorporating both states and events. The core of SE-POR is a synchronous product of an LKS and an SE-BA with the integration of POR and the identification of visible actions with respect to events. In addition, we compare our technique with wSE-POR and combine them to obtain more reduction. The preliminary experimental results illustrate the potential for reduction of SE-POR compared with pure state-based POR and SE-LTL model checking without POR. In the future, we will focus on the selection of visible actions of SE-POR to obtain most reduction as we provide several strategies to identify visible actions. Moreover, we would like to implement our technique using symbolic model checking.

References

1. Beneš, N., Brim, L., Buhnova, B., Černá, I., Sochor, J., Vařeková, P.: Partial order reduction for state/event LTL with application to component-interaction automata. Sci. Comput. Program. **76**(10), 877–890 (2011)
2. Chaki, S., Clarke, E.M., Ouaknine, J., Sharygina, N., Sinha, N.: Concurrent software verification with states, events, and deadlocks. Formal Asp. Comput. **17**(4), 461–483 (2005)
3. Clarke, E.M., Emerson, E.A.: Design and synthesis of synchronization skeletons using branching-time temporal logic. In: Kozen, D. (ed.) Logics of Programs, Workshop, Yorktown Heights, New York. LNCS, vol. 131, pp. 52–71. Springer, Heidelberg (1981)
4. Clarke, E.M., Grumberg, O., Peled, D.A.: Model Checking. MIT Press, Cambridge (1999)
5. Gastin, P., Oddoux, D.: Fast LTL to Büchi automata translation. In: Berry, G., Comon, H., Finkel, A. (eds.) CAV 2001. LNCS, vol. 2102, pp. 53–65. Springer, Heidelberg (2001)
6. Godefroid, P., Wolper, P.: A partial approach to model checking. Inf. Comput. **110**(2), 305–326 (1994)
7. Holzmann, G.J.: Design and Validation of Computer Protocols. Prentice Hall, Upper Saddle River (1990)
8. Holzmann, G.J.: The SPIN Model Checker: Primer and Reference Manual. Addison-Wesley, Boston (2004)

9. Huth, M., Ryan, M.: Logic in Computer Science: Modelling and Reasoning About Systems. Cambridge University Press, Cambridge (2004)
10. Kamel, M., Leue, S.: Formalization and validation of the General Inter-ORB Protocol (GIOP) using PROMELA and SPIN. STTT **2**(4), 394–409 (2000)
11. Kan, S., Huang, Z., Chen, Z., Li, W., Huang, Y.: Partial Order Reduction for Checking LTL Formulae with the Next-time Operator (2016). doi:10.1093/logcom/exw004
12. Lawford, M., Pantelic, V., Zhang, H.: Towards integrated verification of timed transition models. Fundam. Inform. **70**(1–2), 75–110 (2006)
13. Peled, D.: All from one, one for all: on model checking using representatives. In: Courcoubetis, C. (ed.) CAV 1993. LNCS, vol. 697, pp. 409–423. Springer, Heidelberg (1993)
14. Queille, J., Sifakis, J.: Specification and verification of concurrent systems in CESAR. In: Dezani-Ciancaglini, M., Montanari, U. (eds.) International Symposium on Programming. LNCS, vol. 137, pp. 337–351. Springer, Heidelberg (1982)
15. Sun, J., Liu, Y., Dong, J.S., Wang, H.H.: Specifying and verifying event-based fairness enhanced systems. In: Liu, S., Araki, K. (eds.) ICFEM 2008. LNCS, vol. 5256, pp. 5–24. Springer, Heidelberg (2008)
16. Valmari, A.: Stubborn sets for reduced state space generation. In: Rozenberg, G. (ed.) Advances in Petri Nets 1990. LNCS, vol. 483, pp. 491–515. Springer, Heidelberg (1991)

Concolic Unbounded-Thread Reachability
via Loop Summaries

Peizun Liu[⊠] and Thomas Wahl

Northeastern University, Boston, USA
lpzun@ccs.neu.edu

Abstract. We present a method for accelerating explicit-state backward search algorithms for systems of arbitrarily many finite-state threads. Our method statically analyzes the program executed by the threads for the existence of simple loops. We show how such loops can be collapsed *without approximation* into Presburger arithmetic constraints that symbolically summarize the effect of executing the backward search algorithm along the loop in the multi-threaded program. As a result, the subsequent explicit-state search does not need to explore the summarized part of the state space. The combination of concrete and symbolic exploration gives our algorithm a *concolic* flavor. We demonstrate the power of this method for proving and refuting safety properties of unbounded-thread programs.

1 Introduction

Unbounded-thread program verification continues to attract the attention it deserves: it targets programs designed to run on multi-user platforms and web servers, where concurrent software threads respond to service requests of a number of clients that can usually neither be predicted nor meaningfully bounded from above a priori. Such programs are therefore designed for an unspecified and unbounded number of parallel threads as a system parameter.

We target in this paper unbounded-thread shared-memory programs where each thread executes a non-recursive Boolean (finite-data) procedure. This model is popular, as it connects to multi-threaded C programs via predicate abstraction [4,14], a technique that has enjoyed progress for concurrent programs in recent years [7]. The model is also popular since basic program state reachability questions are decidable. They are also, however, of high complexity: the equivalent *coverability problem* for Petri nets was shown to be EXPSPACE hard [6]. The motivation for our work is therefore to improve the efficiency of existing algorithms.

A sound and complete method for *coverability* analysis for *well quasi-ordered systems* (WQOS) is the backward search algorithm by Abdulla [1]. Coverability for WQOS subsumes program state reachability analysis for a wide class of multi-threaded Boolean programs. Starting from the target state whose reachability

---

This work is supported by US National Science Foundation grant no. 1253331.

K. Ogata et al. (Eds.): ICFEM 2016, LNCS 10009, pp. 346–362, 2016.
DOI: 10.1007/978-3-319-47846-3_22

is under investigation, the algorithm proceeds backward by computing *cover preimages*, until either an initial state is reached, or a fixpoint. This search principle is used in several variants, such as the widening-based approach in [16].

In this paper we propose an idea to accelerate backward search algorithms like Abdulla's. The goal is to symbolically *summarize* parts of the finite-state transition system $\mathcal{P}$ (our formal model for Boolean programs) executed by each thread, in a way that reachability in the summarized parts can be reduced to satisfiability of the summary formulas. Prime candidates for such symbolic summaries are *loops* in $\mathcal{P}$. The exploration algorithm may have to traverse them multiple times before a loop fixpoint is reached. We instead wish to summarize the loop statically, obtaining a formula parameterized by the number κ of loop iterations, for the global state reached after κ traversals of the loop.

In order to enable loop summarization, our approach first builds an abstraction $\overline{\mathcal{P}}$ of the transition graph $\mathcal{P}$ (i) that is *acyclic*, and (ii) whose *single-threaded* execution overapproximates the execution of $\mathcal{P}$ by *any* number of threads. Thus, if there is no single-threaded path to the final state in $\overline{\mathcal{P}}$, the algorithm returns "unreachable" immediately. Otherwise, since $\overline{\mathcal{P}}$ is acyclic, there are only finitely many paths that require investigation.

For each such path, we now determine whether it is "summarizable". This is the case if the path either features no loops, or only *simple* loops: single cyclic paths without nesting. We show in this paper how a *precise* summary of the execution of standard backward search across such a path can be obtained as a formula in Presburger arithmetic, the decidable theory over linear integer operations. Conjoined with appropriate constraints encoding the symbolic initial and final states, reachability is then equivalent to the satisfiability of this summary.

Our algorithm can be viewed as separating the branching required in the explicit-state traversal in Abdulla's algorithm [1], and the arithmetic required to keep track (via counting) of the threads in various local states. Structure $\overline{\mathcal{P}}$ is loop-free and can thus be explored path by path. Paths with only simple loops are symbolically summarized into a Presburger formula. The question whether the target state is reachable along this path can then often be answered quickly, in part since the formulas tend to be easy to decide. Other parts are explored using standard explicit-state traversal, restricted to the narrow slice of the state space laid out by this path, which gives our algorithm a *concolic* flavor.

We conclude this paper with experiments that investigate the performance gain of our acceleration method applied to backward search. The results demonstrate that transition systems obtained from Boolean programs, which feature "execution discipline" enforced by the control flow, are better suited to pathwise acceleration than Petri nets, which often encode rule-based (rather than program-based) transition systems and thus feature fewer summarizable paths.

Proofs to claims made in this paper can be found in the Appendix of [21].

2   Thread-Transition Diagrams and Backward Search

We assume multi-threaded programs are given in the form of an abstract state machine called *thread transition diagram* [16]. Such a diagram reflects the

replicated nature of programs we consider: programs consisting of threads executing a given procedure defined over shared ("global") and (procedure-)local
variables. A thread transition diagram (TTD) is a tuple $\mathcal{P} = (S, L, R)$, where

- S is a finite set of *shared* states;
- L is a finite set of *local* states;
- $R \subseteq (S \times L) \times (S \times L)$ is a (finite) set of *edges*.

An element of $V = S \times L$ is called *thread state*. We write $(s_1, l_1) \rightarrow (s_2, l_2)$ for
$((s_1, l_1), (s_2, l_2)) \in R$. We assume the TTD has a *unique* initial thread state,
denoted $t_I = (s_I, l_I)$; the case of multiple initial thread states is discussed in
Appendix A of [21]. An example of a TTD is shown in Fig. 1(a).

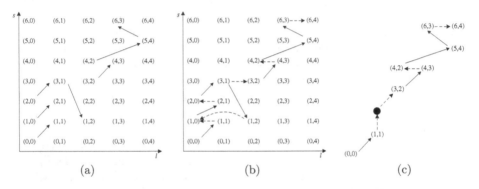

Fig. 1. (a) A thread transition diagram $\mathcal{P}$ (initial state $t_I = (0, 0)$); (b) the Expanded
TTD $\mathcal{P}^+$ with a path σ^+; (c) the SCC quotient graph $\overline{\mathcal{P}}$ of $\mathcal{P}^+$, with quotient path $\overline{\sigma}$.
The black disc represents the loop in σ^+ (the other SCCs are trivial)

A TTD gives rise to a family, parameterized by n, of transition systems
$\mathcal{P}_n = (V_n, R_n)$ over the state space $V_n = S \times L^n$, whose states we write in the
form $(s|l_1, \ldots, l_n)$. This notation represents a global system state with shared
component s, and n threads in local states l_i, for $i \in \{1, \ldots, n\}$. The transitions
of $\mathcal{P}_n$, forming the set R_n, are written in the form $(s|l_1, \ldots, l_n) \rightarrowtail (s'|l'_1, \ldots, l'_n)$.
This transition is defined exactly if there exists $i \in \{1, \ldots, n\}$ such that $(s, l_i) \rightarrow$
(s', l'_i) and for all $j \neq i$, $l_j = l'_j$. That is, our execution model is asynchronous:
each transition affects the local state of at most one thread.[1]

The initial state set of $\mathcal{P}_n$ is $\{s_I\} \times \{l_I\}^n$. A *path* of $\mathcal{P}_n$ is a finite sequence
of states in V_n whose first element is initial, and whose adjacent elements are
related by R_n. A thread state $(s, l) \in S \times L$ is *reachable* in $\mathcal{P}_n$ if there exists a
path in $\mathcal{P}_n$ ending in a state with shared state s and some thread in local state l.

A TTD also gives rise to an infinite-state transition system $\mathcal{P}_\infty = (V_\infty, R_\infty)$,
whose set of states/transitions/initial states/paths is the union of the sets of
states/transitions/initial states/paths of $\mathcal{P}_n$, for all $n \in \mathbb{N}$. We are tackling in this

---

[1] *Dynamic thread creation* is discussed at end of Sect. 6.

paper the *thread state reachability problem*: given a TTD $\mathcal{P}$ and a *final* thread state (s, l_F), is (s, l_F) reachable in $\mathcal{P}_\infty$? It is easy to show that this question is decidable, by reducing $\mathcal{P}_\infty$ to a *well quasi-ordered system* (WQOS) [1]: let the *covers* relation $\succeq$ over V_∞ be defined as follows:

$$(s|l_1, \ldots, l_n) \succeq (s'|l'_1, \ldots, l'_{n'})$$

whenever $s = s'$ and for all $l \in L$, $|\{i : l_i = l\}| \geq |\{i : l'_i = l\}|$. The latter inequality states that the number of threads in local state l "on the left" is at least the number of threads in local state l "on the right". Relation $\succeq$ is a well quasi-order on V_∞, and $(\mathcal{P}_\infty, \succeq)$ satisfies the definition of a WQOS, in particular the *monotonicity* property required of $\succeq$ and $\longmapsto$. The proof of this property exploits the *symmetry* of the multi-threaded system: the threads execute the same program $\mathcal{P}$: a state $(s|l_1, \ldots, l_n)$ can be compressed without loss of information into the counter notation $(s|n_1, \ldots, n_{|L|})$, where $n_l = |\{i : l_i = l\}|$.

The thread state reachability question can now be cast as a *coverability problem*, which is decidable but of high complexity, e.g. EXPSPACE-hard for standard Petri nets [6], which are equivalent in expressiveness to infinite-state transition systems obtained from TTD [16].

A sound and complete algorithm to decide coverability for WQOS is the *backward search* algorithm by Abdulla et al. [1,2], a simple version of which is shown on the right. Input is a WQOS M, a set of initial states I, and a non-initial final state q. The algorithm maintains a work set W of unprocessed states, and a set U of minimal encountered states. It iteratively computes minimal *cover predecessors*

$$\text{CovPre}(w) = \min\{p : \exists w' \succeq w : p \longmapsto w'\} \quad (1)$$

starting from q, and terminates either by backward-reaching an initial state (thus proving coverability of q), or when no unprocessed vertex remains (thus proving uncoverability).

Strongly Connected Components. In this paper we also frequently make use of the following standard notions. Given a directed graph G, a *strongly connected component*

Algorithm 1. $\text{Bws}(M, I, q)$

Input: initial states I,
   final state $q \notin I$
1: $W := \{q\}$; $U := \{q\}$
2: **while** $\exists w \in W$
3:    $W := W \setminus \{w\}$
4:    **for** $p \in \text{CovPre}(w) \setminus \uparrow U$
5:       **if** $p \in I$ **then**
6:          "q coverable"
7:       $W := \min(W \cup \{p\})$
8:       $U := \min(U \cup \{p\})$
9: "q not coverable"

Algorithm 1: Infinite-state backward search. Symbol $\uparrow U$ stands for the *upward closure* of U: $\uparrow U = \{u' : \exists u \in U : u' \succeq u\}$.

(SCC) is a maximal set C of vertices such that for any two vertices c_1 and c_2 in C, there is a path in C from c_1 to c_2. If the subgraph of G induced by C has no edge, C is called *trivial*.

The *SCC quotient graph* $\overline{G}$ of G has exactly one vertex for each SCC of G, and no other vertices; we identify each vertex of $\overline{G}$ with the SCC it represents. An edge (C_1, C_2) exists in $\overline{G}$ whenever $C_1 \neq C_2$ and there is a G-edge from some vertex in C_1 to some vertex in C_2. For a vertex v, we denote by $\overline{v}$ the unique SCC that v belongs to (hence, by identification, $\overline{v}$ is also a vertex in $\overline{G}$). Since each cycle of G is contained entirely in one SCC, and nodes in $\overline{G}$ have no self-loops, $\overline{G}$ is *acyclic*.

3   Pathwise Unbounded-Thread Reachability: Overview

Our approach for accelerating backward reachability analysis is two-phased. The first phase constructs from $\mathcal{P}$ an abstract structure $\overline{\mathcal{P}}$, with the property that any thread state reachable in $\mathcal{P}_\infty$ (i.e., for any number of threads) is also reachable in $\overline{\mathcal{P}}$ **when executed by a single thread**. Structure $\overline{\mathcal{P}}$ thus overapproximates the thread-state reachability problem for $\mathcal{P}$ to a much simpler sequential reachability problem. Technically, the abstraction first adds certain edges to $\mathcal{P}$, and then collapses strongly connected components to obtain $\overline{\mathcal{P}}$, which is hence acyclic. Note that this first phase performs no exploration and is in fact independent of the underlying reachability algorithm being accelerated.

In the second phase, we analyze each path $\overline{\sigma}$ in the acyclic structure $\overline{\mathcal{P}}$ from t_I to t_F separately, if any. We now distinguish: if $\overline{\sigma}$ visits only *simple* SCCs, by which we mean SCCs that represent simple loops, then we call $\overline{\sigma}$ simple, and we precisely summarize the effect of traversing the path using Presburger formulas.[2] Instead of executing Algorithm 1, we solve these Presburger constraints, in effect accelerating the algorithm, losslessly, along loop-free path segments and simple loops. If $\overline{\sigma}$ visits at least one *spaghetti SCC* — an SCC that represents more than a simple loop (e.g. a loop nest) — then we call $\overline{\sigma}$ *spaghetti* as well and explore it using Algorithm 1, restricted to the edges along $\overline{\sigma}$.

At the end of this section we illustrate the overall process in more detail. We first introduce the acyclic quotient structure $\overline{\mathcal{P}}$.

A Single-Threaded Abstraction of $\mathcal{P}_\infty$. A key operation employed during backward search is what we call *expansion* of a global state: the addition of a thread in a suitable local state during the computation of the cover preimage (1). We can simulate the effect of such expansions *without adding threads,* by allowing a thread to change its local state in certain disciplined ways. To this end, we expand the TTD data structure as follows.

Definition 1. *Given a TTD $\mathcal{P} = (S, L, R)$, an **expansion edge** is an edge of the form $((s, l), (s, l'))$ (same shared state) such that $l \neq l'$ and the following holds:*

- *there exists an edge of the form $\ldots \to (s, l)$ in R,* **and**
- *there exists an edge of the form $(s, l') \to \ldots$ in R, or $(s, l') = (s_F, l_F)$.*

*The **Expanded TTD (ETTD)** of $\mathcal{P}$ is the structure $\mathcal{P}^+ = (S, L, R^+)$ with $R^+ = R \cup \{e : e \text{ is an expansion edge}\}$.*

To distinguish the edge types in $\mathcal{P}^+$, we speak of *real edges* (in R) and expansion edges. Intuitively, expansion edges close the gap between two real edges whose target and source, respectively, differ only in the local state. This can be seen in Fig. 1(b), which shows the ETTD generated from the TTD in Fig. 1(a). In

---

[2] Simple SCC nodes (representing a simple loop) are not to be confused with *trivial* SCC nodes (representing a single node). Simple nodes are by definition non-trivial.

the graphical representation, expansion edges run horizontally and are shown as dashed arrows $(s, l) \dashrightarrow (s', l')$.

To facilitate the identification and treatment of loops, we collapse the ETTD $\mathcal{P}^+$ into its (acyclic) SCC quotient graph, denoted $\overline{\mathcal{P}}$. An example is shown in Fig. 1(c). For ease of presentation, we assume that both the initial and final thread states t_I and t_F of $\mathcal{P}$ form single-node SCCs in $\overline{\mathcal{P}}$, i.e. loops occur only in the interior of a path. This can be enforced easily using artificial states.

Being acyclic, the quotient graph $\overline{\mathcal{P}}$ contains only finitely many paths between any two nodes. It also has another key property that makes it attractive for our approach. Let us interpret $\overline{\mathcal{P}}$ as a sequential transition system. That is, when we speak of *reachability of a thread state* and *paths* in $\overline{\mathcal{P}}$, we assume $\overline{\mathcal{P}}$ is executed by a single thread from t_I. (In contrast, the semantics of $\mathcal{P}$ is defined via the unbounded-thread transition system $\mathcal{P}_\infty$.) Given these stipulations, $\overline{\mathcal{P}}$ overapproximates $\mathcal{P}$, in the following sense:

Lemma 2. *If thread state t_F is reachable in $\mathcal{P}_\infty$, then t_F is also reachable in $\overline{\mathcal{P}}$.*

By Lemma 2, if t_F is not reachable from t_I in $\overline{\mathcal{P}}$ (a simple sequential reachability problem), it is not reachable in $\mathcal{P}_\infty$. In that case our algorithm immediately returns "unreachable" and terminates. If t_F is reachable in $\overline{\mathcal{P}}$, we cannot conclude reachability in $\mathcal{P}_\infty$, as can be seen from Fig. 1: thread state $t_F := (6, 4)$ is easily seen to be unreachable in $\mathcal{P}_\infty$, no matter how many threads execute the diagram $\mathcal{P}$ in (a). But t_F is obviously sequentially reachable in $\overline{\mathcal{P}}$ (c). In the rest of this paper we describe how to decide, for each path $\overline{\sigma}$ in $\overline{\mathcal{P}}$ from t_I to t_F, whether it actually witnesses reachability of t_F in $\mathcal{P}_\infty$.

To give an overview of this process, consider a quotient path $\overline{\sigma}$ with one simple SCC node. One such path is schematically depicted in Fig. 2, where we have zoomed in on the SCC node ℓ_i in order to show the simple loop of $\mathcal{P}^+$ collapsed inside it. To analyze reachability of t_F in $\mathcal{P}_\infty$, we first consider the path segment from t_F to the *exit point* of the loop (see Fig. 2). The exit point is the unique node of $\mathcal{P}^+$ abstracted by SCC node ℓ_i that is first encountered when the quotient path $\overline{\sigma}$ is explored *backward*.

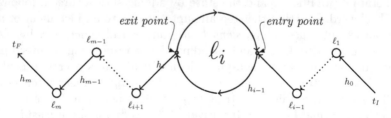

Fig. 2. A path $\overline{\sigma}$ in the acyclic structure $\overline{\mathcal{P}}$ with a non-trivial and magnified SCC node ℓ_i, representing some kind of loop structure in $\mathcal{P}^+$

Our approach builds a symbolic summary for this path segment. We then do the same for the simple loop collapsed inside ℓ_i, and for the path from the *entry point* of the loop back to t_I. These summaries are combined conjunctively into a single Presburger expression φ over a parameter κ that represents the number of iterations through the loop represented by ℓ_i. We now conjoin φ with the constraint that, when backward-reaching t_I along $\overline{\sigma}$, no thread resides in any local state *other than* l_I. This condition ensures that the global state constructed via symbolic backward execution is of the form $\{s_I\} \times \{l_I\}^n$, i.e. it is initial. The claim that t_F is reachable in $\mathcal{P}_\infty$ is then equivalent to the satisfiability of the overall formula; a satisfying assignment to κ specifies how many times the loop in ℓ_i needs to be traversed.

In Sects. 4 and 5 we describe how loop-free path segments and simple loops, respectively, are summarized, to obtain a symbolic characterization.

4   Presburger Summaries for Loop-Free Path Segments

Consider a path segment $\overline{\sigma}$ in $\overline{\mathcal{P}}$ with only trivial (singleton) SCC nodes in its interior; we call such segments *loop-free*. (The start and end state of $\overline{\sigma}$ may still be non-trivial SCC nodes; the loops contracted by these SCC nodes are not considered in this section.) The real and expansion edges along $\overline{\sigma}$ suggest a *firing sequence* of edges during an exploration of $\mathcal{P}_\infty$ using Algorithm 1. Each real edge corresponds to a thread state change for a single thread; each expansion edge corresponds to the expansion of the current global state. More precisely, given a global state of the form $(s'|l'_1, \ldots, l'_n)$, Algorithm 1 computes cover preimages (Eq. (1)), by first firing edges of R backward whose targets equal one of the thread states (s', l'_i). Second, for each edge e whose target (s', l') (with shared state s') does not match any of the thread states (s', l'_i), Algorithm 1 expands the global state, by adding one thread in local state l', followed by firing e backward, using the added thread.[3]

The steps performed by Algorithm 1 can be expressed in terms of updates to local-state counters. Let edge e be of the form $(s, l) \rightarrow (s', l')$. If the current global state $(s'|l'_1, \ldots, l'_n)$ contains a thread in local state l', firing e backward amounts to decrementing the counter $n_{l'}$ for the target l', and incrementing the counter n_l for the source l. If the current global state does not contain a thread in local state l', we first expand the state by adding such a thread, followed by firing e backward. Together the step amounts exactly to an increment of n_l.

We can execute these steps *symbolically*, instead of concretely, by traversing path segment $\overline{\sigma}$ backward and encoding the corresponding counter updates described in the previous paragraph as logical constraints over the local-state counters. The constraints are expressible in *Presburger* (linear integer) arithmetic. To demonstrate this, we introduce some light notation. For $x, y \in \mathbb{Z}$ and $b \in \mathbb{N}$, let $x \oplus_b y = \max\{x+y, b\}$. Intuitively, $x \oplus_b y$ is "$x+y$ but at least b". When $b = 0$, we omit the subscript. We also use $x \ominus_b y$ as a shorthand for $x \oplus_b (-y)$ ($= \max\{x - y, b\}$). For example, $x \ominus 1$ equals $x - 1$ if $x \geq 1$, and 0 otherwise. Neither $\oplus_b$ nor $\ominus_b$ are associative: $(1 \oplus 2) \oplus -3 = 0 \neq 1 = 1 \oplus (2 \oplus -3)$. We therefore stipulate: these operators associate from left to right, and they have the same binding power as $+$ and $-$.

---

[3] We exploit the fact that cover preimages in systems induced by TTDs increase the number of threads in a state by at most 1 (see [20, Lemma 1] for a proof).

Algorithm 2. Summary of a loop-free path segment

Input: path $\overline{\sigma} = t_1, \ldots, t_k$ in $\overline{\mathcal{P}}$, i.e. $(t_i, t_{i+1}) \in R^+$ for $1 \leq i < k$; local state l
1: $e_i := (t_i, t_{i+1})$ **for** $1 \leq i < k$, $(s_i, l_i) := t_i$ **for** $1 \leq i \leq k$
2: summary := "n_l" $\triangleright$ summary is a string
3: **for** $i := k - 1$ **downto** 1
4:     **if** $e_i \in R$ and $l_i = l$ **then**
5:         summary := summary."+1" $\triangleright$. = string concatenation
6:     **if** $e_i \in R$ and $l_{i+1} = l$ **then**
7:         summary := summary."-1"
8:     **if** $e_i \in R^+ \setminus R$ and $l_i = l$ **then**
9:         summary := summary."$\ominus$1+1"
10: **return** summary

Operators $\oplus/\ominus$ in Presburger formulas are syntactic sugar: we can rewrite a formula Γ containing $x \oplus_b y$, using a fresh variable v per occurrence:

$$\Gamma \equiv (\Gamma|_{(x \oplus_b y) \to v}) \wedge ((x + y \geq b \wedge v = x + y) \vee (x + y < b \wedge v = b)) \quad (2)$$

where $\alpha|_{\beta \to \gamma}$ denotes substitution of γ for β in α.

The *summary* of loop-free path segment $\overline{\sigma}$ is computed separately for each local state l: Algorithm 2 symbolically executes $\overline{\sigma}$ backward; for certain edges a "contribution" to counter n_l is recorded, namely for each edge of R^+ that is adjacent to local state l, but only if it is real, or it is an expansion edge that starts in local state l. Note that the three **if** clauses in Algorithm 2 are not disjoint: the first two both apply when edge e_i is "vertical": it both enters and exits local state l. In this case the two contributions cancel out.

The summary of path $\overline{\sigma}$ for local state l defines a function $\Sigma_l : \mathbb{N} \to \mathbb{N}$ that summarizes the effect of path $\overline{\sigma}$ on counter n_l. The summary functions for the short path in Fig. 3 are shown next to the figure. These examples illustrate how we can encode a loop-free quotient path into a quantifier-free Presburger formula. The formula for $\Sigma_0(n_0)$ implies that if we traverse the path backward from a state with $n_0 = 0$ threads in local state 0, at the end there will be $\Sigma_0(0) = 0 \ominus 1 + 1 = 1$ thread in local state 0. If we start with $n_0 = 1$, we also end up with $n_0 = 1$. Note that the path cannot be traversed backward starting with $n_2 = 0$, since its endpoint is thread state $(2, 2)$.

Non-trivial SCC nodes along $\overline{\sigma}$ are contractions of loops in the expanded structure $\mathcal{P}^+$, to the effect that paths in $\mathcal{P}^+$ are no longer finite; their summaries cannot be obtained by symbolic execution. Instead we will determine a precise summary of simple loops that is parameterized by the number κ of times the loop is executed. Spaghetti loops are discussed in Sect. 6.

5   Presburger Summaries for Simple Loops

In this section we generalize path summaries to the case of simple SCCs, formed by a single *simple loop*, i.e., a single cyclic path without repeated inner nodes.

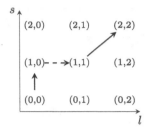

Summary functions for local states $l = 0, 1, 2$:

$$\Sigma_0(n_0) = n_0 \ominus 1 + 1 - 1 + 1 = n_0 \ominus 1 + 1$$
$$\Sigma_1(n_1) = n_1 + 1$$
$$\Sigma_2(n_2) = n_2 - 1$$

Examples:

$$\Sigma_0(0) = 1, \ \Sigma_0(1) = 1, \ \Sigma_1(0) = 1, \ \Sigma_2(1) = 0 .$$

Fig. 3. A loop-free quotient structure $\overline{\mathcal{P}}$ with a vertical real edge

We aim at an exact solution in the form of a closed expression for the value of local state counter n_l after Algorithm 1 traverses the loop some number of times κ.

In this section, since we need to "zoom in" to SCCs collapsed into single nodes in $\overline{\mathcal{P}}$, we instead look at paths in $\mathcal{P}^+$. Recall that for a loop-free path σ^+, the value of counter n_l after Algorithm 1 traverses σ^+ can be computed using σ^+'s path summary function Σ_l, determined via symbolic execution (Algorithm 2). In the case that σ^+ is a loop, we would like to obtain a summary formula parameterized by the number κ of times the loop is executed (we cannot replicate σ^+'s summary function κ times, since κ is a variable).

To this end, let $\sigma^+ = t_1, \ldots, t_k$ with $t_k = t_1$ be a loop in $\mathcal{P}^+$, and define $(s_i, l_i) := t_i$ for $1 \le i \le k$. Let

$$
\delta_l = |\{i : 1 \le i < k : (t_i, t_{i+1}) \in R \wedge l_i \ \ = l\}| - \\
|\{i : 1 \le i < k : (t_i, t_{i+1}) \in R \wedge l_{i+1} = l\}| \tag{3}
$$

be the *real-edge summary* $\delta_l \in \mathbb{Z}$ of σ^+, i.e. the number of *real* edges along σ^+ that start in local state l, minus the number of *real* edges along σ^+ that end in l. Value δ_l summarizes the total contribution by real edges to counter n_l as path σ^+ is traversed backward: real edges starting in l increment the counter, those ending in l decrement it. Let further $b_l = \Sigma_l(1)$ if σ^+ ends in local state l (in this case the backward traversal must start with at least 1 thread in l), and $b_l = \Sigma_l(0)$ otherwise.

Theorem 3. *Let superscript* $^{(\kappa)}$ *denote* κ *function applications. Then, for* $\kappa \ge 1$,

$$\Sigma_l^{(\kappa)}(n_l) = n_l \oplus_{b_l} \delta_l \oplus_{b_l} (\kappa - 1) \cdot \delta_l. \tag{4}$$

Recall that $\oplus$ is not associative (it associates from left to right); the right-hand side of Eq. (4) can generally not be simplified to $n_l \oplus_{b_l} \kappa \cdot \delta_l$. Intuitively, the term $n_l \oplus_{b_l} \delta_l$ marks the contribution to counter n_l of the first loop traversal, while $(\kappa - 1) \cdot \delta_l$ marks the contribution of the remaining $\kappa - 1$ traversals.

Example. We show how the *un*reachability of thread state $(6, 4)$ for the TTD in Fig. 1 is established. For each local state $l \in \{0, \ldots, 4\}$, the following constraints are obtained (after simplifications) from summaries of the loop-free path segment from $(6, 4)$ to $(3, 1)$ ("loop exit point"), the loop inside the SCC node (black disc) using Theorem 3, and the loop-free path segment from $(1, 0)$ ("loop entry point") via $(1, 1)$ to the initial thread state $(0, 0)$. Parameter κ is the number of times the loop is executed:

$$
\begin{array}{llllllll}
n_0 : & 0 \oplus_0 & 0 \oplus_2 & 2 \oplus_2 (\kappa - 1) \cdot & 2 \oplus_3 & 3 & \geq 1 \\
n_1 : & 0 \oplus_1 & 0 \oplus_1 & -1 \oplus_1 (\kappa - 1) \cdot & -1 \oplus_0 & -3 & = 0 \\
n_2 : & 0 \oplus_2 & 2 \oplus_0 & -1 \oplus_0 (\kappa - 1) \cdot & -1 \oplus_0 & 0 & = 0 \\
n_3 : & 0 \oplus_0 & -2 \oplus_0 & 0 \oplus_0 (\kappa - 1) \cdot & 0 \oplus_0 & 0 & = 0 \\
n_4 : & 1 \oplus_1 & 0 \oplus_0 & 0 \oplus_0 (\kappa - 1) \cdot & 0 \oplus_0 & 0 & = 0
\end{array}
$$

The equation for n_4 simplifies to $1 = 0$ and thus immediately yields unsatisfiability. Since there is only one path in $\overline{\mathcal{P}}$, we conclude unreachability of $t_F = (6, 4)$. In contrast, for target thread state $(6, 3)$, the equations for n_3 and n_4 both reduce to *true*. The conjunction of all five equations reduces to $1 \oplus_0 (\kappa - 1) \cdot (-1) = 0$. This formula is satisfied by $\kappa = 2$, witnessing reachability of $(6, 3)$ via a path containing two full iterations of the loop inside the SCC.

6   Pathwise Unbounded-Thread Reachability

Consider an SCC along quotient path $\overline{\sigma}$ that represents several distinct simple loops in $\mathcal{P}^+$. An example is an SCC with two loops A and B that have one point in common and form an "eight" ∞. Such a double loop features paths of the form $(A|B)^*$, where in each iteration there is a choice between A and B. Our loop acceleration technique from Sect. 5 does not apply to such paths.

To solve this problem, we exploit the synergy between the pathwise analysis suggested by the acyclic structure $\overline{\mathcal{P}}$, and the fact that certain — namely, simple — paths can be processed using the technique described in Sects. 4 and 5. Spaghetti paths are explored by Algorithm 1, but restricted to the narrow "slice" of $\mathcal{P}$ marked by the quotient path in $\overline{\mathcal{P}}$.

This algorithm is shown in Algorithm 3. It takes as input the TTD $\mathcal{P}$, as well as the initial and final thread states, t_I and t_F. The algorithm begins by building the quotient structure $\overline{\mathcal{P}}$. This acyclic structure is now analyzed pathwise. For each path $\overline{\sigma}$ from t_I to t_F in $\overline{\mathcal{P}}$, we first decide whether it is spaghetti or simple.

- If $\overline{\sigma}$ is spaghetti (visits some spaghetti SCCs), we explore it using Algorithm 1 (Line 4). More precisely, let $\mathcal{P}|_{\overline{\sigma}}$ be the restriction of the given TTD to the edges along $\overline{\sigma}$, including any edges collapsed inside SCCs. Let further $(\mathcal{P}|_{\overline{\sigma}})_\infty$ be the infinite-state transition system derived from $\mathcal{P}|_{\overline{\sigma}}$ as described in Sect. 2. We pass this transition system to procedure Bws (Algorithm 1), along with the unchanged set of initial states, and the unchanged final state (which is also the end-point of $\overline{\sigma}$). If this invocation results in "coverable", t_F is reachable in $\mathcal{P}_\infty$ from t_I, which is hence returned in Line 5.

Algorithm 3. Pathwise Reachability

Input: TTD $\mathcal{P}$, thread states t_I, t_F
1: $\mathcal{P}^+ :=$ expanded TTD, $\overline{\mathcal{P}} :=$ SCC quotient graph of $\mathcal{P}^+$
2: **for all** path $\overline{\sigma}$ in $\overline{\mathcal{P}}$ from t_I to t_F
3:     **if** $\overline{\sigma}$ is spaghetti **then**
4:         **if** $\text{Bws}((\mathcal{P}|_{\overline{\sigma}})_\infty, \cup_{n \in \mathbb{N}} \{s_I\} \times \{l_I\}^n, t_F) =$ "t_F coverable" **then**
5:             **return** "t_F reachable in $\mathcal{P}_\infty$ from t_I"
6:     **else**
7:         $m :=$ number of non-trivial SCCs visited by $\overline{\sigma}$ $\triangleright$ these SCCs are all simple
8:         $\phi(\kappa_1, \dots, \kappa_m) := $ *Presburger summary for $\overline{\sigma}$* $\triangleright$ Sect. 4, 5
9:         **if** $\phi(\kappa_1, \dots, \kappa_m)$ satisfiable **then**
10:             **return** "t_F reachable in $\mathcal{P}_\infty$ from t_I"
11: **return** "t_F unreachable in $\mathcal{P}_\infty$ from t_I"

- If $\overline{\sigma}$ is simple (does not visit any spaghetti SCCs), we can accelerate exploration along it using the techniques introduced in Sects. 4 and 5. We build a Presburger summary for the path, parameterized by the loop iteration counts κ_i, one for each loop.[4] If this formula is satisfiable, again we have that t_F is reachable in $\mathcal{P}_\infty$ from t_I. The assignment to the κ_i gives the number of times each loop needs to be traversed; from this data a multi-threaded path through $\mathcal{P}$ can easily be constructed.

If none of the paths $\overline{\sigma}$ results in the answer "coverable" by either concrete or symbolic exploration, t_F is unreachable in $\mathcal{P}_\infty$ from t_I, which is hence returned as the answer. Note that this happens in particular if there is no path at all from t_I to t_F in $\overline{\mathcal{P}}$.

Correctness. Algorithm 3 terminates since $\overline{\mathcal{P}}$ is acyclic, so the loop in Line 2 goes through finitely many iterations. Partial correctness follows from the following two claims. Let $\overline{\sigma}$ be a quotient path considered in Line 2.

1. If $\overline{\sigma}$ is spaghetti, then Algorithm 3 outputs "reachable" in Line 5 iff t_F is reachable in $\mathcal{P}_\infty$ along the edges represented by $\overline{\sigma}$.
2. If $\overline{\sigma}$ is simple, then Algorithm 3 outputs "reachable" in Line 10 iff t_F is reachable in $\mathcal{P}_\infty$ along the edges represented by $\overline{\sigma}$.

Claim 1 is proved using soundness and completeness of Algorithm 1. Claim 2 is proved using Theorem 3. Given these claims, we obtain:

Corrolary 4 (Soundness). *If Algorithm 3 returns "reachable" (Line 5 or Line 10) or "unreachable" (Line 11), then t_F is reachable or unreachable, respectively, in $\mathcal{P}_\infty$.*

---

[4] Loop-free paths ($m = 0$) can be processed either using Algorithm 1, or via summaries.

Proof

- If Algorithm 3 returns "reachable", then it does so for some $\bar{\sigma}$, in Lines 5 or 10. The fact that t_F is actually reachable in $\mathcal{P}_\infty$ follows from one of the two claims above, depending on whether $\bar{\sigma}$ is spaghetti or simple.
- If Algorithm 3 returns "unreachable", then it does not reach Lines 5 or 10, for *any* $\bar{\sigma}$. By the above two claims, t_F is not reachable in $\mathcal{P}_\infty$ along the edges represented by any quotient path. The fact that then $\bar{\sigma}$ is not reachable in $\mathcal{P}_\infty$ at all follows from the proof of Lemma 2: the proof shows that, if t_F is reachable, then there exists a quotient path in $\overline{\mathcal{P}}$ from t_I to t_F such that t_F is reachable in $\mathcal{P}_\infty$ along the edges represented by that quotient path.   □

Implementation. Our technique is implemented in a reachability checker named CUTR[5]. We discuss some details on the implementation of Algorithm 3 in CUTR.

Line 2 selects potential paths in $\overline{\mathcal{P}}$. Since we can abort the algorithm once a path is found that witnesses reachability, it makes sense to rank the paths by "promise" of ease of processing: we begin with loop-free paths, i.e. those with only trivial SCCs, followed by paths with simple SCCs whose edges are all real, followed by paths with simple SCCs that feature expansion edges. Finally we select paths with spaghetti loops inside SCCs. The length of a path is secondary.

In order to call BWS in Line 4 on the TTD restricted to the edges represented by $\bar{\sigma}$, there is no need to construct $\mathcal{P}|_{\bar{\sigma}}$ a priori. Instead, when computing cover preimages, we make sure to only fire TTD edges belong $\bar{\sigma}$ and its loops.

To keep our computational model simple, we have excluded from the formalization in Sect. 2 *dynamic thread creation*, where threads are spawned during the execution of the program. This feature does not formally add expressive power, but is often included for its presence in multi-threaded software. Our implementation does support thread creation. Symbolically backward-executing a thread creation edge is straightforward: the counter of the local state of the spawned thread must be decreased, since that thread does not exist in the source state. Our implementation performs some book-keeping to ensure the backward-executability of such an edge: both the local state of the spawned thread, as well as that of the spawning thread must exist in the successor state, since the spawning thread does not change its state (it only side-effects the thread creation).

7 Empirical Evaluation

In this section we provide experimental results obtained using CUTR. The goal of the experiments is to measure the performance impact of the presented approach compared to the backward search Algorithm 1. We expect our approach to improve the latter, as it is short-cutting standard backward exploration across simple loops and linear path segments. The question is whether solving Presburger equations instead of concretely exploring loops actually amounts to speed-up.

---

[5] CUTR "=" **C**oncolic **U**nbounded-**T**hread **R**eachability analysis.

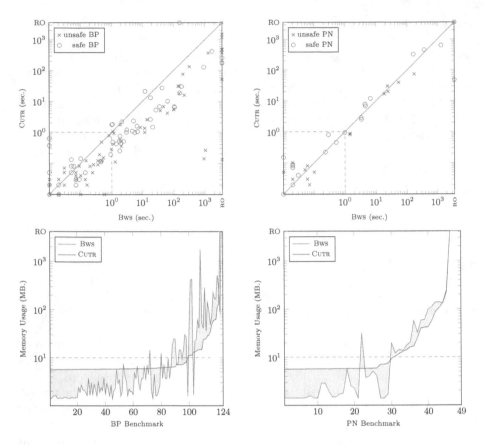

Fig. 4. Performance impact (BP/PN = TTD from BP/PN). RO stands for "out of resources": the run reached the time or the memory limit before producing a result.
• Top row shows the comparisons of execution time. Left: comparison on BPs; Right: comparison on PNs. Each plot represents execution time on one example.
• Bottom row shows the comparison of memory usage. Left: comparison on BPs; Right: comparison on PNs. The curves are sorted by the memory usage of CUTR.

Experimental Setup. We collected an extensive set of benchmarks, 173 in total, which is organized into two suites. The first suite contains 124 TTDs obtained from Boolean programs (BPs), which are in turn obtained from C source programs (taken from [16]) via predicate abstraction. As TTDs are equivalent in expressiveness to certain forms of Petri nets [8,16], we include PN examples in our benchmark collection. The second suite therefore contains 49 TTDs obtained from PNs (taken from [8]). While PNs are not the main focus of this work, we were hoping to get insights into how complex concurrency affects our approach, as the PNs available to us exhibited more challenging concurrent behaviors than the BPs. The table on the right shows size ranges of the benchmarks.

We use Z3 (v4.3.2) [22] as the Presburger solver. For each benchmark, we consider verification of a safety property. In the case of BP examples, the property is specified via an assertion. There are 87 safe instances in total: 56 of the BPs, and 31 of the PNs. All experiments are performed on a 2.3 GHz Intel Xeon machine with 64 GB memory, running 64-bit Linux. Execution time is limited to 30 min, and memory to 4 GB. All benchmarks and our tool are available online[6].

BP	Min.	Max.
$|S|$	5	257
$|L|$	14	4097
$|R|$	18	20608
PN	Min.	Max.
$|S|$	6	18234
$|L|$	6	332
$|R|$	13	27724

Comparison. We first consider TTDs obtained from BPs, the target of this work. The runtime comparison results are given in the top left part of Fig. 4. The results demonstrate that CUTR performs much better than BWS. In some cases, runs that time out in BWS can be successfully solved by CUTR within 30 min; in contrast, there is only one example such that BWS successfully completes while CUTR runs time out. The latter situation can be explained by the path explosion: there are more than 5000 paths for this example.

We now consider TTDs obtained from PNs; see top right of Fig. 4. Here we see little performance difference. Investigating this further, we found that for Petri nets the density of TTD edges is higher (explained by their more complex structure and the relatively less organization and control in the concurrent systems represented by Petri nets, compared to programs). This has two consequences: (i) there are few but large SCCs, and (ii) most of them are spaghetti. As a result, there are few paths through the quotient structure, and almost all of them are explored via calling BWS. This makes the whole process essentially equivalent to a single call to BWS.

The curves at the bottom left of Fig. 4 illustrate that BWS utilizes less memory on small BP benchmarks, an effect can be explained by the overhead of pathwise analysis and Z3. On large examples CUTR tends to need less memory resource than BWS. The memory comparison for PNs shows similar results.

The performance impact of our acceleration approach, on both runtime and memory, can be summarized as follows. Our method analyzes a specific path at a time. If t_F is reachable, there is a good chance CUTR can find a solution early, due to the ranking of paths, some of which permit quick decisions. Although CUTR relies on backward search to cross nested loops, the cost of that is limited as such exploration is confined to a small fragment of the TTD. In the extreme, the entire TTD contains only one path with spaghetti loops. In this case CUTR falls back on backward search.

8   Related Work

Groundbreaking results in infinite-state system analysis include the decidability of coverability in *vector addition systems* (VAS) [17], and the work by German

---

[6] Webpage: http://www.ccs.neu.edu/home/lpzun/cutr.

and Sistla on modeling communicating finite-state threads as VAS [13]. Numerous results have since improved on the original procedure in [17] in practice [11,12,23,24]. Others extend it to more general computational models, including *well-structured* [10] or *well quasi-ordered* transition systems [1,2].

Recent theoretical work by Leroux employs Presburger arithmetic to solve the VAS global configuration reachability (not coverability) problem. In [18], it is shown that a state is *unreachable* in the VAS iff there exists an "inductive" Presburger formula that separates the initial and final states. The theoretical complexity of this technique is mostly left open. Practicality is not discussed and doubted later by the author in [19], where a more direct approach is presented that permits the computation of a Presburger definition of the reachability set of the VAS in some cases, e.g. for *flatable* VAS. Reachability can then be cast as a Presburger decision problem. The question under what exact conditions the VAS reachability set is Presburger-definable appears to be undecided.

The results referenced above are mainly foundational in nature and target generally harder (even undecidable) reachability questions than we do in this paper. We emphasize that our motivation for acceleration is not to ensure convergence of (otherwise possible diverging) fixpoint computations. Instead, our goal here was to show, for the decidable problem of TTS thread state reachability, (i) how to practically compute a Presburger encoding whose satisfiability implies reachability of the thread state, and (ii) that the resulting (quantifier-free) formulas are often easy to decide, thus giving rise to an efficient algorithm. Existing (typically forward) acceleration techniques for infinite-state systems [5,9,15] were inspirational for this paper.

In recent work, Petri net *marking equations* are used to reduce the coverability problem to linear constraint solving [8]. Follow-up work investigates a similar approach for thread-transition systems [3]. Like the present work, these approaches benefit from advances in SMT technology and in fact have proved to be efficient. On the other hand, they are incomplete (the constraints overapproximate coverability). Our goal here was to retain (soundness and) completeness, and to investigate at what cost this can be achieved.

9   Conclusion

In this paper, we have presented an approach for accelerating a widely-applicable infinite-state search algorithm for systems of unbounded numbers of threads. A key ingredient is the construction of an acyclic quotient of the input program, which in turn enables a finite path-by-path analysis. Loop-free paths and paths with only simple loops can be collapsed *without approximation* into Presburger arithmetic constraints that symbolically summarize the effect of executing the backward search algorithm along these paths in the multi-threaded program. Each path passing through loop nests is processed via standard explicit-state backward search but confined to this particular path. We have demonstrated the power of this method for proving and refuting safety properties of an extensive set of TTDs obtained from Boolean program benchmarks. We conclude that partial but exact symbolic acceleration of existing sound and complete infinite-state search algorithms is very much feasible, and in fact very beneficial.

References

1. Abdulla, P.A.: Well (and better) quasi-ordered transition systems. Bull. Symb. Log. **16**(4), 457–515 (2010)
2. Abdulla, P.A., Cerans, K., Jonsson, B., Tsay, Y.K.: General decidability theorems for infinite-state systems. In: LICS, pp. 313–321 (1996)
3. Athanasiou, K., Liu, P., Wahl, T.: Unbounded-thread program verification using thread-state equations. In: Olivetti, N., Tiwari, A. (eds.) IJCAR 2016. LNCS, vol. 9706, pp. 516–531. Springer, Heidelberg (2016)
4. Ball, T., Majumdar, R., Millstein, T., Rajamani, S.K.: Automatic predicate abstraction of C programs. In: PLDI, pp. 203–213 (2001)
5. Bardin, S., Finkel, A., Leroux, J., Schnoebelen, P.: Flat acceleration in symbolic model checking. In: Peled, D.A., Tsay, Y.-K. (eds.) ATVA 2005. LNCS, vol. 3707, pp. 474–488. Springer, Heidelberg (2005)
6. Cardoza, E., Lipton, R.J., Meyer, A.R.: Exponential space complete problems for Petri nets and commutative semigroups: preliminary report. In: STOC, pp. 50–54 (1976)
7. Donaldson, A., Kaiser, A., Kroening, D., Wahl, T.: Symmetry-aware predicate abstraction for shared-variable concurrent programs. In: Gopalakrishnan, G., Qadeer, S. (eds.) CAV 2011. LNCS, vol. 6806, pp. 356–371. Springer, Heidelberg (2011)
8. Esparza, J., Ledesma-Garza, R., Majumdar, R., Meyer, P., Niksic, F.: An SMT-based approach to coverability analysis. In: Biere, A., Bloem, R. (eds.) CAV 2014. LNCS, vol. 8559, pp. 603–619. Springer, Heidelberg (2014)
9. Finkel, A., Leroux, J.: How to compose presburger-accelerations: applications to broadcast protocols. In: Agrawal, M., Seth, A.K. (eds.) FSTTCS 2002. LNCS, vol. 2556, pp. 145–156. Springer, Heidelberg (2002)
10. Finkel, A., Schnoebelen, P.: Well-structured transition systems everywhere!. Theor. Comput. Sci. **256**(1–2), 63–92 (2001)
11. Geeraerts, G., Raskin, J.F., Begin, L.V.: Expand, enlarge and check: new algorithms for the coverability problem of WSTS. J. Comput. Syst. Sci. **72**(1), 180–203 (2006)
12. Geeraerts, G., Raskin, J.-F., Van Begin, L.: On the efficient computation of the minimal coverability set for Petri nets. In: Namjoshi, K.S., Yoneda, T., Higashino, T., Okamura, Y. (eds.) ATVA 2007. LNCS, vol. 4762, pp. 98–113. Springer, Heidelberg (2007)
13. German, S.M., Sistla, A.P.: Reasoning about systems with many processes. J. ACM **39**(3), 675–735 (1992)
14. Graf, S., Saïdi, H.: Construction of abstract state graphs with PVS. In: CAV, pp. 72–83 (1997)
15. Jonsson, B., Saksena, M.: Systematic acceleration in regular model checking. In: Damm, W., Hermanns, H. (eds.) CAV 2007. LNCS, vol. 4590, pp. 131–144. Springer, Heidelberg (2007)
16. Kaiser, A., Kroening, D., Wahl, T.: A widening approach to multithreaded program verification. ACM Trans. Program. Lang. Syst. **36**(4), 14 (2014)

17. Karp, R.M., Miller, R.E.: Parallel program schemata. J. Comput. Syst. Sci. **3**(2), 147–195 (1969)
18. Leroux, J.: The general vector addition system reachability problem by Presburger inductive invariants. In: LICS, pp. 4–13 (2009)
19. Leroux, J.: Presburger vector addition systems. In: LICS, pp. 23–32 (2013)
20. Liu, P., Wahl, T.: Infinite-state backward exploration of Boolean broadcast programs. In: FMCAD, pp. 155–162 (2014)
21. Liu, P., Wahl, T.: Concolic unbounded-thread reachability via loop summaries (extended technical report). CoRR abs/1607.08273 (2016). http://arxiv.org/abs/1505.02637
22. de Moura, L., Bjørner, N.S.: Z3: an efficient SMT solver. In: Ramakrishnan, C.R., Rehof, J. (eds.) TACAS 2008. LNCS, vol. 4963, pp. 337–340. Springer, Heidelberg (2008)
23. Reynier, P.A., Servais, F.: Minimal coverability set for Petri nets: Karp and Miller algorithm with pruning. In: Petri Nets, pp. 69–88 (2011)
24. Valmari, A., Hansen, H.: Old and new algorithms for minimal coverability sets. In: Haddad, S., Pomello, L. (eds.) PETRI NETS 2012. LNCS, vol. 7347, pp. 208–227. Springer, Heidelberg (2012)

Scaling BDD-based Timed Verification with Simulation Reduction

Truong Khanh Nguyen[1], Tian Huat Tan[2], Jun Sun[2], Jiaying Li[2(✉)],
Yang Liu[3], Manman Chen[2], and Jin Song Dong[4]

[1] Autodesk, San Rafael, USA
truong.khanh.nguyen@autodesk.com
[2] Singapore University of Technology and Design, Singapore, Singapore
{tianhuat_tan,sunjun,manman_chen}@sutd.edu.sg,
jiaying_li@mymail.sutd.edu.sg
[3] Nanyang Technological University, Singapore, Singapore
yangliu@ntu.edu.sg
[4] National University of Singapore, Singapore, Singapore
dongjs@comp.nus.edu.sg

Abstract. Digitization is a technique that has been widely used in real-time model checking. With the assumption of digital clocks, symbolic model checking techniques (like those based on BDDs) can be applied for real-time systems. The problem of model checking real-time systems based on digitization is that the number of tick transitions increases rapidly with the increment of clock upper bounds. In this paper, we propose to improve BDD-based verification for real-time systems using simulation reduction. We show that simulation reduction allows us to verify timed automata with large clock upper bounds and to converge faster to the fixpoint. The presented approach is applied to reachability and LTL verification for real-time systems. Finally, we compare our approach with existing tools such as Rabbit, Uppaal, and CTAV and show that our approach outperforms them and achieves a significant speedup.

1   Introduction

Timed automata are an extension of finite automata with clock variables which represent timed constraints [3]. Interesting model checking problems of timed automata, like the verification of the reachability and LTL properties, are shown to be decidable through the construction of region graphs [3]. However, since the size of region graphs grows exponentially with the number of clocks and the maximal clock constants, verification based on region graphs is impractical.

There are two lines of work that are proposed to address this problem. The first line of work is based on *Difference Bound Matrices* (DBMs). DBMs were proposed to represent a set of clock valuations satisfying a set of convex

---

This work is supported by research project T2MOE1303.

K. Ogata et al. (Eds.): ICFEM 2016, LNCS 10009, pp. 363–382, 2016.
DOI: 10.1007/978-3-319-47846-3_23

clock constraints [20] with a zone graph. The resulted zone graph is often much smaller than the region graph, which often results in efficient verification of timed automata models [15]. There are several problems with DBMs. First, it is difficult to verify LTL properties with non-Zeno assumption. A run is called Zeno if there are infinite actions happening in finite time. Zeno runs are unrealistic and therefore should be excluded during the system verification. However, this process has shown to be fairly non-trivial [44]. Second, DBMs cannot represent non-convex zones. Some verification/reduction techniques for timed automata may result in non-convex zones, and novel techniques need to be invented for handling such cases. For instance, with a particular abstraction technique called LU abstraction [7], the resulted zone can be non-convex. In such a case, a convex subset of LU abstraction, called $Extra_{LU}^{+}$ extrapolation [7], needs to be used. Third, since locations and clock valuations are stored separately in zone graphs, state space explosion is often encountered with models having many processes.

The other line of work is based on digitization [30]. It replaces the continuous passage of time with a passage in discrete steps. The advantage of this approach is that it helps transforming the problem to model checking a discrete system and techniques such as BDD-based symbolic model checking [16] can be leveraged. There are several advantages of using BDD-based verification compared to DBMs-based verification. First, checking non-Zenoness with digitization and BDDs is almost trivial. Furthermore, it has been shown to outperform zone-based approach in many existing works (e.g., [5,9,12,15,46]). Second, we can store both locations and clock valuations together symbolically and is not limited to non-convex sets. However, the problem with digitization and the BDD-based approach is that it does not scale for large clock constants. Large clock constants would significantly increase the number of tick transitions which denote the passage of one time unit. As a result, a large number of iterations are often necessary to completely explore the state space.

In this work, we propose the usage of LU simulation to address the aforementioned problem. In particular, we propose two algorithms, based on LU simulation, for model checking reachability and LTL properties respectively. A desired property of LU simulation is that it can be obtained for free in timed automata. Our algorithms depend on two clock bounds: the maximal lower bound and the maximal upper bound (LU bounds) [7]. By leveraging these clock bounds, we could explore the set of all reachable states from initial states in fewer iterations. Intuitively, this is achieved in two ways. First, during the verification, given a set of reachable states S encoded as BDD, we actively enlarge it by adding states which can be simulated by those in S. Thus, we have more states and it is possible to find all the reachable states with fewer iterations. Second, according to LU simulation relation, states with clock value greater than the maximal lower bound can simulate all states with larger clock values. Therefore, our method could perform well even if the maximal upper bound is very large.

In short, we make the following technical contributions in this work:

1. We have applied simulation reduction in a BDD efficient way for both reachability and LTL properties. To the best knowledge of the authors, we are the first to apply LU simulation relation in BDD-based approach model checking of timed automata.
2. We have shown the soundness and completeness of our proposed algorithms. In addition, we further prove that for the algorithm on verifying reachability properties, our approach always requires the same or fewer iterations than classic approaches.
3. We have compared our approaches on verifying reachability and LTL properties with state-of-the-art DBMs-based and BDD-based model checkers, e.g., Uppaal [31] and Rabbit [10] on benchmark systems. The results show that our approach achieves a significant speed up and outperforms other tools.

Related Work. On the effort of improving reachability analysis of timed automata, this work is related to studies on the abstraction techniques [7,13, 27,35] to reduce the number of states in zone graphs. The idea is to enlarge a DBMs without violating the correctness. This work continues the research on using BDDs and BDD-like data structures to improve the verification of real-time systems [5,8,9,12,15,40,46,47].

This work is related to the research on simulation reduction (e.g., [21,22]) as well as research on the emptiness checking of Timed Büchi Automata (TBA). Note that LTL verification on timed automata can be converted to the emptiness checking of TBA. In [44], Tripakis discovered that it is non-trivial to check whether a run in a zone graph can induce a non-Zeno run in the original TBA. In [45], Tripakis questioned whether coarser extrapolation techniques, specifically inclusion abstraction [19] and LU extrapolation [7], can also be used to check TBA emptiness. In [29], Laarman *et al.* showed that inclusion abstraction only preserves the emptiness of TBA in one direction. In [32], Li showed that LU extrapolation indeed preserves the emptiness of TBA. One result of this work is an improved algorithm to solve non-emptiness problem based on BDDs.

This work is closely related to [7,32] and work on using downward closure [22] based on LU simulation relation as an abstraction. While [7,32] both apply LU simulation relation to DBMs ($Extra^+_{LU}$ extrapolation) for reachability analysis and emptiness checking respectively, we apply the LU simulation relation to BDDs for both reachability and emptiness. There are two advantages of our approach. First, given a convex set of clock valuations, $Extra^+_{LU}$ is a subset of LU abstraction. Our approach based on LU abstraction can be more efficient than $Extra^+_{LU}$ [22,27], because a BDD can represent a non-convex set of clock valuations. Second, to handle the non-Zeno condition, [32] relies on the strongly non-Zeno transformation, which requires an additional clock and may result in a zone graph with exponentially more states [25,26]. This work is orthogonal to our previous works of verification [17,43] and synthesis [33] of time requirements for service composition, and can be used to complement our previous works.

Organization. The rest of the paper is organized as follows. Section 2 introduces timed automata and the LU simulation relation in timed automata. Section 3 presents our work on the reachability analysis. Then, Sect. 4 presents our work on the LTL verification. Next, Sect. 5 shows the experimental results. Section 6 discusses our work. Finally, Sect. 7 concludes our paper.

2   Preliminaries

2.1   Timed Automata

In this section we introduce timed automata, arguably one of the most popular modeling languages for real-time systems. We denote the finite alphabet by Σ. Let $\mathbb{R}_{\geq 0}$ be the set of non-negative real numbers. Let X be the set of non-negative real variables called clocks. The set $\Phi(X)$ contains all clock constraints δ defined inductively by the grammar: $\delta := x \sim c \mid x - y \sim c \mid \delta \wedge \delta$ where $x, y \in X$, $\sim \in \{<, \leq, =, \geq, >\}$, and $c \in \mathbb{N}$. Given a set of clocks X, a clock valuation $v : X \to \mathbb{R}_{\geq 0}$ is a function which assigns a non-negative real value to each clock in X. We denote $\mathbb{R}_{\geq 0}^{|X|}$ the set of clock valuations over X. We write $v \models \delta$ if and only if δ evaluates to true using the clock valuation v. We denote as $\mathbf{0}$ the valuation that assigns each clock with the value 0. Given a clock valuation v and $d \in \mathbb{R}_{\geq 0}$, the clock valuation $v' = v + d$ is defined as $v'(x) = v(x) + d$ for all clocks x in X. For $R \subseteq X$, let $[R \mapsto 0]v$ denote the clock valuation v' such that $v'(x) = v(x)$ for all $x \in X \setminus R$ and $v'(x) = 0$ for all $x \in R$.

Definition 1. *A* timed automaton *is a tuple* $A = (\Sigma, X, L, l_0, T, I)$ *where*

- Σ *is the finite alphabet,* X *is the set of clock variables.*
- L *is the set of locations,* $l_0 \in L$ *is the initial location.*
- $T \subseteq L \times \Phi(X) \times \Sigma \times 2^X \times L$ *is the set of transitions* (l, g, e, R, l') *where* l *and* l' *are the source and destination locations of this transition respectively,* $g \in \Phi(X)$ *is a guard,* $e \in \Sigma$ *is an event name, and* $R \subseteq X$ *is a set of resetting clocks.*
- $I : L \to \Phi(X)$ *assigns invariants to locations.*

The (continuous) semantics of a timed automaton $A = (\Sigma, X, L, l_0, T, I)$ is a transition system $CS(A) = (S, s_0, \to)$ where $S = L \times \mathbb{R}_{\geq 0}^{|X|}$ is a set of states, $s_0 = (l_0, \mathbf{0})$ is the initial state, and $\to$ is the smallest labeled transition relation satisfying the following:

- Delay transition: $(l, v) \xrightarrow{d} (l, v + d)$ if $\forall 0 \leq d' \leq d, v + d' \models I(l)$
- Action transition: $(l, v) \xrightarrow{t} (l', v')$ with $t = (g, e, R)$ if there exists $(l, g, e, R, l') \in T$ such that $v \models g$, $v' = [R \mapsto 0]v$, and $v' \models I(l')$

We write $(l, v) \xrightarrow{d} \xrightarrow{t} (l', v')$ if there exists (l_1, v_1) where $(l, v) \xrightarrow{d} (l_1, v_1)$ and $(l_1, v_1) \xrightarrow{t} (l', v')$. A run of A is a sequence $(l_0, v_0) \xrightarrow{d_0} \xrightarrow{t_0} (l_1, v_1) \xrightarrow{d_1} \xrightarrow{t_1} \cdots$. A state (l_n, v_n) is reachable from (l_0, v_0) if there is a run starting from (l_0, v_0)

and ending at (l_n, v_n). The duration of the run is defined as the total delay over this run, $\sum_{i \geq 0} d_i$. A run is called Zeno if there are infinite actions happening in finite time. Given a timed automaton $A = (\Sigma, X, L, l_0, T, I)$ and a location $l \in L$, reachability analysis is to decide whether a given state (l, v) is reachable from the initial state $(l_0, \mathbf{0})$. Next, we define the emptiness checking problem for timed automata. Let $Acc \subseteq L$ be the set of accepting locations. An accepting run of A is a run which visits a state in Acc infinitely often. The language of A over Acc, $\mathcal{L}(A)$, is defined as the set of accepting non-Zeno runs. The emptiness problem is to determine whether $\mathcal{L}(A)$ is empty, i.e., whether there exists an infinite run which is non-Zeno and accepting. We remark that reachability analysis is often used to verify safety problem, whereas algorithms for the emptiness checking problem can often be extended to verify liveness properties like LTL formulae.

In the above semantics, clock values are continuous and events are observed at real time points. Thus, the number of states is infinite and BDDs can not be applied to verify timed automata under this semantics. In the following, we introduce discrete semantics which are based on the assumption that events are observed at integer time points only.

2.2 Discrete Semantics

In discrete semantics, we assume that clock constraints are always closed, i.e., defined by $\delta_c := x \sim_c c \mid x - y \sim_c c \mid \delta_c \wedge \delta_c$ where $x, y \in X$, $\sim_c \in \{\leq, =, \geq\}$, and $c \in \mathbb{N}$. Timed automata with closed constraints are called *closed timed automata* [5,24].

Given any clock $x \in X$, we write $M(x)$ to denote the maximal constant to which x is compared in any clock constraint of A. Given a clock valuation v, $v \oplus d$ denotes the clock valuation where $(v \oplus d)(x) = min(v(x) + d, M(x) + 1)$. Intuitively, for each clock x, once the clock value is greater than its maximal constant $M(x)$, its exact value is no longer important, but the fact $v(x) > M(x)$ matters.

The discrete semantics of a closed timed automaton $A = (\Sigma, X, L, l_0, T, I)$ is a transition system $DS(A) = (S, s_0, \rightarrow)$ where $S = L \times \mathbb{N}^{|X|}$ is a set of states, $s_0 = (l_0, \mathbf{0})$ is the initial state, and $\rightarrow$ is the smallest labeled transition relation satisfying the following condition:

- Tick transition: $(l, v) \xrightarrow{tick} (l, v \oplus 1)$ if $v \models I(l)$ and $v \oplus 1 \models I(l)$
- Action transition: $(l, v) \xrightarrow{t} (l', v')$ with $t = (g, e, R)$ if there exists $(l, g, e, R, l') \in T$ such that $v \models g$, $v' = [R \mapsto 0]v$, and $v' \models I(l')$

It was shown that the discrete semantics preserves untimed properties of closed timed automata [5,24]. Thus, $DS(A)$ can be used in place of $CS(A)$ in the verification of untimed properties like untimed reachability analysis and untimed LTL verification. It follows that BDDs can be used to encode and verify the closed timed automata based on the discrete semantics. In this work, we adopt the approach presented in [9,37] to encode $DS(A)$ in BDD. Given a timed automaton $A = (\Sigma, X, L, l_0, T, I)$, we denote *Init*, *Tick*, and *Trans* the BDD encodings of the initial states, tick transitions, and action transitions of $DS(A)$, respectively. Note that the encoding of the transition relation of $DS(A)$ is the disjunction of $Tick$ and $Trans$. The tick transitions and action transitions are encoded separately for efficiency. The details are discussed in Sect. 3.

2.3   Simulation Relation

Since our model checking algorithms use the simulation relation, we introduce the simulation relation over timed automata in the following.

Definition 2. *Given a timed automaton A, a (location-based) simulation relation over states of $CS(A)$ is a binary relation $\mathcal{R} \subseteq S \times S$ such that for all $((l_1, v_1), (l_2, v_2)) \in \mathcal{R}$,*

- $l_1 = l_2$.
- *if $(l_1, v_1) \xrightarrow{d} (l_1, v_1 + d)$ then there exists d' such that $(l_2, v_2) \xrightarrow{d'} (l_2, v_2 + d')$ and $((l_1, v_1 + d), (l_2, v_2 + d')) \in \mathcal{R}$.*
- *if $(l_1, v_1) \xrightarrow{t} (l'_1, v'_1)$ then there exists (l'_2, v'_2) such that $(l_2, v_2) \xrightarrow{t} (l'_2, v'_2)$ and $((l'_1, v'_1), (l'_2, v'_2)) \in \mathcal{R}$.*

hold. A state (l_1, v_1) is simulated by state (l_2, v_2) denoted as $(l_1, v_1) \preccurlyeq (l_2, v_2)$, if there exists a simulation relation $\mathcal{R}$ such that $((l_1, v_1), (l_2, v_2)) \in \mathcal{R}$. By definition, any state simulates itself. Given a set of states $Q \subseteq S$, we define the downward closure [22] as $Down(Q) = \{s_1 \in S \mid \exists s_2 \in Q.s_1 \preccurlyeq s_2\}$. Intuitively, the downward closure of Q is the set of states which can be simulated by any state in Q. Since the simulation relation is reflexive, it follows that $Q \subseteq Down(Q)$.

For timed automata, there exists a simulation relation called the LU simulation relation [7]. Given a clock x, the maximal lower bound $L(x)$ (respectively maximal upper bound $U(x)$) is the maximal constant k that there exists a constraint $x > k$ or $x \geq k$ in the timed automaton. If such constant k does not exist, we set $L(x)$ to $-\infty$. Then, given two clock valuations v and v', we denote $v \preccurlyeq v'$ if for all clocks $x \in X$, either $v'(x) = v(x)$ or $L(x) < v'(x) < v(x)$ or $U(x) < v(x) < v'(x)$. It shows the relation $\mathcal{R}_{CS} = \{((l, v), (l, v')) \mid v \preccurlyeq v'\}$ is a simulation relation based on $CS(A)$ [7]. The following proposition shows that it is also a simulation relation based on $DS(A)$.

Proposition 1. *The relation $\mathcal{R} = \{((l, v), (l, v')) \mid v, v' \in \mathbb{N}^{|X|} \wedge v \preccurlyeq v'\}$ is a simulation relation of $DS(A)$.*

The proof is the same as Lemma 3 in [7]. For simplicity, we denote $\preccurlyeq$ the BDD encoding of the simulation relation $\mathcal{R}$ defined in Proposition 1.

Algoritm 1: Reachability Analysis

1: **function**
 $IsReach(Init, Tick, Trans, goal)$
2: $Q_p = \emptyset$
3: $Q = Init$
4: $Q = Reach(Q, Trans)$
5: **while** $(Q_p \neq Q)$ **do**
6: $Q_p = Q$
7: $Q = Q \cup Reach($
 $succ(Q, Tick), Trans)$
8: **if** $Q \cap goal \neq \emptyset$ **then**
9:   **return** true
10: **end if**
11: **end while**
12: **return** false
13: **end function**
14:
15: **function** $Reach(Q, R)$
16: $Q_p = \emptyset$
17: **while** $(Q_p \neq Q)$ **do**
18: $Q_p = Q$
19: $Q = Q \cup succ(Q, R)$
20: **end while**
21: **return** Q
22: **end function**

Algoritm 2: Reachability Analysis with Simulation

1: **function**
 $IsReach_{sim}(Init, Tick, Trans, goal)$
2: $Q_p = \emptyset$
3: $Q = Down(Init)$
4: $Q = Reach_{sim}(Q, Trans)$
5: **while** $(Q_p \neq Q)$ **do**
6: $Q_p = Q$
7: $Q = Q \cup Reach_{sim}$
 $(Down(succ(Q, Tick)), Trans)$
8: **if** $Q \cap goal \neq \emptyset$ **then**
9:   **return** true
10: **end if**
11: **end while**
12: **return** false
13: **end function**
14:
15: **function** $Reach_{sim}(Q, R)$
16: $Q_p = \emptyset$
17: **while** $(Q_p \neq Q)$ **do**
18: $Q_p = Q$
19: $Q = Q \cup Down(succ(Q, R))$
20: **end while**
21: **return** Q
22: **end function**

3 Reachability Analysis Algorithm

In this section, we present the reachability analysis algorithm without the simulation reduction and the one with the reduction.

3.1 Algorithm Without Simulation Reduction

Given a set of states *goal*, the reachability analysis is performed by computing the set of reachable states and checking whether it contains any state in *goal*. The problem of efficiently computing the set of reachable states in BDDs for timed systems has been investigated by Beyer in [9,11]. There are two important observations to avoid exploding BDDs. First, separating action and tick transitions is more efficient than unifying them as monolithic transitions. Second, for fix-point computation, applying action transitions before tick transitions can achieve smaller encodings of intermediate reachable states.

Algorithm 1 shows the reachability analysis algorithm based on Beyer's observations, without simulation reduction. The function $IsReach$ takes $Init$, $Tick$, $Trans$, and $goal$ as input. It checks whether a state in $goal$ is reachable from an initial state in $Init$ by transitions in $Tick$ or $Trans$. Moreover, given a set of states Q and a transition relation R, the function $Reach(Q, R)$ computes the set of states reachable from Q by transitions in R. We denote the set of successor

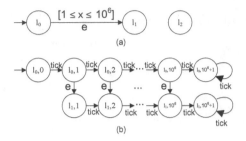

Fig. 1. Timed automaton with large clock constant and the transition system based on discrete semantics

states of Q as $succ(Q, R)$. Intuitively, Q stores the set of states reachable within i time units after i^{th} iteration (lines 5–11). The algorithm reaches the fixpoint if no new state is found in the next time unit.

While Algorithm 1 is relatively efficient in computing the reachable states, it still suffers from large maximal clock constants. Models with large maximal clock constants require a large number of iterations to obtain the fixpoint. Figure 1a presents a timed automaton with a large clock constant, i.e., with a maximal clock constant of 10^6. We remark that in practice, large clock constants are not uncommon because different time units are often used in the same time. Figure 1b is the transition system generated by the discrete semantics. States at location l_2 are ignored in Fig. 1b for simplicity. We denote (l_i, j) the state where the location is l_i and the clock valuation v such that $v(x) = j$. Assume the property is whether location l_2 is reachable. Then, Algorithm 1 requires $10^6 + 2$ iterations to reach the fixpoint to conclude that l_2 is unreachable. Specifically, $10^6 + 1$ iterations to find all the reachable states and the last iteration does not find any new state and concludes that the fixpoint is reached. However, with simulation reduction, our approach can verify whether l_2 is reachable within 3 iterations.

In the next section, we present our improved algorithm by using the simulation relation. We prove that the number of iterations can be reduced, and experimental results given in Sect. 5 confirm that our improved algorithm is much more efficient.

3.2   Algorithm with Simulation Reduction

In this section, we present our improved reachability analysis algorithm. Given a transition system $\mathcal{L}$, a simulation relation $\preceq$ over states of $\mathcal{L}$ and a set of states *goal*, our algorithm determines whether any state in *goal* is reachable. The reachability analysis is performed similarly as Algorithm 1 by computing the reachable states set and checking whether it contains any state in *goal*.

We assume that the simulation on $\mathcal{L}$ is compatible with the set *goal*, i.e., for any $(s_1, s_2) \in \preceq$, $s_1 \in goal \implies s_2 \in goal$. In our reachability verification for timed automata, the LU simulation relation satisfies this condition because the reachability verification is over locations. Effectively, with simulation reduction, we would explore a reduced transition system defined as Definition 3.

Definition 3. *Given the transition system $\mathcal{L} = (C, init_c, \rightarrow)$ and the simulation relation $\preccurlyeq$, we define the transition system $\mathcal{L}' = (C', init'_c, \Longrightarrow)$ such that:*

- *$C' = C$, $init'_c = Down(init_c)$.*
- *Given any state $s'_1, s'_2 \in \mathcal{L}'$, there is a transition $s'_1 \Longrightarrow s'_2$ in $\mathcal{L}'$ if there exists a transition $s'_1 \rightarrow s_2$ in $\mathcal{L}$ and $s'_2 \preccurlyeq s_2$.*

Note that the state space is unchanged. The initial states and transition functions are changed accordingly the simulation relation over the set of states C. Intuitively, for any transition $s'_1 \rightarrow s_2$ in $\mathcal{L}$, we allow other states simulated by s_2 to be successor states of s'_1 in $\mathcal{L}'$. Thus, given a set of states $Q \subseteq C$, $succ(Q, \Longrightarrow) = Down(succ(Q, \rightarrow))$. In the following, we establish that $\mathcal{L}'$ preserves the reachability.

Lemma 1. *Given $q'_1 \preccurlyeq q_1$, if there exists a path with length n, $q'_1 \Longrightarrow q'_2 \Longrightarrow \cdots \Longrightarrow q'_n$ in $\mathcal{L}'$, there exists a path with the same length, $q_1 \rightarrow q_2 \rightarrow \cdots \rightarrow q_n$ in $\mathcal{L}$ such that $q'_i \preccurlyeq q_i$ for all $1 \leq i \leq n$.* □

Theorem 1. *Given the transition systems $\mathcal{L}$, $\mathcal{L}'$, and a set of states goal, goal is reachable in $\mathcal{L}$ if and only if goal is reachable in $\mathcal{L}'$.* □

Based on the relationship between transition systems $\mathcal{L}$ and $\mathcal{L}'$ stated by Theorem 1, we can use $\mathcal{L}'$ as the input for Algorithm 1. However, explicitly computing the transition relation of $\mathcal{L}'$ is computationally expensive. Instead, we apply $Down$ to the result of any call $succ(Q)$ on the fly in Algorithm 1 because $succ(Q, \Longrightarrow) = Down(succ(Q, \rightarrow))$. Algorithm 2 presents our improved reachability analysis algorithm with simulation reduction. We rename the two functions as $IsReach_{sim}$ and $Reach_{sim}$ respectively. The difference between Algorithms 2 and 1 is that in the function $IsReach_{sim}$, we first update $Q = Down(Init)$ at line 3, and subsequently, we call $Reach_{sim}(Q, R)$ and $Down(succ(Q, R))$ instead of $Reach(Q, R)$ and $succ(Q, R)$ respectively. It can be observed that we always apply $Down$ to the results of the $succ$ function.

Theorem 2. *Algorithm 2 is sound and complete.* □

Proof: As we discussed the difference between Algorithms 2 and 1, given a transition system $\mathcal{L}$, while the function $IsReach(Init, Tick, Trans, g)$ checks the reachability of g on $\mathcal{L}$, the function $IsReach_{sim}(Init, Tick, Trans, g)$ actually checks the reachability of g on $\mathcal{L}'$. Thus, the correctness of Algorithm 2 is obtained based on Theorem 1 and the correctness of Algorithm 1.

Our algorithm is similar to the algorithm of antichain of promising states [22]. Note that in [22], the algorithm uses the Min operator while our approach uses the $Down$ operator. We uses $Down$ operator because it is efficient to compute in BDD. This algorithm is also similar to the one in [7], where LU simulation is used to improve zone-based verification of timed automata. However, the $Down$ operator here is coarser than extrapolation used in [7] (any extrapolation must result in convex zones).

Lemma 2. *Assume* $Q' = Down(Q)$, $Q' \cup Reach_{sim}(Down(succ(Q', Tick))$, $Trans) = Down(Q \cup Reach(succ(Q, Tick), Trans))$.

Lemma 3. *Assume* $Q' = Down(Q)$, *after* n *iterations, if* $Reach(Q, R)$ *reaches the fixpoint,* $Reach_{sim}(Q', R)$ *also reaches the fixpoint. Moreover the results of those functions satisfy* $Reach_{sim}(Q', R) = Down(Reach(Q, R))$.

Since the reachability analysis requires many fixpoint computations, the rationale of Algorithm 2 is to converge faster to the fixpoint. In the following, we prove that $Reach_{sim}$ $(Down(Q))$ requires the same or smaller number of iterations to reach the fixpoint than $Reach(Q)$. In our proof, to distinguish with Algorithm 1, given any variable Q appearing in Algorithm 2, we use the prime version Q' to denote that variable in Algorithm 2.

Theorem 3. *Algorithm 2 requires fewer or the same number of iterations than Algorithm 1.*

Proof: By Lemmas 3 and 2, in Algorithms 1 and 2, $Q' = Down(Q)$. So if Algorithm 1 terminates when $Q \cap goal \neq \varnothing$, Algorithm 2 also terminates because $Q' \cap goal \neq \varnothing$. Otherwise if $Q = Q_p$ holds in Algorithm 1, $Q' = Q'_p$ also holds in Algorithm 2.

Example. In the following, we demonstrate how Algorithm 2 works using the example in Fig. 1. The reachability problem is to check whether l_2 is reachable from the initial state l_0. According to timed automaton, we have $L(x) = 1$ and $U(x) = 10^6$. Algorithm 2 only takes 3 iterations to verify l_2 is unreachable, specifically:

- $Q'_0 = \{(l_0, 0)\}$, $Q'_1 = \{(l_0, 0), (l_0, 1), (l_1, 1)\}$
- $Q'_2 = \{(l_0, i) \mid 0 \leq i \leq 10^6 + 1\} \cup \{(l_1, i) \mid 1 \leq i \leq 10^6 + 1\}$, $Q'_3 = Q'_2$

In the 2nd iteration, we have $(l_0, 2), (l_1, 2) \in Q'_2$ at first. Since $(l_0, i) \preccurlyeq (l_0, 2)$ and $(l_1, i) \preccurlyeq (l_1, 2)$ for all $i > 2$, we add all states (l_0, i), (l_1, i) where $i > 2$ to Q'_2 by *Down* function. Thus, finally $Q'_2 = \{(l_0, i) \mid 0 \leq i \leq 10^6 + 1\} \cup \{(l_1, i) \mid 1 \leq i \leq 10^6 + 1\}$.

In this section, we have presented our improved algorithm for reachability verification by using the LU simulation relation. We prove that our approach in Algorithm 2 always uses fewer or the same number of iterations compared with the classic algorithm as in Algorithm 1. In the next section, we continue with presenting our improved emptiness checking algorithm with the simulation relation.

Algorithm 3: Algorithm $IsEmpty$

1: **function** $IsEmpty(Init, Tr, J)$
2:     $old = \varnothing$
3:
4:     $new = Reach(Init, Tr)$
5:     **while** $(new \neq old)$ **do**
6:         $old = new$
7:         **for all** $J_i \in J$ **do**
8:             $new = Reach(new \cap J_i, Tr)$
9:         **end for**
10:        **while** $(new \neq (new \cap$
11: $succ(new)))$ **do**
12:            $new = (new \cap succ(new))$
13:        **end while**
14:    **end while**
15:    **return** $(new = \varnothing)$
16: **end function**

Algorithm 4: Algorithm $IsEmpty_{sim}$

1: **function** $IsEmpty_{sim}(Init, Tr, J)$
2:     $old = \varnothing$
3:     $Init = Down(Init)$
4:     $new = Reach_{sim}(Init, Tr)$
5:     **while** $(new \neq old)$ **do**
6:         $old = new$
7:         **for all** $J_i \in J$ **do**
8:             $new = Reach_{sim}(new \cap J_i, Tr)$
9:         **end for**
10:        **while** $(new \neq (new$
11: $\cap Down(succ(new))))$ **do**
12:            $new = (new \cap Down(succ(new)))$
13:        **end while**
14:    **end while**
15:    **return** $(new = \varnothing)$
16: **end function**

4   Emptiness Checking Algorithm

Under digitization and automata theory, LTL verification can be done by emptiness checking. Thus, the emptiness checking algorithm of Kesten *et al.* [28] can be used. In this section, we first present the algorithm of Kesten. Then, we introduce our improved algorithm by using the simulation relation.

4.1   Algorithm Without Simulation Reduction

Given a transition system and a set of Büchi conditions J where $J_i \in J$ is a set of states, an accepting run is an infinite run which visits a J_i-state (a state in J_i) infinitely often for all $J_i \in J$. The emptiness problem is to check whether this run exists.

For simplicity, in this section, we merge $Trans$ and $Tick$ and assume that Tr is the encoding of the whole transition system. Algorithm 3 [28] presents the symbolic emptiness checking algorithm. Specifically, function $IsEmpty$ takes the set of the initial states $Init$, the transition relation Tr, and a set of Büchi conditions J as input.

In Algorithm 3, function $IsEmpty$ searches for an accepting strongly connected component (SCC) which contains a J_i-state for every Büchi condition $J_i \in J$. The algorithm computes the set of all reachable accepting SCCs. If this set is empty, there is no accepting run in the given transition system. At line 4, new is assigned as the set of all reachable states from the initial states. Then, the while-loop (from line 5 to line 14) continuously refines the set of states new until a fixpoint is reached (i.e., $new = old$ at line 5). Inside this while-loop, first, we backup the current value of new in old (line 6). Then, from line 7 to line 9, we continue to refine new as the set of states reachable by a J_i-state for all $J_i \in J$. Next, in the inner while-loop from line 11 to line 13, we again refine new by successively removing from new states which do not have a predecessor in new

(line 12). This loop is iterated until *new* is closed under predecessor. Thus, *new* is the set of all reachable SCCs. Because of the loop from line 7 to line 9, those SCCs are accepting by contain a state in J_i for all $J_i \in J$. At the end, *new* contains all reachable accepting SCCs in this transition system.

4.2 Algorithm with Simulation Reduction

In this section, we present our improved emptiness checking algorithm of timed automata Algorithm 4, which improves Algorithm 3 by using the simulation relation. We rename the function as $IsEmpty_{sim}$. The difference between Algorithm 4 and Algorithm 3 is that in the function $IsEmpty_{sim}$, we update $Init = Down(Init)$ at line 3 at the beginning, and throughout the algorithm, we call the functions $Reach_{sim}(Q, Tr)$ and $Down(succ(Q))$ instead of $Reach(Q, Tr)$ and $succ(Q)$, respectively. Note that the function $Reach_{sim}(Q, Tr)$ is introduced in Sect. 3. In other words, we always apply the function $Down$ on the results of the $succ$ function. We prove that Algorithm 4 is sound and complete as we did for Algorithm 3. First, we prove that $\mathcal{L}'$ (defined in Definition 3) also preserves the emptiness.

Lemma 4. *Given $q'_1 \preceq q_1$, if there exists a path with length n, $q'_1 \implies q'_2 \implies \cdots \implies q'_n$ in $\mathcal{L}'$, there exists a path with the same length n, $q_1 \to q_2 \to \cdots \to q_n$ in $\mathcal{L}$ such that $q'_i \preceq q_i$ for all $1 \leq i \leq n$.*

Lemma 5. *Given $q'_1 \preceq q_1$, if there exists a cycle $q'_1 \implies \cdots \implies q'_1$ in $\mathcal{L}'$ which contains a J_i-state for all $J_i \in J$, there exists a cycle $q_1 \to \cdots \to q_1$ in $\mathcal{L}$ which contains a J_i-state for all $J_i \in J$.*

Lemma 6. *If there exists an accepting run in $\mathcal{L}'$, there exists an accepting run in $\mathcal{L}$.*

Theorem 4. *Given a transition system $\mathcal{L}$, a set of Büchi conditions J, and a simulation relation $\preceq$ over states of $\mathcal{L}$, $\mathcal{L}$ has an accepting run if and only if $\mathcal{L}'$ has an accepting run.*

Following Theorem 4, we can use the transition system $\mathcal{L}'$ as the input for Algorithm 3. However, explicitly computing the transition relation of $\mathcal{L}'$ is not efficient. Instead, we apply $Down$ for the result of any call $succ(Q)$ on the fly in Algorithm 3 because of the fact that $succ(Q, \implies) = Down(succ(Q, \to))$.

Theorem 5. *Algorithm 4 is sound and complete.*

Proof: As we discussed the difference between Algorithm 4 and Algorithm 3, given a transition system $\mathcal{L}$ with a set of initial states $Init$, the transition relation Tr and a set of Büchi conditions J, while $IsEmpty(Init, Tr, J)$ is checking the emptiness of $\mathcal{L}$, $IsEmpty_{sim}(Init, Tr, J)$ is actually checking the emptiness of the transition system $\mathcal{L}'$. Thus, the correctness of Algorithm 4 is obtained based on Theorem 4.   □

Algorithm 4 does not guarantee that it always takes fewer or the same number of iterations than Algorithm 3. To distinguish between Algorithms 4 and 3, we use new' and new to denote the variable new in Algorithm 4 and Algorithm 3 respectively. Then, the reason that Algorithm 4 might take more iterations is $new' = Down(new)$ is not an invariant during the algorithm. Assume before executing the line 12, it holds that $new' = Down(new)$, then $new' = Down(new)$ may not hold after this line is executed as shown in Lemma 8 in [2]. Thus, $new' = Down(new)$ is not an invariant. Nevertheless, in our evaluation in Sect. 5, Algorithm 4 always outperforms Algorithm 3 and takes less number of $succ$ function calls. The reason is that during the computation of all reachable states from initial states at line 4 and the first run of the while-loop in lines 7–9, Algorithm 4 can take much lesser number of $succ$ function calls than Algorithm 3 as the result of Theorem 3 and Lemma 7 in [7]. Moreover, the computation of all reachable states (line 4) is the most expensive computation in these algorithms.

Algorithm 4 can be adopted to verify the emptiness of TBA straightforwardly. The requirement that the run must visit an accepting location infinite times and contain an infinite number of tick transitions and action transitions is represented as a set of Büchi conditions $J = \{Acc, J_0, J_1\}$ where Acc is a set of accepting locations in $DS(A)$ and J_0 (respectively J_1) is the set of states which are the destination states of the action transition (respectively tick transition). A boolean variable $isTick$ can be introduced during the encoding. For each transition, this variable is updated to false if that is an action transition. Otherwise it is updated to true. Then J_0 is the set of states where $isTick$ is false and J_1 is the set of states where $isTick$ is true.

We have presented our approach on the verification of reachability and LTL properties by using the LU simulation relation. We evaluate them in the next section.

5   Evaluation

We conducted experiments to evaluate our approach. Specifically, we attempted to answer the following research questions:

RQ1: How is the *improvement* in the number of iterations and verification time of our methods, compared to the existing state-of-the-art BDD-based and DBM-based methods, in checking reachability and LTL properties?

RQ2: How *scalable* is our method in size of maximal clock constants and processes?

Our approach has been implemented as a BDD library for the reachability and LTL verification of timed automata in the PAT framework [42]. Our implementation is based on the CUDD package [41], which is a package that provides functions to manipulate BDDs. All of the experiments are performed on a PC with Intel Core i7-2600 CPU at 3.4 GHz and 4 GB RAM.

To answer the research questions, we have conducted four experiments, and the results are shown in Tables 1-4. For all experiments, we measure the number of $succ$ function calls ($\#Succ$), the verification time (in seconds) ($Time$), and

Table 1. Experimental results in the reachability verification with increasing clock constants

		PAT-Sim			PAT-NonSim			Rabbit
	MCC	#Succ	Time	Memory	#Succ	Time	Memory	Time
CSMACD	808	4,369	6	34	17,794	1,563	577	208
CSMACD	1,616	8,721	36	59	-	oot	-	1,494
CSMACD	3,232	17,425	228	181	-	-	-	oot
Fischer	256	796	14	73	2,838	1,033	1,089	58
Fischer	512	1,564	112	252	-	-	oom	1,076
Fischer	1,024	3,100	867	931	-	-	-	oom
Lynch	64	481	12	66	1,347	217	498	256
Lynch	128	929	104	287	2,627	2,163	1,562	oot
Lynch	256	1,825	859	1,003	-	-	oom	oom

Table 2. Experimental results in the reachability verification with increasing number of processes

		PAT-Sim			PAT-NonSim			Rabbit	Uppaal
	#Proc	#Succ	Time	Memory	#Succ	Time	Memory	Time	Time
CSMACD	16	7,377	62	85	-	oot	-	5,638	oom
CSMACD	32	14,289	453	187	-	-	-	oot	-
CSMACD	64	26,801	3,912	477	-	-	-	-	-
Fischer	8	308	52	482	-	oot	-	7,258	0.7
Fischer	16	356	366	1,442	-	-	-	oom	oom
Fischer	32	452	3,351	1,651	-	-	-	-	-
Lynch	8	169	8	72	696	6,203	1,690	2,494	1.1
Lynch	16	217	104	290	-	-	oom	oom	oom
Lynch	32	313	2,971	1,201	-	-	-	-	-

the memory usage of CUDD library (in MB) (*Memory*) over three benchmark systems from [1,15,36]: CSMACD protocol, Fischer's protocol, and Lynch-Shavit protocol. We run PAT in two settings, i.e., with and without simulation, which are referred to as *PAT-Sim* and *PAT-NonSim*. The algorithms for PAT-Sim (PAT-NonSim resp.) on verifying reachability and LTL properties are given in Algorithms 2 and 4 (Algorithms 1 and 3 resp.).

All experiments are conducted with a time limit of 2 CPU hours. An entry 'oot' in the table means that the time limit is reached, and an entry 'oom' means that the program runs out of memory. Given a benchmark system, when a smaller model is running out of time or memory, we omit the evaluation of larger models. An entry '-' means the information is unavailable.

Table 3. Results in the LTL verification with increasing maximal clock constants

		PAT-Sim			PAT-NonSim		
	MCC	#Succ	Time	Memory	#Succ	Time	Memory
CSMACD	404	4,334	5	36	14,169	493	876
CSMACD	808	8,608	18	75	28,257	2,857	1,489
CSMACD	1,616	16,688	35	82	-	-	oom
Fischer	200	979	2	28	2,812	417	1,101
Fischer	400	1,779	3	29	5,412	3,847	1,600
Fischer	800	3,379	8	34	-	oot	-
Lynch	200	6,937	25	53	19,682	2,404	1,434
Lynch	400	13,137	45	62	-	oot	-
Lynch	800	25,537	90	63	-	-	-

Table 4. Results in the LTL verification with increasing number of processes

		PAT-Sim			PAT-NonSim			CTAV
	#Proc	#Succ	Time	Memory	#Succ	Time	Memory	Time
CSMACD	12	22,184	283	1,041	-	oot	-	562
CSMACD	16	28,972	511	756	-	-	-	oom
CSMACD	20	35,760	839	1,063	-	-	-	-
Fischer	8	608	5	39	1,974	10,275	1,689	4
Fischer	12	672	46	208	-	-	oom	oom
Fischer	16	736	310	965	-	-	-	-
Lynch	4	3,591	1	25	10,003	243	329	1
Lynch	8	9,839	42	65	-	-	oom	5
Lynch	12	19,551	585	326	-	-	-	oom

We compare the results to three state-of-the-art model checkers, i.e., DBM-based model checker *Uppaal* [31] and *CTAV* [32], as well as BDD-based model checker *Rabbit* [10]. Although RED [46] and BDD-based version of Kronos [14] are related to our work as real time verification tools using BDD (BDD-like) data structure, Rabbit was shown to outperform them [10]. Therefore, only Rabbit is used in our experiments.

5.1 Evaluation for Reachability Properties

We evaluate our approach with Rabbit and Uppaal in the verification of reachability properties. Since our approach is digitization-based, naturally, the first question is how well the library scales with the number of clock ticks. In the first experiment (cf. Table 1), we exponentially increase the maximal clock constants while keeping the number of processes constant (we set it 4). Since Uppaal is a DBM-based model checker, its performance does not depend on the maximal clock constants; therefore, it is not used in the experiment. The column *MCC* is the maximal clock constant values in the corresponding models. Compared to PAT-NonSim, PAT-Sim takes smaller number of *succ* function calls which can be reduced from 2 to 4 times by using simulation. Compared to Rabbit, PAT-Sim achieves a speedup from 2 to 21 times, and there are five cases where Rabbit runs out of memory or time. As a result, PAT-Sim outperforms both PAT-NonSim and Rabbit and can handle larger maximal clock constants.

In the second experiment (cf. Table 2), we compare PAT, Rabbit, and Uppaal using the same benchmark systems. The column *#Proc* represents the number of processes. In this experiment, we set the maximal clock constants to 64 in Fischer protocol, 16 in Lynch-Shavit protocol, and 404 in CSMACD protocol. Then, we increase the number of processes in each benchmark system to find out which tool can verify the most number of processes. By using simulation, the number of *succ* function calls is reduced. Thus, PAT-Sim is faster and can handle larger number of processes compared to PAT-NonSim. For example, in the Lynch model with 8 processes, PAT-Sim requires 169 *succ* function calls and takes 8 s, while PAT-NonSim requires 696 *succ* function calls and takes 6,203 s. The verification time is thus reduced significantly. According to Table 2, PAT-Sim also outperforms Rabbit and Uppaal. Although Uppaal achieves shorter evaluation time in smaller number of processes, both Rabbit and Uppaal easily run out of memory or time when the number of processes increases. On the contrary, PAT-Sim can still verify models while both other tools are out of memory or time, for example, 64 processes in the CSMACD benchmark.

5.2   Evaluation for LTL Properties

We evaluate our approach with CTAV in the verification of LTL properties under non-Zeno condition. Note that we do not compare with Uppaal since Uppaal does not support the verification of LTL properties under non-Zeno condition. In the third experiment (cf. Table 3), to demonstrate the efficiency of our approach in the handling of large maximal clock constants, we fix the number of processes at 4 and increase the maximal clock constants. We do not compare with CTAV since it is a DBM-based model checker and its performance is not affected by maximal clock constants. According to the results, by using the LU simulation relation, the number of *succ* function calls is reduced significantly. For example, in the Lynch protocol with $MCC = 200$, the number of *succ* calls is reduced from 19,682 to 6,937. As a result, the verification time is improved significantly, from 2,404 s to 25 s.

PAT-Sim outperforms PAT-NonSim on all the models. It is faster and uses less memory. Thus, it can handle models with maximal clock constants up to thousands.

In the fourth experiment (cf. Table 4), to demonstrate the efficiency of our approach in the handling of large number of processes, we fix the maximal clock constant as 808 for CSMACD and 100 for other benchmarks. We increase the number of processes then. In this experiment, we compare our approach with

CTAV tool. The results indicate PAT-Sim approach outperforms PAT-NonSim and CTAV on all the models. Specifically, it is faster and can handle more processes than PAT-NonSim and CTAV. For example, in the CSMACD model with 16 processes, PAT-Sim can verify within 511 s and 756 MB while PAT-NonSim runs out of time, and CTAV runs out of memory.

With the results of four experiments, we answer research questions $RQ1$ and $RQ2$. Our approach improves the performance significantly by reducing the number of iterations. Furthermore, it can handle models with clock constants larger than a thousand.

6   Discussion

Limitation. A limitation of our approach is that when maximal lower and upper bounds are the same, LU abstraction would not provide better performance. This is because our method will take the same number of iterations to achieve the fixpoint, and there are overheads for calling the *Down* operator.

Complexity of Down operator. [7] For checking of reachability properties, given the maximal distance from the initial state to a state in the explored model as N, the complexity is $O(N)$. For checking of LTL properties, the time complexity is linearly dependent upon the size of the symbolic (BDD) representation in terms of the distances between states in the automaton graph, the number and arrangement of the strongly connected components in the graph, and the number of fairness conditions asserted [39]. Overall, *Down* operator can be computed efficiently. In addition, variable ordering could affect the performance of BDD. Overall, the *Down* operator can be computed efficiently. In our implementation, we make use of several well-known heuristics [6,9,23,38] that can produce a fairly good ordering.

7   Conclusion

In this paper, we propose to use the simulation relation to improve the BDD-based model checking for real-time systems. Our approach is applied to verify reachability and LTL properties. Experimental results confirm that our approach achieves a significant speedup and outperforms Rabbit, Uppaal, and CTAV. As future works, first, we plan to investigate the extensibility of our method to other variety of timed automata, such as parametric timed automata [4]. Second, we plan to investigate other reduction techniques, e.g., interpolation [34] or IC3 [18], on top of our proposed techniques.

References

1. MCMT Benchmarks of Timed Automata. http://crema.di.unimi.it/~carioni/mcmt_ta.html
2. Technical Report of Scaling BDD-based Timed Verification with Simulation Reduction. http://tianhuat.github.io/tr_bddsr.pdf

3. Alur, R., Dill, D.L.: A theory of timed automata. Theor. Comput. Sci. **126**(2), 183–235 (1994)
4. Alur, R., Henzinger, T.A., Vardi, M.Y.: Parametric real-time reasoning. In: STOC, pp. 592–601 (1993)
5. Asarin, E., Maler, O., Pnueli, A.: On discretization of delays in timed automata and digital circuits. In: Sangiorgi, D., de Simone, R. (eds.) CONCUR 1998. LNCS, vol. 1466, pp. 470–484. Springer, Heidelberg (1998)
6. Aziz, A., Tasiran, S., Brayton, R.K.: BDD variable ordering for interacting finite state machines. In: DAC, pp. 283–288 (1994)
7. Behrmann, G., Bouyer, P., Larsen, K.G., Pelánek, R.: Lower and upper bounds in zone based abstractions of timed automata. In: Jensen, K., Podelski, A. (eds.) TACAS 2004. LNCS, vol. 2988, pp. 312–326. Springer, Heidelberg (2004)
8. Behrmann, G., Larsen, K.G., Pearson, J., Weise, C., Yi, W.: Efficient timed reachability analysis using clock difference diagrams. In: Halbwachs, N., Peled, D.A. (eds.) CAV 1999. LNCS, vol. 1633, pp. 341–353. Springer, Heidelberg (1999)
9. Beyer, D.: Improvements in BDD-based reachability analysis of timed automata. In: Oliveira, J.N., Zave, P. (eds.) FME 2001. LNCS, vol. 2021, pp. 318–343. Springer, Heidelberg (2001)
10. Beyer, D., Lewerentz, C., Noack, A.: Rabbit: a tool for BDD-based verification of real-time systems. In: Hunt Jr., W.A., Somenzi, F. (eds.) CAV 2003. LNCS, vol. 2725, pp. 122–125. Springer, Heidelberg (2003)
11. Beyer, D., Noack, A.: Efficient verification of timed automata using BDDs. In: FMICS, pp. 95–113 (2001)
12. Beyer, D., Noack, A.: Can decision diagrams overcome state space explosion in real- time verification. In: König, H., Heiner, M., Wolisz, A. (eds.) FORTE 2003. LNCS, vol. 2767, pp. 193–208. Springer, Heidelberg (2003)
13. Bouyer, P.: Forward analysis of updatable timed automata. Formal Methods Syst. Des. **24**(3), 281–320 (2004)
14. Bozga, M., Daws, C., Maler, O., Olivero, A., Tripakis, S., Yovine, S.: Kronos: a model-checking tool for real-time systems. In: Vardi, Y.M. (ed.) CAV 1998. LNCS, vol. 1427, pp. 546–550. Springer, Heidelberg (1998)
15. Bozga, M., Maler, O., Pnueli, A., Yovine, S.: Some progress in the symbolic verification of timed automata. In: Grumberg, O. (ed.) CAV 1997. LNCS, vol. 1254, pp. 179–190. Springer, Heidelberg (1997)
16. Burch, J.R., Clarke, E.M., McMillan, K.L., Dill, D.L., Hwang, L.J.: Symbolic model checking: 10^{20} states and beyond. Inf. Comput. **98**(2), 142–170 (1992)
17. Chen, M., Tan, T.H., Sun, J., Liu, Y., Pang, J., Li, X.: Verification of functional and non-functional requirements of web service composition. In: Groves, L., Sun, J. (eds.) ICFEM 2013. LNCS, vol. 8144, pp. 313–328. Springer, Heidelberg (2013)
18. Cimatti, A., Griggio, A.: Software model checking via IC3. In: Madhusudan, P., Seshia, S.A. (eds.) CAV 2012. LNCS, vol. 7358, pp. 277–293. Springer, Heidelberg (2012)
19. Daws, C., Tripakis, S.: Model checking of real-time reachability properties using abstractions. In: Steffen, B. (ed.) TACAS 1998. LNCS, vol. 1384, pp. 313–329. Springer, Heidelberg (1998)
20. Sifakis, J.: Timing assumptions and verification of finite-state concurrent systems. In: Dill, D.L. (ed.) Automatic Verification Methods for Finite State Systems. LNCS, vol. 407, pp. 197–212. Springer, Heidelberg (1989)
21. Dill, D.L., Hu, A.J., Wong-Toi, H.: Checking for language inclusion using simulation preorders. In: Larsen, K.G., Hu, A.J., Wong-Toi, H. (eds.) CAV 1991. LNCS, vol. 575, pp. 255–265. Springer, Heidelberg (1991)

22. Doyen, L., Raskin, J.-F.: Antichain algorithms for finite automata. In: Esparza, J., Majumdar, R. (eds.) TACAS 2010. LNCS, vol. 6015, pp. 2–22. Springer, Heidelberg (2010)

23. Fujii, H., Ootomo, G., Hori, C.: Interleaving based variable ordering methods for ordered binary decision diagrams. In: ICCAD, pp. 38–41 (1993)

24. Henzinger, T.A., Manna, Z., Pnueli, A.: What good are digital clocks? In: Kuich, W. (ed.) ICALP 1992. LNCS, vol. 623, pp. 545–558. Springer, Heidelberg (1992)

25. Herbreteau, F., Srivathsan, B.: Efficient on-the-fly emptiness check for timed Büchi automata. In: Bouajjani, A., Chin, W.-N. (eds.) ATVA 2010. LNCS, vol. 6252, pp. 218–232. Springer, Heidelberg (2010)

26. Herbreteau, F., Srivathsan, B., Walukiewicz, I.: Efficient emptiness check for timed Büchi automata. In: Touili, T., Cook, B., Jackson, P. (eds.) CAV 2010. LNCS, vol. 6174, pp. 148–161. Springer, Heidelberg (2010)

27. Herbreteau, F., Srivathsan, B., Walukiewicz, I.: Better abstractions for timed automata. In: LICS, pp. 375–384 (2012)

28. Kesten, Y., Pnueli, A., Raviv, L.: Algorithmic verification of linear temporal logic specifications. In: Larsen, K.G., Skyum, S., Winskel, G. (eds.) ICALP 1998. LNCS, vol. 1443, pp. 1–16. Springer, Heidelberg (1998)

29. Laarman, A., Olesen, M.C., Dalsgaard, A.E., Larsen, K.G., van de Pol, J.: Multi-core emptiness checking of timed Büchi automata using inclusion abstraction. In: Sharygina, N., Veith, H. (eds.) CAV 2013. LNCS, vol. 8044, pp. 968–983. Springer, Heidelberg (2013)

30. Lamport, L.: Real-time model checking is really simple. In: Borrione, D., Paul, W. (eds.) CHARME 2005. LNCS, vol. 3725, pp. 162–175. Springer, Heidelberg (2005)

31. Larsen, K.G., Pettersson, P., Yi, W.: UPPAAL in a Nutshell. STTT 1(1–2), 134–152 (1997)

32. Li, G.: Checking timed Büchi automata emptiness using LU-abstractions. In: Ouaknine, J., Vaandrager, F.W. (eds.) FORMATS 2009. LNCS, vol. 5813, pp. 228–242. Springer, Heidelberg (2009)

33. Li, Y., Tan, T.H., Chechik, M.: Management of time requirements in component-based systems. In: Jones, C., Pihlajasaari, P., Sun, J. (eds.) FM 2014. LNCS, vol. 8442, pp. 399–415. Springer, Heidelberg (2014)

34. McMillan, K.L.: Interpolation and SAT-based model checking. In: Hunt Jr., W.A., Somenzi, F. (eds.) CAV 2003. LNCS, vol. 2725, pp. 1–13. Springer, Heidelberg (2003)

35. Møller, J.B., Lichtenberg, J., Andersen, H.R., Hulgaard, H.: Difference decision diagrams. In: Flum, J., Rodríguez-Artalejo, M. (eds.) CSL 1999. LNCS, vol. 1683, pp. 111–125. Springer, Heidelberg (1999)

36. Morbé, G., Pigorsch, F., Scholl, C.: Fully symbolic model checking for timed automata. In: Gopalakrishnan, G., Qadeer, S. (eds.) CAV 2011. LNCS, vol. 6806, pp. 616–632. Springer, Heidelberg (2011)

37. Nguyen, T.K., Sun, J., Liu, Y., Dong, J.S., Liu, Y.: Improved BDD-based discrete analysis of timed systems. In: Giannakopoulou, D., Méry, D. (eds.) FM 2012. LNCS, vol. 7436, pp. 326–340. Springer, Heidelberg (2012)

38. Rice, M., Kulhari, S.: A survey of static variable ordering heuristics for efficient BDD/MDD construction. Technical report, University of California, Riverside (2008)

39. Rozier, K.Y.: Linear temporal logic symbolic model checking. Comput. Sci. Rev. 5(2), 163–203 (2011)

40. Seshia, S.A., Bryant, R.E.: Unbounded, fully symbolic model checking of timed automata using Boolean methods. In: Hunt Jr., W.A., Somenzi, F. (eds.) CAV 2003. LNCS, vol. 2725, pp. 154–166. Springer, Heidelberg (2003)
41. Somenzi, F.: CUDD: CU Decision Diagram Package. http://vlsi.colorado.edu/~fabio/CUDD/
42. Sun, J., Liu, Y., Dong, J.S., Pang, J.: PAT: towards flexible verification under fairness. In: Bouajjani, A., Maler, O. (eds.) CAV 2009. LNCS, vol. 5643, pp. 709–714. Springer, Heidelberg (2009)
43. Tan, T.H., Liu, Y., Sun, J., Dong, J.S.: Verification of orchestration systems using compositional partial order reduction. In: Qin, S., Qiu, Z. (eds.) ICFEM 2011. LNCS, vol. 6991, pp. 98–114. Springer, Heidelberg (2011)
44. Tripakis, S.: Verifying progress in timed systems. In: Katoen, J.-P. (ed.) AMAST-ARTS 1999, ARTS 1999, and AMAST-WS 1999. LNCS, vol. 1601, pp. 299–314. Springer, Heidelberg (1999)
45. Tripakis, S.: Checking timed Büchi automata emptiness on simulation graphs. ACM Trans. Comput. Logic 10(3), 1–19 (2009)
46. Wang, F.: Symbolic verification of complex real-time systems with clock-restriction diagram. In: Kim, M., Chin, B., Kang, S., Lee, D. (eds.) FORTE 2001, vol. 69, pp. 235–250. Springer, Heidelberg (2001)
47. Wang, F.: Efficient verification of timed automata with BDD-like data-structures. In: Zuck, L.D., Attie, P.C., Cortesi, A., Mukhopadhyay, S. (eds.) VMCAI 2003. LNCS, vol. 2575, pp. 189–205. Springer, Heidelberg (2003)

Model Checking Real-Time Properties
on the Functional Layer of Autonomous Robots

Mohammed Foughali[1,2]([⊠]), Bernard Berthomieu[1,2], Silvano Dal Zilio[1,2],
Félix Ingrand[1,2], and Anthony Mallet[1,2]

[1] CNRS, LAAS, 7 Avenue du Colonel Roche, F-31400 Toulouse, France
mfoughal@laas.fr
[2] Univ. de Toulouse, LAAS, F-31400 Toulouse, France

Abstract. Software is an essential part of robotic systems. As robots
and autonomous systems are more and more deployed in human environments, we need to use elaborate validation and verification techniques in
order to gain a higher level of trust in our systems. This motivates our
determination to apply formal verification methods to robotics software.
In this paper, we describe our results obtained using model-checking on
the functional layer of an autonomous robot. We implement an automatic
translation from GenoM, a robotics model-based software engineering
framework, to the formal specification language Fiacre. This translation
takes into account the semantics of the robotics middleware. TINA, our
model-checking toolbox, can be used on the synthesized models to prove
real-time properties of the functional modules implementation on the
robot. We illustrate our approach using a realistic autonomous navigation example.

1 Introduction

Software is an essential part of robotic systems. As robots and autonomous
systems are more and more deployed in human environments (autonomous
cars, coworker robots, surgery robotics, etc.) and/or costly exploration missions
(extraterrestrial rover, deep space mission, etc.), we need to use more elaborated
V&V techniques, in order to gain a higher level of trust in the behavior of such
systems. Indeed, the trust we currently put in robotics software mainly rely on
testing campaigns, best coding practices, and the choice of sound architecture
principles. This does not rise to the level found in many regulated domains, such
as the aeronautic or nuclear industries, where formal methods are routinely used
to check the most vital parts of systems.

On the other hand, robotics software provides new opportunities to apply
formal methods. Indeed, robotics applications are often deployed using model-
based software engineering approaches [14] and described as a set of functional
modules orchestrated by a robotics middleware. These modules, and their interactions, are amenable to an interpretation into formal models.

Autonomous systems are typically organized along layers [13]. The lower one,
the *functional layer*, interacts directly with sensors and actuators and performs

© Springer International Publishing AG 2016
K. Ogata et al. (Eds.): ICFEM 2016, LNCS 10009, pp. 383–399, 2016.
DOI: 10.1007/978-3-319-47846-3_24

the data processing tasks. The *decisional layer* deals with more cognitive activities, such as task planning or monitoring. With respect to V&V, the decisional layer models are often formal and range from planning models (PDDL, ANML, NDDL, etc.) to acting models (TDL, SMach, RMPL, OpenPRS, etc.) or monitoring models (Livingstone, etc.) [22], a fact reflected by a large body of research applying formal V&V approaches to the deliberation functions [1,16,21,29]. In contrast, little has been done to bridge frameworks used to deploy functional level modules with formal methods and their associated V&V tools.

In this paper, we propose to connect a robotics model-based approach (G^{en}oM3) with a formal V&V framework (Fiacre/TINA). We describe how we can automatically synthesize a formal model of robotics functional modules and then use it to prove important behavioral and timed properties of the modules implementation on the robot. We illustrate our presentation with a realistic autonomous navigation example, on which we formally prove properties of interest to the robot programmers.

The paper is organized as follows. After a section on related works focusing on formal verification of the functional level of robotic systems, we introduce (Sect. 3) the Fiacre formal specification language and the TINA model-checking toolbox. We then describe the G^{en}oM3 framework (Sect. 4), used to specify functional level modules for robotic systems. In Sect. 5, we illustrate our robot navigation example as specified in G^{en}oM3. Section 6.1 gives examples on how we map GenoM modules constituents into Fiacre so as to automatically synthesize formal models. Before concluding, Sect. 7 discusses some examples of properties formally checked on our navigation modules.

2   Related Work

An early work on formal verification in robotics is presented in [19]. It proposes the verification of robotics applications specified in Orccad [30]. Behavioral properties are checked with Mauto after translating Orccad descriptions into the ESTEREL synchronous language [12], with time-related constraints translated into logical events. Timed properties are checked with Kronos, a TCTL model-checker, after translating the specification into Timed-Argos [25], an extension of the synchronous language Argos with delays.

Brat et al. [13] describe an approach to verify autonomous systems with planning, execution and functional layers. They propose a modular verification approach combining compositional techniques (assume-guarantee), static analysis, testing and model checking to assert safety properties. No timing constraints are taken into account.

In [32], the authors attempt to prevent state explosion while model-checking large systems through a compositional approach (inferring properties of the system from the properties of its constituents). They succeed to assert some properties of low-level controllers. Not all properties are amenable to compositional verification, however. They suggest to combine model checking and automated theorem proving to benefit from their respective strengths.

BIP [4], a modeling framework based on automata, is used in the joint verification effort presented in [2]. The functional modules, written in $G^{en}oM$, of an outdoor robot with two navigation modes, are modeled in BIP. The invariant extractor and SAT-solving tool D-Finder [5] is used to check, offline, the absence of deadlocks within the BIP model. Additional safety constraints can be added and automatically translated from logical formulae into BIP. The resulting model is run within the BIP Engine on DALA, an iRobot ATRV (All-Terrain Robotic Vehicle), and the constraints are consequently enforced at runtime. Timing constraints are not considered.

In [20], the MAUVE framework is used to build functional level components for a P3DX mobile robot. The schedulability of the different components is formally verified. Execution scenarios are manually translated into Fiacre [6] models and behavioral properties are asserted on them.

This list is far from being exhaustive. Indeed, we only mentioned methods comparable to ours, omitting for instance those relying on hybrid formal models like [17] or on pure theorem proving as in [31]. Our approach is the closest in spirit to that of [19] and relies on model-checking. Formal models are automatically synthesized and all properties are checked in the same verification framework, including timed properties.

3   Fiacre and TINA

Fiacre [6] is a specification language for describing compositionally both the behavioral and timing aspects of embedded and distributed systems. It has a formal semantics and can be used as an input format for formal verification tools (mainly real-time model-checkers) as well as for simulation purposes.

Fiacre stems from several projects involving industrial and academics partners. Besides the applications described in this paper, Fiacre has been used in a variety of applicative domains, like telecoms, avionics or robotics systems [7,11,20,28]. In this work, we use Fiacre specifications with the model-checking toolbox TINA.

3.1   The Fiacre Language

Fiacre descriptions are made of processes and components, both parameterizable by values, value locations (shared variables) and interaction labels (for communication or synchronization).

Processes describe sequential behaviors; they specify a set of control states and a set of transitions, each expressing a state change by a statement built from deterministic constructs (assignments, conditionals, loops, and sequential composition), nondeterministic constructs (nondeterministic choice and assignments), interaction statements and jump statements. Several examples of Fiacre processes are shown in Sect. 6.1.

Components describe in a hierarchical manner the architecture of the system; a system is a parallel composition of process or component instances. Components also specify the interactions between the constituting processes or components, and possibly constrain these interactions with timing and/or priority requirements.

Apart from its ability to model priorities and timing constraints (using a dense time model), a distinctive feature of Fiacre is to include a rich set of datatypes: booleans, integers and integer ranges, records, tagged unions, arrays and queues. The language is statically typed, with depth subtyping to handle integer ranges. In terms of process interactions, Fiacre supports both the classical paradigms of shared variables and synchronous message passing à la process calculi. Shared variables and interaction ports are created local to components. Finally, Fiacre provides functions, native or imported. Some introductory material and examples can be found on the Fiacre site (www.laas.fr/fiacre).

Semantics. Classically for a timed language, the semantics of a Fiacre description is a timed transition system, that is a transition system with two kinds of transitions: discrete transitions resulting from discrete state changes and continuous transitions resulting from time elapsing. The semantics of a component is the synchronized product of the semantics of its subcomponents, further constrained by time and priority constraints on their interactions, if any.

Verification. Fiacre descriptions can be complemented by declarations of properties. Atomic properties include the states of process instances, predicates on the values of variables and Fiacre events (interactions). The Fiacre observables are boolean combinations of atomic properties. They can be combined to form property patterns in the style of [18]. For checking real-time properties, these patterns are enriched with time constraints [3]. For verification, the real-time patterns are translated by the Fiacre compiler into LTL properties on the Fiacre description instrumented with observers.

As an illustration, this is how a "leadsto within" timed property is handled. The property is written in Fiacre as (*source* **leadsto** *target* **within** $[d1, d2]$), where *source* and *target* are some observables and $[d1, d2]$ is a time interval. The property asserts that along each path some state obeying *target* occurs within a delay in interval $[d1, d2]$ after each state obeying *source*. This property is encoded using a Fiacre process (an observer) given in the listing below; the process is connected with the main Fiacre program through two transition guards on the *source* and *target* observables. With this observer, the property is to show that the state **error** of the observer is unreachable.

```
process LeadsToWithin is
    states idle, start, watch, error
    from idle
      on source; to start
    from start
      wait [d1,d1]; to watch
    from watch
```

```
select
    on target; wait [0,0]; to idle
unless
    wait ]Δ,...[; to error /* where Δ = d2 − d1 */
end
```

3.2   The TINA Toolbox

TINA [9] is a toolbox for the analysis and verification of Time Petri nets (possibly) enriched with priorities, stopwatches and/or data processing. It is freely available at www.laas.fr/tina.

Time Petri nets. Together with Timed Automata, Time Petri nets [26] (*TPN* for short) are a prominent model for analysis of real-time systems. Time Petri nets enrich Petri nets with time intervals associated with the transitions of the net specifying the possible time delays between last enabledness of these transitions and their activation (or firing in Petri net terminology).

Due to the dense nature of time considered in *TPN*, their state spaces are typically infinite, but finite abstractions of these are available since [8], known as *State Classes*. State Classes provide a finite time-abstracted representation of the behavior of bounded *TPN* preserving their markings and traces. A state class associates a marking of the *TPN* with a system of difference constraints (a DBM) capturing the times in the future at which the transitions enabled at that marking can fire.

Since it preserves markings and traces, the state classes construction is suitable for LTL model-checking. A simple variation of the construction (reducing classes by inclusion) only preserves markings and is typically coarser; it is the method of choice for reachability analysis.

In contrast with the well known zone constructions for Timed Automata, state classes do not capture clock domains for the enabled transitions, but potential firing times in the future (called firing domains). For these reasons, state class constructions are typically coarser than zone constructions preserving the same properties. But zone constructions are also applicable to *TPN* and are indeed necessary to handle some *TPN* extensions like priorities.

A description of available abstraction methods for *TPN* can be found in [9, 10]. TINA offers all constructions discussed in these papers, as well as several constructions relying on discrete time and a number of constructions specific to Petri nets.

Enriching TPN. TPN can be conveniently enriched by a number of features enhancing their expressiveness like *priorities* expressing that some transitions should be favored over others when fireable at the same instant, *stopwatches* allowing to encode preemption, or *data-processing* consisting of synchronizing the evolution of the *TPN* with computations on a set of variables in some programming notation. TINA provides state class constructions for such enriched *TPN*.

Verification in TINA. The TINA toolbox provides state space generators and offline model-checkers for LTL and modal μ-calculus. The generators produce compressed representations of state spaces into files. Some classes of properties can also be checked on the fly when building state spaces. When a property reveals false, a counter example scenario is generated as a timed trace and can be replayed in a simulator.

Verification of Fiacre Descriptions. For their verification, Fiacre descriptions are translated into enriched *TPN* as defined above by an optimizing compiler. The compiler, `frac`, performs syntax analysis and type checking, then encodes the description into an enriched *TPN* for TINA preserving its semantics. The compilation process includes a model optimization pass that simplifies redundant transitions, removes dead code and abstracts some variables, retaining only those contributing to the state (unlike e.g. those only used as temporaries). This optimization pass helps reduce the size of the state space.

The `frac` compiler also translates the properties declared in the description into properties in the format supported by the TINA model checkers. Verifications of Fiacre properties are then carried out exactly like verification of TINA models properties; in case of failure, a timed scenario can be computed, corresponding to a Fiacre scenario.

4 G^{en}_oM3

Functional modules are the building block of LAAS robot architecture functional level [23]. Each module is in charge of a specific function on the robot, from controlling a low-level driver (e.g. motors), a sensor (e.g. laser, camera, etc.), up to more complex functionalities (e.g. motion planning, Simultaneous Localization And Mapping "SLAM", etc.). These modules are controlled by a supervisor (e.g. OpenPRS[1], eltcsh[2], etc.).

G^{en}_oM3 [24] is a tool that parses a specification language for functional modules. It provides a template-based generator to synthesize code, libraries, models, etc., from the specification.

A G^{en}_oM3 module (Fig. 1) is specified in the language with the following elements:

- an internal data structure (IDS), shared among the services S.
- execution tasks ET_i aperiodic or with a period (p_i); each runs the active activity services associated with it.
- services S, that can be of three different types: *attribute* (to set or get an element of the IDS), *function* (for a quick and simple computation) or more interestingly *activity*.
- ports P, *in* or *out*, depending on whether the module reads or writes them.
- a list of exceptions for non nominal executions.

---

[1] https://git.openrobots.org/projects/openprs.
[2] https://www.openrobots.org/wiki/eltclsh.

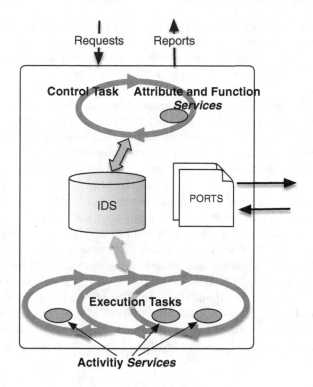

Fig. 1. A generic G$^{en}_o$M3 module.

Services can take parameters and return values. Each *Activity* executes in an execution task *ET* that it specifies. It also defines an automaton that specifies for each state:

- the codel[3] to execute in this state, taking as arguments the elements in and out from the IDS, and the ports in and out it needs for its execution.
- the list of states it yields to.
- the WCET (Worst Case Execution Time) of the codel.

All activities have a **start** state-codel, which is the entry point in the automaton, and an **ether** state which is a sink (terminal) state. At runtime, the codel associated with a state must return the state to which it will transition, or throw an exception. An activity thus terminates (transitions to **ether**) either with an exception or with a nominal end. In both cases, exception or return values are reported to the client that requested the activity. A service may have a **validate** codel to validate the *in* arguments before it runs. Any service may be incompatible with a list of services that need to be interrupted before it executes (including itself if e.g. at most one instance of the same service may run at any time). Interrupted activities execute directly their **stop** codel, if defined, otherwise they transit to **ether**.

---

[3] Codels (code elements) are the programmer implementation of the specified service, broken down to small chunks of C or C++ code.

Each module has an implicit aperiodic control task CT, in charge of the module I/O. The CT handles requests from clients as well as the reports upon execution of services. CT is also responsible for executing attributes and functions, and instructing the different ET_i of the activity instances to run or interrupt.

Templates Mechanism. The $G^{en}{}_oM3$ parser builds an abstract syntax tree and converts it into a suitable representation for the scripting language of the template interpreter (TCL). Then, every file of the template is read by $G^{en}{}_oM3$ and interpreted within this representation. Special markers in the file are detected and their content replaced in a manner similar to how a PHP script is embedded into an HTML page. The scripted code has access to all the information of the module description file. A typical template will consist of regular code, mixed with scripted loops on e.g., services that generate calls to functions of the core libraries. Since the interpreter relies on a complete scripting language, there are virtually no restrictions on what a template can express and synthesize.

There are already templates to synthesize: the module itself for various middleware (e.g., PocoLibs[4], ROS-Com [27], Orocos [15]); client libraries to control the module (e.g., JSON, C, OpenPRS), etc. The template we developed in this work maps the PocoLibs module implementation of any set of modules specified in $G^{en}{}_oM3$ into their timed Fiacre model. From now on, when we refer to a $G^{en}{}_oM3$ module, we implicitly mean the $G^{en}{}_oM3$ PocoLibs implementation of the module.

5 Illustrative Example

To illustrate our approach, we introduce a realistic example of a robot navigation implementation (Fig. 2a). This navigation remains generic, in the sense that it could be instantiated with different sensors, motion planners, etc. Yet, the modules, the ports they share, the periods of their internal tasks, the services, their automata and the WCETs associated to their codels are the same as the ones of the real navigation running on our RMP 400[5] robot, Mana.

Figure 2a presents the four modules in charge of the navigation:

ROBLOCO is in charge of the robot low-level controller. It has a track task (period 50 ms) associated to the activity *TSStart* (TrackSpeedStart, interruptible by the function *TSStop*) that reads data from the **speed** port and sends it to the motor controller. In parallel, one of the odo task (period 50 ms) associated activities, namely *OdoStart* (interruptible by the function *OdoStop*), reads the encoders on the wheels and produces a current position on the **pos** port.

ROBLASER is in charge of the laser. It has a scan task (period 50 ms) associated, *inter alia*, to the *StartScan* activity (interruptible by the function *StopScan*). The latter produces, on the port **scan**, the free space in the laser's range tagged with the position where the scan has been made (read on **pos**).

---

[4] https://git.openrobots.org/projects/pocolibs/gollum/index.

[5] http://rmp.segway.com/tag/rmp400/.

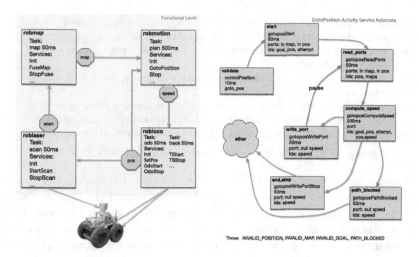

(a) The robot navigation with its four G^{en}₀M3 modules, their tasks and a partial list of their services (activities are in *italic*)

(b) The GotoPosition activity automaton.

Fig. 2. Modules and an activity service.

ROBMAP aggregates the successive **scan** data in the **map** port. A fuse task (period 50 ms) and *FuseMap*, one of its activities, perform the computation. The function *FuseStop* interrupts the activity *FuseMap*.

ROBMOTION has one task plan (period 500 ms) which, given a goal position (via the activity *GotoPosition*), computes the appropriate speed to reach it and writes it on **speed**, using the current position (from **pos**), and avoiding obstacles (from **map**). *GotoPosition* interrupts itself, so a new request will cancel the currently running one (if it exists) and force the execution of its **stop** state. Similarly, The *Stop* service (function) interrupts *GotoPosition*.

Each activity introduced above has its own automaton. Figure 2b presents the automaton of *GotoPosition*. For each state, we define a codel, its WCET, the ports and the elements of the IDS it needs (in and out). Listing 1 presents the G^{en}₀M3 specification of this activity.

```
activity GotoPosition (in robloco::position goto_position)
  { validate controlPosition (in goto_position) wcet 10 ms;
    codel <start> gotoposStart(in goto_position, port in pos, port in map,
    ids out goal_pos, ids out attempts) yield read_ports, ether wcet 50 ms;
    codel <read_ports> gotoposReadPorts(ids out pos, ids out explored_map,
    port in pos, port in map) yield compute_speed wcet 50 ms;
    codel <compute_speed> gotoposComputeSpeed(ids in goal_pos, ids in pos,
    ids in explored_map, ids in verbose, /* This codel takes a long time */
    ids out speed, ids inout attempts) /* we make sure no ports are locked */
    yield write_port, end, path_blocked wcet 200 ms;
```

```
codel <write_port> gotoposWritePort(ids in speed, port out speed)
yield pause::read_ports wcet 50 ms; /* enforces task cycle termination */
codel <end,stop> gotoposWritePortStop(ids out speed, port out speed)
yield ether wcet 50 ms;
codel <path_blocked> gotoposPathBlocked(ids out speed, port out speed)
yield ether wcet 50 ms;
interrupts GotoPosition; /* a new instance interrupts a running one */
task plan; /* the execution task in which the activity will execute */
throw Invalid_Position, Invalid_Map, Invalid_Goal, Path_Blocked; };
```

Listing 1. The G^{en}_oM3 specification of the GotoPosition activity.

Activities are executed in their respective execution tasks. For example, *GotoPosition* executes in the plan task along its period. It begins with executing the state **start** associated codel (**gotoposStart**), and transitioning to the state returned by such an execution (see Sect. 4). It continues until a transition labeled with *pause* occurs (e.g., Fig. 2b the transition from **write_port** to **read_ports**) or the activity terminates. In either case, the control is given back to the execution task which will then execute the other active instances, if any, or otherwise wait for the next period signal.

For the sake of simplicity, our description of the mechanisms offered by G^{en}_oM3 to specify and deploy functional modules remains partial. Still, one can see the complexity raised by running these 4 modules, with 9 threads, 27 services including 10 activities with their respective automata and overall more than 35 codels with their WCET.

The PocoLibs implementation of the module offers a high level of parallelism while preserving shared data access with proper locking. However, it does not offer any guarantee on crucial properties such as schedulability of tasks, boundedness in time of ports updates, proper termination of services, absence of deadlock due to sharing resources, etc.

6   Mapping and Automatic Synthesis

An important step of this work is to automatically synthesize a Fiacre model of any G^{en}_oM3 module. All the generic software components (tasks, services, automata, ports, etc.) potentially present in G^{en}_oM3 modules are formalized into Fiacre. In this section, we analyze through a few illustrative examples how we map some of the G^{en}_oM3 module software component into Fiacre processes/-components. We then briefly discuss the integration of such a mapping into the translator.

6.1   Mapping

Periodic Execution Tasks. Most G^{en}_oM3 specifications include periodic execution tasks in charge of executing the activities they manage. We model a periodic execution task with two Fiacre processes. The first one is a simple one-state **timer**. It is in charge of scheduling a **manager** process that manages the execution of the activities. The **timer** (Listing 2–left) assigns, every new time period PERIOD, the value true to the variable tick that it shares with the **manager**. The **manager** starts only when tick is true and switches this flag to false. If there are active activities in this task, it transitions to the state manage and executes them accordingly (Sect. 5). It does not transition back to its initial state, start, unless all eligible executions in this cycle have ended.

```
process timer (&tick: bool) is      process Manager (&tick: bool, ...) is
  states start                        states start, manage
  from start                          from start
    wait [PERIOD,PERIOD];               wait [0,0];
    tick := true;                       on tick;
    to start                            tick := false;
                                        if (...) /* no active activity */
                                        then to start
                                        else to manage end
                                      from manage
                                        wait [0,0];
                                        ... /* execute one active activity
                                              */
                                        if (...) /* no more activities */
                                        then to start
                                        else to manage end
```

Listing 2. Fiacre models of an execution task timer and manager (simplified)

State-Codels, WCETs and Concurrency. PocoLibs ensures proper locking of the resources the state-codels share (in the IDS for each module and among ports across multiple modules). In this context, state-codels are categorized as either **thread-safe** or **non-thread-safe**. A thread-safe state-codel runs with no condition on resources availability (e.g., it uses no shared resources or uses some of them exclusively) while a non-thread-safe one needs to have all the resources it accesses unlocked so it can execute. A thread-safe state-codel is mapped into a single Fiacre state with every transition out of it associated with the firing interval]0,WCET]. The target states correspond to the yield values of the state-codel (Sect. 4). In contrast, we map a non-thread-safe state-codel into two Fiacre states (Listing 3), the first for waiting and the second for executing. The transition from the first to the second fires providing no conflicting state-codel (i.e. potentially locking at least one of the needed resources) is in its Fiacre executing state.

```
from NTS_WAITING
  wait [0,0];
  on CONFLICT_1 = NOT_RUNNING and CONFLICT_2 = NOT_RUNNING ...;
  NTS := RUNNING;
  to NTS_EXECUTING
from NTS_EXECUTING
```

```
wait ]0,WCET];
NTS := NOT_RUNNING;
... /* possible transitions */
```

Listing 3. Fiacre model of a non-thread safe state-codel (simplified)

Activities. A G^{en}ₒM3 activity is mapped into a Fiacre process. The latter is constituted of the states corresponding to the activity state-codels and the transitions corresponding to their yield values. The task manager (Sect. 6.1) communicates with the activities to ensure a correct execution of active instances (Sect. 5). This communication, not shown in our listings for the sake of simplicity, also includes the proper handling of potential interruptions. Listing 4 is a simplified, symbolic, view of the Fiacre process corresponding to the *GotoPosition* activity (Sect. 5, start state-codel only).

```
process GotoPosition_plan (.../*shared variables*/) is
  states start, start_2, read_ports, ...
  from start_waiting
    wait [0,0];
    on (...) /* wait until the manager allows me to run */
    if (...) /* interruption signal (by manager) */ then to stop_
    /* otherwise, nominal execution: */
    else on (GetGoalPosition = NOT_RUNNING and ... );
    GotoPosition_plan_start := RUNNING;
    to start_executing
    end
  from start_executing
    wait ]0,0.05]; /* the WCET of the Start codel */
    /* back to not running when leaving: */
    GotoPosition_plan_start := NOT_RUNNING;
    select
      /* non determinism. Either to read_ports: */
      to read_ports_waiting
      /* or to ether */
    [] ... /* back to the manager */; to start_waiting /*
        terminate */
    end
  from read_ports_waiting
    ...
```

Listing 4. Extract from the GotoPosition Fiacre process (simplified)

6.2 Automatic Synthesis

For producing Fiacre models from G^{en}ₒM3 descriptions, we rely on the generic template mechanism provided by the G^{en}ₒM3 environment (Sect. 4). Fiacre models are generated fully automatically from unrestricted G^{en}ₒM3 descriptions.

The mappings from $G^{en}_o M3$ to Fiacre, some of which are discussed in Sect. 6.1, have been carefully chosen so that the behavior of the generated Fiacre models faithfully represents that of the $G^{en}_o M3$ module. The translation of $G^{en}_o M3$ descriptions into Fiacre gives them a formal semantics, which enables verification of real-time properties as illustrated in the next section. This constitutes the very first formalization of $G^{en}_o M3$ specifications.

7 Experiments and Discussion

In this section, we rely on the automatically generated Fiacre models (Sect. 6) of our $G^{en}_o M3$ modules (Sect. 5) to express and assert various temporal/timed properties using, respectively, Fiacre and TINA (Sect. 3) on each individual module but also on all the four modules together with a realistic navigation scenario. We assume that the targeted robotics platform is real-time, has enough cores to run all the tasks in parallel[6] and that the affinity is set to one core per task. All experiments are carried out on a typical mid-range computer; Intel Core i5 2.7 GHz with 8 GB of RAM.

7.1 Single Module Verification

The Fiacre model of a module cannot be analyzed without embedding it in a "system model", i.e., we need a "client" to synthesize the possible requests the module may serve. For this, the template automatically produces a Fiacre process able to send any type of request at any given time. Clearly, the Fiacre model of the module and that of its client form a system that will cover all the reachable states the real module may encounter when evolving alone (no interactions through ports).

Schedulability. We refer to an execution task as **schedulable** if it never overruns its period. We start with the most complex module, ROBLOCO (Sect. 5), involving three tasks running in parallel and a number of services. The modeling choice made in Sect. 6.1 for periodic tasks permits an easy expression of the property for both execution tasks. E.g. for task **odo**:

```
property sched_odo is always ((robloco/odo_manager/state manage) ⇒
    not (robloco/odo_manager/value tick_odo))
```

The idea is that a period is violated only if a new period tick occurs while an activity is being executed (see Sect. 6.1). This modeling choice makes it easy to express schedulability properties not with timed properties (implying a larger state space to analyze) but with reachability properties (which do not involve traces). Thus, we can use the coarser TINA construction that does not preserve firing sequences (smaller state space). We end up with a manageable state space (built in about 18 mn) with 10 857 940 classes all obeying the property, for both tasks. We then assert the truth of the same property on the remaining modules execution tasks in less than 1 mn overall.

---

[6] The template still provides the user with the possibility to specify their hardware constraints.

Safe End. Let us consider the module ROBMAP (Sect. 5). We assert the following safety property: when the module terminates following a *kill* request, all services have properly terminated. This translates in Fiacre to: for all execution paths, if the process *timer* is in state *shutdown*, then the function *running* returns false for all services instances:

```
property safeshut is always ((robmap/timer/state shutdown) ⇒
    not (robmap/manager/value (running (.../*all services
        instances*/))))
```

Indeed, our unique execution task's timer transits to the state *shutdown* when the module is killed, and the function **running** evaluates to true only if at least one of the services is running or being interrupted. Again, this property is an invariant and does not rely on traces. In our experiment, this property can be checked true by exploring a state class graph with 125 606 classes and 102 512 markings, computed in 4 s.

7.2 Full Perception-Plan-Action Loop Verification

We synthesize the global Fiacre model for the four modules communicating through ports. We then add a Fiacre client defining a full-navigation scenario.

Schedulability of Tasks and Progress of Activities. One of the properties we succeeded to verify in Sect. 7.1 is the tasks schedulability. However, this property is not necessarily preserved when the modules evolve altogether. Indeed, ports, properly synthesized in the Fiacre model of the four modules, constitute another shared resource that codels use concurrently. Since we already saw how to express the schedulability properties in Fiacre, we will skip directly to the results. Interestingly, no task respects its period anymore, except for the task plan of the module ROBMOTION.

These results lead us to further investigation. For the tasks becoming non schedulable, could it be possible that some activities are infinitely blocked while waiting for some ports to be free. Once more, our modeling choices, particularly the ones pertaining to periodic tasks and their associated activities (Sect. 6.1), allow an easy and quick verification of such a property. Using the Fiacre pattern **leadsto** (Sect. 3), we simply check that none of the involved tasks is forever blocked in its state **manage**. E.g. for the task **track**:

```
property no_block_track is (navigation/robloco/track_manager/state
    manage) leadsto (navigation/robloco/track_manager/state start)
```

The property holds for all the concerned tasks. Since no activity is infinitely blocked, which would be definitely worrying, the programmer has to decide whether it is critical for this application to have all the tasks schedulable. If yes, they may consider tuning the different periods while watching the effects on the robot performance. Our experiments show that, for instance, doubling the period of the task **track** renders it schedulable. All results are obtained in less than 40 s overall.

Speed/pos *Update Bounded in Time.* One important aspect in our navigation would be the time elapsed between a **pos** update, and the next **pos** update following a **speed** update with all the ports properly updated in-between (**scan**, **map**). We proceed by first checking upper bounds on each part of the whole loop between the subsequent events, using the Fiacre timed pattern **leadsto within** (Sect. 3), then summing these bounds. We consider all scenarios including a blocked path or a reached goal. The state spaces computation time range from 10 s to 30 s. The result is 1.274 s, which is acceptable considering the maximum speed of the robot and its laser range.

Safe Stop. We extend the client providing the navigation scenario to generate, at any given moment, a *TSStop* (Sect. 5) request. We again rely on the pattern **leadsto within** (Sect. 3) to formally prove that the generation of such a request leads to the termination of the running instance of *TSStart* in a maximum duration. We proved that this duration amounts to 72 ms with the model checker succeeding to find a counterexample for the next smaller value (i.e. 71 ms). Since the end of *TSStart* (through an interruption) means necessarily sending a null speed to the motor controller, the programmer may deduce critical information from this current setup, e.g., that the robot driving at 2 m/s will advance at least 0.14 m before a full stop. The reachability graph features 1 484 091 classes built in about 3 mn.

8 Conclusion

We formally check important real-time properties on the navigation modules of our RMP 400 robot. Our results compare favorably with previous works. In contrast to [2,13], we take all time constraints into account. Also, unlike the related works cited in Sect. 2 ([2] aside), we provide a fully automatic translation from G^{en}_oM3 specifications to the equivalent Fiacre model. Finally, and compared to [19], our experiments tackle examples of a high complexity and a maximum level of parallelism. We succeed to check nontrivial timed properties; no property verification lasted more than 18 mn (including the time needed to generate the reachability graph). These promising results are mainly due to careful modeling choices (Sects. 6 and 7) and optimized state space generation techniques implemented in TINA.

Formalizing G^{en}_oM3 specifications (Sect. 6) remains the hardest part of our effort. Several PocoLibs/G^{en}_oM3 aspects were not trivially expressible in Fiacre. Moreover, avoiding the combinatory explosion of model checking was challenging. Modeling choices were systematically assessed considering, despite their correctness, the ability to express and verify important properties on them. Many of such choices were thus discarded or refined throughout the process. As a consequence, the resulting models for our experiments remain scalable.

An unexpected result from this work is that transforming a G^{en}_oM3 specification and its PocoLibs implementation in a language like Fiacre, with a clear formal semantics, forced us to clarify some of the implementation choices and fix bugs.

A limitation of our approach in its current setting is that we need a fine knowledge of the Fiacre model produced by the translator from G^{en}_oM3 in order to express properties. For the robot programmers, it would be more convenient to express the properties within G^{en}_oM3, in a language they are familiar with. As a next step, the template will include the translation of properties expressed in G^{en}_oM3 into Fiacre/TINA properties. As for the verification results, when TINA evaluates the property to false, it would be equally important to automatically interpret the counterexample into what the robot programmers would easily grasp (that is at G^{en}_oM3 level), so they can act accordingly.

Last, robotic platforms seldom offer enough cores/processors to run all the tasks/threads of a realistic application in parallel. Thus, we now aim to verify real-time properties while taking into consideration the actual hardware constraints.

Acknowledgement. This work was supported in part by the EU CPSE Labs project funded by the H2020 program under grant agreement No. 644400.

References

1. Abdeddaïm, Y., Asarin, E., Gallien, M., Ingrand, F., Lesire, C., Sighireanu, M.: Planning robust temporal plans: a comparison between CBTP and TGA approaches. In: ICAPS (2007)
2. Abdellatif, T., Bensalem, S., Combaz, J., de Silva, L., Ingrand, F.: Rigorous design of robot software: a formal component-based approach. Robot. Auton. Syst. **60**, 1563–1578 (2012)
3. Abid, N., Dal Zilio, S., Le Botlan, D.: A formal framework to specify and verify real-time properties on critical systems. Int. J. Crit. Comput. Based Syst. **5**(1), 4–30 (2014)
4. Basu, A., Bozga, M., Sifakis, J.: Modeling heterogeneous real-time components in BIP. In: SEFM, pp. 3–12 (2006)
5. Bensalem, S., Bozga, M., Nguyen, T.-H., Sifakis, J.: D-Finder: a tool for compositional deadlock detection and verification. In: Bouajjani, A., Maler, O. (eds.) CAV 2009. LNCS, vol. 5643, pp. 614–619. Springer, Heidelberg (2009)
6. Berthomieu, B., Bodeveix, J.-P., Farail, P., Filali, M., Garavel, H., Gaufillet, P., Lang, F., Vernadat, F.: Fiacre: an intermediate language for model verification in the topcased environment. In: ERTS, HAL - CCSD, Toulouse (2008)
7. Berthomieu, B., Dal Zilio, S., Fronc, Ł.: Model-checking real-time properties of an aircraft landing gear system using fiacre. In: Boniol, F., Wiels, V., Ait Ameur, Y., Schewe, K.-D. (eds.) ABZ 2014. CCIS, vol. 433, pp. 110–125. Springer, Heidelberg (2014)
8. Berthomieu, B., Menasche, M.: An enumerative approach for analyzing time Petri nets. IFIP Congr. Ser. **9**, 41–46 (1983)
9. Berthomieu, B., Ribet, P.-O., Vernadat, F.: The tool TINA - construction of abstract state spaces for Petri nets and Time Petri. Int. J. Prod. Res. **42**(14), 2741–2756 (2004)
10. Berthomieu, B., Vernadat, F.: State Space Abstractions for Time Petri Nets. Handbook of Real-Time and Embedded Systems. CRC Press, Boca Raton (2007)

11. Bourdil, P.-A., Berthomieu, B., Jenn, E.: Model-checking real-time properties of an auto flight control system function. In: IEEE ISSREW (2014)
12. Boussinot, F., de Simone, R.: The ESTEREL Language. In: Proceeding of the IEEE, pp. 1293–1304, September 1991
13. Brat, G., Denney, E., Giannakopoulou, D., Frank, J., Jónsson, A.K.: Verification of autonomous systems for space applications. In: IEEE Aerospace Conference (2006)
14. Brugali, D.: Model-driven software engineering in robotics. IEEE Robot. Autom. Mag. **22**(3), 155–166 (2015)
15. Bruyninckx, H.: Open robot control software: the OROCOS project. In: IEEE International Conference on Robotics and Automation (2001)
16. Cimatti, A., Roveri, M., Bertoli, P.: Conformant planning via symbolic model checking and heuristic search. Artif. Intell. **159**, 127–206 (2004)
17. Dolginova, E., Lynch, N.: Safety verification for automated platoon maneuvers: a case study. In: Maler, O. (ed.) HART 1997. LNCS, vol. 1201, pp. 154–170. Springer, Heidelberg (1997)
18. Dwyer, M.B., Avrunin, G.S., Corbett, J.C.: Patterns in property specifications for finite-state verification. In: ICSE (1999)
19. Espiau, B., Kapellos, K., Jourdan, M.: Formal verification in robotics: why and how? In: Giralt, G., Hirzinge, G. (eds.) Robotics Research. Springer, London (1996)
20. Gobillot, N., Lesire, C., Doose, D.: A modeling framework for software architecture specification and validation. In: Brugali, D., Broenink, J.F., Kroeger, T., MacDonald, B.A. (eds.) SIMPAR 2014. LNCS, vol. 8810, pp. 303–314. Springer, Heidelberg (2014)
21. Hähnel, D., Burgard, W., Lakemeyer, G.: GOLEX—bridging the gap between logic (GOLOG) and a real robot. In: Herzog, O. (ed.) KI 1998. LNCS, vol. 1504, pp. 165–176. Springer, Heidelberg (1998)
22. Ingrand, F., Ghallab, M.: Deliberation for autonomous robots: a survey. Artif. Intell. 1–40 (2014). Elsevier
23. Ingrand, F., Lacroix, S., Lemai-Chenevier, S., Py, F.: Decisional autonomy of planctary rovers. J. Field Robot. **24**(7), 559–580 (2007)
24. Mallet, A., Pasteur, C., Herrb, M., Lemaignan, S., Ingrand, F.: GenoM3: building middleware-independent robotic components. In: IEEE ICRA (2010)
25. Maraninchi, F.: Operational and compositional semantics of synchronous automaton compositions. In: Cleaveland, W.R. (ed.) CONCUR 1992. LNCS, vol. 630, pp. 550–564. Springer, Heidelberg (1992)
26. Merlin, P.M., Farber, D.J.: Recoverability of communication protocols: implications of a theoretical study. IEEE Trans. Commun. **24**(9), 1036–1043 (1976)
27. Quigley, M., Gerkey, B., Conley, K., Faust, J., Foote, T., Leibs, J., Berger, E., Wheeler, R., Ng, A.Y.: ROS: an open-source Robot Operating System. In: IEEE ICRA (2009)
28. Rangra, S., Gaudin, E.: SDL to Fiacre translation. In: Embedded Real-Time Software and Systems, Toulouse (2014)
29. Simmons, R., Pecheur, C.: Automating model checking for autonomous systems. In: AAAI Spring Symposium on Real-Time Autonomous Systems (2000)
30. Simon, D., Joubert, A.: ORCCAD: towards an open robot controller computer aided design system. Technical report, Research report 1396, INRIA (1991)
31. Täubig, H.H., Frese, U., Hertzberg, C., Lüth, C., Mohr, S., Vorobev, E., Walter, D.: Guaranteeing functional safety: design for provability and comp uter-aided verification. Auton. Robots **32**(3), 303–331 (2011)
32. Wongpiromsarn, T., Murray, R.M.: Formal verification of an autonomous vehicle system. In: Conference on Decision and Control, May 2008

Decision Problems for Parametric Timed Automata

Étienne André[1,2(✉)], Didier Lime[1], and Olivier H. Roux[1]

[1] École Centrale de Nantes, IRCCyN, CNRS, UMR 6597, Nantes, France
eandre93430@lipn13.fr
[2] Université Paris 13, Sorbonne Paris Cité, LIPN, CNRS, UMR 7030,
Villetaneuse, France

Abstract. Parametric timed automata (PTAs) allow to reason on systems featuring concurrency and timing constraints making use of parameters. Most problems are undecidable for PTAs, including the parametric reachability emptiness problem, *i.e.*, whether at least one parameter valuation allows to reach some discrete state. In this paper, we first exhibit a subclass of PTAs (namely integer-points PTAs) with bounded rational-valued parameters for which the parametric reachability emptiness problem is decidable. Second, we present further results improving the boundary between decidability and undecidability for PTAs and their subclasses.

1 Introduction

Timed automata (TAs) [1] are a powerful formalism that extend finite-state automata with clocks (real-valued variables evolving linearly) that can be compared with integer constants in locations ("invariants") and along transitions ("guards"); additionally, some clocks can be reset to 0 along transitions. Many interesting problems for TAs (including the reachability of a location) are decidable. However, the classical definition of TAs is not tailored to verify systems only partially specified, especially when the value of some timing constants is not yet known.

Parametric timed automata (PTAs) [2] leverage this problem by allowing the specification and the verification of systems where some of the timing constants are parametric. PTAs extend TAs by allowing the use of integer- or rational-valued parameters in place of timing constants in guards and invariants. PTAs were used to verify a variety of case studies, from hardware circuits to communication protocols (see [3]). This expressive power comes at the price of the undecidability of most interesting problems. The EF-emptiness problem ("does there exist a parameter valuation such that a given location is reachable?") is

---

This work is partially supported by the ANR national research program "PACS" (ANR-14-CE28-0002).

K. Ogata et al. (Eds.): ICFEM 2016, LNCS 10009, pp. 400–416, 2016.
DOI: 10.1007/978-3-319-47846-3_25

undecidable in general [2], even when parameters are bounded [15], even when only strict inequalities are used [11], and with a single integer-valued parameter [8].

In [13], L/U-PTAs are introduced as a subclass of PTAs where each parameter is either always compared to a clock as a lower bound in guards and invariants, or always as an upper bound. The EF-emptiness problem is decidable for L/U-PTAs. In [10], further results are proved for L/U-PTAs with integer-valued parameters: emptiness, finiteness and universality of the set of parameter valuations for which there exists an infinite accepting run are decidable. The AF-emptiness problem ("does there exist a parameter valuation for which a given location is eventually reached for any run?") is undecidable for L/U-PTAs [14]. It is also shown in [14] that the synthesis of the parameters reaching a given location in an L/U-PTA is intractable in practice. Two further subclasses have been defined in [10]: L-PTAs and U-PTAs, where all parameters are always lower bounds and upper bounds respectively.

In [14], PTAs with bounded integer-valued parameters are considered. The problem of finding parameter valuations such that a given location is reachable or unavoidable becomes decidable, and two algorithms are provided that compute the exact such sets of integer valuations in a symbolic manner, *i.e.*, without performing an exhaustive enumeration. In [6], it is shown that computing a parametric extrapolation of the integer hull of symbolic states allows one to synthesize (rational-valued) parameter valuations for bounded PTAs, guaranteeing the synthesis of at least all integer-valued valuations, but also sometimes most or even all rational-valued valuations.

Contribution. L/U-PTAs is the only non-trivial[1] subclass of PTAs for which the EF-emptiness problem is decidable for an arbitrary number of clocks and parameters. However, other results are disappointing: undecidability of AF-emptiness, intractability of the synthesis [14]. It is hence important to look for further subclasses of PTAs for which problems may be decidable. It is shown in [6,14] that integer points play a key role in decidability. Hence, our first contribution here is to investigate integer-points PTAs (IP-PTAs), that are PTAs where each symbolic state contains at least one integer point (*i.e.*, an integer valuation of the clocks and the parameters). Our intuition is successful: we prove that the EF-emptiness problem is decidable for bounded IP-PTAs (*i.e.*, with a bounded parameter domain), even when parameters are rational-valued. Although we show that it cannot be decided whether a bounded PTA is a (bounded) IP-PTA, we give two sufficient syntactic conditions: we show that bounded L/U-PTAs with non-strict inequalities are IP-PTAs and, more interestingly, we introduce a new subclass of "reset-PTAs", that are also IP-PTAs, and for which, when bounded, the EF-emptiness problem is hence decidable too. This class is only the second syntactic subclass of PTAs (after L/U-PTAs) for which this problem is decidable.

---

[1] The bounded integer PTAs of [14] are arguably a trivial such subclass (even though the associated analysis techniques are not).

Our second main contribution is to study several open problems for PTAs and several known subclasses (as well as the new class of IP-PTAs): we study here the emptiness and universality of reachability (EF), as well as unavoidability emptiness (AF). Emptiness is of utmost importance as, without decidability of the emptiness, exact synthesis is practically ruled out. Universality checks whether all parameter valuations satisfy a property, which is important for applications where the designer has no power on some valuations; this is the case of networks, where some latencies (e.g., the transmission time of some packets) may be totally arbitrary. Among our results, we prove in particular that AF-emptiness is undecidable for both bounded IP-PTAs and bounded L/U-PTAs. Overall, we significantly enhance the knowledge we have of decidability problems for PTAs and subclasses.

Outline. We first recall the necessary definitions in Sect. 2. Then, we introduce in Sect. 3 a new proof for the undecidability of the EF-emptiness problem for PTAs with a single rational-valued parameter; whereas this result is not essentially new (it has been known since [15]), our original proof will be used in several other results of this paper. In addition, we extend this result (using a variant of our proof) to bounded PTAs with only non-strict inequalities which, to the best of our knowledge, is an original result. Then, we introduce the new class of IP-PTAs in Sect. 4, and study its properties. Finally, in part by using this new class, we prove in Sect. 5 several open results for L/U-PTAs and PTAs. We conclude in Sect. 6.

2 Preliminaries

2.1 Clocks, Parameters and Constraints

Let $\mathbb{N}$, $\mathbb{Z}$, $\mathbb{Q}_+$ and $\mathbb{R}_+$ denote the sets of non-negative integers, integers, non-negative rational numbers and non-negative real numbers respectively.

Throughout this paper, we assume a set $X = \{x_1, \ldots, x_H\}$ of *clocks*, i.e., real-valued variables that evolve at the same rate. A clock valuation is a function $w : X \to \mathbb{R}_+$. We identify a clock valuation w with the *point* $(w(x_1), \ldots, w(x_H))$. An integer clock valuation is a valuation $w : X \to \mathbb{N}$. We write $\mathbf{0}$ for the valuation that assigns 0 to each clock. Given $d \in \mathbb{R}_+$, $w + d$ denotes the valuation such that $(w + d)(x) = w(x) + d$, for all $x \in X$.

We assume a set $P = \{p_1, \ldots, p_M\}$ of *parameters*, i.e., unknown constants. A parameter *valuation* v is a function $v : P \to \mathbb{Q}_+$. We identify a valuation v with the *point* $(v(p_1), \ldots, v(p_M))$. An *integer* parameter (resp. clock) valuation is a valuation that assigns an integer value to each parameter (resp. clock).

In the following, we assume $\prec \in \{<, \leq\}$ and $\bowtie \in \{<, \leq, \geq, >\}$. *lt* denotes a linear term over $X \cup P$ of the form $\sum_{1 \leq i \leq H} \alpha_i x_i + \sum_{1 \leq j \leq M} \beta_j p_j + d$, with $x_i \in X$, $p_j \in P$, and $\alpha_i, \beta_j, d \in \mathbb{Z}$. *plt* denotes a parametric linear term over P, that is a linear term without clocks ($\alpha_i = 0$ for all i). A *constraint* C over $X \cup P$ is a conjunction of inequalities of the form $lt \bowtie 0$ (i.e., a convex polyhedron). Given a parameter valuation v, $v(C)$ denotes the constraint over X obtained by replacing each parameter p in C with $v(p)$. Likewise, given a clock valuation w, $w(v(C))$ denotes the expression obtained by replacing each clock x in $v(C)$ with $w(x)$. We say that v *satisfies* C, denoted by $v \models C$, if the set of clock valuations satisfying $v(C)$ is nonempty. Given a parameter valuation v and a clock valuation w, we denote by $w|v$ the valuation over $X \cup P$ such that for all clocks x, $w|v(x) = w(x)$ and for all parameters p, $w|v(p) = v(p)$. We use the notation $w|v \models C$ to indicate that $w(v(C))$ evaluates to true. We say that C is *satisfiable* if $\exists w, v$ s.t. $w|v \models C$. An *integer point* is $w|v$, where w is an integer clock valuation, and v is an integer parameter valuation. We define the *time elapsing* of C, denoted by $C^\nearrow$, as the constraint over X and P obtained from C by delaying all clocks by an arbitrary amount of time. Given $R \subseteq X$, we define the *reset* of C, denoted by $[C]_R$, as the constraint obtained from C by replacing with 0 the value of the clocks in R, and keeping the value of other clocks unchanged. We denote by $C\downarrow_P$ the projection of C onto P, i.e., obtained by eliminating the clock variables (*e. g.*, using the Fourier-Motzkin algorithm).

A *guard* g is a constraint over $X \cup P$ defined by inequalities of the form $x \bowtie z$, where z is either a parameter or a constant in $\mathbb{Z}$.

A *zone* is a polyhedron over a set of variables V (usually clocks) in which all constraints on variables are of the form $x \bowtie k$ (rectangular constraints) or $x_i - x_j \bowtie k$ (diagonal constraints), where $x_i \in V$, $x_j \in V$ and k is an integer. Operations on zones are well-documented (see *e. g.*, [9]).

A *parametric zone* is a convex polyhedron over $X \cup P$ in which all constraints on variables are of the form $x \bowtie plt$ (parametric rectangular constraints) or $x_i - x_j \bowtie plt$ (parametric diagonal constraints), where $x_i \in X$, $x_j \in X$ and plt is a parametric linear term over P.

2.2   Parametric Timed Automata

Definition 1. *A PTA $\mathcal{A}$ is a tuple $\mathcal{A} = (\Sigma, L, l_0, X, P, I, E)$, where: (i) Σ is a finite set of actions, (ii) L is a finite set of locations, (iii) $l_0 \in L$ is the initial location, (iv) X is a finite set of clocks, (v) P is a finite set of parameters, (vi) I is the invariant, assigning to every $l \in L$ a guard $I(l)$, (vii) E is a finite set of edges $e = (l, g, a, R, l')$ where $l, l' \in L$ are the source and target locations, $a \in \Sigma$, $R \subseteq X$ is a set of clocks to be reset, and g is a guard.*

We say that a PTA is *closed* if all its guards and invariants use only non-strict constraints. Note that the grammar of constraints does not include negation so this restriction is meaningful, and that $=$ defines closed constraints.

Given a parameter valuation v, we denote by $v(\mathcal{A})$ the non-parametric timed automaton where all occurrences of a parameter p_i have been replaced by $v(p_i)$.

Definition 2 (Concrete Semantics of a TA). *Given a PTA $\mathcal{A} = (\Sigma, L, l_0, X, P, I, E)$, and a parameter valuation v, the concrete semantics of $v(\mathcal{A})$ is given by the timed transition system $(S, s_0, \rightarrow)$, with*

$-\ S = \{(l, w) \in L \times \mathbb{R}_+^H \mid w|v \models I(l)\}$, $s_0 = (l_0, \mathbf{0})$

- $\rightarrow$ consists of the discrete and (continuous) delay transition relations:
  - discrete transitions: $(l, w) \xrightarrow{e} (l', w')$, if $(l, w), (l', w') \in S$, there exists $e = (l, g, a, R, l') \in E$, $\forall x \in X : w'(x) = 0$ if $x \in R$ and $w'(x) = w(x)$ otherwise, and $w|v \models g$.
  - delay transitions: $(l, w) \xrightarrow{d} (l, w + d)$, with $d \in \mathbb{R}_+$, if $\forall d' \in [0, d], (l, w + d') \in S$.

Moreover we write $(l, w) \xmapsto{e} (l', w')$ for a sequence of delay and discrete transitions where $((l, w), e, (l', w')) \in \mapsto$ if $\exists d, w'' : (l, w) \xrightarrow{d} (l, w'') \xrightarrow{e} (l', w')$.

Given a TA $v(\mathcal{A})$ with concrete semantics $(S, s_0, \rightarrow)$, we refer to the states of S as the *concrete states* of $v(\mathcal{A})$. A concrete run of $v(\mathcal{A})$ is an alternating sequence of concrete states of $v(\mathcal{A})$ and edges starting from the initial concrete state s_0 of the form $s_0 \xmapsto{e_0} s_1 \xmapsto{e_1} \cdots \xmapsto{e_{m-1}} s_m$, such that for all $i = 0, \ldots, m-1$, $e_i \in E$, and $(s_i, e_i, s_{i+1}) \in \mapsto$. Given a concrete state $s = (l, w)$, we say that s is reachable (or that $v(\mathcal{A})$ reaches s) if s belongs to a concrete run of $v(\mathcal{A})$. By extension, we say that l is reachable in $v(\mathcal{A})$.

Symbolic Semantics. Let us now recall the symbolic semantics of PTAs (see *e. g.*, [4]). A symbolic state is a pair (l, C) where $l \in L$ is a location, and C its associated parametric zone. The initial symbolic state of $\mathcal{A}$ is $\mathbf{s}_0 = (l_0, (\bigwedge_{1 \le i \le H} x_i = 0) \nearrow \wedge I(l_0))$.

The symbolic semantics relies on the Succ operation. Given a symbolic state $\mathbf{s} = (l, C)$ and an edge $e = (l, g, a, R, l')$, $\mathsf{Succ}(\mathbf{s}, e) = (l', C')$, with $C' = ([(C \wedge g)]_R \wedge I(l'))\nearrow \wedge I(l')..$

A symbolic run of a PTA is an alternating sequence of symbolic states and edges starting from the initial symbolic state, of the form $\mathbf{s}_0 \xRightarrow{e_0} \mathbf{s}_1 \xRightarrow{e_1} \cdots \xRightarrow{e_{m-1}} \mathbf{s}_m$, such that for all $i = 0, \ldots, m-1$, $e_i \in E$, and $\mathbf{s}_{i+1}$ belongs to $\mathsf{Succ}(\mathbf{s}_i, e)$. Given a symbolic state $\mathbf{s}$, we say that $\mathbf{s}$ is reachable if $\mathbf{s}$ belongs to a symbolic run of $\mathcal{A}$. In the following, we simply refer to symbolic states belonging to a run of $\mathcal{A}$ as symbolic states of $\mathcal{A}$.

2.3   Subclasses of PTAs

In this paper, we will sometimes consider *bounded* PTAs, *i.e.*, PTAs with a bounded parameter domain that assigns to each parameter a minimum integer bound and a maximum integer bound. That is, each parameter p_i ranges in an interval $[a_i, b_i]$, with $a_i, b_i \in \mathbb{N}$. Hence, a bounded parameter domain is a hyperrectangle of dimension M.

Let us now recall L/U-PTAs [10, 13].

Definition 3 (L/U-PTA [13]). *An L/U-PTA is a PTA where the set of parameters is partitioned into lower-bound parameters and upper-bound parameters. A lower- (resp. upper-)bound parameter is a parameter p that is used only in guards and invariants of the form $p \prec x$ (resp. $x \prec p$), where x is a clock.*

2.4   Decision Problems

Let $\mathcal{P}$ be a given a class of decision problems (reachability, unavoidability, etc.).

$\mathcal{P}$-emptiness problem:
INPUT: A PTA $\mathcal{A}$ and an instance ϕ of $\mathcal{P}$
PROBLEM: Is the set of parameter valuations v such that $v(\mathcal{A})$ satisfies ϕ empty?

$\mathcal{P}$-universality problem:
INPUT: A PTA $\mathcal{A}$ and an instance ϕ of $\mathcal{P}$
PROBLEM: Are all parameter valuations v such that $v(\mathcal{A})$ satisfies ϕ?

Emptiness is the most basic parametric question: is there at least one parameter valuation such that the property holds? Universality gives a robustness quality to the property and permits to effectively abstract an infinite number of verifications with concrete values.

In this paper, we mainly focus on reachability and unavoidability properties, and call them EF and AF respectively. For example, given a PTA $\mathcal{A}$ and a subset G of its locations, EF-universality asks: "are all parameter valuations v such that G is reachable in $v(\mathcal{A})$ from the initial state?" And AF-emptiness asks: "is the set of valuations v such that G is unavoidable in $v(\mathcal{A})$ empty?"

3   Undecidability of EF-Emptiness

Let us first recall the following classical result for PTAs.

Theorem 1 [15]. *The EF-emptiness problem is undecidable for bounded PTAs.*

We provide an alternative and original proof of this result. This new construction is similar to that of Miller [15], but it might be seen as a bit simpler and we will provide a complete proof. And above all, it allows us to extend it to obtain several of the main results of this paper.

Proof. We build a PTA that encodes a 2-counter machine (2CM) [16], such that the machine halts iff there exists some valuation of the parameters of the PTA such that it reaches a specific location.

Recall that such a machine has two non-negative counters C_1 and C_2, a finite number of states and a finite number of transitions, which can be of the form:

- when in state s_i, increment C_k and go to s_j;
- when in state s_i, decrement C_k and go to s_j;
- when in state s_i, if $C_k = 0$ then go to s_j, otherwise block.

The machine starts in state s_0 and halts when it reaches a particular state l_{halt}. The halting problem for 2-counter machines is undecidable [16].

Given such a machine $\mathcal{M}$, we now provide an encoding as a PTA $\mathcal{A}(\mathcal{M})$: each state s_i of the machine is encoded as a location of the automaton, which we also call s_i.

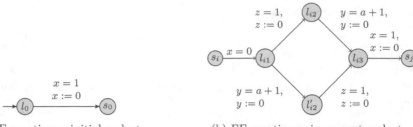

(a) EF-emptiness: initial gadget   (b) EF-emptiness: increment gadget

Fig. 1. EF-emptiness: gadgets

The counters are encoded using clocks x, y and z and one parameter a, with the following relations with the values c_1 and c_2 of counters C_1 and C_2: in any location s_i, when $x = 0$, we have $y = 1 - ac_1$ and $z = 1 - ac_2$. Note that all three clocks are parametric, i.e., are compared with a in some guard or invariant. We will see that a is a rational-valued bounded parameter, typically in $[0, 1]$. The main idea of our encoding is that, to correctly simulate the machine, the parameter must be sufficiently small to encode the maximum value of the counters, i.e., for $1 - ac_1$ and $1 - ac_2$ to stay non-negative all along the execution of the machine.

We initialize the clocks with the gadget in Fig. 1a. Clearly, when in s_0 with $x = 0$, we have $y = z = 1$, which indeed corresponds to counter values 0.

We now present the gadget encoding the increment instruction of C_1 in Fig. 1b. The transition from s_i to l_{i1} only serves to clearly indicate the entry in the increment gadget and is done in 0 time unit.

Since we use only equalities, there are really only two paths that go through the gadget: one going through l_{i2} and one through l'_{i2}. Let us begin with the former.

We start from some encoding configuration: $x = 0$, $y = 1 - ac_1$ and $z = 1 - ac_2$ in s_i (and therefore the same in l_{i1}). We can enter l_{i2} (after elapsing enough time) if $1 - ac_2 \leq 1$, i.e., $ac_2 \geq 0$, which implies that $a \geq 0$, and when entering l_{i2} we have $x = ac_2$, $y = 1 - ac_1 + ac_2$ and $z = 0$. Then we can enter l_{i3} if $1 - ac_1 + ac_2 \leq 1 + a$, i.e., $a(c_1 + 1) \geq ac_2$. When entering l_{i3}, we then have $x = a(c_1 + 1)$, $y = 0$ and $z = a(c_1 + 1) - ac_2$. Finally, we can go to s_j if $a(c_1 + 1) \leq 1$ and when entering s_j we have $x = 0$, $y = 1 - a(c_1 + 1)$ and $z = 1 - ac_2$, as expected.

We now examine the second path. We can enter l'_{i2} if $1 - ac_1 \leq a + 1$, i.e., $a(c_1 + 1) \geq 0$, and when entering l'_{i2} we have $x = a(c_1 + 1)$, $y = 0$ and $z = 1 - ac_2 + a(c_1 + 1)$. Then we can go to l_{i3} if $1 - ac_2 + a(c_1 + 1) \leq 1 + a$, i.e., $a(c_1 + 1) \leq ac_2$. When entering l_{i3}, we then have $x = ac_2$, $y = ac_2 - a(c_1 + 1)$ and $z = 0$. Finally, we can go to s_j if $ac_2 \leq 1$ and when entering s_j we have $x = 0$, $y = 1 - a(c_1 + 1)$ and $z = 1 - ac_2$, as expected.

Remark that exactly one path can be taken depending on the respective order of $c_1 + 1$ and c_2, except when both are equal or $a = 0$, in which cases both paths lead to the same configuration anyway.

Decrement is done similarly by replacing guards $y = a + 1$ with $y = 1$, and guards $x = 1$ and $z = 1$ with $x = a + 1$ and $z = a + 1$, respectively.

From s_i, to encode zero-testing C_1 and going to s_j, we only need to add a transition from s_i to s_j with guard $y = 1 \wedge x = 0$.

All those gadgets also work for C_2 by swapping y and z.

Finally, we add another location l'_{halt} and a transition from l_{halt} to l'_{halt} with guard $0 < x < 1$ and $x = a$. This implies the constraint $0 < a < 1$ when reaching l'_{halt}. This is important, in order to remove the $a = 0$ value, which does not encode the counters properly. (Note that we could also do this as early as the initialization gadget; however, it is convenient to leave it here for the subsequent proofs reusing this proof.) Removing the value $a = 1$, which would be possible if both counters are always 0, is not necessary but it will be useful in subsequent proofs.

Let us now prove that the machine halts iff there exists a parameter valuation p such that $p(\mathcal{A})$ can reach l'_{halt}. Consider two cases:

1. Either the machine halts, then the automaton can go into the l'_{halt} location, with constraints $0 < a < 1$ and, if c is the maximum value of both C_1 and C_2 over the (necessarily finite) halting run of the machine, and if $c > 0$, then $a \leq \frac{1}{c}$. The set of such valuations for a is certainly non-empty: $a = \frac{1}{2}$ belongs to it if $c = 0$ and $a = \frac{1}{c}$ does otherwise;
2. Or the machine does not halt. There are two subcases:
   (a) either the counters stay bounded. Let c be their maximal value. As before, if $c = 0$ and $0 < a \leq 1$ or $c > 0$ and $ca < 1$, then the machine is correctly encoded and the PTA cannot reach l'_{halt}. Otherwise, at some point during an incrementation of, say, C_1 we will have $a(c_1 + 1) > 1$ when taking the transition from l_{i2} to l_{i3} and the PTA will be blocked;
   (b) or one of the counters is not bounded, say C_1. Then whatever the value of $a > 0$, we have the same situation as in the previous item: the automaton blocks during some incrementation.
   In both subcases, the automaton cannot reach the l'_{halt} location and the set of parameters such that it does is obviously empty.

$\square$

Remark 1. We use guards with constraints $y = a+1$ while our definition of PTAs, following [2], only allows comparisons of a clock with a single parameter. Note however, and that will be true for all subsequent constructions, that transitions with $y = a + 1$ guards and $y := 0$ reset can be equivalently replaced by one transition with an $y = 1$ guard and a reset of some additional clock w, followed by a transition with a $w = a$ guard and the $y := 0$ reset (and similarly for x and z is the decrement gadget). This allows the proof to work without complex parametric expressions in guards and uses only one parametric clock and three normal clocks, with one parameter, matching the best known results with that respect [15].

Now, by reusing the previous proof, we can show that the EF-emptiness problem is undecidable for closed bounded PTAs. To the best of our knowledge, this is an original result, as all existing results with bounded PTAs (*e. g.,* [11, 15]) require strict inequalities.

Theorem 2. *The EF-emptiness problem is undecidable for closed bounded PTAs.*

4   Integer-Points Parametric Timed Automata

In this section, we introduce integer-points parametric timed automata (IP-PTAs for short), *i.e.*, a subclass of PTAs in which any symbolic state contains at least one integer point. Our first result is to prove the decidability of the EF-emptiness problem for bounded IP-PTAs (Sect. 4.1). Then, we compare IP-PTAs with L/U-PTAs and show that the class of bounded IP-PTAs is strictly larger than bounded L/U-PTAs with non-strict inequalities (Sect. 4.2). We then show that synthesis is intractable in practice, and that the same holds for bounded L/U-PTAs (Sect. 4.3). Finally, although we prove that the membership problem is undecidable for IP-PTAs, we exhibit a syntactic sufficient condition, that provides a new subclass of PTAs for which the EF-emptiness problem is decidable (Sect. 4.4).

Definition 4. *A PTA $\mathcal{A}$ is an* integer points PTA *(in short IP-PTA) if, in any reachable symbolic state (l, C) of $\mathcal{A}$, C contains at least one integer point.*

4.1   A Decidability Result for Bounded IP-PTAs

Our main positive result is that the EF-emptiness problem is decidable for bounded IP-PTAs.

Theorem 3. *The EF-emptiness problem is decidable (and PSPACE-complete) for bounded IP-PTAs.*

Proof. We first need to recall two lemmas relating symbolic and concrete runs (proved in [4,13]).

Given a concrete (respectively symbolic) run $(l_0, \mathbf{0}) \overset{e_0}{\mapsto} (l_1, w_1) \overset{e_1}{\mapsto} \cdots \overset{e_{m-1}}{\mapsto} (l_m, w_m)$ (respectively $(l_0, C_0) \overset{e_0}{\Rightarrow} (l_1, C_1) \overset{e_1}{\Rightarrow} \cdots \overset{e_{m-1}}{\Rightarrow} (l_m, C_m)$), we define the corresponding discrete sequence as $l_0 \overset{e_0}{\Rightarrow} l_1 \overset{e_1}{\Rightarrow} \cdots \overset{e_{m-1}}{\Rightarrow} l_m$. Two runs (concrete or symbolic) are said to be equivalent if their associated discrete sequences are equal.

Lemma 1. *Let $\mathcal{A}$ be a PTA, and v be a parameter valuation. Let ρ be a run of $\mathcal{A}$ reaching a symbolic state (l, C). Then, there exists an equivalent run in the TA $v(\mathcal{A})$ reaching a concrete state (l, w) (for some w) iff $v \models C{\downarrow_P}$.*

Lemma 2. *Let $\mathcal{A}$ be a PTA, and v be a parameter valuation. Let ρ be a run of the TA $v(\mathcal{A})$ reaching a concrete state (l, w). Then there exists an equivalent run in $\mathcal{A}$ reaching a symbolic state (l, C), for some C such that $v \models C{\downarrow_P}$.*

Let $\mathcal{A}$ be a bounded IP-PTA. EF-emptiness is false for $\mathcal{A}$ iff there exists a valuation v such that a run of $v(\mathcal{A})$ reaches a location in some predefined set G. Assume there exists a valuation v such that a run of $v(\mathcal{A})$ reaches l, with $l \in G$. From Lemma 2, there exists a symbolic run of $\mathcal{A}$ reaching a symbolic state (l, C), for some C. Since $\mathcal{A}$ is an IP-PTA, C contains at least one integer point. Hence there exists an integer parameter valuation $v' \models C{\downarrow}_P$; hence from Lemma 1, there exists a concrete run of $v'(\mathcal{A})$ reaching l. This gives that EF-emptiness is false for $\mathcal{A}$ iff there exists an integer valuation v' such that a run of $v'(\mathcal{A})$ reaches a location in G.

Hence, deciding whether some valuation permits to reach l reduces to deciding whether some *integer* valuation permits to do so, which, for bounded PTAs, is PSPACE-complete [14]. □

In practice, [14] proposes efficient symbolic algorithms to synthesize all the integer parameter valuations that permit to reach some given location, and thus to solve EF-emptiness for IP-PTAs.

4.2   Comparison with L/U-PTAs

Let us now compare IP-PTAs and L/U-PTAs. We first need the following lemma, stating that any reachable symbolic state of an L/U-PTA contains an integer parameter valuation.

Lemma 3. *Let (l, C) be a reachable symbolic state of an L/U-PTA. Then $C{\downarrow}_P$ contains at least one integer point.*

Proof. Consider a (non-empty) reachable symbolic state (l, C) of an L/U-PTA. Let $v \models C{\downarrow}_P$. From the well-known monotonicity property of L/U-PTAs (exhibited in [13]), any parameter valuation such that the lower-bound parameters p_i^- are lower or equal to $v(p_i^-)$ and upper-bound parameters p_j^+ are greater than or equal to $v(p_j^+)$ also belong to $C{\downarrow}_P$. In particular, this is the case of the integer parameter valuation assigning 0 to all lower-bound parameters, and assigning to upper-bound parameters p_j^+ the smallest integer greater than or equal to $v(p_j^+)$. □

The previous lemma that ensures the presence of an integer parameter valuation in any symbolic state does not guarantee that an L/U-PTA is an IP-PTA, because clocks may have non-integer values.

Proposition 1. *The class of IP-PTAs is incomparable with the class of L/U-PTAs.*

Proof

– Consider an L/U-PTA with a transition guarded by $x > 0$ and resetting no clock, followed by a second location with invariant $x < 1$; then, necessarily, the symbolic state associated with this second location contains no integer point (as $x \in (0, 1)$ in that symbolic state).

– It is easy to exhibit an IP-PTA that is not an L/U-PTA. This is for example the case of a simple PTA with only one location, one clock x and one parameter p with a self-loop with guard $x = p$ and resetting x.   □

However, we can prove that any *closed* L/U-PTA, *i.e.*, with only non-strict inequalities, is an IP-PTA. In order to show that the class of closed L/U-PTAs is included in IP-PTAs, we need the following lemma.

Lemma 4. *Let $\mathcal{A}$ be a PTA with only non-strict inequalities. Let $\mathbf{s} = (l, C)$ be a symbolic state of $\mathcal{A}$. Then if $C{\downarrow}_P$ contains at least one integer parameter valuation, then C contains an integer point.*

Proof. Since there is at least one integer parameter valuation v in $C{\downarrow}_P$, then $v(C)$ is not empty. Since v is an integer valuation, $v(C)$ is a zone of a timed automaton with integer constants, so the vertices of $v(C)$ are integer points. Finally, there is at least one vertex in $v(C)$ because all clocks are nonnegative (and hence are bounded from below by 0), and this vertex does belong to $v(C)$ because it is topologically closed due to the non-strict constraints. So C contains at least one integer point.   □

Proposition 2. *The class of IP-PTAs is strictly larger than the class of closed L/U-PTAs.*

Proof. From Lemmas 3 and 4, and Proposition 1 ($\Leftarrow$).   □

The previous result also holds for bounded PTAs:

Proposition 3. *The class of bounded IP-PTAs is strictly larger than the class of closed bounded L/U-PTAs.*

Proof. Lemma 3 extends to bounded L/U-PTAs, since the bounds are integers (this would not hold otherwise). Then, the proof of Proposition 1 ($\Leftarrow$) holds with bounded IP-PTAs and closed bounded L/U-PTAs. Applying Lemma 4 concludes the proof.   □

Proposition 4. *The class of bounded IP-PTAs is incomparable with the class of bounded L/U-PTAs. The class of bounded IP-PTAs is incomparable with the class of L/U-PTAs.*

Proof. The proof of Proposition 1 can be applied with bounded PTAs on either side.   □

Since bounded IP-PTAs are incomparable with L/U-PTAs (for which the EF-emptiness problem is known to be decidable), and since L/U-PTAs are the only non-trivial subclass of PTAs for which this problem is known to be decidable, then Theorem 3 strictly extends the subclass of PTAs for which this problem is decidable.

4.3   Intractability of the Synthesis

Although the EF-emptiness problem is decidable for L/U-PTAs [13], the synthesis seems to pose practical problems: it was shown in [14] that the solution to the EF-synthesis problem for L/U-automata, if it can be computed, cannot be represented using any formalism for which emptiness of the intersection with equality constraints is decidable. In particular, this rules out the possibility of computing the solution set as a finite union of polyhedra.

  We reuse the intuition of this result and extend it to closed bounded L/U-PTAs.

Theorem 4. *If it can be computed, the solution to the EF-synthesis problem for closed bounded L/U-automata cannot be represented using any formalism for which emptiness of the intersection with equality constraints is decidable.*

Proof. We reuse the idea of [10] used for proving that constrained emptiness for infinite runs acceptance properties is undecidable, and reused in [14, Theorem 2]. Suppose that the solution to the EF-synthesis problem for closed bounded L/U-PTAs can be represented using a formalism for which emptiness of the intersection with equality constraints is decidable. Assume a closed bounded PTA $\mathcal{A}$; for each parameter p_i of $\mathcal{A}$ that is used both as an upper bound and a lower bound, replace its occurrences as upper bounds by a fresh parameter p_i^u and its occurrences as lower bounds by a fresh parameter p_i^l. We therefore obtain a closed bounded L/U-PTA. Assume we can derive a solution to the EF-synthesis problem for this closed bounded L/U-PTA, and let K be that solution. Then, by hypothesis, we can decide whether $K \wedge \bigwedge_i p_i^l = p_i^u$ is empty or not; hence, we can solve the EF-emptiness for $\mathcal{A}$, which contradicts the undecidability of EF-emptiness for closed bounded PTAs (from Theorem 2). □

Corollary 1. *If it can be computed, the solution to the EF-synthesis problem for IP-PTAs cannot be represented using any formalism for which emptiness of the intersection with equality constraints is decidable.*

Proof. From the fact that a closed bounded L/U-PTA is an IP-PTA. □

4.4   Membership

We first show that it cannot be decided in general whether a PTA is a (bounded) IP-PTA.

Theorem 5. *It is undecidable whether a PTA is an IP-PTA, even when bounded.*

Proof. Let us consider the PTA $\mathcal{A}(\mathcal{M})$ encoding the 2-counter machine $\mathcal{M}$ proposed in our proof of Theorem 1. The PTA $\mathcal{A}(\mathcal{M})$ has only one parameter a and all the symbolic states of $\mathcal{A}(\mathcal{M})$ contain the integer value $a = 0$ except the states corresponding to the location l'_{halt}. Since all constraints are non-strict, except that of the transition leading to l'_{halt}, all reachable symbolic states, except those associated with l'_{halt}, contain an integer point. Then the PTA $\mathcal{A}(\mathcal{M})$ reaches the location l'_{halt} if and only if $\mathcal{A}(\mathcal{M})$ is not an IP-PTA. As a consequence, this PTA is an IP-PTA iff the 2-counter machine does not halt. Finally, note that this PTA can be bounded by $0 \leq a \leq 1$, without any change in the reasoning above.   □

Nevertheless, Proposition 2 provides a sufficient syntactic membership condition, since any closed L/U-PTA is an IP-PTA. In addition, we now define another new non-trivial set of restrictions leading to IP-PTAs:

Definition 5 (Reset-PTA). *A reset-PTA is a PTA where:*

- *all guards and invariants are conjunctions of constraints of the form $x \leq p+k$, $x \geq p+k$, $x \leq k$, or $x \geq k$, with x a clock, p a parameter, and k an integer;*
- *and all clocks are reset to 0 on any transition with a guard or a source location invariant in which a parameter appears.*

This kind of restriction is somewhat reminiscent of those enforced by *initialized* hybrid automata [12] to obtain decidability. We now prove that reset-PTAs are IP-PTAs, which in turn means that the EF-emptiness problem is decidable for bounded reset-PTAs. It is worth noting that, to the best our knowledge, bounded reset-PTAs and L/U-PTAs are the only non-trivial sets of syntactic restrictions of PTAs making the reachability emptiness problem decidable.

Theorem 6. *Any reset-PTA is an IP-PTA.*

Recall that the synthesis is intractable for bounded IP-PTAs (from Corollary 1) and for bounded L/U-PTAs. In contrast, and although studying reset-PTAs in detail goes beyond the scope of this work, we highly suspect that exact synthesis can be computed for reset-PTAs (see remarks in Sect. 6).

5   New (Un)decidability Results for PTAs

In this section, we take advantage of the newly introduced class of IP-PTAs to solve several open problems on the more general class of PTAs; these results allow us to draw a better cartography of several subclasses of PTAs.

5.1   Undecidability of EF-Universality

We show below that, unlike L/U-PTAs, the EF-universality problem is undecidable for IP-PTAs even bounded. This result differentiates the classes of (bounded) L/U-PTAs and bounded IP-PTAs, and helps to understand better the boundary between decidability and undecidability for subclasses of PTAs.

Theorem 7. *The EF-universality problem is undecidable for bounded IP-PTAs.*

Corollary 2. *The EF-universality problem is undecidable for IP-PTAs, for bounded PTAs, and for PTAs.*

Proof. From Theorem 7 and from the fact that a bounded IP-PTA is an IP-PTA, is a bounded PTA, and is a PTA.   □

5.2   Undecidability of AF-Emptiness

It is known that AF-emptiness is undecidable for L/U-PTAs [14]; reusing the encoding of the 2-counter machine proposed in our proof of Theorem 1, we now show that this result holds even for bounded L/U-PTAs.

Theorem 8. *The AF-emptiness problem is undecidable for bounded L/U-PTAs.*

Corollary 3. *The AF-emptiness problem is undecidable for bounded IP-PTAs, for IP-PTAs and for bounded PTAs.*

Proof. The AF-emptiness problem is undecidable for bounded L/U-PTAs (Theorem 8), which immediately gives the undecidability for bounded PTAs.

Furthermore, the PTA used in the proof of Theorem 8 only uses non-strict inequalities; furthermore, $a^- = 0$ and $a^+ = 1$ is a parameter valuation solution of any symbolic state. Hence, from Lemma 4, this PTA is a bounded IP-PTA, which gives the result for bounded IP-PTAs. As a consequence, the result also holds for general IP-PTAs.   □

5.3   Summary

Before being able to summarize our results in Table 1, we need to prove two further missing results.

Theorem 9. *The EF-emptiness problem is undecidable for IP-PTAs.*

Proof. The proof of the undecidability of the EF-emptiness problem for general PTAs in [2] can be interpreted over integer parameter valuations. Any symbolic state contains at least one integer parameter valuation (the one that is large enough to correctly encode the value of the two counters), as well as all larger parameter valuations. Furthermore, since the proof only uses non-strict inequalities (in fact only equalities), from Lemma 4, all symbolic states contain at least one integer point. Hence the PTA used in [2] to encode the 2-counter machine is an IP-PTA.   □

Finally, we show below (without surprise) that the EF-emptiness problem (shown to be decidable for L/U-PTAs [13]) and the EF-universality problem (shown to be decidable for integer-valued L/U-PTAs [10]) are also decidable for bounded L/U-PTAs.

Table 1. Decidability results for PTAs and some subclasses

Class	bL/U-PTAs	bIP-PTAs	L/U-PTAs	IP-PTAs	bPTAs	PTAs
EF-empt.	**Th. 10**	**Th. 3**	**[13]**	Th. 9	[15]	[2]
EF-univ.	**Th. 10**	Th. 7	**[10]**	Cor. 2	Cor. 2	Cor. 2
AF-empt.	Th. 8	Cor. 3	**[14]**	Cor. 3	Cor. 3	[14]

Theorem 10. *The EF-emptiness and EF-universality problems are decidable for bounded L/U-PTAs.*

Proof. In [10,13], it is shown that decreasing a lower-bound parameter p_i^- or increasing an upper-bound parameter p_j^+ in an L/U-PTA $\mathcal{A}$ can only add behaviors. Hence, deciding EF-emptiness can be done by testing the reachability of the location in the TA obtained from $\mathcal{A}$ by instantiating all p_i^-s with 0 and all p_j^+s with ∞. (Recall that testing the reachability of a location in a TA is decidable [1].) For a bounded L/U-PTA, this can be done in a similar manner, by testing the reachability of the location in the TA obtained from $\mathcal{A}$ by instantiating all p_i^-s with their minimal value and all p_j^+s with their maximal value in the (closed) bounded parameter domain.

EF-universality can be solved similarly, except that p_i^-s are replaced with their upper bound and p_j^+s are replaced with their lower bound.   □

We give a summary in Table 1. We give from left to right the (un)decidability for bounded L/U-PTAs, bounded IP-PTAs, L/U-PTAs, IP-PTAs, bounded PTAs, and PTAs. Decidability is given in bold green, whereas undecidability is given in thin red. Our contributions are depicted using a plain background, whereas existing results are depicted using a light background.

We give another summary in Fig. 2. Note that bounded L/U-PTAs and L/U-PTAs are in fact incomparable of terms of expressiveness [7]; they are therefore not included into each other in the figures. Decidability (resp. undecidability) is depicted in plain green (resp. dashed red); open problems are depicted in dotted black. Our contributions are depicted in thick.

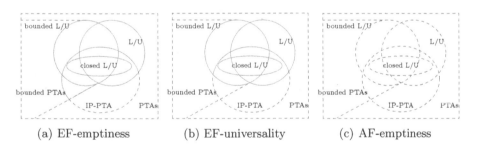

(a) EF-emptiness   (b) EF-universality   (c) AF-emptiness

Fig. 2. Decidability results for PTAs and subclasses (Color figure online)

6   Conclusion

In this paper, we exhibited a new subclass of PTAs (namely bounded IP-PTAs) for which the EF-emptiness problem is decidable. By showing that bounded IP-PTAs are incomparable with L/U-PTAs, we strictly extend the set of PTAs for which this problem is decidable. Although we showed that it cannot be decided whether a PTA is an IP-PTA, we introduced a new syntactic subclass of IP-PTAs, namely reset-PTAs, for which, when bounded, the EF-emptiness problem is decidable. It is worth noting that, to the best our knowledge, there is no other non-trivial set of syntactic restrictions making the reachability emptiness problem decidable for PTAs (aside from L/U-PTAs, of course).

In a second part, we considered three decision problems, and contributed in solving several open problems for PTAs and subclasses: this was achieved thanks to the results proved for IP-PTAs, and to (variations of) an original proof for the undecidability of the EF-emptiness problem for general PTAs with a single bounded rational-valued parameter and only non-strict constraints.

Future Works. Our new class of reset-PTAs seems promising in terms of synthesis, as the symbolic states have a very special form. Using a proper extrapolation, exact synthesis might be achievable. In addition, we are interested in extending this class to hybrid systems, and combining its restrictions with the condition of initialized hybrid automata [12]. The AF-universality problem is not treated in this paper, as it connects in an interesting manner with the problems of the existence of deadlocks or livelocks, which warrants a study on its own: in [5], we show in particular that the AF-universality problem is decidable for bounded L/U-PTAs with a closed parameter domain, and becomes undecidable if we lift either the assumption of boundedness or of closedness. Finally, all problems undecidable for L/U-PTAs remain open for L-PTAs and U-PTAs.

References

1. Alur, R., Dill, D.L.: A theory of timed automata. TCS **126**(2), 183–235 (1994)
2. Alur, R., Henzinger, T.A., Vardi, M.Y.: Parametric real-time reasoning. In: STOC, pp. 592–601. ACM (1993)
3. André, É.: What's decidable about parametric timed automata? In: Ölveczky, P.C., Artho, C. (eds.) Formal Techniques for Safety-Critical Systems. CCIS, vol. 596, pp. 1–17. Springer, Heidelberg (2015)
4. André, É., Chatain, T., Encrenaz, E., Fribourg, L.: An inverse method for parametric timed automata. IJFCS **20**(5), 819–836 (2009)
5. André, É., Lime, D.: Liveness in L/U-parametric timed automata (2016, submitted). https://hal.archives-ouvertes.fr/hal-01304232
6. André, É., Lime, D., Roux, O.H.: Integer-complete synthesis for bounded parametric timed automata. In: Bojanczyk, M., et al. (eds.) RP 2015. LNCS, vol. 9328, pp. 7–19. Springer, Heidelberg (2015). doi:10.1007/978-3-319-24537-9_2
7. André, É., Lime, D., Roux, O.H.: On the expressiveness of parametric timed automata. In: Fränzle, M., Markey, N. (eds.) FORMATS 2016. LNCS, vol. 9884, pp. 19–34. Springer, Heidelberg (2016). doi:10.1007/978-3-319-44878-7_2
8. Beneš, N., Bezděk, P., Larsen, K.G., Srba, J.: Language emptiness of continuous-time parametric timed automata. In: Halldórsson, M.M., Iwama, K., Kobayashi, N., Speckmann, B. (eds.) ICALP 2015. LNCS, vol. 9135, pp. 69–81. Springer, Heidelberg (2015)
9. Bengtsson, J.E., Yi, W.: Timed automata: semantics, algorithms and tools. In: Desel, J., Reisig, W., Rozenberg, G. (eds.) Lectures on Concurrency and Petri Nets. LNCS, vol. 3098, pp. 87–124. Springer, Heidelberg (2004)
10. Bozzelli, L., La Torre, S.: Decision problems for lower/upper bound parametric timed automata. Formal Methods Syst. Des. **35**(2), 121–151 (2009)

11. Doyen, L.: Robust parametric reachability for timed automata. Inf. Process. Lett. **102**(5), 208–213 (2007)
12. Henzinger, T., Kopke, P., Puri, A., Varaiya, P.: What's decidable about hybrid automata? J. Comput. Syst. Sci. **57**, 94–124 (1998)
13. Hune, T., Romijn, J., Stoelinga, M., Vaandrager, F.W.: Linear parametric model checking of timed automata. JLAP **52–53**, 183–220 (2002)
14. Jovanović, A., Lime, D., Roux, O.H.: Integer parameter synthesis for timed automata. Trans. Softw. Eng. **41**(5), 445–461 (2015)
15. Miller, J.S.: Decidability and complexity results for timed automata and semi-linear hybrid automata. In: Lynch, N.A., Krogh, B.H. (eds.) HSCC 2000. LNCS, vol. 1790, pp. 296–309. Springer, Heidelberg (2000)
16. Minsky, M.L.: Computation: Finite and Infinite Machines. Prentice-Hall Inc., Upper Saddle River (1967)

Verifying Nested Lock Priority Inheritance in RTEMS with Java Pathfinder

Saurabh Gadia[1], Cyrille Artho[2,3](✉), and Gedare Bloom[4]

[1] University of Southern California, Los Angeles, CA, USA
[2] National Institute of Advanced Industrial Science and Technology, Osaka, Japan
[3] KTH Royal Institute of Technology, Stockholm, Sweden
artho@kth.se
[4] Howard University, Washington DC, USA

Abstract. Scheduling and synchronization algorithms for uniprocessor real-time systems benefit from the rich theory of schedulability analysis, and yet translating these algorithms to practical implementations can be challenging. This paper presents a Java model of the priority inheritance protocol for mutual exclusion, as implemented in the RTEMS open-source real-time operating system. We verified this model using Java Pathfinder to detect potential data races, deadlocks, and priority inversions. JPF detected a known bug in the RTEMS implementation, which we modified along with the Java model. Verification of the modified model showed the absence of data races, deadlocks, and established nine protocol-specific correctness properties.

Keywords: Java Pathfinder · RTEMS · Priority inheritance

1 Introduction

Real-time application correctness depends on a bound on the amount of interference that high-priority tasks can cause to lower-priority tasks. When a high-priority task preempts the low-priority task and executes, the response time of the low-priority task is delayed by the preemption. Schedulability analysis considers the interference caused by such preemption: given a set of tasks, their execution times, job releases and deadlines, and priorities, one may calculate whether the tasks will be schedulable under a given scheduling algorithm. Two key assumptions made during schedulability analysis is that tasks are preemptable and do not share resources.

In case tasks share resources (e.g., shared memory) that require synchronization, the inclusion of critical sections complicates the schedulability analysis. The usual approach to create a critical section is with a semaphore or mutex lock, which leads to a priority inversion problem in which a low-priority task holding a lock interferes with any higher-priority tasks waiting on the lock, until the low-priority task eventually releases the lock. The usual assumption in real-time systems is that a lock holder can hold the lock no longer than its worst-case

© Springer International Publishing AG 2016
K. Ogata et al. (Eds.): ICFEM 2016, LNCS 10009, pp. 417–432, 2016.
DOI: 10.1007/978-3-319-47846-3_26

execution time, and therefore the lock is released eventually. However, if middle-priority tasks preempt and starve the low-priority task, the high-priority task may be blocked indefinitely since the low-priority task continues to hold the lock while the middle-priority tasks execute. Priority inversions are solved by using the priority inheritance protocol (PIP) or priority ceiling protocol (PCP) [15].

PIP works by promoting the priority of a lock holder to that of the highest-priority task waiting for the lock. Hence, when a task fails to acquire a lock, the lock holder will inherit the task's priority until the lock is released. PIP ensures that a middle-priority task cannot indefinitely block higher-priority tasks by starving low-priority lock holders. The lock holder's priority is restored to the previous value when releasing the lock. Although PIP works well for single lock acquire and release, some real-time applications require mutual exclusion for multiple resources at a time. Hence, multiple locks are acquired, one for each resource. We say these locks are *nested*. The proper implementation of PIP with nested resources requires that each time a lock is released, the lock holder's priority should be changed to that of the highest priority task still blocked on any lock held by the releasing task, or to the lock holder's normal priority, i.e., the priority it held when entering the outermost lock.

RTEMS is an open-source real-time operating system with an implementation of PIP. However, RTEMS implementation of the PIP for nested locks is incorrect. When a nested lock is obtained and priority is inherited, the task's current priority is saved. When the nested lock is released, the current priority is restored without checking what the highest priority is on the outer lock. Therefore, a task could be blocked on the outer lock with a higher-priority than the task that just released the inner lock, thus creating a priority inversion. Currently, this inversion is avoided by retaining the highest inherited priority until all locks are released, which has a different problem in that schedulability analysis needs to account for interference caused by all critical sections of any lower-priority tasks that may outer-nest a lock shared with a high priority task.

In this paper, we present our experience creating and model-checking a Java model of the locking and scheduling algorithms from the implementations in RTEMS relevant to PIP with nested resources. Our model detects priority inversion conditions via exhaustively searching through the lock and scheduler data structures. We passed the Java model through the Java Pathfinder (JPF) model checker [16] to detect potential deadlocks, data races, and priority inversions. After confirming the priority inversion in the existing RTEMS nested resource locking, we model-checked an alternative algorithm, which we then implemented in RTEMS. In our model analysis, we use intelligent pre-processing to reduce the size of the state space by a factor of 158, which made it possible to check the model repeatedly for different versions of our algorithm.

This paper is organized as follows: Sect. 2 provides the necessary background and shows related work. Section 3 shows how we modeled the relevant parts of the RTEMS kernel for verification with JPF. Section 4 shows the flaw we found in the adaption of PIP in RTEMS, and our fix. The final results of the verification with JPF are shown in Sects. 5 and 6 concludes.

2   Background

2.1   RTEMS

The Real-Time Executive for Multiprocessor Systems (RTEMS) [1] is an open-source real-time operating system (RTOS) that provides essential RTOS services with support for POSIX interfaces. RTEMS is used in particle accelerators, satellite instruments, medical devices, military systems, robotics, and other data acquisition and real-time control applications. RTEMS has been an open-source project since 1988 and is widely used in academic, government, and private sectors around the world.

2.2   Model Checking

Model checking is a technique to analyze a formal description of a system (the model) against all possible outcomes, starting from a given initial state. The system to be analyzed is usually represented by a transition system [4].

A *model checker* is a tool that verifies the model against given properties [4]. Traditionally, model checking has been used to verify hardware or protocols. Models are usually described in a domain-specific language, and properties are often expressed in temporal logics such as linear temporal logics [14]. Model checkers may explicitly construct the entire state space in memory [7] or use a symbolic representation of multiple states as a set of states [11].

2.3   Java Pathfinder

In contrast to traditional model checkers, *software model checkers* analyze an actual application (as source code or executable) code instead of a model [6,16].

Java Pathfinder (JPF) is such a software model checker. It implements a Java Virtual Machine (JVM) that is capable of executing the full bytecode instruction set [16], and is designed to explore the full state space of a Java bytecode application. Unlike in a traditional model checker, the state space is not known a priori. Instead, the state space is derived from the execution of the system under test (SUT). The SUT is executed by JPF until an action occurs in which the outcome under different thread schedules may vary. At that point, JPF stores a copy of the full program state comprising memory and thread states, and explores the next available choice. When a given choice leads to the end of program execution, it backtracks to an earlier program states by restoring that state from the saved copy. (JPF uses depth-first search by default; other search strategies are supported as well.) A state in JPF therefore corresponds to a full program state—with the heap and the states of each thread—and a transition corresponds to a sequence of instruction executions by a thread [16].

By default, JPF checks an execution against uncaught exceptions, assertion failures, and deadlocks. It also has a built-in data race detector, which allows a user to find problematic data accesses even if no property checking the output of the program has been written. This is useful because it is difficult to write properties checking the outcome of each operation that may be affected by shared memory access.

For our work, we chose Java Pathfinder because the input language (Java) is much closer to C than the input languages of other model checkers, such as Promela used by SPIN [7]. Furthermore, many locking features used by the RTEMS kernel have close equivalents in Java or JPF, which makes it easier to model RTEMS in JPF than on other platforms (see Sect. 3).

2.4   Related Work

Klein et al. verified a general-purpose operating system microkernel [8] that includes thread management and many other features. The kernel has been implemented in 10,000 lines of C code; properties were verified using a theorem prover with about 480,000 lines of Isabelle [13] proofs that were developed over ten years [8]. In contrast to that, the core of RTEMS is about 34,000 lines of C code, with the part implementing mutual exclusion weighing in at about 730 lines. Our model is about the size same as that part of the C code (600 lines of code for the model, 130 lines of code for the helper program that generates all test settings), and verification is fully automatic after we apply symmetry reduction to our environment model.

The idea of symmetry-based state space reduction is common [3]. Compared to previous work, we take a staged approach, where we first pre-process the parameters of the model to reduce the state space, and then use these parameters to generate different settings at run-time. Compared to "classical" model checking [4], where a model is expressed in a domain-specific language, we express our model in Java, which is richer than other modeling languages. Verification is performed using Java Pathfinder, which executes the model as program code and generates the state space by exploring different outcomes of non-determinism at run-time [16]. This is different from most other tools, where the state space is generated as a graph structure a priori [4].

Java Pathfinder is typically used to explore different interleavings in concurrent software, to analyze whether functional properties hold for all possible interleavings [16]. For applications written in Java, Java Pathfinder can determine the worst-case execution time (WCET) of a program by assigning a cost to each instruction, and calculating the maximal total cost [10]. This previous work was not applicable to estimate the worst-case execution time in the RTEMS kernel, as it would have required a complete model of the kernel in Java, together with accurate execution cost weights that reflect the true execution cost of the original RTEMS code on different platforms. Our work checks the correctness, but not WCET, of the priority inheritance protocol in RTEMS.

Lui Sha et al. discusses that synchronization primitives can lead to uncontrolled priority inversion problem [15]. They showed that two priority inheritance class protocols called basic priority inheritance protocol and priority ceiling protocol solved this priority inversion problem. This original publication does not explicitly mention the priority inversion problem caused in basic priority inheritance protocol if a task inheriting priority is owner of more than one mutex that we found in RTEMS. As a result, we cannot rule out that a direct application of that algorithm may have the same issue.

Linux makes use of data structure called plist—'priority sorted linked list'— for implementation of real time mutex design. Every task in Linux has pi_list data structure that stores all top waiters of the mutexes that are owned by the task. Whenever a task releases any mutex, it always ensures that its priority is set to the top priority waiting task in its pi_list. This way it rules out the problem of priority inversion in case of task owning multiple mutexes.

3   Modeling RTEMS Locks and Scheduling in Java

This section describes the Java model of locking in RTEMS [5].

3.1   Mapping RTEMS Kernel Constructs to JPF

The POSIX threads (Pthreads) standard is a widely used standardized interface that provides concurrency primitives, in particular locking, thread creation and control, and the use of condition variables and signaling [12]. Java has been designed to allow a virtual machine to implement the thread constructs in Java readily using Pthreads; each basic Java concurrency feature can be mapped to Pthreads [2].

Table 1. RTEMS kernel data structures and constructs in Java and JPF.

RTEMS resource	Java/JPF equivalent
Lock usage	`synchronized` block usage
Thread signaling	`wait` and `notify`
Priority queue	`java.util.PriorityQueue`
Global scheduler lock	`gov.nasa.jpf.vm.Verify.beginAtomic` and `endAtomic`

The RTEMS kernel also exhibits similarities to the Pthreads interface, and by extension Java concurrency features: see Table 1 for a high-level mapping. We employ nested locking and unlocking implemented in a straightforward way using `synchronized` blocks in Java; non-nested locking could be supported using extra libraries [9]. Thread signaling and condition variables use the same semantics as in POSIX. Furthermore, priority queues in the RTEMS kernel are modeled using priority queues from the Java base library.

For uniprocessor systems, RTEMS has a mechanism that temporarily disables the scheduler making a block of code behave atomically. Java has no direct construct for such scheduler disabling, and while a global lock can be used, it only guarantees mutual exclusion with respect to other global locks. Fortunately, Java Pathfinder has a construct that provides atomic sections: `Verify.beginAtomic` and `endAtomic`. These two functions are not available in standard Java.

Another modeling problem is that the Java scheduler does not obey thread priorities strictly, but thread priorities in RTEMS are strict, and a higher-priority thread is always scheduled before lower-priority threads. Although Java Pathfinder allows a user to provide a custom scheduler, which we could have used to model the RTEMS scheduler in addition to its locking implementation, we chose not to do so for two reasons. First, writing a custom scheduler in JPF is more difficult than writing a model in Java. Second, we wanted our lock model to be correct under any scheduler, not just under the current scheduler used by RTEMS.

3.2   Design of the Lock Model

We designed and implemented a Java model of the locking and scheduling algorithms of RTEMS so that JPF could be used to model check the current and alternative solutions for PIP. Our scheduler model uses a task control block (TCB) that inherits from the Java Thread Class and adds two priority fields, for the initial and current priority, and a linked list to track the mutex locks held by the thread.

To model mutex locks in Java we created a Lock class that uses Java's `synchronized` and JPF's `Verify.beginAtomic` and `Verify.endAtomic` to construct critical sections. The Lock class also adds a `validator` routine that executes on every mutex release to check whether there exists any priority inversion by iterating through all the remaining mutex locks held by the releasing thread checking that it has a higher priority than all threads waiting on any remaining mutexes it holds.

In the course of our work, we experimented with several variants of possible implementations of PIP:

1. A model using a global lock. Using a global lock facilitates a correct implementation at the expense of performance. We used this model to focus on correct thread priorities in an initial version of the model.
2. A uniprocessor model using a global scheduler lock (see above), which is derived from the first model.
3. A model using multiple fine-grained locks, allowing for more parallelism and thus better performance on a real system.

3.3   Test Harness

Java Pathfinder explores the state space of a program by starting from its `main` method, as in a normal execution under the Java VM. To analyze the implementation of a multi-threaded program, and our lock implementation in particular, we need a test harness.

Our test harness creates three threads with a given thread priority, each of which locks and unlocks two locks. Each lock is chosen from three distinct candidate locks.[1] We test reentrant locking by assigning the same candidate

---

[1] This design guarantees a certain degree of overlapping lock usage between threads, without which there would be no need for mutual exclusion.

```
public class TestThread extends RTEMSThread {
  Lock availableLocks[] = {createLock(0), createLock(1), createLock(2)};

  public TestThread(int idx[], int priority) {
    super(priority); // initialize thread with given priority
    locks = new Lock[idx.length];
    for (int i = 0; i < idx.length; i++) {
      locks[i] = availableLocks[idx[i]]; // use given locks permutation
    }
  }

  public void run() {
    for (int i = 0; i < idx.length; i++) {
      locks[i].lock();
    }
    for (int i = idx.length-1; i>= 0; i--) {
      locks[i].unlock();
    }
    assert currentPriority==realPriority;
  }
}
```

Fig. 1. Test thread using a given priority and nested locks.

lock to multiple slots in the same test thread. Each thread is also assigned a
priority chosen from three values, representing high, medium, and low priority.
We currently do not test non-nested locking and unlocking, which could however
be achieved by permuting the order of unlock operations (Fig. 1).

The test harness includes a main method that parses arguments from the
command line, which indicate the lock indices and thread priorities. Because
some types of cyclic deadlocks require three threads, we wanted to simulate at
least as many threads in our model. In doing, so, we ran into the state space
explosion problem: If each thread non-deterministically uses two locks (out of
three candidate locks), and a non-deterministic priority setting taken from three
possible values, we have a total of $(3^2)^3$(2 locks per thread) $* 3^3$(priorities) =
$3^9 = 19683$ combinations.

Encoding all these options as non-deterministic choices would be extremely
inefficient for the following reasons:

1. A lot of symmetries exist in the state space, some of which would not be
   recognized by JPF and explored redundantly.
2. Exploring the entire state space at once increases memory usage and may
   cause JPF to run out of memory or trigger garbage collection excessively
   often.
3. Debugging a failed test (from a faulty model) is more difficult because the
   error trace by JPF does not show the lock indices or thread priorities as such.
   They could be made visible in other ways, through listeners or printing them
   on the screen, but the latter option would print a lot of clutter during the
   state space exploration.

3.4   State Space Preprocessing

The full state space is too large to be explored by JPF if equivalent configurations are not taken into account. We present an algorithm to remove redundant lock set configurations, and show how the number of thread priority configurations can be minimized.

Lock Sets. We define A to be the alphabet of lock indices; in our case $A = 0, 1, 2$. A *lock set configuration* is a list of n elements, each being a sequence of m lock indices.

To reason about lock indices, we observe the following properties:

1. Locks are symbolic objects. Any configuration l' where all lock indices in l are replaced with a permutations of the indexes in A, yields a heap structure that is isomorphic to l. For example, $(00, 00, 01)$ and $(11, 11, 10)$ are isomorphic.
2. Between threads, permutations of lock index sequences are also isomorphic; e.g., $(00, 00, 01)$, $(00, 01, 00)$, and $(01, 00, 00)$ are isomorphic.

Algorithm 1 computes the set of all relevant lock permutations, based on these two observations. It starts by initializing the output sets F and B and generating all possible isomorphic mappings I. For three indices, six isomorphisms exist: $I = \{\{0 \rightarrow 0, 1 \rightarrow 1, 2 \rightarrow 2\}, \{0 \rightarrow 1, 1 \rightarrow 2, 2 \rightarrow 0\}, \ldots\}$. The algorithm reduces the set of all possible permutations C of lock indices, to topologically distinct ones.

Based on Property 1, the algorithm then proceeds to generate all morphisms M from C (step 4a). Property 2 allows us to ignore different permutations of lock index sequences between threads (step 4b); the sequences are filtered by sorting. For example, the sorted list of subsequences in $(12, 01, 00)$ is $(00, 01, 12)$. These two steps are sufficient to reduce the set of 729 lock permutations to only 31 truly distinct settings.

---

1. Let F be the set of final candidates, and B be the set of "bad" lock permutations that result in a deadlock.
2. Generate the set I of all isomorphic mapping functions (permutations of symbols identifying locks) $p_i \in I$ with $i_k = A \mapsto A$ for all lock indices in A.
3. Generate all lock permutations, called the *candidates* C.
4. For each candidate $c \in C$:
   (a) Generate all isomorphic variants M of c, for each permutation in I:
       $\forall iso \in I, M = M \cup iso(c)$.
   (b) For each isomorphic candidate $m \in M$, sort the lock index sequences of all threads: $S = \text{sorted}(M)$.
   (c) We add all items in S to F: $F = F \cup S$.
5. For each unique permutation $f \in F$, check if the lock indices form a cycle between all threads; if so, add that permutation to B: $\forall f \in F, B = B \cup f$ if cyclic(f).
6. Output the set of "good" candidates, $F \setminus B$, and "bad" candidates B.

Algorithm 1. Algorithm to compute all relevant lock permutations.

However, some lock set configurations contain a cyclic dependency between locks. For example, if thread t_1 owns lock a and tries to obtain lock b, and thread t_2 owns lock b and tries to obtain lock a, a deadlock occurs. The deadlock is due to the cyclic lock dependency between the threads. A test using such a configuration may deadlock, and if JPF is used, it will always find and report such a possibility. We can either ignore such cases or ensure that JPF actually detects a deadlock. To distinguish between "good" (deadlock-free) and "bad" (deadlocking) cases, we check the lock configuration for such cyclic dependencies (step 5 in Algorithm 1). This splits the set of 31 configurations into 25 deadlock-free and 6 deadlocking configurations (see Table 2).

Thread Priorities. We also consider the impact of different thread priorities on the outcome. As only the relative priority between all three threads matters, we consider only these four cases:

1. All threads have the same priority.
2. Two threads have the same priority, one has a lower priority than the others.
3. Two threads have the same priority, one has a higher priority than the others.
4. All threads have a different priority.

We implement this as a non-deterministic choice between four settings that reflect these cases, as opposed to a non-deterministic priority choice for each thread in isolation. This reduces the thread priority state space from $3^3 = 27$ settings to just four.

The combined state space reduction from both optimizations is from 19863 to $31 * 4 = 124$ configurations, a reduction of almost 160 times. The fact that configurations for Java Pathfinder can be parameterized on the command line makes it easy to generate the parameter state space with a preprocessor, and supply it to Java Pathfinder in a second phase.

3.5   Properties

By default, JPF reports a deadlock where the program cannot proceed with execution, such as when multiple threads have a cyclic lock dependency. It can also be configured to report data races. A data race exists if at least two threads access the same memory location without mutual exclusion, and at least one of these accesses is a write access. We used deadlock and data race detection along with model-specific properties in our verification.

Specific properties are encoded as assertions (safety properties) in our model [5], and cover the following:

Property 1. The priority of a thread waiting for a lock corresponds to its actual (original) priority.

Property 2. A thread is in the correct state when acquiring a new mutex.

Property 3. A newly acquired mutex is not held by another thread, and its lock count is zero.

Table 2. Model checking time, number of states, and number of instructions for all distinct scenarios. Lock usage is shown as a triple of sequences (of length two) of lock IDs. These IDs correspond to the two locks used by the test harness of each thread. Each lock configuration was tested for all relevant priority settings.

Deadlock-free configurations			
Lock configuration	Time	Number of states	Number of instructions
(00,00,00)	00:05:51	3,597,839	39,134,614
(00,00,01)	00:08:31	5,359,776	53,499,140
(00,00,10)	00:29:50	20,530,383	158,243,065
(00,00,11)	00:22:19	15,321,110	117,084,710
(00,00,12)	00:31:16	21,614,670	159,649,787
(00,01,01)	00:10:26	7,277,751	71,695,034
(00,01,02)	00:10:21	7,277,751	71,695,034
(00,01,11)	00:25:07	17,704,921	137,981,768
(00,01,12)	00:37:20	26,655,214	198,517,948
(00,01,20)	00:46:39	32,883,641	249,273,627
(00,01,21)	00:49:55	35,524,795	262,654,448
(00,01,22)	00:34:44	23,805,000	181,621,827
(00,10,10)	00:27:31	19,231,201	164,864,689
(00,10,12)	00:38:42	27,290,669	221,112,177
(00,10,20)	02:06:17	93,616,077	713,877,172
(00,10,21)	01:41:56	72,693,793	556,663,234
(00,10,22)	01:33:02	66,929,870	529,446,674
(00,11,22)	01:27:25	61,758,697	504,124,972
(00,12,12)	00:45:33	32,800,449	266,311,244
(01,01,01)	00:11:18	9,172,281	90,384,827
(01,01,02)	00:13:13	9,327,571	91,742,294
(01,01,12)	00:41:50	29,339,526	222,928,606
(01,01,20)	00:52:03	45,084,155	339,817,731
(01,01,21)	01:04:19	50,192,733	371,521,061
(01,02,12)	00:40:47	38,795,617	290,831,840
Deadlock-prone configurations			
Lock configuration	Time	Number of states	Number of instructions
(00,01,10)	00:00:01	8,486	270,677
(00,12,21)	00:00:01	8,486	270,677
(01,01,10)	00:00:01	8,486	271,022
(01,02,10)	00:01:37	940,738	7,995,738
(01,10,20)	00:02:21	1,402,381	11,219,277
(01,12,20)	00:03:22	2,062,672	16,476,034

Property 4. The lock count of a lock being released is greater than zero. After a lock is released, there is no holder registered anymore for it.

Property 5. If there is another thread waiting on a just-released lock, that thread must be in the waiting state.

Property 6. The thread releasing a lock must contain a matching lock entry at the head of the list maintained in that thread's TCB.

Property 7. The thread releasing a lock must not contain any higher-priority threads linked from the list of lock entries in the thread's TCB.

Property 8. The promotion of a thread's priority is caused by a different thread.

Property 9. The priority of a thread is correctly reverted to the original priority after all locks have been released.

4   Fixing PIP in RTEMS

Priority inversion occurs if a higher-priority task is blocked by a lower-priority task. Ideally, a higher-priority task should be blocked no longer than the time for the lower-priority task to complete its critical section. Lui Sha et al. demonstrated that practically this blocking period of higher-priority task can be arbitrarily long and unpredictable [15]. They showed that two priority inheritance class protocols, basic PIP and priority ceiling protocol, can rectify uncontrolled priority inversion. We extend basic PIP for the case when a task inheriting priority is the owner of more than one mutex, which we found in RTEMS, and we propose an algorithm to solve uncontrolled priority inversion problem in this case.

4.1   RTEMS Data Structures Involved in PIP

In RTEMS, associated with each mutex is a linked list *CORE_mutex_order_list*, which contains *priority_before*, a field to store the priority of the acquiring task. This field is used to restore the task's priority to what it was before acquiring that mutex, in case the priority of the task is temporarily increased due to the PIP. Each task control block (TCB) stores a last-in first-out (LIFO) linked list of acquired mutexes, which is the expected order of lock release. This is a doubly linked list, *Chain_Control*, consisting of nodes of type *Chain_Node* (see Fig. 2).

4.2   Uncontrolled Priority Inversion Problem for PIP in RTEMS

The following example demonstrates the uncontrolled priority inversion problem:

1. Consider three tasks T_0, T_1, and T_2 in descending order of priority with T_0 having highest priorities of 0 and T_2 having lowest priority of 2.
2. Initially, we only have task T_2 executing in our system. T_2 acquires mutex m_0 followed by m_1 to access some shared data structure. The linked list of mutexes in T_2's TCB contains m_0 and m_1 with associated priority 2 (Fig. 3).

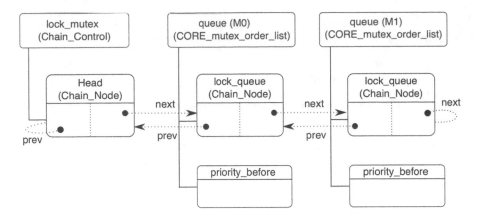

Fig. 2. Data structures linking the mutexes with the lock queues.

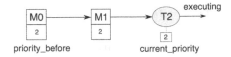

Fig. 3. Initial system state

3. Task T_0 is created and being a higher-priority task it preempts task T_2. T_0 attempts to acquire m_0 and hence the PIP will promote the priority of T_2 to be that of T_0, i.e., 0. This is the classic example of basic PIP rectifying priority inversion problem. This system state is free from priority inversion and deterministic as we are certain that task T_0 will be waiting till task T_2 releases m_0.

4. Another task T_1 is created, with medium priority. It will be in waiting state as task T_2 has the highest priority. When T_2 releases m_1, the priority stored in the mutex data structure for m_1 is written into the TCB of T_2, restoring T_2's priority to 2. Task T_1 preempts task T_2. We are now uncertain of blocking period of task T_0 (see Fig. 4) and thus the system is in uncontrolled priority inversion state.

Fig. 4. Uncontrolled priority inversion

4.3   Solution to Uncontrolled Priority Inversion

Avoiding uncontrolled priority inversion calls for more intelligence when restoring the priority of a task. Algorithm 2 imparts this intelligence when a task

```
1: function UPDATEPRIORITY(holder, queue, priority)
2:     // holder is the TCB for the owner of the mutex being acquired
3:     // queue is the CORE_mutex_order_list of the mutex
4:     // priority is the priority of the thread trying to acquire the mutex
5:
6:     head_node ← (&holder→lock_mutex)→Head
7:     next_node ← (&queue→lock_queue)→next
8:     change_priority ← True
9:     while next_node ≠ head_node do
10:        queue ← next_node→CORE_mutex_order_list
11:        if queue→priority_before ≤ priority then
12:            change_priority ← False
13:            Break
14:        end if
15:        queue→priority_before ← priority
16:        next_node = next_node→next
17:    end while
18:    return change_priority          ▷ if True, then holder thread priority is checked
19: end function
```

Algorithm 2. Algorithm for updating priority

attempts to acquire a busy mutex. Whenever a task attempts to acquire a busy mutex, this task may update the holder task's priority and the priorities of mutexes held by that holder. Updating the priority of holder is done as usual for PIP. The updates of the held mutexes occur by traversing the linked list of mutexes stored in the holder's TCB. If the recorded priority of a mutex is lower than the priority of the acquiring task, then the recorded priority is updated. The traversal stops at an equal or higher priority, or at the head of the list.

Applied to the above example, Algorithm 2 works as follows:

1. When task T_0 attempts to acquire mutex m_0, it traverses the acquired mutex list of holder task T_2. Traversal moves to the mutex next in the list from m_0, which is m_1, towards the head of the list. The recorded priority of m_1 is 2, lower than T_0's priority 0, so is changed to 0 before going to the next mutex in the list. The head of the list is reached, therefore the priority of T_2 is compared with that of T_0 and is boosted to 0, and the algorithm is finished. T_2 will resume executing at its new, higher priority (see Fig. 5).
2. When T_2 releases m_1, the priority stored in the mutex data structure for m_1 is written into the TCB of T_2, restoring T_2's priority to 0. At this point, task T_1 is waiting as T_2 still has the highest priority in the system. This way our algorithm ensures there is no priority inversion in the system (see Fig. 6).
3. Note that if T_2 was blocking on another mutex (see Fig. 7), it would be reblocked after potentially boosting priority of that mutex's owner through a transitive call to Algorithm 2. Hence, we always have a system which is free from priority inversion and in deterministic state.

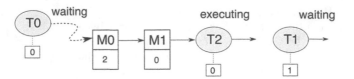

Fig. 5. Priority update as per proposed algorithm

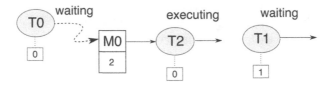

Fig. 6. Deterministic system with no priority inversion

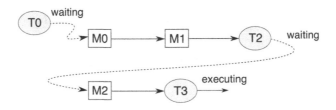

Fig. 7. Nested priority inversion

5   Model-Checking Results Using JPF

We used Java PathFinder version 8.0, rev. 28, to analyze the Java models of
RTEMS locking, after eliminating redundant configurations in the parameter
state space by preprocessing it (see Sect. 3). We ran the experiments on a Mac
Pro with two 3.7 GHz quad-core Intel Xeon E5 CPUs. This allowed us to use
multiple cores at once, speeding up the verification of 31 different lock set configurations. Table 2 shows the results of the experiments on the final, correct
version of the model.

In configurations that do not cause deadlocks, JPF has to explore the entire
state space of the model. Configurations with few locks preclude much possible
parallelism, and lock priority changes, in the behaviors. Their state space is
therefore much smaller than the state space of more complex settings. Because
of this, verification runs for a given lock set configuration ranges between barely
six minutes and over two hours; the number of explored program states, and
executed bytecode instructions, is proportional to the analysis time (see Table 2,
top). Deadlock-prone configurations have at least one possible interleaving that
leads to a deadlock due to a cyclic lock dependency. JPF sometimes finds such
a deadlock immediately and aborts the search after one second; in other cases
the search takes a few minutes, but still finds the bug after only a small fraction
of the state space has been searched (see Table 2, bottom).

The results of our experiments confirm that our revised implementation of PIP in the RTEMS kernel is free of data races, deadlocks, and incorrect priority assignments. Deadlock-prone lock usage of application-level tasks is also detected as expected. In total, verification of the improved PIP implementation took 11 h and 43 min of CPU time, which translated to about three hours of real time when running 5–6 instances in parallel on eight cores.

6 Conclusion

Despite the rich, robust theoretical frameworks that have been built around real-time scheduling, the correctness of scheduler design and implementation—especially with synchronization—is challenged by system complexity. In this paper, we have presented a Java model of a real-time operating system's PIP implementation that we model-checked in JPF to look for deadlocks, race conditions, and priority inversions, the latter by way of nine correctness properties that were encoded as assertions in the Java model. Key to the efficient model checking is the state space preprocessing of Algorithm 1, which reduces JPF's search space. JPF found a potential priority inversion, a correctness error, that was known to exist in the C language implementation. We further proposed a fix to the PIP implementation and validated it to be free of potential deadlocks, race conditions, and priority inversions. Future work may consider validating multi-core scheduling algorithms, which are even more complex and less well-understood than the established uniprocessor algorithms.

Acknowledgments. This material is based upon work supported by the Google Summer of Code program, the National Science Foundation under Grant No. CNS 0934725, and the Office of Naval Research under ONR Award No. N00014-14-1-0386. Any opinions, findings, and conclusions or recommendations expressed in this material are those of the authors and do not necessarily reflect the views of Google, NSF, or ONR.

References

1. RTEMS real time operating system (RTOS) (2016). https://www.rtems.org/
2. Artho, C., Hagiya, M., Leungwattanakit, W., Tanabe, Y., Yamamoto, M.: Model checking of concurrent algorithms: from Java to C. In: Hinchey, M., Kleinjohann, B., Kleinjohann, L., Lindsay, P.A., Rammig, F.J., Timmis, J., Wolf, M. (eds.) DIPES 2010. IFIP AICT, vol. 329, pp. 90–101. Springer, Heidelberg (2010)
3. Clarke, E., Enders, R., Filkorn, T., Jha, S.: Exploiting symmetry in temporal logic model checking. Form. Methods Syst. Des. 9(1), 77–104 (1996)
4. Clarke, E., Grumberg, O., Peled, D.: Model Checking. MIT Press, Cambridge (1999)
5. Gadhia, S., Artho, C., Ramirez, D.: Model locks with thread priority from RTEMS (2015). https://github.com/saurabhgadia4/lock-model
6. Henzinger, T.A., Jhala, R., Majumdar, R., Sutre, G.: Software verification with BLAST. In: Ball, T., Rajamani, S.K. (eds.) SPIN 2003. LNCS, vol. 2648, pp. 235–239. Springer, Heidelberg (2003)

7. Holzmann, G.: The SPIN Model Checker. Addison-Wesley, Reading (2004)
8. Klein, G., Andronick, J., Elphinstone, K., Murray, T., Sewell, T., Kolanski, R., Heiser, G.: Comprehensive formal verification of an OS microkernel. ACM Trans. Comput. Syst. **32**(1), 2:1–2:70 (2014)
9. Lea, D.: Concurrent Programming in Java, 2nd edn. Addison-Wesley, Reading (1999)
10. Lindstrom, G., Mehlitz, P.C., Visser, W.: Model checking real time Java using Java PathFinder. In: Peled, D.A., Tsay, Y.-K. (eds.) ATVA 2005. LNCS, vol. 3707, pp. 444–456. Springer, Heidelberg (2005)
11. McMillan, K.: Symbolic Model Checking. Springer, Heidelberg (1993)
12. Nichols, B., Buttlar, D., Farrell, J.: Pthreads Programming. O'Reilly, Beijing (1998)
13. Nipkow, T., Paulson, L.C., Wenzel, M.: Isabelle/HOL - A Proof Assistant for Higher-Order Logic. LNCS, vol. 2283. Springer, Heidelberg (2002)
14. Pnueli, A.: The temporal logic of programs. In: IEEE Proceedings of 17th Annual Symposium on Foundations of Computer Science (FOCS), Rhode Island, USA, pp. 46–57. IEEE Computer Society Press (1977)
15. Sha, L., Rajkumar, R., Lehoczky, J.P.: Priority inheritance protocols: an approach to real-time synchronization. IEEE Trans. Comput. **39**(9), 1175–1185 (1990)
16. Visser, W., Havelund, K., Brat, G., Park, S., Lerda, F.: Model checking programs. Autom. Softw. Eng. J. **10**(2), 203–232 (2003)

An SMT-Based Approach to the Formal Analysis of MARTE/CCSL

Min Zhang[1]($\boxtimes$), Frédéric Mallet[1,2,3], and Huibiao Zhu[1]

[1] Shanghai Key Laboratory of Trustworthy Computing, ECNU, Shanghai, China
{zhangmin,hbzhu}@sei.ecnu.edu.cn
[2] University of Nice Sophia Antipolis, I3S, UMR 7271 CNRS, Nice, France
Frederic.Mallet@unice.fr
[3] INRIA Sophia Antipolis Méditerranée, Valbonne, France

Abstract. MARTE (abbreviated for Modeling and Analysis of Real-Time and Embedded systems) is a UML profile which provides a general modeling framework to design and analyze real-time embedded systems. CCSL (abbreviated for Clock Constraint Specification Language) is a formal language companion to MARTE, used to specify the constraints between the occurrences of events in real-time embedded systems. Many approaches have been proposed to the formal analysis of CCSL such as simulation and model checking. We propose in this paper an SMT-based approach to the formal analysis of CCSL. It is well-known that the SMT-based approach can effectively overcome the state-explosion problem for model checking, and can also be used for theorem proving. The latter feature allows us to prove the invalidity of CCSL constraints, which most of the existing approaches lack. We implement the proposed approach in a prototype tool clyzer on top of $\mathbb{K}$ framework and use Z3 as the underlying SMT solver.

Keywords: MARTE/CCSL · SMT · Z3 · $\mathbb{K}$ framework, Model checking

1 Introduction

Logical clock, as defined by Lamport [9], gives a flexible abstraction to compare and order the occurrences of events, and is useful for the design of distributed systems and real-time embedded systems. In order to facilitate the design of real-time embedded systems, a general modeling framework MARTE [1] is proposed by extending UML. A time model has been adopted in MARTE to support different forms of time such as discrete, dense, chronometric or logical. Clock Constraint Specification Language (CCSL) is originally proposed as an annex of the MARTE specification to express constraints between clocks in MARTE models, and has evolved and been developed independently of the UML. Although it is still an

This research work was supported by National Natural Science Foundation of China (NSFC) projects: No. 61502171, No. 61361136002, and China HGJ Project: No. 2014ZX01038-101-001.

© Springer International Publishing AG 2016
K. Ogata et al. (Eds.): ICFEM 2016, LNCS 10009, pp. 433–449, 2016.
DOI: 10.1007/978-3-319-47846-3_27

open problem of checking the existence of schedules for a given set of CCSL constraints, it is desirable to perform formal analysis of CCSL constraints such as to simulate a schedule that satisfies all the constraints with certain policy and to verify if a given set of constraints satisfy some properties. Many efforts have been made in this direction, relying on the transformation into automata and other specific formats [11,14]. However, successive intermediate transformation is prone to introduce accidental complexity. In this paper, we propose an SMT-based approach to the formal analysis of CCSL constraints. In our approach, CCSL constraints are naturally transformed into SMT formulas. It is well-known that SMT-based approaches can effectively overcome the notorious state-explosion problem in model checking, and can also be used for theorem proving. The former feature helps improve the efficiency when CCSL constraints are verified by model checking. The latter one allows to prove the invalidity of CCSL constraints by means of theorem proving, which most of the existing approaches lack.

Among the properties of CCSL constraints, periodicity is a basic but important one with the fact that real-time embedded systems are inherently periodic and it is a crucial task of designing correct periodic schedules for such systems. Given a set of CCSL constraints, it is desired to know if there exists periodic schedules of a given set of CCSL constraints. In our earlier work [16], we proposed a sufficient condition to periodic scheduling of CCSL constraints, and a state-based approach to search all the schedules to find one that satisfies the condition. The approach is applicable when the number of schedules of the given constraints is reasonably small and the condition is satisfied at early step, but becomes less efficient otherwise due to state explosion. In this paper, we propose a less constraining sufficient condition and encode it into SMT formulas, with which we can find periodic schedules of given CCSL constraints by SMT solvers such as Z3 [12] and verify their properties by bounded model checking.

Execution trace analysis is another important application of CCSL constraints. In the scheme of MARTE/CCSL, execution trace analysis is an effective way to design and debug real-time embedded systems [5]. Execution traces are produced by instrumented code. Events in the generated traces are extracted and then analyzed to check if they satisfy initial constraint specification. One of the most challenging problems with execution trace analysis is to find an efficient way of checking if a trace satisfies the predefined constraints. We show the SMT-based approach to be proposed is also suited to execution trace analysis.

We implement a prototype tool using the K framework [13] for the transformation from CCSL constraints into SMT formulas and Z3 as its underlying SMT solver. K is a rewrite-based executable semantic framework in which programming languages, type systems and formal analysis tools can be defined. We choose Z3 because it also accepts and can work with formulas that use quantifiers. Although it is no longer a decision procedure for formulas with quantifiers in general, it is often able to handle formulas involving quantifiers. Thus, Z3 could return answers to some formulas with quantifiers that are transformed from CCSL constraints even if no bound is set.

In summary, the contributions of this paper are multifold:

1. An approach is proposed to transform CCSL constraints into SMT formulas for formal analysis of CCSL constraints. The transformation approach is straightforward and hence reduces both effort on the transformation and probability of introducing accidental complexity.
2. Applications of the SMT-based approach are demonstrated, including periodic scheduling and trace analysis by means of bounded model checking, and invalidity proving by means of theorem proving.
3. A prototype tool based on the approach is implemented, and experimental results show the feasibility of the proposed approach and the improvement of the efficiency for formal analysis of CCSL constraints.

The rest of this paper is organized as follows: Sect. 2 briefly introduces CCSL language and some existing work on its periodic scheduling; Sect. 3 presents the transformation approach from CCSL constraints to SMT formulas. Section 4 shows the applications of the SMT-based approach to invalidity proving, periodic scheduling, execution trace analysis, etc. Section 5 describes the prototype tool and some concrete examples. Section 6 compares our approach with other existing ones and Sect. 7 finally concludes the paper.

2   CCSL and Its Extension to Periodic Constraint

In CCSL, clocks are used to measure the occurrence time of events in a system. Each event is associated to a clock. Time is represented in a logical way as a sequence of discrete steps, instead of physical time. Thus, clocks are called logical clocks. The constraints between clocks can be interpreted as the relations between events, e.g., some event must occur earlier than another. Event relations are usually established at early design stage in the development of a real-time and embedded system.

Definition 1 (Logical clock). *A logic clock c is an infinite sequence of ticks $(c^i)_{i \in \mathbb{N}+}$, where each c^i can be tick or idle, representing that the event associated to c occurs or not at step i.*

In [11], clock relations are divided into two classes, i.e., CCSL constraints and clock definitions. There are four primitive constraint operators which are binary relations between clocks, and five kinds of clock definitions. The four constraint operators are called *precedence, causality, subclock* and *exclusion*; and the five clock definitions are called *union, intersection, infimum, supremum,* and *delay*. Besides, we introduce a new clock definition called *periodic filter*, which is used to define the periodicity between two clocks. The meanings of the ten primitive operators are given by *schedule* and *history*. Intuitively, a schedule is used to record the clocks that tick at each given step, and a history is used to record the number of ticks of each clock before it reaches a given step.

Definition 2 (Schedule). *Given a set C of clocks, a schedule of C is a total function $\delta : \mathbb{N}^+ \to 2^C$ such that for any i in $\mathbb{N}^+$, $\delta(i) = \{c | c \in C \wedge c^i = tick\}$ and $\delta(i) \neq \emptyset$.*

Intuitively, $\delta(i)$ is the subset of all the clocks in C which tick at step i. Note that we have the condition $\delta(i) \neq \emptyset$ in the definition of δ, which says that at any step there must be at least one clock ticking. The condition excludes from schedules those steps where no clocks tick. They are called *empty steps* which are trivial in that adding them to and removing them from a schedule do not affect the logical relations among the clocks. Thus, we exclude the empty steps from schedules.

Definition 3 (History). *Given a set C of clocks, and a schedule $\delta : \mathbb{N}^+ \to 2^C$, a history of δ over C is a function $\chi : C \times \mathbb{N}^+ \to \mathbb{N}$ such that for any clock $c \in C$ and $i \in \mathbb{N}$:*

$$\chi(c, i) = \begin{cases} 0 & \textit{if } i = 1 \\ \chi(c, i - 1) & \textit{if } i > 1 \wedge c \notin \delta(i - 1) \\ \chi(c, i - 1) + 1 & \textit{if } i > 1 \wedge c \in \delta(i - 1) \end{cases}$$

Obviously, $\chi(c, i)$ is the number of the ticks that clock c has ticked immediately before it reaches step i.

We use $\delta \models \phi$ to denote that schedule δ satisfies constraint ϕ. Figure 1 shows the definition of the satisfiability of a constraint ϕ with regards to a schedule δ. We take the definition of precedence for example. $\delta \models c_1 \prec c_2$ holds if and only if for any n in $\mathbb{N}^+$, c_2 must not tick at step n if the number of the ticks of c_1 is equal to the one of c_2 immediately before they reach step n. Precedence and causality are asynchronous constraints and they forbid clocks to tick depending on what has happened on other clocks in the earlier steps. Subclock and exclusion are synchronous constraints and they force clocks to tick or not depending on whether another clock ticks or not.

1. $\delta \models c_1 \prec c_2$	$\iff \forall n \in \mathbb{N}^+. \chi(c_2, n) = \chi(c_1, n) \Rightarrow c_2 \notin \delta(n)$	(Precedence)
2. $\delta \models c_1 \preceq c_2$	$\iff \forall n \in \mathbb{N}^+. \chi(c_1, n) \geq \chi(c_2, n)$	(Causality)
3. $\delta \models c_1 \subseteq c_2$	$\iff \forall n \in \mathbb{N}^+. c_1 \in \delta(n) \Rightarrow c_2 \in \delta(n)$	(Subclock)
4. $\delta \models c_1 \# c_2$	$\iff \forall n \in \mathbb{N}^+. c_1 \notin \delta(n) \vee c_2 \notin \delta(n)$	(Exclusion)
5. $\delta \models c_1 \triangleq c_2 + c_3$	$\iff \forall n \in \mathbb{N}^+. (c_1 \in \delta(n) \iff c_2 \in \delta(n) \vee c_3 \in \delta(n))$	(Union)
6. $\delta \models c_1 \triangleq c_2 \times c_3$	$\iff \forall n \in \mathbb{N}^+. (c_1 \in \delta(n) \iff c_2 \in \delta(n) \wedge c_3 \in \delta(n))$	(Intersection)
7. $\delta \models c_1 \triangleq c_2 \wedge c_3$	$\iff \forall n \in \mathbb{N}^+. \chi(c_1, n) = max(\chi(c_2, n), \chi(c_3, n))$	(Infimum)
8. $\delta \models c_1 \triangleq c_2 \vee c_3$	$\iff \forall n \in \mathbb{N}^+. \chi(c_1, n) = min(\chi(c_2, n), \chi(c_3, n))$	(Supremum)
9. $\delta \models c_1 \triangleq c_2 \$ d$	$\iff \forall n \in \mathbb{N}^+. \chi(c_1, n) = max(\chi(c_2, n) - d, 0)$	(Delay)
10. $\delta \models c_1 \triangleq p \bowtie c_2$	$\iff \forall n \in \mathbb{N}^+. c_1 \in \delta(n) \iff c_2 \in \delta(n) \wedge \exists m \in \mathbb{N}^+. \chi(c_2, n) = m * p$	(Periodicity)

Fig. 1. Definition of the 10 primitive CCSL operators

Clock definitions from 5 to 10 are used to define new clocks such that the clock c_1 at the left-hand side of "$\triangleq$" is uniquely determined by the clock(s) at the right-hand side. By union it defines a clock c_1 which ticks whenever c_2 or c_3 ticks, and by intersection it defines a clock c_1 which ticks whenever both c_2 and c_3 tick. Supremum is used to define the slowest clock c_1 which however is faster than both c_2 and c_3, and infimum is used to define the fastest clock c_1 which however is slower than both c_2 and c_3. By delay it defines the clock c_1 which is delayed by c_2 with d steps, and by periodicity it defines the clock c_1 which ticks once every after c_2 ticks p times.

Given a set Φ of CCSL constraints and definitions, we use $\delta \models \Phi$ to denote that the schedule δ satisfies all the constraints in Φ, and $\delta; k \models \Phi$ with $k \in \mathbb{N}^+$ to denote that δ satisfies all the constraints in Φ at step k. It is obvious that $\delta \models \Phi$ if and only if $\forall k \in \mathbb{N}^+.\delta; k \models \Phi$.

Definition 4 (Satisfiability problem of CCSL). *Given a set Φ of CCSL constraints, does there exist a schedule δ such that $\delta \models \Phi$?*

The satisfiability problem of CCSL is still open, and there has not been a decision procedure proposed to it so far. Nevertheless, the satisfiability problem of some subclass of CCSL constraints has been studied [11]. For instance, the satisfiability problem of CCSL constraints without operators $\prec$, $\wedge$, and $\vee$ is decidable. The CCSL operators except $\prec$, $\wedge$, and $\vee$ can be encoded as finite-state transition systems [11], and the satisfiability problem of a given subclass of CCSL constraints is transformed into the reachability problem of the synchronized product of finite-state transition systems, which is decidable. The three operators $\prec$, $\wedge$, and $\vee$ cannot be encoded as finite-state transition systems if no extra information such as counter is provided. They are called *unsafe* operators in [11] in that they may cause non-terminating of composing state transition systems. To solve the satisfiability problem of CCSL constraints with unsafe operators, we can set an upper bound to schedules in that we are only concerned with the schedules within a bounded step. In [16], we call them *bounded schedules*.

Definition 5 (Bounded schedule). *Given a set Φ of clock constraints on clocks in C, and a function $\delta : \mathbb{N}^+_{\leq n} \to 2^C$, δ is called an n-bounded schedule if for any $i \leq n$, $\delta; i \models \Phi$.*

In most of the cases, bounded schedule is too restrictive in practice for real-time systems, because real-time systems are assumed to run infinitely until they are shut down. We consider a special class of infinite schedules by which each clock ticks periodically from a pragmatic point of view. We call such schedules *periodic schedules*. Periodic schedules are useful in practice based on the fact that periodicity is one of the intrinsic features of real-time embedded systems.

Definition 6 (Periodic schedule). *A schedule δ is called periodic if there exist k, p in $\mathbb{N}^+$ such that for any $k' \geq k$, $\delta(k' + p) = \delta(k')$, and p is called a period of δ.*

Definition 6 means that after step k the schedule δ repeats every p steps. p is called the smallest period of δ if there does not exist p' in $\mathbb{N}^+$ such that p' is also a period of δ and $p' < p$.

It is also an open problem of deciding the existence of a periodic schedule for a given set of CCSL constraints. In [16] we proposed an approach to extend a bounded schedule to a periodic one and a sufficient condition under which the approach can be applied. We omit the extension approach here due to space limitation. Interested readers are referred to the work [16] for the details of the approach. In this paper, we propose a less constraining sufficient condition than the one in the work [16].

Theorem 1. *Given a bounded schedule* $\delta : \mathbb{N}^+_{\leq n} \to C$ *of a set* Φ *of* CCSL *constraints,* δ *can be extended to a periodic one if there exist two natural numbers* $k, k' \leq n$ *and* $k < k'$ *such that the following five conditions are satisfied:*

1. $\delta(k) = \delta(k')$;
2. *If* ϕ *is in form of* $c_1 \prec c_2$ *or* $c_1 \preccurlyeq c_2$, *then* $\chi(c_1, k') - \chi(c_1, k) \geq \chi(c_2, k') - \chi(c_2, k)$;
3. *If* ϕ *is in form of* $c_1 \triangleq c_2 \$ d$, *then* $\chi(c_2, k) \geq d$ *and* $\chi(c_1, k') - \chi(c_1, k) = \chi(c_2, k') - \chi(c_2, k)$;
4. *If* ϕ *is in form of* $c_3 \triangleq c_1 \wedge c_2$ *or* $c_3 \triangleq c_1 \vee c_2$, *then* $\chi(c_1, k') - \chi(c_1, k) = \chi(c_2, k') - \chi(c_2, k) = \chi(c_3, k') - \chi(c_3, k)$;
5. *If* ϕ *is in form of* $c_1 \triangleq p \bowtie c_2$, *then there exists* $m \in \mathbb{N}^+$ *such that* $(\chi(c_2, k') - \chi(c_2, k)) = m \times p$.

Intuitively, Condition 1 says that the clocks that tick at step k are the same as those at step k'; Condition 2 means from the step k to k', c_1 must tick faster than or at the same speed as c_2 if c_1 and c_2 satisfy precedence or causality; and Condition 3 says that for the constraint that a clock c_1 is delayed d steps by c_2 the number of ticks of c_2 immediately before step k must be greater than or equal to d and c_1 and c_2 must tick the same steps from step k to k'. Condition 4 requires that for the three clocks i.e. c_1, c_2 and c_3 that are constrained by infimum or supremum, they must tick the same number of ticks from step k to k'. The last condition says that between k and k' there must be m times p steps ticking of c_2.

The above conditions are less constrained than the ones in our earlier work [16] in that by the new conditions all the clocks do not necessarily need to tick the same number of ticks from step k to k', which is required by the conditions in the work [16]. With the new sufficient condition, we may find more periodic schedules for a given set of CCSL constraints. Theorem 1 can be proved by case analysis on CCSL constraints. We omit the proof in the paper due to space limitation.

3   Encoding CCSL Constraints into SMT Formulas

In this section we introduce an approach for encoding CCSL constraints and the sufficient condition of periodic scheduling proposed in Sect. 2 into SMT formulas.

The generated formulas may contain quantifiers, linear integer arithmetic and uninterpreted functions, and hence belongs to UFLIA (abbreviated for the linear fragment of theory of integer arithmetic with free sort and function symbols) logic according to SMT-LIB standard [2].

CCSL constraints can be straightforwardly encoded as SMT formulas. Given a set Φ of CCSL constraints on a set C of clocks, a schedule δ of Φ can be encoded by a finite set $\mathcal{T} = \{t_c : \mathbb{N}^+ \to \text{Bool} | c \in C\}$ of functions such that for any c in C and n in $\mathbb{N}^+$, $c \in \delta(n) \iff t_c(n)$. The functions in $\mathcal{T}$ are uninterpreted functions. Given a set Φ of CCSL constraints, finding a schedule of Φ is equal to giving interpretations to these uninterpreted functions.

We introduce another set $\mathcal{H} = \{h_c : \mathbb{N}^+ \to \mathbb{N} | c \in C\}$ of functions in order to encode CCSL constraints into SMT formulas. Each function in $\mathcal{H}$ takes a natural number n as its argument, and returns the number of steps that its associated clock has ticked immediately before the clock reaches step n. That is, for any c in C and n in $\mathbb{N}$, there is $h_c(n) = \chi(c, n)$. According to Definition 3, the functions in $\mathcal{H}$ must satisfy the following two formulas:

$$\bigwedge_{c \in C} h_c(1) = 0 \tag{F1}$$

$$\bigwedge_{c \in C} \forall n \in \mathbb{N}^+.(\neg t_c(n) \Rightarrow h_c(n+1) = h_c(n)) \land (t_c(n) \Rightarrow h_c(n+1) = h_c(n)+1) \tag{F2}$$

With $\mathcal{T}$ and $\mathcal{H}$, we replace $c \in \delta(n)$ by $t_c(n)$ and $\chi(c, n)$ by $h_c(n)$ in the definition of the ten primitive CCSL constraints in Fig. 1, and consequently obtain the ten corresponding formulas as shown in Fig. 2. Given a CCSL constraint ϕ, we denote its corresponding formula by $[\![\phi]\!]$.

According to Definition 2, a schedule must return a non-empty set of clocks at each step. Correspondingly, for each i in $\mathbb{N}^+$ there must exist at least one function t_c in $\mathcal{T}$ such that $t_c(i)$ is true. Thus, the functions in $\mathcal{T}$ must satisfy the following formula:

$$\forall n \in \mathbb{N}^+. \bigvee_{c \in C} t_c(n) \tag{F3}$$

1. $c_1 \prec c_2 \iff \forall n \in \mathbb{N}^+.h_{c_1}(n) = h_{c_2}(n) \Rightarrow \neg t_{c_2}(n)$ (Precedence)

2. $c_1 \preceq c_2 \iff \forall n \in \mathbb{N}^+.h_{c_1}(n) \geq h_{c_2}(n)$ (Causality)

3. $c_1 \subseteq c_2 \iff \forall n \in \mathbb{N}^+.t_{c_1}(n) \Rightarrow t_{c_2}(n)$ (Subclock)

4. $c_1 \# c_2 \iff \forall n \in \mathbb{N}^+.\neg(t_{c_1}(n) \land t_{c_2}(n))$ (Exclusion)

5. $c_1 \triangleq c_2 + c_3 \iff \forall n \in \mathbb{N}^+.t_{c_1}(n) \iff t_{c_2}(n) \lor t_{c_3}(n)$ (Union)

6. $c_1 \triangleq c_2 \times c_3 \iff \forall n \in \mathbb{N}^+.t_{c_1}(n) \iff t_{c_2}(n) \land t_{c_3}(n)$ (Intersection)

7. $c_1 \triangleq c_2 \land c_3 \iff \forall n \in \mathbb{N}^+.(h_{c_2}(n) \geq h_{c_3}(n) \Rightarrow h_{c_1}(n) = h_{c_2}(n)) \land (h_{c_2}(n) < h_{c_3}(n) \Rightarrow h_{c_1}(n) = h_{c_3}(n))$ (Infimum)

8. $c_1 \triangleq c_2 \lor c_3 \iff \forall n \in \mathbb{N}^+.(h_{c_2}(n) \geq h_{c_3}(n) \Rightarrow h_{c_1}(n) = h_{c_3}(n)) \land (h_{c_2}(n) < h_{c_3}(n) \Rightarrow h_{c_1}(n) = h_{c_2}(n))$ (Supremum)

9. $c_1 \triangleq c_2 \$ d \iff \forall n \in \mathbb{N}^+.(h_{c_2}(n) \geq d \Rightarrow h_{c_1}(n) = (h_{c_2}(n) - d)) \land (h_{c_2}(n) < d \Rightarrow (h_{c_1}(n) = 0))$ (Delay)

10. $c_1 \triangleq p \bowtie c_2 \iff \forall n \in \mathbb{N}^+.((t_{c_1}(n) \iff t_{c_2}(n)) \land h_{c_2}(n) \neq 0 \land h_{c_2}(n)\%p = 0)$ (Periodicity)

Fig. 2. Encoding CCSL constraints into SMT formulas

A set $\Phi = \{\phi_1, \ldots, \phi_m\}$ of m $(m > 0)$ CCSL constraints can be encoded as a set $\{\![\Phi]\!\}$ of SMT formulas such that $\{\![\Phi]\!\} \triangleq \{[\![\phi_1]\!], [\![\phi_2]\!], \ldots, [\![\phi_m]\!], F1, F2, F3\}$.

4 Applications of SMT-based Formal Analysis

The SMT formulas that are transformed from CCSL specifications contain uninterpreted functions and quantifiers. As there can be no decision procedure for first-order logic, we may not get an answer to the problem that whether there exists a model satisfying generated SMT formulas. Nevertheless, there are still multiple applications of the SMT-based approach to the formal analysis of CCSL specifications such as invalidity proving, periodic scheduling, bounded model checking and execution trace analysis.

4.1 Invalidity Proving

In the work [11], a set Φ of CCSL constraints is called *invalid* if there does not exist any schedule δ such that $\delta \models \Phi$. Namely, there does not exist a set $\mathcal{T}$ of functions such that $\mathcal{T}$ satisfies all the formulas in $\{\![\Phi]\!\}$, i.e., $\{\![\Phi]\!\}$ is not satisfiable. Consequently, we have the following proposition hold:

Proposition 1. *A set Φ of* CCSL *constraints is valid iff $\{\![\Phi]\!\}$ is satisfiable.*

By the above proposition, we can conclude that Φ is valid once we find a solution, i.e., a set $\mathcal{T}$ of functions, to the satisfiability problem of $\{\![\Phi]\!\}$. As mentioned in Sect. 3, the formulas in $\{\![\Phi]\!\}$ are in UFLIA logic and hence its satisfiability problem is undecidable. If an upper bound is set to the universally quantified variable n in each formula in $\{\![\Phi]\!\}$, the satisfiability problem becomes decidable because the quantifiers in the formulas can be eliminated. We denote the set of formulas in $\{\![\Phi]\!\}$ with a common upper bound u for each n in the formulas by $\{\![\Phi]\!\}_{\leq u}$. If $\{\![\Phi]\!\}_{\leq u}$ is unsatisfiable, by Proposition 1 we can immediately conclude that Φ must be invalid because the unsatisfiability of $\{\![\Phi]\!\}_{\leq u}$ implies that $\{\![\Phi]\!\}$ is also unsatisfiable.

Invalidity proving is also useful to prove automatically the derivation of a constraint ϕ from a set Φ of CCSL constraints.

Definition 7. *A constraint ϕ is derived from a set Φ of* CCSL *constraints if for any schedule δ, $\delta \models \Phi$ implies $\delta \models \phi$.*

Let $\mathcal{T}_\delta$ be the set of functions that represent δ. $\delta \models \Phi$ implies that $\mathcal{T}_\delta$ is a solution of $\{\![\Phi]\!\}$. By Definition 7, $\mathcal{T}_\delta$ must be a solution of $[\![\phi]\!]$ if ϕ can be derived from Φ. That is, for any solution of $\{\![\Phi]\!\}$, it must be a solution of $[\![\phi]\!]$. Namely, $\{\![\Phi]\!\} \implies [\![\phi]\!]$ is valid. Thus, we have the following proposition hold:

Proposition 2. *A constraint ϕ is derived from a set Φ of* CCSL *constraints if and only if $[\![\Phi]\!] \implies [\![\phi]\!]$ is valid.*

By Proposition 2, to prove the derivation of ϕ from Φ is equivalent to prove that the formula $\neg(\{\!\![\Phi]\!\!\} \implies [\![\phi]\!])$ is unsatisfiable, which generally is undecidable. However, we can assign a value to n, and check if $\neg(\{\!\![\Phi]\!\!\}_{\leq n} \implies [\![\phi]\!]_{\leq n})$ is unsatisfiable. We repeat until some n is found such that $\neg(\{\!\![\Phi]\!\!\}_{\leq n} \implies [\![\phi]\!]_{\leq n})$ is unsatisfiable or abort when n exceeds a predefined bound.

The aforementioned approach can be also applied to verification of CCSL constraints' properties that are expressed in temporal logic such as LTL and CTL. Let $\mathcal{P}$ be a property, and we use $\Phi \models \mathcal{P}$ to denote that the constraints in Φ satisfy $\mathcal{P}$, i.e., for any schedule that satisfies Φ, it must satisfy $\mathcal{P}$. We assume that a property $\mathcal{P}$ is encoded to be an SMT formula $[\![\mathcal{P}]\!]$. Then, to verify $\Phi \models \mathcal{P}$ is equivalent to prove that $\{\!\![\Phi]\!\!\} \cup \{\neg[\![\mathcal{P}]\!]\}$ is unsatisfiable. If $\{\!\![\Phi]\!\!\} \cup \{\neg[\![\mathcal{P}]\!]\}$ is proved to be satisfiable, a solution of it can be considered as a counterexample, i.e., a witness to the violation of $\mathcal{P}$ by Φ. Due to the undecidability of the problem, we may not be able to prove that $\{\!\![\Phi]\!\!\} \cup \{\neg[\![\mathcal{P}]\!]\}$ is unsatisfiable or find a solution using existing SMT solvers. If $\mathcal{P}$ is an invariant property, that is, a property stating that something bad should never happen [3], we can do bounded model checking of $\mathcal{P}$ by setting an upper bound to the number of steps. If a counterexample is found, $\mathcal{P}$ must not be satisfied by Φ. However, bounded model checking cannot be directly applied to liveness properties.

4.2 Verification of Periodic Scheduling

The SMT-based approach can be applied to formal analysis of periodic scheduling of CCSL constraints, such as the existence of periodic schedules and model checking of temporal properties of periodic schedules.

By Theorem 1, we can conclude there must be a periodic schedule of a given set Φ of CCSL constraints once we find two natural numbers k and k' ($k, k' \leq n$ and $k < k'$) for an n-bounded schedule of Φ such that k, k' satisfies the five sufficient conditions. The problem of finding k, k' is a satisfiability problem by transforming the five sufficient conditions into corresponding SMT formulas. We declare two free integer constants k, k'. As argued above, k, k' should satisfy the formula $k < k' \wedge k' \leq n \wedge k > 0$. The five conditions are transformed straightforwardly into SMT formulas as follow:

1. Condition 1 is equivalent to the following formula:

$$\bigwedge_{c \in C} t_c(k) \iff t_c(k') \tag{C1}$$

2. For each constraint in form of $c_1 \prec c_2$ or $c_1 \preccurlyeq c_2$:

$$h_{c_1}(k') - h_{c_1}(k) \geq h_{c_2}(k') - h_{c_2}(k) \tag{C2}$$

3. For each constraint in the form of $c_1 \triangleq c_2 \$ d$:

$$h_{c_2}(k) \geq d \wedge h_{c_1}(k') - h_{c_1}(k) = h_{c_2}(k') - h_{c_2}(k) \tag{C3}$$

4. For each constraint in form of $c_3 \triangleq c_1 \wedge c_2$, or $c_3 \triangleq c_1 \vee c_2$:

$$h_{c_1}(k') - h_{c_1}(k) = h_{c_2}(k') - h_{c_2}(k) \wedge h_{c_2}(k') - h_{c_2}(k) = h_{c_3}(k') - h_{c_3}(k) \text{(C4)}$$

5. For each constraint in form of $c_1 \triangleq p \bowtie c_2$:

$$(h_{c_2}(k') - h_{c_2}(k))\%p = 0 \tag{C5}$$

Let $\{\![\Phi]\!\}_p = \{\![\Phi]\!\} \cup \{C1, \ldots, C5\}$. If $\{\![\Phi]\!\}_p$ is satisfiable, there exists a periodic schedule for Φ. By existing SMT solvers we can find solutions to k and k' and n-bounded schedule of a given set of CCSL constraints, and then obtain the periodic schedule by extending the bounded schedule in the aforementioned way.

There can be more than one periodic schedule for a given set of CCSL constraints. We may need some specific properties which should be satisfied by the returned periodic schedule, e.g., a fixed period n. In that case, we only need to transform these properties into SMT formulas. For instance, the property of fixed period n can be expressed as $k' - k = n$. Another example is that all the clocks should tick infinitely often, which is a common requirement for real-time and embedded systems. The requirement can be encoded as the following formula:

$$\bigwedge_{c \in C} \exists i \in \mathbb{N}^+.t_c(i) \wedge \forall j \in \mathbb{N}^+.\exists j' \in \mathbb{N}^+.(j' > j) \wedge (t_c(j) \implies t_c(j'))$$

The formula says that for each clock c it much tick at some step i, and for any step j if c ticks at step j there must be a forthcoming step j' where c also ticks. For a periodic schedule, it suffices to define a formula $\bigwedge_{c \in C} \exists i \in \mathbb{N}^+.(k \leq i < k') \wedge t_c(i))$, which says that each clock c must tick at least once in a period. By specifying these specific constraints, we can obtain desired periodic schedules.

We can also verify if all the periodic schedules of a given set of CCSL constraints satisfy some desired properties by bounded model checking. For the periodicity, we can verify even liveness properties of periodic schedules. For some liveness properties, it suffices to verify if they are satisfied before the step k' where all the clocks start a new period. The approach to bounded model checking of a property with respect to periodic schedules is the same as the one described in the previous subsection.

4.3 Execution Trace Analysis

The proposed approach can be also used for execution trace analysis. An execution trace is a sequence of sets of events that occur each step. A trace is produced during the execution of real-time embedded systems by the code that is instrumented in the systems. Thus, each trace is finite in that the number of the steps that clocks tick is finite. A finite trace with length n is essentially an n-bounded schedule. A bounded schedule can be encoded as quantifier-free formulas. Given an n-bounded schedule δ on a set C of clocks, δ can be transformed into a quantifier-free formula as follows:

$$\bigwedge_{c \in C} \bigwedge_{i=1,\ldots,n} .t_c(i) = x \tag{F4}$$

where x is true if $c \in \delta(i)$, and false otherwise.

An execution trace is finite. Supposing that the length of a trace is n, it suffices to check if the corresponding schedule satisfies all the constraints in Φ in the first n steps. Namely, we only need to check the satisfiability of $\{[\Phi]\}_{\leq n} \cup \{F4\}$. All the formulas are quantifier-free and built over linear integer arithmetic, i.e., in QF_LIA logic. The satisfiability problem in QF_LIA logic is decidable. Thus, it is decidable to check if an execution trace satisfies a set Φ of CCSL constraints.

Listing 1.1. $\mathbb{K}$ definition of CCSL syntax of constraints

```
1 syntax ClockRel ::= Clock"<" Clock
2         | Clock"<="Clock
3         | Clock"->"Clock
4         | Clock"#" Clock
5         | Clock"=" Clock"+" Clock
6         | Clock"=" Clock"*" Clock
7         | Clock"=" Clock"/\"Clock
8         | Clock"=" Clock"\/"Clock
9         | Clock"=" Clock"$" Int
10        | Clock"=" Int  "~" Clock
```

Listing 1.2. $\mathbb{K}$ rule for translating causality without bound constraint

```
1 rule <k> ((C1 <= C2) => .) ... </k>
2 <bound> 0 </bound>
3 <consts>
4   (.List => ListItem(C1 <= C2)) ...
5 </consts>
6 <out> ...
7   (.List =>
8    ListItem(smtsPrettyPrint(assert(
9      causUnbd(C1,C2)))))
9 </out>
```

5 A Prototype Tool and Examples

In this section, we introduce a prototype analyzer of CCSL language which is developed based on the proposed approach and show some experimental results. All the experiments are conducted on a Linux desktop operating system (Ubuntu 16.04) with an Intel 8-Core CPU (i7-4790 model, 3.60 GHz) and 12 GB memory.

5.1 CCSL Analyzer: clyzer

We implement a prototype tool clyzer (abbreviated for CCSL analyzer) for the formal analysis of CCSL constraints. The tool consists of a translator for the transformation from CCSL constraints in SMT problems, and a backend SMT solver Z3.

The translator is implemented in the $\mathbb{K}$ framework. $\mathbb{K}$ is a rewrite-based executable semantic framework which is mainly used to formalize the operational semantics of programming languages, type systems and define formal analysis tools. By defining the operational semantics of a programming language such as C [6], $\mathbb{K}$ automatically generates an interpreter which can execute programs of the language, and also provides exhaustive state exploration and LTL model checking facilities to verify properties of programs [13]. In our earlier work [16], we have defined the operational semantics of CCSL using Maude [4], the backend language of $\mathbb{K}$. $\mathbb{K}$ also provides APIs to interact with Z3. These features allow us to develop in $\mathbb{K}$ an integrated environment for both the state-based approach and the SMT-based approach to the formal analysis of CCSL constraints, which is one piece of our future work.

At present, we use $\mathbb{K}$ only as a pretty-printer (translator) to print out an SMT script, which can be fed into Z3. In $\mathbb{K}$ the syntax of a programming language is naturally defined in a standard Backus-Naur Form (BNF), and the transformation is implemented by $\mathbb{K}$ rules. Listing 1.1 shows the $\mathbb{K}$ definition of CCSL syntax. The translation of CCSL constraints are defined in $\mathbb{K}$ as a state transition system. A state is represented as a labeled and potentially nested cell structure in XML style, which is called a *configuration*. A $\mathbb{K}$ rule specifies the information change of each cell. For instance, Listing 1.2 shows the $\mathbb{K}$ rule which formalizes the translation of a causality constraint, e.g., C1 <= C2 in the k cell, into a corresponding formula. Function smtsPrettyPrint prints out the formula as an SMT assertion that conforms to the syntax of SMT-LIB standard. The value in **bound** cell is 0, indicating that the variable in the generated formula is not bounded but universally quantified in $\mathbb{N}^+$.

Listing 1.3. The command that is used to prove $a \prec b$ implies $a \preccurlyeq b$

```
1 Clock a
2 Clock b
3 a < b
4 //prec.ccsl is a file for the code
5 clyzer -f prec.ccsl -b 10 -c a<=b
```

Listing 1.4. The command used to prove alternation implies exclusion

```
1 Clock a b c
2 a < b
3 c = a $ 1
4 b < c
5 clyzer -f alter.ccsl -b 7 -c a#b
```

5.2   Examples of Invalidity Proving

Mallet et al. proved that precedence is a stronger form of causality, i.e., for any two clocks a, b, $a \prec b$ implies $a \preccurlyeq b$ [11]. As an example, we show that it can be automatically proved in the proposed approach using Z3.

Listing 1.3 shows the code and command used to prove $a \prec b$ implies $a \preccurlyeq b$ in our tool clyzer. The tool clyzer takes a file where a set Φ of CCSL constraints are declared, an optional argument for bound, and a target CCSL constraint ϕ, which is going to be proved. In this example, it returns **unsat** with the above command, which means that $\neg(\llbracket a \prec b \rrbracket_{\leq 10} \implies \llbracket a \preccurlyeq b \rrbracket_{\leq 10})$ is unsatisfiable. By the argument in Sect. 4, we can conclude that precedence is a stronger form of causality. We need a bound e.g., 10, because the underlying SMT solver Z3 times out without outputting any result if no bound is given.

Another example is that alternation implies exclusion, i.e., if two clocks tick alternatively, then they must satisfy the exclusion constraint. Alternation can be represented by the combination of precedence and delay. For instance, if clock a alternates with clock b, it is represented as a set Φ_{alt} of constraints such that $\Phi_{alt} \triangleq \{a \prec b, c \triangleq a \$ 1, b \prec c\}$. We prove that Φ_{alt} implies $a \# b$ with the code and command shown in Listing 1.4. Z3 returns **unsat** if the bound is set to an odd number e.g., 7. If the bound is set an even number, e.g. 6, Z3 returns the following solution to the formula $\neg(\{\llbracket \Phi_{alt} \rrbracket\}_{\leq 6} \implies \llbracket a \# b \rrbracket_{\leq 6})$:

$$t_a(i) = \begin{cases} idle \text{ if } i \in \{2,4\} \\ tick \text{ if otherwise} \end{cases} t_b(i) = \begin{cases} tick \text{ if } i \in \{2,4,6\} \\ idle \text{ if otherwise} \end{cases} t_c(i) = \begin{cases} tick \text{ if } i \in \{3,5\} \\ idle \text{ if otherwise} \end{cases}.$$

By the solution, at step 6 clock a ticks but clock c idles, which violates the constraint $c \triangleq a \$ 1$ at step 7 where $\chi(a,7) = 4$ but $\chi(c,7) = 2$. However, by definition of the delay, we have $\chi(c, 7) = \chi(a, 7) - 1$, which is obviously violated by the solution. The reason for the spurious solution is that for some constraints such as delay, infimum and supremum, a clock depends on its ticking history to determine whether it should tick next step. Because of the bound, it is not required that all the constraints should be satisfied after the step exceeds the bound. Thus, the schedule may not be correct at the step which is equal to the bound. For instance, clock a should not tick at step 6, although it ticks according to the returned solution.

There are also cases when Z3 returns result even if no bound is given. For instance, we can prove that for any two clocks a and b if b is delayed by a with one step, a must precede b, i.e., $b \triangleq a \, \$ \, 1$ implies $a \prec b$. Z3 returns unsat even if no bound is given.

We finally show an example on the verification of temporal properties of CCSL constraints by bounded model checking. We verify that the constraints defined in Φ_{alt} satisfy *one-step alternation*, i.e., two clocks tick alternatively by a single step. One-step alternation can be represented as an LTL formula $\Box((tick(a) \implies \bigcirc tick(b)) \land (tick(b) \implies \bigcirc tick(b)) \land (tick(a) \oplus tick(b)))$, where $\Box$ and $\bigcirc$ are *globally* and *next* operators in LTL, and $tick$ is a parameterized state predicate which returns true in a state for a clock a if a ticks in that state and otherwise false. The LTL formula can be equivalently translated into the following formula in first-order logic:

$$\forall i \in \mathbb{N}^+.(t_a(i) \implies t_b(i+1)) \land (t_b(i) \implies t_a(i+1)) \land t_a(i) \oplus t_b(i) \quad (A1)$$

Similar to the proof of $a \, \# \, b$, Z3 returns unsat when the bound is set an odd number, and returns a spurious counterexample when the bound is an even number. The reason for the occurrence of spurious counterexample is the same as one for the occurrence of spurious solution. If no bound is given, Z3 times out without outputting any result.

5.3 Examples of Periodic Scheduling Analysis

We show in this section some applications of the proposed approach to the analysis of periodic scheduling. The first application is to check if there exists a periodic schedule for a given set of CCSL constraints. Let us consider the constraints in Φ_{alt}. We use the command clyzer -f alter.ccsl -p to find a periodic schedule for Φ_{alt}. However, Z3 cannot return any result and times out. We need to set a bound to make the problem decidable.

Table 1 shows the experimental results with different bounds. When the bound is less than or equal to 4, Z3 returns unsat which means that no periodic schedule is found. When the bound is set 5, a periodic schedule is returned with $i = 2$ and $j = 4$, that is, the period is 2. Table 1(b) shows the returned schedule, by which each clock starts to repeat step 2 and step 3 from step 4. By increasing the bound, the values of i and j are different, but the returned periodic schedule has the same period, as shown in Table 1(a). Actually, Z3 returns the same periodic schedule when the bound is set 5, 10 and 100 respectively.

Next, we show that the returned periodic schedule satisfies the one-step alternation property. As mentioned in Sect. 4, it suffices to verify the property is satisfied by a single period, e.g. from step 2 to 3. That is, the formula to be verified is that $\neg(\{\![\Phi_{alt}]\!\}_{\leq 5} \implies A1_{2 \leq i \leq 3})$, where $A1_{2 \leq i \leq 3}$ represents the formula A1 with the quantified variable i range from 2 to 3, instead of $\mathbb{N}^+$. Z3 returns unsat, which means the property is verified.

We finally consider a more complex set of CCSL constraints which are abstracted from an application for Flow Latency Analysis (FLA) on AADL (abbreviated for Architecture Analysis & Design Language) specifications [7]. Figure 4 shows the clocks and the constraints denoted by Φ_{fla} among them in the application. There are eight clocks, each of which is associated to an event. Clocks in_1 and in_2 stand for two inputs, based on which some calculations are performed at $step_1$ and $step_2$ respectively. At $step_3$ the calculation results are synthesized and the final result is output at out. Clocks tmp_1 and tmp_2 are two intermediate clocks which are used to represent the alternation constraint between $in_1 \vee in_2$ and out.

We try to find periodic schedules that satisfy the constraints in Φ_{fla}. Table 2 shows the returned results with different bounds. No periodic schedule is found in the first 4 steps. With the increase of the bound, different periodic schedules are found. Note that when the bound is set to 5 and 8, the same schedule is returned. It is obvious that for the periodicity a periodic schedule that satisfies the constraints within 5 steps must also satisfy within 8 steps. We can also give a specific period p so that the returned schedule must have the period p. A different schedule whose period is 3 is returned when the bound is set to 10. In particular, a schedule whose period is 31 is found when the bound is 100.

Table 1. Experimental results for periodic scheduling checking of Φ_{alt}

(a) The results with different bounds

Bound	i	j	Time (sec)
≤ 4	unsat		≤ 0.011
5	2	4	0.018
10	5	7	0.028
100	97	99	2.042

(b) The periodic schedule found with bound 5

Clock/Step	1	2	3	4	5
a	t	i	t	i	-
b	i	t	i	t	-
c	i	i	t	i	-

Fig. 3. Clocks and the constraints Φ_{fla} among them in the FLA example

Table 2. Experimental results for periodic scheduling checking of Φ_{fla}

Bound	i	j	Time (sec)
≤ 4	unsat		≤ 0.033
5	2	4	0.071
8	4	6	0.206
10	5	8	0.274
100	52	83	102.994
110	4	6	183.122

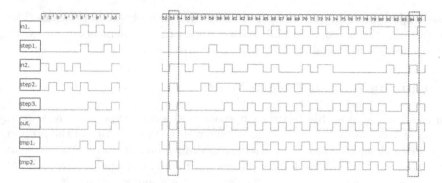

Fig. 4. The periodic schedule with period 31 found by clyzer

Figure 3 depicts the periodic schedule. The period is much longer than what we expected and is not founded by any other existing approaches.

6 Related Work

Many efforts have been made to the formal analysis of CCSL constraints and several approaches have been proposed. André defined the operational semantics of CCSL as a set of rewrite rules and built a simulation engine that can perform the clock calculus dynamically on the fly [10]. Gascon et al. proposed to encode CCSL specifications as Büchi automata and compare its expressiveness with temporal logic [8]. Yin et al. proposed to transform CCSL specifications into Promela and perform model checking using Spin [15]. In all of their approaches, only a safe subset of CCSL operators were taken into consideration, i.e., the underlying state space is finite. Mallet et al. proposed a state-based semantics of CCSL and encoded each constraint as a transition system [11]. However, some CCSL constraints such as precedence, supremum and infimum cannot be represented as a finite-state transition system, which may lead to non-termination of the synchronization of transition systems. Suryadevara et al. proposed to encode CCSL as timed automata and showed that clocks of CCSL were complementary to real-valued clocks of timed automata [14]. In our earlier work [16], we defined an executable semantics of CCSL in Maude and showed its applications to both simulation and model checking. The above-mentioned approaches can be used to boundedly model check those unsafe specifications by setting a bound to the steps that the clocks can proceed, which is similar to our SMT-based approach to bounded model checking.

Compared with the above existing approaches, the main advantage of the SMT-based approach proposed in this paper is that it is more suited to verifying the invalidity of CCSL constraints and finding bounded and periodic schedules even for unsafe CCSL constraints. Moreover, the direct interpretation of CCSL constraints as SMT formulas makes the transformation easier to implement than other state-based approaches. From the efficiency perspective SMT-based approaches are generally more efficient than state-based approaches. These features make the proposed SMT-based approach complementary to existing approaches to the formal analysis of CCSL constraints.

7   Conclusion and Future Work

We have proposed an SMT-based approach and a prototype tool clyzer to the formal analysis of CCSL constraints. We showed the applications of the proposed approach to invalidity proving, periodic scheduling, bounded model checking and trace analysis. Some examples were presented to demonstrate the feasibility and experimental results showed the efficiency of the proposed approach.

Based on the proposed approach, more work is required to do, e.g., how to guide the choice of bounds for a given example, how to translate CTL or LTL properties of CCSL constraints into SMT formulas for model checking, and how to detect whether a returned model is spurious. Besides, more complex case studies will be conducted to check the scalability of proposed approach.

References

1. André, C., Cuccuru, A., Dekeyser, J.L., et al.: MARTE: a new OMG profile RFP for the modeling and analysis of real-time embedded systems. In: Proceedings of the 2nd UML-SoC Workshop (2005)
2. Barrett, C., Fontaine, P., Tinelli, C.: The SMT-LIB standard (version 2.5) (2015)
3. Clarke, E.M., Grumberg, O., Peled, D.A.: Model Checking. MIT Press, Cambridge (2001)
4. Clavel, M., Durán, F., Eker, S., Lincoln, P., Martí-Oliet, N., Meseguer, J., Talcott, C. (eds.): All About Maude - A High-Performance Logical Framework: How to Specify, Program and Verify Systems in Rewriting Logic. LNCS, vol. 4350. Springer, Heidelberg (2007)
5. Ebeid, E., Fummi, F., Quaglia, D.: HDL code generation from UML/MARTE sequence diagrams for verification and synthesis. Des. Autom. Embed. Syst. **19**(3), 277–299 (2015)
6. Ellison, C., Roşu, G.: An executable formal semantics of C with applications. In: Proceedings of the 39th POPL, pp. 533–544. ACM (2012)
7. Feiler, P., Hansson, J.: Flow latency analysis with the architecture analysis and design language (AADL) (2007)
8. Gascon, R., Mallet, F., DeAntoni, J.: Logical time and temporal logics: comparing UML MARTE/CCSL and PSL. In: Proceedings of the 18th TIME, pp. 141–148. IEEE CS (2011)
9. Lamport, L.: Time, clocks, and the ordering of events in a distributed system. Commun. ACM **21**(7), 558–565 (1978)
10. Mallet, F., André, C.: On the semantics of UML/MARTE clock constraints. In: Proceedings of ISORC, pp. 305–312. IEEE CS (2009)
11. Mallet, F., de Simone, R.: Correctness issues on MARTE/CCSL constraints. Sci. Comput. Program. **106**, 78–92 (2015)
12. de Moura, L., Bjørner, N.S.: Z3: an efficient SMT solver. In: Ramakrishnan, C.R., Rehof, J. (eds.) TACAS 2008. LNCS, vol. 4963, pp. 337–340. Springer, Heidelberg (2008)

13. Roşu, G., Şerbănută, T.F.: An overview of the $\mathbb{K}$ semantic framework. J. Logic Algebraic Program. **79**(6), 397–434 (2010)
14. Suryadevara, J., Seceleanu, C., Mallet, F., Pettersson, P.: Verifying MARTE/CCSL mode behaviors using UPPAAL. In: Hierons, R.M., Merayo, M.G., Bravetti, M. (eds.) SEFM 2013. LNCS, vol. 8137, pp. 1–15. Springer, Heidelberg (2013)
15. Yin, L., Mallet, F., Liu, J.: Verification of MARTE/CCSL time requirements in Promela/SPIN. In: Proceedings of the 16th ICECCS, pp. 65–74. IEEE CS (2011)
16. Zhang, M., Mallet, F.: An executable semantics of clock constraint specification language and its applications. In: Artho, C., et al. (eds.) FTSCS 2015. CCIS, vol. 596, pp. 37–51. Springer, Heidelberg (2016). doi:10.1007/978-3-319-29510-7_2

Checking SysML Models for Co-simulation

Nuno Amálio[1]([⊠]), Richard Payne[2], Ana Cavalcanti[3], and Jim Woodcock[3]

[1] Birmingham City University, Birmingham, UK
nuno.amalio@gmail.com
[2] Newcastle University, Newcastle upon Tyne, UK
richard.payne@newcastle.ac.uk
[3] University of York, York, UK
{ana.cavalcanti,jim.woodcock}@york.ac.uk

Abstract. Cyber-physical systems (CPSs) are often treated modularly to tackle both complexity and heterogeneity; and their validation may be done modularly by *co-simulation*: the coupling of the individual subsystem simulations. This modular approach underlies the FMI standard. This paper presents an approach to verify both healthiness and well-formedness of an architectural design, expressed using a profile of SysML, as a prelude to FMI co-simulation. This checks the *conformity of component connectors* and the absence of *algebraic loops*, necessary for co-simulation convergence. Verification of these properties involves theorem proving and model-checking using: FRAGMENTA, a formal theory for representing typed visual models, with its mechanisation in the Isabelle/HOL proof assistant, and the CSP process algebra and its FDR3 model-checker. The paper's contributions lie in: a SysML profile for architectural modelling supporting multi-modelling and co-simulation; our approach to check the adequacy of a SysML model for co-simulation using theorem proving and model-checking; our verification and transformation workbench for typed visual models based on FRAGMENTA and Isabelle; an approach to detect algebraic loops using CSP and FDR3; and a comparison of approaches to the detection of algebraic loops.

Keywords: Co-simulation · FMI · CSP · SysML · Algebraic loops

1 Introduction

Cyber-physical systems (CPSs) are designed to actively engage with the physical world in which they reside. They tend to be heterogenous: their subsystems tackle a wide variety of domains (such as, mechanical, hydraulic, analogue and a plethora of software domains) that mix phenomena of both continuous and discrete nature, typical of physical and software systems, respectively.

CPSs are often handled modularly to tackle both heterogeneity and complexity. To effectively separate concerns, the global model of the system is decomposed into subsystems, each typically focussed on a particular phenomenon or domain and tackled by the most appropriate modelling technique. Simulation,

© Springer International Publishing AG 2016
K. Ogata et al. (Eds.): ICFEM 2016, LNCS 10009, pp. 450–465, 2016.
DOI: 10.1007/978-3-319-47846-3_28

the standard validation technique of CPSs, is often carried out modularly also, using co-simulation [18] – the coupling of subsystem simulations. This constitutes the backdrop of the industrial Functional Mockup Interface (FMI) standard [4,5] for co-simulation of components built using distinct modelling tools.

This paper presents an approach to formally verify the well-formedness and healthiness of SysML CPS architectural designs as a prelude to co-simulation. The designs are described using INTO-SysML [3], a profile for multi-modelling and FMI co-simulation. The well-formedness checks verify that designs comply with all the required constraints of the INTO-SysML meta-model; this includes *connector conformity*, which checks the adequacy of the connections between SysML blocks (denoting components) with respect to the types of the ports being wired. The healthiness checks concern detection of *algebraic loops*, a feedback loop resulting in instantaneous cyclic dependencies; this is relevant because a desirable property of co-simulation, which often reduces to coupling of simulators, is *convergence* – whether numerical simulations approximates the solution –, which is dependent on the structure of the subsystems and cannot be guaranteed if this structure contains algebraic loops [6,18]. The work presented here demonstrates the capabilities of our verification workbench for modelling languages and engineering theories, which rests on FRAGMENTA [2], a theory to formally represent designs of visual modelling languages, and its accompanying mechanisation in the Isabelle proof assistant [22], and the CSP process algebra [13] with its accompanying FDR3 refinement-checker [12].

Contributions. The paper's contributions are as follows:

- A novel SysML profile for architectural modelling of CPSs that tackles heterogeneity by providing support for multi-modelling and co-simulation in compliance with the FMI standard.
- An approach to statically check the adequacy of a SysML architectural model for co-simulation, supporting connector conformity and algebraic loops detection, by using a theorem prover and a model-checker.
- A prototyping environment for FRAGMENTA [3], a mathematical theory to represent typed visual models, based on the proof assistant Isabelle/HOL that enables model verification and transformation.
- A CSP-based solution to the detection of algebraic loops, which is based on a novel approach to represent graphs in CSP.
- An evaluation of approaches to the detection of algebraic loops.

Outline. The remainder of the paper gives some background on FRAGMENTA and CSP (Sect. 2). It presents our approach to represent architectural designs in INTO-SysML, highlighting verification of well-formedness (Sect. 3), and our approach for representing directed graphs in CSP and detecting algebraic loops through a FDR3 refinement check (Sect. 4). It evaluates our CSP-based approach (Sect. 5). Finally, the paper discusses its results (Sect. 6), compares them against related work (Sect. 7) and draws the conclusions (Sect. 8).

2   Background

We give some background on two main ingredients of the work presented here:
FRAGMENTA and CSP.

2.1   Fragmenta and Its Isabelle Mechanisation

FRAGMENTA [2] is a graph-based theory to represent modularised (or frag-
mented) typed class models. It is based on the algebraic theory of graphs and
their morphisms [8]. FRAGMENTA represents designs of visual modelling languages whose structure is defined by class metamodels – domain-specific languages (DSLs) – and their resulting instance models. Its overall models are a
collection of sub-models called *fragments*. Type and instance models are related
through morphisms. A major novelty lies in FRAGMENTA's *proxies* – representatives of other nodes. A fragment is as a graph that supports proxies.

Figure 1 portrays five fragments and one global fragment graph (GFG) from
INTO-SysML's metamodel. It highlights how fragments build up on other fragments either in a bottom-up (through imports) or top-down (through continues) fashion and the use of proxies for inter-fragment referencing. Importing
is bottom-up because the bigger fragments are built from smaller ones. Continuation is top-down because it starts by specifying a summary model (or a
skeleton) with points of continuation, represented as proxies, to be continued

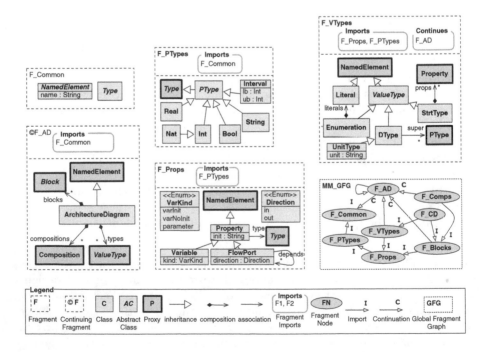

Fig. 1. Some fragments of metamodel of INTO-SysML.

by other fragments. Fragment F_PTypes is an increment to F_Common; node Type from F_Common is referenced through the proxy with same name; likewise in F_Props with proxy NamedElement. Fragment F_AD, which summarises metamodel of INTO-SysML architecture diagrams (ADs), is a continuing fragment; F_VTypes continues F_AD. The GFG (MM_GFG) describes the continues and imports relations between fragments.

FRAGMENTA proposes two composition operators: (a) union composition ($\cup_F$) merges fragments without resolving the proxies, and (b) colimit composition (based on category theory) joins fragments by resolving the proxies.

The theory introduces the following sets (see [2] for details):

- Fr, of well-formed fragments, requires that: (a) the underlying graph is well-formed, (b) the inheritance hierarchy is acyclic, (c) the source of composition relations has multiplicity 1 or 0 .. 1 and (d) proxies do not inherit[1]. All fragments in Fig. 1 are members of Fr.
- $GFGr$, of acyclic GFGs – MM_GFG (Fig. 1) $\in GFGr$.
- Mdl, of all well-formed models, requires that the model's fragments are disjoint. A model M is a tuple (GFG, fd), made up of a $GFG \in GFGr$ and a total function $fd : Ns_{GFG} \rightarrow Fr$ mapping GFG nodes to fragments. INTO-SysML's metamodel, partially described in Fig. 1, is a member of Mdl.
- $F_1 \rightarrow_F F_2$, of all well-formed fragment morphisms, which impose the required graph commuting constraints in the setting of fragments.
- $FrTy$, of well-formed typed fragments $FT = (F, TF, ty)$; F and TF are instance and type fragments, respectively: $F, TF \in Fr$, and $ty \in F \rightarrow_F TF$.
- $FrTyConf$, of conformant fragments, a subset of $FrTy$, imposes the following constraints on instances: abstract nodes may not have direct instances, containments are not shared, instance relations satisfy metamodel multiplicities, and instances of containments form a forest.
- $MdlTy$, of all well-formed typed models $MT = (M, TM, ty)$, where M and TM are instance and type models – $M, TM \in Mdl$ –, and the type morphism is conformant – $(UFs\ M, UFs\ TM, ty) \in FrTyConf$, where UFs makes a single fragment out of the union of model fragments.

FRAGMENTA's Isabelle mechanisation[2] provides a verification and transformation environment for metamodel designs. One can check that:

- The individual fragments of both model and metamodel are locally consistent and well-formed. For fragment F_Common of Fig. 1, for instance, we need to prove $\vdash F\_Common \in Fr$[3]; likewise for the remaining fragments.
- GFGs are well-formed also. For GFG of Fig. 1: $\vdash MM\_GFG \in GFGr$.
- Overall models and metamodels are also consistent and well-formed. For the metamodel $INTO\_SysML$ of Fig. 1: $\vdash INTO\_SysML \in Mdl$.
- Instance models conform to the constraints imposed by the type model.

Section 3 gives further details on INTO-SysML inside FRAGMENTA/Isabelle.

---

[1] A local check that ensures the compositionality of FRAGMENTA's union operator.

[2] Available at https://github.com/namalio/Fragmenta.

[3] Such membership predicates are represented in Isabelle as functions to booleans and they capture the well-formedness constraints associated with a FRAGMENTA set.

2.2   CSP and FDR3

The CSP process algebra [13] describes communicating processes and interaction-driven computations. CSP's major structuring concept, the process, represents a self-contained component made up of interfaces to enable interaction with a multitude of environments.

Processes communicate by transmitting information along channels. A CSP channel carries messages and has, therefore, a set of associated events, corresponding to all messages that may be transmitted. Process expressions are built using a number of operators, which include:

- Event prefixing, expressed as $e \rightarrow P$, describes a process that expects event e and then behaves as process P.
- External choice, $P_1 \,\square\, P_2$, gives the environment the choice of events offered by P_1 and P_2. Replicated external choice $\square \; i : \mathbb{N} \bullet P(i)$ composes the resulting processes using external choice.
- Internal choice, $P_1 \,\sqcap\, P_2$, non-deterministically chooses to act like P_1 or P_2.
- Parallel composition, $P_1 \parallel_{A} P_2$, executes the two processes in parallel synchronising on the set of events A.

FDR3 [12] is CSP's refinement checker. It checks refinement according to CSP's denotational models (including traces, failures and failures-divergences), and other properties, including deadlock- and livelock-freedom, and determinism.

3   Architectural Modelling in INTO-SysML

The Systems Modelling Language (SysML) [25] is a general-purpose notation for systems engineering that builds up on the Unified Modelling Language (UML). The INTO-SysML profile [3] customises SysML for architectural modelling in a setting of multi-modelling and FMI co-simulation. It embraces the many themes of the INTO-CPS project[4], namely, tool interoperability, heterogeneity, holistic modelling and co-simulation, and constitutes the gateway into modelling in the INTO-CPS approach.

The profile introduces specialisations of SysML blocks (known as stereotypes) to represent different types of CPS components, constituting the building blocks that enable a hierarchical description of the CPS architectures that we need. A component is a logical or conceptual unit of the system, corresponding to a software or a physical entity. The profile's component constructs comprise: System, EComponent (encapsulating component) and POComponent (part-of component). A system is decomposed into subsystems (represented as EComponents), which are further decomposed into POComponents. EComponents and POComponents may be further classified as Subsystem (a collection of inner components), Cyber (an atomic unit that inhabits the digital or logical world) or Physical (an atom

---

[4] The INTO-CPS project aims to create an integrated "tool chain" for comprehensive model-based design of CPSs. For further information, see http://into-cps.au.dk/.

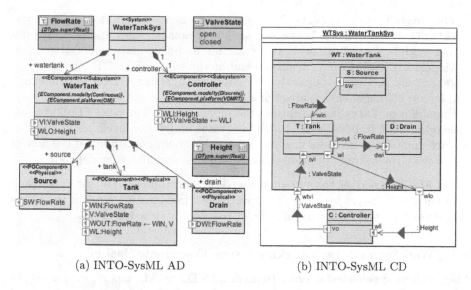

(a) INTO-SysML AD   (b) INTO-SysML CD

Fig. 2. The INTO-SysML model of the water tanks system

unit pertaining to the physical world). Furthermore, their characterising phenomena may be classified as `discrete` or `continuous`.

Currently, INTO-SysML comprises two diagram types: *architecture diagrams* (ADs) and *connections diagrams* (CDs), specialising SysML block definition and internal block definition diagrams, respectively. They are as follows (see Fig. 2):

- ADs (see Fig. 2a) describe a decomposition in terms of the types of system components and their relations. They emphasise multi-modelling: certain components encapsulate a model built using some modelling tool (such as VDM/RT [20], 20-sim [17] or Open Modelica [11]).
- CDs (see Fig. 2b) are AD instances. They convey the configuration of the system's components, highlighting flow and connectedness.

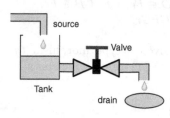

Fig. 3. Water tanks system.

The water tanks system, sketched in Fig. 3, is this paper's running example. A source of water fills a tank whose water outflow is controlled by a valve; when the valve is open the water flows into the drain. The valve, managed by a software controller, is opened or closed depending on the tank's water level. We also consider a variant of this system with the drain connected to the tank.

Figure 2 portrays the architectural model of water tanks, built using INTO-SysML's Modelio implementation[5]. The AD of Fig. 2a is as follows:

---

[5] Available from http://forge.modelio.org/projects/intocps-modelio34.

- The overall system (WaterTankSys) comprises two major subsystems, WaterTank and Controller, which are EComponents – they encapsulate separate models. WaterTank deals with continuous phenomena modelled in Open Modelica. Controller is discrete and modelled in VDM/RT.
- WaterTank has three physical sub-components: Source, Tank and Drain – they are POComponents (part-of of a subsystem).
- Enumeration ValveState captures the valve's state. Unit types FlowRate and Height, built from reals, deal with flow rates and water levels.
- Each component provides flow ports to enable communication and the flow of material; the outputs indicate the inputs ports on which they depend.

CD of Fig. 2b describes the system instance (WTSys) composed of one WaterTank (WT) with its sub-components. The Controller instance (C) receives the water height from WT and, in return, directs WT to open or close the valve.

3.1   Well-Formedness Checking Using Fragmenta/Isabelle

Many things are checked in order to deem a INTO-SysML model, such as one of Fig. 2, consistent, well-formed and type conformant. Such checks are performed on the FRAGMENTA typed representation illustrated in Fig. 4. Figure 4b gives the FRAGMENTA representation of CD in Figs. 2b and 4a is the metamodel of INTO-SysML CDs; the correspondence from CD to metamodel, entailed by the type morphism, is represented as labels with numbers. In Fig. 4b, the proxies reference elements from the AD of Fig. 2a, nodes labelled 4 correspond to the connectors of the CD, and those labelled 5 correspond to ports.

From the FRAGMENTA base sets of Sect. 2.1, we build a set of well-formed INTO-SysML models $INTO\_Mdls$, catering for all profile-specific invariants. The AD invariants are: (i) there is one system block, (ii) EComponents are not nested, and (iii) POComponents are contained by EComponents. The CD invariants are: (iv) instance ports are correctly typed with respect to AD flow ports, (v) connection's flow types correspond to types consistent with the ports being connected (conformity of connectors), and (vi) the CD satisfies multiplicities imposed by AD.

The model of Fig. 2, referred as M_WTs, is subject to the following checks:

- Fragments of AD and CD are well-formed: $\vdash F\_AD \in Fr, \vdash F\_CD \in Fr$.
- The model's GFG is well-formed: $\vdash GFG\_WTs \in GFGr$.
- Overall model is well formed: $\vdash M\_WTs \in Mdl$.
- M_WTs must be a valid INTO-SysML model. Given a type morphism ty (illustrated in Fig. 4b), we prove: $\vdash (M\_WTs, ty) \in INTO\_Mdls$, which entails $\vdash (M\_WTs, INTO\_SysML, ty) \in MdlTy$.

These are the checks required for any INTO-SysML model.

3.2   Fragmenta/Isabelle as a Transformation Engine

To enable usage of model-checkers, FRAGMENTA/Isabelle is used as a transformation engine in the algebraic loops check, which finds cycles in a topology of dependencies in instantaneous component communication (Fig. 5).

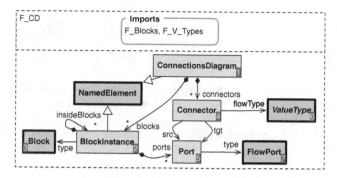

(a) Metamodel of INTO-SysML CDs

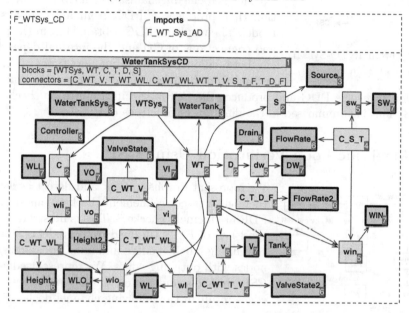

(b) INTO-SysML CD of water tanks system (Fig. 2b) in FRAGMENTA

Fig. 4. Metamodel, models and typing morphism (numbered labels) in FRAGMENTA illustrated with INTO-SysML CDs

Figure 5a portrays a self-cycle component that is algebraic loop free. Output y1 of A is connected to A's input u2, but this does not entail an algebraic loop. The topology in Fig. 5b, on the other hand, contains an algebraic loop.

Finding algebraic loops equates to detecting cycles in a directed graph describing port dependancy relations. An edge between two ports indicates that the target node is instantaneously dependent on the source. This constitutes a *port dependancy graph* (PDG), illustrated in Fig. 5c, which portrays a PDG with an algebraic loop corresponding to the variant of the INTO-SysML model of Fig. 2 that connects the Drain to the Tank (dwo to win).

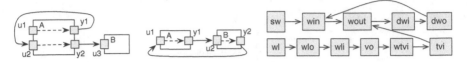

(a) A topology without (b) A topology with an (c) PDG of a variant of Fig. 2
algebraic loops   algebraic loop   with algebraic loop

Fig. 5. The algebraic loops check is about finding cycles in a system topology emphasising component communication

Fig. 6. From INTO-SysML models to CSPm

The Isabelle mechanisation introduces a function that produces a PDG from a INTO-SysML model. The resulting PDG, obtained from the ports and connections of CD and the internal dependancies between output and input port types of AD, is derived from both metamodel and model. Another function takes the PDG and produces the CSPm specification to be checked in FDR3. This is summarised in the diagram of functions of Fig. 6.

4   Algebraic Loop Verification Using CSP

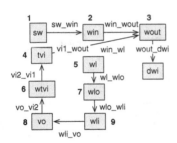

Fig. 7. A PDG with labelled nodes and edges

We represent graphs in CSP and detect cycles on them via a traces-refinement check executed in the FDR3 refinement checker[6]. This is illustrated with the PDG of Fig. 7 (derived from model of Fig. 2), containing labelled edges and numbers assigned to nodes with outgoing edges. We represent edges as CSP channels and nodes as CSP processes. The edges result in the following channel declaration:

channel $sw\_win, win\_wout, wout\_dwi, tvi\_wout,$
$wtvi\_tvi, vo\_wtvi, wli\_vo, \ldots$

The overall graph is a CSP process constructed from sub-processes representing each node. The node processes are an external choice of CSP prefixed expressions for each edge that starts at the node. They offer the events on the corresponding channel and then behave as the process at the end of the edge. An edge to a sink node (no outgoing edges) results in a transition to *SKIP*. The main process is the external choice of all sub-processes. The process for PDG of Fig. 7 is:

$$PortDependancyGraph =$$
$$\text{let } P(1) = sw\_win \rightarrow P(2)$$

---

[6] https://www.cs.ox.ac.uk/projects/fdr/.

$$P(2) = win\_wout \rightarrow P(3)$$
$$P(3) = wout\_dwi \rightarrow SKIP$$

$$\vdots$$

$$\text{within } \square \, i : 1..9 \bullet P(i)$$

Cycles are detected through traces refinement. The abstract CSP process to be refined defines all finite paths whose size is at most the number of edges in the graph (those that can be built by combining the graph's edges):

$$edges = \{sw\_win, win\_wout, wout\_dwi, tvi\_wout, wtvi\_tvi, vo\_wtvi, \ldots\}$$
$$Limited =$$

$$\text{let } Limited0(E, n) =$$

$$\text{if } n > 0 \rightarrow \square \, e : E \bullet e \rightarrow Limited0(E, n - 1) \sqcap SKIP \text{ else } STOP$$

$$\text{within } Limited0(edges, 9)$$

The traces refinement check to be executed in FDR3 is then:

$$\textbf{assert } Limited \sqsubseteq_{T} PortDependancyGraph$$

All counter-examples are cycles. The function $toCSP$ of FRAGMENTA/Isabelle (Sect. 3.2) yields CSP specifications as outlined above. For the PDG of Fig. 7, FDR3 gives no counter-examples; for Fig. 5c FDR3 yields one counter-example.

5   Evaluation

FDR3 is a tool based on model-checking, a verification technique whose drawback is scalability. We compare our CSP approach to detect algebraic loops (Sect. 4) against one approach based on Alloy [14] and one graph algorithm [15], to gauge scalability.

5.1   Experimental Setup

Scalability is evaluated against growing PDGs based on the water tanks running example (Fig. 3). We keep adding tanks to a base water tanks systems to produce systems of cascading water tanks having two versions: one with algebraic loops (drain is connected to first tank) and one without (as per Fig. 3).

The generation of files to execute in either FDR3, Alloy 4[7] or the implementation of Johnson's algorithm in JGraphT[8], involves Isabelle functions that yield PDGs given the number of tanks. We then define functions from PDGs to the abstract syntax of CSP (as per Sect. 4), Alloy (see below) and Graph ML[9] as per diagram of Fig. 8[10].

---

[7] http://alloy.mit.edu/alloy/download.html.

[8] A Java library of graph algorithms – https://github.com/jgrapht/jgrapht.

[9] A standard for graphs exchange that enables a direct representation of PDGs – http://graphml.graphdrawing.org/.

[10] The Isabelle file that performs the generation, the actual generated files, and the Java code that runs the three approaches, can be found at http://bit.ly/1WKTIC7.

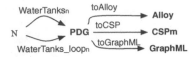

Fig. 8. The experiment's generation functions

The graph checks and data collection were performed by a Java program that reads the files and calls either Alloy 4 (using the minisat SAT solver), FDR3 or JGraphT, executed on a MacBook Pro with a 2.5 GHz Intel core i7 processor and 16 GB RAM memory. The resulting data was subject to a statistical analysis carried out in the R statistical package [24].

5.2 The Alloy Model

Alloy [14] is a declarative modeling language based on first-order logic with transitive closure. It is used for data modelling and provides an automatic bounded analysis of a model. Our Alloy model of PDGs is based on the signature *Port*:

```
abstract sig Port {tgt : set Port}{tgt ≠ this}
```

Above, we declare a set of `Port` instances – `abstract` says that `Port` has no instances of its own and that all its instances belong to its extensions (subsets) – with the relation `tgt` between `Ports` declared to be non-reflexive: the `tgt` of some `Port` cannot be itself (`this`).

The actual nodes of the PDG of Fig. 7 extend `Port`:

```
one sig sw, win, wout, dwi, wl, wlo, wli, vo, wlvi, tvi
    extends Port   {}
```

Above, the nodes are singletons (constraint `one`) that subset `Port(extends)`.

The following Alloy fact defines the edges of the graph:

```
fact {sw.tgt = win
    win.tgt = wout
    wout.tgt = dwi
    no dwi.tgt ... }
assert AcyclicTgt {no ^tgt & iden}
check AcyclicTgt for 10
```

Above, each edge is declared through relation `tgt`: `sw.tgt =win` says that there is an edge from `sw` to `win` – operator . is the relational image –, `win.tgt =wout` says that there is an edge from `win` to `wout`, and `no dwi.tgt` says that `dwi` has no outgoing edges (set is empty).

Finally, we assert the acyclicity of the relation `tgt` representing the PDG and declare the command to check the assertion:

```
assert AcyclicTgt {no ^tgt & iden}
check AcyclicTgt for 10
```

Above, the assertion says that there can be no elements (operator `no`) in the set resulting from the intersection (operator `&`) of the relation's transitive closure (`^tgt`) with the identity relation (`iden`). The `check` command includes a scope declaration: the analysis should consider at most 10 PDG nodes.

5.3   Comparisons

The plots of Fig. 9 depict the data obtained from running the experiments. They display the number of nodes of the analysed graph in the abscissa and the duration of the check (in seconds) in the ordinate.

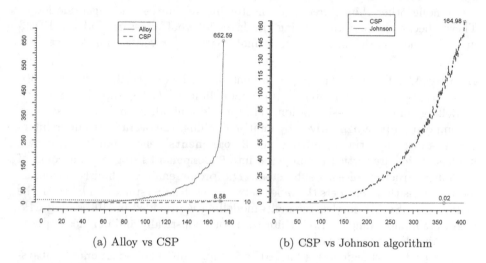

(a) Alloy vs CSP   (b) CSP vs Johnson algorithm

Fig. 9. The performances of the Alloy and CSP solutions (seconds on the ordinate and number of nodes of a graph on the abscissa)

Figure 9a shows that there is an overwhelming difference in favour of CSP against Alloy. CSP's maximum duration is 8.58 s, Alloy's is 652.59 s. The two approaches start to diverge with small to medium size graphs (number of nodes >17). The p-value, obtained from the paired data plotted in Fig. 9a using the Wilcoxon statistical test[11], of $<2.2^{-16}$ (<0.001) indicates a very large difference. We derived estimates of functions that fit the data of both Alloy and CSP to yield estimates of time complexity: Alloy has complexity $O(Exp)$, whereas CSP has complexity $O(n^3)$ – n is number of nodes of graph.

Figure 9b, on the other hand, shows that Johnson's algorithm performs substantially better than CSP. The former's maximum duration is 0.02 s, CSP's is 164.98 s. The p-value of $<2.2^{-16}$ (<0.001) signals a very large difference. The estimated function that fits the data endorses the algorithm's linearity claim.

6   Discussion

The following discusses the results presented in the paper.

---

[11] It is a non-parametric test that compares the two sampled distributions without assuming that they follow the normal distribution.

A Prelude to Co-simulation. The work presented here statically checks an architectural design of a CPS in preparation for co-simulation. This is done at the high-level architectural design to provide early warnings of any issues so that the appropriate remedial action can be taken. It is a preliminary check – done before delving into the details of global co-simulation and local modelling and analysis of each component – to ensure that the models to be co-simulated are, among other things, free of connector inconformities and algebraic loops. These checks are performed using the Isabelle proof assistant and the FDR3 model-checker; both constitute an intimate part of our verification toolset.

Into-SysML Profile. The paper presents a profile of SysML (defined in [3]), designed as a DSL, for architectural modelling of CPSs supporting multi-modelling and FMI co-simulation. The profile embodies an implicit systems decomposition paradigm driven by multi-modelling: the overall system architecture is a decomposition of subsystems (`E-components`), encapsulating their own models, which are further decomposed into `POComponents` to give an account of the inner structure of each subsystem. The profile enables a holistic algebraic loop analysis that considers the inner details of each subsystem. Guidance on the definition of SysML models for multi-modelling is provided in [10], aiding CPS engineers in modelling a CPS architecture both holistically and in a decomposed form suitable for co-simulation.

The profile's design caters for FMI co-simulation. The `E-component` subsystems of the architecture result in FMI's Functional Mock-up Units (FMUs) to be co-simulated; FMUs are generated by the corresponding modelling framework.

FRAGMENTA/Isabelle as Prototyping Environment. The profile's DSL design was brought to life by FRAGMENTA and its accompanying Isabelle mechanisation. FRAGMENTA/Isabelle, built as part of the work presented here, constitutes a prototyping environment built on top of FRAGMENTA's mathematical theory that provides reasoning and transformation capabilities for metamodels and their instances. As this paper demonstrates, it can be used in real-world settings; ideally, however, FRAGMENTA designs should be specialised and optimised as part of fully fledged visual modelling environments.

Algebraic Loops. The algebraic loops healthiness check is performed on a graph describing the instantaneous dependencies between ports extracted from INTO-CPS architectural models; external port connections are derived from the CD and internal ones from the AD. Internal and external port dependencies of the INTO-SysML model must be consistent with the underlying model equations.

It is interesting to contrast the two model-based approaches to check algebraic loops. Alloy represents a graph directly (Sect. 5.2) as a relation between nodes; the property to check is stated as an ordinary relational calculus formula. The CSP approach (Sect. 4), on the other hand, is edge-oriented to suit CSP's communication model based on channels; a graph is the communications established between nodes (CSP processes) chosen from the environment (external choice); the property is expressed in an ingenious, but less evident way: through an abstract process and a traces refinement check.

FDR3 and Alloy 4 are both based on model-checking; however, the CSP solution outperforms Alloy overwhelmingly. Alloy's exponential time complexity is attributed to the complexity of SAT whose worst-case time complexity is exponential [19,21] – the Alloy solution resorts to the transitive closure, a computationally demanding operation (specialised algorithms do it in $O(n^3)$). An important factor in CSP's lower $O(n^3)$ time complexity lies in the use of traces refinement, founded on the simplest denotational model of CSP and with the least expensive time complexity – polynomial according to [16].

Our CSP solution is beaten by Johnson's algorithm, but it is used in our verification approach, which employs FDR3 for more sophisticated checks of FMI co-simulations [1]. It is difficult for general-purpose model-checking to outperform specialised algorithms taking advantage of problem specificities.

The experimental setup varies size but not structure, which remains essentially the same throughout the different water tanks systems. However, as the results show, this is enough to expose differences; furthermore, as discussed above, the obtained results are consistent with theoretical results.

7   Related Work

Feldman et al. [9] generate FMI model descriptions from Rhapsody SysML models and FMUs from statecharts to enable integration with continuous models. Unlike our work, this does not define a profile embodying a paradigm designed for multi-modelling and FMI-co-simulation; furthermore, formal static checks covering connector conformity and absence of algebraic loops are not covered. Pohlmann et al. [23] propose a UML-based DSL for real-time systems; FMI FMUs are generated from model components described as real-time statecharts; our work specialises the SysML block diagrams, a standard notation for architectural modelling, and supports multi-modelling.

This paper applies the FRAGMENTA theory presented in [2] to a real-world problem. This required an extension to the Isabelle/HOL theory of [2], developed to prove that paper's main theorem. This extension builds an infrastructure to support automated verification and transformation for visual modelling languages. FRAGMENTA/Isabelle constitutes a prototyping environment supporting all the novel aspects of FRAGMENTA, namely: a formal theory of proxies and its verified theory of decomposition and the support for fragmentation strategies. This is the first time that the novel theory of modularity with its Isabelle mechanisation is applied to a real-world application. To our knowledge, this is also the first prototyping environment based on a proof assistant that provides formal reasoning and transformation capabilities for visual models.

The approach to connector conformity used here is based on typing. It supports sub-typing according to the inheritance relations specified in the metamodel; for instance, in INTO-SysML, natural numbers may be used when integers are expected because the metamodel says that the former is a subtype of the latter. This is checked as part of FRAGMENTA's typing morphisms. This is different from the *connector compatibility* of [7], which performs validations based on interface contracts, a relation between allowed inputs and outputs [26].

Broman et al. [6] require that FMI component networks are algebraic-loop free as a pre-condition to the deterministic composition results of their FMI master algorithms, proposing port-dependency graphs as a means to perform such checks. Unlike the work presented here, [6] does not study different approaches to detect algebraic loops; it suggests algorithms that topologically sort a graph, which yield an error if the graph has a cycle. Our algebraic loop analysis provides actual cycles as feedback to designers.

8 Conclusions

This paper has presented our approach to check a SysML model in preparation for co-simulation. This involves checking the consistency and well-formedness of the INTO-SysML model, which involves checking the conformance of the model with respect to its metamodel based on FRAGMENTA's representation. The actual checks are carried out using FRAGMENTA's Isabelle mechanisation, ensuring, among other things, connector conformity. The paper then showed how the INTO-SysML models could be transformed into other modelling languages to perform a check for the absence of algebraic loops using FRAGMENTA's Isabelle mechanisation as a transformation engine. The paper presented a novel CSP approach to detect algebraic loops by checking a traces refinement in FDR3. The paper's evaluation highlighted how our CSP approach based on refinement-checking performs well when compared with an Alloy SAT-based model-checking approach, but that it does not perform better than a special-purpose graph algorithm. The work presented in this paper is done in tandem with the effort on the formal semantics of FMI in CSP [1].

Acknowledgements. This work was supported by the EU project INTO-CPS (Horizon 2020, # 644047, http://into-cps.au.dk/). Thanks are due to Etienne Brosse, who implemented the INTO-SysML profile in the Modelio tool, and Bernhard Thiele, who provided useful feeedback on the work presented here.

References

1. Amalio, N., Cavalcanti, A., König, C., Woodcock, J.: Foundations for FMI co-modelling. Technical report, INTO-CPS Deliverable, D2.1d, December 2015
2. Amálio, N., de Lara, J., Guerra, E.: FRAGMENTA: a theory of fragmentation for MDE. In: MODELS 2015. IEEE (2015)
3. Amalio, N., Payne, R., Cavalcanti, A., Brosse, E.: Foundations of the SysML profile for CPS modelling. Technical report, INTO-CPS Deliverable, D2.1a, December 2015
4. Blochwitz, T., Otter, M., Akesson, J., Arnold, M., Clauss, C., Elmqvist, H., Friedrich, M., Junghanns, A., Mauss, J., Neumerkel, D., Olsson, H., Viel, A.: The functional mockup interface 2.0: the Standard for tool independent exchange of simulation models. In: Modelica Conference, Munich, Germany (2012)

5. Blochwitz, T.: Functional mock-up interface for model exchange and co-simulation, July 2014. https://www.fmi-standard.org/downloads (Blochwitz, T. (ed.))

6. Broman, D., Brooks, C., Greenberg, L., Lee, E., Masin, M., Tripakis, S., Wetter, M.: Determinate composition of FMUs for co-simulation. In: EMSOFT (2013)

7. Dragomir, I., Preoteasa, V., Tripakis, S.: Compositional semantics and analysis of hierarchical block diagrams. In: Bošnacki, D., Wijs, A. (eds.) SPIN 2016. LNCS, vol. 9641, pp. 38–56. Springer, Heidelberg (2016). doi:10.1007/978-3-319-32582-8_3

8. Ehrig, H., Ehrig, K., Prange, U., Taentzer, G.: Fundamentals of Algebraic Graph Transformation. Springer, Heidelberg (2006)

9. Feldman, Y., Greenberg, L., Palachi, E.: Simulating rhapsody SysML blocks in hybrid models with FMI. In: Modelica Conference, pp. 43–52 (2014)

10. Fitzgerald, J., Gamble, C., Payne, R., Pierce, K.: Method guidelines 1. Technical report, INTO-CPS Deliverable, D3.1a, December 2015

11. Fritzson, P.: Principles of Object-Oriented Modeling and Simulation with Modelica 2.1. Wiley-IEEE Press, Hoboken (2004)

12. Gibson-Robinson, T., Armstrong, P., Boulgakov, A., Roscoe, A.W.: FDR3 — a modern refinement checker for CSP. In: Ábrahám, E., Havelund, K. (eds.) TACAS 2014 (ETAPS). LNCS, vol. 8413, pp. 187–201. Springer, Heidelberg (2014)

13. Hoare, T.: Communication Sequential Processes. Prentice-Hall International, Englewood Cliffs (1985)

14. Jackson, D.: Software Abstractions: Logic, Language, and Analysis. MIT Press, Cambridge (2012)

15. Johnson, D.B.: Finding all the elementary circuits in a directed graph. SIAM J. Comput. 4(1), 77–84 (1975)

16. Kanellakis, P.C., Smolka, S.A.: CCS expressions, finite state processes, and three problems of equivalence. Inf. Comput. 86(1), 43–68 (1990)

17. Kleijn, C.: Modelling and simulation of fluid power systems with 20-sim. Int. J. Fluid Power 7(3), November 2006

18. Kübler, R., Schiehlen, W.: Two methods of simulator coupling. Math. Comput. Model. Dyn. Syst. 6(2), 93–113 (2000)

19. Kullmann, O.: New methods for 3-SAT decision and worst-case analysis. Theor. Comput. Sci. 223(1–2), 1–72 (1999)

20. Larsen, P.G., Battle, N., Ferreira, M., Fitzgerald, J., Lausdahl, K., Verhoef, M.: The overture initiative - integrating tools for VDM. SIGSOFT Softw. Eng. Notes 35(1), 1–6 (2010)

21. Monien, B., Speckenmeyer, E.: Solving satisfiability in less than 2n steps. Discret. Appl. Math. 10(3), 287–295 (1985)

22. Nipkow, T., Klein, G.: Concrete Semantics: with Isabelle/HOL. Springer, Switzerland (2014)

23. Pohlmann, U., Schäfer, W., Reddehase, H., Röckemann, J., Wagner, R.: Generating functional mockup units from software specifications. In: Modelica Conference (2012)

24. R Core Team: R: A Language and Environment for Statistical Computing. R Foundation for Statistical Computing, Vienna, Austria (2015). https://www.R-project.org/

25. OMG Systems Modeling Language (OMG SysML™). Technical report version 1.3, SysML Modelling Team, June 2012. http://www.omg.org/spec/SysML/1.3/

26. Tripakis, S., Lickly, B., Henzinger, T.A., Lee, E.A.: A theory of synchronous relational interfaces. ACM TOPLAS 33(4), 14 (2011)

A CEGAR Scheme for Information Flow Analysis

Manuel Töws[(✉)] and Heike Wehrheim

Paderborn University, Paderborn, Germany
manuel.toews@uni-paderborn.de

Abstract. Information flow analysis studies the flow of data between program entities (e.g. variables), where the allowed flow is specified via *security policies*. Typical information flow analyses compute a conservative (over-)approximation of the flows in a program. Such an analysis may thus signal non-existing violations of the security policy.

In this paper, we propose a new technique for inspecting the reported violations (counterexamples) for spuriousity. Similar to counterexample-guided-abstraction-refinement (CEGAR) in software verification, we use the result of this inspection to improve the next round of the analysis. We prove soundness of this scheme.

1 Introduction

Information flow analysis aims at finding data leaks in programs. More precisely, it analyses whether information flows from a private, confidential source to a public sink. Information flow *control* should thus provide *confidentiality* of data: access to confidential information is only given in ways allowed by specified security policies (or security *lattices*). A typical policy is the explicit division of variables into *low* (L) and *high* (H) ones, disallowing flow of data from high to low.

A large number of information flow analyses exist today. These are e.g. based on type systems [12,18], logic [1,7,13], theorem proving [7], dependency analysis that operates either on the control flow [1] or on program dependence graphs [11]. A good survey of the known approaches is given by *Sabelfeld and Myers* [15]. Most of these approaches are computing overapproximations of the actual information flow in program executions, thereby potentially raising *false alarms*. As a large number of false alarms makes such an analysis practically useless, a lot of approaches try to get rid of false alarms by making the analysis itself more precise, e.g. by augmenting it with costly points-to analysis. A different approach is taken by the path conditions of [16]: path conditions encode the potential flow of information from a source to a sink as a logical formula and use SMT solvers

---

This work was partially supported by the German Research Foundation (DFG) within the Collaborative Research Centre "On-The-Fly Computing" (SFB 901).

© Springer International Publishing AG 2016
K. Ogata et al. (Eds.): ICFEM 2016, LNCS 10009, pp. 466–483, 2016.
DOI: 10.1007/978-3-319-47846-3_29

```
1: if (v_h == 1)
2:     v_i = v_i+2;
3: else
4:     v_i = v_i+2;
5: fi
6: v_l = v_i;
7:
```

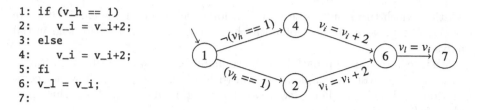

Fig. 1. Running example of a secure program and its control flow automaton

to derive feasibility of the flow. As these path conditions are abstractions of the actual paths as well, a further specialisation of this technique provides for a *refinement* of path conditions [17]. The refinement is based on actual program executions monitoring the raised, potential information flow. Thus this technique provides for a CEGAR scheme (counterexample guided abstraction refinement) in information flow analysis.

This approach can, however, only tackle one source of imprecision, namely that of infeasibility of a flow. The ultimate objective of showing *non-interference*, i.e., the property that a program started with the same public (low) input – but potentially different secret (high) input – should not terminate with different public output, cannot always be achieved with path condition refinement. To see this, consider the small code snippet in Fig. 1, which is intentionally kept simple for illustration purpose. Variables indexed with h are considered secret (high), those indexed with l are public (low) and variable v_i is neither secret nor public (internal). The security policy states that flow from high to low variables is disallowed. A standard flow analysis, even when enhanced with path condition refinement, will compute a dependency of v_l on v_h and thus of v_l on v_h and v_i. Still, this program possesses our key objective of *non-interference*: the values of the two low variables do not depend on variable v_h since the branches of the if-statement do not differ. Our technique aims at detecting and eliminating such false alarms.

The basis of our approach is a standard static analysis computing dependencies between variables for every location in the control flow graph of a program. Upon detection of a potential leak (a flow of data to a variable v at location l from some non-allowed variable set V), it first computes a *candidate* subset of these dependencies $V' \subseteq V$ for the variable v at l, only containing allowed accesses. It then builds a logical formula encoding not the flow (like path conditions do) but the wanted non-interference property for this candidate: the formula describes two program runs up to l with identical initial values for variables in V', arbitrary initial (possibly different) values for the other variables and different final values for v at l. If this formula is unsatisfiable, non-interference holds for v at ℓ.

We memorize for this combination of variable and location the modified dependencies (as the candidate has been shown to be sound), and use this information when computing dependencies for other variables and locations. This technique is repeated until no more violations are detected or until we find a violation which turns out to be real, i.e., for which none of the candidates are correct. We prove soundness of both this refinement step and for the initial analysis.

We integrated our approach into the configurable software verification framework CPACHECKER. Its implementation within CPACHECKER allows for combinations with several other software analyses, e.g. predicate analysis which provides path sensitivity.

2   Background

We start with defining the programs which we consider in this paper. For the formal treatment, we restrict ourselves to simple imperative programs; the implementation treats a larger class. In the following, x is a variable (of type integer or boolean) and $a \in AExpr$, $b \in BExpr$ are arithmetic and boolean expressions, respectively.

$$Stmt ::= \quad skip; \quad | \quad x := a; \quad | \quad Stmt; \; Stmt \quad | \quad \text{if} \,(b)\, \text{then} \, Stmt \, \text{else} \, Stmt \, \text{fi} \quad |$$
$$\text{while} \,(b)\, \text{do} \, Stmt \, \text{od}$$

Programs are either given in the syntax of above or directly as control-flow automata (*CFAs*). A control-flow automaton $CFA = (L, G, l_0)$ consists of a set of locations L, a set of control flow edges $G \subseteq L \times Ops \times L$ and a program entry location $l_0 \in L$ where

$$Ops ::= skip \mid assume(b) \mid x := a$$

describe assignments, assume (i.e., conditions of if and while) and skip statements. We let V denote the set of all program entities (variables[1]) that occur in any operation $op \in Ops$ of any edge $(\cdot, op, \cdot) \in G$. We say that a location $l \in L$ *occurs inside a loop* if l is on a cycle of the control flow graph. Every program can be transformed into a control flow automaton by assigning names to its program locations. We therefore often directly give programs with their location names. Figure 1 describes our running program and its control flow automaton.

The semantics of a control-flow automaton (and thus of a program) (L, G, l_0) is defined by a transition system $T = (C, \rightarrow, c_0)$. In this, the *concrete data state* $C: V \rightarrow \mathbb{Z} \cup \{true, false\}$ of a program is a total (type-correct) function that maps every variable from the set V to a concrete integer or boolean value, $c_0 \in C$ is the initial state and $\rightarrow \subseteq C \times G \times C$ is a transition between states. Note that initial states may vary and thus a number of transition systems can be assigned to a program.

A tuple $(c, (l, op, l'), c') \in \rightarrow$ describes that at location l with state c the operation op can be applied and thereby location l' with state c' is reached.

---

[1] We consider V in general as variables, however, objects, function identifiers etc. are also possible as entities used in security policies.

Therein, the semantics of the transition is given by the following constraints:

$$(c, (l_i, skip, l_j), c') \in \rightarrow \text{ then } c' = c$$

$$(c, (l_i, x := a, l_j), c') \in \rightarrow \text{ then } c'(y) = \begin{cases} c(y) & \text{if } x \neq y \\ c(a) & \text{if } x = y \end{cases}$$

$$(c, (l_i, assume(b), l_j), c') \in \rightarrow \text{ then } c(b) = true \wedge c' = c$$

Note that we use in the semantics two evaluation functions $c \colon AExpr \rightarrow \mathbb{Z}$ and $c \colon BExpr \rightarrow \{true, false\}$ to evaluate expressions. A *feasible path* to a location $l_k \in L$ in $T = (C, \rightarrow, c_0)$, is a sequence of concrete states and transitions a program can pass through, starting in location l_0 with concrete state c_0 and ending in location l_k with concrete state c_k:

$$Paths(T) = \{(c_0, (l_0, op_0, l_1), c_1), (c_1, (l_1, op_1, l_2), c_2), .., (c_{k-1}, (l_{k-1}, op_{k-1}, l_k), c_k) \mid$$
$$\forall 0 \leq i < k : \exists l_i \in L, \exists c_i \in C, \exists op_i \in Ops \text{ s.t. } (l_i, op, l_{i+1}) \in G$$
$$\wedge (c_i, (l_i, op, l_{i+1}), c_{i+1}) \in \rightarrow\}$$

2.1 Security Policies

The allowed flow of information in programs is specified by so called *security policies* based on the generalization used by *Foley* [9]. For this, let S denote a set of *security classes*. We assume every program variable to have an assigned security class given by a mapping $SC \colon V \rightarrow S$ (*security class mapping*). This mapping classifies the confidentiality level of the entity. For our example in Fig. 1 the mapping is $SC(v_h) = h, SC(v_i) = i$ and $SC(v_\ell) = \ell$.

A security policy P is a collection of pairs of the form $S \times 2^S$. We call an element $(a, A) \in P$ in general a *security state*. An element (a, A) describes that a program entity with security level a is allowed to depend on information equal to the security classes A. For technical reasons we furthermore demand that $a \in A$ holds (which is similar to reflexivity) and that for each $b \in A$ there exists at least one state $(b, B) \in P$.

Definition 1. *Let S be a set of security classes. The set of feasible policies over S, $Pol(S)$, is defined as*

$$Pol(S) := \{P \colon S \times 2^S \mid \forall a \in S, \forall A \in 2^S : ((a, A) \in P \Rightarrow (a \in A \wedge \forall b \in A \, \exists B \in 2^S : (b, B) \in P))\} .$$

In this paper, we use a standard policy for illustration of our technique. To simplify policy specification on a set of security classes S, we use some auxiliary operations according to [9]:

$$\bot := \{(a, A \cup \{a\}) \mid a \in S; A \in 2^S\}$$

$$d \leftsquigarrow D := \{(a, \{a\}) \mid a \in S\} \cup \bigcup_{A \in 2^D} \{(d, A \cup \{d\})\}$$

$\perp$ describes a policy that allows anything, while $d \rightsquigarrow D$ describes a policy where only an entity of security class d is allowed to depend on entities with security classes equal to any subset of D unified with $\{d\}$. Given a security policy $P \in Pol(S)$, three sets are important for our analysis:

$$\perp \quad \text{(Set of all possible states)}$$
$$P \quad \text{(Set of secure states)}$$
$$N(P) = \perp \setminus P \quad \text{(Set of non-secure states)}$$

As recurring example, we use a policy that consists of three security classes: l *(low)*, h *(high)* and i *(internal)*. We aim at a security policy where the security class h is used for entities that contain secret information that should not be observed directly, while l declares entities that contain public information and that can be observed at several program states. The last security class i is used for internal entities and entities that do not directly contain secret information and that should not be observed directly. Nevertheless, we do not want that information of security class h can flow via these entities into entities of security class l. This policy is defined in Definition 2 as *LHI*.

Definition 2. *Let* $S = \{\ell, h, i\}$ *be a set of security classes. The LHI-policy is defined as*

$$LHI := \left(\ell \rightsquigarrow \{\ell, i\}\right) \cup \left(i \rightsquigarrow \{\ell, h, i\}\right) \cup \left(h \rightsquigarrow \{\ell, h, i\}\right).$$

The security states can be ordered in a partial order $\sqsubseteq$: $(S \times 2^S) \times (S \times 2^S)$ with $((a, A), (b, B)) \in \sqsubseteq$ iff $(a = b) \wedge A \subseteq B$. All secure states for entities in the *LHI*-Policy can be found in Fig. 2 ordered by $\sqsubseteq$.

The two states $(\ell, \{\ell, h\})), (\ell, \{\ell, h, i\}) \in N(LHI)$ are non-secure states for the security class ℓ and signal a policy violation.

The *LHI*-Policy belongs to a special family of security policies, the *aggregation policies* [8]. These are policies with the following aggregation property: if a security class a is allowed to access combined elements (where a is included), it is also allowed to access the information of any subsets of the security classes that include at least a itself. Formally,

$$(a, B) \in P \Rightarrow (a, A) \in P \tag{1}$$

holds for $a \in A \subseteq B \subseteq S$. Our CEGAR technique depends on this property of policies.

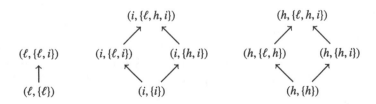

Fig. 2. The secure states of the *LHI*-policy ordered according to $\sqsubseteq$.

2.2   Security

Having stated our security policies, we can next define non-interference. The *non-interference* property [10] is a well-known standard security concern. Informally, it says that a program executed twice with the same public input should not behave observably distinguishable on the public output channels even when the secret information differs. Many authors consider policies that consist of only one public (low) and one secret entity (high). We will define something similar but consider security policies in general. First of all we define non-interference of entities:

Definition 3. *Non-interference to an entity at a location*
    Let (L, G, l_0) be a program and $T = (C, \rightarrow, c_0)$ and $T' = (C, \rightarrow, c'_0)$ be two transition systems (differing in the initial state) for this program. Furthermore, let V be the set of entities that occur in the CFA. An entity $w \in V$ does not interfere with an entity $v \in V$ at location $l \in L$, l being a location not inside a loop, iff the following holds

$$\Xi_l(v, w) ::= \forall \pi = ((c_0, g_0, c_1), .., (c_{j-1}, (l_{j-1}, op_{j-1}, l), c_j)) \in Path(T),$$
$$\forall \pi' = ((c'_0, g'_0, c'_1), .., (c'_{k-1}, (l'_{k-1}, op'_{k-1}, l), c'_k)) \in Paths(T'),$$
$$\forall z \in V \setminus \{w\} : c_0(z) = c'_0(z) \Rightarrow c_j(v) = c'_k(v) .$$

For each $v \in V$ and $l \in L$ we can separate the set of all entities into the following two disjoint sets:

$$Noninterferences_l(v) = \{w \in V \mid \Xi_l(v, w)\}$$
$$Interferences_l(v) = \{w \in V \mid \neg\Xi_l(v, w)\}$$

We demand for the final location $l \in L$ of the two paths π and π' not to be inside a loop. For the while-language this means it is not inside the loop body of a while-statement. Omitting this restriction would in general cause a violation for this location even if two program runs are identical the same with the same initial values $c_0 = c'_0$. To see this, consider the example in Fig. 3: Each loop iteration will decrease at location 3 the concrete state of the variable $v_\ell \in V$ by one and therefore, differ to the previous loop iteration. However, even for two paths with $c_0(v_\ell) = c'_0(v_\ell) > 1$ the concrete states for location 3 will differ after the first (c_4) and the second iteration (c'_6) and therefore $\Xi_3(v_\ell, v_h)$ does not hold and signals an interference to v_h although there is no influence for any computation in the loop.
    Nevertheless, all other locations occurring before l in the paths π and π' are without restriction allowed to be part of loops and to occur in a loop more than once. With these definitions at hand we can fix our non-interference security property:

Definition 4. *Security at a location*
    Let $P \in Pol(S)$ be a security policy, let $CFA = (L, G, l_0)$ be a program and let V be the set of entities that occur in the CFA. The program is secure

```
1: v_h=0
2: while (v_l > 0) do
3:     v_l = v_l-1;
4: od
5:
```

$$c_0 = c_0'$$
$$c_0(v_\ell) \mapsto 3 \quad c_0'(v_\ell) \mapsto 3$$
$$c_0(v_h) \mapsto 7 \quad c_0'(v_h) \mapsto 7$$

$$2 = c_4(v_\ell) \neq c_6'(v_\ell) = 1$$

$$\pi = ((c_0, (1, \text{skip}, 2), c_1), (c_1, (1, v_h = 0, 2), c_2), (c_2, (1, \text{assume}(v_\ell > 0), 3), c_3),$$
$$(c_3, (1, v_\ell = v_\ell - 1, 2), c_4)$$
$$\pi' = ((c_0', (1, \text{skip}, 2), c_1'), (c_1', (1, v_h = 0, 2), c_2'), (c_2', (1, \text{assume}(v_\ell > 0), 3), c_3'),$$
$$(c_3', (1, v_\ell = v_\ell - 1, 2), c_4'), (c_4', (1, \text{assume}(v_\ell > 0), 3), c_5'), (c_5', (1, v_\ell = v_\ell - 1, 2), c_6'))$$

Fig. 3. Small example that explains why locations like 3 are excluded from the non-interference definition. If not, location 3 would signal for v_ℓ an interference of v_h and conclude a violation.

at location $l \in L$ wrt. P, l being a location not inside a loop, iff $\forall v \in V$: $(SC(v), SC(v) \cup \bigcup_{w \in Interferences_l(v)} SC(w)) \in P$ holds.

Stated the other way round: The occurrence of an entity $v \in V$ such that $(SC(v), SC(v) \cup \bigcup_{w \in Interferences_l(v)} SC(w)) \notin P$ constitutes a violation of the security policy. The program in Fig. 1 is secure at all locations like illustrated in Table 1.

Next, we present an analysis which aims at detecting security violations.

Table 1. The program in Fig. 1 is secure at all locations according to the definition.

Location l	Concrete states c_l	$Interferences_l(*)$	Security
1, 2, 4	$v_\ell \mapsto c_0(v_\ell)$	$v_\ell \mapsto \{v_\ell\}$	$(\ell, \{\ell\}) \in LHI$
	$v_h \mapsto c_0(v_h)$	$v_h \mapsto \{v_h\}$	$(h, \{h\}) \in LHI$
	$v_i \mapsto c_0(v_i)$	$v_i \mapsto \{v_i\}$	$(i, \{i\}) \in LHI$
3, 5, 6	$v_\ell \mapsto c_0(v_\ell)$	$v_\ell \mapsto \{v_\ell\}$	$(\ell, \{\ell\}) \in LHI$
	$v_h \mapsto c_0(v_h)$	$v_h \mapsto \{v_h\}$	$(h, \{h\}) \in LHI$
	$v_i \mapsto c_0(v_i) + 2$	$v_i \mapsto \{v_i\}$	$(i, \{i\}) \in LHI$
7	$v_\ell \mapsto c_0(v_i) + 2$	$v_\ell \mapsto \{v_i\}$	$(\ell, \{\ell, i\}) \in LHI$
	$v_h \mapsto c_0(v_h)$	$v_h \mapsto \{v_h\}$	$(h, \{h\}) \in LHI$
	$v_i \mapsto c_0(v_i) + 2$	$v_i \mapsto \{v_i\}$	$(i, \{i\}) \in LHI$

3   Dependency Analysis

We base our technique for analysing programs with respect to security (as given in Definition 4) on a forward dataflow analysis. It computes the set of interferences over program entities based on the ideas of Amtoft and Banerjee [1]), i.e., it computes for every location l and pair of variables v and w, whether v might depend on w's value at program start. A small difference to [1] is that we aim at computing the set of interferences while they aim at computing the set of non-interferences.

We intend to compute an abstract state space of *dependencies*. Dependencies are specific to the program part which has already been executed. After the execution of a statement, these dependencies can differ. Let V again describe the set of all program entities of a program CFA. The total mapping $Dep: Stmt \times V \to 2^V$ is the sole attribute of an abstract state where the idea is that for each entity a set of those entities is described it depends on. E.g., an expression $Dep(st, v) = \{w, z\}$ stands for the case that an entity v – after having executed the statements $st \in Stmt$ – depends on the initial values of the entities w and z.

We define $Dep(st, v)$ by induction on the structure of programs where we assume the initial dependencies of an empty program, $Dep(skip, v) = \{v\}$, to be the identity function. The remaining cases are given in Fig. 4 where st_0, st_1, st_2, $lst \in Stmt$. Furthermore, $fv(e) \subseteq V$ defines the set of all free variables occuring in an expression $e \in AExpr \cup BExpr$. For while statements, an iterative computation of dependencies until a fixpoint is reached is needed. Since there are only finitely many variables, a fixpoint always exists.

Skip Statement

$$Dep([st_0; \text{skip}], v) = Dep(st_0, v)$$

Assignment

$$Dep([st_0; x := a;], v) = \begin{cases} Dep(st_0, v) & \text{if } x \neq v \\ \bigcup_{z \in fv(a)} Dep(st_0, z) & \text{if } x = v \end{cases}$$

If Statement

$$Dep([st_0; \text{if}(b) \text{ then } st_1 \text{ else } st_2 \text{ fi}], v) = Dep([st_0; st_1], v) \cup Dep([st_0; st_2], v)$$
$$\cup \bigcup_{z \in fv(b)} Dep(st_0, z)$$

While Statement

$$Dep([st_0; \text{while } (b) \text{ do } lst \text{ od}], v) = \bigcup_{i=0}^{\infty} D([st_0; lst^i], v)$$

$$\text{where } D([st_0; lst^0], v) = Dep(st_0, v)$$

$$D([st_0; lst^i], v) = D([st_0; lst^{i-1}], v) \cup \bigcup_{z \in fv(b)} D([st_0; lst^{i-1}], z)$$

Fig. 4. Dependencies between program variables

The mapping Dep gives us the dependencies between variables. For the running example from Fig. 1 (called Ex) we list in Table 2 all the dependencies that will be computed during the analysis. Our interest is, however, in the security classes of these dependencies. The mapping $CSC: Stmt \times V \to 2^S$ (*security classes of the*

Table 2. Computed dependencies *Dep* during the analysis

	$Dep(*,*)$	Computed security
$Ex_1 = [\text{skip}]$	$Dep(*, v_\ell) = \{v_\ell\}$	$(\ell, \{\ell\}) \in LHI$
	$Dep(*, v_h) = \{v_h\}$	$(h, \{h\}) \in LHI$
	$Dep(*, v_i) = \{v_i\}$	$(i, \{i\}) \in LHI$
$Ex_2 = [v_i = v_i + 2]$	$Dep(*, v_\ell) = \{v_\ell\}$	$(\ell, \{\ell\}) \in LHI$
	$Dep(*, v_h) = \{v_h\}$	$(h, \{h\}) \in LHI$
	$Dep(*, v_i) = \{v_i\}$	$(i, \{i\}) \in LHI$
$Ex_3 = [\text{ if } (v_h == 1) \text{ then } \{ v_i = v_i + 2 \}$	$Dep(*, v_\ell) = \{v_\ell\}$	$(\ell, \{\ell\}) \in LHI$
$\text{else } \{ v_i = v_i + 2 \} \text{ fi }]$		
	$Dep(*, v_h) = \{v_h\}$	$(h, \{h\}) \in LHI$
	$Dep(*, v_i) = \{v_i, v_h\}$	$(i, \{i, h\}) \in LHI$
$Ex = [\text{ if } (v_h == 1) \text{ then } \{ v_i = v_i + 2 \}$	$Dep(*, v_\ell) = \{v_i, v_h\}$	$(\ell, \{\ell, h, i\}) \notin LHI$
$\text{else } \{ v_i = v_i + 2 \} \text{ fi}; v_\ell = v_i]$		
	$Dep(*, v_h) = \{v_h\}$	$(h, \{h\}) \in LHI$
	$Dep(*, v_i) = \{v_i, v_h\}$	$(i, \{i, h\}) \in LHI$

content in the entity) is a function that associates to each program entity a set of security classes that classifies the current content stored in the entity. We base the semantics of *CSC* for a program entity on the dependencies (see Sect. 3) to other entities and the security level of the union of these dependencies. Therefore this mapping can and will vary between different abstract program states:

$$CSC(st, v) = \bigcup_{w \in Dep(st,v)} SC(w) \cup SC(v)$$

We will check security of a program *st* by checking that $SC(v), CSC(st, v)) \in P$ holds for all $v \in V$. This procedure is similar to Definition 4 with the only difference that the computed set *Dep* takes the place of *Interferences*. This is a sound procedure, which we show in Theorem 1. To get a correspondence between a location and statements we use the notation $[l : st; l' :]$ where $l \in L$ stands for the location right before and $l' \in L$ labels the location right after the statement.

Theorem 1. *Soundness of Analysis*

For all aggregation policies $P \in Pol(S)$, all programs $[st; l :] \in Stmt$ with l being the location label after *st*, the following holds:

If $[st; l :]$ is not secure at l wrt. P, then $(SC(v), CSC([st; l :], v)) \notin P$ holds.

Proof. We only give a proof sketch here. We prove this property by induction, and show that for each location $l \in L$ following a statement $st \in Stmt$

$$Interferences_l(v) \subseteq Dep([st; l :], v)$$

holds. As induction hypothesis we use that for statements $[st'; l_0 :]$ – which consist of a sequence of at most k statements – for any variable $v \in V$

$Interferences_{l_0}(v) \subseteq Dep([st'; l_0 :], v)$ holds. The base clause for the induction is given by the empty program $[\text{skip}; l :]$ where $Interferences_l(v) = \{v\} \subseteq \{v\} = Dep([\text{skip}; l :], v)$ holds.

As induction step, we show that this relation still holds if we extend the sequence $[st'; l_0 :]$ of k to $k + 1$ statements by adding a st after st': $[st'; l_0 : st; l :]$. Then the relation can be straightforward shown by considering all possible cases that can occur for $Interferences$ and Dep by using the definition from Definition 3 and Fig. 4 per each case of statements (namely skip, assignment, if and while). Comparing these two sets will lead to a proof of the $\subseteq$ relation. □

This theorem states that we are computing a conservative overapproximation of the actual dependencies: whenever a program is not secure, we will detect this. However, our technique can raise false alarms: for the program of Fig. 1, the dependencies $Dep(Ex, v_\ell) = \{v_i, v_h\}$ will cause a violation since $(SC(v_\ell), CSC(Ex, v_\ell)) = (\ell, \{\ell, h, i\}) \notin LHI$ (see Table 2). This is a spurious counterexample. We next see how we can detect such false alarms and can use the detection to further improve our analysis.

4   Checking Spurious Counter Examples

The main reason we are using the dependency analysis is that we consider the evaluation of the formula representing the definition of *Security* from *Definition* 3 as too costly to be applied for every entity and every security state at every location. The analysis stated in the previous Sect. 3 though is conservative and not precise with respect to the security definition. In this section, we explain how we can refine the analysis results for the usage in a CEGAR scheme. In principle we will do this by applying the mentioned costly evaluation of the formula representing security when we detect a possible violation. So we evaluate this formula not on all locations, but only when needed.

Given this counter example from the previous Sect. 3, our next step is to show that there are no violations by refining the dependencies. We do this by first determining a set of possible *candidates* for a refinement of the security class mapping. Let $P \in Pol(S)$ be an aggregation policy. We define the set of next feasible security states for a given non-secure state $(a, A) \notin P$ by

$$X_P((a, A)) := \{(a, B) \mid B \subseteq A \land (a, B) \in P \land (\exists x \in A \setminus B : (a, B \cup \{x\}) \notin P)\}$$

This set determines possible candidates for a refinement of the security states of the counter example. For our detected possible violation $(\ell, \{\ell, h, i\}) \notin LHI$, this set consists of two elements:

$$X_{LHI}((\ell, \{\ell, h, i\})) = \{(\ell, \{\ell\}), (\ell, \{\ell, i\}))\}$$

This is also illustrated in Fig. 6. Now let $l' \in L$ be the (potentially insecure) location after execution of program st, and $w \in V$ be the variable which causes the violation, i.e., $(SC(w), CSC([l : st; l'], w)) \notin P$. Next we take a logical encoding

```
1:          if (< v_h, 0 >== 1)
2:                  < v_i, 2 >=< v_i, 0 > +2;
3:          else
4:                  < v_i, 4 >=< v_i, 0 > +2;
5:          fi
5.1:       < v_i, 5 >= φ(< v_i, 2 >, < v_i, 4 >)
6:         < v_l, 6 >=< v_i, 5 >;
7:
```

Fig. 5. Running example of the secure program in SSA-form

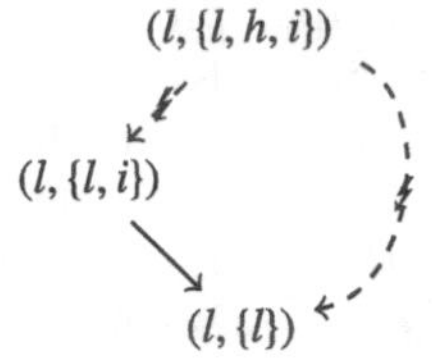

Fig. 6. Possible downgrading candidates of $(l, \{l, h, i\})$ are the next states below which are secure

of the program $\Psi([l : st; l' :])$ leading to l'. The encoding of the program as formula assumes an SSA-form (static single assignment) [6] of variables which we below mimic by using a renaming into unique SSA names for variables in the form $\langle v, l \rangle$ (variable plus location), where $l \in L$ is the location the variable was last assigned to. For example, a variable $x \in V$ in a statement $[l : x = a; l' :]$ with location $l \in L$ before and $l' \in L$ afterwards will be renamed to a pair $\langle x, l \rangle$. For joining variables in SSA-form, we use the standard technique of inserting ϕ-functions which join variables after two branches have merged. Notationally, the ϕ-functions in if statements appear after the if and those for while in a square bracket before the loop condition.

$$st_0; \text{if}\,(b)\,\text{then}\,st_1\,\text{else}\,st_2\,\text{fi}; \langle x_1, l' \rangle = \phi(\langle x_1, l_1^1 \rangle, \langle x_1, l_1^2 \rangle); \ldots; \langle x_k, l' \rangle = \phi(\langle x_k, l_k^1 \rangle, \langle x_k, l_k^2 \rangle)$$

$$st_0; \text{while}[\langle x_1, l \rangle = \phi(\langle x_1, l_1^0 \rangle, \langle x_1, l_1^l \rangle); \ldots; \langle x_k, l \rangle = \phi(\langle x_k, l_k^0 \rangle, \langle x_k, l_k^l \rangle);]\,(b)\,\text{do}\,lst\,\text{od}$$

In this, l_i^1, l_i^2, l_i^0 and l_i^l denotes the location where x_i was written the last time in $[st_0; st_1]$, $[st_0; st_2]$, $[st_0;]$ and $[lst;]$, respectively. The SSA-form of the running example program is illustrated in Fig. 5. SSA-forms are automatically generated.

Based on the SSA-form, we define the program encoding Ψ as depicted in Fig. 7. Each statement for Ψ is encoded according to its semantics, except for the while-loop. For while-loops there exist in general several possibilities for handling the unknown number of loop iterations. Common variants are the bounded unrolling of the loop of at most k rounds or the use of invariants. At the moment we encode a loop as two cases. One is that the loop condition is not fulfilled at the beginning and the loop body will not be iterated. In the second case, we completely ignore the current state of the variables appearing in the loop and iterate the loop body only once. The idea is here to make an encoding which models a run through the loop in an arbitrary start state, and thus to overapproximate all finite loop iterations. We do so by substituting every loop variable $\langle x_i, l \rangle$ with a new fresh variable $\langle a_i, l \rangle$ in both the formula encoding of the loop body as well as of the loop condition (see Fig. 7, while statement).

As we now aim at checking non-interference, we evaluate another formula $\Phi: (Stmt \times V \times (S \times 2^S)) \to \{true, false\}$ for unsatisfiability. For this, we use the above mentioned program encoding twice as $\Psi(l : st : l'])$, $\Psi'(l : st; l'])$, where in Ψ' all variable names are renamed disjoint to Ψ (i.e., variable v occurs as v').

<u>Empty Program</u>

$$\Psi(\text{skip};) = \textit{true}$$

<u>Skip Statement</u>

$$\Psi(st_0; \text{skip};) = \Psi(st_0;)$$

<u>Assignment</u>

$$\Psi(st_0; l : \langle x, l \rangle = a;) = \Psi(st_0;) \wedge (\langle x, l \rangle = a)$$

<u>If Statement</u>

$$\Psi(st_0; \text{ if } (b) \text{ then } st_1 \text{ else } st_2 \text{ } l' : \text{fi}; \langle x_1, l' \rangle = \phi(\langle x_1, l_1^1 \rangle, \langle x_1, l_1^2 \rangle); \dots ; \langle x_k, l' \rangle = \phi(\langle x_k, l_k^1 \rangle, \langle x_k, l_k^2 \rangle)) =$$

$$(\Psi(st_0;) \wedge b \wedge \Psi(st_1;) \wedge \bigwedge_{i=1}^{k} \langle x_i, l' \rangle = \langle x_i, l_i^1 \rangle)$$

$$\vee (\Psi(st_0;) \wedge \neg b \wedge \Psi(st_2;) \wedge \bigwedge_{i=1}^{k} \langle x_i, l' \rangle = \langle x_i, l_i^2 \rangle)$$

<u>While Statement</u>

$$\Psi(st_0; l : \text{ while}[\langle x_1, l \rangle = \phi(\langle x_1, l_1^0 \rangle, \langle x_1, l_1^1 \rangle); \dots ; \langle x_k, l \rangle = \phi(\langle x_k, l_k^0 \rangle, \langle x_k, l_k^1 \rangle)] (b) \text{ do } lst \text{ od}) =$$

$$\Psi(st_0;) \wedge \neg b \wedge ((\bigwedge_{i=1}^{k} \langle x_i, l \rangle = \langle x_i, l_i^0 \rangle) \vee (\bigwedge_{i=1}^{k} \langle x_i, l \rangle = \langle x_i, l_i^1 \rangle \wedge b_{[\langle x_i, l \rangle / \langle a_i, l \rangle]} \wedge \Psi(lst;)_{[\langle x_i, l \rangle / \langle a_i, l \rangle]}))$$

Fig. 7. Encoding of candidate check

Let $w \in V$ be the entity for which we detected the spurious counter example $(a, A) \in P$ as violation. Let $V_B = \{v \in V \mid SC(v) \in B\} \subseteq V$. For all $(a, B) \in X_P((a, A))$, we then do an evaluation according to the security Definition 4 and check whether

$$\Phi(l : st; l' :, w, (a, B)) = \bigwedge_{v \in V_B} \langle v, 0 \rangle = \langle v', 0 \rangle \wedge \Psi(l : st; l') \wedge \Psi'(l : st; l' .) \wedge \neg(\langle w, l_{st}^w \rangle = \langle w', l_{st}^w \rangle)$$

is unsatisfiable. In this, we use l_{st}^w as the location in st where w is last written to, which is unique since we operate on SSA-forms. Intuitively, the formula states that upon two executions to the location l started in initial states which agree on the values of variables which w is allowed to depend on, the value of w at the end is not the same. If this evaluation leads to a proof of unsatisfiability, we detect that we were too conservative (w at l does not depend on secret information) and can downgrade to this secure state B. If there are more $B_1, B_2, .. \in X_P((a, A))$ candidates where $\phi_l(B_i)$ is unsatisfiable, we can downgrade to the intersection $\bigcap_{\phi_l(B_i) \text{ unsat}} B_i$. This is a sound joining, since the property of aggregation policies is that intersection of secure states can only result in secure states.

Theorem 2. *Soundness of Encoding*
    Let $v \in V$ be a variable, $l \in L$ a location, P an aggregation policy, $(a, B) \in X_P((a, A))$ a candidate with $V_B = \{v \in V \mid SC(v) \in B\} \subseteq V$. Then:

$$\Phi(st; l :, w, (a, B)) \text{ unsatisfiable} \Rightarrow V \setminus V_B \subseteq \textit{Noninterferences}_l(w)$$

Proof. We only give a proof sketch here. We will show this theorem by an indirect proof. Assume $\Phi(st; l :, w, (a, B))$is unsatisfiable and $V \setminus V_B \not\subseteq Noninterferences_l(w)$. This means, there is a $z \in V \setminus V_B$ such that $\Xi_l(w, z)$ is satisfiable. We argue that in this case for the search space – Φ explores to proof unsatisfiablity – contains always the search space that $\Xi(w, z)$ explores.

Because of the satisfiability of $\Xi_l(w, z)$, there exist two paths π, π' (corresponding to those in the formula $\Xi_l(w, z)$) where the initial concrete states of the paths are restricted by $\forall v \in V \setminus \{z\} : c_0(v) = c_0'(v)$ and the end states differ for w: $\neg(c_j(w) = c_k'(w))$. First we argue that the domain of initial concrete states of Ξ is contained in Φ, since $V \setminus V_B \subseteq V \setminus \{z\}$ implies that by the subformula $\bigwedge_{v \in V_B} \langle v, 0 \rangle = \langle v', 0 \rangle$ in Φ at least all these concrete initial states of Ξ are modelled.

Let us consider the path π (π' is analogous) defined in Ξ. We argue that in the program encoding of the subformula Ψ of Φ each path π of Ξ is modelled. That means if the path π exists, the formula Ψ will evaluate to true. That is because skip, assignment and if-statements are represented one to one to its correlating semantics. The encoding of while-statements in Ψ covers more since we ignore restriction to the concrete states of those entities rewritten in the loop body before entering the while-statements. However, π is also contained in the encoding of Ψ. On the one hand a path that does not enter the loop body is directly represented in Ψ. On the other hand each path that iterates several times the loop body before leaving it is covered by the other branch of Ψ which represents the last iteration by simultaneously ignoring the past of in the loop rewritten variables (further restriction to concrete states of these variables).

We can conclude, that Φ explores all possible paths of $\Xi_l(w, z)$ and considers also all domains of initial concrete states that are considered by $\Xi_l(w, z)$. So if π, π' would result for $\Xi_l(w, z)$ to be evaluated to satisfiable, Φ would have recognized these two paths too and would also be evaluated to satisfiable. This contradicts the assumption.   □

For our example Ex, the unprimed formula is

$$\Psi(Ex; 7 :) = [[(\langle v_h, 0 \rangle = 1 \wedge \langle v_i, 2 \rangle = \langle v_i, 0 \rangle + 2 \wedge \langle v_i, 5 \rangle = \langle v_i, 2 \rangle)]$$
$$\vee [(\neg(\langle v_h, 0 \rangle = 1) \wedge \langle v_i, 4 \rangle = \langle v_i, 0 \rangle + 2 \wedge \langle v_i, 5 \rangle = \langle v_i, 4 \rangle)]]$$
$$\wedge \langle v_\ell, 6 \rangle = \langle v_i, 5 \rangle.$$

The primed formula $\Psi'(Ex; 7 :)$ looks similar. Like previously mentioned, for Ex our dependency analysis determined a spurious counterexample as a pair $(v_\ell, Dep(v_\ell) = \{v_i, v_h\})$ with the conclusion $(\ell, \{\ell, h, i\}) \notin LHI$. The two candidates for downgrading of the violation $(\ell, \{\ell, h, i\})$ are $(\ell, \{\ell\}), (\ell, \{\ell, i\}) \in X_{LHI}((\ell, \{\ell, h, i\}))$. We will then check the following two formulas for unsatisfiability:

$$\Phi([Ex;7:],v_\ell,(\ell,\{\ell,i\})) = (\langle v_\ell,0\rangle = \langle v'_\ell,0\rangle) \wedge (\langle v_i,0\rangle = \langle v'_i,0\rangle)$$
$$\wedge \Psi(Ex;7:) \wedge \Psi'(Ex;7:) \wedge \neg(\langle v_\ell,6\rangle = \langle v'_\ell,6\rangle)$$
$$\Phi([Ex;7:],v_\ell,(\ell,\{\ell\})) = (\langle v_\ell,0\rangle = \langle v'_\ell,0\rangle)$$
$$\wedge \Psi(Ex;7:) \wedge \Psi'(Ex;7:) \wedge \neg(\langle v_\ell,6\rangle = \langle v'_\ell,6\rangle)$$

The formula $\Phi([Ex;7:],v_\ell,(\ell,\{\ell,i\}))$ is unsatisfiable, but $\Phi([Ex;7:],v_\ell,(\ell,\{\ell\}))$ is satisfiable. So v_ℓ depends only on variables with security classes of ℓ and i but not on h like the result of the dependency analysis claimed. We will therefore try to modify our dependencies to accomplish this first element as the result. We achieve this now by modifying the dependencies by removing the dependencies to entities that are too restrictive. The set Δ defines for a spurious counterexample $(a,A) \in P$ at location $l \in L$ for variable w the difference of security classes of the aimed refinement to the spurious counterexample:

$$\Delta_l(w,(a,A)) := A \setminus \bigcap_{\substack{(a,B)\in X_P((a,A)) \\ \Phi_l(w,(a,B)) \ unsat}} B$$

Furthermore based on this set Δ_l, the set R_{Δ_l} describes the set of entities that has to be removed for making the result more precise:

$$R_{\Delta_l}(w,(a,A)) := \{v \in V \mid SC(v) \in \Delta_l(w,(a,A))\}$$

The refinement will then be achieved by taking

$$Dep'([l:st;l':],w) := Dep([l:st;l':],w) \setminus R_{\Delta_{l'}}(w,(a,A))$$

as new analysis result for w. We can memorize this information as triple $(l,w,Dep'([l:st;l':],w))$ to avoid this spurious counter example to be found again and again. If we run the dependency analysis at $[l:st;l']$ with memorizing this information $(l,w,Dep'([l:st;l':],(w)))$, we directly use it without re-computation. The result will then also be applied for the computation of dependencies of succeeding locations.

Back to our example with the policy LHI:

$$\Delta_7((\ell,\{\ell,h,i\})) = \{h\}$$
$$R_{\Delta_7}((\ell,\{\ell,h,i\})) = \{v_h\}$$
$$Dep'([Ex:7],v_\ell) = Dep([Ex:7],v_\ell) \setminus R_{\Delta_7}(v_\ell,(\ell,\{\ell,h,i\})) = \{v_i,v_h\} \setminus \{v_h\} = \{v_i\}$$

Since we memorize $(7,v_\ell,\{v_i\})$ for further iterations, the same counter examples will not appear again. In this case, no other violation is detected and hence the program is proven secure. In general, several iterations of the checking and refinement procedure might be necessary to finally state security or report a real violation.[2]

---

[2] As additional remark we want to clarify that the refinement technique is able to handle more complex examples than the illustrated implicit flow example. E.g. in examples like $[v_\ell = v_h; v_\ell = v_\ell - v_h$]the firstly computed dependency to v_h will be recognized as nonexistent as well.

5 Implementation

We implemented our approach within the CPACHECKER framework [3–5][3]. This is a framework for specifying a configurable program analysis – a unification which allows both model checking approaches as well as data flow analysis.

The implementation of our approach is divided into three interleaved separate configurable program analysis which are

1. Dependency Analysis,
2. ControlContext Analysis, and
3. PolicyChecker.

The task of the *Dependency Analysis* is to determine the dependencies corresponding to Sect. 3. This is done with the help of an auxiliary analysis called *ControlContext Analysis* which is used for making the dependencies more precise using the control context. The class of programs covered by our analysis is larger than given here. E.g. we also consider function calls, and we are using for instance dominators for the control context analysis to determine further control dependencies instead of only considering the control dependence of if and while-statements.

The *PolicyChecker* is the actual security analysis. Its task is to validate whether the dependencies of the abstract state space computed by *Dependency Analysis* lead to a security violation wrt. a beforehand specified policy P and security mapping SC. Unlike described so far, we do not check each entity on each location, but we divide the entities $V = I \dot\cup E$ further into two sets: In those that can potentially violate security on every location (e.g. by writing on a public output console) which is the set I, and those that can only be observed after the program execution which is the set E. The security of I will be checked on every location whereas the security of E is only checked on end locations. The PolicyChecker thus needs user defined input which is

– the security mapping SC
– security policy P,
– immediate violation set I.

The set SC can be partial defined instead of a total function. The analysis will expand the function to a total mapping by setting all not specified entities to a security class $s \in S$ that can be given as additional input. The set $E = V \setminus I$ is implicit.

The usage of the CPACHECKER framework allows for an easy combination of our approach with different already integrated program analysis, in particular the possibility of using information of other analyses for improving precision of our own analysis. We can for instance use a standard *Points-to-Analysis* [2] to improve precision of the *Dependency Analysis* or a *Predicate Analysis* [5] to eliminate dead paths.

---

[3] https://cpachecker.sosy-lab.org/.

6   Conclusion

We presented a CEGAR Scheme for information flow analysis that is based on a conservative dependency analysis. In this, we inspect counter examples for their spuriousity by an evaluation of a program encoding that overapproximates the underlying security concern – non-interference. Soundness of both the dependency analysis and refinement triggered by the evaluation of the program encoding is shown by Theorems 1 and 2.

As an advantage we can process arbitrary security policies, with the only restriction that the joining of several secure states (for the dataflow analysis) has to result in a secure state. Resting the security upon the dependency analysis result allows an exchange of the security policy without the need of recomputing the dependencies (but in some circumstances to use the CEGAR scheme to make the dependencies more precise).

Related Work. The approach most similar to ours is that of Taghdiri et al. [17]. Both their and our analysis perform a security analysis on the basis of a dependency analysis with CEGAR aspects. While they generate and use a conservative program dependence graph to signal dependencies, we compute conservative dependencies with a dataflow analysis to use it in the CPAChecker framework together with other software analysis that can refine the dependencies. The aggregation policies we consider in this paper are equal in expressiveness to the lattices they consider as policies. However, the CEGAR schemes differ. Their analysis marks the nodes on a path in the PDG with ascending security classes according to their lattice. Such a path can be a spurious counter example they plan to eliminate, where they use a path encoding to validate whether this path is possible. In our CEGAR scheme, the computed security classes that an entity contains can violate the security at a location. We then use an encoding of the paths to this location for the purpose of evaluating the non-interference property for a smaller subset that would imply a secure state. If that is the case we refine the dependencies.

For our dependency analysis we use a forward dataflow analysis on aggregation policies, which has similarities to the forward analysis of Amtoft and Banarjee [1]. While they consider independences of variables, we consider dependencies.

Darvas et al. [7] use a theorem proving approach where they evaluate two variants of program encodings of non-interference in dynamic logic. One of the evaluation examples is similar to ours. However, they only validate the program as a whole and not per location of interest, and they consider only the standard policy (bipartition in high and low entities).

The policy specification is based on the framework used by Foley [8,9]. Mantel [14] gives a good overview of formalizing security concerns – including non-interference – based on the specification of a general policy. However, they consider more security concerns like e.g. separability, perfect security etc. which are ordered in a hierarchy and are expressed as formulas. At the moment, we consider as security concern non-interference only. We could also think about varying the security concerns and use one of these other concerns.

Future Work. We use general security policies which are only restricted by sound joining of secure states, because of the underlying forward data flow analysis. By using a model checking approach instead, we could allow arbitrary feasible policies with no further restriction since joining of states would not be needed. For this case, we have to extend the definition of refinement candidates X_P from Sect. 4 to each maximal state of context change between secure and non-secure states with respect to the $\sqsubseteq$ relation. For the downgrading of security states, a spurious counter example refinement would then have to consider not only false negatives but false positives as well, and has to choose the maximal candidate that holds.

Another aspect is the program encoding we use for while-loops to overapproximate the non-interference definition. At the moment we consider only the last iteration with arbitrary concrete states for the rewritten variables. A next step would be to allow further subformulas at the beginning of the loop iteration encoding to make the allowed concrete states more precise while retaining the conservativeness of the approach, which will be similar to loop invariants.

References

1. Amtoft, T., Banerjee, A.: Information flow analysis in logical form. In: Giacobazzi, R. (ed.) SAS 2004. LNCS, vol. 3148, pp. 100–115. Springer, Heidelberg (2004)
2. Andersen, L.O.: Program analysis and specialization for the C programming language. Ph.D. thesis, University of Cophenhagen (1994)
3. Beyer, D., Henzinger, T.A., Théoduloz, G.: Configurable software verification: concretizing the convergence of model checking and program analysis. In: Damm, W., Hermanns, H. (eds.) CAV 2007. LNCS, vol. 4590, pp. 504–518. Springer, Heidelberg (2007)
4. Beyer, D., Henzinger, T.A., Théoduloz, G.: Program analysis with dynamic precision adjustment. In: ASE 2008, pp. 29–38. IEEE Computer Society (2008)
5. Beyer, D., Keremoglu, M.E., Wendler, P.: Predicate abstraction with adjustable-block encoding. In: Bloem, R., Sharygina, N. (eds.) FMCAD 2010, pp. 189–197. IEEE (2010)
6. Cytron, R., Ferrante, J., Rosen, B.K., Wegman, M.N., Zadeck, F.K.: Efficiently computing static single assignment form and the control dependence graph. ACM Trans. Program. Lang. Syst. **13**(4), 451–490 (1991)
7. Darvas, Á., Hähnle, R., Sands, D.: A theorem proving approach to analysis of secure information flow. In: Hutter, D., Ullmann, M. (eds.) SPC 2005. LNCS, vol. 3450, pp. 193–209. Springer, Heidelberg (2005)
8. Foley, S.N.: Unifying information flow policies. Technical report, DTIC Document (1990)
9. Foley, S.N.: Aggregation and separation as noninterference properties. J. Comput. Secur. **1**(2), 159–188 (1992)
10. Goguen, J.A., Meseguer, J.: Security policies and security models. In: 1982 IEEE Symposium on Security and Privacy, pp. 11–20. IEEE Computer Society (1982)

11. Hammer, C., Snelting, G.: Flow-sensitive, context-sensitive, and object-sensitive information flow control based on program dependence graphs. Int. J. Inf. Sec. **8**(6), 399–422 (2009)
12. Hunt, S., Sands, D.: On flow-sensitive security types. In: Morrisett, J.G., Jones, S.L.P. (eds.) POPL 2006, pp. 79–90. ACM (2006)
13. Joshi, R., Leino, K.R.M.: A semantic approach to secure information flow. Sci. Comput. Program. **37**(1–3), 113–138 (2000)
14. Mantel, H.: On the composition of secure systems. In: 2002 IEEE Symposium on Security and Privacy, pp. 88–101. IEEE Computer Society (2002)
15. Sabelfeld, A., Myers, A.C.: Language-based information-flow security. IEEE J. Sel. Areas Commun. **21**(1), 5–19 (2003)
16. Snelting, G., Robschink, T., Krinke, J.: Efficient path conditions in dependence graphs for software safety analysis. ACM Trans. Softw. Eng. Methodol. **15**(4), 410–457 (2006)
17. Taghdiri, M., Snelting, G., Sinz, C.: Information flow analysis via path condition refinement. In: Degano, P., Etalle, S., Guttman, J. (eds.) FAST 2010. LNCS, vol. 6561, pp. 65–79. Springer, Heidelberg (2011)
18. Volpano, D.M., Irvine, C.E., Smith, G.: A sound type system for secure flow analysis. J. Comput. Secur. **4**(2/3), 167–188 (1996)

Erratum to: Formal Availability Analysis Using Theorem Proving

Waqar Ahmad[(✉)] and Osman Hasan

School of Electrical Engineering and Computer Science,
National University of Sciences and Technology (NUST), Islamabad, Pakistan
{waqar.ahmad,osman.hasan}@seecs.nust.edu.pk

Erratum to:
Chapter "Formal Availability Analysis Using
Theorem Proving" in: K. Ogata et al. (Eds.):
Formal Methods and Software Engineering, LNCS,
DOI: 10.1007/978-3-319-47846-3_15

The original version of this chapter contained an error. The name of the author Waqar Ahmad was spelled incorrectly as Waqar Ahmed in the original publication. The original chapter was corrected.

The updated original online version for this chapter can be found at
DOI: 10.1007/978-3-319-47846-3_15

© Springer International Publishing AG 2017
K. Ogata et al. (Eds.): ICFEM 2016, LNCS 10009, p. E1, 2016.
DOI: 10.1007/978-3-319-47846-3_30

Author Index

Printed in the United States
By Bookmasters

Printed in the United States
By Bookmasters